Crime Classification Manual

A Standard System for Investigating and Classifying Violent Crime

Third Edition

John E. Douglas, Ann W. Burgess,
Allen G. Burgess, and Robert K. Ressler

WILEY

Published by John Wiley & Sons, Inc., Hoboken, New Jersey

Published simultaneously in Canada

For general information about our other products and services, please contact our Customer Care Department within the United States at (800) 762-2974, outside the United States at (317) 572-3993 or fax (317) 572-4002.

Wiley publishes in a variety of print and electronic formats and by print-on-demand. Some material included with standard print versions of this book may not be included in e-books or in print-on-demand. If this book refers to media such as a CD or DVD that is not included in the version you purchased, you may download this material at http://booksupport.wiley.com. For more information about Wiley products, visit www.wiley.com.

Library of Congress Cataloging-in-Publication Data:
Douglas, John E.
  Crime classification manual : a standard system for investigating and classifying violent crimes / John E. Douglas, Ann W. Burgess, and Allen G. Burgess. – Third Edition.
      pages cm
  Includes bibliographical references and index.
  ISBN 978-1-118-30505-8 (pbk.)
  1. Crime–Classification–Handbooks, manuals, etc. 2. Crime–United States–Classification–Handbooks, manuals, etc. I. Burgess, Ann Wolbert. II. Burgess, Allen G. III. Title.
  HV6253.C75 2013
  364.01'2–dc23
                                                                         2012048961

Printed in the United States of America

10 9 8 7 6 5 4 3 2 1

Contents

Preface   *vii*

PART I   CRIME ANALYSIS AND INVESTIGATION

1 *Crime Classification: Past and Present*   3

2 *Criminal Investigative Concepts in Crime Scene Analysis*   21
John E. Douglas and Lauren K. Douglas

3 *The Impact of the Internet, Technology, and Forensics on Crime Investigation*   39
John E. Douglas, Lauren K. Douglas, and Stefan R. Treffers

4 *Local, Federal, and International Agencies*   59

5 *Classifying Crimes by Severity From Aggravators to Depravity*   91
Michael Welner

PART II   THE CLASSIFICATIONS

6 *Criminal Enterprise Homicide*   111

7 *Personal Cause Homicide*   165

8 *Sexual Homicide*   205

9 *Extremist and Medical Homicide*   237

10 *Group Cause Homicide*   263

11 *Arson/Bombing*   277

12 *Rape and Sexual Assault*   307

13 *Nonlethal Crimes*   367

14 *Computer Crimes*   399
Allen G. Burgess

15 *Increased Globalization of Crime*   431
Stefan R. Treffers

16 *Mass and Serial Homicide*   471

17 *Poison and Biological Agents as Weapons*   491
Arthur E. Westveer, John P. Jarvis, Carl J. Jensen, III,
and Anne M. Berger

PART III   LEGAL ISSUES

18 *Interviewing, Interrogation, and
Criminal Confessions*   507
Gregory M. Cooper, Michael P. Napier,
and Susan H. Adams

19 *Wrongful Convictions: Causes, Solutions,
and Case Studies*   527
Peter Shellem

About the Editors   545
About the Contributors   549
Citation Index   551
Name Index   555
Subject Index   557

We dedicate this edition to chapter contributors

Peter Shellem, B. S. (1960–2009)
award-wining crime investigative reporter
in Pittsburgh, PA

and

Arthur E. Westveer, M.L.A. (1936–2010)
retired FBI supervisory special agent

Preface

Criminal trials in 2012 saw former Penn State assistant football coach Jerry Sandusky convicted of child sexual abuse and sanctions brought against the university. Drew Peterson was charged and convicted of killing his third wife, Kathleen Savio with no physical evidence linking Peterson to Savio's death, relying instead on a heavily circumstantial case on hearsay statements that Peterson threatened to kill Savio. Joran van der Sloot, a 23-year-old Dutchman, confessed to the slaying of a 21-year-old Peruvian business student Stephany Flores on May 30, 2010, after she used his laptop to find out about his involvement in the case of Natalee Holloway, an 18-year-old Alabama student who vanished in Aruba in May 2005. van der Sloot said he did not want to do it but the girl intruded into his private life.

The year 2012 also witnessed horrific mass shootings in the United States. Just minutes into a midnight showing on opening day of the latest Batman movie on July 20, 2012, a man dressed in tactical gear with bright dyed orange hair opened fire inside the Century 16 movie theater in Aurora, Colorado. Some initially thought it was a prank—smoke filled the theater, but then, shots were fired. Twelve people were killed and 58 injured. 24-year-old James Holmes was arrested minutes later outside. But right after the arrest, police went to his apartment, which they'd found rigged with explosives.

On August 6, 2012, there was a mass shooting by 40-year-old Wade Michael Page at the Sikh Temple in Oak Creek, Wisconsin. Six people died, and three people were injured before the gunman took the 9-millimeter handgun he had purchased just one week earlier to himself.

On December 14, 2012 a 20-year-old gunman, Adam Lanza, murdered his mother at home first, and then went into Sandy Hook Elementary School in Newtown, Connecticut where he shot 20 children and six adults, and finally, killed himself before police arrived.

This textbook is about classifying crime. Professions develop and advance their science, as they are able to organize and classify their work. The nature of science started when organisms began to generalize, to see similarities between themselves and members of their own species or to see differences and other similarities between other species and themselves. Thus, the nature of science requires that one first observe and then attempt to categorize, compare and classify observations. Classification is a process in data collection and analysis in which data are grouped according to previously determined characteristics.

The past four decades have witnessed the major advancement in investigative science. A series of FBI studies conducted in the 1980's on sexual murderers, rapists, child molesters and abductors, and arsonists described and identified critical characteristics of these crimes. These characteristics were initially used for profiling techniques. An additional use of the research findings has now been compiled into a crime classification manual. The advent of technology and forensic science has also strengthened the investigative skills for solving crime.

This is the third edition of the *Crime Classification Manual*, better known simply as CCM-III. The development of this manual over the years has received notice from FBI investigative profilers, law enforcement officers, corrections and parole staff, mental health staff and students in forensic studies and criminal justice studies.

The purpose of this manual is fourfold:

1. To standardize terminology within the criminal justice field;
2. To facilitate communication within the criminal justice field and between criminal justice and mental health;
3. To educate the criminal justice system and the public at large to the types of crimes being committed; and
4. To develop a database for investigative research.

In the development of the manual, a decision was made to base the classification on the primary intent of the criminal. The intent categories include: (1) criminal enterprise, (2) personal cause, (3) sexual intent, and (4) group cause.

Task force groups chaired by supervisory special agents at the FBI's National Center for the Analysis of Violent crime worked on refining the crime categories for the first edition. The preliminary draft of the manual was presented to an Advisory Committee who provided additional comments and suggestions for refinement of the manual.

The second edition of the CCM includes three new classifications contributed by experts in their field. Michael Welner, MD contributed the classification of Religion-Inspired Homicide and Neonaticide, Mark Safarik contributed Elder Sexual Homicide classification and Allen G. Burgess classified Computer Crimes.

The third edition includes three new chapters on the Impact of Internet, Technology & Forensics, Local, Federal and International Agencies, and Global Crimes.

Definitions

For the purposes of this book, the crime definitions are as follows:

Murder is the willful (nonnegligent) killing of one human being by another. The classification of this offense, as for all other Crime Index offenses, is based solely on police investigation as opposed to the determination of a court, medical examiner, coroner, jury, or other judicial body. Not included in this classification are deaths caused by negligence, suicide, or accident; justifiable homicides; and attempts to murder or assaults to murder, which are scored as aggravated assaults.

In December 2011, FBI Director Robert S. Mueller III, approved revisions to the Uniform Crime Reporting (UCR) Program's 80-year-old definition of rape. As approved, the UCR Program's definition of rape is the penetration, no matter how slight, of the vagina or anus with any body part or object, or oral penetration by a sex organ of another person, without the consent of the victim. In January 2013 the FBI began collecting data using the new definition of rape.

Arson, as defined by UCR, is any willful or malicious burning or attempt to burn, with or without intent to defraud, a dwelling house, public building, motor vehicle or aircraft, personal property of another. Bombing has been added to the classification.

Computer crimes include crimes whereby the computer is the target or the mechanism for committing the crime or the computer user is the target. It also includes crimes committed over the Internet or whereby the Internet plays a role in the commission of the crime.

Organization of the Manual

This third edition of the Crime Classification Manual is divided into three major sections. The first section of the manual contains five chapters on Crime Analysis and Investigation. Part II includes the classification categories of Homicide, Arson/Bombing, Rape and Sexual Assault, Nonlethal Crimes, Computer Crimes, Global Crimes, Mass and Serial Homicide and Poisoning and Biological Agents as Weapons. Part III includes Legal Issues of Interviewing, Interrogation and Confessions, and Wrongful Convictions.

Our results have implications not only for law enforcement personnel who are responsible for the investigation of a crime, but for professionals in other disciplines who address the crime problem. These groups include criminal justice professionals directly involved with the legal aspects of crime; correction institution administrators and staff personnel, who not only have custody of criminals but also are responsible for decisions regarding these individuals' return to society; for mental health professionals, both those involved with offender treatment and those assisting victims and families affected by these crimes; for social service personnel working with juveniles, as they detect early signs and characteristics of violent individuals and seek to divert these individuals from criminal activity; for criminologists who study the problem of violent crime; and for public policymakers who attempt to address the problem through their decisions. It is our hope that this book will advance the knowledge base of these professionals as they seek increased understanding of the nature of crime and of the individuals who commit such crime.

Acknowledgments

Many people have helped with this project over the years. We wish to acknowledge past FBI Director William H. Webster and Executive Assistant Director John E. Otto for their early support of the criminal investigative research project efforts of the Behavioral Science Unit, as well as Director William S. Sessions for his continued support. We also wish to acknowledge Anthony Daniels, Assistant Director of the FBI Training Division, and Deputy Assistant Director of Training for their encouragement of the crime classification project.

We are especially appreciative for the grant monies received from the Department of Justice. We are indebted to many Department of Justice officials, including Robert W. Sweet, Jr., Administrator, Office of Juvenile Justice and Delinquency Prevention for the release of monies to study serial child molesters, abductors and murderers of children; Robert O. Heck for his belief in the criminal profiling concept and the Violent Criminal Apprehension Program.

In particular our thanks are extended to major contributors to the first edition, especially Corinne M. Munn, the Classification Coordinator and Research Associate and Classification Committee chairmen SA James Wright, SA Judson Ray, SA Greg McCrary, and Dr. David Icove.

And we wish to acknowledge the people who assisted with this 3rd edition: Stefan Treffers for his research of crime statistics and contributions to three new chapters, Sarah Gregorian for her assistance with the preparation of the manuscript and study guides, and the contributors of cases who are acknowledged with the case.

PART I

Crime Analysis and Investigation

Chapter 1

Crime Classification: Past and Present

Within hours, on July 23, 2011, the Internet detailed the crimes of a 32-year-old Norwegian, Anders Behring Breivik, who was accused of (and later confessed to) killing 77 people. He portrayed his acts as "atrocious" yet "necessary."

It took police over an hour to stop the massacre because of the problems with transport out to the island. Witnesses said the gunman, wearing a police uniform, was able to shoot unchallenged for a prolonged period, forcing youngsters to scatter in panic or to jump into the lake to swim for the mainland.

Breivik gave himself up after admitting to a massacre in which mostly young people died while attending a summer camp of the youth wing of Norway's ruling Labour Party on a peaceful island. Breivik was also arrested for the earlier bombing of Oslo's government district that killed seven people hours earlier.

A video posted to the YouTube Web site showed several pictures of Breivik, including one of him in a Navy Seal–type scuba diving outfit pointing an automatic weapon. "Before we can start our crusade we must do our duty by decimating cultural Marxism," said a caption under the video called "Knights Templar 2083" that also provided a link to a 1,500-page electronic manifesto stating that Breivik was the author.

Breivik, tall and blond, owned an organic farming company called Breivik Geofarm, which a supply firm said he had used to buy fertilizer—possibly to make the Oslo bomb. On August 23, 2012, a Norwegian court found that Anders Behring Breivik was sane when he killed 77 people in a bombing and shooting rampage, and sentenced him to a maximum of 21 years for "terrorist acts" (Criscione, 2012).

This case illustrates the planning, motive, and horrific actions of a mass murderer and the abject terror and panic in the words of the surviving victims. This type of antigovernment militant is not unique. It has struck also in the United States. Timothy McVeigh, 33, killed 168 people, between the ages of 4 months and 73 years, with a truck bomb in Oklahoma City in November 1995. Fort Hood, located near Killeen, Texas, was the site of another mass shooting on

October 16, 1991, when George Hennard, 35, drove his pickup truck through the windows of Luby Cafeteria's restaurant and shot and killed 23 people before turning the gun on himself. He also wounded 20 people. On November 8, 2009, a U.S. Army psychiatrist, Major Nidal Malik Hasan, 39, opened fire inside Fort Hood in Texas. Thirteen people were killed, and 30 people were injured.

When measuring crime and its victims, these four mass murderers claimed the lives of 281 victims. And for all the victims who died, many more were serious injured physically and, along with their families, were predicted to have long-lasting traumatic memories. Domestic terrorism, as a crime classification of extremist homicide, is increasing.

Violent crimes of murder and rape continue to be of increasing concern in our society. They represent serious interpersonal assaultive behaviors, and law enforcement officials feel public pressure to apprehend the perpetrators as quickly as possible.

Traditionally, most violent crimes such as murder were fairly easy for law enforcement to solve and make an arrest. However, there has been a changing nature of violent crime itself over the past several decades and law enforcement's ability to make arrests following crimes appears to have significantly diminished in recent years. This is especially true for homicide: From 1980 to 1996, the rate at which homicide cases were cleared nationally decreased more than 7% (Brown & Langan, 2001).

Clearance rates for murder and nonnegligent manslaughter, according to the Uniform Crime Reports, declined from 93% in 1961 to 65% in 1993. The most prevalent type of homicide 30 years ago was acquaintance homicide, involving the victim's knowing the assailant in some way. While the overall clearance rate of acquaintance homicide is increasing, the same cannot be said of stranger-to-stranger homicide. A wide range of social stressors, including guns and drugs, contribute to the rising incidence of stranger-to-stranger homicides. Investigators are faced with a type of homicide that has a high likelihood of never being solved (Richardson & Kosa, 2001).

A study of San Diego homicide trends between 1970 and 1980 (Gilbert, 1983) identified a marked increase in stranger-to-stranger homicides. While the proportion of acquaintance homicides decreased from 67% of all homicide cases in 1970 to 34% in 1980, the rate of felony homicides, specifically robbery-related homicides, increased significantly. The study concluded that the decline of homicide clearance rates can be attributed to an increase in stranger-to-stranger homicides.

Historical Perspective

Understanding behavior and methodology has been a challenge to the civilized world. The term *dangerous class* has been used throughout history to describe individuals who are deemed a threat to law and order. Initially, the term described the environment in which one lived or was found to be living in versus the type of crime being committed. An example of this occurred in England at the end of the Hundred Years' War with France. The demobilization of thousands of soldiers, coupled with the changing economic trade market, saw the homeless population increase nationwide with the displacement of farmers (Rennie, 1977). During the reign of England's Henry VIII, 72,000 major and minor thieves were hanged. Under his daughter, Elizabeth I, vagabonds were strung up in rows, as many as 300 or 400 at a time (Rennie, 1977).

Categorizing these individuals began to change in 1838 when the winning entry at the French Académie des Sciences Morales et Politiques, the highly competitive academic society, was titled "The Dangerous Classes of the Population in the Great Cities, and the Means of Making Them Better" (Rennie, 1977). The term *dangerous class* was then used to describe individuals who were criminals or had such potential. Initially, these were the poor, homeless, and unemployed in the large cities.

Classification of offenders began with the work of statistics. This early work permitted a comparison of the incidence of crime with factors, such as race, age, sex, education, and geography (Rennie, 1977). Cesare Lombrosos, the famed Italian physician, is generally credited with launching the scientific era in criminology. In 1872 he differentiated five types of criminals—the born criminal, the insane criminal, the criminal by passion, the habitual criminal, and the occasional criminal (Lindesmith & Dunham, 1941)—based on Darwin's theory of evolution. The operational definitions for the five groups that were developed allowed subsequent investigators to test Lombrosos's formulations empirically. A majority of his hypotheses and theories proved to be invalid, but the fact that they were testable was an advancement for the science (Megargee & Bohn, 1979).

Englishman Charles Goring refuted the Lombrosian theory of the degenerate "criminal man" in 1913, concluding, "The one vital mental constitutional factor in the etiology of crime is defective intelligence" (Goring, 1913, p. 369). This concept persisted for several decades. Henry Goddard, who did his early work on feeblemindness in 1914, reported that 50% of all offenders were defective (Goddard, 1914). As psychometric techniques improved, the finding of mental deficiency changed. Murchison in 1928 concluded that those in "the criminal group are superior in intelligence to the white draft group of WWI" (Bromberg, 1965). As studies progressed, it became obvious that a disordered personality organization (including psychoses, neuroses, and personality problems) was a more significant factor in crime than feeblemindedness.

With increasing rapidity, from the late 1930s to the World War II years to the present, interest has shifted away from insanity and mental defectiveness to personality disturbances in analyzing the genesis of crime. In the decades before the report of Bernard Glueck (1918) from Sing Sing Prison in New York State, the focus in crime study was on subnormal mentality.

In 1932 the Psychiatric Clinic of the Court of General Sessions in New York began to classify each offender according to a personality evaluation, thus combining the insights of psychoanalysis, descriptive psychiatry, and behavioral phenomenology. Each convicted offender presented was analyzed in relation to four categories: (a) presence or absence of psychosis, (b) intellectual level, (c) presence of psychopathic or neurotic features and/or personality diagnosis, and (d) physical condition.

Typologies of crime traditionally have been developed addressing the criminal offense. The psychiatric perspective to understanding crime has used two approaches: scrutiny of the inner (mental and moral) world of the criminal offender and examination of the external (social) world in which he lives (Bromberg, 1965).

A project at the Bellevue Psychiatric Hospital in New York City, spanning 1932 to 1965 (Bromberg, 1965), found that the personality patterns of criminals far outshadowed the significance of psychotic or defective diagnoses in terms of analyzing criminal behavior and in assisting the court and probation department in estimating the potential or deficits of the individual offender. Fifteen personality diagnoses were established by this project.

The investigation of the psychological motivations and social stresses that underlie crime has proved that the behavior patterns involved in criminal acts are not far removed from those of normal behavior. Studies indicate that criminal behavior, as is true of all other behavior, is responsive to inner and outer stresses. The external realities of mental life—social pressures, cultural emphases, physical needs, subcultural patterns of life—precipitate criminal action. The inner realities of behavior—neurotic reactions, impulses, unconscious motivations, preconscious striving, eruption of infantile aggressions—represent a precondition to criminal acts. Criminal behavior is suggested to derive from three behavioral areas: (a) the aggressive tendency, both destructive and acquisitive; (b) passive, or subverted, aggression; and (c) psychological needs (Bromberg, 1965).

Several research-based classification typologies for offenders have been developed. Julian Roebuck in 1967 provided rules to classify offenders based on the frequency and recency of their offenses during their criminal career. According to this system, an offender can be classified into a single offense pattern. The function of his typology was in terms of explanatory theory rather than in terms of diagnostic systems used in treatment. Investigation into the offender's arrest history, regardless of length, was the primary tool used in developing a classification system. The total of known arrests, included with behavior, allowed for the observance of a pattern, if one existed. One basic assumption used was that the arrest pattern would indicate a pattern of behavior or criminal career. The most frequent charge or charges in the history was the basis for classification (Roebuck, 1967). An obvious weakness is that not all criminals have accurate arrest histories.

Classification of criminal offenders has been and is an important component in correctional facilities throughout the United States. In 1973 the National Advisory Commission called for criminal classification programs to be initiated throughout the criminal justice system (Megargee & Bohn, 1979). This has not been an easy task. The correctional system is a complex, expanding, expensive operation that has accountability to society, individual communities, correctional staff, and the inmates themselves. The current trend within the correctional system has been growth of the inmate population with a modest growth in facilities. As the population within the system is faced with economic and now medical issues (such as AIDS), classification is a cost-effective and efficient management and treatment tool. It provides a common language for the various professional groups to communicate among themselves.

Megargee and Bohn (1979) found during their research project that a comprehensive classification system must take into account many different components of the criminal population. They stressed that an important element in any such system is the personality and behavioral pattern of the individual offender.

In the 1980s, a research team at the Massachusetts Treatment Center in Bridgewater, Massachusetts, began a research program to classify sexual offenders (Knight, Rosenberg, & Schneider, 1985). Their application of a programmatic approach to typology construction and validation has produced taxonomic systems for both child molesters and rapists. The classification for child molesters has demonstrated reasonable reliability and consistent ties to distinctive developmental antecedents. In addition, results of a 25-year recidivism study of child molesters indicate that aspects of the model have important prognostic implications (Knight & Prentky, 1990).

The classification of Internet child pornography in the 21st century indicates an increasing number of child pornography possessors who are being caught in a concerted effort to apprehend offenders. It is suggested that a "perfect i-storm," is being created characterized by a large but crudely estimated number of pedophiles involved in organized pornography rings, estimated between 50,000 and 100,000 worldwide, with roughly one third being in the United States (Wortley & Smallbone, 2006).

Crime Characteristics and Crime Classification Today

Crime statistics provide one type of social indicator for a community to assess its safety. The Wickersham Commission in 1929 worked two years and published in 14 volumes the first U.S. comprehensive national study of crime and law enforcement. The work led to the development of a federal reporting system under the FBI as the Uniform Crime Report (UCR) (National Commission on Law Observance and Enforcement, 1931).

The UCR collects data on five general reporting forms: offenses known to police; property stolen and recovered; supplementary homicide report; age, sex, race, and ethnic origin of persons arrested; and police employees. These forms are completed monthly, submitted to the FBI or state-level UCR programs, and published yearly.

Cases can be cleared or closed in one of two ways: by arrest or by exceptional means. Three specific conditions need to be met for an offense to be cleared: (a) at least one person has been arrested; (b) the person has been charged with the offense; and (c) the person turned over to the court for prosecution.

Cases are cleared by exceptional means when there are factors beyond an agency's control preventing law enforcement from formally charging an offender. These conditions include: (a) the offender has been identified; (b) there is sufficient information upon which to make an arrest; (c) the location of the offender is known; and (d) there is a circumstance beyond the control of law enforcement that prohibits the agency from arresting, charging, and prosecuting the offender.

Crime victim surveys entered the criminology field in the mid-1960s with the goal to reduce the number of cases that were eluding police. Of note, the first victimization survey pilot indicated that, depending on the type of crime, there were 3 to 10 times as many crimes reported by victims than there were recorded by law enforcement through the UCR.

The National Crime Victims Survey (NCVS), now in its fourth generation of design, includes four primary objectives: (a) to develop detailed victim information and consequences of crime; (b) to estimate the number and types of crimes not reported to the police; (c) to provide uniform measures of selected types of crimes; and (d) to permit comparisons over time and types of areas.

The NCVS focuses on certain criminal offenses, completed or attempted, that are of major concern to the general public and law enforcement authorities. These are the personal crimes of rape, robbery, assault, and larceny and the household crimes of burglary, larceny, and motor vehicle theft. Definitions of the measured crimes generally are compatible with conventional use and with the definitions used by the FBI in its annual publication, *Crime in the United States: Uniform Crime Reports*. The NCVS reports on characteristics of personal crime victims, victim–offender relationships, offender characteristics in personal crimes of violence, and crime characteristics. The results of the NCVS indicated improved data regarding the victim–offender relationships when a crime was a nonstranger type.

CLASSIFICATION BY MOTIVATION

Identifying motivations in the investigation of a crime is a standard procedure for law enforcement. Typically, motivation provides police with the means to narrow the potential suspect pool. The classification of motivations should focus on observable behavior at the crime scene.

The work of investigative analysts at the FBI Academy with the large number of cases seen weekly has led to an expansion of these traditional crime categories. The *Crime Classification Manual* (CCM) makes explicit crime categories that have been used informally and attempts to standardized the language and terminology used throughout the criminal justice system. It classifies the critical characteristics of the perpetrators and victims of major crimes—murder, arson, sexual assault, and nonlethal acts—based on the motivation of the offender.

Douglas & Olshaker (1995), writing on the motivation for writing the CCM, observed that law enforcement had long tried to rely on the psychiatric *Diagnostic and Statistical Manual of Mental Disorders* (DSM) for guidance and definition about what constituted a serious mental disorder and what did not. But many at the FBI Academy found little value in understanding criminals through the DSM. A team of collaborators set out to organize and classify serious crimes by their behavioral characteristics and explain them in a way that a strictly psychological approach could not do. For example, the type of murder scenario of which O. J. Simpson was accused would not be found in the DSM, but it could be found in the CCM. The team's goal was to separate the wheat from the chaff as far as behavioral evidence was concerned and to help investigators and the legal community focus in on which considerations could be relevant and which could not (Douglas & Olshaker, 1995, p. 347).

Jim Clemente, FBI retired special agent, describes the best way that agents in the FBI Behavioral Analysis Unit (BAU) view all human behavior on a continuum or spectrum of behavior. At any given time, an offender may find himself anywhere along that spectrum. He may change positions on that spectrum as time and circumstances change for him. Humans are not behaviorally stagnant. And it is important to remember that the classifications are not simply an intellectual exercise. They are meant as a way to help law enforcement understand pre-, post-, and offending behavior in an effort to identify and apprehend criminals.

Crime Classification: The Decision Process

To classify a crime using the CCM, an investigator needs to ask questions about the victim, the crime scene, and the nature of the victim–offender exchange. The answers to these questions will guide the investigator toward making a decision on how best to classify the offense. However, the optimum use of this manual depends on the quality of information the investigator has concerning the crime.

DEFINING CHARACTERISTICS

The defining characteristics of each offense need to be as comprehensive and complete as possible. Victimology is an essential step in arriving at a possible motive. An investigator who fails to obtain complete victim histories may be overlooking information that could quickly direct the investigation to a motive and suspects.

As one looks through the classification sections in this book, it becomes apparent a blend of motivations inspires many violent crimes. This is especially true when multiple offenders are involved. There may be as many different reasons for the crime as there are offenders.

The approach taken in the CCM for multiple motives is to classify the offense according to the predominant motive. Consider a case in which a husband kills his wife for insurance money. He then attempts to cover the murder with a fire. In addition, he was having an affair, and his wife would not give him a divorce. This homicide has criminal enterprise (financial gain) and personal cause (domestic) motives. It also can be classified as crime conceal-ment under the arson section. The financial considerations should be the primary criteria for classifying this crime. The other applicable categories would be subclassifications. So, once classified, this homicide would appear as follows. For example, the number 107 refers to the category "insurance-related death"; the subcategory of 107.01 refers to "individual profit motive." The number 122 refers to "domestic murder" and the 122.02 refers to "staged domestic homicide." The number 231 refers to the category "crime conceal-ment, murder."

107.01 Individual profit motive
122.02 Staged domestic homicide
231.00 Crime concealment, murder

The investigator will now be able to consult the investigative considera-tions and search warrant suggestions for each of these categories for possible guidance. Prosecutors will also benefit from having all aspects of the crime detailed. Later, other investigators working cases with one or more elements of this offense can use this case or any others with the applicable heading for reference.

The main rule when several of the categories apply (e.g., murder and sexual assault, or sexual assault and arson) is to lead with the crime of highest lethality.

Homicide takes precedence. Next comes arson/bombing and then sexual assault, if applicable.

The following sections describe each of the key elements in categorizing a crime: victimology, crime scene indicators frequently noted, staging, common forensic findings, and investigative considerations.

VICTIMOLOGY

Victimology is the complete history of the victim. (If the crime is arson, then victimology includes targeted property.) It is often one of the most beneficial investigative tools in classifying and solving a violent crime. It is also a crucial part of crime analysis. Through it, the investigator tries to evaluate why this particular person was targeted for a violent crime. Often, just answering this question will lead the investigator to the motive, which will lead to the offender.

Was the victim known to the offender? What were the victim's chances of becoming a target for violent crime? What risk did the offender take in perpetrating this crime? These are some of the important questions investigators should keep in mind as they analyze the crime.

One of the most important aspects of classifying an offense and determining the motive is a thorough understanding of all offender activity with the victim (or targeted property). With sexual assault, this exchange between the victim and offender includes verbal interchange as well as physical and sexual activity.

The tone of the exchange between an offender and a victim of sexual assault is extremely helpful in directing the investigator to an appropriate classification. Excessively vulgar or abusive language, scripting, or apologetic language is common to a certain type of rapist.

A comprehensive victimology should include as much as possible of the information on the victim listed in the sample worksheet.

CRIME SCENE INDICATORS

Of the many elements that constitute the crime scene, not all will be present or recognizable with every offense. The following sections describe the major points investigators should consider when looking at the crime scene, especially as it pertains to crime classification.

Phases of a Crime   A crime can generally be divided into four phases. The first is the precrime stage, which takes into account the "antecedent behavior" of the offender. Often, this is the last stage to obtain knowledge, although it is first in temporal sequence. The second phase is the actual commission of the crime. In this stage there is victim selection as well as the criminal acts themselves, which may include abduction, torture, or rape, as well as the killing. The third phase is the disposal of the body. Some murderers do not display any concern about having the victim's body found, while others go to great lengths to avoid its discovery. The fourth and final phase is postcrime behavior, which in some cases can be important, as some offenders attempt to interject themselves into the investigation of the murder or otherwise keep in touch with the crime to continue the fantasy that started it.

How Many Crime Scenes   How many crime scenes are involved with the offense? There may be one site, as in group excitement homicide. In contrast, the product tamperer may taint the product at one location and then put it on shelves in several stores. The victim may consume the product in one location but die in another location. In this case, there are at least four crime scenes.

The use of several locales during the commission of an offense frequently gives the investigator significant insight into the nature of the offender. One example is the disorganized sexual killer who may confront, assault, kill, and leave the body all in the same location. In contrast, the organized killer may abduct, assault, kill, and dispose of the victim using separate locations for each event.

Environment, Place, and Time   The environment of a crime scene refers to the conditions or circumstances in which the offense occurs. Is it indoors or outside? Was it during daylight hours or in the middle of the night? Did it happen on a busy street or a deserted country road? Answering these questions not only assists in defining the classification of an offense but also provides an assessment of the offender risk. Gauging these risk factors usually offers insight into an offender's motivations and behavioral patterns.

With some offenses, location may have more obvious bearing on the motive and classification than others. An example is street gang murder, in which the homicide is commonly a so-called drive-by in an area of known gang conflict. In other offenses, like arson for excitement, the investigator may not know that the typical location of this crime scene is residential property, as opposed to vandalism arson, which usually involves educational facilities. Adding this information to other characteristics of the arson will often lead the investigator to the classification and, most important, possible motives.

How long did the offender stay at the scene? Generally, the amount of time the offender spends at the scene is proportional to the degree of comfort he feels committing the offense at that particular location. Evidence of a lingering offender will often assist the investigation by directing it toward a subject who lives or works near the crime scene, knows the neighborhood, and consequently feels at ease there.

How Many Offenders?   The answer to this question will help the investigator determine whether to place the offense into the criminal enterprise category or the group cause category. The motive in criminal enterprise murders is for profit. The motive in group cause is based on ideology. The offenses included in both groupings involve multiple offenders.

Organized or Disorganized, Physical Evidence, and Weapon   The general condition of the crime scene is important in classifying a crime. Is it like a group excitement killing: spontaneous and disarrayed with a great deal of physical evidence at the scene? Or does the crime scene reflect a methodical, well-organized subject who did not leave a single print or piece of physical evidence behind? The latter may be seen with an organized crime hit, as in the criminal competition category.

The amount of organization or disorganization at the crime scene will tell much about the offender's level of criminal sophistication. It will also demonstrate how well the offender was able to control the victim and how much premeditation was involved with the crime. It should be emphasized that the crime scene will rarely be completely organized or disorganized. It is more likely to be somewhere on a continuum between the two extremes of the orderly, neat crime scene and the disarrayed, sloppy one.

Another aspect of crime scene examination concerns the weapon. Questions the investigator needs to answer about the weapon include the following: Was it a weapon of choice, brought to the crime scene by the offender? Or was it a weapon of opportunity acquired at the scene? (With arson, did the fire start from materials at hand, or did the offender bring accelerants to the scene?) Is the weapon absent from the crime scene, or has it been left behind? Was there evidence of multiple weapons and ammunition? Multiple weaponry does not always signify multiple offenders. Authority killing and nonspecific motive killing are examples of offenses that often involve the use of multiple firearms and ammunition by a lone offender.

Body Disposition   Was the body openly displayed or otherwise placed in a deliberate manner to ensure discovery? Or was the body concealed or buried to prevent discovery? Did the offender seem to have no concern as to whether the body would be discovered? These are some questions whose answers will aid the classification of a homicide. Certain homicides (disorganized sexual homicide, for example) may involve the intentional arranging of the body in an unnatural or unusual position. In some homicides, like cult murder or drug murder, the body may be left in a degrading position or in a location to convey a message.

Items Left or Missing   The addition or absence of items at the crime scene often assists the investigator in classifying the offense. The presence of unusual artifacts, drawings, graffiti, or other items may be seen with offenses such as extremist murder or street gang murder. Offender communication (such as a ransom demand or extortion note) frequently is associated with the crime scene of a kidnap murder or product tampering.

Items taken from the scene as a crime scene indicator is found in felony murder, breaking and entering, arson for crime concealment, and felony sexual assault. A victim's personal belongings may be taken from the scene of a sexual homicide. These so-called souvenirs (photos, a driver's license, or costume jewelry, for example, all belonging to victim) often may not be monetarily valuable.

Other Crime Scene Indicators   There are other crime scene indicators common to certain offenses that help investigators classify crimes and motives. Examples are wounded victims, no escape plan, and the probability of witnesses. The nature of the confrontation between the victim and offender is also important in determining the motive and classification. How did the offender control the victim? Are restraints present at the scene, or did the offender immediately blitz and incapacitate the victim?

STAGING

Staging is the purposeful alteration of a crime scene. For example, clothing on a victim may be arranged to make it appear to be a sexual assault. The detection and characteristics of staging are covered in Chapter 2.

FORENSIC FINDINGS

Forensic findings are the analysis of physical evidence pertaining to a crime, evidence that is used toward legal proof that a crime occurred. This evidence is often called a silent witness, offering objective facts specific to the commission of a crime. The primary sources of physical evidence are the victim, the suspect, and the crime scene. Secondary sources include the home or work environment of a suspect; however, search warrants are necessary for the collection of such evidence (Moreau, 1987).

Medical reports provide important evidence. These reports include toxicological results, X-ray films, and autopsy findings. In homicide cases, the forensic pathologist identifies and documents the postmortem findings present and interprets the findings within the context of the circumstances of death (Luke, 1988).

Cause of Death   The mechanism of death is often a determining factor when attempting to classify a homicide. The victim of a street gang murder almost always dies from gunshot wounds. Explosive trauma is a frequent forensic finding with many criminal competition and extremist murders. Strangulation is common to the more personal crimes such as domestic murder and sexual homicide.

Trauma The type, extent, and focus of injury sustained by the victim are additional critical factors the investigator uses when classifying a crime. Overkill, facial battery, torture, bite marks, and mutilation are examples of forensic findings that will often lead the investigator to a specific homicide category and, thus, a possible motive for the offense.

Sexual Assault Evidence of assault to the victim's sexual organs or body cavities has great bearing on motive and classification. The type and sequence of the assault is important, as well as the timing of the assault (before, during, or after death).

The investigator should remember that the apparent absence of penetration with the penis does not mean the victim was not sexually assaulted. Sexual assault also includes insertion of foreign objects, regressive necrophilia, and many activities that target the breasts, buttocks, and genitals.

INVESTIGATIVE CONSIDERATIONS AND SEARCH WARRANT SUGGESTIONS

Once the investigator has classified the offense (and thus the motive), the investigative considerations and search warrant suggestions can be used to give direction and assistance to the investigation. It should be emphasized that the considerations examined here are general suggestions and not absolutes that apply in every case.

There are 10 basic steps to a crime scene search:

1. Approach the scene.
2. Secure and protect the scene.
3. Conduct a preliminary survey.
4. Narratively describe the scene.
5. Photograph the scene.
6. Sketch the scene.
7. Evaluate latent fingerprint evidence and other forms of evidence.
8. Conduct a detailed search for evidence, and collect, preserve, document the evidence.
9. Make the final survey.
10. Release the scene.

The forensic analysis of physical evidence of hair and fibers, blood, semen, and saliva can provide the basis for critical testimony in court.

Exhibit 1.1 is a worksheet that outlines the defining characteristics of each of the categories. Under each characteristic are some of the aspects that will assist investigators in classifying the offense.

Classification by Type, Style, and Number of Victims

Crimes may be classified by type, style, and number of victims. Using the homicide classification as an example, the following definitions are used by the FBI BAU.

Single murder: Unlawful killing of one victim.

Double murder: Unlawful killing of two victims at the same location in a single continuous criminal episode.

Triple murder: Unlawful killing of three victims at the same location in a single continuous criminal episode.

Mass murder: Unlawful killing of four of more victims by the same offender(s) acting in concert, at one location in a single continuous event that may last minutes, hours, or days.

Serial murder: The unlawful killing of two or more victims by the same offender(s) in separate events. [A qualitative rather than a quantitative term related to the motivation and intent of the offender. It is time and circumstance dependent. That is, over time the number of victims may rise as the circumstances are such that a victim is available, vulnerable, and desirable and the offender is able to carry out his intended crimes. Research definitions may vary depending on available data sets and goals.] The "cooling off" period is now considered a historical term.

Spree murder: A historical term used to describe the killing of two or more victims in a single, extended criminal event at two or more locations over an uninterrupted period of time; typically, the killings serve a common purpose such as sensationalism, evading capture, and/or suicide by cop. [The uninterrupted period of time may vary in length, with the determinative factor being the ongoing nature of the crimes. One crime typically runs into the next, separated only by distance and travel time, forming an unbroken chain of criminal events.]

Serial killing: Title 18 USC: . . . A pattern of three or more murders, not less than one of which was committed within the United States, having common characteristics such as to suggest the reasonable possibility that the crimes were committed by the same actor or actors. [This statutory definition was created by Congress for the purpose of setting the jurisdictional standards for federal involvement in investigations of this nature.] (FBI BAU, 2008)

Crime Classification Numbering System

The numbering system for classifying crimes uses three digits, with the first digit representing the major crime category. All possible codes are not currently assigned in anticipation of future editions. There are five major crime categories in this edition: homicide, arson/bombing, rape and sexual assault, nonlethal crimes, and computer crime, with the last two new to this edition. The homicide category is identified by the number 1 (codes 100 to 199), arson/bombing by the number 2 (codes 200 to 299), rape and sexual assault by the number 3 (codes 300 to 399), nonlethal crimes by the number 4 (codes 400 to 499), computer crimes by the number 5 (codes 500 to 599), and global crimes by the number 6 (codes 600 to 699). As other major crimes categories are classified, they will be assigned appropriate identification codes.

The second digit of the code represents further grouping of the major crimes. Homicides are divided into four groups: criminal enterprise (100 to 109), personal cause (120 to 129), sexual (130 to 139), and group cause (140 to 149). There are unassigned numbers that allow for future editions within specific categories and additional groups within a major category. The third digit of the code represents specific classifications within these groups.

Individual classifications within these groups are further divided into subgroups using two additional digits following a decimal point after the code. The division into subgroups occurs when there are unique characteristics within a factor that clearly identify a major difference with the group. For example, domestic homicide (code 122) has two subgroups: spontaneous domestic homicide (122.01) and staged domestic homicide (122.02). Additional codes are added after the subgroup to identify crimes by the type of victim (child, adolescent, adult ages 20 to 59, and elder adults age 60 and over) if there are unique characteristics associate with the age of victims.

Exhibit 1.1

   I. Victimology: Why did this person become the victim of a violent crime?
      A. About the victim
         Lifestyle
         Employment
         Personality
         Friends (type, number)
         Income (amount, source)
         Family
         Alcohol/drug use or abuse
         Normal dress
         Handicaps

Transportation used

Reputation, habits, fears

Marital status

Dating habits

Leisure activities

Criminal history

Assertiveness

Likes and dislikes

Significant events prior to the crime

Activities prior to the crime

B. Sexual assault: verbal interaction

Excessively vulgar or abusive

Scripting

Apologetic

C. Arson and bombing: targeted property

Residential

Commercial

Educational

Mobile, vehicle

Forest, fields

II. Crime scene

How many?

Environment, time, place

How many offenders?

Organized, disorganized

Physical evidence

Weapon

Body disposition

Items left/missing

Other (e.g., witnesses, escape plan, wounded victims)

III. Staging

Natural death

Accidental

Suicide

Criminal activity (i.e., robbery, rape/homicide)

IV. Forensic findings

A. Forensic analysis

Hair/fibers

Blood

Semen

Saliva

Other

B. Autopsy results

Cause of death

Trauma (type, extent, location on body)

Overkill

Torture

Facial battery (depersonalization)

Bite marks

Mutilation

Sexual assault (when, sequence, to where, insertion, insertional necrophilia)

Toxicological results

V. Investigative considerations

A. Search warrants

Home

Work

Car

Other

B. Locating and interviewing witnesses

References

Bromberg, W. (1965). *Crime and the mind: A psychiatric analysis of crime and punishment.* New York, NY: Macmillan.

Brown, J. M., & Langan, P. A. (2001). Policing and Homicide, 1976–98: Justifiable Homicide of Felons by Police and Murder of Police by Felons. Bureau of Justice. Retrieved December 5, 2012, from http://bjs.ojp.usdoj.gov/index.cfm?ty=pbdetail&iid=829

Criscione, V. (2012). Found sane, Norway killer Breivik gets 21 years in prison. *Christian Science Monitor.* Retrieved August 24, 2012, from www.csmonitor.com/World/Europe/2012/0824/Found-sane-Norway-killer-Breivik-gets-21-years-in-prison-video

Douglas, J. D., & Olshaker, M. (1995). *Mindhunter: Inside the FBI's elite serial crime unit.* New York, NY: Scribner.

Federal Bureau of Investigation, Behavioral Analysis Unit. (2008). *Serial murder: Multi-disciplinary perspectives for investigators.* Washington, DC: Author. Retrieved August 22, 2012, from www.fbi.gov/stats-services/publications/serial-murder/serial-murder-july-2008-pdf

Federal Bureau of Investigation, Uniform Crime Reports. (2001). *Crime in the United States, 1976–98.* See also www.ojp.usdoj.gov/bjs/homicide/addinfo.htm

Gilbert, J. N. (1983). A study of the increased rate of unsolved criminal homicide in San Diego, CA, and its relationship to police investigative effectiveness. *American Journal of Police: An Interdisciplinary Journal of Theory and Research, 2*(2) [149–166].

Glueck, B. (1918). 608 admissions to Sing Sing. *Mental Hygiene, 2,* 85.

Goddard, H. H. (1914). *Feeblemindness: Its cause and consequences.* New York, NY: Macmillan.

Goring, C. (1913). *The English convict.* London, England: H. M. Stationary Office.

Knight, R. A., & Prentky, R. A. (1990). Classifying sexual offenders: The development and corroboration of taxonomic models. In W. L. Marshall, D. R. Laws, & H. E. Barbaree (Eds.), *Handbook of sexual assault.* New York, NY: Plenum.

Knight, R. A., Rosenberg, R., & Schneider, B. A. (1985). Classification of sexual offenders: Perspectives, methods, and validation. In A. W. Burgess (Ed.), *Rape and sexual assault.* New York, NY: Garland.

Lindesmith, A. R., & Dunham, H. W. (1941). Some principles of criminal typology. Social Forces, 19, 307–314.

Luke, J. L. (1988). The role of forensic pathology in criminal profiling. In R. Ressler, A. Burgess, & J. Douglas (Eds.), *Sexual homicide.* Lanham, MD: Lexington Books.

Megargee, E. I., & Bohn, M. J. (1979). *Classifying criminal offenders: A new system based on the MMPI.* Thousand Oaks, CA: Sage.

Moreau, D. (1987). Concepts of physical evidence in sexual assault investigations. In R. Hazelwood & A. W. Burgess (Eds.), *Practical rape investigation: A multidisciplinary approach.* New York, NY: Elsevier.

National Commission on Law Observance and Enforcement. (1931). *Guide to federal records in the National Archives of the United States.* Compiled by Robert B. Matchette et al. Washington, DC: National Archives and Records Administration, 1995. Retrieved July 4, 2012, from www.archives.gov/research/guide-fed-records/groups/010.html

Rennie, Y. (1977). *The search for criminal man: The dangerous offender project.* Lanham, MD: Lexington Books.

Richardson, D. A., & Kosa, R. (2001). *An examination of homicide clearance rates: Foundation for the development of a homicide clearance model.* Washington, DC: Police Executive Research Forum.

Roebuck, J. B. (1967). *Criminal typology* (2nd ed.). Springfield, IL: Charles C. Thomas.

Wortley, R., & Smallbone, S. (2006, May). *Child pornography on the Internet. U.S. Department of Justice, Office of Community Oriented Policing Services. Problemspecific Guides Series No. 41.* Retrieved July 4, 2012, from www.cops.usdoj.gov

Chapter 2

Criminal Investigative Concepts in Crime Scene Analysis

John E. Douglas and Lauren K. Douglas

In 1989 Chuck and Carol Stuart were on their way home from a prenatal birthing class when, according to Chuck, a 5 foot 5 inch Black man weighing 150 to 165 pounds abducted the couple, forcing them to drive to Mission Hill, a racially mixed Boston neighborhood where drug abuse and crime are common. After robbing the couple, said Stuart, the perpetrator shot Carol in the head and then shot Chuck in the stomach. Carol died that night in the hospital; their infant, who was delivered by cesarean section, died 17 days later. The story was covered heavily by the media, with commentators pronouncing how fortunate Chuck was to be alive.

As part of the investigation, police began to stop Black men randomly on the streets in the hope of eventually finding the killer. A few days after the shooting, police arrested William Bennett for a video store robbery. Bennett soon became the prime suspect in Carol Stuart's murder. Chuck even identified Bennett as the perpetrator in a police lineup.

As investigators began to explore Chuck's background, however, rumors flew that he was having money troubles, had a girlfriend, and had taken out a life insurance policy on his wife. Investigators became suspicious of Chuck's recount of the abduction and murder. Chuck had told the police that the perpetrator had shot him and his wife from the back seat of his car. Investigators were curious how the offender was able to shoot Chuck in the stomach from such an odd angle. The question was also raised as to why Chuck chose to call 911 first before attempting to help his dying pregnant wife. Chuck's brother would later identify Chuck as the actual killer. Chuck had shot his pregnant wife and then himself, staging the crime scene to look as though a third party were responsible. Chuck Stuart ended up committing suicide, and William Bennett was a free man.

Behavior reflects personality. Everything observed at a crime scene tells a story and reflects something about the unknown subject (UNSUB) who committed the crime. The crime scene and forensic evidence contain messages that will lead to the answers the investigators need to solve the crime. By studying crimes and talking to perpetrators who have committed violent crimes, investigators can learn to apply and solve the equation of Why + How = Who. During this process, investigators attempt to interpret clues left by the UNSUB at the scene, similar to a doctor who evaluates symptoms to diagnose a particular disease or condition. As a doctor begins forming a diagnosis and treatment plan based on his or her experience, an investigator correspondingly conducts crime analysis when he or she sees patterns emerge. Based on the analysis, leads and tactics can be developed to help investigators identify the UNSUB.

A major part of the process of crime scene analysis depends on the analyst's insight into the dynamics of human behavior. Speech patterns, writing styles, verbal and nonverbal gestures, and other traits and patterns compose human behavior. This combination causes every individual to act, react, function, or perform in a unique and specific way. This individualistic behavior usually remains consistent, whether it concerns keeping house, selecting a wardrobe, or raping and murdering.

The commission of a violent crime involves all the same dynamics of normal human behavior. The same forces that influence normal everyday conduct also influence the offender's actions during an offense. The crime scene usually reflects these behavior patterns or gestures. Learning to recognize the crime scene manifestations of this behavior enables an investigator to discover much about the offender. Due to the personalized nature of this behavior, the investigator also has a means to distinguish among different offenders committing the same offense.

This chapter discusses the investigative concepts of modus operandi, signature, personation, and staging that form the foundation for identifying patterns of criminal behaviors.

The Assessment

One aspect of interpreting the behavior patterns of an offense depends on attention to details. These details often escape notice during the initial phase of protecting and preserving the crime scene. A violent crime may not only emotionally detach the investigator from the offense, but it may also desensitize that investigator to minute clues offered by the crime scene. Another pitfall that obscures these important details is the inability of the investigator to achieve a comfortable distance from the crime. Identification with the victim, perhaps relating the victim to a family member, prevents detachment from the crime, and judgment may become clouded by emotion. By taking quality crime scene photographs, investigators will be in a better position to detach themselves from a highly emotional situation.

The assessment phase of crime analysis attempts to answer several questions. What was the sequence of events? Was the victim sexually assaulted before or after death? Was mutilation before or after death? Observations like this can offer important insights into an offender's personality. How did the encounter between the offender and victim occur? Did the offender blitz-attack the victim, or did he use verbal means (the con) to capture her? Did the offender use ligatures to control the victim? Finally, any items added to or taken from the crime scene require careful analysis.

The Modus Operandi

Modus operandi (MO) is learned behavior, what the perpetrator does to commit the crime. It is dynamic—that is, it can change as the perpetrator progresses in his criminal career and realizes that one action or technique works better for him than another.

The MO has great significance when investigators attempt to link cases. An appropriate step of crime analysis and correlation is to connect cases due to similarities in MO. However, an investigator who rejects an offense as the work of a serial offender solely on the basis of disparities in MO has made a mistake. What causes an offender to use a certain MO? What influences shape it? Is it static or dynamic? The answers to these questions help investigators avoid the error of attributing too much significance to MO when linking crimes.

Actions taken by an offender during the perpetration of a crime in order to perpetrate that crime form the MO. MO is a learned set of behaviors that the offender develops and sticks with it because it works, but it is dynamic and malleable. In any criminal career, no matter what the circumstances, the MO will evolve with the criminal. Every criminal makes mistakes, but most learn from them and try to get better with time, as the following example shows.

Late one night, a novice prowler prepared to enter a house through a basement window to burglarize it. The window was closed and locked, so the prowler shattered the window to gain access to the house. He had to rush his search for valuables because he feared the breaking window had awakened the residents of the home. For his next late-night residential burglary, he brought tools to force the lock and keep the noise to a minimum. This allowed him more time to commit the crime and obtain a more profitable haul. However, he was still nervous about the prospect of waking the residents of his target home, so he began targeting unoccupied homes and switched to midmorning break-ins. This also allowed him better light by which to see the valuables he was after, an added advantage.

This offender's original MO was to break and enter through the window of a residence at night, then steal valuables and escape. Through experience, his MO evolved to forcing the lock on windows in unoccupied homes during the day. He refined his breaking and entering techniques to lower his risk of apprehension and increase his profit. This is very common among offenders who repeatedly commit property crimes. He saw challenges to his enterprise, figured out how to overcome them, and incorporated the techniques into his MO. He might have found another way to avoid the noise of a broken window; for example, he might have watched for the location of a hidden door key and used that to gain entrance or begun targeting unguarded and unoccupied offices at night instead of residences.

The offender learns from challenges that trip him up as well. Had that original broken window resulted in his arrest and incarceration, he would have tried not to repeat that mistake if he chose to return to burglary after his release.

In violent crimes, victims' responses can significantly influence the evolution of an offender's MO. If a rapist has problems controlling a victim, he will modify his MO to accommodate and overcome resistance. He may bring duct tape or other ligatures, he may use a weapon, or he may blitz-attack the victim and immediately incapacitate her. If such measures are ineffective, he may resort to greater violence, including killing the victim.

The Signature Aspect

Signature, while it may evolve, does not change radically. It is what the perpetrator has to do to fulfill himself. For example, a single bullet or other "clean kill" would be considered MO. A savage "overkill" would be a signature element.

The violent serial offender often exhibits another element of criminal behavior during an offense: his signature, or calling card. This criminal conduct goes beyond the actions necessary to perpetrate the crime—the MO—and points to the unique personality of the offender.

Unlike MO, a serial offender's signature will never change at its core. Certain details may be refined over time (e.g., the lust murderer who performs greater postmortem mutilation as he progresses from crime to crime), but the basis of the signature will remain the same (performing postmortem mutilations in this example).

What makes up this signature? Surviving victims or witnesses sometimes attest to the behavioral elements of the signature. For example, a rapist may demonstrate part of his signature by engaging in acts of domination, manipulation, or control during the verbal, physical, or sexual phase of the assault. Exceptionally vulgar or abusive language or scripting is a verbal signature. When the offender scripts a victim, he demands a particular verbal response from her (e.g., "Tell me how much you enjoy sex with me" or "Tell me how good I am"). A rapist might also stick to his own sort of script by engaging in phases or types of sexual activities in a set order with different victims.

The crime scene can include aspects of an offender's signature in, for instance, evidence of excessive force. A large amount of blood ranging around the home in which a violent crime occurred might demonstrate that the victim was moved or dragged around the area as the offender used more force than necessary to subdue (in the case of rape) or kill (in the case of murder).

The signature is not necessarily evident in each of a serial offender's crimes. Contingencies can arise, such as interruptions or unexpected victim responses, that cause the offender to abandon these unnecessary steps. In such instances, the offender will be much less satisfied or gratified by his offense.

Why is this? Violent crimes often originate with offender fantasies. This is particularly true for serial offenders. As they brood and daydream, they develop a more and more compelling need to express their violent fantasies. When they finally act out, some aspects of the crime will demonstrate their unique personal expression based on these fantasies. This is *personation*. As an offender acts out again (and again), this personation will be repeated and is his signature. The elements that comprise signature are the most specific manifestations of his fantasies; they are therefore the most meaningful to him.

Another reason for the absence of signature elements in some crimes committed by serial offenders is that the investigator does not always have a surviving victim or even a crime scene to work with. Violent offenses often involve high-risk victims, which may mean no one reports them missing, so there is no search for them or their bodies. Many offenders dump bodies outside, away from the scene of the crime and in an isolated spot. This may result in a great deal of decomposition, which obscures signs of signature on the victim's body and clothing. And if the body has been dumped, the actual crime scene is somewhere else, along with most of the indicators of signature.

Nevertheless, although detecting a signature or calling card is a challenge, it can be the biggest piece of the puzzle in identifying a serial offender. It is an unfortunate truth that the more victims there are, the more indicators of signature there are. Investigators want to stop violent serial offenders, but it often takes evidence gathered from multiple victims, crime scenes, dump sites, witnesses, and so on to identify signature elements that will link the crimes to a serial offender.

Modus Operandi or Signature?

A rapist entered a residence and captured a woman and her husband. The offender ordered the husband to lie on his stomach on the floor. He then placed a cup and saucer on the husband's back. "If I hear that cup move or hit the floor, your wife dies," he told the husband. He forced the wife into the next room and raped her. In another situation, a rapist entered a house and ordered the woman to phone her husband and use some ploy to get him home. Once the husband arrived, the offender tied him to a chair and forced him to witness the rape of his wife.

The rapist who used the cup and saucer had developed an effective MO to control the husband: he had dealt with the obstacle that stood between him and his goal. The second rapist went beyond this. The full satisfaction of his fantasies required not only raping the wife, but also finding, summoning home, humiliating, and dominating the husband. The first rapist dealt with the husband because he was there; he kept him from witnessing or interfering with the rape. The second rapist needed the husband to be there and, furthermore, needed him to witness the rape. His personal needs compelled him to perform this signature aspect of crime.

In Michigan, a bank robber made the tellers undress during a robbery. In Texas, another bank robber also forced the bank employees to undress; in addition, he made them pose in sexually provocative positions as he took photographs. Do both crimes demonstrate a signature aspect?

The Michigan robber used a very effective means to increase the odds of his escape. He probably guessed or knew that the tellers would get dressed before calling the police. When interviewed, these employees offered vague, meager descriptions because their embarrassment had prevented eye contact with the perpetrator. This subject had developed a clever MO. The Texas robber, however, went beyond the required actions to perpetrate his crime. The act of robbing the bank did not gratify his psychosexual needs. He felt compelled to enact the ritual of posing the tellers and taking pictures, leaving his signature on the crime. The distinction between MO and signature can go a long way in understanding the actions and motivation of a particular perpetrator.

Linking Cases

In September 1989, a Shreveport, Louisiana, man named Nathaniel Code Jr. stood trial for murder. The jury determined Code had murdered eight people between 1984 and 1987. These eight homicides took place during three different events: one murder in 1984, four in 1985, and three in 1987. There were several disparities in modus operandi (actions taken by an offender during the perpetration of a crime in order to perpetrate that crime) and victimology (characteristics of the victims) among the three crime scenes.

Could one man be linked to the murders at all three scenes? With differences in modus operandi (MO) and victimology, what could link Code with each of these eight homicides? MO and victimology are important factors in an investigation, but they are often somewhat generalized and offer less information about the subtle details of personality and, ultimately, identity that are often necessary to track down an offender. However, personation, that is, the offender's signature, or his "calling card," is an individualized set of indicators that can point specifically to an offender's personality. In the case of multiple crimes committed by the same (or serial) offender, there is often repeated personation. This was true in the case of Nathaniel Code. He left his signature—gags, duct tape, and bodies with gunshot wounds and slashed throats—at each of the three crime scenes. This linked Code with all eight murders.

No one in contemporary law enforcement would dispute that our society has far too many Nathaniel Codes. The increase of violent crime has compelled law enforcement to develop new measures to address it. One important step is the recognition of the serial offender, who often crosses jurisdictional boundaries. Any effective effort among local, state, and federal agencies depends on early recognition of a serial offender as such; different jurisdictions looking for the same offender need to recognize that they are after the same person and cooperate with one another. But the common crossing of multiple jurisdictional lines by offenders makes this a great challenge. Comprehensive analysis of victimology, crime scene, and forensics, as well as the careful interview and examination of any living victims to gather information about the offender's verbal and nonverbal behavior, can help an agency discover a serial offender within its own jurisdiction or among several others.

The MO has great significance when investigators attempt to link cases. An appropriate step of crime analysis and correlation is to connect cases due to similarities in MO. However, an investigator who rejects an offense as the work of a serial offender solely on the basis of disparities in MO (as in the Code cases) has made a mistake. What causes an offender to use a certain MO? What influences shape it? Is it static or dynamic? The answers to these questions help investigators avoid the error of attributing too much significance to MO when linking crimes.

When investigators attempt to link cases, MO plays an important role. However, MO should not be the only criterion used to connect crimes, especially with repeat offenders who alter the MO through experience and learning. The first offenses may differ considerably from later ones; nevertheless, the signature aspect remains the same, whether it is the first offense or one committed 10 years later. The ritual may evolve, but the theme persists.

The signature aspect also should usually receive greater consideration than victimology (this should not be discounted, however) when investigators attempt to link cases to one another or to a specific serial offender. For instance, physical similarities among victims may not be significant indicators when crimes are motivated by anger; in such cases, the signature will tell investigators much more about the offender than victimology will.

Cases Linked by Offender Signature

RONNIE SHELTON

During the 1980s, Cleveland, Ohio, was terrorized by a man who became known as the West Side Rapist. When he was finally caught, Ronnie Shelton was found guilty of 49 rapes, 29 aggravated burglaries, 18 felonious assaults, 60 counts of gross sexual imposition, 12 kidnappings, 19 counts of intimidation, 3 counts of cutting telephone lines, 2 thefts, and 27 aggravated robberies. He was convicted on 220 counts of the indictment. The judge gave him 3,198 years, the longest sentence in Ohio history.

Shelton's MO included entering the victim's dwelling through a window or patio facing a wooded area or bushes offering concealment. He wore a ski mask, stocking, or scarf. He was initially violent, threatening the victim, throwing the victim to the floor, or holding a knife to her throat. But he would then calm her down by convincing her he was not there to rape but to rob her, saying, "I just want money," or something similar. When he had the victim under control, he would return to the violent mode. Shelton would use such phrases as, "Keep your eyes down," "Cover your eyes," or "Don't look at me and I won't kill you [or hurt your kids]." Before he left, he would verbally intimidate the victim with warnings such as, "Don't call the police or I'll come back and kill you."

It was in his verbal approach and the nature of his sexual assaults that Shelton's signature was evident. He was verbally degrading and exceptionally vulgar. He also would say such things as, "I have seen you with your boyfriend," "I've seen you around," or "You know who I am." He would rape the victim vaginally, withdraw, and ejaculate on the victim's stomach or breasts. He would then frequently masturbate over the victim or between her breasts. He often used the victim's clothing to wipe off his ejaculate. Shelton forced many of his victims to perform oral sex on him and then insisted they swallow the ejaculate. He would also force them to masturbate him manually. A combination of these acts was Shelton's signature.

One puzzling element of the assaults was that the rapist's earlier victims described a bump on the rapist's penis, while later victims did not. Shelton's signature linked him with all the assaults, despite the difference in descriptions. Had his signature not been recognized, he might not have been punished for many of his crimes.

As it turned out, there was a simple explanation for the difference in physical descriptions: Shelton had undergone a procedure to remove genital warts, so the "bump" had been removed before the later victims were assaulted.

Serial Killers and Signature Crime

STEVEN PENNELL

Steven Pennell was a sexual sadist who murdered at least three victims. His MO involved using duct tape and ligatures to control his victims while he tortured them. He used hammer blows to kill them (Douglas, 1989).

Pennell's signature could be seen in the nature of the wounds inflicted on his victims. He targeted the buttocks and breasts, beating and pinching them with tools, including a hammer and pliers. The victims were kept alive during these assaults because Pennell derived sexual gratification from their response to torture. Autopsy results confirmed that none of the victims had been sexually assaulted.

The victims also had ligature marks around their necks, although the blunt-force trauma to the head was the cause of death. Pennell enjoyed tightening the ligature to the point of near strangulation. Because he required his victims to be alive and conscious during torture, he did not kill them this way. Strangulation was part of his signature, not the MO. It was a method to cause extreme suffering in order to fulfill his sadistic fantasy.

Body disposal was similar for the victims. Pennell left their bodies in full view, dumped with cold indifference by roadsides. The absence of remorse demonstrated by Pennell's body disposal methods can be considered another aspect of his calling card.

The violence escalated as Pennell's ritual matured and his fantasies seasoned. The last victim suffered the greatest amount of antemortem trauma and postmortem mutilation. Again, Pennell targeted the breasts. But in this victim's case, there was postmortem mutilation to the breasts rather than antemortem mutilation, as had been evident with his other victims. This caused some to debate whether this victim bore Pennell's signature and whether she had in fact been killed by him.

There were two reasons that this case could be linked to Pennell. His signature was still evident with this victim. First, he had inflicted a great deal of injury to the victim's buttocks while she was alive. Therefore, the signature aspect of torturing a live victim was present, but it was evolving. With each victim, the torture became more brutal. As stated earlier, interference with the ritual due to contingencies arising will alter an offender's ritual. This victim probably died before Pennell completed his ritual mutilations, so the signature appeared to be somewhat different but actually was the same. Second, victimology strengthened the connection between these victims and Pennell. The victims were all high risk: they were prostitutes or had a history of drug abuse, or both. They disappeared from the same area, a state highway, and police recovered the bodies within a few miles of each other.

Personation

Most violent crime careers have a quiet, isolated beginning within the offender's imagination. The subject fantasizes about raping, torturing, killing, building bombs, setting fires, or any combination of these violent acts. When the offender translates these fantasies into action, his emotional needs compel him to exhibit violent behavior during the commission of a crime.

One of the first cases brought to the National Center for the Analysis of Violent Crime (NCAVC) was the 1979 homicide of a 26-year-old White female on the roof of her apartment in New York City. The cause of death was ligature strangulation. The UNSUB left the victim's body face up and positioned her body to resemble a Jewish religious medal. He carefully removed her earrings and placed them on either side of her head. He cut her nipples off and placed them on her chest. The offender also inserted her umbrella into the vagina and placed her comb into the pubic hair. He then placed the victim's nylons around her wrists and ankles. He scrawled a derogatory message to police on her body using her pen. Finally, he left a pile of his feces, covered with her clothing, a few feet from the body. The NCAVC assessed all of this activity as being postmortem. A few inexpensive articles of jewelry were missing, including the Jewish religious medal that resembled the body's positioning.

This crime scene displayed some unusual input by this offender. The perpetration of this crime did not require the positioning of the body, the postmortem mutilation, insertion and removal of items, and use of postmortem ligatures. The significance of this behavior was not readily apparent to the investigator. The act of sexual assault and murder had little to do with most of this offender's behavior at the crime scene. His behavior went far beyond the actions necessary to carry out this offense (the MO) because assault and murder alone would not satisfy his needs.

Personation is unusual behavior by an offender, beyond that necessary to commit the crime. The offender invests intimate meaning into the crime scene (e.g., by posing the victim, mutilation, items removed or left, or other symbolic gestures involving the crime scene). Only the offender knows the meaning of these acts. Signature is when a serial offender demonstrates repetitive ritualistic behavior from crime to crime. The signature aspect of a crime is simply repetitive personation.

Undoing represents a form of personation with more obvious meaning. Undoing frequently occurs at the crime scene when there is a close association between the offender and the victim or when the victim represents someone of significance to the offender.

The following case exemplifies undoing. A son stabbed his mother to death during a fierce argument. After calming down, the son realized the full impact of his actions. First, he changed the victim's bloodied shirt and then placed her body on the couch with her head on a pillow. He covered her with a blanket and folded her hands over her chest so she appeared to be sleeping peacefully. This behavior indicated his remorse by attempting to emotionally undo the murder. Other forms of undoing may include the offender's washing up, cleaning the body, covering the victim's face, or completely covering the body. The offender engages in these activities not because he is attempting to hide the victim but because he may be feeling some degree of remorse.

Staging

Staging is someone's purposely altering the crime scene prior to the arrival of police. There are two reasons that someone employs staging: to redirect the investigation away from the most logical suspect or to protect the victim or victim's family.

When a crime is staged, the responsible person is not someone who just happens upon the victim. It is usually someone who had some kind of association or relationship with the victim. This offender will further attempt to steer the investigation away from him by his conduct when in contact with law enforcement. Thus, investigators should never eliminate a suspect solely on the grounds of that person's overly cooperative or distraught behavior.

A double homicide case that received national publicity involved Susan Smith, the mother of Alex and Michael, who purposely let her car, with her two small sons inside, roll into John D. Long Lake in Union, South Carolina. Smith first went to a nearby home, where she banged on the door, screaming, "He's got my kids and he's got my car. A Black man has got my kids and my car." The homeowners called 911. Smith told police that she was stopped at a red light when a Black man jumped in her car and told her to drive. Eventually, Smith said, the man told her to get out of the car and he proceeded to drive off with her children.

Smith attempted to steer the investigation away from her by creating a false scenario to detract police. She was interviewed on many occasions, and police began to catch the inconsistencies in her story. In addition, the manner in which she spoke of her children's disappearances made police question her as a potential suspect. During numerous interviews, Smith spoke about her sons in the past tense; at one point she said, "No man would ever make me hurt my children." This statement told police that she believed her children were not alive. Police began to focus the investigation on Smith, who ultimately confessed during an interview with an investigator.

A landmark case for the NCAVC in the use of signature analysis was the 1991 trial of George Russell Jr., charged with the bludgeoning and strangulation murder of three women in Seattle. Each victim was blitz-attacked, with all three killings happening over a seven-week period. All three women were left naked and posed provocatively and degradingly. The sexual content of the posed scene escalated from one victim to the next. The first victim was posed with hands clasped and legs crossed at the ankles and left near a sewer grate and trash dumpster. The second victim was posed on a bed with a pillow over her head, her legs bent out to each side, a rifle inserted into her vagina, and red high heels on her feet. The final victim was posed on her bed with her legs spread, with a dildo in her mouth, and a copy of *The Joy of Sex* placed under her left arm.

The blitz attacks were necessary to kill these women; the degrading posing was not. One of the chapter authors (J.E.D.) would testify at the hearing, advising jurors of the fact that there are not many cases of posing, that is, when the offender treats the victim like a prop to leave a specific message. These crimes are usually crimes of anger and of power. It is the thrill of the hunt, the thrill of the kill, and the thrill afterward of how the offender leaves the victim that makes the offender feel as though he has beaten the system. Douglas, relying on the signature aspects of the crimes, believed that whoever killed one of these victims killed all three. A jury ultimately found Russell guilty of one count of first-degree murder and two counts of aggravated first-degree murder. He was sentenced to life in prison without possibility of parole.

Increasing numbers of anti-Semitic hate crimes show staging. In March 2004, Kerri Dunn, a professor at Claremont McKenna College, reported her car had been vandalized in the campus parking lot. The police report confirmed her car windows had been broken; the tires slashed; and a swastika, "Kike Whore," and "Nigger Lover" painted on the doors and hood of the vehicle. The Jewish community was understandably upset by the incident and demanded that the college administration take some action to prevent this type of behavior from occurring in the future. The upheaval ended when two students told investigators they witnessed Dunn vandalizing her own car. It was known that Dunn was in the process of converting from Catholicism to Judaism, which may be one of the reasons that she committed the act. There was also speculation that perhaps it was a mandatory initiation rite. A jury ultimately found Dunn guilty of staging the anti-Semitic hate crime.

Another reason for staging is to protect the victim or victim's family and is employed most frequently with rape–murder crimes or autoerotic fatalities. The offender of a sexual homicide frequently leaves the victim in a degrading position. One can hardly fault a family member's protective staging behavior, but the investigator needs to obtain an accurate description of the body's condition when found and exactly what that person did to alter the crime scene.

This type of staging is also prevalent with autoerotic fatalities. The victim may be removed from the apparatus that caused death (e.g., cut down from a noose or device suspending the body). In many cases, the victim wears a mask or costume. The costume often involves cross-dressing, so not only does the person discovering the body have to endure the shock of finding the victim dead, but also the shock of finding the victim in female dress. To prevent further damage to the victim's or family's reputation or to protect other family members, the person discovering the body may redress the victim in men's clothing or dress the nude body. He or she will often stage the accident to look like a suicide, perhaps writing a suicide note. This person may even go as far as staging the scene to appear as a homicide. Nevertheless, scrutiny of forensics, crime scene dynamics, and victimology probably will reveal the true circumstances surrounding death. Evidence of previous autoerotic activities (bondage literature, adult "toys," eyebolts in the ceiling, worn spots from rope on beams) in the victim's home also will help determine if an autoerotic activity caused death.

Finally, the investigator should discern whether a crime scene is truly disorganized or whether the offender staged it to appear careless and haphazard. This determination not only helps direct the analysis to the underlying motive, but also helps to shape the offender profile. However, the recognition of staging, especially with a shrewd offender, can be difficult. The investigator must scrutinize all factors of the crime if there is reason to believe it has been staged. Forensics, victimology, and minute crime scene details become critical to the detection of staging.

CRIME SCENE RED FLAGS

An offender who stages a crime scene usually makes mistakes because he stages it to look the way he thinks a crime scene should look. While doing this, the offender experiences a great deal of stress and does not have time to fit all the pieces together logically. Inconsistencies thus begin appearing at the crime scene, with the forensics, and with the overall picture of the offense. These contradictions often serve as the red flags of staging and prevent misguidance of the investigation.

These red flags often occur in the form of crime scene inconsistencies. The investigator should scrutinize all crime scene indicators individually and then view them in the context of the whole picture. Several important questions need to be asked during crime scene analysis. First, did the subject take inappropriate items from the crime scene if burglary appears to be the motive?

In one case submitted to the NCAVC, a man returning home from work interrupted a burglary in progress. The startled burglars killed the man as he attempted to flee. A later inventory revealed the offenders had not stolen anything, but it appeared they had begun taking apart a large stereo and TV unit for removal. Analysis of the crime scene indicated the offenders passed over smaller items, including jewelry and coin collections, of greater worth. With further investigation, police discovered that the victim's wife had paid the offenders to stage the burglary and kill her husband. She was having an affair with one of the offenders.

Second, did the point of entry make sense? For example, an offender enters a house by a second-story window despite the presence of easier, less conspicuous entry points.

Third, did the perpetration of this crime pose a high risk to the offender? In other words, did it happen during daylight hours, in a populated area, with obvious signs of occupation at the house (lights on, vehicles in the driveway), or involving highly visible entry points? The following case illustrates some of these points.

In a small northeastern city, an unknown intruder attacked a man and his wife one Saturday morning. The offender had placed a ladder against the house, climbed up to a second-story window, and entered after removing the screen. This all occurred in a residential area during a time when the neighbors were awake. The husband had peered outside his bedroom door and saw a figure going downstairs; he then followed with a gun. He claimed the offender struck him on the head after a struggle and then returned upstairs and killed his wife by manual strangulation. The victim's body was found with her nightgown pulled up around her waist, implying she had been sexually assaulted.

As the detectives processed the crime scene, they noted that the offender's weight on the ladder had left no impressions in the ground. However, when the police investigator placed one foot on the bottom rung, the ladder left an impression. In addition, the offender had positioned the ladder backward, with the rungs going in the wrong direction. Many of the rotted rungs could never have supported even 50 pounds of weight. It was observed that the offender neither left foot impressions nor was debris transferred from the rungs to the roof, where he supposedly gained entrance through a second-story window.

Why didn't the offender choose an entrance through a first-story window? This would have decreased the chance of detection from both the occupants and the neighbor. Why burglarize on a Saturday morning in an area full of potential witnesses? Why choose a house obviously occupied, with several vehicles in the driveway? If the criminal intent was homicide, why didn't the intruder seek his intended victims immediately? Instead, he went downstairs first. If he intended to murder, why didn't he come equipped to kill? Why did the person posing the greatest threat to the intruder receive only minor injuries? When an investigator analyzes a crime scene demonstrating a great deal of offender activity and no clear motive for this activity, the statements of the victim or witness should be questioned. In this case, the victim's husband was charged with and convicted of homicide.

Another red flag apparent with many staged domestic murders is the fatal assault of the wife or children, or both, by an intruder while the husband escapes without injury or with nonfatal injury. This was seen in the Stuart case at the beginning of the chapter. If the offender does not initially target the person posing the greatest threat or if that person suffers the least amount of injury, the police investigator should reexamine all other crime scene indicators. In addition, the investigator should scrutinize forensics and victimology (e.g., were there any recent insurance policies on the victim?) with particular attention.

FORENSIC RED FLAGS

Do the injuries fit the crime? Forensic results that do not fit the crime should cause the investigator to think about staging. The presence of a personal-type assault using a weapon of opportunity when the initial motive for the offense appears to be for material gain should raise suspicion. This type of assault also includes manual or ligature strangulation, facial beating (depersonalization), and excessive trauma beyond that necessary to cause death (overkill). Generally, the more evidence there is of overkill, the closer the relationship is between the victim and the offender.

Sexual and domestic homicides demonstrate forensic findings of this type: a close-range, personalized assault. The victim (not money or goods) is the primary focus on the offender. This type of offender often attempts to stage a sexual or domestic homicide to appear motivated by criminal enterprise. This does not imply that personal-type assaults never happen during the commission of a property crime, but usually the criminal enterprise offender prefers a quick, clean kill that reduces time at the scene. Any forensic red flags should be placed in context with victimology and crime scene information after careful analysis.

Other discrepancies may arise when the account of a witness or survivor conflicts with forensic findings. In one case, an estranged wife found her husband, a professional golfer, dead in the bathroom tub with the water running. Initially, it appeared as if the golfer had slipped in the tub, struck his head on the bathroom fixture, and drowned. However, the autopsy began to raise suspicion. Toxicology reports revealed a high level of Valium in the victim's bloodstream at the time of death. The autopsy also revealed several concentrated areas of injury or impact points on the head, as if the victim had struck his head more than once. Later, investigators learned the wife had been with him the night of his death. The wife later confessed that she had made dinner for her husband and had laced his salad with Valium. After her husband passed out, she let three men she hired into the house to kill him and make the death look accidental.

Investigators often find forensic discrepancies when a subject stages a rape–murder. The offender frequently positions the victim to imply that sexual assault has occurred. An offender who has a close relationship with the victim will often only partially remove the victim's clothing (e.g., pants pulled down, shirt or dress pulled up). He rarely leaves the victim totally nude. Despite the body's positioning and the partial removal of clothes, the forensic examination demonstrates a lack of sexual assault. The investigator should remember that sexual assault can take many forms, including exploratory probing, regressive necrophilia, and insertion of objects. With a staged sexual assault, there is usually no evidence of any sexual activity and an absence of seminal fluids in the body orifices.

An investigator who suspects a staged crime scene should look for other signs of close offender association with the victim, such as washing up or any other indications of undoing. In addition, when an offender stages a domestic homicide, he frequently plans and maneuvers a third-party discovery of the victim. The case that involved the husband staging his wife's murder to appear as the work of an intruder illustrates this point. Instead of going upstairs to check on his wife and daughter, he called his brother, who lived across the street. The husband stayed downstairs in the kitchen while the brother ran upstairs and discovered the victim. Offenders often manipulate the victim's discovery by a neighbor or family member or will be conveniently elsewhere when the victim is discovered.

Objectivity

It is imperative in any case analysis to remain objective and not be placed in a position whereby one may be influenced by investigators working the case. This is particularly important if the analysis may possibly be used not just as an investigative tool in a case but in courtroom testimony when an expert is called on for an opinion. The only way to remain objective at the onset of the analysis is with an UNSUB case. If investigators have already identified a suspect, this fact should not be made available during crime scene analysis. The only information furnished for crime scene analysis should be a synopsis of the crime and a description of the crime scene, including, if applicable, weather conditions; political and social environment; a complete background of the victim; forensic information to include autopsy and toxicology and serology reports, autopsy photographs, and photographs of the cleansed wounds; crime scene sketches showing distances, directions, and scale; and maps of the area.

Until the analysis of the crime is complete, having suspect information will directly prejudice the analyst's conclusions and may even consciously or subconsciously cause one to tailor an analysis that steers the investigation toward the investigator's primary suspect. Strict adherence to this procedural rule must be followed. Crime analysis is not a substitute for a thorough and well-planned investigation. Over the years, it has proven to be a viable investigative tool when the standards for analysis have been carefully followed and the crime scene analyst's opinions have not been contaminated by having prejudicial information.

Conclusion

Behavior reflects personality, and to understand the criminal, the investigator must be able to detach himself or herself emotionally from the violent offense. There is a fine line between being detached versus being observant and sensitive to minute forensic details left by the UNSUB at the scene. Investigators should recognize offender behavioral patterns such as MO, personation, undoing, and staging. If investigators approach each crime scene with an awareness of these factors they will improve their abilities to solve the equation, Why + How = Who.

References

Douglas, J. E. (1989). Expert witness testimony. *State of Delaware v. Steven B. Pennell.* State v. Pennell, 584 A.2d 513 (Del. Super., 1989).

Chapter 3

The Impact of the Internet, Technology, and Forensics on Crime Investigation

John E. Douglas, Lauren K. Douglas, and Stefan R. Treffers

The Internet has meant that old concepts of boundaries and borders and limitations are gone. People are no longer doing things at the speed of physically transmitting messages from one place to another, but trading their thoughts, their emotions, their images, and their desires at the speed of light. The human imagination seems to be freed from the constraints of the past. When you go online, you can be anyone you wish to be.

The Internet is both a vast research tool into every possible subject and a gateway to information. It provides services as varied as how to adopt a child from the United States or another country, how to trade stocks or collect coins, and how to stalk an unsuspecting person. The Internet features bomb-making techniques and other information used by terrorists, both domestic and foreign. America's radical groups have been linked by computer networks since the mid-1980s. And international terrorists are linked to their followers worldwide by e-mail and zip files.

The Internet has opened new ways to do business, new ways to find or generate information, and new ways to meet potential mates or partners. Online personal ads and chat rooms become contemporary bars and singles clubs, but instead of having access to a few people in a physical setting, anyone can now access potential partners worldwide. In years past, when people met, interacted with, and assessed each other, eye contact, body language, and appearance came into play. Our combined human and animal instincts were the best gifts to protect us from danger. The fight-or-flight response is most effective on a visual basis, and intuition is a valuable tool in selecting potential partners or mates. Both of these skills are dramatically reduced when communicating on the Internet.

What often started out online as an exciting way to meet new people sometimes led to more serious consequences. Stories began to surface everywhere about relationships and marriages dissolving because of cyber-romance. On the Net, personal interactions can quickly move from casual e-mails to intimate e-mails to sensual and sexual communications to the exchange of pictures to the decision to meet physically, to having an affair, to planning on marriage—and then on to divorce and breaking up households. As soon as online love became popular, services popped up offering to track spouses on the Internet without ever being detected in order to see whom he or she was meeting in cyberspace. Private investigation began to take on a new meaning.

As the Internet entered tens of millions of American homes, criminals began using the new technology to commit fraud, theft, and many other violations of the law. At the same time, both law enforcement and private agencies were beginning to study behavior—particularly sexual behavior—on the Internet and developing statistics about their findings. The results revealed that huge numbers of people used the Internet for some form of sexual exploration. The Internet seems to have freed something that had previously been repressed in the human mind or the unconscious or in the body itself. Self-imposed restrictions or controls were fading, and people often did things in cyberspace they might have never done anywhere else. The online world had become a new fraudulent, sexual, and violent playground for countless Americans.

A radically altered reality had arrived at the end of the 20th century. It is most frequently compared to the Old West, where many people were armed and dangerous and where lawmen struggled to maintain order and protect the citizens of the new frontier. That era was sometimes wild and lawless, but it was not driven by a rapidly growing, ever-changing technology. Horses dominated the western landscape, and both criminals and sheriffs used the same animals in their chosen line of work. The outlaws and peacekeepers were fairly evenly matched. When automobiles came along in the early 20th century, criminals quickly adapted them to fit their needs, and once again law enforcement easily made the same adaptation. In the online world, the old patterns do not apply. Technology was changing so fast that the authorities simply could not keep up during the first few years in which the Internet exploded. By the mid-1990s, when law enforcement began to realize how many different kinds of crime were being committed in cyberspace and how insidious some of those crimes were, they had barely started to train or employ enough experts to fight back. They needed money for education and for more sophisticated equipment because the technology turned over so fast, and they needed time to absorb what they were learning. Whenever they made progress, the technology surged forward again and was often being used for illegal activities.

Never had those involved in finding and catching criminals been faced with such a challenge. Never had they required more resources or knowledge.

They were playing catch-up against a foe that had infiltrated every corner of the Internet. The following case of one of the first Internet serial murderers illustrates this challenge.

Internet Serial Murder Case: John E. Robinson Sr.

In the spring of 2000, Vicki Neufield, a clinical psychologist from Texas, came to Olathe, Kansas, a suburb of Kansas City, for an encounter with a man she had met online. Vicki was there to seek employment in the Kansas City area and to explore a possible personal relationship with John Robinson, who had presented himself as a successful businessman with local contacts that could further her career. When they were alone in the motel room, he assaulted her and took nude photographs. After the attack, she was horrified and anxious to notify police about Robinson, but she hesitated. She was, after all, compromised by the photos and her sexual encounter with the man. When she had threatened him with exposure, he counter-threatened to reveal the photos. As she struggled with her options, another woman, Jeanna Milliron, met Robinson in a different Kansas City motel. She, too, had come to the Midwest after answering Robinson's Web site for employment and looking for a sexual relationship with him. Her encounter also ended badly, with unwanted pictures and a beating. Milliron wanted to call the police, but she was reluctant to reveal her own participation with Robinson. Both women eventually contacted law enforcement.

On March 1, 2000, the Olathe, Kansas, animal control officers learned about a pair of Pekingese dogs running loose at Robinson's mobile home. The dogs were traced to Suzette Trouten, a Michigan woman who had met Robinson online and had moved to Olathe after he had promised her a job taking care of his elderly father, traveling, and earning $60,000 a year. Not long after coming to Olathe, Trouten was reported missing. After the dogs were picked up, they were scheduled to be euthanized, but that did not happen because they were now being viewed as potential evidence in Trouten's disappearance and possible death.

The investigation of John Robinson eventually led authorities to many more women around the country whom he had met online. When making contact with them in chat rooms, he called himself John or "JT" or "JR" or "Jim Turner" and said he was a wealthy entrepreneur. Almost every woman he encountered responded favorably to his financial condition as he presented it. To some, he hinted at an interest in the world of sadomasochism, and a few of the women were not put off by this. But he usually presented a wholesome image. He sent out pictures of himself dressed like a cowboy: dark western hat cocked jauntily, shiny black cowboy boots, crisply pressed blue jeans, denim shirt, and bolo tie. He wore a friendly grin and leaned against a post on farmland he owned in Linn County, Kansas. He was soon attracting women from all over. He met one named "Lauralei" from Kentucky, who had gone online looking for someone who was "over 45 and was sure of himself and secure financially." Her main concern was not becoming involved with someone she would have to support. She and "JT" flirted and did some sexual role-playing online. He presented himself as divorced (which was false) and as having an open and caring heart. When Lauralei's brother died, he expressed great sympathy and began phoning her regularly. He asked to meet her in Kansas City, but she was one of the fortunate ones who declined. Several women who had come into contact with Robinson could no longer be found in cyberspace—or anywhere else.

The Robinson investigation spread to his isolated farm on the Kansas–Missouri border, holding a prefab structure surrounded by fields of corn, beans, and alfalfa. His primary residence was in Olathe, where he had lived with his wife of 36 years while raising four grown children, but lately he needed another address to escape to where he could engage in his secret Internet life. The countryside surrounding his farm looked as innocently pastoral as the photos that Robinson took of himself and sent to women online. But his rural outpost held secrets of its own. As the combined task forces of Missouri and Kansas investigators moved onto his property, they searched the structure, dug into his land with shovels, and set loose dogs to sniff out clues. The police soon found two 85-gallon sealed barrels. Inside each was the crumpled body of a woman who had suffered a severe blow to the head.

Law enforcement quickly traced more missing women to Robinson. Among them was a young mother; Robinson had talked the woman into giving her four-month-old baby to him, and he then sold the infant to his brother for $5,500. The mother was never found, and the police would eventually charge Robinson with this murder and kidnapping. Other women who vanished were a Polish college student from Purdue, a woman and her disabled daughter from California, and a prison librarian from Missouri.

In addition to being a sexual predator, Robinson had for years been running financial scams on women by collecting checks from their commercial mailboxes. He had gained their confidence by offering them "exciting overseas jobs" and "education opportunities for unwed mothers." Using an Internet service that would postmark envelopes from anywhere in the world, Robinson would send the victim's relatives a letter signed by the victim asking them to send money to a stated address. Robinson would then cash the checks the family sent. Concerned relatives of the missing simply assumed their loved ones were employed or traveling abroad. One victim, Beverly Bonner, a former prison librarian, had rented a storage locker in Cass County, Missouri, in suburban Kansas City. Robinson himself used the storage facility and sometimes joked with the proprietor that his "sister" Beverly was having such a great time overseas she might never return.

By the late spring of 2000, investigators had learned that at least 11 women who had been involved with Robinson had vanished. The police search eventually led them to the storage locker John Robinson had rented in Bonner's name. When authorities opened it, they saw three more sealed 85-gallon barrels. Inside each was a dead woman who had been beaten and killed. The bodies had apparently been there for years. One was Bonner. Five corpses had now been recovered, but six were unaccounted for. Police were asking for the public's help in linking Robinson to anyone associated with his scams or sexual activities, but many people were reluctant to come forward and share information about their involvement. The only thing as powerful as the desires that drove sex in cyberspace was the desire to keep this part of their life secret.

In June 2000, Robinson was arrested and held for sexual assault on the two women he had recently taken to Kansas City motels. Using their information and other leads, prosecutors built their case and soon charged Robinson with five capital murders: two in Kansas and three in Missouri. Bond was set at $5 million, and he was appointed three death-penalty lawyers. Thirty task force members, half in Kansas and half in Missouri, kept working the case, which took them to Florida, California, and other venues. It was the largest investigation ever done on an individual for computer-related crimes, and the police put together 11,000 pages of information detailing Robinson's long criminal history, his numerous cyber relationships, and his connection with the dead women.

The case had the potential of becoming even bigger and more complicated.

"There's a sex angle to this case," said Johnson County, Kansas, district attorney Paul Morrison, who would be prosecuting Robinson. "There's an Internet angle to this case. And there's also a developing financial angle on this case that ultimately will be a very large part of it."

Robinson maintained his innocence, and so did his wife and children. They released several public statements expressing their support for the defendant and denying his involvement in the crimes. They claimed never to have seen the side of Robinson that law enforcement said had killed at least six females. The accused man's neighbors told the media that he was a quiet fellow who kept a statue of the Virgin Mary in his back yard and always put up wonderful holiday decorations. A few women in the neighborhood said that he had made suggestive remarks but they had warded off his advances.

The balding, pudgy, bespectacled Robinson looked as unthreatening as the cornfields around his home country. When he first appeared in court following his arrest, he wore a tailored blue suit and seemed self-contained. He appeared well mannered and bland.

"He cleans up well," said a lawyer in the Johnson County courthouse that morning, "but his appearance is totally deceiving. If he hadn't done jail time in the last decade, I think he would have killed a lot more women than he did. He was a monster on the Net."

As Robinson sat in jail in Olathe and his attorneys worked on a defense, local, state, and federal investigators continued to pursue information from across the nation as they hunted for more missing women and more bodies.

The first trial for John Robinson began October 7, 2002, in Olathe. On November 19, the jury found him guilty of capital murder for the deaths of Suzette Trouten, age 27, and Izabela Lewicka, age 21. He was also convicted of first-degree murder for the death of Lisa Stasi, age 19, whose body was never found, and of arranging the fraudulent adoption of her four-month-old baby. The same jury that convicted Robinson recommended that he be put to death. District Judge John Anderson III sentenced him January 21, 2003.

While Robinson was on death row in Kansas, Missouri continued pursuing the three murders that were discovered across the state line. Robinson's attorneys negotiated with the Missouri prosecutor, Chris Koster, in an attempt to get Robinson to lead them to the bodies of Lisa Stasi, Paula Godfrey, and Catherine Clampitt. Eventually, Koster and his team became convinced the women's remains would not be found, and he and the victim's families agreed to accept the guilty pleas in exchange for life without parole sentences.

In mid-October 2003, Robinson acknowledged that Koster had enough evidence to convict him of capital murder for the deaths of the three women. He demanded the unusual plea agreement because an admission of guilt in Missouri might have been used against him in Kansas. Kansas prosecutor Morrison said he was not convinced the murders actually occurred in Koster's jurisdiction. Although Morrison said he supported Koster's deal to end the mystery of what happened to the women, he said John Robinson, the Internet's first serial killer, was a "gamesman to the end." He gave no hint at what prompted his homicidal acts.

Advances in Technology

The Internet has broadened the potential for possible victims and has also made law enforcement's job increasingly difficult. Persons who engage with strangers on the Internet are not likely to tell anyone about the communications for fear of embarrassment. Also, unlike a traditional crime where there are eyewitnesses, no one can see a crime taking place on the Internet. Not only does the Internet produce a larger pool of potential victims, it also attracts individuals who would never think about committing a crime outside cyberspace. These individuals feel they have anonymity on the Internet and feel an increased sense of security about committing a crime. These facts make the investigative process more critical and complicated.

Technological innovations have created new avenues for criminal activity, especially with the diversification of communication technologies, the anonymity of the Internet, and the devices developed to evade police. Various means of communication such as wireless broadband, peer-to-peer, voice over Internet protocol (IP), and third-party applications (e.g., Skype) have allowed potentially dangerous communications between criminals and terrorists to go undetected (Caproni, 2011; Dunn & Meller, 2009). Devices such as smartphones have allowed criminals to eavesdrop on police radios as a means to avoid capture (Tucker, 2011). As criminals become more technologically advanced and equipped, law enforcement agencies must also evolve to level the playing field. New technologies have been developed for law enforcement to enhance their surveillance capabilities by adopting technologies formerly developed for military use. Cameras that penetrate clothing and walls are beginning to transition into police forces as they become more affordable. Global positioning system (GPS) devices are used to track subjects and can be deployed in very innovative ways. Automated data analysis and mining have enabled agencies to detect suspicious criminal and terrorist activity that would not have otherwise been recognizable by human analysts. Communications also have experienced major improvements as law enforcement has moved away from traditional analog radio systems. A new encouragement of collaboration, cooperation, and coordination has facilitated the development of partnerships between law enforcement agencies based on information sharing all as a result of technological advances in computer software and voice communication.

Communication can serve as an important psychological strategy between a criminal and law enforcement. For example, why do serial predatory offenders do what they do? It is because this act of manipulation, domination, and control—be it rape, murder, arson, or any other criminal enterprise—gives them a communication of power, satisfaction, and fulfillment that they achieve nowhere else in life. For this one moment, a "loser" or "nobody" who feels that he has no power or influence in normal life can exert the ultimate power over another human being, can make that other human being suffer and bend to his will, can decide whether that other human being will live or die. For this type of individual, there is no greater sense of empowerment.

So vital is the sense of self-importance derived by some offenders and the need for recognition that it can lead directly or indirectly to their apprehension. The self-styled "BTK Strangler" terrorized Wichita, Kansas, beginning in January 1974. The name originated with communications he sent to law enforcement and media, proudly explaining that his technique was to bind, torture, and kill. After a period of years, the case went cold and the killings ceased. His last communication was 1979. Then, in 2004, the communications began again, containing information that appeared to authenticate the sender as BTK, including crime scene photographs of an unsolved murder. There had been no official police photos of this scene due to the quick removal of the body, but this communication confirmed the statement in the author's original profile of BTK that sketches included in the early communications signified that he was photographing his victims as "trophies."

Dennis Rader, a former municipal ordinance official from nearby Park City was arrested and charged several months after the communications resumed. Among the pieces of evidence that led to his arrest was the tracing of an electronic imprint on a computer disk he had sent to a local television station (Douglas & Olshaker, 1999). In a similar manner, Theodore J. Kaczynski was identified as the notorious Unabomber in 1996 after his brother, David, recognized familiar phrasing in an extensive rambling manifesto the subject insisted be published in national newspapers (Bouton, 1990).

The following research outlines some of the top technologies that have been adopted for use in intelligence gathering and communication within law enforcement.

DATA MINING AND AUTOMATED DATA ANALYSIS

Data mining is a technology that has many different applications in law enforcement and can provide automated analysis of data and sorting tasks that would be difficult if not impossible for human analysts to carry out (DeRosa, 2004). These programs are able to find patterns that would otherwise go undetected. Automated data analysis can achieve accurate identifications by examining whether records represent the same or different people. The same program can access public records or collections of data to find links between a subject and other relevant information such as an address or other subjects. A hindsight automated analysis revealed that many of the terrorists of the September 11 attacks had been placed on watch lists, had identical contact addresses, or had lived with other identified terrorists (DeRosa, 2004). In addition, data can be analyzed for patterns in behavior. For example, identifying people who have entered the country under a temporary visa and have purchased abnormally large amounts of fertilizer, which could be used for developing bombs, would send out an alert of suspicious terrorist activity (DeRosa, 2004). Data mining also has very useful applications in identifying Internet search strings or terrorist communication revealed in e-mail messages, which alert the program based on certain keywords (DeRosa, 2004).

SURVEILLANCE

Possibly the most impressive of all the technological innovations within law enforcement in the past decade may be the development of surveillance systems capable of penetrating clothing, vehicles, and even walls. Concealed weapon detection (CWD) is an example of a technology that allows law enforcement officers to detect dangerous weapons or explosives that are concealed in clothing or objects from a safe distance. The most promising devices proposed to detect weapons use passive millimeter wave and terahertz radiation technologies, which have the ability to penetrate through nonmetallic objects and leave a silhouette of a weapon under clothing. CWD devices allow officers to detect weapons by less physically invasive measures and minimal or no cooperation of a suspect when necessary (Tillery, 2007).

Through-the-wall surveillance (TWS) is based on similar technology and can be used to detect movement, conduct searches, map interiors of a building, and find weapons by penetrating through walls using ultra-wideband radar technology (Miles, 2007). Initially developed for use in the military, TWS technologies can be applicable in intelligence gathering or special weapons and tactics (SWAT) operations and will become more common as the technology becomes more affordable to law enforcement agencies (Miles, 2007). The technology has great promise but is still in its infancy as further research and development is required for law enforcement to adopt TWS as a staple in their arsenal of tools.

GPS AND GIS SYSTEMS

Geographic information systems (GISs) are capable of organizing geographic data in datasets that can be used to analyze crime patterns, allocate enforcement resources, and plan strategic operations. Pin-mapping capabilities can display crime, arrest, and quality-of-life data in comparative charts and tables as well as identify hot spots that may require increased patrol resources. In addition, information from other agencies may be integrated to provide a broader map of data (Garson & Vann, 2001; Hoover, Zhang, & Zhao, 2010). GISs enable users to access and fully organize data in real time during patrol, superseding traditional pin maps on the station house walls. Global positioning systems (GPSs) reveal satellite-derived information about location, speed, and direction of a target. The applications of GPS technology in law enforcement range from navigation to monitoring and intelligence gathering. GPS devices have been attached to sex offenders to monitor their location, to vehicles to intercept crimes, to targets that have led law enforcement to crime locations such as drug development labs, and even to fleeing vehicles involved in high-speed chases via air gun–launched darts. Cell phones have also been tracked by law enforcement agencies to identify a suspect's location (Smith, 2011). In fact, during 2009, Sprint revealed that within a one-year period, the company had received over 8 million government requests for location information (Abdo & Shamsi, 2011). However, some applications of GPS technology in law enforcement have been criticized for violating the Fourth Amendment and have been argued to be consistent with facilitating a "surveillance state" (Abdo & Shamsi, 2011; Liptak, 2011). Most of these claims have involved the erosion of privacy by tracking individuals without a warrant.

WIRELESS COMMUNICATIONS

Newer wireless radio communication used in public safety today functions on a system that records audio optimized for human speech and transmits a digital audio stream to a receiver. The system distinguishes itself from the older analog radios in its design to prevent eavesdropping through encryption of the digital audio stream. Agencies that value transparency over security issues may feel that encryption on a case-by-case basis would better suit their operations (Tucker, 2011). The use of other wireless communication devices such as smartphones is becoming more common and allows police officers to operate outside their vehicles. The Baltimore Police Department participated in a pilot study in 2010 where Blackberry smartphones equipped with PocketCop software were distributed to more than 2,000 officers. The devices allowed officers to share information, take photographs at the crime scene, use GPS navigation, and access information without having to rely on dispatchers (National Law Enforcement and Corrections Technology Center, 2011). As police officers acquire tools that enable a higher degree of mobility, they are more capable of serving outside the isolation of the patrol car and in the community.

COMMUNICATION INTEROPERABILITY

The ability for law enforcement agencies to coordinate activities or emergency responses with other law enforcement and first responders relies heavily on the compatibility of communication systems across agency and jurisdictional boundaries. Commonly referred to as *interoperability*, the ability of agencies to work together toward common ends is facilitated by connecting similarly integrated systems and coordinating communications over radio or other voice communication technologies (Hawkins, 2006). It was noted that during the Oklahoma City bombing and the attacks of September 11, emergency agencies experienced difficulties communicating with each other as a result of incompatible radio systems that operated on different radio frequencies (U.S. General Accounting Office, 2004). As a result, the national SAFECOM Program was initiated by the Department of Homeland Security to improve multijurisdictional and intergovernmental communications interoperability through planning, research, development, testing, guidance, and support to agencies applying for federal grant funding (Hawkins, 2006). The program would aim to address barriers identified the National Task Force on Interoperability such as incompatible and aging communication equipment, limited and fragmented funding, limited planning, lack of coordination and cooperation, and a shortage of radio frequencies of the radio spectrum (Hawkins, 2006). Programs like these take into consideration that, as technology advances, agencies will experience diminished interoperability resulting from varying needs of different community agencies and an increased availability of communication choices.

INFORMATION SHARING

Interoperability is also associated with information-sharing capabilities and the compatibility of data sources, which may differ in software, hardware, and design. To encourage electronic information sharing between justice agencies, the Global Justice Information Sharing Initiative was created and provided a common standard that could be used for data exchanges as well as data dictionaries, which define common terminologies. COPLINK serves as an integrated information system that allows the sharing of information between police departments through a user-friendly database, and also provides shared crime pattern information (Holmes, Comstock-Davidson, & Hayen, 2007).

Advances in Forensics

The forensic sciences have played a key role in criminal investigations for many years. Recently, there has been increased attention on the forensic sciences by law enforcement, prosecutors, and the general public. Particularly in high-profile cases, intense media coverage concerning evidence issues and the work of crime laboratories has served to heighten this interest.

In the past two decades, there have been tremendous technological advances in the laboratory testing of forensic samples. There have also been a number of improvements in the identification and collection of evidence at the crime scene, through innovative processing and evidence collection methods. Together, these advances allow for a greater probability of successful recovery and analysis of evidence than was previously possible. There is also growing recognition by criminal justice professionals of the wider scope of forensic techniques and available tests.

The field of forensic deoxyribonucleic acid (DNA) analysis and the legislation that allows DNA testing on a broader number of offenders has made some of the more remarkable advances. DNA testing now allows much smaller samples of biological material to be analyzed and the results to be more discriminating. DNA testing of forensic crime scene samples can now be compared against a database of known offenders and other unsolved crimes. The most common method of DNA profiling involves the use of polymerase chain reaction (PCR) technology, which mimics DNA replication on specific regions of interest. In addition, analysis of short repeated sequences of DNA known as short tandem repeats (STRs) can be used to discriminate between DNA belonging to different individuals. A hallmark of this technology is its ability to amplify small amounts of DNA that may have been degraded by decomposition or other crime scene factors (Sapse, 2011).

Forensic botany, the science behind plants as applied to the crime scene, is an emerging field that has proven to be an asset in crime reconstruction. Early applications of forensic botany have relied on morphological characteristics of plant evidence, including plant structure and physical form; however, the field has increasingly involved the identification of genus and species of plants microscopically. Once a plant species is identified, this information may be able to link a suspect or victim within a specific location or to a broader geographical region. Forensic teams may also analyze succession patterns where the ground has been disturbed, indicating the potential burial of a body. Forensic botanists may also study samples of freshwater plants such as algae found in the lungs of drowned victims for the purpose of assessing the time and location of death (Wallace, 2011). The closely related field of forensic entomology has also been helpful in piecing together a crime scene. The study of insects, more commonly carrion breeding insects, has been used primarily to estimate time of death. The ability of investigators to do this is dependent on distinct developmental timelines of certain insects and the fact that particular species have been found to be attracted to specific states of decomposition and decay. Forensic entomology has been coupled with modern DNA identification methods including PCR, restriction fragment length polymorphism (RFLP) analysis, and mitochondrial DNA sequencing (Wallace, 2011).

Advances in forensic technology have also enabled law enforcement to better respond to biological warfare. The field of microbial forensics has experienced tremendous advances from technologies that historically relied on light microscopy, biochemical tests, and staining procedures. More modern techniques include variations of mass spectroscopy, which determines the elemental composition and chemical structures of molecules based on mass of particles. Each type of microorganism extracted from a biological sample has a unique profile that can be compared and identified. Molecular techniques using quantitative PCR technology can be used to identify certain genetic markers in DNA that may be indicative of a certain microorganism. All of these techniques are primarily used to identify the type of biological agent in order for law enforcement and public health agencies to formulate an appropriate response (Wallace, 2011).

DNA analysis has also been used to detect enzymes, transporters, and receptors that are involved in the metabolism of drugs (Allorge & Tournel, 2011). Such testing plays an important role in identifying drugs administered to victims, identifying drugs that have led to an overdose, as well as supporting or denying a person's statement regarding whether they have taken drugs. Nuclear magnetic resonance (NMR) spectroscopy has allowed forensic toxicologists to perform drug analysis with a reduced preanalytical preparation time and the ability to screen for a spectrum of drugs (Champeil, 2011; Komoroski, Komoroski, Valentine, Pearce, & Kearns, 2000).

Forensic laboratories have developed advanced analytical techniques through the use of computer technology. Systems such as the Combined DNA Index System (CODIS), various Automated Fingerprint Identification

Systems (AFISs), and the National Integrated Ballistics Identification Network (NIBIN), were identified by the symposium as beneficial to serial murder investigations, by providing links between previously unrelated cases.

CODIS is a national automated DNA information processing and tele-communications system that was developed to link biological evidence (DNA) in criminal cases, among various jurisdictions around the United States. Samples in CODIS include DNA profiles obtained from persons convicted of designated crimes, DNA profiles obtained from crime scenes, DNA profiles from unidentified human remains, and DNA from voluntary samples taken from families of missing persons (see Chapter 4).

Forensic science assumes an important role in the recovery and examination of trace evidence. Trace evidence is described as small, often microscopic material. It commonly includes hair and fiber evidence but may encompass almost any substance or material. Trace evidence may provide important lead information pertaining to offender characteristics, vehicle and tire descriptors, and environmental clues that relate to killing scenes and modes of transportation used to move bodies.

A skilled trace evidence examiner can compare the trace evidence from multiple victims in a case, in an effort to identify evidence common to all of the victims. This trace evidence will reflect a "common environment" with which all of the victims were in contact. This common environment will repeat in objects in the serial offender's world, such as his vehicles and/or residence. This can demonstrate that all of the victims had contact with the offender at the same location(s) (FBI Behavioral Analysis Unit [BAU], 2008).

Recent improvements of technologies that analyze trace evidence have given investigators increasingly powerful tools in the analysis of crime scene evidence. For example, the use of micro spectrophotometry and thin-layer chromatography allow for the comparison of dyes used in colored fabrics. The comparison of dye components and their relative ratios within fabrics can serve to determine whether two pieces of fabric evidence have a common origin. X-ray diffraction can be used to reveal spaces between atoms that are characteristic of certain arrangements of atoms and molecules, ultimately leading to the identification and origin of trace evidence. The ability of forensic investigators to discriminate between three forms of titanium dioxide has been an important function in paint analysis (Lewis & Sigman, 2007). Furthermore, analysis of gunshot residue has been critical to determining whether a particular suspect had fired a weapon. The mixture of organic and inorganic materials originating from the discharge of a weapon can be found on the hands, face, hair, or clothing of individuals, including suspects and victims, who are in close proximity. Usually, a positive sample will include barium and antimony found together above the baseline level. This determination is aided by a range of technologies including instrumental neutron activation analysis, graphite furnace atomic absorption, and inductively coupled atomic emission spectroscopy. The main objective of these technologies is to extract an elemental profile of the suspected residue and confirm or deny the presence of gunshot residue based on its composition (Lewis & Sigman, 2007).

FORENSIC EVIDENCE CASE VIGNETTE

The case of serial child murderer Richard Mark Evonitz highlights the variety of forensic testing that may be utilized to solve difficult cases. In 1996 and 1997, in Spotsylvania County, Virginia, three young girls were abducted from their residences, sexually assaulted, and killed. The first case occurred on September 9, 1996, when Sophia Silva disappeared from the front porch of her house. She was found in October of 1996, in a swamp, 16 miles from her residence. A suspect was arrested and charged for her murder, based on a faulty trace evidence examination conducted by a state laboratory.

On May 1, 1997, two sisters, Kristin and Kati Lisk, disappeared from their residence after returning home from school. Their bodies were discovered five days later in a river, 40 miles from their residence. After an examination by an FBI Laboratory examiner yielded trace evidence that positively linked the Silva and Lisk homicides to a common environment, the suspect arrested in the Silva case was subsequently released.

The investigation continued for an additional five years, until a girl was abducted in South Carolina. The victim was able to escape, and she identified Richard Mark Evonitz as her attacker. Evonitz fled South Carolina and was sighted in Florida. After a high-speed chase with police, Evonitz committed suicide. The investigation revealed that Evonitz had lived in Spotsylvania in 1996 and 1997.

Forensic searches were conducted on Evonitz's residence in South Carolina; his former residence in Spotsylvania, Virginia; and his car. A detailed trace examination of the evidence from these searches and the evidence obtained from the three victims revealed a number of hair and fiber matches, providing sufficient evidence to tie Evonitz to the three murders.

The following trace examinations linked Evonitz to all three homicide victims:

- Fibers from a bath mat.
- Fibers from an afghan.
- Fibers from two separate carpets in Evonitz's former home in Virginia.
- Carpet fibers from the trunk of Evonitz's car.
- Head hair consistent with Evonitz.

A trace examination also linked fibers from a pair of fur-lined handcuffs to the three homicide victims and the surviving victim. Latent fingerprints belonging to Kristin Lisk were located on the inside of the trunk lid of Evonitz's car, five years after the fact (FBI BAU, 2008).

Solving Homicides by Virtual Crime Scene Analysis

For crime scene investigators around the world, information technology is becoming an invaluable tool for cracking tough cases. Whether these crime scenes are virtual or physical, law enforcement is learning to use data-replication devices, specialized search tools, and virtualization software to get the drop on the perpetrators.

Technology is also being brought to bear on more traditional crime scenes. Police are using the virtual reality scenes to reenact crime scenes, which helps preserve the integrity of the scene and can be used further to evaluate the reliability of a suspect's deposition.

Police investigators and forensics specialists face challenging conditions when examining a crime scene. Often, the site of a crime can only be preserved for a short time, particularly if it's in a public area. Investigators must gather as much information as quickly as possible while doing their best not to disturb the scene itself. Also, crime photographers have to shoot scenes from multiple angles while attempting to preserve a sense of scale to ensure that the pictures are meaningful—both to investigators and to a future courtroom.

Today, some police forces are using virtual reality technology to capture and recreate a crime scene digitally. Several companies have developed numerous methods investigators can use when at the scene of a crime. Some replicate crime scenes with computer graphics similar to what you might find in a virtual reality video game. Other systems assemble photographs into a 360-degree virtual environment just like the photographic walkthroughs you may have seen on hotel and real estate Web sites. Police forces around the world have discovered that, if used properly, virtual environments can help the investigation process from its earliest stages all the way to a courtroom conviction (Strickland, 2012).

At Boston College, a forensic lab was developed to allow students to enter a virtual environment of an actual crime scene where they could interact with a game-based interface to the actual crime scene. When inspecting or photographing the crime scene, the actual crime scene photographs are viewed. Students are allowed to interact with all aspects of the crime scene in a correct or incorrect manner. Students learn how to secure a crime scene, how to search for signs of forced entry, how to collect evidence, and how to correctly take crime scene photos. Students are asked to analyze the crime scene to determine interaction between the offender and the victim. In selecting possible offenders they are asked to describe the interaction and what evidence supports their analysis and judgment.

Students also record crime scene photographs including the scientific rationale in a photo log and send it to the instructor for grading for each assigned task, such as where would you look for fingerprints, locate and analyze all the blood spatter, and so on.

Actual cases are set online to replicate a real crime scene using virtual gaming software. The following cases are part of the training lab for the *Crime Classification Manual*. Information on how to access the software for the crime scenes and the outcome of the cases can be found at www.diiforensics.com.

Virtual Cases

Case 1: The Z Case—False Confession or Murder?

The case begins with the actual 911 call that was made by a 78-year-old man who said he found his wife murdered. Indeed, police arrived and did find his 74-year-old wife dead in the kitchen. The caller, however, was unable to remember any details of the crime. He remembered that day, shopping, dinner, and watching television with his wife, retiring to bed at 9:30 p.m., but nothing else until he came across his wife's body at midnight. The Forensic Virtual Lab takes the student through the crime scene and helps the student with critical thinking in solving this crime.

Forensic science students access the virtual lab on the Boston College web, answer the following questions, and compose a virtual photo log to justify their answers. What was the state of the crime scene (i.e., organized, disorganized, or mixed)? What was the cause of death (i.e., strangulation, stabbing, gunshot, blunt-force trauma)? What type of weapon was used (i.e., hands, tool, knife, or gun)? Was the weapon one of opportunity or brought to the scene? What is the motive for the crime (i.e., criminal enterprise, personal cause, sexual homicide, or group cause)? Who committed the crime (i.e., spouse, family member, neighbor/acquaintance, or stranger)? Forensic science lab students would answer these additional questions. What areas would you dust for fingerprints? What does the blood spatter tell you? How was the victim approached? Did she move, struggle, or resist? How many crime scenes were there?

Case 2: Tinsel Man

This case reviews the principles and tests for forensic evidence involving the murder of a 19-year-old man whose body had been wrapped and moved several times to various building locations. Tinsel Man is a murder case that was unsolved for two years before a suspect was identified.

The lab is designed to provide the student the simulated experience in the collection of evidence in three locations—the body location, an apartment, and the basement of the apartment building. Once the evidence is collected at all sites, it is taken back to a virtual crime lab, where the student simulates using crime lab equipment to perform comparisons and analysis of the evidence collected to the actual lab equipment printouts.

Case 3: Serial Murder Case

Ten women in Charlotte, North Carolina, were raped and murdered over a two-year period starting in 1992. There was no forced entry into the women's apartment, indicating that the offender probably knew his victims and killed in a specific way, although the crime scenes included outdoors, indoors, and water.

This lab is designed to provide the student the simulated experience in determining if this is a serial killer, and if so, which cases are linked and how. The student photographs the evidence and prepares the motivation of the killer. More than 10 crime scenes are shown, and the student identifies and provides rationale to explain the pseudo crime scenes.

Case 4: The Child Abducted From Home

A three-year-old girl was reported missing to her father by her six-year-old brother at 7:50 a.m. in 2004. After checking with neighbors for his daughter, the father called the police dispatcher on 411 to report his missing daughter. Later that afternoon, the child's body was found in a creek about three miles from the parents' home. She had been bound, gagged, sexually assaulted, and then drowned. Police immediately suspected the father, and five months later they extracted a confession from him. The father was held in jail for eight months before DNA evidence exonerated him.

This lab requires the student to review the crime scene of the home and room of the abduction, the wooded area where she was raped, and the creek where she was found. The student identifies and photographs potential evidence found at the crime sites and presents a profile of a likely suspect. This profile is compared to the actual killer, who was identified years later.

Case 5: The Abducted Girls

An eight-year-old girl was riding her bicycle with her nine-year-old friend in Illinois on Mother's Day in May 2005. She was reported missing when she did not return home that evening. Early the next morning, the father and grandfather of one of the girls started searching and found the two bodies of the missing girls in a remote area in a nearby park. The eight-year-old girl had 20 stab wounds in the neck, the abdomen, and once in each eye. DNA evidence was found on the ground and on her underwear. The nine-year-old had been stabbed 11 times. The father of the eight-year-old was interrogated for over 20 hours and finally gave a confession. He was later exonerated by DNA evidence after he spent five years in jail.

This lab requires the student to review the outdoor crime scene where the bodies were found, the forensic reports on the evidence, and the father's confession. The student then classifies the crime and prepares a profile of a person of interest that is then compared with the actual murderer.

Case 6: The Murdered Sports Writer

A 48-year-old sports editor for a Missouri newspaper was found dead on October 31, 2001, at 2:20 a.m. in the parking lot 20 minutes after he had left his office. Two years later, police followed a tip that a young college student said he'd told friends that he'd had a dream in which he and his friend killed the man. The two young men were juniors in high school when the murder happened. In exchange for a lighter sentence, one man pleaded guilty and testified against the other man and received 25 years, while the other man received a 40-year sentence. Years later, two primary witnesses recanted and the case was appealed.

This lab requires the student to review the parking lot crime scene; determine the sequence of the 20-minute encounter of the killer and the victim; and answer questions as to the number of assailants, the structure of the crime, and the motive and classification.

Case 7: Rape and Murder Capital Case

A woman called emergency dispatchers at 6:30 a.m. in 2010 after finding her sister unresponsive in her bed and her head bloodied. The EMTs arrived not knowing this was a crime scene. The woman had had facial surgery the day before and the bleeding was initially attributed to surgical complications. The woman died several days later. After learning that a rape had also occurred, investigators returned to the home to take crime scene photographs. Investigators collected DNA samples from men who lived near the victim's home, asking them to voluntarily stand for swabbing. Months later, a DNA link led to the arrest of a 29-year-old man, and he was charged with capital murder.

This lab requires the student to collect evidence in the bedroom, the house, and the outside perimeter. It also requires analysis of crime scene data to determine how the suspect gained access to the house and bedroom while another female was present. The student will critique the suspect arrest, classify the crime, and determine a defense for the death penalty charge.

Conclusion

The Internet has made the search for unsuspecting individuals easier than ever before. With just a touch of a button, subjects can enter a special interest chat room, for example, a sadomasochistic chat room, and have potential victims at their disposal. Criminals are now using the Internet to convince and lure individuals to meet them in person. However, advances in technologies have assisted law enforcement enabling the acquisition of new tools to use in investigations and daily operations. This is especially true for agencies that increasingly find themselves at a disadvantage as a result of outdated communication equipment and ineffective surveillance equipment, or lack the means to police new frontiers of criminal activity such as the Internet. The improvement of technologies with forensic applications has seen tremendous growth and its appeal to law enforcement lies in its ability to provide significantly accurate results from limited amounts of biological evidence. As a result of increasing accuracy in the analysis of crime scene evidence, forensic sciences related to DNA typing, botany, and entomology have particularly experienced increased judicial acceptance.

Technology and the forensic sciences have significantly strengthened evidence collection that serves as a major asset in court proceedings. For the educational component, the addition of virtual crime labs for online study has raised the learning level for investigators and students.

References

Abdo, A., & Shamsi, H. (2011). Privacy and surveillance post-9/11. *Human Rights, 38*(1), 5–9.

Allorge, D., & Tournel, G. (2011). Role of pharmocogenetics in forensic toxicology. In D. Sapse & L. Kobilinsky (Eds.), *Forensic science advances and their application in the judiciary*. Boca Raton, FL: CRC Press.

Bouton K. (1990, February 25). The prosecutor: Linda Fairstein vs. rape. *New York Times Magazine*, pp. 21–23, 58–60.

Caproni, V. (2011, February 17). Going dark: Lawful electronic surveillance in the face of new technologies: Testimony. Federal Bureau of Investigation. Retrieved on January 11, 2012, from www.fbi.gov/news/testimony/going-dark-lawful-electronic-surveillance-in-the-face-of-new-technologies

Champeil, E. (2011). Magnetic resonance spectroscopy: A powerful tool for the identification and quantitation of drugs and drugs of abuse in biofluids. In D. Sapse & L. Kobilinsky (Eds.), *Forensic science advances and their application in the judiciary*. Boca Raton, FL: CRC Press.

DeRosa, M. (2004). *Data mining and data analysis for counterterrorism*. Washington, DC: CSIS Press. Retrieved on January 12, 2012, from http://csis.org/files/media/csis/pubs/040301_data_mining_report.pdf

Douglas, J., & Olshaker, M. (1999). *The anatomy of motive* (pp. 34–35). New York, NY: Scribner.

Dunn, J. E., & Meller, P. (2009). Skype calls may be tapped in police crackdown on criminal groups. *IT Business Newsletter*. Retrieved on January 12, 2012, from www.itbusiness.ca/it/client/en/home/News.asp?id=52126

Federal Bureau of Investigation, Behavioral Analysis Unit. (2008). Serial murder: Multi-disciplinary perspectives for investigators. Retrieved August 8, 2012, from www.fbi.gov/stats-services/publications/serial-murder/serial-murder-1

Garson, D. G., & Vann, I. B. (2001). *Geographic information systems for small and medium law enforcement jurisdictions: Strategies and effective practices*. Retrieved on January 12, 2012, from www.gcc.state.nc.us/gispage/ep1.htm

Hawkins, D. (2006). *Law enforcement tech guide for communications interoperability: A guide for interagency communications projects*. U.S. Department of Justice. Retrieved on January 9, 2012, from www.search.org/files/pdf/CommInteropTechGuide.pdf

Holmes, M. C., Comstock-Davidson, D. D., & Hayen, R. L. (2007). Data mining and expert systems in law enforcement agencies. *Issues in Information Systems, 8*(2), 329–335.

Hoover, L., Zhang, Y., & Zhao, J. S. (2010). *Geographic information systems and their effects on police efficacy: A Campbell systematic review*. Sam Houston State University. Retrieved on January 11, 2012, from www.campbellcollaboration.org/lib/download/989/

Komoroski, E. M., Komoroski, R. A., Valentine, J. L., Pearce, J. M., & Kearns, G. L. (2000). The use of nuclear magnetic resonance spectroscopy in the detection of drug intoxication. *Journal of Analytical Toxicology, 24*(3), 180–187.

Lewis, L. A., & Sigman, M. E. (2007). Forensic analysis of dyes in fibers via mass spectrometry. In R. D. Blackledge (Ed.), *Forensic analysis on the cutting edge: New methods for trace evidence analysis*. Hoboken, NJ: Wiley-Interscience.

Liptak, A. (2011). Court case asks if "Big Brother" is spelled GPS. *New York Times*. Retrieved on January 11, 2012, from www.nytimes.com/2011/09/11/us/11gps.html?_r=1

Miles, C. A. (2007). Through-the-wall surveillance: A new technology for saving lives. *National Institute of Justice Journal, 258*, 20–25.

National Law Enforcement and Corrections Technology Center. (2011). Smartphones and law enforcement. National Institute of Justice. Retrieved on January 12, 2012, from www.justnet .org/TechBeat%20Files/SmartphonesandLawEnforcement

Sapse, D. (2011). Scientific evidence. In D. Sapse & L. Kobilinsky (Ed.), *Forensic science advances and their application in the judiciary*. Boca Raton, FL: CRC Press.

Smith, A. M. (2011). *Law enforcement use of global position (GPS) devices to monitor motor vehicles: Fourth amendment considerations*. CRS Report for Congress. Retrieved on January 11, 2012, from www.fas.org/sgp/crs/misc/R41663.pdf

Strickland, J. (2012). *How virtual crime scenes work*. Howstuffworks. Retrieved August 29, 2012, from http://people.howstuffworks.com/vr-csi.htm

Tillery, C. (2007). Detecting concealed weapons: Directions for the future. *National Institute of Justice Journal, 258*(1), 26–28.

Tucker, E. (2011, November, 20). *Police using technology to shield internal communications*. Associated Press. Retrieved on January 12, 2012, from www.msnbc.msn.com/id/45376345/ns/technology_ and_science-tech_and_gadgets/#.TxnKOuzNTy2

U.S. General Accounting Office. (2004). *Project Safecom: Key cross-agency emergency communications effort requires stronger collaboration*. Retrieved on January 9, 2012, from www.gao.gov/new .items/d04494.pdf

Wallace, M. (2011). New frontiers in molecular forensics: Identification of botanical, entomological, and microbial material. In D. Sapse & L. Kobilinsky (Eds.), *Forensic science advances and their application in the judiciary*. Boca Raton, FL: CRC Press.

Chapter 4

Local, Federal, and International Agencies

In 1998, the U.S. Customs Service broke up a large Internet child porn ring. It was called "Wonderland" and involved buyers and sellers in at least 12 countries and 32 American cities. Numerous professional people were involved in the ring, and some of them could not cope with the consequences of their actions. Within a few days of their arrests, four men associated with Wonderland—a veterinarian and former military officer among them—committed suicide. Some 750,000 indecent images of children were recovered worldwide, and there have been 50 convictions of Wonderland members in Britain, America, Scandinavia, Europe, and Australia.

In September 1999, an even larger bust occurred when a team of computer specialists and U.S. postal inspectors entered the home of Thomas and Janice Reedy of Fort Worth, Texas. The team soon determined that the Reedy's Internet business, Landslide Productions, provided access to 300 child porn sites around the globe and reached thousands of people across the United States and 320,000 clients worldwide. The Reedys, parents of a nine-year-old daughter, were earning $1.4 million a month from Landslide. The uncovering of this business caused postal inspectors to create Operation Avalanche, a much larger investigation into online child pornography, and a year later the operation led to 100 more arrests of people allegedly in possession of child pornography. The porn sites were run by operators in Russia and Indonesia.

Thomas Reedy was the main focus of the allegations and was given the opportunity to work with the FBI to catch other child pornographers in exchange for a 20-year sentence. He declined the offer and went to trial. He was convicted on 89 counts and his wife on 87, although she was viewed as an accomplice and received only a 14-year sentence. He received 1,335 years in prison—the first life sentence ever given in a federal child pornography case where the defendant was not accused of actual molestation. With the Reedy arrest and subsequent conviction, the government had made a huge statement to potential online predators: they could be imprisoned for the rest of their lives even without harming children physically; that could happen just by buying or selling pictures on the Internet.

Crime that occurs on the Internet has made the job of prosecuting and defending these cases extremely difficult. The Constitution considers crime to be a local matter, reserved to individual states, not the federal government. In the light of this new type of crime, many states are changing laws and creating statutes to include crimes carried out through the use of the Internet. Nevertheless, states are unsure about and unfamiliar with how to settle jurisdiction issues of cybercrime. Traditionally, when a crime is committed, it is prosecuted within the state where it occurred. The type of crime decides whether that case will be handled by a state or federal court. For example, if a perpetrator crosses state lines after committing a crime, a federal court handles the case. Now the legal implications have changed, and dealing with cybercrime is not straightforward. Law enforcement and the government must adapt to this new realm. Just as law enforcement caught up with the criminals who began using cars to aid in their crimes in the early 20th century, they now are catching up with the criminals who are using the Internet.

This chapter reviews some of the types of law enforcement agencies available in the United States and internationally to work cases. There are agencies whose mission is to provide a law enforcement function, and there are also agencies that have a law enforcement department or component within a larger agency. And some cases, as in the cases cited, involve local, state, federal, and international law enforcement agencies.

Types of U.S. Law Enforcement Agencies

There are basically three types of U.S. law enforcement agencies: local, state, and federal. Local law enforcement agencies include police and sheriff departments. State agencies include the state or highway patrol. Local law enforcement agencies include city police departments, county sheriff office or department, transit authority police, school district police, housing authority police, district attorney's office investigators, airport police, hospital police, and university police.

The types of names of U.S. law enforcement agencies can vary greatly from state to state. Most states have a state police department of highway patrol. Some have a state bureau of investigation. The state police are unique to each U.S. state, as Table 4.1 illustrates.

Cooperation Between Local, State, and Federal Agencies: Operation Melting Pot.

On November 5, 2010, a sweeping federal and state firearm and drug trafficking investigation led to dozens of arrests on the North Shore of Massachusetts. Forty-eight members and affiliates of Lynn-based street gangs

Table 4.1 Types of Law Enforcement by State

State Police	Highway Patrol or DPS
Alaska State Troopers	Alabama Highway Patrol
Arkansas State Police	California Highway Patrol
Colorado State Patrol	Florida Highway Patrol
Connecticut State Police	Kansas Highway Patrol
Delaware State Police	Mississippi Highway Patrol
Georgia State Patrol	Missouri Highway Patrol
Idaho State Police	Montana Highway Patrol
Illinois State Police	Nebraska State Patrol
Indiana State Police	Nevada Highway Patrol
Iowa State Patrol	North Carolina State Highway Patrol
Kentucky State Police	North Dakota Highway Patrol
Louisiana State Police	Ohio State Highway Patrol
Maine State Police	Oklahoma Highway Patrol
Maryland State Police	South Carolina Highway Patrol
Massachusetts State Police	South Dakota Highway Patrol
Michigan State Police	Tennessee Highway Patrol
Minnesota State Patrol	Texas Highway Patrol
New Hampshire State Police	Utah Highway Patrol
New Jersey State Police	Wyoming Highway Patrol
New Mexico State Police	**Department of Public Safety**
New York State Police	Arizona Department of Public Safety
Oregon State Police	Hawaii Department of Public Safety
Pennsylvania State Police	
Rhode Island State Police	
Vermont State Police	
Virginia State Police	
Washington State Patrol	
West Virginia State Police	
Wisconsin State Patrol	

were charged with gun and drug trafficking offenses. These charges in federal and state court brought to 61 the total number of individuals charged to date in the multiphase investigation dubbed "Operation Melting Pot, The press release from the USDOJ US Attorney's Office for the District of Massachusetts (2010) presented the following facts.

Local, state, and federal law enforcement arrested 37 individuals on state and federal drug and gun charges and executed four search warrants. Three state and federal defendants were fugitives. The remaining 21 defendants were already in state and federal custody.

Operation Melting Pot was a wide-ranging investigation of leaders, members, and associates of the Avenue King Crips, the Bloods, the Gangsta Disciples, the Deuce Boyz, and the Latin Kings, primarily in Lynn and also Lowell.

The Bloods and Avenue King Crips had been involved in a violent war for a 10-year period, emerging as the two most powerful street gangs in Lynn. Over the past several years, there had been a number of murders, armed assaults, and other violence in Lynn, which investigators believed were gang related.

During the course of investigation, authorities seized 34 guns, including two SKS rifles, two Tech-9 semiautomatic machine guns, a Mac 11 semiautomatic machine gun, two sawed-off shotguns, a .40 caliber submachine gun, an AR-15 assault rifle, and a 50-caliber handgun. Over a kilogram of crack, two kilograms of cocaine, a half kilogram of heroin, approximately seven pounds of marijuana, and approximately $40,000 in cash were also purchased or seized. During the last arrest, authorities seized an additional seven guns, drugs including cocaine base and marijuana, and an indeterminate amount of cash.

"The people of Lynn deserve a safe community in which to live and raise their children. Unfortunately, there are a few individuals, often belonging to violent street gangs, whose illegal activities diminish the quality of life for all. We hope that this well-coordinated effort will bring peace to the streets of Lynn," said U.S. Attorney Carmen M. Ortiz. "We also want to assure all the citizens of Massachusetts that we will continue to work closely with our federal, state, and local partners to disrupt and dismantle violent street gangs in Lynn or anywhere in Massachusetts."

Richard DesLauriers, special agent in charge of the FBI, said, "Since the inception of the FBI-led North Shore Gang Task Force, it has generated remarkable results. Today is clear evidence of that success. Neighborhoods in Lynn and Lowell are much safer today than they were yesterday. No longer will senseless violence from a decade-long feud keep the community hostage. This investigation, previous ones, and those ongoing reflect our collective dedication to deterring gang activity. Though our resolve is apparent in the number of arrests made by the task force over the last 12 years—in Operation Melting Pot alone the task force made nearly 60 arrests—we will continue to actively identify individuals throughout the Commonwealth involved in unlawful gang activity."

Chief Kevin F. Coppinger of the Lynn Police Department said the suspects that were arrested had been identified as "impact players" that had negatively affected public safety in Lynn. The arrests significantly reduced the level of violence in the city and the number of violent offenses that had been committed by these individuals did drop significantly.

Law enforcement officers emphasized that the message being sent was that gang-related activities would not be tolerated and would be actively pursued through the support and cooperative efforts of federal, state, and local law enforcement agencies. Also, citizens were reminded that there were a wide range of dangerous drugs available on the streets, including meth and gamma-hydroxybutyrate (GHB) cocaine, heroin, marijuana, and other widely known narcotics. The gun and drug nexus fueled substantial violence throughout the

Commonwealth, which created quality-of-life issues for the residents of Lowell. Anything that could be done to mitigate the effects of gun and drug trafficking was worthwhile, and would hopefully stem the tide of violence in the community.

Operation Melting Pot was investigated for 12 years by members of the FBI's North Shore Gang Task Force inclusive of members of the Massachusetts State Police, Essex County Sheriff's Office, Lynn Police Department, and Chelsea Police Department. The Task Force also received assistance from the Bureau of Alcohol, Tobacco, Firearms and Explosives; the Massachusetts Department of Corrections; and the Middlesex County Sheriff's Office. The federal cases are being prosecuted by members of the Attorney General Ortiz's Organized Crime Strike Force Unit. The state cases are being prosecuted by the Essex County District Attorney's Office and Middlesex County District Attorney's Office.

Federal Bureau of Investigation (FBI)

In 1908, Attorney General Charles J. Bonaparte organized a small force of investigators under the name of the Bureau of Investigation (BOI) to handle all Department of Justice (DOJ) investigative matters, except certain bank frauds. This work expanded to include interstate prostitution and interstate auto theft. World War I in April 1917 saw added responsibility for espionage, sabotage, sedition, and selective service matters. In 1920, bank robbers, bootleggers, and kidnappers took advantage of jurisdictional boundaries by crossing state lines to elude capture because there was no federal law for the BOI authority to tackle this new criminal culture. Please see Table 4.2 for a listing of FBI Directors.

In 1924, John Edgar Hoover was appointed director of the FBI and served until 1972 when he died. Hoover reinstated merit hiring, introduced professional training of new agents, instituted regular inspections of all Bureau operations, and required strict professionalism in the Bureau's work.

Hoover expanded and combined fingerprint files in the Identification Division to compile the largest collection of fingerprints to date. In 1932, he also expanded the FBI's recruitment and hiring, and created the FBI Laboratory, a division established to examine evidence.

In 1973, Clarence M. Kelley became director of the FBI for four years following Hoover's death. He was the first director of the FBI to be appointed through the nomination and confirmation process. Kelley was credited with helping to modernize crime-fighting techniques, such as using computers to track criminals, and won praise as an administrator who identified with street officers working the trenches. Kelley allowed agents to develop more undercover investigations and sting operations for which the FBI since has become known.

Table 4.2 Directors of the FBI

Date	Attorney General	Director	Legislative Action
1908 AG Charles J. Bonaparte ordered new unit	Small investigative unit to report to DOJ	Became Bureau of Investigation in 1909 1910 "White-Slave Traffic" Act, added interstate prostitution; and the 1919 Dyer Act, for interstate auto theft	Investigated antitrust cases, land fraud, copyright violations, peonage, and some 20 other matters
1924 Attorney General Harlan Stone appointed John Edgar Hoover as Director (1924–1972)	Sixth director of the Bureau	Identification Division created in 1924 Technical Crime Laboratory created in 1932 Federal Kidnapping Act 1932 FBI National Academy opened in 1935 1968 Omnibus Crime Control and Safe Streets Act and the 1970 Organized Crime Control Act Racketeering and Corrupt Organizations (RICO) Act	Provided U.S. police a means to identify criminals across jurisdictional boundaries Provided forensic analysis and research for law enforcement Lindbergh kidnapping Provided standardized professional training for America's law enforcement FBI had effective weapons with which to attack organized criminal enterprises Title III provided warrants for wiretaps
Director Clarence M. Kelley (1973–1977)	Refocused FBI investigative priorities for less emphasis on having a high number of cases and to focus more on the quality of cases handled	Cases like ABSCAM (1980), Greylord (1984), and UNIRAC (1978); in 1983, new concerns about terrorist acts grew	New guidelines for investigative techniques like wiretaps, informants, and undercover agents *(continued)*

Table 4.2 (*Continued*)

Date	Attorney General	Director	Legislative Action
Director William H. Webster (1978–1987)	Three priority programs—white-collar crime, organized crime, and foreign counterintelligence; later, illegal drugs (1982), counterterrorism (1982), and violent crimes (1989) were also identified	Success in white-collar crime in investigations like ILLWIND (1988) and Lost Trust (1990), and in organized crime cases like BRILAB (1981) and Pizza Connection (1985)	Investigations into drugs, counterterrorism, and violent crimes Approved the criminal research personality study at the FBI Academy
Director William S. Sessions (1987–1993)	1992 confrontation at Ruby Ridge, Idaho	An unarmed Vicky Weaver was shot dead by an FBI sniper	Investigation continued into Freeh's term
Director Louis Freeh 1993–2001	1992 Ruby Ridge sniper shooting 1993 Branch Division compound in Waco, TX 1996 Kobar Towers bombings 2001, Robert Hanssen arrested	Paramilitary hostage rescue team ATF served a warrant Terrorist group detonated a truck bomb; Hanssen, a 25-year veteran of the FBI, charged with spying for the Soviet Union and Russia	Investigations into the cases
Director Robert S. Mueller III, 2001–	9/11/2001 terrorist attacks; anthrax-filled letters sent to American media outlets and to two U.S. senators	Permit domestic warrantless eavesdropping program On October 26, 2001, President George W. Bush signed into law the USA PATRIOT Act.	Al-Quada terrorists killed included Osama Bin Laden, American-born cleric Anwar al-Awlaki; Al Qaeda's No. 2 leader, Atiyah Abd al-Rahman

Kelley inherited an agency shaken by the Watergate scandal and one still in transition after the death of Hoover a year earlier. The FBI had two acting directors—L. Patrick Gray III and William D. Ruckelshaus—before Kelley was confirmed as director.

President Jimmy Carter appointed William H. Webster as director of the FBI in 1978, and he served until 1987. Then, in 1987, President Ronald Reagan chose him to be director of the Central Intelligence Agency (CIA). He was a former federal judge who ascended to the CIA after his successful coups against the New York mafia families while director of the FBI. Judge Webster is the only American to serve as director of both the CIA and the FBI.

President Ronald Reagan nominated William Steele Sessions (1987–1993) to succed William Webster in 1987. Sessions was seen as combining tough direction with fairness and applauded for pursuing a policy of broadening the FBI to include more women and minorities. He served five years.

In 1993, President Clinton nominated Louis J. Freeh to be director. The threat of international and domestic terrorism came with the 1993 bombing of the World Trade Center in New York and the 1995 bombing of the Alfred P. Murrah Federal Building in Oklahoma City. The FBI responded to the emerging international face of crime by aggressively building bridges between U.S. and foreign law enforcement.

Under the leadership of Director Louis J. Freeh (1993–2001), the Bureau dramatically expanded its legal program (39 offices by the fall of 2000); provided professional law enforcement education to foreign nationals through the International Law Enforcement Academy (ILEA) in Budapest (opened in 1994) and other international education efforts; and created working groups and other structured liaisons with foreign law enforcement.

Former U.S. Attorney Robert S. Mueller III was nominated to be director of the FBI by President George W. Bush in 2001. He was sworn in as director with a mandate to address a number of tough challenges: upgrading the FBI's information technology infrastructure, addressing records management issues, and enhancing the Bureau's foreign counterintelligence analysis and security in the wake of the damage done by former special agent and convicted spy Robert S. Hanssen. Mueller took office a week before the terrorist attacks on the United States on September 11, 2001. Since then, he has overseen the expansion of the FBI from an agency dedicated to criminal investigations to one taking a major role in the nation's global antiterrorism effort.

Director Mueller led the FBI's massive investigative efforts in partnership with all U.S. law enforcement, the federal government, and our allies overseas. The investigation of the attacks was the largest in FBI history. Director Mueller focused the Bureau on prevention of terrorist attacks, on countering foreign intelligence operations against the United States, and on addressing cyber-based attacks and other high-technology crimes. This change in course was in part a response to accusations of the FBI's mishandling of crucial intelligence prior to the September 11 attacks.

FBI Director Mueller was set to step down as FBI director in August 2011 owing to a law that set a 10-year term limit for the position. In July, however, Congress approved a bill, which was subsequently signed by President Obama, that allowed Mueller to serve for another two years. Later that month, he was unanimously confirmed by the Senate for the additional term.

Table 4.3 FBI Directors, Then and Now

Robert S. Mueller, III 2001–Present
Thomas J. Pickard, 2001
Louis J. Freeh, 1993–2001
Floyd I. Clarke, 1993
William S. Sessions, 1987–1993
John E. Otto, 1987
William H. Webster, 1978–1987
James B. Adams, 1978
Clarence M. Kelley, 1973–1978
William D. Ruckelshaus, 1973
L. Patrick Gray, 1972–1973
J. Edgar Hoover, 1924–1972
William J. Burns, 1921–1924
William J. Flynn, 1919–1921
William E. Allen, 1919
Alexander B. Bielaski, 1912–1919
Stanley W. Finch, 1908–1912

Source: www.fbi.gov/about-us/history/directors/directors_then_and_now

The FBI has been led by a single person since it was established in 1908. The first leadership title was "Chief," but that was changed to "Director" in the term of William Flynn. Since 1920, the Director of FBI answers to the attorney general. Under the Omnibus Crime Control Act and Safe Streets Act of 1968, Public Law 90-3351, the Director is appointed by the U.S. President and confirmed by the Senate. On October 15, 1976, in reaction to the 48-year term of J. Edgar Hoover, Congress passed Public Law 94-503, limiting the FBI Director to a single term of no longer than 10 years. See Table 4.3.

FBI's Behavior Science Unit

The Behavioral Science Unit (BSU) was established in 1972 at the FBI Academy in Quantico, Virginia. Through its legacy of training, research, and consultation activities, the BSU developed techniques, tactics, and procedures that have become a staple of behavior-based programs that support law enforcement, intelligence, and military communities. It is here that the term *serial killer* was coined and where criminal investigative analysis and "profiling" were developed under the leadership of unit chief John Douglas. Many of these programs eventually developed into stand-alone programs, units, and centers, such as the National Center for the Analysis of Violent Crime (NCAVC), Undercover Safeguard Unit, Crisis Negotiation Unit, Hostage Rescue teams, and Employee Assistance Unit (O'Block, 2010).

In 1977, John Douglas and Bob Ressler begin their research project on interviewing criminals in prison. Douglas suggested to Ressler that they ask them why they did the crime and find out what it was like through their eyes. The first felon they decided to interview was Ed Kemper, who was serving multiple life sentences in California. They began the interview by telling Kemper that they had carefully researched his file so they would know if he was trying to con them.

Kemper talked for hours and provided important details and motives of his crime (Douglas & Olshaker, 1995, pp. 113–115). The first important teaching point the agents identified was that manipulation, domination, and control were the three watchwords of violent serial offenders. Everything they do and think about, according to Douglas, was directed toward assisting them in filling their otherwise inadequate lives. Second, the single crucial factor in the development of a serial rapist or killer was the role of fantasy. Kemper's fantasies developed early and involved the relationship between sex and death. The game he made his sister play with him involved binding him to a chair as if he were in a gas chamber.

Third, there was a several-step escalation from fantasy to reality, often fueled by pornography, morbid experimentation on animals, and cruelty to peers. This last trait was seen by the subject as "getting back" at them for bad treatment. In Kemper's case, he was shunned and tormented by other children because of his size and personality. He had already dismembered two family cats and beheaded his sister's doll, practicing what he was planning for his victims.

At another level, Kemper's overriding fantasy was to be rid of his domineering, abusive mother. But rarely does the offender direct his anger at the focus of his resentment. In Kemper's case, he murdered his grandparents, served time, was released, then murdered many coeds, and finally his mother and her friend.

Douglas and Ressler used the Kemper case to break down the components of a crime into pre- and postoffense behavior. Kemper had mutilated his victims, which at first suggested a sexual sadist. On interview, however, dismemberment was analyzed more to be a fetish act than sadistic and had more to do with the possession part of the fantasy. His handling and disposing of the bodies also had meaning. The early victims had been carefully buried far from the mother's home, but the later ones—his mother and her friend—had been virtually left out in the open. That, combined with Kemper's extensive driving around town with bodies and body parts in the car, seemed to be a taunting of the community that had taunted and rejected him.

John Douglas makes the point that if you want to understand the artist, look at his work. The successful serial killers plan their work as carefully as a painter plans his canvas. An evaluation comes from meeting the offender and interacting with him and the rest comes from studying and understand his work, that is, the crime scene (Douglas & Olshaker, 1995, p. 116).

The lessons learned from the 10 to 12 research interviews were accumulating. The agents were able to correlate what was going on in an offender's mind with the evidence he left at the crime scene. In 1979 the unit received about 50 requests for profiles, and by the next year the caseload had doubled. Soon, John Douglas had a newly created title of "criminal-personality profiling program manager" and started working with FBI field offices to coordinate the submission of cases by local police departments for profiling.

History of VICAP*

Although the Violent Criminal Apprehension Program (VICAP) is a program funded, staffed, and supported by the Critical Incident Response Group (CIRG) of the FBI, the initiating concept of VICAP was the idea of a sworn officer in local law enforcement: Detective Pierce Brooks, of the Los Angeles Police Department's Robbery–Homicide Squad (Egger, 1990; Keefer, 1998; Taylor, 1998; Witzig, 2006).

Brooks conceived of VICAP while working the case of serial killer Harvey Glatman. In the early 1950s, Glatman moved to Los Angeles from New York State, where he had served time for robbery (Newton, 1990). He opened a television repair service and made a house call at the home of his first murder victim, Judy Dull, then only 19 years of age. Photography was Glatman's hobby, and he convinced Dull to come to his home for a photo shoot. On August 1, 1957, after taking a few detective magazine–style photographs, he bound Dull and raped her. Later, he took her to the desert outside Los Angeles, where he took a few more pictures of her and then strangled her to death. He left her in a shallow grave (Newton, 1990).

Glatman's second victim was Shirley Bridgeford. He met her through a lonely hearts club and convinced her to pose for a few photographs. In March 1958, she too was taken to the desert, bound, photographed, raped, and strangled to death (Newton, 1990).

The third victim was Ruth Mercado. On July 23, 1958, she came to Glatman's apartment, where photographs were taken and she was raped. She was taken to the desert and strangled.

Brooks became involved in the cases of Dull and Bridgeford. He examined both cases and observed that the victims were bound with excessive amounts of rope, far more than would be needed to restrain them. Moreover, the bindings were neatly arranged, with the coils of rope resting tightly against each other.

Brooks noted that the neatly applied, excessive bindings on the first two victims suggested strongly that these were not the killer's first victims or his last. He thought that finding other victims of one killer would be easier if

---

* Sections on the history of VICAP were written by Eric W. Witzig.

information about all of the city's homicides and homicides from other jurisdictions could be stored in one place. Perhaps a new machine that the federal government used to tally the 1950 census would be useful: a computer. He investigated buying a computer for the city but found that it would be half as large as city hall and cost half as much (Taylor, 1998).

Brooks employed an elementary form of VICAP in order to solve his problem. For a year and a half, he went to the central library in Los Angeles on his days off and began to read out-of-town newspapers. He found a newspaper reporting a homicide remarkably similar to the two he was investigating. Brooks contacted the police department handling the out-of-town case and, combining their investigative information with the information gleaned from his own cases, three murders were closed with the arrest of Harvey Glatman (Witzig, 1995).

In 1981, Brooks wrote a plan for VICAP that was submitted to the Law Enforcement Assistance Administration:

> VI-CAP [the hyphen was dropped in 1984], a product of ICAP (the Integrated Criminal Apprehension Program), is a program designed to integrate and analyze, on a nationwide basis, all aspects of the investigation of a series of similar pattern deaths by violence, regardless of the location or number of police agencies involved. The overall goal of the VI-CAP is the expeditious identification and apprehension of the criminal offender, or offenders, involved in multiple murders. [Cited in Egger, 1990, p. 191]

In 1981 and 1982, the Law Enforcement Assistance Administration (LEAA) funded a series of VI-CAP planning meetings. In 1983, a series of meetings were held at the Sam Houston State University to plan for an entity to be called the National Center for the Analysis of Violent Crime (NCAVC), which would be located at the FBI's Training Division in Quantico, Virginia. Planning included VICAP as part of NCAVC (Egger, 1990). In 1983, Brooks testified before Congress and presented his theory of VICAP. Two years later, in 1985, the director of the FBI, William Webster, credited Brooks for his assistance in the creation of the NCAVC (Keefer, 1998; Taylor, 1998).

VICAP went online May 29, 1985, with Pierce Brooks at the keyboard of a terminal linking the NCAVC to the FBI's mainframe computer located in the J. Edgar Hoover headquarters building in Washington, D.C. Brooks was VICAP's first program manager. His presence ensured that VICAP, as implemented, matched his vision.

VICAP'S Mission

When VICAP began in 1985, its purpose was to

> collect data for analyses which will lead to the identification of patterns of violent crime throughout the country. Although the completion of the [VICAP] Report and

the submission of cases is voluntary, the importance of doing so cannot be over emphasized. A single report received and analyzed by the VICAP staff could initiate a coordinated effort among law enforcement agencies hundreds or even thousands of miles apart and expedite the apprehension of a violent serial offender. (Brooks, Devine, Green, Hart, & Moore, 1988, p. 2)

In the mid-1990s the VICAP mission statement was streamlined: "VICAP's mission is to facilitate communication, cooperation, and coordination between law enforcement agencies and provide support in their efforts to investigate, identify, track, apprehend, and prosecute violent serial and repeat offenders" (VICAP, 2002, p. 2).

VICAP Case Types

The types and kinds of cases accepted, and sought, by VICAP since its beginning have changed little. VICAP works well for the following kinds of cases:

- Solved or unsolved homicides or attempts, especially those that involve an abduction; are apparently random, motiveless, or sexually oriented; or are known or suspected to be part of a series.
- Missing persons, where the circumstances indicate a strong possibility of foul play and the victim is still missing.
- Unidentified dead bodies where the manner of death is known or suspected to be homicide (Howlett et al., 1986)
- Abductions of children or attempts.
- Solved or unsolved sexual assaults or attempts.

HOMICIDE OR ATTEMPTS

After 20 years of VICAP operation, confusion remains in the law enforcement community about the types and kinds of cases that can, and should, be forwarded to the national VICAP database. There is a popular misconception that VICAP is interested only in unsolved, recent homicides. Those cases should be entered, of course, but so too should older homicides because the value of information in the case never diminishes.

For example, one eastern state police agency sent in the solved murder of an eight-year-old girl. The defendant had been convicted and was incarcerated. When the case was sent to the VICAP database, almost 45 years had passed since the murder. Nonetheless, the case was entered. A year or two later, a state police agency in the Midwest forwarded an unsolved murder of a seven-year-old girl. A VICAP crime analyst compared the two cases in terms of victimology and offender modus operandi (MO). The analyst noted that the two cases presented with similarities and notified investigators. Reopening their cold case, state investigators developed probable cause to believe that the incarcerated offender had committed the murder in their state. After 45 years, the child's parents, now in their 60s, could be told that the police had solved their daughter's murder. Clearly, older homicides, those solved and those unsolved, should be included in the database.

Death investigators typically think that solved cases are of little interest to their colleagues. In fact, in addition to providing object lessons for the solution of murder, solved cases provide information about offenders, victims, and MO—all invaluable when contrasting and comparing cases in an effort to seek possible matches between or among cases. Once an offender is identified and it is determined or believed that he killed more than once, a database search for other, unsolved (or possibly cases where an arrest was made or an indictment handed up, causing authorities to believe the case was solved) cases can be accomplished with information about the offender, his victim, and his MO.

Reporting of attempted homicides is important for two reasons. First, attempted homicides can be instrumental to the solution of a series of murders, and a record of the attempts should be forwarded to the VICAP database. Harris, Thomas, Fisher, and Hirsch (2002) noted that medicine is more successful than ever before in treating victims of violent crime and saving their lives. They wrote that between 1960 and 1999, the fraction of criminal assaults resulting in death dropped by 70%. In other words, it is not that the offender did not try hard enough to kill the victim; it is simply that the victim would not die or that medical attention saved him or her.

Second, the reporting of attempted homicides is important because not everyone who comes into the sphere of control of a killer is killed. Survivors of a serial killer can provide police with invaluable information that can be used to cut short the killer's violent career. For police, the difficulty comes in associating the correct attempted murder, out of a set of many possible attempted murders, with the correct series of homicides. In retrospect, connecting cases is not always easy; the art of analysis and case matching is in knowing which facets of the case are to be connected, how to make those facets pop out of the background noise of all of the facts, or even if all of the facts are present.

For example, the late Theodore Bundy did not kill all potential victims. Robert D. Keppel (1995) wrote that in mid-July 1974, Bundy was hunting for victims around Lake Sammamish near Seattle, Washington. Bundy, wearing a cast on his left arm, approached a young woman and asked her to help him load something into his car. She walked with him to his car but declined to get in and walked away from Bundy. Later, witnesses placed Bundy with another woman, Janice Ott, who was never again seen alive. Still later in the day, Bundy was seen chatting with several women. In the end, he met young Denise Naslund. She too was never seen again alive.

Robert Yates of Spokane, Washington, is another example. He pleaded guilty in October 2000 to the murders of 13 women in and around Spokane but was not always successful when he tried to kill a woman (Fuhrman, 2001). Yates patronized prostitutes on Spokane's East Sprague Street and murdered some of them. In August 1998, he picked up Christine Smith. Both were in the back of Yates's van when she received a tremendous blow to the head. She fled from Yates and the van and received medical attention. A year later, an X-ray taken of her head during the course of medical treatment revealed that what Smith thought was a blow to the head from Yates was actually a gunshot wound. Subsequently, the police searched a van that Yates owned and found a .25 caliber shell casing and an expended bullet (Fuhrman, 2001). Smith was able to provide authorities with information concerning her assailant, who turned out to be Yates.

Subsequent to his guilty pleas in Spokane County, Yates was brought to trial in Pierce County, Washington, for two murders: Melinda Mercer, whose body was found December 7, 1997, and Connie LaFontaine Ellis, whose body was found October 13, 1998. Yates was found guilty of the murders, and the jury sentenced him to death.

MISSING PERSONS AND ABDUCTIONS

Among the difficult decisions that law enforcement officers and officials face is the handling of missing persons matters. One of the many considerations in these cases is the age and vulnerability of the missing person to be a victim of abduction and become the target of sexual or homicidal assault. The Child Abduction Response Plan makes this clear:

> Often the most challenging task at hand upon receipt of a missing child complaint is determining whether it is an actual abduction, runaway child, lost child, thrown away child, or fictitious report to cover up the death of the child or other family problem. This crucial assessment of the initial facts will dictate what actions the responding law enforcement agency will perform. (U.S. Department of Justice, 1998, p. 1)

Once an assessment of the missing person is completed and the appropriate law enforcement responses have been made, if the person, juvenile or adult, has not been located, then a report should be forwarded to VICAP for inclusion in the database. In 1985, Detective David Reichert of the King County, Washington, Sheriff's Office and a member of the Green River Task Force said that once the offender's victim selection preferences were identified, the task force paid particular attention to other missing persons with the same characteristics. The task force assembled as much information as possible about missing persons, including individual medical information, dental charts, and

X-rays. When victims of the Green River Killer were discovered, their remains were typically little more than skeletons. However, task force preparation paid off, and recovered remains were compared with missing person reports, with identification achieved in only a day or two.

Case Example: 3-D Facial Reconstruction and DNA Help Identify 12-Year-Old Case of a Jane Doe From Utah

Identifying missing persons is often a joint effort among multiple law enforcement agencies. Special acknowledgment is given to the detectives and investigators with the Midvale and Salt Lake City police departments and local medical examiner's office in Salt Lake; Gina McNeil with the Utah State Clearinghouse; and the National Center for Missing and Exploited Children's (NCMEC) forensic artist, J. Mullins, for their diligent work in resolving this 12-year-old case. Thanks to their dedication and hard work, the remains were positively identified, bringing closure to a searching family.

Nikole Bakoles, or Niki as her friends and family called her, was only 19 years old when she was last seen by her mother in October 1999, boarding a flight to Salt Lake City. Niki had traveled to Washington with her infant daughter to visit her mother. Originally from Washington State, she had relocated to Utah with her boyfriend in 1997. The two had a very tumultuous relationship and, shortly after arriving in Utah, began using drugs. After a couple of run-ins with law enforcement, Niki sought out help and completed a drug treatment program. She had gone back to Washington and seemed "like a new person," says her mother. But soon after, Niki began receiving phone calls from her ex-boyfriend asking that she return. Pregnant and still deeply in love with her boyfriend, Niki eventually decided to go back. Two months later, Niki and her boyfriend welcomed a baby girl.

Initially, everything seemed fine and Niki visited her mother with her infant daughter a couple of times. But during her last visit to Washington, Niki's mother sensed something was wrong. Niki had begun using drugs again and had recently been arrested twice by police in Utah. In early 2000, Niki lost custody of her infant daughter after social services removed the child from the couple's home in Midvale. Niki last spoke to her mother over the phone in March 2000, to discuss the pending custody situation. That was the last time anyone heard from Niki. She simply disappeared and was never seen again.

For several years, Niki's mother tried to follow up on leads and reached out to family and friends to see if anyone had seen or heard from Niki. With no information about her daughter, she eventually filed a missing persons report with police in 2003. For almost 10 years, Niki's mother continued looking for her daughter and searched the Internet for any information about her.

In late 2011, while searching through Utah's Missing Persons Web site, Niki's mother came across a facial reconstruction of unidentified remains located in October 2000, in an area referred to as Saltair on the southern shore of the Great Salt Lake. The remains were believed to be of a young White female between the ages of 17 and 20. She had long, wavy light brown hair that fell slightly below her shoulders. The images of the unidentified female featured a second three-dimensional facial reconstruction created in 2009, by NCMEC's forensic artist as part of the NCMEC's initiative to assist with long-term missing persons cases. After seeing the image, Niki's mother contacted the Utah Clearinghouse and informed officials that she thought the remains found in Saltair could be those of her daughter. On July 24, 2012, University of Northern Texas confirmed that the unidentified remains and the missing person were a match through DNA results (NCMEC, 2012).

Source: National Center for Missing and Exploited Children. Permission to cite the case given on August 11, 2012, by NCMEC.

UNIDENTIFIED DEAD

Matters involving unidentified dead persons can be thought of as the mirror image of missing person cases. It is very difficult to begin the homicide investigation of an unidentified victim. The body recovery site of an unidentified victim may suggest its connection to a multiple murderer. Fuhrman (2001) wrote that during the Spokane series of murders, the bodies of Laurie A. Wason and Shawn McClenahan were found on top of one another in a vacant lot in Spokane. He also wrote that in the early 1970s, Ted Bundy engaged in similar behavior: he kidnapped two women on one day and killed both at the same location.

Failing the certainty of connection with an ongoing serial event, where to begin in a murder investigation is far more easily determined if the victim is identified. To that end, it makes investigative sense to enter the cases of unidentified dead into the VICAP database.

SEXUAL ASSAULT

For a number of years, sexual assaults were not included in VICAP. But in 2004, the VICAP Crime Analysis Report was revised to include data collection fields suitable for these types of offenses. The questions were based on the Behaviorally Oriented Interview of the Rape Victim proposed by Robert Roy Hazelwood and were reviewed in July 2002 by a VICAP working group (Hazelwood & Burgess, 2009). In December 2002, the VICAP advisory board added their review and approval to the enhanced data collection variables.

VICAP EVALUATION

In 1995, after 10 years of operation, VICAP's program delivery was evaluated with a business analysis. The examination revealed four points (Meister, 1998):

- Only 3 to 5% of the 21,000 to almost 25,000 homicides committed each year were submitted to VICAP.

- There was an "urban void" of submissions. Case submissions ranged from 150 (in 1985, the first half-year) to almost 1,400 per year in 1995. This was but a fraction of the total number of homicides reported for those years (24,526 murders were recorded in 1991 alone). Cities and urban areas that were recording large numbers of homicides were not submitting the cases to the national database, indicating an urban void.
- Users reported that the VICAP Crime Analysis Report had too many questions, was too complicated, and took too long to complete. In 1986, the VICAP report form was reduced in size from three volumes to a 15-page, 190-question, check-the-block, forced-choice instrument (Howlett et al., 1986, p. 17). This was the report form that users in 1995 found too difficult.
- Users reported the perception of a "black hole." VICAP users had the perception that VICAP was like an astronomical black hole, where the force of gravity is so intense that nothing escapes, not even light. The perception was that data went to VICAP, and nothing was ever heard about this information again. VICAP did little to close the communication loop.

1994 CRIME LEGISLATION

The first and major stimulus for change of VICAP was the Violent Crime Control and Law Enforcement Act of 1994, which provided funding for VICAP to develop a pilot program. The goal was to create an intelligent information system to collect, collate, organize, and analyze information about violent serial crime. Congressional funding allowed VICAP to embark on the next change.

VICAP crime analysts began a detailed examination of the crime analysis report to reduce questions from 190 to 95. Moreover, with the aid of color printing technology not available in 1986 and intelligent layout and design, the new VICAP form looked less imposing and more like an attractive, easy-to-use reporting instrument.

By the mid-1990s, tremendous advances had been made in computing. Advances in hardware and software made possible the shift of VICAP software from a mainframe platform to a desktop platform. Data accessible only by a few VICAP Case Analysts could now be accessed by anyone in law enforcement equipped with VICAP software written for the client–server environment.

THE NETWORK

VICAP engaged contractors outside the FBI to write the client–server software application for New VICAP. (Use of the lowercase "i" in ViCAP became the official choice in the late 1990s. A standard spelling, VICAP, is used in this chapter to reduce confusion.) VICAP software is now distributed to participating agencies so that they can perform their own analyses with direct access to all of the data they enter into the system. A networked version of New VICAP software allows the exchange of violent crime information within a police department, a county, a state, or across the nation.

When an intranet is not available for data transmission, the utility of another FBI-sponsored initiative is used: Law Enforcement Online (LEO). LEO is accessible to members of law enforcement entities on application. After an applicant's law enforcement agency status is confirmed, LEO issues software, a sign-on, and a password. The LEO e-mail tool provides an encrypted conduit for information exchange. Through LEO, VICAP users ensure that their transmitted data will not be read by others.

The change in New VICAP utility was the movement of the software from a mainframe platform to a user-friendly, client–server environment that can be delivered to any law enforcement entity. Briefly, New VICAP software permits users to:

- Match violent crime cases.
- Perform cold case analysis.
- Identify trends.
- Learn the "how" and "why" of violence.
- Provide agency administrators with a violent crime reporting system.

CRIME CASE MATCHING

New VICAP software provides state and local agencies with the same type and kind of crime case matching capability enjoyed at the national level by the VICAP Unit. Any data that a user enters into the system are retrievable. Much of the information is captured through the use of pull-down menus, reducing the amount of typing necessary for data entry and the potential for misspelled words (which make data retrieval difficult when correctly spelled words are used in a computer retrieval statement). Dialogue boxes capture hand-entered data. Provision was made for a narrative to be included as part of the data. In an effort to avoid double data entry, the narrative portion accepts text that can be applied in a cut-and-paste style from other word processing programs.

These details of data entry are important because only the data entered into a New VICAP database can be extracted, but all of the data in the database, forced choice or text, can be retrieved for crime case comparison. A CA can select facts or behaviors from an offense and query the database for cases exhibiting similar characteristics. This is the way that CAs in the FBI's VICAP Unit check for two or more cases that may have been committed by the same offender, or match open, unsolved cases to a known offender's timeline of travels and activities.

Another feature of New VICAP software is the ability to enter victim or crime scene photographs into the database and have them associated with a particular case. A written description cannot capture the details of bindings applied to a victim, but a photograph can do so with great clarity. Moreover, although case jackets and photographs can disappear over time, data entered into the New VICAP database are not lost and are available for later retrieval and analysis.

COLD CASE ANALYSIS

During the 20 years that VICAP has been in operation, an entire generation of detectives has moved from the start of their careers to retirement. Experience teaches us that when seasoned homicide detectives leave the unit, all of their case knowledge goes with them. But a computer database never forgets. Data entered (and properly backed up) are never lost. The answer to the question, "What are the facts of the murder committed six years ago in the alley, the rear, of the 200 block of Tennessee Avenue, Southeast?" is always available.

Turner and Kosa (2003) offered that cold case squads are formed because

> law enforcement agencies, regardless of size, are not immune to rising crime rates, staff shortages, and budget restrictions. Rising crime rates can tax the investigative and administrative resources of an agency. More crime may mean that fewer cases are pursued vigorously, fewer opportunities arise for followup, or individual caseloads increase for already overworked detectives. Transfers, retirements, and other personnel changes may force departments to rely on younger, less experienced investigators to work cases, often unsuccessfully. (p. 1)

The VICAP tool allows storage of old, cold cases for reassessment and work at a later date. Moreover, the evidence-tracking capability of VICAP affords instant recall of evidence collected for examination by new and enhanced laboratory techniques available at some future date.

VICAP Today

Today's VICAP is still located within CIRG and is part of NCAVC, along with BAU 1, which handles terrorism threats; BAU-2, which handles crimes against adults; BAU-3, which handles crimes against children; and the Behavioral Research Group, serving as the center's research component. The NCAVC provides assistance to law enforcement entities at all levels and around the world in these types of cases:

- Child abduction or mysterious disappearance of a child
- Serial murder

- Single murder
- Serial sexual assaults or rapes
- Extortion
- Threats
- Kidnapping
- Product tampering
- Arson and bombing
- Weapons of mass destruction
- Public corruption
- Domestic and international terrorism

In summary, VICAP maintains the largest investigative repository of violent crime cases in the United States. It is a Web-based data information center designed to collect and analyze information about homicides, sexual assaults, missing persons, and unidentified human remains. VICAP Web users compare information in an attempt to identify similar cases and help move investigations forward.

VICAP's mission is to facilitate cooperation and coordination between law enforcement agencies and to provide support to those agencies in their efforts to apprehend and prosecute violent serial offenders, especially those who cross jurisdictional boundaries.

Since its creation by the Department of Justice in 1985, more than 4,000 law enforcement agencies have submitted cases to VICAP, and there are currently over 84,000 cases in the database. More than 4,000 investigators and analysts are registered users of the system, and together they forge a powerful nationwide network of professionals collaborating on a daily basis.

In the summer of 2008, the VICAP program made its database available to all law enforcement agencies through a secure Internet link. This allows for real-time access to the database and allows agencies to enter and update cases directly into the database. VICAP analysts, as part of the Highway Serial Killings Initiative, have created a map of over 500 cases that mark where bodies have been found along highways over the past 30 years.

Additional Federal Agencies

DEPARTMENT OF HOMELAND SECURITY

Shortly after the terrorist attacks on September 11, 2001, President George W. Bush announced his plans to create what later would become the Department of Homeland Security (DHS). His intentions for the cabinet department would be to establish a national strategy to protect the country from future terrorist attacks (Borja, 2008). In March 2003, a reorganization of agencies took place, with the DHS absorbing 22 existing agencies (Viotti, Opheim, & Bowen, 2008). The mega-agency of the DHS had been developed in response to a perceived lack of intelligence sharing, coordination, and cooperation among federal agencies that were made particularly apparent after the September 11 attacks (Ward, Kiernan, & Mabrey, 2006). The primary missions outlined by the agency included the prevention of terrorist attacks within and against the United States, the reduction of the country's vulnerability to terrorism, and the mitigation and minimization of damage from potential terrorist attacks and natural disasters (Ward et al., 2006).

The bulk of the DHS and a major portion of its expenditures include roles related to port and border security, immigration and customs, and investigations regarding immigration laws (Viotti et al., 2008). The U.S. Immigration and Customs Enforcement (ICE) is the principal investigative branch of the DHS and is also responsible for the enforcement of immigration and customs laws within the United States (U.S. ICE, 2012). Within ICE, the Homeland Security Investigations (HSI) directorate investigates immigration crimes, human rights violations, financial crimes, cybercrimes, and crimes involving the illegal movement of drugs, weapons, and people. The Enforcement and Removal Operations (ERO) is responsible for apprehension and deportation of illegal aliens and convicted criminals who pose a threat to national security (U.S. ICE, 2012).

Regarding border enforcement and inspections at ports of entry, the U.S. Customs and Border Protection (CBP) assumed former responsibilities from Customs Service, Immigration and Naturalization Service, and the Department of Agriculture as a result of the Homeland Security Act of 2002. Although CBP is responsible for the overall border enforcement, CBP officers are assigned to points of entry for immigration, customs, and agricultural inspections. In contrast, U.S. Border Patrol (USBP) officers carry out enforcement duties between points of entry and have a primary focus on preventing illegal entry into the United States and movement of contraband across the border (Haddal, 2010). Migrants wishing to become citizens through lawful immigration will contact the U.S. Citizenship and Immigration Services (USCIS), which processes citizenship, residency, and asylum requests (U.S. CIS, 2012).

The DHS was also structured to respond to natural and man-made disasters through merged agencies under the Emergency Preparedness and Response Directorate. The Federal Emergency Management Agency (FEMA) formed a major component of the DHS's emergency response and was responsible for coordinating an integrated national effort to respond and lessen the impacts of disasters by reducing risks and minimizing damage and losses (Viotti et al., 2008). FEMA is not regarded as a first responder, but rather as a coordinating agency that provides funding for emergency planning, financial assistance to rebuild after disasters, and training to first responders (Ward et al., 2006). However, many have been critical of FEMA's ability to coordinate and organize strategic response operations in the event of disaster. In fact, it has been stated that the transition of the agency into the Department of Homeland Security realigned its main focus on rooting out terrorists and homeland security while ignoring the strategic level of reorganization that was required to respond effectively to natural disasters (Viotti et al., 2008).

Other components of the DHS include the Coast Guard, Secret Service, Transportation Security Administration, intelligence agencies, and defense agencies involved in countermeasures against chemical, biological, radiological, and nuclear warfare.

Bureau of Alcohol, Tobacco, and Firearms (ATF)

The ATF has its roots in the nation's first excise tax collection duties, which can be traced back to more than 200 years ago. After having been a part of the Department of Treasury for more than 80 years, the ATF was transferred to the Department of Justice under the Homeland Security Act of 2002. Included in the transition were the removal of tax collection duties on alcohol products and an increased focus on investigations into violations of firearm, cigarette, and alcohol regulations as well as problems involving explosives (U.S. Department of Justice, 2009). These violations have commonly included the illegal manufacture, sale, and transfer of tobacco, alcohol, firearms, and explosives. Also included in the ATF mandate is the prevention of terrorist attacks through the interdiction of illegal trafficking operations that may be potential sources for funding terrorist activity (Krouse, 2011).

A major focus of ATF is the reduction of firearms-related violence through the enforcement of firearm laws across the United States. However, additional appropriations have been given to the ATF by Congress to combat gun trafficking, with a heightened focus on the Southwest border between the United States and Mexico, a project that has been called Project Gunrunner. In an attempt to reduce illegal gun transactions and movement of arms from the United States to Mexico, the ATF has also developed cooperative partnerships with the Mexican government. The ATF also participates in a nationally coordinated strategy to combat drug and arms trafficking and its associated violence under the Mérida Initiative. Under the initiative, appropriations were given to the ATF that allowed the agency to distribute a Spanish version of the firearms trace software (e-Trace) and facilitated the establishment of a U.S.–Mexico ballistic evidence exchange program (Krouse, 2011). Another major responsibility of the ATF is the inspections of federal firearms licensees to ensure their compliance with firearm distribution regulations as a means to prevent the diversion of guns to illegal markets. Consistent with firearm-associated violence is the agency's involvement in Project Safe Neighborhoods, which aims to investigate and prosecute violent, armed offenders; infiltrate violent criminal groups; determine the origins of illegally acquired guns; and develop and promote community outreach efforts within the United States (Krouse, 2011).

The ATF also has the responsibility of investigating arson cases, responding to arson and explosive incidents, and enforcing federal laws dealing with the manufacture, distribution, and importation of explosives. The agency has been given the responsibility of maintaining records of all arson and explosive incidents and making them available to first responders across the United States. In addition, under the Safe Explosives Act, the ATF is responsible for investigations of explosive thefts, background check to prevent prohibited persons from acquiring explosives, and compliance inspections of licensees and permittees every three years to ensure that proper storage guidelines are followed (Krouse, 2011).

Tobacco and alcohol diversion enforcement by the ATF are generally regarded as lower priority responsibilities due to the usually nonviolent nature of the crimes. In addition, the transfer of the ATF from the Department of Treasury to the Department of Justice was characterized by a lesser focus on enforcing laws relating to alcohol manufacturing and distribution, as many of these duties were assumed by the Alcohol and Tobacco Tax and Trade Bureau (TTB) of the Treasury. Despite that, the ATF has been involved in ongoing investigations into tobacco-smuggling operations of large criminal networks that have used cigarette bootlegging as a means to finance other criminal activities. Other responsibilities regarding tobacco diversion include coordinating with other law enforcement agencies, assisting in the procurement of funding for large-scale investigations, and coordinating with industry officials to obtain products for undercover or "fronting" operations (U.S. Department of Justice, 2009).

International Agencies

SCOTLAND YARD/METROPOLITAN POLICE SERVICE

Maintaining law and order had become a matter of public concern as London was expanding in the 18th and 19th centuries. In 1828, Sir Robert Peel and his committee introduced his police bill, which led to an organized police service in London. Ten years later, the Marine Police and Bow Street Runners were incorporated into the Metropolitan Police Service. In 1914, the Women Police was formed.

The McNaughton case served as the basis for first famous legal test for insanity in 1843. Daniel McNaughton, a Scottish woodworker, killed the prime minister's secretary, Edward Drummond, mistaking him for Prime Minister

Robert Peel, because he believed that the prime minister was conspiring against him. The court acquitted McNaughton "by reason of insanity," and he was laced in a mental institution for the rest of his life. However, the case caused a public uproar, and Queen Victoria ordered the court to develop a stricter test for insanity.

The "McNaughton rule" was a standard to be applied by the jury, after hearing medical testimony from prosecution and defense experts. The rule created a presumption of sanity, unless the defense proved that the accused, at the time of committing the act, was laboring under such a defect of reason, from disease of the mind, as not to know the nature and quality of the act he was doing or, if he did know it, that he did not know what he was doing was wrong.

Scotland Yard, the headquarters for London's Metropolitan Police Service (MPS) is responsible for law enforcement within Greater London. The police force is the oldest and one of the largest in the world and has become an international symbol of policing. In addition to regular local policing responsibilities, the MPS carries out national duties such as the protection of royalty, ex-members of the government, and diplomats, as well as counter-terrorism functions.

One of the most famous cases investigated by Scotland Yard was the Jack the Ripper case. A serial killer is believed responsible for the murders of five women in East London between August and November 1888. In 1988, the century anniversary year of the case, John Douglas was invited to participate in Peter Ustinov's television special and offer a profile. In his book, *Cases That Haunt Us*, Douglas presents his behavioral profile of the killer and his choice from the suspects (Douglas & Olshaker, 2000, pp. 62–80).

INTERPOL

The INTERPOL organization is an intergovernmental agency, stationed in Lyon, France, which helps facilitate international police cooperation between 190 member countries in order to combat and prevent international crimes (INTERPOL, 2012). It was established as the International Criminal Police Commission (ICPC) in 1923 and adopted its telegraphic address as its common name in 1956.

The agency helps bridge gaps in information sharing and communication that result from incompatible information systems and language barriers. Through the maintenance of a police communications and support system called I-24/7, INTERPOL is able to share vital data with authorized law enforcement agencies. This data helps to determine the identity of a suspect, their location and assists law enforcement agencies in their apprehension. These suspects may be responsible for international violations that warrant their arrest, may be involved in crimes committed in multiple countries, or may have escaped across a border after committing an offense (Central Bureau of

Investigation, 2012). INTERPOL has outlined its priorities in identifying and facilitating the apprehension of criminals involved in drugs and organized crime, financial and high-tech crime, public safety and terrorism, trafficking in human beings, and corruption, as well as fugitives who have escaped arrest (United Nations, 2007). An additional function of INTERPOL is emergency and crisis response enabling the deployment of incidence response teams to provide investigative and analytical support in the event of a crisis (United Nations, 2007).

In order to maintain as politically neutral a role as possible, INTERPOL's constitution forbids it to undertake any interventions or activities of a political, military, religious, or racial nature. INTERPOL agents do not make arrests themselves, and there is no single INTERPOL jail where criminals are taken. Rather, the agency provides communication and database assistance between the law enforcement agencies of the member countries.

A major advantage of INTERPOL's databases is to help law enforcement see the big picture of international crime. Although other agencies have their own extensive crime databases, the information rarely extends beyond one nation's borders. INTERPOL can track criminals and crime trends around the world.

Case Study: INTERPOL and the Pink Panthers

Responsible for at least 100 jewel heists worldwide during the past 10 years, a group called the "Pink Panthers" has been a major focus of INTERPOL. The group is believed to be made up of Serbian ex-military who fought in the Balkan Wars, with a majority originating from the Serbian city of Nis (Quinn, 2009). In the eyes of their fellow citizens, members of the group are seen as heroes who have been able to take millions of dollars' worth of jewels from luxury stores (Oliver, 2008; Quinn, 2009). Officials describe the group as very fast and very well organized, as demonstrated by their heists, which usually last less than three minutes, as evidenced in a recent heist in a shopping mall located in Dubai (Papenfuss, 2010). They are also well connected, as the Balkan Wars enabled network building and friendships (McAllester, 2010). In February 2011, police officers from almost 30 countries came together to collaborate and share information on investigations and successful arrests regarding the gem thieves (INTERPOL, 2011). INTERPOL developed the Pink Panthers project in 2007 to facilitate the identification, location, and apprehension of members of the group through network building and data sharing and analysis among local law enforcement agencies (INTERPOL, 2011). In the previous year, 36 members of the group were arrested; however, other individuals in the group remain elusive. Although some stolen items have been recovered, a majority of the stolen jewels are usually cut to look different and resold for around 25% of their retail value (McAllester, 2010).

EUROPOL

Europol is the European Union's criminal intelligence agency established under the Treaty on European Union in 1993. It became fully operational in 1999. Its mission is to make Europe safer by assisting the Member States of the European Union in their fight against serious international crime and terrorism. Large-scale criminal and terrorist networks pose a significant threat to the internal security of the EU and to the safety and livelihood of its people. The biggest security threats come from terrorism, international drug trafficking and money laundering, organized fraud, counterfeiting of the euro currency, and people smuggling. There are also dangers in the form of cybercrime, trafficking in human beings, and other modern-day threats. This is a multibillion-euro business, quick to adapt to new opportunities and resilient in the face of traditional law enforcement measures.

The agency uses its unique information capabilities and the expertise of 700 staff to identify and track the most dangerous criminal and terrorist networks in Europe. Law enforcement authorities in the EU rely on this intelligence work and the services of Europol's operational coordination center and secure information network, to carry out almost 12,000 cross-border investigations each year. These have led to the disruption of many criminal and terrorist networks, the arrest of thousands of dangerous criminals, the recovery of millions of euro in criminal proceeds, and the recovery from harm of hundreds of victims, including children trafficked for sexual exploitation. Europol also acts as a major center of expertise in key fields of law enforcement activity and as a European center for strategic intelligence on organized crime. Its Organised Crime Threat Assessment is a seminal product for EU policymakers and police chiefs.

Europol Cases Reported During June 2012   An international investigation carried out under the leadership of the Police of the Czech Republic, with the support of Europol, has succeeded in dismantling a large network of cocaine smugglers.

Judicial and law enforcement authorities in four countries (France, Bulgaria, Poland, and Belgium) successfully conducted a joint operation—supported and coordinated by Eurojust and Europol—against a trafficking in human beings (THB) criminal network operating in several Member States.

An international organized crime group, responsible for payment card fraud and illegal online purchases, has been successfully disrupted during a raid in Romania, with the support of Europol and Eurojust.

An international people-smuggling ring, bringing illegal immigrants from the Philippines to France and other European countries, was dismantled by French police authorities on Monday, with the support of Europol and Eurojust.

Combating Cybercrime

As crime has spread across the Internet, law enforcement has begun to catch up with those using the Internet for illicit purposes. In 1996, the Computer Crime and Intellectual Property Section of the U.S. Department of Justice created the Infotech Training Working Group to investigate online violations of the law. This office evolved into the National Cybercrime Training Partnership (NCTP). The NCTP worked with all levels of law enforcement to develop long-range strategies, raise public awareness, and build momentum to combat this problem on many fronts. The National White Collar Crime Center (NW3C) based in Richmond, Virginia, offered operational support to the NCTP and functioned as an information clearinghouse for cybercrime. These agencies worked together to generate more funding to help law enforcement keep up with the ever-changing computer world. Those in charge of policing the Net looked on their mission as a battle that they could not afford to lose.

One problem for the authorities was the difficulty of police departments to compete with private companies, when it came to paying those with computer expertise. Trained technical personnel could usually earn far more money in the private sector than working for public agencies. Near the end of his second term as president, Bill Clinton took measures to alleviate the situation by announcing plans for congressional funding that offered scholarships to those who studied computer security and then agreed to join the "Federal Cyber Service" after graduation. The program was modeled after a military program that had been successfully used by the Reserve Officers Training Corps on college campuses.

In early 1999, the Training and Research Institute of NW3C conducted an in-depth survey on white-collar violations of the law. It found that in part because of the recent emergence of the Internet, one in three American households were now the victims of white-collar crime. Traditional street crimes were falling in many places around the nation, but high-tech crimes were on the rise. The institute also found that only 7% of these online victims contacted a law enforcement agency. In order to boost these figures, in May 2000, the FBI, the Department of Justice, and the NW3C announced the creation of the Internet Fraud Complaint Center (IFCC), established to provide a vehicle for victims nationwide to report incidents of online fraud.

In early 2001, the IFCC issued its first study on Internet fraud: in the first six months of operation, the IFCC received 20,014 fraud complaints, and 6,087 of those were referred to law enforcement agencies throughout the nation. Of those, 5,273, or well over 80%, involved fraud that was perpetrated in cyberspace. California ranked first in Internet fraud victims and criminals, followed by Texas, Florida, Pennsylvania, and New York.

Later in 2001, the NCTP held a number of focus group meetings and found that electronic crime is having a profound effect on law enforcement.

After conducting a survey of 31 state and local law enforcement agencies responsible for training more than 84,000 people to combat Internet crime, the NCTP called for more program coordination, fast-track implementation, and skills training.

In May 2001, as a result of the growing sophistication on the part of law enforcement, the FBI, the Department of Justice, and the NW3C announced that criminal charges were being brought against nearly 90 individuals and companies accused of Internet fraud. The massive investigation, called Operation Cyber Loss, was initiated by the IFCC and included charges of online auction fraud, systemic nondelivery of merchandise purchased over the Internet, credit and debit card fraud, bank fraud, investment fraud, money laundering, multilevel marketing, Ponzi/pyramid schemes, and intellectual property rights violations. Altogether, these frauds victimized 56,000 people who lost in excess of $117 million.

Government groups were not the only ones sending out warning signals about the Net. Two Virginia-based private organizations, the National Law Center for Children and Enough Is Enough, provided information to parents; teachers; and local, state, and federal employees about the dangers of child pornography, while supporting legislative efforts to control or get rid of it. Written material produced by Enough Is Enough described child porn as a billion-dollar-a-year industry that was a threat to children both morally and physically. Any child with a computer can simply access and print out pornographic pictures. The literature described in detail how child predators used the Internet to find victims before meeting them in person and molesting them.

The Patriot Act, passed after the September 11, 2001, attacks, greatly increased U.S. law enforcement's authority to fight terrorism at home and abroad. Law enforcement officials were given expanded authority to gather and share evidence, especially relating to wire and electronic communications.

The Cyber Security Enhancement Act, part of the Homeland Security Act, was passed in 2002. The law helps deter cybercrime by subjecting hackers to harsher sentences based on the hacker's intent, sophistication, violation of privacy rights, and actual loss sustained by the crime.

In October 2004, the Secret Service arrested 30 people and issued 30 search warrants as part of Operation Firewall. The operation involved 18 Secret Service offices and 11 international law enforcement organizations. In all, Operation Firewall involved 2,000 terabytes of data and was the first use of a wiretap on a computer network.

The FBI's 2005 Cyber-Crime Survey was developed and analyzed with the help of leading public and private authorities on cybersecurity. The survey is based on responses from a cross-section of more than 2,000 public and private organizations in four states. The results of the survey estimated that $65 billion was lost to cybercrime in 2005 alone.

Media Strategy Case Vignette

The BTK case is an example of how a proactive media strategy among law enforcement agencies contributed to the capture of a serial murderer. The BTK killer first emerged in 1974 and, over time, killed a total of 10 victims. From 1974 until 1988, BTK sent a series of five communications to the media, citizens, and the police, in which he not only named himself BTK (Bind them, Torture them, and Kill them) but also claimed credit for killing a number of the victims. He abruptly stopped communicating in 1988. He reemerged in 2004 by sending a new communication to the media. The Wichita Police Department formed a task force with the Kansas Bureau of Investigation, the FBI, and other agencies. The FBI's BAU-2 was contacted and provided a proactive media strategy that was utilized throughout the case. This strategy involved using the lieutenant in charge of the investigation to provide written press releases at critical times, which resulted in 15 press releases during the course of the investigation. BTK provided 11 communications to police and the media during the 11-month investigation. The last communication BTK sent included a computer disk, containing information that eventually identified Dennis Rader as BTK. During Rader's interrogation, he commented positively on the press releases and his perceived relationship with the investigative lieutenant who issued the press statements (FBI BAU, 2008).

Conclusion

The Internet, forensic science, and advances in technology present an endless opportunity to improve our lives and the way in which we conduct business. Criminals have seized this moment and opportunity to take advantage of unsuspecting victims. Cybercriminals are not confined by state borders. Equipped with just a computer, a cybercriminal can use the Internet to commit a variety of crimes, from violent crimes to crimes against e-commerce. Federal, state, and local law enforcement in the United States and abroad must coordinate their efforts to fight cybercrime. Law enforcement officials should be given the necessary procedural authority through the development of uniform laws to act against this crime. In addition, law enforcement should create task forces whose primary task will be to investigate and prosecute cybercrimes. Awareness and coordination of law enforcement efforts, both nationally and internationally, can begin to prevent the abuses of the Internet.

References

Borja, E. C. (2008). *Brief documentary history of the Department of Homeland Security 2001–2008*. Department of Homeland Security History Office. Retrieved February 2, 2012, from www .dhs.gov/xlibrary/assets/brief_documentary_history_of_dhs_2001_2008.pdf

Brooks, P. R., Devine, M. J., Green, T. J., Hart, B. L., & Moore, M. D. (1988). Multi-agency investigative team manual. Washington, DC: Government Printing Office.

Central Bureau of Investigation. (2012). *Interpol guide—What is Interpol?* CBI India. Retrieved February 14, 2012, from http://cbi.nic.in/interpol/interpol.php

Douglas, John E., Mark Olshaker. (1995). *"Mindhunter: Inside the FBI's Elite Serial Crime Unit."* New York, NY: Scribner.

Douglas, John E., Mark Olshaker. (2000). *"The Cases That Haunt Us."* New York, NY: Scribner.

Egger, S.A. (1990) Serial murder—An elusive phenomenon. CT: Praeger.

Federal Bureau of Investigation, Behavioral Analysis Unit. (2008). *Serial murder: Multi-disciplinary perspectives for investigators.* Retrieved August 8, 2012, from www.fbi.gov/stats-services/publications/serial-murder/serial-murder-1

Fuhrman, M. (2001). Murder in Spokane. New York, NY: HarperCollins.

Haddal, C. C. (2010). *Border security: The role of the U.S. border patrol.* Congressional Research Service. Retrieved January 27, 2011, from www.fas.org/sgp/crs/homesec/RL32562.pdf

Harris, A. R., Thomas, S. H., Fisher, G. A., & Hirsch, D. J. (2002). Murder and medicine: The lethality of criminal assault, 1960–1999. Homicide Studies, 6, 128–166.

Hazelwood, R. R., & Burgess, A. W. (2001). Practical aspects of rape investigation (3re ed.). Boca Raton, FL: CRC Press.

Hazelwood, R. R. (2009). Analyzing the rape and profiling the offender. In R. R. Hazelwood & A. W. Burgess (Eds.), *Practical aspects of rape investigation* (4/ed.). New York, NY: Elsevier.

Howlett, J.B., Hanfland, K.A., & Ressler, R.K. (1986, December). The Violent Criminal Apprehension Program: A progress report. Law Enforcement Bulletin, 14.

INTERPOL. (2011). *Pink Panthers' investigators come together to share cases and experiences.* Retrieved February 15, 2012, from www.interpol.int/News-and-media/News-media-releases/2011/N20110214a

INTERPOL. (2012). *Priorities.* Retrieved February 14, 2012, from www.interpol.int/About-INTERPOL/Priorities

Keefer, B. (1998, March 1). Distinguished homicide detective dies at 75. Eugene (Ore.) Register-Guard, p. 1.

Keppel, R. D. (1995). The riverman. New York, NY: Pocket Books.

Krouse, W. J. (2011). *The Bureau of Alcohol, Tobacco, Firearms and Explosives (ATF): Budget and operations for FY2011.* Congressional Research Service. Retrieved January 28, 2011, from www.fas.org/sgp/crs/misc/R41206.pdf

McAllester, M. (2010). *Inside a world-class ring of diamond thieves.* GlobalPost International News. Retrieved on February 15, 2012, from www.globalpost.com/dispatch/europe/100116/pink-panthers-jewel-thieves?page=0,4

Meister, A. P. (1998). VICAP presentations.

National Center for Missing & Exploited Children (2012). Alexandria, VA.

Newton, M. (1990) Hunting humans. WA: Loompanics Unlimited.

O'Block, R. (2010). Meet the FBI's behavioral science unit. *The Forensic Examiner 9*(3): 1–10.

Oliver, W. (2008). *Brazen "Pink Panther" heists stir ire, admiration of cops.* Newser LLC. Retrieved February 15, 2012, from www.newser.com/story/45287/brazen-pink-panther-heists-stir-ire-admiration-of-cops.html

Papenfuss, M. (2010). *Interpol hunts bold Pink Panthers gem gang.* Newser LLC. Retrieved February 15, 2012, from www.newser.com/story/98783/interpol-hunts-bold-pink-panthers-gem-gang.html

Quinn, R. (2009). *Bold gem heist gang is toast in Serbia*. Newser LLC. Retrieved February 15, 2012, from www.newser.com/story/65545/bold-gem-heist-gang-is-toast-of-serbia.html

Taylor, M. (1998, March 1). Pierce Brooks. San Francisco Chronicle.

Turner, R., & Kosa, R. (2003, July). Cold case squads: Leaving no stone unturned. Washington, DC: U.S. Department of Justice.

United Nations. (2007). *International Criminal Police Organization (INTERPOL)*. Fifth special meeting of the Counter-Terrorism Committee with International, Regional and Subregional Organizations in Nairobi, Kenya. Retrieved February 14, 2012, from www.un.org/en/sc/ctc/specialmeetings/2007-nairobi/docs/icpo_background-Information.pdf

U.S. Citizenship and Immigration Services. (2012). Retrieved January 28, 2011, from www.uscis.gov/portal/site/uscis

U.S. Department of Justice. Federal Bureau of Investigation. (1998). *Child abduction response plan*. Washington, DC: Government Printing Office.

U.S. Department of Justice. (2009). *The Bureau of Alcohol, Tobacco, Firearms and Explosives' efforts to prevent the diversion of tobacco*. Report by the Office of the Inspector General. Retrieved January 28, 2011, from www.justice.gov/oig/reports/ATF/e0905.pdf

USDOJ. (2010). Forty-eight alleged Lynn Gang members and associates charged in sweeping federal and state firearm and drug trafficking investigation. The United States Attorney's Office: District of Massachusetts (press release). November 12, 2010. http://www.justice.gov/usao/ma/news/2010/November/PressRelease.html.

U.S. Attorney's Office of District of Massachusetts. (November 5, 2010). Forty-eight alleged Lynn gang members and associates charged in sweeping federal and state firearms and drug trafficking investigation. Retrieved December 8, 2012, from www.justice.gov/usao/ma/news/2010/November/PressRelease.html

U.S. Immigration and Customs Enforcement. (2012). Retrieved January 28, 2011, from www.ice.gov/

VICAP. (2002, April). The victim's voice brochure. Washington, DC: VICAP.

Viotti, P., Opheim, M., & Bowen, N. (2008). Terrorism and homeland security: Thinking strategically about policy. Boca Raton, FL: CRC Press.

Ward, R. H., Kiernan, K., & Mabrey, D. (2006). *Homeland Security: An introduction*. Southington, CT: Anderson Publishing.

Witzig, E. W. (1995). Observations on the serial killer phenomenon: An examination of selected behaviors of the interstate offender contrasted with the intrastate offender. Unpublished master's thesis, Virginia Commonwealth University.

Witzig, E. (2006). VICAP: The violent criminal apprehension program unit. In: Douglas, J. E., Burgess, A. W., Burgess, A. G., & Ressler, K. (Eds): Crime Classification Manual: A Standard System for Investigation and Classifying Violent Crimes, 2e (pp. 73–90). NY: John Wiley & Sons, Inc.

Chapter 5

Classifying Crimes by Severity From Aggravators to Depravity

Michael Welner

Which is a worse assault scenario—attacking a stranger for fun or colliding a car into another stranger while driving recklessly? Which qualities of a homicide are worse—bombing a building in the middle of the night, wanting to watch a victim suffer, victimizing someone who is disabled, or being able to carry out regular activities after a crime as if nothing happened? Is there specific intent that is more culpable, more severe, than intent to carry out the crime?

Consider the following case of Christopher James Hyden (*State of Minnesota v. Christopher James Hyden*, 2011).

The Crime

D. B., her fiancé, and their two children, six-year-old V. B. and two-year-old M. B., lived in a rental home in Clinton, Minnesota. In the summer of 2008, the owner of the home hired Christopher James Hyden to do occasional maintenance work and house upkeep. As the months passed, Hyden developed a good relationship with the family and often played with the two children.

On August 1, 2008, Hyden took V. B. for a ride on his four-wheeler just as he had done many times before. This time, however, Hyden drove the six-year-old to a remote area of the grounds. He forced her to the ground and raped her, causing injuries throughout her vaginal wall and tearing the hymen at the vaginal opening. Hyden then cut V. B.'s throat with a knife, leaving her to die before fleeing the scene. V. B., however, did not die. Somehow, she was able to walk nearly one mile in search of help.

Meanwhile, Hyden drove back to the house to find D. B. He pulled out a pocketknife and began stabbing D. B. several times, causing multiple injuries that included two deep lacerations on her neck. During the assault, Hyden repeatedly told D. B. that he *had* to kill her. Fortunately, D. B.'s friend interrupted the assault when she arrived at the home, and Hyden fled the scene on his four-wheeler.

Police caught up with Hyden, who had driven into a nearby cornfield. Hyden eventually surrendered and confessed to committing the crimes.

The Appeal

The charges made against Hyden included attempted first-degree murder, attempted second-degree murder, and first-degree criminal sexual conduct. In their decision, the district court noted that the state had proven the existence of two heinous elements relating to the first-degree criminal sexual conduct. Hyden received a sentence of life without possibility of release.

Under Minnesota law, heinous element exists when (a) the offender tortured the complainant, (b) the offender intentionally inflicted great bodily harm upon the complainant, or (c) the offender exposed the complainant to extreme inhumane conditions. On appeal, Hyden did not challenge the district court's finding of exposure to extreme inhumane conditions, but argued that the district court erred in using infliction of great bodily harm as a heinous element.

On appeal, Hyden argues that because the act of cutting the victim's throat was "sufficiently related to the sexual assault, it was part of the personal injury element of the first-degree criminal sexual conduct charge" and therefore not a heinous element. The appellate court found no merit in Hyden's argument, ruling instead that the throat slashing plainly constituted great bodily harm, and the infliction of great bodily harm is plainly not an element of first-degree criminal sexual conduct. Because two heinous elements were present, the district court upheld the original sentence, finding that there was no error or abuse of discretion in sentencing Hyden to life in prison without possibility of release.

Even as Minnesota listed factors of a crime that classify it as a heinous offense, how clearly can these be proven or disproven? Are there qualities of the crime that were key to the court's decision that are common to attempted murder, or did the court reserve exceptional sentence for exceptional reasons? Are there other features of Hyden's actions that Minnesota law and this court should have considered heinous? For example, is Hyden's exploited good rapport with the family significant? Did he exploit V. B.'s trust when he took her out that day? How about V. B.'s physical helplessness to escape or resist Hyden? Hyden partially blamed a previous investigation for the commission of this crime. Is Hyden's blaming others an element of depravity?

A juror confronts these realities in order to consider the true nature of a crime such as this. Although courts determine depravity based on the *events* of the crime, as the Minnesota court did, the question becomes *which* specific type of actions warrant aggravating terms in attempted murder? Is there a place in these determinations for the perpetrator's intent and attitude about his crime?

Crime classification highlights the often overlooked reality that each murder, rape, arson, and other criminal act distinguishes itself. Contract killing is quite obviously different from sexual homicide, for example.

Crime-solving considerations force investigators to appreciate the differences between offenses according to the perpetrator's background, crime scene evidence, victimology, and forensic findings. Distinguishing subtypes of crime enables various organs of law enforcement to effect justice.

To be involved in the justice system is to be humbled by one's Lilliputian role in a process that extends well beyond a suspect's arrest. Is justice served merely when a suspect is taken into custody? What if a manslaughterer is charged as a murderer? What if a cold-blooded killer is prosecuted as a battered woman? Is that justice? Obviously not.

Nor is it justice to presume that even among all types of offenders, each is as blameworthy as the next. Experience in murder, sexual assault, and even property crime reinforces the understanding that some crimes separate themselves from others as the worst of the worst.

The final leg of the justice system is punishment. Totalitarian societies and fascist theocracies need not concern themselves with nuances of justice. They have the luxury of applying absolute state power that has less to do with justice and more to do with who is deciding another's fate. Crime classification in these systems does not value individual liberties, and if unsystematic and unscientific crime investigation leads to penalizing the wrong person, or overpenalizing a perpetrator, it is of little consequence.

Likewise, court systems modeled on rehabilitating offenders do not apply punishment for its deterrent effect and therapeutic consolation to victims and their families. Those societies, afflicted with boundless rationalizations for predatory elements, relegate punishment's impact on promoting prosocial behavior for the pursuit of universal compassion. At the expense of accountability for war criminals and other unthinkable offenders nevertheless nurtured in their midst, the courts of such countries opt to cover their eyes so as to preserve the delusions of their society's pacifism.

The utility of and need for punishment carves out a coexistence with compassion and rehabilitative goals.

Numerous factors, termed mitigating factors, diminish punishment, or the severity of sentencing, in American courts. An offender's previous history, social disadvantage, mental illness, or possibility of coinciding intoxication, lesser role in a crime, stature in the community, and negative impact of the punishment on others are examples of qualities that mitigate punishment. When these factors distinguish an individual, American courts may choose to mete out a less severe sentence to a convicted offender. Mitigating factors primarily relate to context, such as who the offender is and why the crime was committed.

Factors that aggravate punishment in criminal courts have been distinguished as well.

Aggravating factors, like mitigators, relate to who an offender is. Many, however, focus attention on the crime itself—what the person did.

Aggravators Relating to the Crime Itself

Of all the themes of aggravating factors, aggravators linked to what a person did in the course of carrying out a crime most protect the justice system from bias, prejudice, privilege, and other unintended inequalities in sentencing. Nothing speaks for a crime like the crime itself.

Each state, along with the federal system, has its own criminal codes and sentencing guidelines. These codes, enacted by legislative initiative and interpreted by courts, contribute to distinct applications of justice. This decentralization also means that identical crimes, prosecuted in different jurisdictions, are punished based on different factors. Depending on the level of judicial initiative in giving jury instructions, even more variable outcomes are possible for each case.

State and federal criminal sentencing guidelines enumerate a host of aggravators relating to the specifics of a crime, as listed in Table 5.1. Aggravators arise from the perpetrator's intent, the perpetrator's actions, and attitudes about the crime, including behavior after the fact. Victimology also provides a basis for aggravating factors.

While most aggravating factors are easy to define, one aggravator—that a crime was "heinous, atrocious, and cruel"—means many things to many people. What is a "horribly inhuman," "vile," "depraved" crime—basically, the worst of the worst? The answer has bedeviled many courts.

DISTINGUISHING SEVERITY: ITS RELATIONSHIP TO CONSTITUTIONALITY

Use of terms such as *heinous, atrocious, cruel, wanton,* and other analogs of these has withstood repeated court challenge. In *Gregg v. Georgia* (1976), the Court upheld the Georgia aggravator of "heinous," "atrocious," and "cruel" as constitutional, but noted that a jury would have difficulty deciding this issue. Writing for the majority, Justice Potter Stewart noted:

> Sentencing authorities are apprised of any information relevant to the imposition of the sentence and *provided with standards to guide* the use of the information. . . . [T]he problem of jury inexperience in sentencing is alleviated if the *jury is given guidance* regarding the *factors about the crime and the defendant* that the state, representing *organized society, deems particularly relevant* to the *sentencing decision* [emphasis added; p. 192].

Table 5.1 Criminal Sentencing Aggravators Categorized by Intents, Actions, Attitudes, and Victimology

Aggravator	Intents	Actions	Attitudes	Victimology
Created grave risk of death to others		X		
Capital crime in conjunction with rape, robbery, kidnapping, or other crimes		X		
Preventing arrest or escaping custody	X			
Pecuniary gain or ransom	X			
Disrupt the government or enforcement of law	X			
Heinous, atrocious, cruel, depraved, wanton, vile, outrageous	X	X	X	X
Contract killing or hiring of contract killer		X		
Vulnerable victim due to old age or youth				X
Vulnerable victim due to handicap, mental illness or infirmity				X
Death of multiple victims		X		
Use of deadly weapon or dangerous instrument		X		
Presence of an accomplice or defendant as leader		X		
Property damage		X		
Physical, emotional, or financial torture to victim or victim's family	X	X		
Death of unborn child or victim was pregnant				X
Hate crime: race, sexual orientation, religion, nationality, or other	X			
Lying in wait for the victim; ambushing victim		X		
Act committed in presence of child or family member	X			
Retaliating against a former witness or judicial or enforcement officer	X			
Killing a witness to obstruct testimony	X			
Impersonating a peace officer		X		
Destructive device, bomb, explosive		X		
Victim was a peace officer, law enforcement officer, judge, etc.				X
Murder by poison or lethal substance		X		
Murder by firearm out of motor vehicle		X		
Murder against someone used as shield or hostage	X	X		
Act required substantial planning and premeditation	X			

(continued)

Table 5.1   (*Continued*)

Aggravator	Intents	Actions	Attitudes	Victimology
Exploiting a position of trust to commit criminal act	X	X		
Inducing a minor to commit criminal act				X
Act resulted in victim's obtaining a sexually transmitted disease or becoming pregnant		X		
Committed in cold, calculating manner without moral justification	X			X
Defendant demonstrated utter disregard for human life				X
Murder committed as result of hijacking of plane, bus, train, ship, for example		X		
Murder committed in conjunction with an act of terrorism	X	X		
Defendant dismembered body or caused permanent debilitation, disfigurement		X		
Administered sedation drug to victim before act		X		
Murder committed to avoid detection of crime	X			
Offense committed with intent to obstruct human or animal health care or agricultural or forestry research or commercial production	X			
Wearing a disguise during commission of crime		X		

In another relevant decision 14 years later, the Court, in *Walton v. Arizona* (1990), clarified that aggravating factors needed to be identified through objective circumstances.

Despite those allowances, inconsistency in defining the worst of crimes has handicapped numerous cases. The U.S. Supreme Court in *Godfrey v. Georgia* (1980), for example, reversed a capital sentence, stating, "There is nothing in these few words, standing alone, that implies any inherent restraint on the arbitrary and capricious infliction of the death sentence." Any sensible person could "fairly characterize almost every murder as outrageously or wantonly vile, horrible and inhuman." Jury instructions in Godfrey, ruled the Court, gave no guidance or explanation concerning the meaning of that aggravating factor, leading to what the Court called "the standardless and unchanneled imposition of the death sentences" (p. 429).

Newman, Rayz, and Friedman (2004) coined the notion of *super-aggravators:* those aggravators that, when present, were more likely to result in a death sentence in a capital-eligible case in Pennsylvania:

- The victim was a prosecution witness to a crime committed by the defendant and was killed to prevent his or her testimony.
- Torture.
- Significant history of felony convictions for acts of violence.
- Prior convictions for which sentences of life imprisonment or death were imposable.
- Prior murder convictions.

Newman et al. (2004) were not able to determine that other aggravators were not charged in some cases where their super-aggravator factors were present. Moreover, because prosecutors may have selected defendants for capital prosecution because of these aggravators, the findings may say more about prosecutors than jurors or a fair, unbiased system.

Litigation very much uses tried-and-true experiences; it is also possible that since prosecutors in Newman and colleagues' sample found any of these factors to have been successful in capital prosecution, they chose future capital prosecution solely because of the presence of any of these super-aggravators in the case history. The research does not demonstrate, however, any aggravators that prosecutors selected that were not often associated with a death penalty. Without accounting for selection bias by prosecutors, therefore, conclusions that can be made about jurors and the general public are limited.

HEINOUS, ATROCIOUS, AND CRUEL: CHALLENGES

While courts have upheld the distinction of crimes for their severity, several challenges confound justice in this endeavor.

Any killing, one might argue, is emotionally painful to the victim. Or consider cases that reflect overkill; perhaps they involve an assailant naive to how quickly lethal blows kill. The killer is not a medical examiner, and may leave a crime scene of overkill that therefore suggests it is heinous when compared to other killings.

In current approaches to labeling crimes as heinous, courts place a heavier emphasis on actions and victimology than on intents and attitudes (Welner, 2003). This reflects the paucity of evidence presented to courts to reflect on intent and attitudes. Clearly, however, both intent and/or attitudes may distinguish crimes from one another.

Furthermore, unless one can estimate the sequence leading to death, it is especially challenging to presume the nature of the suffering of a victim.

A review of court decisions upholding findings of heinous crimes also found that killing using instruments other than guns was heavily represented (Welner, 2003). But do such trials explore whether killers who use knives and hammers choose them because there are no other weapons available?

Ambiguity is present even in some killings of children. Was the small victim nevertheless a witness to another crime and eliminated for crime concealment (which would otherwise have also been done to an adult witness), as opposed to the handiwork of a predator victimizing a child by design?

A lack of clarification to law enforcement and defense investigators as to what evidence is relevant to depravity means that much less factual information about a crime is available to a jury. Without guidance, the jury may be forced to make an uninformed decision, not only for lack of definition but for lack of evidence demonstrating or refuting depraved intents, actions, victimology, or attitudes. With no guidance, as the U.S. Supreme Court has noted, distinguishing the worst of crimes is arbitrary. Arguments readily play to the fact finder's emotions, diverting them to unremarkable aspects of a case and risking the overemphasis of select details or wholesale dismissal of many pertinent pieces of factual evidence.

By now, we have all come to appreciate the role of the press in setting the tone for a case through its coverage and interest. The theater of competitive and intense news coverage creates the risk that judgments will be made based on a person, not the person's acts, as the issue. High-profile cases particularly fuel such dynamics for distortion.

Finally, consideration of the worst of crimes most frequently attaches itself to murder. Yet there are kidnappings that distinguish themselves as the worst of their ilk, just as there are robberies or even property crimes that may be particularly heinous relative to other property crimes.

Legislatures have thus codified that evil crimes exist. But without guidance, jurors struggle to distinguish qualities of a heinous crime. The inspiration for establishing standards for the worst of crimes and for providing guidance to jurors therefore engages the challenge of what crimes are depraved and what it is about those crimes that makes them depraved.

A Framework for Defining the Worst of Crimes

Many of the aggravators noted denote behavior that distinguishes a particularly unusual criminal at work. As such, perpetrators who meet such aggravators earn membership in a narrowed class of defendants. Other aggravators, however, speak more to the goals of society than the exceptional nature of the crime. A police officer is armed, for example, and engages with criminals and in hazardous duty. Society has an interest in protecting law enforcement. Yet when a perpetrator kills a police officer in attempting to escape, that clearly does not reflect an unusual criminal mentality or ensure that such a crime was anything more than a spontaneous, if dramatic, choice. In other words, some aggravators, such as killing in the course of committing a felony, attach themselves to deterrence goals, such as the protection of police officers. Other aggravators distinguish what are truly unusual, and the worst of the worst crimes.

Toward a Depravity Standard for Criminal Sentencing

The Depravity Standard research, initiated in 1998 and supported by The Forensic Panel, has embarked on a series of protocols designed to create a standardized methodology for distinguishing the worst of crimes in any given category (see www.depravityscale.org). The research delineates features that would distinguish crimes in which those items were present as depraved, heinous, and the worst of the worst.

Given this challenge, the Depravity Standard methodology committed to accomplish the following in order to establish a standard that would unfailingly contribute to justice:

- Can the standard be inclusive, to be applicable to the range of all possible crimes?
- Can the standard emphasize evidence over impressionism?
- Can its items ensure that such determinations are color, diagnosis, race, religion, nationality, and socioeconomic blind?
- Can its items control for cultural distinctions?
- Can the standard be neither pro prosecution nor pro defense?
- Can its items incorporate the range of values of a free society?
- Can items bridge society's judgments with psychiatry's?
- Can the items incorporate established diagnostic understandings of the worst of behavior?
- Can this be done in a way that does not disproportionally target those labeled undesirable?
- Can the standard ensure fairness rather than arbitrariness?
- Can science contribute to the standard, without stifling the law?
- Can the standard be measurable, in order to enable comparison?
- Can it be applied in a way that is not cumbersome?
- Can it distinguish a narrow class of offenders within categories of offenses?
- Can it be protected from abuse?
- Can it assist jurors without replacing their decision making?
- Can it be utilized in a way that ensures consistent application to justice?

The research began by identifying numerous examples of intent, actions, and attitudes that appellate courts have upheld as reflecting heinous, atrocious, cruel, vile, inhuman, wanton, or horrible crimes (Welner, 1998). This included a victimology of the worst of crimes as well.

In order to distinguish depraved features from those items earning aggravator status to serve the aims of public policy—but that do not uniformly distinguish a heinous or evil act (examples include using a deadly weapon, ambushing, killing a witness to disrupt testimony, and preventing arrest or escaping custody)—the intents, actions, attitudes, and victimologies of those upheld appellate cases were distilled and organized under headings shaped by psychiatric diagnoses associated with the most pernicious behavior (see Table 5.2).

Thus, a given fact pattern might relate very much to sadism and yet would be limited to an even more distinct "actions that cause a victim emotional suffering." Or a perpetrator who enlists followers into active criminality may be, according to the construct of antisocial by proxy, represented well by "involving another person in the crime in order to maximize destructiveness."

After expanding the list of potential intents, actions, and attitudes to encompass the range of potential crimes, the Depravity Standard research project identified 26 items for closer study (Welner, 2001). These items focus on

Table 5.2 Diagnoses Associated With Criminally Depraved Acts

Diagnosis (Source)	Characteristics
Antisocial personality disorder	History of conduct disorder in youth; adult pattern of irresponsibility and rule breaking; exploitativeness for money, sex, and other primitive needs
Conduct disorder	Childhood/adolescence of truancy, lying, fighting, destruction of property, fire setting, impulsivity, and cruelty to animals
Narcissistic personality disorder	Grandiosity, entitlement, haughtiness, envy, intense anger
Psychopathy	Brazenness; manipulative, callus, self-centered, grandiose personality, plus antisocial behavior
Sexual sadism	Sexual arousal through coercion and control, including through the infliction of pain
Sadism	The desire to inflict pain irrespective of sexual satisfaction
Necrophilia	Infatuation with death and decay
Malignant narcissism	Antisocial behavior, sadism, paranoia, more ideological and more likely to attach to groups; experience others as threatening enemies rather than merely objects to be exploited
Antisocial personality by proxy	Predator; physically or materially unable to carry out an antisocial impulse, so manipulates a vulnerable and less inhibited person to do so

"what" is depraved about the crime. The items are event, history, and fact driven. Questions of who is depraved, or evil, are more diagnostic and addressed through the psychiatric diagnoses or theological sources. Questions of why, or context, are well addressed in mitigation evidence and its rebuttal. The Depravity Standard is not intended to replace these elements of a case, as it confines itself to the circumstances of the crime.

In addition, the Depravity Standard items were developed in such a way as to apply with equal relevance to murder as to robbery or other crimes. "Intent to maximize damage," for example, is as applicable to the planting of a computer virus as it is to a mass casualty terror plot. Moreover, items are worded in order to ensure the instrument is blind to race, religion, politics, or socioeconomic status. At the same time, "intent to terrorize" works with defined terrorism, something many societies refuse to do for fear of self-incrimination.

In order that the research yield results that reflect societal attitudes, in keeping with U.S. Supreme Court directives, the next phases of the research explored which of the 26 intents, victimologies, actions, and attitudes would draw a consensus of support from the general public, regardless of demographic or background, as representative of a depraved crime.

This Internet-based phase of the research, www.depravityscale.org, was constructed to survey the general public randomly in a secure, confidential, and replicable manner. The Depravity Scale research was the first systematic academic effort to engage citizen input to shape a criminal sentencing instrument for legislatures and courts.

Data from the Depravity Scale survey have contributed to establishing the intents, victimology, actions, and attitudes to be included in a Depravity Standard. Data collection is ongoing at www.depravityscale.org, for societal attitudes evolve. The methodology enables the standard to reflect updated societal attitudes, even many years after a valid scale began to be used as an instrument of justice.

Most of the studied items, in research involving thousands of participants to date, have drawn an overwhelming endorsement for being especially or somewhat representative of depravity. There is, notwithstanding differences among the cultures of different states, remarkable consistency of data across American states.

Some distinctions have emerged in data comparison between American respondents and residents of Great Britain and other countries. Nevertheless, this phase of the research has demonstrated that no matter what the differences are among us personally, ethnically, or spiritually, consensus can be achieved as to what intents, victimology, actions, and attitudes distinguish a heinous or depraved crime. Indeed, 16 of the 26 items originally under study garnered over 90% agreement that they were at least somewhat depraved. Strong support for most of the remaining items emerged as well (Welner, 2009).

One of the items, for whom definition proved to be potentially confusing, was dropped from further consideration.

Aided by an advisory board of judges, prosecutors and defense attorneys, professors, forensic scientists, statisticians, and other professionals, the research team then devised a follow-up phase of the research, in which the general public is tasked with assessing relative depravity among the remaining 25 items. Each of the items is randomly sorted into groups of five, in which participants have the difficult exercise of comparing the severity of one element to another. Through this refinement, Depravity Standard items emerge that, no matter the circumstances or prospective juror, weigh heaviest in societal appraisal of the worst elements of crime. Please see Table 5.3 for a list of Depravity Standard Items.

Our research has demonstrated not only that a consensus can be established for characterizing heinous elements of a crime, but even what qualities of crime are the worst. Revealed in Table 5.4 are the five items of the Depravity Scale to which respondents attached the highest degree of depravity.

The Depravity Standard research is now in its final stage of validation, conducting analysis of entire samples of adjudicated murder cases from cities and communities spanning a given period. The analysis probes investigative reports, autopsy reports, indictment sheets, witness statements, ballistics information, and other pertinent reports from all areas of forensic science (Welner & Mastellon, 2010). The presence and absence of the items of the Depravity Standard are being recorded for each case.

Weighting, from the data gathered from the public surveys, will provide statistical analysis of the elements of each case. A subset of killings will ultimately separate itself from other murders for having elements of crime that weigh as most depraved, or having multiple elements of depravity. These crimes will, statistically, demonstrate themselves to be the worst of the worst.

Defining the Depravity Standard Items: Implications for Investigators

Items of the Depravity Standard have been carefully defined in order to inspire evidence-based determinations of whether an item is present. What denotes, for example, "actions that cause grotesque suffering?" Given the ramifications of a jury finding that such actions were a feature of the crime, determination of this item must be evidence driven. In order to reduce risk of arbitrariness in decision making, description of this and all other items must ensure consistent examination in court cases everywhere.

Detailed descriptions of items are important guidelines to law enforcement and investigators. Those who investigate crimes have the greatest proximity to evidence that reflects on the required evidence for items such as "disrespect for the victim after the fact" or evidence that such an item is not present.

Table 5.3 Depravity Standard Items

Item 1	Intent to emotionally traumatize the victim, maximizing terror, through humiliation, or intent to create an indelible emotional memory of the event
Item 2	Intent to maximize damage or destruction, by numbers or amount if more than one person is victimized, or by degree if only one person is victimized
Item 3	Intent to cause permanent physical disfigurement
Item 4	Intent to carry out a crime for excitement of the criminal act
Item 5	Targeting victims who are not merely vulnerable, but helpless
Item 6	Exploiting a necessarily trusting relationship to the victim
Item 7	Influencing depravity in others in order to destroy more
Item 8	Crime reflects intent of progressively increasing depravity
Item 9	Carrying out a crime in order to terrorize others
Item 10	Carrying out a crime in order to gain social acceptance or attention, or to show off
Item 11	Influencing criminality on others to avoid prosecution or penalty
Item 12	Disregarding the known consequences to the victim
Item 13	Intentionally targeting victims based on prejudice
Item 14	Prolonging the duration of a victim's physical suffering
Item 15	Unrelenting physical and emotional attack; amount of attacking
Item 16	Exceptional degree of physical harm; amount of damage
Item 17	Unusual and extreme quality of suffering of the victim, including terror and helplessness
Item 18	Indulgence of action, inconsistent with the social context
Item 19	Carrying out attack in unnecessarily close proximity to the victim
Item 20	Excessive response to trivial irritant; actions clearly disproportionate to the perceived provocation
Item 21	Pleasure in response to the actions and their impact
Item 22	Falsely implicating others, knowingly exposing them to wrongful penalty and the stress of prosecution
Item 23	Projecting responsibility onto the victim; feeling entitlement to carry out the action
Item 24	Disrespect for the victim after the fact
Item 25	Indifference to the actions and their impact

Table 5.4 Five Qualities Ranked Highest for Level of Depravity (as of July, 2012)

1. **Actions** that cause unusual quality of suffering of the victim
2. **Actions** that prolong the duration of a victim's physical suffering
3. **Intent** to emotionally traumatize the victim
4. **Intent** to cause permanent physical disfigurement
5. **Targeting** victims who are not merely vulnerable but helpless (victimology)

Many forensic science methodologies do not reliably guarantee that the same conclusions will be generated by qualified professionals conducting a given examination. This challenge is carefully addressed in the definitions and thresholds of items of the Depravity Standard (Welner, 2005).

The descriptions of items also aim to preserve a narrowed class of individuals who truly meet criteria of a Depravity Standard item. These specific parameters preserve the constitutionality of the standard. One item was ultimately dropped from consideration despite the overwhelming support of participants that it was representative of depravity: Our research team concluded that evidence for this item would be too difficult to distinguish consistently and scientifically (Welner & Mastellon, 2010).

Using the Depravity Standard

What an offender did can be notable for being unremarkable, just as a crime can distinguish itself as unforgettable. Once formulas are calculated to account for the weights of items, the Depravity Standard will be available for use in courts, parole, tribunals, and by policymakers and academics gathering and probing evidence from crimes across the spectrum.

The Depravity Standard is meant only to guide, not to replace, a trier of fact. In order to protect the responsibility of the jurors, crimes will, according to the weights of items present, be classified relative to other such crimes as "low depravity," "medium depravity," or "high depravity," rather than presenting to the court a numerical threshold of "depraved" or "not depraved."

With a validated and reliable Depravity Standard, prosecuting authorities will be required to distinguish a basis for charging a crime as depraved, heinous, or evil. If the evidence collected by investigators points to "exploiting an emotionally vulnerable or trusting relationship," only then can depravity be considered. The defense will have an opportunity to present its own evidence that, for example, "exploiting an emotionally vulnerable or trusting relation-ship" did not distinguish that crime and therefore depravity is not present.

The availability of substantive evidence to be considered by a sentencing authority weighing depravity is paramount. If no evidence is available with which to assert the presence of an item of the Depravity Standard, then a claim that a crime was evil, heinous, vile, or the like cannot be made in a just system.

Once in use, the Depravity Standard will inform juries with a valid, evidence-based means of appraising relative depravity with far greater fair-ness. The Depravity Standard will work as a guide that focuses litigation of the heinousness of the crime to the evidence for and against the actual items present. Jurors receiving more informed guidance will then make decisions based more on whether these evidentiary burdens of proof are satisfied and less on visceral emotion.

A collateral benefit of the Depravity Standard will be the necessary additional investigative scrutiny to the elements of crime, beyond guilt. More culpable qualities will be identified that underscore the merits or lack of a punitive court. At the same time, a paucity of evidence relating to intent, actions, and attitudes may one day be the first sign that a defendant is altogether innocent. Greater investigative scrutiny at a pretrial phase benefits all parties of the justice system.

Investigators of the depravity of a crime must be mindful of a number of key subtleties. Determination of intent has always been the most elusive aspect of crime. Examination of possible depraved intent must rely on evidence, not presumption. This challenge compels the investigator to use evidence available from diverse forensic sciences, from forensic pathology to forensic anthropology, to forensic psychiatry. Forensic psychiatric interviewing of defendants and other witnesses may provide particularly key evidence relating to depraved, heinous, atrocious, or horribly inhuman intent and attitude items.

With respect to Depravity Standard actions, forensic pathology, emergency medicine, radiology, anthropology, and criminalistics are particularly important contributors. Not surprisingly, analysis of actions in a crime must control for a prolonged confrontation in which damage and injuries multiply while a struggle occurs, as opposed to an unopposed sequence of attack. These forensic sciences contribute to understanding what weapon was used, how it was used, and how often it was used.

Crime investigation often focuses least on the attitudes of a criminal about his crime. Commonly, the absconding offender is not witnessed or communicating his attitudes. Postcrime communications, which police and forensic psychiatric investigation may elicit from interviewing skills, are often the most useful evidence with which to consider attitude items.

Consider the following case.

The Crime (*In re Michael Jay Loveless on Habeas Corpus*, 2011)

Michael Jay Loveless, Robert Allen, and George Layton planned to burglarize Robert DeRungs's home, after hearing that DeRungs had "large sums of money" in his house. Throughout January 1986, the three men visited the home on numerous occasions in order to assess the property and plan the robbery.

On January 31, 1986, at approximately 10:00 p.m., the men approached the home, disguised in theatrical makeup and armed with guns. The men knocked on the door and immediately forced DeRungs to lie on the floor when he answered. Allen searched the home and found DeRungs's 14-year-old son sleeping in his bedroom. He brought DeRungs's son into the room with Loveless and forced him to lie next to his father. Loveless stood over DeRungs, pointing a gun at his head, with the gun cocked and loaded and Loveless's finger on the trigger. Allen began to tie DeRungs up when Loveless shot him in the back of the head. Loveless apologized to Allen, stating that the gun slipped and he did not mean to shoot DeRungs.

As his father lay dying on the floor, the men asked the young boy where they kept the money in the house. DeRungs's son explained that any money would be in his father's wallet. While Allen searched the home again, Loveless tied up the boy, instructing Loveless, upon his return, to shoot him because he had witnessed the murder. The men ultimately left the home without shooting DeRungs's son and divided the $110 from DeRungs's wallet between them.

Loveless entered a negotiated guilty plea to second-degree murder and was sentenced to 15 years to life in prison.

The Parole Hearing and Writ of Habeas Corpus

On January 31, 2008, the 22nd anniversary of DeRungs's death, Loveless came up for a parole hearing. After reviewing his case, the board found that the offense displayed an "exceptionally callous disregard for human suffering." The Board determined that Loveless would pose an unreasonable risk to society and denied him parole.

Loveless challenged this decision, petitioning the superior court for a writ of habeas corpus. The Board reevaluated Loveless's case and noted that the crime was committed "in an especially heinous, atrocious or cruel manner" (§ 2402, subd. (c)(1)). The Board argued that the crime was especially cruel and heinous because the motive for killing the victim ($110) was extremely trivial. Additionally, Loveless and Allen acted in a "cold and calculating manner," creating roles and arming themselves, as well as bringing DeRungs's innocent son into the room and discussing the murder in his presence. The Board again reached the conclusion that Loveless is unsuitable for parole and denied his release. The trial court issued a new order to deny Loveless's petition for writ of habeas corpus.

Did Loveless's expression of regret after shooting the victim reflect remorse or frustration for ineptitude? How does demanding the son's direction to money in the home after witnessing his father's murder speak to this? Or did assailants merely capitalize on the heightened terror of the son? What is the significance of assailants' discussing the prospect of shooting the surviving son and of then not shooting him? Would evidence prove this to reflect remorse or indifference? How about the perpetrators' decision to tie up the son next to the body of his murdered father?

Investigation of attitude about the crime focuses on the offense's oft-overlooked aftermath. The Depravity Standard investigation uses a model of the life cycle of a crime (that is, before, during, and after the crime) to ascertain evidence relating to intents, victimology, actions, and attitudes.

The higher scrutiny prompted by the standard's use in sentencing enables a closer scrutiny of crimes and further protects against key evidence being overlooked.

The more consistently and fairly courts distinguish the worst of crimes, the more readily they balance the aims of punishment with sensitivity and understanding. Once again, classification serves the interest of justice at every stage.

References

Godfrey v. Georgia, 446 U.S. 429 (1980).

Gregg v. Georgia, 428 U.S. 153 (1976).

In re Michael Jay Loveless on Habeas Corpus, 192 Cal; LEXIS 110 (January 7, 2011). Reprinted with permission from www.depravityscale.org

Newman, S., Rayz, E., & Friedman, S. (2004). Capital sentencing: The effect of adding aggravators to death penalty statues in Pennsylvania. *University of Pittsburgh Law Review,* 65, 457–506.

State of Minnesota v. Christopher James Hyden, Minn; LEXIS 90 (January 25, 2011). Case is reprinted with permission from www.depravityscale.org

Walton v. Arizona, 497 U.S. 639 (1990).

Welner, M. (1998). Defining evil: A depravity scale for today's courts. *Forensic Echo* 2(6), 4–12.

Welner, M. (2001, May). *The Depravity Scale: Development and potential.* Paper presented at the American Psychiatric Association Annual Meeting, New Orleans, LA.

Welner, M. (2003, May). *Frontiers in standardizing the definition of evil in criminal law.* Paper presented at the American Psychiatric Association Annual Meeting, San Francisco, CA.

Welner, M. (2005). The Depravity Standard: A future role of forensic and behavioral evidence analysis. In W. Petherick (Ed.), *The science of criminal profiling* (pp. 150–152). London, England: Barnes & Noble.

Welner, M. (2009). The justice and therapeutic promise of science-based research on criminal evil. *Journal of the American Academy of Psychiatry and the Law,* 37(4), 442–449.

Welner, M., & Mastellon, T. (2010). The Depravity Standard: A call for large scale homicide research. *Empire State Prosecutor,* pp. 14–17.

PART II

The Classifications

Chapter 6

Criminal Enterprise Homicide

100: Criminal enterprise
101: Contract murder (third party)
102: Gang-motivated murder
103: Criminal competition
104: Kidnap murder
105: Product tampering
106: Drug murder

107: Insurance-related death
   107.01: Individual profit
   107.02: Commercial profit
108: Felony murder
   108.01: Indiscriminate murder
   108.02: Situational murder

Murder is the unlawful taking of human life. It is a behavioral act that terminates life in the context of power, personal gain, brutality, and sometimes sexuality. Murder is a subcategory of homicide, which also includes lawful taking of human life, such as manslaughter, deaths resulting from criminal and non-criminal negligence, and unpremeditated vehicular deaths (Megargee, 1982). Although a distinction is made in the literature among homicide, murder, and killing, for the purpose of this book, the terms are used interchangeably.

The Uniform Crime Reporting Program

The earliest system for classification of homicide is the Uniform Crime Reports (UCR). The UCR, prepared by the FBI in conjunction with the U.S. Department of Justice, presents statistics for crimes committed in the United States within a given year. Recognizing a need for national crime statistics, the International Association of Chiefs of Police formed the Committee on Uniform Crime Records in the 1920s to develop a system of uniform police statistics. Seven offenses were chosen to serve as an index for gauging fluctuations in the overall volume and rate of crime. Known collectively as the crime index, these offenses were the violent crimes of murder and nonnegligent manslaughter, forcible rape, robbery, and aggravated assault, and the property crimes of burglary, larceny theft, and motor vehicle theft. By congressional mandate, arson was added as the eighth index offense in 1979.

A survey of the figures reported in the UCR for all murders committed between 1976 and 2003 shows that the number of murders in the United States has fluctuated from 16,605 in 1976 to a peak of 21,860 in 1980, dropping to 20,613 in 1986 and up to 21,500 in 1989 to a low of 16,503 in 2003 (U.S. Department of Justice, 1976–1989, 2003). The UCR also cites information about age, race, and sex of victims and offenders; types of weapons used; and situations in which killings took place.

The current UCR classifies murders as follows:

- Felony murder (occurs during the commission of a felony).
- Suspected felony murder (elements of felony are present).
- Argument-motivated murder (noncriminally motivated).
- Miscellaneous or nonfelony types (any known motivation not included in previous categories).
- Unknown motives (motive fits into none of the above categories).

An estimated 14,748 persons were murdered nationwide in 2010. This was a 4.2% decrease from the 2009 estimate, a 14.8% decrease from the 2006 figure, and an 8.0% decrease from the 2001 estimate.

In 2010, there were 4.8 murders per 100,000 inhabitants, a 4.8% decrease from the 2009 rate. Compared with the 2006 rate, the murder rate decreased 17.4%, and compared with the 2001 rate, the murder rate decreased 15.0%.

Nearly 44% (43.8) of murders were reported in the South, the most populous region, with 20.6% reported in the West, 19.9% reported in the Midwest, and 15.6% reported in the Northeast. See Table 6.1 for Victim Characteristics.

Table 6.1 Victim Characteristics

Murder-Victim Situation	Single victim, single offender (48.4%)
	Single victim, unknown offender(s) (29%)
	Single victim, multiple offenders (12.6%)
	Multiple victims, single offender (5.8%)
	Multiple victims, multiple offenders (1.5%)
	Multiple victims, unknown offender(s) (2.7%)
Age of Victim (Total: 6,284)	Under 18 (665)
	18 and over (5,558)
	Unknown (61)
Race (Total: 12,996)	6,043 were White, 6,470 were Black, 331 were other, and 152 were unknown

Sources: UCR 2010 (Extracted from FBI, 2010); Bureau of Justice Statistics: Data from Supplementary Homicide Reports (Cooper & Smith, 2011)

Long-Term Trends in Homicide Rates

- The homicide rate doubled from the early 1960s to the late 1970s peaking at 10.2 per 100,000 in 1980 and then falling to 7.9 per 100,000 in 1984. The homicide rate rose again from the late 1980s and early 1990s to a peak of 9.8 per 100,000 in 1991.
- The homicide rate fell to 4.8 per 100,000 in 2010. Between 1999 and 2008, the homicide rate remained relatively constant.

From 1980 to 2008

- Blacks were disproportionately represented as homicide victims and offenders with a victimization rate of 27.8 per 100,000 (whereas Whites had a rate of 4.5 per 100,000).
- Males represented 77% of homicide victims and nearly 90% of homicide offenders.
- The 18 to 24-year-old age group had the highest rate of homicide victims (17.1) and homicide offenders (29.3).
- The victim/offender relationship was 21.9% stranger, 10% spouse, 12.4% other family, 6.3% boyfriend/girlfriend, 49.4% other acquaintance.
- Compared to homicides by intimates or a family member, homicides committed by a friend/acquaintance or stranger were more likely to involve a gun.

Percentages for all categories of murder except the unknown motives category have decreased. In 2003, there were 14,054 murders categorized. The number of murders classified in the category, however, has risen dramatically. In 2003, there were 4,476 murders categorized in the unknown category out of the 14,054 murders. This trend is particularly noteworthy in that it suggests both the heterogeneity of motives that give rise to murder and the clear inadequacy of a system that partitions murder essentially into three categories: felony, noncriminal, and miscellaneous. The miscellaneous and unknown motives categories represent wastebasket classifications. A classification system that fails to capture 40 to 50% of the cases (other and unknown) clearly is suboptimal in its ability to explain the universe of behavior.

The FBI estimated that in 2002 the clearance rate for reported murders in the United States was 64%, for reported rapes 45%, for reported burglaries 13%, and for reported auto thefts 14%.

Homicide Classification by Victims, Type, and Style

The FBI Academy's Behavioral Science Unit at Quantico, Virginia, began contributing to the literature on the classification of homicide with the Hazelwood and Douglas (1980) publication on typing lust murderers. The classifying of homicides by number of victims, type, and style was first published by Douglas, Ressler, Burgess, and Hartman in 1986. A *single homicide* is defined as one victim and one homicidal event. The November 2, 2007 murder of Meridith Kercher where Amanda Knox and Raffaele Sollecito were convicted of the murder and later acquitted is an example of a single homicide (Errickson, 2011). A *double homicide* is defined as two victims who are killed at one time in one location. The January 27, 2001, murder of Dartmouth College professors Half and Susanne Zantop by teenage classmates James Parker and Robert Tulloch is an example of a double homicide. This case was solved by investigators who traced the knives to Parker, who bought them online. A *triple homicide* is defined as three victims who are killed at one time in one location. On July 24, 2007, the wife and two daughters of a prominent Connecticut endocrinologist, Dr. William Petit, were killed by two men who invaded their suburban home in Cheshire, held them hostage for hours, set fire to the house, and then rammed three police cars with the family's sport utility vehicle before they were arrested.

Mass murder is described as a number of murders (four or more) occurring during the same incident, with no distinctive time period between the murders. These events typically involve a single location, where the killer murders a number of victims in an ongoing incident (e.g., the 1984 San Ysidro McDonald's incident in San Diego, California; the 1991 Luby's Restaurant massacre in Killeen, Texas; and the 2007 Virginia Tech murders in Blacksburg, Virginia).

There are two subcategories of mass murder: classic mass murder and family mass murder. A *classic mass murder* involves one person operating in one location at one period of time, which could be minutes or hours or even days. The prototype of a classic mass murder is a mentally disordered individual whose problems have increased to the point that he acts out against groups of people who are unrelated to him or his problems, unleashing his hostility through shootings and stabbings. One classic mass murderer was Charles Whitman, who in 1966 armed himself with boxes of ammunition, weapons, ropes, a radio, and food; barricaded himself in a tower at the University of Texas at Austin; and opened fire for 90 minutes (see Chapter 16). The second type of mass murder is *family mass murder*. If four or more family members are killed and the perpetrator takes his own life, it is classified as a mass murder–suicide. Without the suicide and with four or more victims, the murder is classified as family mass murder. An example is John List, an insurance salesman who killed his entire family in 1972. List disappeared after the crime, and his car was found at an airport parking lot. He was located 17 years later following a television program describing the murders.

A *spree murder* is a historical term defined as a single event with two or more locations and no emotional cooling-off period between murders. The single event in a spree murder can be of short or long duration. On September 6, 1949, spree murderer Howard Unruh of Camden, New Jersey, took a loaded

German Luger with extra ammunition and randomly fired the handgun while walking through his neighborhood, killing 13 people and wounding 3 in about 20 minutes. Although Unruh's killing took a short length of time, it was not classified as a mass murder because he moved to different locations (Ressler, Burgess, & Douglas, 1988).

Serial murder was initially defined as three or more separate events in three or more separate locations with an emotional cooling-off period between homicides. The term *cooling-off period* is now considered a historical term. There has been at least one attempt to formalize a definition of serial murder through legislation. In 1998, a federal law was passed by the U.S. Congress, titled Protection of Children from Sexual Predator Act of 1998 (Title 18, United States Code, Chapter 51, and Section 1111). This law includes a definition of serial killings:

> The term "serial killings" means a series of three or more killings, not less than one of which was committed within the United States, having common characteristics such as to suggest the reasonable possibility that the crimes were committed by the same actor or actors.

Although the federal law provides a definition of serial murder, it is limited in its application. The purpose of this definition was to set forth criteria establishing when the FBI could assist local law enforcement agencies with their investigation of serial murder cases. It was not intended to be a generic definition for serial murder (FBI, 2008).

At a 2005 FBI symposium on serial murder, discussion focused on the number of events needed for classification as serial. The definition agreed upon at the conference was serial murder is *the unlawful killing of two or more victims by the same offender(s), in separate events.* The serial murder is hypothesized to be premeditated, involving offense-related fantasy and detailed planning. Ted Bundy is an example of a serial murderer. Bundy killed 30 or more times over a period of many years in at least five different states. Symposium attendees agreed that there is no single identifiable cause or factor that leads to the development of a serial killer. Rather, there are a multitude of factors that contribute to their development. The most significant factor is the serial killer's personal decision in choosing to pursue his or her crimes.

There are other differences that are hypothesized to distinguish the mass and serial murderers. The classic mass murderers are not concerned with knowing who their victims are; they will kill anyone who comes in contact with them. In contrast, the serial murderer usually selects a type of victim. He thinks he will never be caught, and sometimes he is right. A serial murderer carefully monitors his behavior to avoid detection, whereas a mass murderer, who often has been identified and is being closely pursued by law enforcement, is usually unable to control the course of events. The serial killer, by contrast, plans and chooses victim and location, sometimes stopping the act of murder if it is not meeting his requirements. With a sexually motivated murderer, the offense may be classified as any of the aforementioned types (FBI, 2008).

Investigative Profiling

Crime classification assists investigative profiling, a step within Investigative Considerations. *Investigative profiling* is best viewed as a strategy enabling law enforcement to narrow the field of options and generate educated guesses about the perpetrator. It has been described as a collection of leads (Rossi, 1982), as an informed attempt to provide detailed information about a certain type of criminal (Geberth, 1981), and as a biological sketch of behavioral patterns, trends, and tendencies (Vorpagel, 1982). Geberth (1981) has noted that the investigative profile is particularly useful when the criminal has demonstrated some clearly identifiable form of psychopathology. In such a case, the crime scene is presumed to reflect the murderer's behavior and personality in much the same way as furnishings reveal a homeowner's character.

Profiling is, in fact, a form of retroclassification, or classification that works backward. Typically, we classify a known entity into a discrete category, based on presenting characteristics that translate into criteria for assignment to that category. In the case of homicide investigation, we have neither the entity (e.g., the offender) nor the victim. It is thus necessary to rely on the only source of information that typically is available: the crime scene. This information is used to profile, or classify, an individual. In essence, we are forced to bootstrap, using crime scene–related data, to make classifications. This bootstrapping process is referred to as profiling. There have been no systematic efforts to validate these profile-derived classifications.

Beginning in the summer of 1979, a number of victims—mostly women—disappeared while hiking and were subsequently found murdered in the area of Mount Tamalpais Park, north of San Francisco. The unknown subject (UNSUB) was dubbed the Trailside Killer by the local media (Douglas & Olshaker, 1995).

In these cases, victims were stabbed and/or strangled and shot to death on remote park trails, which would, in the case of female victims, suggest an intention on the offender's part for sexual assault. There were conflicting witness sightings of possible suspects, which is not unusual. The fact that each murder site was remote and heavily wooded, accessible only on foot and involving a considerable hike, suggested that the killer was local and intimately familiar with the area.

Douglas profiled that the multiple stabbings and blitz-style attacks from the rear indicated an asocial type who was withdrawn, unsure of himself, and incapable of engaging his victims in conversation with the intent of seducing or conning them. The victims were physically fit hikers, and the blitz attack was an indication that the only way he could control an intended victim was to devastate her before she could respond. These were not the crimes of someone who knew his victims. The sites were secluded and protected from view, which meant the killer essentially had as much time as he wanted to act out his fantasy with each victim. Yet he still felt the need for a blitz attack. There was handling of the bodies postmortem, and probably masturbation in addition to any sexual assault. The victims represented a range of ages and physical types, indicating a nonpreferential killer. The profile concluded with the prediction that the killer would have a speech impediment. This was met with considerable skepticism by the investigating task force.

Yet when the suspect, David Carpenter, was apprehended after a complex investigation that included the tracing of eyeglass frames the killer had inadvertently left at one of the murder scenes, the 50-year-old industrial arts teacher did indeed have a stutter, which became pronounced under stress. The reason for including such an odd trait in the profile was that this subject clearly did not feel comfortable taking his time or striking up a conversation with his intended victim. Despite the unlikelihood of interference in so secluded a setting, he did not have confidence in his ability to control the victim through words and manner. This suggested someone with a serious self-image/self-confidence problem. The most logical reason for this would be some sort of disfigurement or speech problem. Had there been disfigurement, it is likely that one or more witnesses would have made mention of a subject fitting this description. As none had, a speech impediment became the more likely factor.

Upon his arrest, Carpenter was found to be the product of a domineering and physically abusive mother and an at least emotionally abusive father. He was a child of well above average intelligence who was picked on because of his severe stuttering. His childhood was also marked by chronic bed-wetting and cruelty to animals. In adult life, his anger and frustration turned into fits of unpredictable, violent rage. He had been convicted of a previous attack on a woman using a knife and hammer, which occurred following the birth of his child into an already strained marriage. During the brutal assault itself, that victim reported, the terrible stutter disappeared.

This case emphasizes that while violent perpetrators can be classified according to type and manner of crime, as well as motive, it is critical to evaluate each incident and each offender on an individual basis, just as it is critical to so evaluate and support each victim.

The Trailside murders would be mixed sexual homicides because (a) the sexual element is the motivating factor and (b) while planning and stalking of the victim are traits of an organized offender, the style of attack was a blitz and no attempt was made to conceal the bodies—traits of a disorganized offender.

Criminal investigative analysis, also called *criminal profiling,* is the overall process whereby crimes are reviewed in their totality from a behavioral and investigative perspective. The behavior is analyzed before, during, and after the crime. From that data, strategies and profiles are developed on the UNSUB. Then the suspects are assessed and interrogation techniques developed. A major task is to be able to identify with both the victim and the suspect, in order to answer the investigative of formula of Why + How = Who.

The criminal profiling process alone cannot convict anyone. The process is to support and help focus the investigation. The foundation of any case must be properly conducted, thorough, and well planned. If the investigation is flawed, the results will be tainted. Garbage in, garbage out!

CCM: A Motivational Model for Classification of Homicide

The first published FBI Behavioral Science Unit system for typing lust murder (Hazelwood & Douglas, 1980), which Megargee (1982) properly described as a syndrome rather than a typology, delineated two categories, the organized nonsocial category and the disorganized asocial category, that were not intended to embrace all cases of sexual homicides. This early work on lust murder evolved into a programmatic effort to devise a classification system for serial sexual murder (Ressler et al., 1988). In the late 1980s, the agents from the Investigative Support Unit at the FBI Academy joined with the Behavioral Science Unit to begin working on a crime classification manual, using as a guide the *Diagnostic and Statistical Manual of Mental Disorders* of the American Psychiatric Association (2006). Work groups were assigned to the major crime categories of murder, arson, and sexual assault. An advisory committee representing federal and private associations was formed.

Although many of the conceptual and theoretical underpinnings of this model derive from earlier writings on the subject, the study of violent crime has advanced and thus new crime classifications have been added.

In the *Crime Classification Manual* (CCM), classification of homicide by motive has 4 major categories. The criminal enterprise category has 8 subcategories: contract murder (third party), gang-motivated murder, criminal competition, kidnap murder, product tampering, drug murder, insurance-related murder (individual profit or commercial profit), and felony murder (indiscriminate or situational). The personal cause category has 11 subcategories: erotomania-motivated murder, domestic homicide (spontaneous, staged, or neonaticide), argument/conflict murder, authority murder, revenge, nonspecific motive murder, extremist homicide (political, religious, or socioeconomic), "mercy/hero" homicide, and hostage murder. The sexual homicide category has 5 subcategories: organized crime scene murder, disorganized crime scene murder, mixed crime scene murder, sadistic murder, and elder female sexual homicide. The group cause category has 3 subcategories: cult murder, extremist homicide (political, religious, or socioeconomic murder [paramilitary or hostage]), and group excitement.

100: Criminal Enterprise

Criminal enterprise homicide is a motivation in which the offender benefits in status or monetary compensation by committing murder that is drug, gang, or organized crime related for material gain. This may include money, goods, territory, favors, or anything else perceived to have value to the individual. This category is further subdivided into contract (third-party) killing, gang-motivated murder, criminal competition homicide, kidnap murder, product-tampering homicide, drug murder, insurance inheritance–related death (individual profit murder and commercial profit murder), and felony murder (indiscriminate felony murder and situational felony murder).

101: Contract Murder (Third Party)

A contract killer is one who kills by secret assault or surprise. He is a murderer who agrees to take the life of another person for profit; that is, he is a hit man. There is usually an absence of relationship (personal, familial, or business) between killer and victim.

Defining Characteristics

VICTIMOLOGY

The victim of a contract killer is perceived by the person hiring the killer as an obstruction or hindrance to the attainment of a goal. This goal could be a financial one (collecting life insurance or controlling a business) or it could be personal (an extramarital affair, a refusal of divorce).

The victim's risk is situational. It is the offender's perception of the victim as an obstacle that puts the victim at risk. The risk for the offenders (contractor and killer) is dependent on their relationship with each other and the experience and expertise of the offender who is committing the murder.

CRIME SCENE INDICATORS FREQUENTLY NOTED

The offender usually spends a minimum of time at the scene. A quick, fast killing is usually opted for.

Several factors at the scene are indicative of offender sophistication. One index of this professionalism is the weapon that is used. Customized suppressors, handguns, or other instruments of death often indicate a specialist who is comfortable with killing. The crime scene may reflect this in other ways, including little or no physical evidence left at the scene, effective staging, elaborate body disposal, and a crime scene that shows a systematic, orderly approach before, during, and after the crime.

The weapon may be chosen based on its availability, lack of traceability, or inability of making a bullet match from it (.22 caliber). The offender often will drop the weapon or leave it at the crime scene with the body to lessen the possibility of being apprehended with it in his possession. Firearms used for a contract killing are often stolen or not registered.

Arson is sometimes used to conceal the contract murder. (Refer to section 231 for further information.)

STAGING

If staging is absent, there will be no other crime indicators: for example, nothing will be missing, and there will be no sexual assault. Secondary criminal activity may mean that the offender is youthful, an amateur, or of low intelligence.

The counter to this is a crime scene with complex staging, such as cut brake lines or aircraft malfunction, to make the death look accidental. Secondary criminal activity to confuse the primary motive of murder may include the appearance of a robbery or breaking and entering that went wrong, or a kidnapping. The body may be positioned to imply that a sexually motivated homicide occurred. Actual sexual assault is a variable depending primarily on offender professionalism.

COMMON FORENSIC FINDINGS

Just as staging and other crime scene indicators reflect the offender's level of experience, forensic findings can also offer distinguishing features. The veteran professional killer, for example, may choose a weapon that is difficult to trace and focus the area of injury to the victim's vital organs, especially the head. Usually, there are a minimal number of wounds; overkill is rare. A blitz or ambush style of attack is also common to this type of killing.

Investigative Considerations

Most contract killings have some evidence of premeditation. The killer may stalk the victim. An individual with preexisting, intact criminal connections will be able to contract a murder more easily and with less of a conspiratorial trail than an individual without established criminal connections. While the latter individual's conspiratorial trail may be more easily detected, the nature of the crime ensures the existence of a conspiracy for all offenders. Scrutiny of a suspect's preoffense contacts, discussions, and communications may provide evidence of the conspiracy (telephone and financial records should be reviewed for such evidence).

The contractor (the party engaging the killer) will have a history of personal conflict or business competition with the victim. However, he or she may exhibit a preoffense behavior change that frequently includes an apparent improvement in relationship with the victim. This improvement is often deliberately made apparent to relatives, friends, and business associates. The offender's motivation for projecting an image of caring and concern toward the victim is to lure the victim into a false sense of security while convincing those around him that he is above suspicion once the investigation has begun. Interviews with those close to the offender and victim may reveal this type of preoffense behavior. Additional preoffense behavior that others may observe is a nervousness or preoccupation on the part of the contractor.

Postoffense, the offender (contractor) will often demonstrate selective recall. He or she will have an uncharacteristically detailed, precise, airtight alibi for the period during which the homicide occurred. The investigator will be able to specify the offender's activities and the exact times these occurred from receipts and other evidence; however, his actions before and after the offense will be harder to pinpoint. The contractor will most likely be highly visible during the time of the offense (at a public place or party, for example).

Search Warrant Suggestions

Telephone records, emails, and other communications, financial records showing transfers of money, travel records, receipts (for rental cars or motels, for example), and weapons are all important search warrant suggestions.

Case Study 101: Contract Murder

Victimology

U.S. District Court Judge John Wood was known as "Maximum John" to members of the legal and law enforcement society in Texas. His reputation for handing out the stiffest penalties possible for drug offenders had brought him to the attention of the criminal community as well. Judge Wood had made serious inroads into the organized drug trade of the southern and western areas of Texas where drug flow across the Mexican border into this region had made trafficking a lucrative business.

Jamiel Charga (known as Jimmy) especially seemed to be benefiting from the drug business, as evidenced by his lifestyle: he had lost $1.1 million during a three-day Las Vegas gambling trip. Jimmy's brother, Lee, who had also been implicated in drug trafficking (and who was murdered on December 23, 1978), often expressed feelings of persecution at the hands of federal representatives like Judge Wood and the assistant U.S. attorney, James Kerr Jr. (Kerr was the object of an attempted assassination in November 1978.)

Jimmy Charga, who was already in prison, shared his brother's animosity of Judge Wood, imagining that he was the object of the judge's personal vendetta. He was also convinced that he would be given a life sentence by Judge Wood if he were convicted of the five counts of drug trafficking he faced in Wood's court.

At approximately 8:40 a.m., on May 29, 1979, Judge Wood called good-bye to his wife as he walked out the front door of their apartment. Ten to 15 seconds later, as he walked from the brick condominium to his green Chevrolet, he was struck in the back by a single gunshot. Mrs. Wood came out of the apartment after hearing the noise she had immediately identified as a gunshot. She found her husband lying near his car and attempted to help him. Wood was transported to Northeast Baptist Hospital, San Antonio, where he was pronounced dead on arrival at 9:30 a.m.

Judge Wood was placed at a high risk because of the stance he took when sentencing drug traffickers. Typically, he would not have been considered a high-risk victim when considering other factors that rate a victim's risk level (lifestyle and income, for example). However, his occupation and intolerance of drug offenders, in addition to his flippant attitude toward the threats against his life (he had ended the protection given him by federal marshals and had stopped carrying the gun they had given him), elevated his risk.

Relating Judge Wood to the victimology of a contract killing shows that his risk was situational. He was viewed as an obstruction to Jimmy Charga's freedom and his drug enterprise.

Crime Scene Indicators

Judge Wood's body was lying three and a half feet from his car at a 45-degree angle with the feet pointing northwest, the head southeast, and the arms outstretched to the side.

The witnesses who saw the judge struck by the bullet and fall to the ground never saw the gunman. There was no physical evidence (no shell casings or fingerprints, for example). The exact location of the sniper was not known. There were reports of several different strangers at the apartment around the time of the murder, but none led to any substantial suspect information.

The fast method of killing meant a minimum of time at the crime scene for the offender. The apparent ease of the killer to slip in, shoot the judge, and escape undetected (especially with a police patrol within two blocks responding at 8:41 a.m.) are all indicators of careful premeditation by an experienced hit man.

Forensic Findings

The bullet entry point was to the lower back, left of center, with a trajectory through the body of less than 15 degrees. It immediately hit the spine, causing fragmentation of the bullet and disintegration. These bullet fragments resulted in wounds throughout the abdomen and internal organs.

Ballistics revealed that the bullet was a .240 caliber or 6mm. Based on the rifling marks, it was concluded that two kinds of common rifles could have fired the bullet: the Browning Lever-Action and the Interarms Mark X.

The ambush, sniper style of attack on Judge Wood, requiring only one shot to kill almost instantly, is forensics information typical of the more experienced contract killer.

Investigation

The investigation of Judge Wood's murder became the largest federal investigation since John F. Kennedy's assassination. Due to the professionalism of the killer (as evidenced by the lack of forensics and witnesses), the direction of the investigation depended greatly on the history of conflict between Judge Wood and Jimmy Charga. In addition, the conspiratorial trail was less visible due to Charga's criminal contacts. This minimized the effort to seek a hit man, therefore minimizing the number of conspirators who could later become damaging witnesses.

The combination of extensive investigation with all of Charga's business associates, family, and friends, combined with intelligence derived from informants, began to focus attention on Charles Voyde Harrelson. On June 24, 1979, Charga's wife, Elizabeth, had paid $150,000 to Harrelson's stepdaughter in Las Vegas for the completed contract killing. Harrelson acknowledged receiving the money but said it was for a drug deal. The conspiratorial trail finally began to emerge after examination of telephone bills that linked Harrelson with Charga through family members.

Charga's wife was audiotaped while visiting her husband in Leavenworth Prison. "Yeah, go ahead and do it," she said, when the couple discussed plans to kill Judge Wood. They were repeating a previous conversation that had taken place before Wood was murdered. Elizabeth Charga also wrote a letter to Mrs. Wood in which she acknowledged making the payoff, but she denied involvement in the conspiracy.

Mrs. Harrelson admitted buying the .240 caliber Weatherby Mark V, the murder weapon, using a false name and giving it to her husband. The rifle butt with the Weatherby trademark was only partly recovered, making a ballistic match impossible (another indicator of some criminal sophistication). Harrelson's placement near the crime scene, in contrast to his claim of being 250 miles away the day of the killing, was solidified when a series of witnesses testified he was at motel in North San Antonio the night before the murder.

Outcome

Charles Harrelson was convicted of the 1979 murder and conspiracy to murder and sentenced to two consecutive life sentences without parole.

He appealed his case in 1998 to the Supreme Court. On March 29, 2004, Harrelson, father of actor Woody Harrelson, lost his Supreme Court appeal. Jimmy Charga was convicted of obstructing justice in the Wood investigation. He was also convicted of conspiracy to commit murder in relation to the attempt made on assistant U.S. attorney James Kerr. Kerr, who often tried drug cases in Wood's court, barely escaped injury from a barrage of bullets by ducking under his car dashboard in November 1978. Charga was also convicted of continuing criminal enterprise, conspiring to import marijuana, and tax fraud.

Elizabeth Charga was originally charged with murder conspiracy, convicted, and sentenced to 30 years. This was later overturned because the judge had not instructed the jury that her guilt had to be based on joining the conspiracy with malicious intent. She was also convicted of obstructing justice and tax fraud and received a five-year sentence.

Jo Ann Harrelson was convicted of perjury before the grand jury, during her own trial, and to FBI agents. Also convicted for their part in the assassination were Joe Charga, Jimmy's brother, and Theresa Jasper, Harrelson's stepdaughter.

102: Gang-Motivated Murder

A street gang is an organization, association, or group of three or more people, whether formal or informal, that has as one of its primary activities the commission of antisocial behavior and criminal acts, including homicide.

Gangs in one form or another have been around for hundreds of years, with pirates probably some of the original gangs. The groups that traditionally come to mind are the Crips and the Bloods from California, whose origins can be traced to the late 1960s. According to the Los Angeles Police Department, as of 2006, Los Angeles is now home to 463 gangs, up from 300 in 1990. The city has an estimated 40,000 gang members. And as another example, gang-related graffiti, robberies, shootings, and stabbings are on the rise in Utah after a decade of decline.

Street gangs were first formed in response to territorial struggles with rival neighborhoods. Fatalities that were associated with gang activity were largely based on these territorial conflicts. Contemporary gangs are demonstrating signs of evolution from loosely knit gangs to more established, organized crime groups. The flourishing cocaine market has been the propelling force behind this evolutionary process. Because the drug enterprise is now the heart of gang existence, drug-related homicide and street gang murder are becoming synonymous.

Defining Characteristics

VICTIMOLOGY

The victims of street gang homicide are usually members or associates of a gang. Gangs generally have a leader or group of leaders who issue orders and reap the fruits of the gang's activities. A gang may also wear "colors," that is, certain types of clothing, tattoos, and brands imprinted with the gang's name, logo, or other identifying marks. Many gangs also adopt certain types of hairstyles and communicate through the use of hand signals and graffiti on walls, streets, their own schoolwork, and school property.

Innocent bystanders are peripheral victims in some drive-by shootings. Local businessmen being extorted by gangs also become homicide victims, but this is usually restricted to Asian gangs. Filipino gangs in Hawaii use firearms as a currency in the drug trade; therefore, these gangs target victims to obtain guns that include military and law enforcement personnel. Violence involving street gangs most often includes minority male victims and offenders.

CRIME SCENE INDICATORS FREQUENTLY NOTED

The homicide scene is usually an open, public place within gang territory. Frequently, the site of the killing is in front of or near the victim's residence. Drive-by killings are the most frequent tactic employed by gangs. This mobile, public clash has a much greater prevalence over the one-on-one confrontation. Drive-by killings often involve more than one car.

The crime scene is disarrayed, with no concern for the body. It is not concealed and may even be displayed and positioned in a specific manner if a message is intended by the killing. Symbolic items may be left, such as the colors representing a gang or graffiti messages. Sometimes gang members involved with the offense will yell another gang name at the scene to misdirect law enforcement and focus retaliation on another gang.

The weapon is bought to the scene and is often concealed. Frequently, there are additional victims injured and associated offenses related to the homicide.

STAGING

Staging is generally absent.

Common Forensic Findings

Firearms are the weapons of choice with most gangs. The typical gang arsenal includes assault rifles, fully automatic weapons, semiautomatic handguns, and shotguns. Knife attacks are rare.

Multiple wounds from multiple-round weapons characterize a common forensic finding of the gang homicide. The offender often empties the gun's magazine into the victim. Such wounds are usually manifested in two ways. For optimum lethality, the offender targets the victim's head and chest. And for a ritualistic attack (especially prevalent with a retaliatory killing), there is methodical shooting of arms, knees, groin, and legs first, then chest and head.

An execution style of shooting is one other method employed with gang murder. There are isolated incidents of torture, but these are rare and usually occur only with an intragang conflict.

The victims who had gang involvement often have tattoos. Hispanic gangs especially tend to have many intricate tattoos.

Investigative Considerations

"Intelligence is the basis for success of the entire investigation," according to Joe Holmes of the Lynwood sheriff station Gang Unit. Known gang conflicts may also give direction to the investigation. Geographical considerations quickly help classify a homicide: an area of concentrated activity will increase the likelihood that the killing was gang motivated. Because gang killings are usually public, there are frequently witnesses.

The type of homicide perpetrated by street gangs is reflecting their emergence as more organized criminal operants. Some gangs are functioning as contract killers. The largest percentage of gang killings are motivated by drugs, with territory disputes and retaliatory killings the second and third most common motives. One other motive for gang homicide is the intermingling of a female from one gang or territory with the male of another.

Although many studies note that the average gang is composed of males between the ages of 12 and 21 who reside in poor, central areas of cities with populations of more than 200,000, girl membership in gangs has been increasing. Surveys of gangs in large cities indicate a wide variance in ethnicity, including African Americans, Hispanics, Asians, and Caucasians.

The law enforcement officer should attempt to keep a log of the addresses of gang members frequently seen together. Gang members often exchange stolen goods, guns, and clothing that may connect them to an offense. If possible, the officer should keep field information cards (FICs) and have gang members sign the back of this card with their moniker (gang nickname) and logo. Usually, gang members are proud of this and will volunteer to do so. The investigator should also have the gang member initial, sign, and draw his gang graffiti on the back of the rights card when being interviewed. This can prove helpful during prosecution for establishing the subject's membership or involvement with a gang.

Known gang conflicts may also give the investigator direction. For example, Bloods do not fight each other, but Crips will fight each other. Also, Black versus Hispanic conflict is becoming more prevalent. The two groups used to coexist peacefully.

Search Warrant Suggestions

Search warrant suggestions for gang-motivated murder include the following:

- Firearms, ammunition.
- Graffiti: walls, garage, books, papers, anywhere in a house.
- Pictures with guns and gang members, photo albums.
- Other items of gang association: clothing with colors, insignias, monikers, pagers, nice cars, jewelry (especially gold).

Multiple addresses should be listed on the search warrant, including gang members recently seen with the offender, due to the exchange of stolen property, guns, and clothing between gang members.

Case Study: 102: Gang-Motivated Murder

Background

As a group of friends from a Los Angeles neighborhood were piling into their cars to go to a movie, someone shouted, "Get down, get down!" Everyone scrambled for safety as gunfire filled the air. The shots were being fired from a car filled with Black males. When the attack was over, two Hispanic males aged 17 and 18 were dead. In addition, a 4-year-old child died several hours later at the hospital.

Victimology

Both teenage victims had an extensive history of gang involvement common to the victims of street gang homicide. The 18-year-old had been jailed several times as a juvenile for assault with a deadly weapon and drug possession charges. The 17-year-old also was involved with the same gang for over three years. He too was well known to the police for being involved with gang conflicts. He had been implicated in a recent drive-by shooting of a rival member, but no action had been taken.

The child victim was typical of many victims of street gang killings: he was an innocent bystander who happened to be playing on his porch at the wrong time.

Crime Scene Indicators

The area of the shooting had a reputation for being the location of many gang-related conflicts. The crime scene was in an open public place, in front of the child's house and next to the house of the 18-year-old. The killing involved a drive-by assault in which the offenders brought their weapons with them. The bodies were left where they fell until paramedics responded. There were witnesses, but most were gang members who preferred to exact their own form of justice, so they were not cooperative with the police.

Forensic Findings

All three victims sustained lethal wounds to the chest area and died of massive blood loss. The 17-year-old also had gunshot wounds to the left arm and left side of his neck. Investigators determined from the forensics that at least two weapons had been involved: a 9mm and a shotgun. The 18-year-old was killed from a shotgun blast. The targeting of vital organs and presence of multiple gunshot wounds are both common forensic findings with gang murder.

Investigation

Through the use of informants, the investigator learned that the 17-year-old victim had been involved in the earlier fatal attack on some rival gang members. He had been recognized and targeted by that gang for retaliation. Investigators were able to come up with three suspects of the four or five gang members believed to be involved. A search warrant produced one of the murder weapons, a 9mm fully automatic MAC-10. Two subjects were charged with murder, and a third was charged with his part in the killings, driving the car.

Outcome

All have been convicted of their respective charges. All of the offenders were sentenced to 20 years to life.

103: Criminal Competition

Death in this type of homicide is a result of organized crime conflict over control of territory.

Defining Characteristics

VICTIMOLOGY

Generally, the victim is a prominent or known organized crime figure or member of the hierarchy. Both intragroup and intergroup conflicts are prevalent prior to the homicide, with the victim generally reflecting this conflict. Innocent bystanders may become unintentional victims.

CRIME SCENE INDICATORS FREQUENTLY NOTED

The crime scene represents a well-planned crime and reflects the evidence consciousness of the offender. The scene may appear to pose a high risk to the offender, but because there are built-in safeguards (like an escape plan), the risk is considerably lowered. An example of this escape plan is the use of a decoy car that runs interference by blocking traffic, feigning car trouble, or causing an accident while the offender escapes.

The killing is done expeditiously, which keeps the time spent at the scene to a minimum. The offender usually is experienced and brings a weapon of choice to the scene.

Body disposal tends to be at opposite ends of the spectrum. The offender will either go to great lengths to conceal and dispose of the body or leave it wantonly displayed at the murder scene.

STAGING

Staging is usually not present.

Common Forensic Findings

Weaponry or the method of killing used depends on the intent of the offender. If he is sending a message or making a statement, bombing, a public killing, or an execution-style shooting (head wounds) will be seen. If the murder is one of elimination, then a small-caliber, untraceable weapon will be more prevalent. Vital organs are targeted in both cases.

Investigative Considerations

The use of intelligence obtained from gangland informants is a fundamental consideration that is especially appropriate with this classification of homicide. Intelligence regarding such matters as rival groups and internal power struggles should be explored.

Search Warrant Suggestions

Search warrant suggestions for the suspect's residence include weapons, guns, spent cartridges, clothing similar to that reported by witnesses, communication records (telephone, letters, tapes), and financial records.

Case Study: 103: Criminal Competition

Background

John T. Scalish was the last great don of the Cleveland mafia. On May 26, 1976, at the age of 63, he faced heart bypass surgery. The man who had possessed the power to decide others' fate with the nod of his head was now helpless to control his own.

Despite the benefit of Cleveland's best heart specialists, Scalish died a few hours after surgery.

Scalish's untimely death created a crucial hole in mob leadership because he had not picked a successor. The battle that was ignited by those struggling to fill that void became one of the bloodiest in 50 years of Cleveland's mafia history.

Victimology

One of the casualties of the mob's leadership transition was Daniel Greene. Born to Irish American parents in 1929, he was placed in an orphanage as a young child when his father either left or died. Greene was schooled in a tough Italian neighborhood that spawned a lifelong hatred of the people who would play a central role in his life.

Greene did a stint in the Marines, where he boxed and became an expert marksman. During the early 1960s, he worked on the Cleveland docks and took over the leadership of the International Longshoreman's Union. He exercised his authority by skimming union funds, extorting money from workers through beatings and threats, and attempted routine shakedowns of employees.

Greene was forced out of the union and convicted in federal court of embezzlement, which was overturned on appeal. He pleaded guilty to a lesser charge of falsifying union records and was fined. He never paid the fine and never saw any prison time for this offense.

Greene started his own business, Emerald Industrial Relations, with which he would have union friends stall or cause trouble on a construction site. He would then offer to settle the dispute for a fee. In addition, he started a business of waste removal by consolidating rubbish haulers, forcing any of the reluctant to join through bombing, burning, and pouring acid on their equipment. Newspaper exposure eventually forced him out of the Solid Waste Guild.

It was during this period that Greene began to make connections with Cleveland's organized crime scene. In 1971, he was implicated in what became the first of a long line of bombings to eliminate threats and further his delusions of a Cleveland-based Celtic crime organization.

At the time of Danny Greene's death, he fit the victimology of being a prominent organized crime figure and representative of one at odds with those in power. He also had a history of being an FBI informant.

Crime Scene Indicators

After John Scalish died, James Licavoli (alias Jack White) reluctantly took charge of the Cleveland mafia. Danny Greene began to methodically kill White's associates in an attempt to overthrow him. Cleveland was in the throes of a full-scale bombing war as a result of Greene's ambitions and White's retaliations.

There were several unsuccessful attempts on Greene's life; he walked away from one bombing that demolished his apartment with only a few broken ribs. Because Scalish had bequeathed White a weak organization, he had no single hit man who could eliminate Greene. To compensate for this deficit, White contacted every thug he knew for the job.

On October 16, 1977, as Greene entered his car after a dentist appointment, Ronald Carabbia sat nervously clutching an airplane transmitter 50 yards away as his accomplice, Ray Ferritto, slowly cruised toward the freeway. The transmitter's target was a platter directional bomb that was planted in the passenger door of a Trojan horse. (Trojan horse is the name given to a nondescript vehicle that has a bomb planted in it. It is parked next to the target's car and is detonated by remote control when the intended victim comes near it.) Once Greene was between his vehicle and the Trojan horse, Carabbia pushed the button that detonated the directional explosive device. The explosion sent a red ball of fire into the air and blasted debris over the entire parking lot.

Greene's clothing was torn off, except his brown zip-up boots and black socks. His left arm landed a hundred feet from the bomb site. A blue Adidas duffel bag he was carrying containing a 9mm pistol, two magazines full of bullets, notebooks, and a list of license plates driven by his enemies was found nearly intact.

Traces of the bomb's components (the explosives, the container, and the detonator) were found at the crime scene but were not traceable to their source. No latent prints were found on the Trojan horse.

By noting the fragment patterns and direction, and the intensity of damage from the blast and the heat and fire, investigators were able to determine where the bomb was (the seat of the blast is where the most damage is).

Forensic Findings

Greene's back was torn apart by the blast. His left arm was severed from his body, as previously mentioned. The cause of death was from massive internal destruction due to both blunt-force trauma and penetrating injury.

Investigation

A woman driving with her husband to an art gallery allowed a blue Plymouth to turn in front of her. For an instant, she and the Plymouth's driver, Ray Ferritto, stared directly at each other. She also noticed a man in the car's backseat staring at the parking lot where Danny Greene was just climbing into his car. The next instant, pieces of Greene's car were flying at the couple, who followed the Plymouth onto the freeway, making note of driver, car, and license plate. The female eyewitness was a commercial artist and was able to sketch a picture of both suspects. In addition, both witnesses later identified Ferritto and Carabbia from photos.

The license plates of the Trojan horse played an important role in the investigation. When agents went to the department of motor vehicles to check registrations, they went to the original files rather than the computer. Immediately before and after the Trojan horse plates were plates that were registered to the same person. One name was a phony, but the other was the true name. The clerk remembered the man who had filed the tags since he acquired two sets of plates with different names. The car was also eventually traced to a dealership that was known to be involved with the Cleveland mafia.

Outcome

Ronald Carabbia was indicted and found guilty of murder. His original sentence was the death penalty, but that was later commuted to life in prison without parole when the state supreme court ruled the death penalty unconstitutional.

Ferritto became a protected government witness and served a five-year term. Another man, Butchy Cisternino, also was convicted for his part in Greene's death by making the bomb.

Jack White was found not guilty during the first state trial. Jury tampering was strongly suspected. At the second state trial, all those involved were found guilty. In federal court, White was convicted of murder among other charges and given a 45-year prison sentence. He died in prison around 1986.

104: Kidnap Murder

Kidnap murder pertains to a person abducted for ransom and killed whether the ransom is paid or not. It is important to know what designates a kidnapping as opposed to a hostage/barricade situation. A kidnapping involves the seizing and detainment or removal of a person by unlawful force or fraud, often with a demand of ransom. The victim has been taken against his or her will by a possibly unknown subject and is detained at a location unknown to the authorities. Negotiations involving a kidnap situation may include the victim's family, government officials, business leaders, law enforcement authorities, and the offender.

A hostage/barricade situation is when a person is held and threatened by an offender to force the fulfillment of substantive demands made on a third party (see classification 129, which deals with hostage murder). The person being held in a hostage situation is at a location known to the authorities. This is the major difference between these two situations.

Defining Characteristics

VICTIMOLOGY

The victim of a kidnap murder has an elevated level of risk due to offender perception. A victim who would be considered low risk due to lifestyle or occupation will have this risk elevated due to his or her socioeconomic background or availability of resources to meet possible ransom demands. Resistance and control considerations are also a factor affecting risk. The elderly and the very young are at higher risk due to their inability to resist the offender as effectively as a healthy adult could.

CRIME SCENE INDICATORS FREQUENTLY NOTED

There may be multiple crime scenes: the location of the abduction, the death scene, and the body disposal site. The victim is usually alone when the abduction occurs. Furniture may be upset, the victim's belongings scattered in a way that indicates sudden interruption of activities, and doors may be left open. The ransom note may be left at the scene. Future communication from the offender, and possibly the victim, is possible. There may be evidence of multiple offenders.

STAGING

No staging is present.

COMMON FORENSIC FINDINGS

Analysis of the ransom note or recording and victim communication are the prime pieces of forensic evidence. Technical enhancement of recordings should be used to amplify background noise and recording techniques. This information may assist in locating where the recording was made. The method of communication (computer, paper, tape, writing) should be analyzed. The authenticity of both offender and victim communication should be established. Gunshot wounds are often noted that are contact or near contact to the head and other vital areas.

Investigative Considerations

Items that should be scrutinized when dealing with a kidnap murder are telephone and financial records. Prior employees should be considered. The possibility that multiple offenders were involved also should be kept in mind. A telephone trap and trace is usually indicated.

The offender's preoffense surveillance, efforts to trace the victim's movement, and routine may help produce witnesses who observed strangers or suspicious persons in the victim's neighborhood or other locations that were part of their routine. Analysis of the offender and victim communication using threat assessment may prove advantageous. Threat assessment is the process of determining validity and potential source of threats received by individuals, groups, or companies. If the threat is determined to be real, countermeasures are developed to protect the potential victim. The analysis of threat communication, based on the psychology and psychodynamics of the threat, may denote personality traits of the suspect. Preoffense publicity of the victim or other types of victim visibility may provide leads to victim select and targeting.

Search Warrant Suggestions

Search warrant suggestions include communication records such as telephone records. In addition, pictures of the victim; audio or video recordings of the victim; and diaries, journals, and travel-related data such as airplane tickets should be considered.

Case Study: 104: Kidnap Murder

Background

Eight-year-old Leiby Kletzky went missing Monday, July 11, 2011, while walking home from the first day of a religious day camp. His disappearance sparked a joint search by New York City police and a block-by-block search by up to 5,000 Orthodox Jewish volunteers from New York and other states coordinated by the Brooklyn South Shomrim volunteer civilian patrol. The kidnapper was located early Wednesday morning after examination of videos from surveillance cameras along the boy's route showed him meeting and entering a man's vehicle.

By that time, the disappearance had sparked a major search effort in his insular community in Borough Park. The boy's picture was plastered on light posts around the area.

The case has drawn comparisons to the 1979 kidnapping and murder of Etan Patz, a six-year-old resident who was kidnapped from a lower Manhattan area while walking to his school bus for the first time.

Victimology

Yehudah Kletzky, known as "Leiby," was the third of six children and only son of Nachman Kletzky and Esti Forster Kletzky. He was a Hasidic Jewish boy.

Leiby had asked his parents to let him walk home from the day camp instead of taking the school bus. It was the first time that his parents allowed him to walk alone, and they had practiced the route the day before; his mother planned to wait for him at a predetermined point a few blocks from their home.

When the boy was still not home at 6:00 p.m. that evening, Esther Kletzky, the boy's mother, made a missing person call to Jewish first responders in their neighborhood of Boro Park.

Crime Scene Indicators

There were three crime scenes: the abduction of the boy into the car, traveling in the car, and the offender's home. The abduction took place outside between 5:00 and 6:00 p.m. on a busy street on a Monday. It was high risk for the offender.

The indoor crime scene was disorganized, with bloody knives and towels in full view for the police. The body had been dismembered and concealed to prevent discovery.

Forensic Findings

The medical examiner's office reported that Aron had given the boy a toxic mix of prescription drugs and over-the-counter drugs before smothering him. Severed feet were found wrapped in plastic in Aron's freezer. A cutting board and three bloody carving knives were found in the refrigerator.

In Aron's confession, he denied ever tying up the boy, though marks were found on his body.

Investigators pulled dozens of bags of evidence out of Aron's home in Kensington, Brooklyn. Some of the bags contained children's clothing and a pillow, spoon, and cup.

Investigation

Police and volunteer searchers found various surveillance videos of the route the boy took to walk home. It showed the wrong turn Leiby took and him talking to a man who then crossed the street and entered a dentist's office. When the man came out, Leiby followed him and appeared to get into his car. Police located the dentist who provided the name of the man who had come in to pay his bill. The man was Levi Aron.

The neighborhood where both Aron and Kletzky lived was a tight-knit Orthodox Jewish community. Leiby was an example of a victim whose risk level became heightened when he became lost outside of his neighborhood.

Investigators determined the car in the surveillance video was a 1990 gold Honda Accord. The car was spotted by volunteers, and when police went to the door, Levi Aron showed them the blood-soaked carving knives and bloody towels in bags.

Aron kept the boy with him, in his car and in his apartment, for two days before getting scared about the manhunt, according to his in-court confession. He claimed to have intentions of taking him back to his home the next day, but when he saw the missing flyers, he panicked. The child remained at the apartment alone all day while Aron was at work. When Aron returned, he took a bath towel and smothered the boy. Aron said his fear led him to drug, kill, and dismember Leiby because he did not know what to do with the body. Aron directed investigators to a trash bin where he dumped a red suitcase containing body parts.

Outcome

On August 9, 2012, Levi Aron, the Brooklyn man accused of killing eight-year-old Leiby Kletzky, pleaded guilty to charges of second-degree murder and kidnapping. Originally, he had pleaded not guilty to eight counts of murder and kidnapping. Levi Aron agreed to a prison sentence of 25 years to life on a conviction of murder in the second degree, and to a sentence of 15 years to life for kidnapping in the second degree, with the sentences to be served consecutively.

Psychiatric evaluations of Levi Aron indicated an adjustment disorder and a personality disorder with schizoid features. While giving authorities conflicting accounts of his life and his mental and physical history, he did say that his younger sister died while institutionalized with schizophrenia. Of the 35-year-old Aron, the psychologist wrote, "His mood is neutral, practically blank. The only time he seems to show any emotional response is when he is asked difficult questions about the reason for his incarceration."

The evaluation offers little details on a possible motive and does not delve much into the crime. Aron admitted knowing the charges against him were serious, and acknowledged that people are angry with him.

The records filled in a few blanks about Aron's life, which was lived mostly alone except for a few impulsive decisions, such as moving to Memphis to get married to a woman he met online and had met in person only twice. They divorced after a few years. Aron was employed as a hardware clerk, and earlier as a supermarket worker and a caterer. Aron spent much of his time online, and made audio and video recordings of himself doing karaoke. He lived in a home owned by his father and stepmother; his brother lived in a separate apartment. His mother died in 2004. His sister was institutionalized with schizophrenia and died at age 24. Both the psychiatrist and psychologist described Aron as reserved, apathetic, sad, and cooperative.

Sources: Goldman, 2011; Sidman, 2011; Tannenbaum, 2011

105: Product Tampering

In this type of homicide, death results from contact with a commercial product, sabotaged by the offender for the purpose of achieving financial gain. There are three primary offender strategies used for achieving financial gain: litigation on behalf of the victim (wrongful death), extortion, and business operations. The last method includes damaging a competing business through sabotage of its product or manipulating the stock market as a result of negative publicity.

Violation of the Federal Anti-Tampering Act occurs when any product has been affected by the actions of the perpetrator. With a business attack, tainting or switching labels may happen on a retail level. Elements of this crime include the involvement of a consumer product such as a drug; the tainting of that product or the switching of product labels to make them materially false; and intent to cause serious injury to the business of a person.

The extortion method also can be tied into the business manipulation approach. An example is a crime involving a protection racket, in which the taint is tied to a demand for payments under threat of closing down the store or causing grave damage to the reputation of the business.

Defining Characteristics

VICTIMOLOGY

The victim of product tampering may be random or specific, dependent on the product's distribution, the product's use, and the offender strategy. Sabotaged baby food, brake lines, and soft drinks will involve a particular age group or class of people. Some sabotaged products will be distributed only on a local scale, so the victimology will be more confined. The localization of victims can also help establish whether the product is being tampered with at a retail stage or at the manufacturer's level. Random victimology is likely to be seen with extortion or with intent to damage a competitor.

The more specific victim is seen when the offender employs litigation for wrongful death. The victim will be a family member or one closely associated with the offender. Random victims are observed when this type of offender wants to remove suspicion from himself or herself and stages the crime to look like the work of an indiscriminate killer.

CRIME SCENE INDICATORS FREQUENTLY NOTED

Multiple crime scenes usually are involved with this homicide: the site where the product is altered, the location where the product is procured by the victim, the place of use or consumption, and the death scene. The location of alteration may offer evidence of the tampering involved. If it is mechanical sabotage, tools particular to that alteration will be present. Chemicals, poisons, and medicines may be found if this type of tampering is employed.

Tampered-product locations and the proximity of victims to sites will aid in deciding the scope and movement of the offender as well as origin of the product. At the death scene, the proximity of the victim to the altered product can aid the investigator in reconstructing the product's path. In addition, communication from the offender may be found at any of the scenes involved.

STAGING

Staging is crucial if the offender is using the litigation strategy. The offender must make it appear as if the family member or close associate was a victim of either a random killer or a company's faulty product. For the first set of circumstances, there could be other random victims selected to give the appearance of an indiscriminate saboteur at work. The other situation may require the death to look like an accident (e.g., a defective automotive part or short-circuited power tool that causes the fatal accident). Fire started by apparently faulty wiring that burns a house down with the victim inside is another illustration of a staged product tampering. The initial impression derived from the crime scene of a staged tampering homicide ranges from violent death to a medical emergency of some kind, without any obvious indicators of a homicide.

COMMON FORENSIC FINDINGS

Examination of the product is one of the fundamental considerations of product tampering. There may be visible signs of tampering, such as clearly discolored capsules. The type of analysis done on the product and victim will depend on the instrument of death.

Suspicion of poisoning requires toxicological and chemical analysis of the product and victim to determine if products of the same lot were involved. Because toxicological analysis is not routine in postmortem examination, exhumation of the victim may be necessary to detect poisoning. This, along with the distribution of victims, will help decide if the source of tampering is at the retail or manufacturer level. Type of poison and consistent or varying levels of poison in each tainted product reflect the resources and sophistication of the offender. The packaging of the product will also be revealing of offender sophistication: this includes absence or presence of fingerprints, repackaging, and the appearance of the tainted items.

The analysis of offender communication would be approached in the same manner as in kidnap murders (see classification 104). If the communication is verbal, a verbatim set of the caller's comments and information about speech patterns and accent are vital to threat assessment.

Investigative Considerations

Threat assessment of offender communication may be helpful. If there is no extortion demand associated with the death and civil litigation has been initiated, the litigant should be scrutinized. The litigant's financial status (beneficiary to insurance claims or inheritance, along with problems such as outstanding debts, for example), relationship with the victim (problems, extramarital affairs), and preoffense and postoffense behavior should be examined.

Although the primary motivation is financial gain, the offender who targets a family member for death often has concurrent secondary motivations or goals that will be equally well served by the victim's death. Avenues such as domestic problems and extramarital affairs should be explored. Because product-tampering deaths are relatively rare, early allegations of such by anyone who stands to benefit from the victim's death should be viewed cautiously and evaluated carefully.

Cyanide is often the poison of choice because it is easily available at chemical and photographic supply houses and in college and high school laboratories. It can also be ordered through the mail. One ounce can kill 250 people, so its potency makes it a popular choice with product-tampering offenders. An important investigative tool in cases of an offender who has used cyanide is a complex instrument in use at the Food and Drug Administration's Cincinnati district laboratory. It can track down the source of the cyanide and identify the supplier, who can find the geographical customer list rather quickly. This may help narrow the list of typical suspects (chemical firms, grocery clerks, the enemies of deceased victims, or a store's terminated personnel file) and further isolate the offender.

Search Warrant Suggestions

Search warrant suggestions for this type of crime include financial records, materials specific to the tampering (e.g., tools, electronic devices, chemicals, drugs, literature pertaining to drugs, manuals), and any related products (other analgesics, empty capsules). Evidence of tampering practice and other tainted products should also be considered.

Product-Tampering Cases

Bromo-Seltzer (United States, 1899)

Harry Cornish, director of New York's Knickerbocker Athletic Club, received a package on Christmas Eve 1899 that contained a silver bottle holder and a Bromo-Seltzer bottle. No card was inside, and Cornish thought it was a hint to avoid excessive drinking over the holidays.

A few nights later, a relative of Cornish's who had admired the bottle holder, awoke with a headache. Katherine Adams took some of the Bromo-Seltzer, which she said tasted bitter. Cornish also took a sip. It was later determined that cyanide had been added to the Bromo-Seltzer.

An hour later, Adams was dead. Although sickened, Cornish survived. In November, another club member, Henry Barnet, had died under similar circumstances. The police investigation focused on Roland Molineux, who had feuded with Cornish and had been Barnet's romantic rival. The three-month trial was one of the longest in New York history to that date. Molineux was found guilty of Adams's murder. He appealed and won a new trial because of evidentiary error. The prosecution had linked Molineaux to Barnet's death even though he was not charged.

The Court of Appeals ruling was a landmark in U.S. law because it established that the presumption of innocence means that previous crimes cannot be used as evidence in an unrelated case in the second trial. The jury took 12 minutes to deliberate. Molineux was found not guilty. Today, in New York State when there is a pretrial hearing on the admissibility of evidence, it is called a Molineux hearing (CBC, updated 8/2/2012).

Tylenol (United States, 1982)

This case changed the way drugs are packaged and led to new product-tampering laws in the United States. Seven people died in the Chicago area after taking Extra-Strength Tylenol that had been laced with cyanide. The case remains unsolved, with no known crime scene or motive despite more than 100 police investigators following over 6,500 leads and 400 possible suspects.

Tylenol was recalled from store shelves and its market share plummeted; however, after a few years, it had regained its lead in analgesics in the United States.

James W. Lewis was charged with extortion in the case. Lewis, a former tax consultant, had moved from Chicago to New York in September 1982. He had sent a letter to Tylenol's manufacturer demanding $1 million to "stop the killing." Lewis spent 11 years in prison.

There were 270 cases of suspected product tampering in the months following the Tylenol murders. In 1986, Tylenol began manufacturing tamper-resistant packaging. However, in February 1986, Diane Elsroth died after taking a cyanide-laced Tylenol. That case also remains unsolved (CBC, updated 8/2/2012).

Oronamin C (Japan 1986)

In 1985, as many as 12 people in Japan began dying after drinking popular drinks dispensed from vending machines. The most frequently tampered drink was Oronamin C, an energy drink with added vitamins. The drinks had been laced with Paraquat, an herbicide. At the time, the vending machines would give out two drinks as a marketing strategy.

Police suspected that the killer usually left the poison drink in the machines' dispenser slot. Police also speculated that some of the deaths might have been suicides or the work of copycat killers. In 1998, Japan had another wave of poisonings of drinks sold in vending machines and convenience stores (CBC, updated 8/2/2012).

Sudafed (United States, 1991)

Kathleen Daneker and Stanley McWhorter died in Washington State after taking cyanide-laced Sudafed, a decongestant. Burroughs Wellcome & Company, Sudafed's manufacturer, recalled the product across the United States. Three other tampered bottles of Sudafed were found on store shelves.

On February 2, 1991, before the deaths, Jennifer Meling took a Sudafed that her husband, Joseph, had given her to stop her snoring. Soon after she became unconscious, Joseph called 911 and Jennifer was rushed to the hospital. She survived. In August 1991, police arrested Joseph Meling after determining he had purchased sodium cyanide weeks before the poisonings. Using a false name, Meling's motive was believed to have been to collect insurance money for his wife's death. He worried he would be a suspect in the poisoning so he planted five other bottles to deflect suspicion. Meling was convicted and sentenced to life in prison.

Case Study: 105: Product Tampering

Background

Stella Maudine Nickell's husband, Bruce, came home from work with a headache. After he had given his wife of 10 years a kiss, he went into their kitchen and reached for a bottle of Extra-Strength Excedrin. He swallowed four capsules and sat down to watch television. Stella remembers that Bruce then decided to go for a walk out on the patio. Suddenly, she heard Bruce call to her that he felt like he was going to pass out. Within the next minute, he collapsed and was unable to speak. Stella called the paramedics, and Bruce was taken to Harborview Medical Center in Seattle. He died a few hours later, never regaining consciousness.

Six days later, on June 11, 1986, Sue Snow started her day by taking two Extra-Strength Excedrin capsules, as was her habit. The caffeine in the capsules was like her morning cup of coffee. Fifteen minutes later, her daughter, Hayley, found her sprawled unconscious on the bathroom floor. By noon, she was dead.

Victimology

At the time of his death, Bruce Nickell was 52. When he married Stella, he was a hard-drinking heavy-equipment operator, which suited Stella since she had a fondness for bar hopping. Nickell had recently taken stock of his life and decided to dry out by attending a rehabilitation program. Stella attended a few sessions with him. Before his death, Bruce was often unemployed, which had begun to get on Stella's nerves.

Sue Snow was 40 years old at the time of her death. She had dropped out of high school to marry but had turned her life around through hard work. She had become the assistant vice president at a branch of the Puget Sound National Bank and was happily married to Paul Webking. They were rarely apart and "madly in love," according to Webking.

Both victims were users of the product. Nickell and Snow had never met; Snow was an example of the random victim that is common to many product-tampering murders.

Crime Scene Indicators

Five bottles of tainted Extra-Strength Excedrin came from Johnny's Food Center in Kent, a Seattle, Washington, suburb, and a Pay 'N' Save store in Auburn. Two contaminated containers were found in the Nickell household. Seals on the containers were cut or missing, and the boxes, which had been reglued, demonstrated obvious signs of tampering. The victims lived within five miles of each other, a factor that was significant to investigators devising the area of offender operation.

Staging

Sue Snow became a victim because of staging. Stella Nickell was very disappointed with the medical examiner's initial decision that her husband had died from emphysema and not cyanide poisoning. Her husband's death meant $105,000 to her in addition to the damages she expected to get from Bristol-Myers when his death was declared by poisoning. Someone else had to die to alert the authorities that a random cyanide killer was at work in King County. So Stella Nickell poisoned the three bottles of Excedrin and slipped them onto the shelves of area stores, one of which was bought by Snow. This set the scene for Nickell to approach officials with her suspicions that her husband had fallen to a cyanide murderer as well as giving her grounds to sue Bristol-Myers.

Forensic Findings

The initial cause of death listed on Bruce Nickell's death certificate was pulmonary emphysema because the coroner had failed to detect the cyanide in his body. It was not until after Snow's death, when Stella Nickell came forward with the hesitant suggestion that her husband also had been the victim of a random cyanide killer, that the true cause of death was determined. At that time, tissue samples demonstrated cyanide poisoning. Sue Snow had levels of cyanide that were easily detected by medical examiners.

After analysis of the tampered bottles, it was established that a random selection of pills had been poisoned. Some capsules contained more than three times the lethal adult dose of potassium cyanide. Others were not contaminated; Paul Webking took two capsules from the same bottle that proved fatal to Sue Snow 20 minutes later.

The exterior carton and bottle tampering was artless. The boxes were reglued in an amateur manner, exhibiting minimal sophistication on the part of the offender.

Investigation

Stella Nickell had a restless yearning to buy the property the Nickell trailer stood on and open a tropical fish store. Her ambitions were becoming insistent. At the age of 44, she had an increasing awareness of the gap between her dreams and reality. To her, the gap seemed to be widening faster as each year passed. That her husband was frequently unemployed reinforced her belief that if she did not act soon, her dreams would slip away for good. In addition, she felt her husband was not much fun since he had stopped drinking.

In the fall of 1985, Nickell took out a $40,000 life insurance policy on her husband, naming herself as sole beneficiary. Bruce Nickell also held a state employee policy that paid $31,000, with an additional $107,000 awarded in the event of an accidental death. To Nickell, $176,000 could easily make her dreams into reality.

Nickell's daughter, Cynthia, who was living with the Nickells at the time of the murder, eventually came forward and told about the conversations she had had with her mother during the five years leading to the offense. Bruce Nickell's death was a popular topic of conversation with Stella Nickell.

Cynthia testified in court that her mother had studied library books on poisons and experimented with toxic seeds, either hemlock or foxglove. Bruce's only reaction was to become lethargic. When Stella learned that a recovering alcoholic was susceptible to other addictive substances, she discussed the idea of killing him with heroin, cocaine, or speed, so it would appear to be just an accidental overdose.

According to Cynthia, her mother expressed great interest in the Tylenol murders of Chicago in 1982. Using the same plan, she could not only collect life insurance but file suit against the responsible company, Bristol-Myers (which she did), for wrongful death. She felt this was a viable alternative to get her fish store and live in the comfort she had always dreamed about.

These discussions between Cynthia and her mother show how scrutiny of a suspect's preoffense conversations may be helpful in establishing motive and premeditation. There was not enough evidence to bring Stella in until Cynthia decided to talk.

Outcome

Stella Maudine Nickell was convicted of five counts of product tampering and two counts of causing the death of another by product tampering (the first conviction using a federal law enacted in 1983). On June 17, 1988, she was sentenced to 90 years. She will not be eligible for parole until 2018.

106: Drug Murder

Drug murder is defined as the murder of an individual where the primary cause is to remove an obstruction and facilitate the operation of the drug business.

Defining Characteristics

Victimology

The victimology of drug-related homicide is dependent on the motive of the offender. The homicides are categorized into five motive groups: discipline, informant, robbery, territory infringement, and antidrug advocate.

The victim of a discipline-motivated homicide is being punished for breaking the rules of a drug distribution group by which he is employed. Examples of these infringements include skimming money or drugs, stealing customers, or in some other way hindering, obstructing, or impeding the operation. The informant supplies information on the criminal enterprise to law enforcement or competing dealers. A robbery-motivated homicide usually deals with a rip-off of drugs, money, or other goods (especially gold jewelry) related to the sale of drugs from customers, traffickers, or dealers. A drug trafficker who infringes on the territory of another drug dealer may become the victim of a drug murder. Victims of these four types of murder are commonly known to law enforcement as having a history of association with the drug trade. They may have an arrest record, reflecting a history of drug use, robberies, and assaultive behavior relating to this involvement, or at least an association with known drug offenders.

The last type of victim can be anyone, from the neighborhood antidrug crusader to a law enforcement officer. These victims may be social workers or clergy who are offering treatment to drug abusers and thus usurping customers of the dealers. Judges who impose stiff penalties, politicians who vigorously campaign against drugs, and witnesses testifying against drug offenders are other examples of this victimology. All of these victim types are individuals opposed to the drug trade and viewed as an obstruction, real or symbolic, the offender wants removed.

CRIME SCENE INDICATORS FREQUENTLY NOTED

Drug-related homicide often occurs in a public place if the death of the victim is intended to be a message. The body is usually not concealed but is left at the scene with a wanton indifference. Evidence such as drugs or money may be removed from the scene. The weapon used is frequently one of choice that is brought to the scene and taken from it by the offender. Drugs or drug proceeds removed from the scene or missing from an obvious or known victim trafficker are another indicator that might be apparent at the scene of a drug murder.

STAGING

Staging is usually not present.

COMMON FORENSIC FINDINGS

The weapon used is predominantly a firearm, often large caliber and semi-automatic. Occasionally, knife wounds or blunt-force trauma will be present, but these injuries are not as prevalent. A high lethality of injury will be seen in which vital organs (chest and head) are targeted. Overkill involving multiple wounds can be seen.

A drug screen done on the victim may help establish possible victim use and connections to the drug business. Sometimes the mode of death might be an overdose, or so-called hotshot, especially if the victim is a user.

The investigator should make sure a latent print process is attempted on the body. Physical contact commonly occurs between the offender and victim of a drug murder before death.

Investigative Considerations

The offender will almost always have a known association with the drug trade as a user, manufacturer, or distributor. This subject commonly will be associated with a street gang, since gangs are immersed in drug trafficking (see classification 102).

This homicide appears opportunistic, with rip-offs, territory infringements, and some discipline-motivated killings. Informant and antidrug advocate hits usually are setups that demonstrate some degree of organization and planning. Although informant use is a fundamental consideration with many investigations, the use of intelligence information is especially valuable with drug-related murder. Use of prison informants might also prove helpful with this type of homicide.

Offenders may exhibit displays of wealth even though they have no legitimate source of money. They have expensive clothing, vehicles, and jewelry yet are unemployed or have a job that is inconsistent with their apparent finances.

Search Warrant Suggestions

Search warrant suggestions include large amounts of money, clothing, electronic equipment, and so on reflective of a possible illegitimate money source; drug paraphernalia, that is, items that link the offender to the drug trade; firearms; phone records; rental contracts; address books; financial records and bank records; transaction records, computerized records, and ledgers; packing materials (packaging from drug shipments, processing, lab setups, distribution [dividing into smaller parcels for street sale]); and photos (of using, manicuring, and preparing drugs).

Two case examples are given. The first illustrates a scene where all persons present were killed. The second case illustrates a dual drug murder.

Case Study: 106: Drug Murder

Background

By the time he was 23, Daniel A. Nicoll had a thriving drug trade that required bimonthly trips to Florida in his 1978 Ford pickup. Although Nicoll did not live in a mainstream drug trade city, he was important enough to be the target of a unified task force consisting of Drug Enforcement Administration (DEA), state, and local law enforcement.

When he was not making Florida trips or selling the drugs he bought there, Nicoll tended bar at the Club California in Buffalo, New York. It is there he met Laura Osborn. As their personal relationship developed, Nicoll began supplying her with cocaine and marijuana for personal use as well as dealing.

Victimology

Donald and Claire Nicoll referred to their son's drug dealings as "dirty business" and as the reason their son was no longer residing with them. Nicoll was arrested by the police in Buffalo, New York, for possession of methadone, unlawful possession of a controlled substance (PCP), and unlawful possession of marijuana. The case was not disposed of prior to the murder.

Nicoll had had some close calls before his death. He returned from one Florida trip with an injury above his eye, attributing it to a drug rip-off. He had also been threatened with a gun when he was suspected of a drug rip-off on another occasion.

Nicoll demonstrated a fitting picture of the drug murder victim. His history of a drug-related arrest and the fact that his reputation in the drug business had reached a federal level with DEA involvement offered further illustration of this victimology. In addition, Nicoll had a history of previous threatening drug-related confrontations.

Laura Osborn had met Nicoll while bar hopping in 1975, and they had maintained a steady relationship for about four years. Osborn benefited from Nicoll's prosperous drug trade personally as well as financially by dealing herself. She had no arrest record but was under the same DEA investigation as Nicoll.

Osborn paid a price for her involvement with Nicoll. She was the victim of his abuse, seen on occasion with bruises around her face. Another time, Nicoll explained a head injury that Osborn suffered as a suicide attempt. However, Osborn claimed that Nicoll had struck her on the head with a bottle. Neighbors had witnessed the assault, but no legal action was ever taken.

Osborn epitomized the drug murder victim for the same reasons Nicoll did: she was known to law enforcement as being associated indirectly (relationship with Nicoll) and directly (through her active dealings) with the drug business.

Crime Scene Indicators

There were two crime scenes involved with these homicides. The first one was on a back road where the victims were parked, waiting for the offender, who was going to buy drugs from them. The offender, Larry Rendell, pulled his truck alongside Nicoll's truck, facing the opposite direction, so that the two drivers were facing each other. Larry then shot both Nicoll and Osborn from his truck. Nicoll fell over unconscious into Osborn's lap. Osborn was still alert, having been shot in the arm while trying to protect herself.

Rendell climbed into the truck and drove it to another road. Osborn pleaded for her life, assuring Rendell she would tell no one about what had happened. She then asked Rendell for some cocaine. It was at this time Nicoll stopped breathing.

Osborn got out of the truck and began to walk away, taking her shoes off as she walked. Rendell felt he could not afford to let Osborn live, so he shot her from the truck and then went over to complete the job.

Both bodies were dragged over an embankment and covered with leaves. Rendell then drove Nicoll's truck into a gully off a nearby road.

Forensic Findings

Later, Rendell told his brother that he tore the truck apart to remove any shell casings from the 10 to 12 shots he fired at Osborn and Nicoll. Confiscated at his apartment were clogs and a green jacket with lettering that he wore at the time of the murder. Both items were soiled with blood from each victim.

Cause of death for Daniel Nicoll was multiple gunshot wounds to the head, causing massive cerebral hemorrhage. Osborn also died of massive cerebral hemorrhage from multiple gunshot wounds. She had been struck at least six times by the .22-caliber rifle.

Investigation

Lawrence K. Rendell had several reasons for killing Nicoll and Osborn. He claimed that Nicoll had shorted him on a previous marijuana deal and Nicoll had ignored his protests. He also owed Nicoll anywhere from $450 to $1,000 for past drug deals and was constantly hassled by the victim to pay up. Rendell had instructed Nicoll to bring his supply of cocaine the day of the murders because he claimed to have a buyer. Rendell had decided that killing Nicoll served a threefold purpose of settling his debts, evening the score from the previous rip-off, and providing him with drugs. In addition to the other physical evidence linking Rendell to the crime, two speakers from Nicoll's truck were found in his apartment during the search.

Outcome

Larry Rendell was convicted of two counts of second-degree murder.

107: Insurance-Related Death

A victim is murdered for insurance or inheritance purposes. There are two subcategories for this type of homicide: individual profit murder and commercial profit murder.

107.01: Individual Profit

The individual profit murder is defined as one in which the murderer expects to gain financially by the victim's death. Examples of these types of crimes are "black widow" killings, robbery homicides, or multiple killings involving insurance or welfare fraud.

Defining Characteristics

VICTIMOLOGY

The victim of an insurance or inheritance death for individual profit has a close relationship with the offender. This includes family members, business associates, and live-in partners.

Many victims of this category are not typically characterized as high-risk targets. In fact, their lifestyles, occupation, and living circumstances often classify them as very low risk. However, because of the offender's perception of them as an avenue to his or her financial goals, their risk is greatly elevated.

CRIME SCENE INDICATORS FREQUENTLY NOTED

Usually, the body is not concealed but is left in the open or somewhere that discovery is probable. The nature of the crime scene, or where it falls in the continuum between organized and disorganized, depends on the amount of the offender's planning and his or her capacity.

An example of one extreme of this continuum is the spontaneous offense committed by a youthful, impulsive, or less intelligent subject. This crime scene would contain more physical evidence, such as fingerprints or footprints. The weapon would be one of opportunity acquired and left at the scene. The crime scene would be chaotic, with evidence of sudden violence to the victim (a blitz-style attack). The body would be left at the assault site with little or no effort to conceal it.

The other extreme of this crime scene would be the offense committed by the calculating, proficient offender who has mapped out all aspects of the crime ahead of time. This methodical approach is represented by an orderly crime scene in which there is minimal physical evidence present. The weapon is one of choice, brought to and removed from the scene by the offender.

STAGING

Staging is often employed with this type of homicide. Its complexity can reflect offender capability, resources, and premeditation. The crime scene will most frequently be staged to give investigators the impression that death resulted from natural or accidental causes or from criminal activity. Suicide staging is also possible, especially in the light of the more liberal standards of some insurance policies.

COMMON FORENSIC FINDINGS

Asphyxial or chemical modalities are common because these deaths are often not considered untimely and therefore not investigated within the medical–legal system. Toxicological studies of the blood, liver, hair, and so on are essential to determine if poisoning was used. Exhumation may be necessary.

The staging used will determine the forensic findings; for example, a staged robbery–murder victim might have gunshot wounds, as opposed to the seemingly accidental drowning victim who has pulmonary edema and blood-streaked foam present in the nose and mouth. Therefore, the variance of forensic findings is vast.

Investigative Considerations

The mechanism of money transfers, whether insurance document or wills, should be checked to determine the authenticity of the victim's signature. Any recent beneficiary change or increase in insurance premiums or new policy procurement justifies further probing into the victim–beneficiary relationship. Many of the components that are detailed in the discussion of domestic homicide (see classification 122) are pertinent with this investigation, especially since multiple motives are often involved (extramarital affairs, irreconcilable conflicts, and so forth).

Precipitating events may be seen as external stressors, such as financial problems, marital discord, dissension with the victim due to job, or alcohol. There may be a change in preoffense behavior toward the victim, often in the form of apparent relationship improvement. Offender nervousness or preoccupation may also be observed by others.

The offender often has an uncommonly detailed, steadfast alibi with selective recall. The offender also may delay reporting the murder, especially if he or she desires a third party to discover the body. A comprehensive examination of the physical and psychological records and history of the victim should be done when the investigator suspects the offender has employed suicide or death-from-natural-causes staging.

Search Warrant Suggestions

Financial records of the victim and offender should be scrutinized. If the death was staged to appear natural, medications, poisons, or drugs of any kind should be looked for. Any indicators that would support the precipitating events (e.g., offender in debt or extramarital affairs) should be sought.

107.02: Commercial Profit

Commercial profit homicide is murder to gain control of a business or to profit from the business.

Defining Characteristics

VICTIMOLOGY

Victimology is the primary point that contrasts this type of murder with individual profit murder (classification 107.01). The victim in this type of murder is more likely to have a partner or professional relationship with the offender; however, this does not exclude a familial or personal relationship with the offender.

CRIME SCENE INDICATORS FREQUENTLY NOTED

Crime scene indicators are the same as those for individual profit murder: a continuum from the spontaneous and haphazard murder to the well-executed one.

STAGING

Staging is the same as for individual profit murder. It depends on the resources, sophistication, and degree of premeditation of offender.

COMMON FORENSIC FINDINGS

Forensic findings range from violent to accidental to natural death.

Investigative Considerations

In a commercially motivated homicide, the business relationship and corporate structure should be checked. As in individual profit murder, the offender's preoffense financial status should be examined. In addition, the victim's preoffense status should be checked because motive for the killing could be that the victim was costing the company money (through faulty investments, ineffectual business decisions, or alcohol problems, for example).

The net worth of the victim, as well as the net worth solvency of the business, is important. For example, a business having difficulties may be bailed out by a business partner's life insurance. This may be seen by a correlation of impending business failure with purchase of the policy.

Search Warrant Suggestions

Business records and the suspect's and victim's financial records are search warrant suggestions. Additional suggestions are those presented for individual profit murder (see classification 107.01).

Case Study: 107.02: Commercial Profit

Background

On the morning of July 9, 1991, 34-year-old Steven Benson surprised everyone by showing up early at his mother's home. He had made arrangements the night before to accompany his family to look at some property that morning. No one really expected him, as it was out of character for him to be up early. Nevertheless, he appeared at his mother's home at 7:30 a.m. Soon after he arrived, he took her Chevrolet Suburban to buy some doughnuts and coffee but took almost an hour and half to return.

After his return, Benson convinced his mother and his brother, Scott, to come along on the outing, despite his mother's brief resistance to the idea. Benson arranged the seating, placing Scott in the driver's seat, the spot he usually occupied. He placed his mother in the front passenger seat where his sister, Carol Lynn, usually sat because she had a problem with carsickness. He placed Carol Lynn in the back, behind Scott.

Just as Benson ran into the house to get something he had forgotten, the Suburban was engulfed by a thunderous explosion and an orange fireball. Benson ran out of the front door, only to immediately return and shut the door behind as a second explosion rocked the house. Of the car's occupants, 63-year-old tobacco heiress Margaret Benson and her 21-year-old adopted son, Scott, were killed instantly. Forty-one-year-old Carol Lynn sustained serious injuries.

Victimology

After Margaret Benson's husband, Edward, had died in 1980, her estate was estimated to be around $9 million. This did not include the millions more she would eventually inherit from her father, Harry Hitchcock. By July 1985 Margaret suspected that her son, Steven, had squandered at least $2.5 million of her money on his many imprudent business deals. In addition to the numerous times she had to bail Steven out of financial disasters, she suspected he was now embezzling money to support his extravagant lifestyle. In part, this extravagance was prompted by the demands of his domineering wife, Debby. Steven lived in fear that if he denied her anything, she would take their three children and leave him, as she had done once before.

By July 1985 Margaret had finally endured enough of Steven's sapping her money. In addition, she had suffered nothing but disrespect and cruelty from both Steven and his wife. The day before her death, she had summoned her lawyer from Pennsylvania to look at the company's books and "finally do something about Steven." She discovered Steven had bought a luxurious home by siphoning money from their joint business, which she had financed and managed. He had also opened up another office in nearby Fort Myers, Florida, that was much more luxurious than the trailer office in Naples. With just one glance at the books, the lawyer was able to tell that here were many improprieties with Steven's bookkeeping.

Once Steven realized what his mother was doing, Margaret's victim risk level skyrocketed. Her lifestyle and personality would normally have put her at very low risk for becoming the victim of a violent crime, but because of her situation, her risk was considerably elevated.

If Margaret discovered the extent of Steven's embezzlement, she might have eliminated his inheritance or severely reduced it. In addition, she was already planning to put a lien on his new home and close down his Fort Myers office. The benefits of killing his mother were obvious. By including Scott and Carol Lynn in the fatal explosion, Steven hoped to secure the entire inheritance and family business for himself. Scott and Carol Lynn's inheritance from Harry Hitchcock would be his. Margaret, Scott, and Carol Lynn became high-risk victims because of their brother's perception of them as obstacles to his absolute control of the family business and money.

Crime Scene Indicators

The first blast blew the car windshield out and both doors open. It also peeled back the top of the car toward the rear. The explosion blasted Margaret and Scott out of the vehicle. Margaret's body landed in the grass alongside the driveway. Scott was thrown away from the house and landed on the driveway. Carol Lynn survived because her door had been open. She jumped out of the car, which was engulfed in flames, and tried to get her shirt off. Both her shirt end her hair were on fire.

When agents from the Bureau of Alcohol, Tobacco, and Firearms (ATF) examined the crime scene, they noted that debris was scattered a hundred feet in all directions. There were two distinct blast areas in the vehicle, signifying there were probably two devices. Because the floor had been blasted downward, the agents concluded that the devices had been placed inside the vehicle. From the blast pattern, it appeared that one device had been between the two front seats and the other was under the passenger seat directly behind the driver, where Steven had placed Carol Lynn. The injuries on the bodies were also consistent with this placement to the bombs. Fragments from the scene revealed that the devices were pipe bombs.

Forensic Findings

Scott Benson had sustained massive injury to his entire right side. The right side of his trunk was laid open from the waist to the shoulder, with most the internal organs exposed. A knifelike piece of shrapnel had penetrated his skull.

Margaret Benson's right foot had been destroyed. It appeared she had been resting her left hand on the console over one of the devices because that hand had been completely blown off. Her face had been obliterated from the forehead down. In addition, the left side of her body had sustained heavy damage.

Carol Lynn lost most of her right ear. She sustained gaping shrapnel wounds to the leg and smaller wounds to the arms and shoulder of her right side. Her chin was gashed and the side of her face seared. Severe burns covered her right arm and parts of her body. In addition, a neighbor who was running to the scene to help was hit by shrapnel from the second blast, which severed the end of his nose.

Investigation

The investigation focused on Steven Benson as investigators learned from Margaret Benson's lawyer how upset she had been with Steven. Information began surfacing very early in the investigation that strengthened the suspicion of ATF agents and the Collier County sheriff's department: Benson had the motive end opportunity (being the last person to drive the vehicle) to place the two pipe bombs in the vehicle.

Next, the investigative team needed to determine whether Benson had the ability to make the bombs. Several people were able to answer this. Benson had the reputation of being an electronics whiz. He owned a burglar alarm company so was familiar with wiring electrical devices and circuits.

One damaging piece of evidence was in the form of two receipts from a supply company located around the corner from Benson's workplace. One was for four end caps, and one was for two four- by twelve-inch pipes, both components of the two devices recovered from the scene. Both receipts were made out to a construction company spelled differently on each one. Even more damaging were the two palm prints lifted from the receipts that matched Benson's.

Outcome

Steven Benson was convicted of two counts of first-degree murder and one count of attempted murder. He was sentenced to serve a minimum of 50 years and will not be eligible for parole until the year 2036.

108: Felony Murder

Property crime (robbery, burglary) is the primary motivation for felony murder, with murder the secondary motivation. During the commission of a violent crime, a homicide occurs. There are two types of felony murder: indiscriminate felony murder and situational felony murder.

108.01: Indiscriminate Murder

An indiscriminate felony murder is a homicide that is planned in advance of committing the felony without a specific victim in mind.

Defining Characteristics

VICTIMOLOGY

The victim of an indiscriminate felony murder is a potential witness to the crime. The victim appears to be no apparent threat to the offender. He or she offers no resistance to the offender but is killed anyway, a victim of opportunity—for example, walking into the store or house at the wrong time or having his or her shift coincide with the robbery.

There are occupations, shifts, and environments that elevate a victim's risk factor. Working the night shift alone at a 24-hour gas station or convenience store is one example. This situation elevates the chance of a person's becoming a victim of felony murder (indiscriminate or situational) compared to the department store clerk who works days. Environmental factors that elevate victim risk factor are locations within high crime areas, working in establishments that enhance crime commission (views obstructed by advertising or product shelves, poorly lit, no alarms or intercom systems linking them to local law enforcement stations, one-clerk staffing, especially at night), and establishments with cash readily available, such as liquor stores.

It is also possible for a victim to elevate risk by attitude and behavior. A careless, naive, or flippant approach to personal safety heightens the chance of being targeted for robbery and, subsequently, felony murder, situational or indiscriminate.

CRIME SCENE INDICATORS FREQUENTLY NOTED

The location of the crime is usually the source of the cash. The weapon is bought to the scene and is most likely removed with the offender. The amount of physical evidence found at the scene is dependent on the offender's mastery and adeptness and the time available.

This offender tends to spend more time at the crime scene, so there will be signs of interaction between the offender and victim. There are generally indications of a completed burglary or robbery. The crime scene commonly is controlled and orderly: The offender is not surprised by the events that surround and include the killing. In most cases, little or no effort is expended to conceal the body.

STAGING

If staging is present, arson is frequently used to conceal the felony murder. (See classification 230, which discusses crime concealment arson.) If the motive seems to be monetary, investigators should require a sexual assault examination of the victim.

COMMON FORENSIC FINDINGS

Most often, the manner of death involves the use of firearms. There can be blunt trauma or battery present. There may also be evidence of restraints used (handcuffs, gags, blindfolds, or something else) evidenced by ligature marks. Sexual assault may also occur.

Investigative Considerations

It is important to work the case as a robbery and not a murder. Any known robbery suspects with a similar modus operandi (MO) should be scrutinized. The offender of an indiscriminate felony murder is usually a youthful male with a criminal history (history of auto theft appears especially prevalent). This offender often travels on foot to the crime scene because he lives in the area of the crime.

Search Warrant Suggestions

The victim's possessions (wallets, watches, jewelry) should be included in any search. Signs of the career criminal such as stereos and other expensive possessions that do not appear appropriate in the light of the offender's finances based on the legitimate sources are also important. Additional search warrant suggestions include possessions common to a burglar, such as burglary tools, police scanners, or a ski mask or stocking mask, and drugs or evidence of drug use.

Case Study: 108.01: Indiscriminate Murder

Background

On April 22, 1974, airmen Dale Pierre and William Andrews decided to rob a stereo shop in Ogden, Utah. They entered the store and forced the clerks into the basement, tying them up. Over the next few hours, three more people happened into the shop, only to become victims of Pierre and Andrews.

Victimology

The five victims involved in this incident were low-risk victims. The two store clerks had a slightly higher chance of becoming victims of a violent crime because of their job. But Ogden, Utah, did not have much violent crime, so this additional occupational risk was negligible. The other victims fit the victimology of felony murder because they were potential witnesses to the robbery.

    None of the victims posed an apparent threat to the offenders since they were immediately tied up and placed face down in the basement. Pierre and Andrews maintained complete control of the victims throughout the entire offense. None of them offered any resistance.

Crime Scene Indicators

Stan Walker and Michelle Ansley were the clerks working at the time of the holdup. Pierre and Andrews tied up Walker and Ansley after forcing them down into the basement. Just then, Cortney Naisbitt, age 16, entered the store to thank Walker for allowing him to park by his store. He was also taken to the basement and tied up.

    Pierre and Andrews had been loading stereo equipment into their van for about an hour when they heard footsteps approaching the back door. It was Stan Walker's father, Orren, who was worried because he knew the stereo shop had been closed for two hours, yet his son had not come home or called. Pierre and Andrews hid in the basement as the sound of the footsteps came closer. As soon as he appeared at the basement door, Pierre brandished a gun and forced him down the stairs. Stan moaned aloud and asked his father, "Why did you come down here, Dad?" As soon as Stan spoke, the sound of gunshots rang out. In a sudden frenzy, Pierre had fired two rounds into the basement wall. With the explosion of gunfire, Michelle and Cortney began to plead with their captors for their life. "I am just 19, I don't want to die," Michelle cried out. Stan and Orren Walker kept telling Pierre and Andrews to just take the merchandise and leave; they would not identify the offenders.

At Pierre's bidding, Andrews brought a bottle wrapped in a paper bag in from their van. Pierre poured a thick blue liquid from the container into a plastic green cup. He told Orren Walker to give it to the three young people lying on the floor. When Walker refused, Pierre forced him onto his stomach next to Michelle and Stan and bound his hands and feet.

At that moment, Cortney Naisbitt's mother, Carol, entered the store in search of her son. Carol was soon tied hand and foot and lying on the basement floor next to Cortney. Next, Pierre propped Carol into the sitting position and held the small green cup to her lips. When she questioned him about the blue liquid, Pierre stated it was vodka and a German drug that would make them sleep for a while.

One by one, Pierre forced the victims to drink the blue liquid. Each victim violently coughed and choked, spewing liquid from their nose and mouth. Orren Walker was the only one who did not drink the liquid. He feigned swallowing and then imitated the other victims' frantic choking. As Pierre filled Cortney's mouth to overflowing, the liquid spilled down his neck, immediately burning his skin. As he swallowed, he felt the liquid scorching all the way into his stomach. He began to retch and vomit, as were the others, who were now being given their second dose of the liquid. Because of the damage it was doing to the victims' stomachs, they were all vomiting. Pierre tried to remedy this situation by sealing the victims' mouths with tape, but because of the blistering around their mouths, the tape would not stick very well.

Next, Pierre went one by one to each victim with his gun. Cortney saw the man lean over his mother and put the muzzle to the back of her head. He heard the bullet enter his mother's head and watched helplessly as her blood spurted onto the carpet a few feet away. Next, he felt the hot muzzle pressed against his own skull. The air seemed to explode around him as he went limp.

Pierre walked over to Orren Walker and fired a shot that missed his head by inches. He then bent over Stan Walker and fired a bullet into his head. Mr. Walker could hear his son say, "I've been shot," in a low but clear voice. Pierre returned to Orren and aimed more carefully this time. Orren fought to stay lucid as his head rang and his shoulder burned from where the caustic liquid had dripped.

Orren Walker heard Pierre untie Michelle. She was still pleading for her life as he led her to the far end of the basement, where he forced her to undress and raped her for 20 minutes. When he was done, Pierre brought Michelle back and forced her down on her stomach. All of this time, Orren Walker had been pretending to be dead. Pierre returned with a flashlight to check for a pulse on Orren Walker. After he had done this, he shot Michelle in the head.

Before he left, Pierre returned to Orren Walker twice. Once he attempted to strangle him. Orren Walker had expanded the muscles in his neck, giving him enough room to breath once Pierre dropped his body back to floor. The second time,

Pierre inserted a pen into Orren's ear and stomped on it until Orren felt the tip poke through the inside of his throat. Finally satisfied, Pierre left the basement and joined Andrews outside in the van.

As they were pulling out, Cortney began moving. Orren saw him begin crawling toward the stairs in the darkness. He made it only to the foot of the stairs before lapsing into unconsciousness.

Around 10:30 p.m. the police were summoned to the shop by Orren Walker's wife and his youngest son. They had begun to worry when Orren had not shown up for dinner.

Pierre and Andrews came to this crime scene well prepared to murder. They had brought the drain cleaner with the intent to kill the victims: they had obtained the idea from a movie.

Forensic Findings

All of the victims sustained gunshot wounds to the head. Stan, Michelle, and Carol died from massive brain injury from these wounds. Carol lived barely long enough to make it to the hospital, where she died. Michelle and Stan were dead at the scene. Michelle had also been sexually assaulted.

The blue liquid was drain cleaner containing hydrochloric acid. The mouths, esophagus, and stomach of each victim except Orren Walker had been severely burned. Orren's shoulder and chin were blistered and burned from the drain cleaner. The pen that had been shoved into his ear had penetrated five inches and caused ear damage. Cortney Naisbitt required 266 days of hospitalization due to the combination of brain damage from the gunshot and reconstructive surgeries for the damage from the drain cleaner.

Investigation

The investigation of the robbery and murders was given direction almost immediately by an informant. Several months before the murders, Andrews had told another airman that he and Pierre were planning something big, like a robbery. Andrews had then told the airman, "One of these days I'm going to rob a hi-fi shop, and if anybody gets in the way, I'm going to kill them."

Within hours of the informant's call, two young boys found purses and wallets belonging to the victims in a dumpster just outside the barracks where Pierre and Andrews lived. After their arrest, a search warrant produced flyers from the stereo shop and a rental agreement for a commercial storage unit. The search of the storage unit produced stereo equipment worth $25,000 from the shop. In addition to the stolen merchandise, police found a small green drinking cup and a half-full bottle of drain cleaner.

Outcome

Dale Pierre and William Andrews were charged and subsequently convicted for the murders. Both men received the death penalty. Despite efforts by the NAACP and Amnesty International, Pierre and Andrews were both put to death by lethal injection—Pierre on August 28, 1987, and Andrews five years later, in 1992.

108.02: Situational Murder

A situational felony murder is unplanned prior to committing the felony. The homicide is committed out of panic, confusion, or impulse.

Defining Characteristics

VICTIMOLOGY

The victim is one of opportunity. All of the victimology features detailed for indiscriminate felon murder apply to this category also. The fundamental difference is that the offender perceives the victim as a threat or an impediment to a successful robbery.

CRIME SCENE INDICATORS FREQUENTLY NOTED

The victim is more often attacked by a blitz-style or surprise assault than is the victim of an indiscriminate felony murder. There are fewer signs of interaction between offender and victim. The victim may have been surprised while going about his or her normal routine. This would be manifested at the crime scene by a spilled purse, car keys on the floor, or a body that is near a room entrance.

The offender may have made small attempts to conceal his identity, like blindfolding the victim, but the sequence of events culminates with the triggering event: the surprise or panic of the offender and the subsequent murder.

There are often paradoxical elements present at the crime scene. Entry into the residence or business may be skillful and meticulous, in contrast with a hasty, panicked retreat that leaves physical evidence such as fingerprints and footprints, often depicting a running retreat. There would be uncompleted acts—for example, stereos unhooked and pulled out from wall units, jewelry, and money on the victim, all left behind.

The situational felony murder tends to offer more evidentiary items, but this is dependent on the level of disorganization or organization of the offender, as well as the nature of the triggering event.

STAGING

If staging is present, arson may be used to conceal this situational felony murder.

COMMON FORENSIC FINDINGS

Nonspecific traumatic modalities may be employed, ranging from blunt trauma to sharp instrument use. If firearms are used, the wounds are often contact or near-contact wounds.

Investigative Considerations

The investigative considerations of this homicide are similar to indiscriminate felony murder, with a few exceptions. The perpetrators of this type of crime are usually in the earlier stages of their criminal career. They are often more youthful and inexperienced, with a history of alcohol or drug abuse that increases their already volatile nature.

Some outside influence will often trigger the killing—an alarm sounds, a spouse comes home, or a victim screams, for example. If several offenders are involved, there is a tremendous motivation for the nontrigger-puller participant to confess if he is approached properly.

Search Warrant Suggestions

The victim's possessions (wallets, watches, jewelry) should be included in any search. Signs of the career criminal such as stereos and other expensive possessions that do not appear appropriate in the light of the offender's finances based on the legitimate sources are also important. Additional search warrant suggestions include possessions common to a burglar, such as burglary tools, police scanners, or a ski mask or stocking mask, and drugs or evidence of drug use.

Case Study: 108.02: Situational Murder

Case Contributed by Kendall McLane

Background

In late March 1978, Willie Bosket brutally murdered two men and assaulted multiple others during attempted robberies in New York City. Bosket, 15 years old at this time, had a long rap sheet and had been in and out of detention centers since he was 9 years old. He was a troubled youth with a family history of violence and crime.

On March 19, 1978, Willie encountered Noel Perez on a subway train. Willie planned to rob Perez of his gold watch while he was sleeping until he noticed Perez's sunglasses, which reminded him of those worn by a counselor at juvenile hall whom he particularly despised. Willie became enraged and shot Perez in the right eye. When Perez woke up and started screaming, Willie feared that he would not die, so he shot him again through the right temple. He searched Perez and stole $20 and a ring, along with the originally intended watch. For Willie, the fatal encounter was his destiny. He now knew what it was like to take a life and it was empowering. He had gotten away with murder and felt that it was no big thing to kill a man. Now he was "bad"—as bad as he had told everyone he would be one day. This earned him street credibility.

On March 23, Willie and his cousin Herman Spates spotted Anthony Lamorte finishing up his shift in the train yard. Lamorte had a CB radio that Willie suspected would sell on the street. When the pair approached Lamorte, he told the boys to get out of the train yard since they had no business there. Willie ignored the warning and shot Lamorte in the shoulder; the wounds proved nonfatal.

Over the next three nights, the boys committed three more violent robberies. After shooting one man, Matthew Connolly, Willie was grabbed and searched by a Transit Authority police officer who missed the gun in his pocket. Getting away with the crime made Willie felt even more invincible, as if he were "smarter than the law."

On March 27, Willie and Herman came across Moises Perez on the train. They approached him for money, but when Perez said that he had no money, Willie shot and killed him. They stole Perez's wallet, took the two dollars it contained, and discarded it in a nearby trash can. Willie was proud of getting away with this murder, bragging about the newspaper clippings to his little sister.

Willie Bosket and Herman Spates were linked to Moises Perez's murder when latent fingerprints were lifted off Perez's wallet. Law enforcement officers ran the prints through the computers and found matches (both young men had been fingerprinted during previous periods of incarceration in juvenile hall). When interviewed, Spates initially insisted that he was at the movies asleep during the time of the murder. The questioning officer told him that Willie had already implicated him in the crime; consequently, Herman insisted that Willie had shot Perez. He also told them about the murder of Noel Perez (no relation) and gave the whereabouts of the gun. Officers obtained a search warrant for Bosket's house and found the gun. Ballistics tests linked the gun to the Moises Perez murder.

Willie Bosket descends from a long line of violent men. His grandfather, James, was reputed to be a violent man who was respected through fear. Butch, Willie's father, was frequently beaten by James and other members of his family. After Butch was convicted of a series of petty crimes, the courts decided that they could not handle him and sent him to the Wiltwych School for Boys. His initial diagnosis of childhood schizophrenia was later changed to conduct disorder. One report said that he was on his way to becoming a psychopath. As an adult, Butch was diagnosed with antisocial personality disorder. Just before Willie's birth, Butch was sent to jail for stabbing and killing two men in a pawnshop. He was sentenced to life in prison.

Willie was born into a single-parent household with few adequate role models; his mother brought in a rotating cast of boyfriends, one of whom sold Willie the gun he used to murder two men for $65. He held his father to hero status and aspired to be as "bad" as he was. When evaluated at the age of 11, Willie already displayed many behaviors that are antecedent to violent crime. He was "an angry, hostile, homicidal boy whom no one could reach. He showed grandiosity, narcissism, poor impulse control, infantile omnipotence, and a history of suicide attempts and daily threats against others." He was diagnosed with antisocial behavior, one step below the diagnosis of antisocial personality disorder that his father was given. One counselor even predicted that he would commit murder sometime in the future. Other predictors of his potentially violent behavior include family history of violence and abuse, including sexual abuse by his grandfather at the age of nine, histories of childhood violence and torture of animals, and an intense interest in and adoration of violent persons.

The first murder Willie Bosket committed would be classified as situational felony murder (108.02). The victim was one of opportunity, and the murder was committed out of panic and impulse. The primary crime was robbery, with a secondary crime of murder when Willie became agitated by the victim's response. The subsequent murder and attempted murder were classified as indiscriminate felony murder (108.01). After his first murder, Bosket knew that he could kill and actually enjoyed it because it made him feel like a man. Although his primary motive was always to rob the victim, he planned to kill them even though they were no threat to him personally. When indicted, Willie Bosket was charged with two counts of murder and one count of attempted murder. These three different charges necessitated three separate trials. Although there were no witnesses to any of the crimes, fingerprint evidence placed Bosket at the scene of the crime, and his cousin, Herman Spates, implicated him during his interview. Bosket approached his trial with an air of detachment. He seemed to think that he was untouchable in court. Surprisingly, just before the trial began, he told his lawyer to plead guilty to all three counts. Because he was a juvenile, he was sentenced to the maximum sentence of five years at the Division of Youth. He would be freed when he turned 21 years old.

This sentence was met with great controversy and publicity because it was an election year. Governor Hugh Carey, criticized for his laxness concerning juvenile crime, came out publicly against the sentence, referring to it as "a breakdown of the system." The trial contributed directly to the passing of the Juvenile Offender Act of 1978, which allowed adolescents as young as 13 to be tried as adults for violent crimes like rape and murder.

Willie was freed from prison at the age of 21. He succeeded in following in his father's footsteps and committed two subsequent felonies and returned to prison, where he stabbed a guard in the heart. A few months after he was sentenced for stabbing the guard, he bashed another guard in the head and received an additional life sentence. Next, he threw hot water in the face of a guard. He soon came to be known as the most dangerous criminal in the New York system and is now kept in a specially constructed isolation cell. Guards are forbidden to speak to him. He has no electrical outlets, no television, and no newspapers. Behind the bars of his cell is a sheath of acrylic plastic sheets. Four video cameras keep him under surveillance at all times. Whenever he goes out, he is shackled with an automobile tow chain. The Juvenile Offender Act is still frequently referred to as Willie Bosket's Law in New York State.

Case Study: 108.02: Situational Murder, Elder

Victimology

Alfred Prochair, age 82, lived and cared for his wife of 58 years who had early dementia. On a Saturday morning, a woman came to door claiming car trouble and asked to use the phone. Mr. Prochair said, "Of course, come in." Mrs. Prochair, who was in bed, saw the woman in her room but was confused and went back to sleep. Later, she entered the living room and found her husband dead. She called 911 and the emergency medical technicians received a confused message but did get an address. They arrived to find the husband dead, but because of the wife's confusion, they dismissed her statement, "She was looking for something," which had been on the 911 tape.

Investigation

Alfred Prochair was pronounced dead with cause of death by natural causes. An autopsy was waived, and cremation plans were made for Tuesday afternoon in San Diego. On Tuesday morning, a Bank of America analyst in Arizona was reviewing credit card transactions. She called the Prochairs because she noted that too many transactions had been made. She asked if Alfred was making them but was told that Alfred had died on Saturday. Cremation was immediately stopped and an autopsy ordered. The results indicated that Alfred Prochair had been murdered by strangulation. Bruising and defense wounds were noted on his hands, arms, and body.

Police began to check pawnshops and learned one shopkeeper took fingerprints because of the suspicious woman pawning "old-looking" rings. The fingerprints were tied to Yolanda Huff. A record check noted her to have many prior arrests for robbery and burglary. However, Mrs. Prochair could not identify her own rings. Family photographs were reviewed, and one was enlarged to show her wearing the rings that had been pawned.

Outcome

Yolanda Huff was convicted of first-degree murder with special circumstances (robbery was part of the crime, and the victim was an elderly person).

References

American Psychiatric Association. (2006). *Diagnostic and Statistical Manual of Mental Disorders* (4th ed., Text Revision). Washington, DC: Author.

CBC. (1899, Updated 8/2/2012). *Five major product tampering cases.* Retrieved August 10, 2012, from http://News.Ca.msn.com/top-stories/five-major-product-tampering-cases

Cooper, A., & Smith, E. L. (2011). *Homicide trends in the United States, 1980–2008.* Bureau of Justice Statistics. Retrieved March 16, 2012, from http://bjs.ojp.usdoj.gov/content/pub/pdf/htus8008.pdf

Douglas, J., & Olshaker, M. (1995). *Mindhunter: Inside the FBI's elite serial crime unit* (pp. 152–159). New York, NY: Scribner, 1995.

Douglas, M. S., Ressler, R. K., Burgess, A. W., & Hartman, C.R. (1986). Criminal profiling from crime scene analysis. *Behavioral Sciences, 4,* 401–421.

Errickson, E. (2011). *Unarresting the Arrested: FBI profiler John Douglas on the case against Amanda Knox & Raffaele Sollecito.* Ground Report. Retrieved August 25, 2012, from www.groundreport.com/World/Unarresting-the-Arrested-FBI-Profiler-John-Douglas_1/2941619

Federal Bureau of Investigation. (2003). *Crime in the United States 2002*. Washington, DC: Uniform Crime Reports.

Federal Bureau of Investigation. (2008). *Serial murder: Multi-disciplinary perspectives for investigators*. Washington, DC. Retrieved August 22, 2012, from http://www.fbi.gov/stats-services/publications/serial-murder/serial-murder-july-2008-pdf

Federal Bureau of Investigation. (2010). *Crime in the United States 2009: Murder*. Retrieved March 16, 2012, from www.fbi.gov/about-us/cjis/ucr/crime-in-the-u.s/2010/crime-in-the-u.s.-2010/violent-crime/murdermain

Geberth, V. J. (1981). Psychological profiling. *Law and Order*, 56, 46–49.

Goldman, Ari L. (2011, July 19). Haredi sensitivity. *The Jewish Week*. Retrieved July 20, 2012, from www.thejewishweek.com/news/new_york/haredi_sensitivity

Hazelwood, R. R., & Douglas, J. E. (1980). The lust murderer. *FBI Law Enforcement Bulletin*, 49 (3), 18–22.

Megargee, E. I. (1982). Psychological determinants and correlates of criminal violence. In M. E. Wolfgang & N. A. Weiner (Eds.), *Criminal violence*. Thousand Oaks, CA: Sage.

Ressler, R., Burgess, A., & Douglas, J. (1988). *Sexual homicide: Patterns and motives*. New York, NY: Simon & Schuster.

Rossi, D. (1982). Crime scene behavioral analysis: Another tool for the law enforcement investigator. *Police Chief*, 57, 152–155.

Sidman, F. (2011). Psychiatrists say Levi Aron has "personality disorder." *Free Daily Israel Report*, A7. Retrieved August 10, 2012, from www.israelnationalnews.com/News/News.aspx/146614

Tannenbaum, G. (2011, July 20). Leiby Kletzky (2002–2011). *The Jewish Press*. Retrieved July 21, 2011, from www.jewishpress.com/pageroute.do/49093

Vorpagel, R. E. (1982). Painting psychological profiles: Charlatanism, charisma, or a new science? *Police Chief*, 49, 156–159.

U.S. Department of Justice. Federal Bureau of Investigation. (1976–1989). *Uniform crime reports: Crime in the United States*. Washington, DC: Government Printing Office.

U.S. Department of Justice. (2003). *Uniform crime reports*. Washington, DC. http://www.ojp.usdoj.gov/bjs/pubalp2.htm

Chapter 7

Personal Cause Homicide

120: Personal cause homicide
121: Erotomania-motivated murder
122: Domestic homicide
    122.01: Spontaneous domestic homicide
    122.02: Staged domestic homicide
    122.03: Neonaticide

123: Argument/conflict murder
    123.01: Argument murder
    123.02: Conflict murder
124: Authority murder
125: Revenge
126: Nonspecific motive murder
    126.01: Nonspecific religion-inspired homicide

120: Personal Cause Homicide

Homicide motivated by personal cause is an act ensuing from interpersonal aggression and results in death to persons who may not be known to each other. This homicide is not motivated by material gain or sex and is not sanctioned by a group. It is the result of an underlying emotional conflict that propels the offender to kill.

This category is divided into erotomania-motivated killing (i.e., growing out of a fantasy based on perceived idealized romantic involvement or spiritual union with the victim), domestic homicide (spontaneous domestic homicide and staged domestic homicide), argument/conflict murder, authority killing, revenge killing, nonspecific motive killing, extremist homicide (political extremist homicide, religious homicide, and socioeconomic extremist homicide), mercy/hero homicide, and hostage murder.

121: Erotomania-Motivated Murder

In erotomania-motivated murder, the murder is motivated by an offender–victim relationship based on the offender's fixation. This fantasy is commonly expressed in such forms as fusion (the offender blends his personality into victims) or erotomania (a fantasy based on idealized romantic love or spiritual union of a person rather than sexual attraction). This preoccupation with the victim becomes consuming and ultimately leads to his or her death. The drive to kill arises from a variety of motives, ranging from rebuffed advances to internal conflicts stemming from the offender's fusion of identity with the victim.

Defining Characteristics

VICTIMOLOGY

The distinguishing characteristic of this type of murder is found in the victimology. The victim targeted is often a person with high media visibility of local, national, or international scope. Through this exposure, the victim comes to the attention of the offender. Other victims include superiors at work or even complete strangers. The victim almost always is perceived by the offender as someone of higher status.

When erotomania is involved, the victim (usually someone unattainable to the offender) becomes the imagined lover of the offender through hidden messages known only to the offender. The offender builds an elaborate fantasy revolving around this imagined love. Male erotomaniacs tend to act out this fantasy with greater force. When this acting out is rebuffed, the erotomaniac decides to guarantee no one else will steal his or her imagined lover. If this idealized person will not belong to him or her, the offender ensures that the victim will not be given the chance to belong to anyone.

Fusion of identity occurs when an individual identifies so completely with another person that his or her imitation of that person becomes excessive. The person emulated is endangered when the imitator feels his own identity is threatened by the existence of the person he has patterned his life after or when the offender feels the person he has imitated no longer lives up to the offender's ideals. The person this offender chooses to imitate usually is perceived as someone of higher status just as with erotomania.

CRIME SCENE INDICATORS FREQUENTLY NOTED

The greater the distance there is between the offender and victim at the time of the killing, the more planning and less spontaneous the crime is. This will be manifested by lack of fingerprints and footprints at the scene. A removed location from the victim also signifies that the offender had to take the time to check out this vantage point and must have been familiar with the victim's routine.

The majority of these erotomania-motivated murders are close range and confrontational. The offender may even remain at the scene. These close-range assaults tend to be a more spontaneous killing, as reflected by a more haphazard approach to the killing: evidence is left, and there are likely to be witnesses. This does not mean the offender did not fantasize, premeditate, and plan the killing; all of these elements characterize this homicide. It means the actual act is usually an opportunistic one. The offender takes advantage of the opportunity to kill as it is presented to him.

STAGING

Staging is not usually present.

COMMON FORENSIC FINDINGS

Firearms are the most common weapons used, especially with a distance killing. Ballistics and the trajectory of projectiles recovered will be of importance. The sophistication and type of weapon and whether it was left at the scene will help establish the degree of offender sophistication.

The vital organs, especially the head and chest, are most frequently targeted. Occasionally, the offender will use a sharp-edged weapon such as a knife.

Investigative Considerations

The offender almost always surveys or stalks the victim preceding the homicide. Therefore, the availability of the victim's itinerary and who may have access to it is one investigative consideration. There is a likelihood of preoffense attempts by the offender to contact the victim through telephone calls, letters, gifts, and visits to the victim's home or place of employment. There may even be an incident whereby law enforcement or security officers had to remove the offender from the victim's residence or workplace.

The offender's conversation often will reflect this preoccupation or fantasy life with the victim. When those associated with the offender are interviewed, they will most likely recall that much of the offender's conversation focused on the victim. He or she may have claimed to have had a relationship with the victim and may have invented stories to support this encounter.

Search Warrant Suggestions

The primary items to search for are pictures, literature (newspaper articles, books, magazine articles), and recordings concerning the victim. Diaries or journals detailing the offender's preoccupation or fantasy life with the victim may also be found. Other items to look for are evidence of contact or attempted contacts with the victim: telephone records, returned letters or gifts, motel receipts, gas bills, rental agreements, or airline, bus, or train tickets implying travel to locations where the victim has been. Credit card records also may be helpful in this regard.

Case Study: 121: Erotomania-Motivated Murder

Background

At 11:00 p.m. on December 8, 1980, John Lennon, lyricist, lead singer, and composer for the Beatles, was returning home with his wife, Yoko Ono, from a recording studio. As Lennon exited his car, Mark David Chapman, for whom Lennon had autographed an album hours before, stepped out of the darkness and said, "Mr. Lennon?" As Lennon turned, Chapman fired his .38-caliber Charter Arms revolver five times at point-blank range. Although four bullets hit Lennon in the chest, he was able to reach the foyer of the apartment before collapsing. Lennon died soon after his arrival at the hospital.

Victimology

In the late 1950s, John Lennon had started the group that was later to become one of the most popular music groups of all times. He was a driving force in the Beatles until it disbanded in 1970. Lennon became known as a social and political activist and an especially outspoken proponent of the peace movement. After the Beatles dissolved, he continued to write music until 1975, when he went into retirement. His reentry into the music world was cut short by his assassination. Throughout his career, even during his period of musical inactivity, Lennon's fame and popularity barely waned, which contributed to high media visibility.

Crime Scene Indicators

Although it appeared that Chapman had planned to assassinate Lennon as early as September 1980, he chose to approach Lennon and kill at close range probably because Lennon was not easily accessible for a long-range assassination. Chapman chose the common weapon of assassins, a firearm. The weapon remained at the scene, as did Chapman (calmly reading *Catcher in the Rye* by J. D. Salinger). Chapman had been a security guard at a Honolulu condominium development; therefore, his weapon of choice was one with which he was comfortable: a .38-caliber revolver. Ballistics confirmed his responsibility for Lennon's death.

Forensic Findings

Lennon died from massive blood loss as a result of the chest wounds he sustained.

Investigation

In September 1980, Chapman sold a Norman Rockwell lithograph for $7,500. He paid off a number of debts and kept $5,000 for a "job" he had to do. He contacted the Federal Aviation Administration to inquire about transporting his gun by plane.

Because Chapman was advised that the change in air pressure that his baggage would be subjected to could damage the bullets, he opted to pack his gun without bullets. When Chapman left his security guard job for the final time, he signed the log "John Lennon."

On October 29, he flew to New York from Honolulu, only to return in frustration on November 12 or 13. He had been unable to gain access to Lennon, who lived in New York City. He made an appointment at the Makiki Mental Health Clinic but failed to keep it.

On December 6, Chapman returned to New York. Two days later, he waited outside the Dakota apartment building for Lennon. At 4:30 p.m. Lennon and his wife exited the building and were approached by Chapman, who had a copy of Lennon's recent album, *Double Fantasy*. Lennon autographed it as Chapman held it out to him. Chapman then lingered at the apartment entrance. When questioned by the doorman, he said he was waiting to get Yoko Ono's autograph. Chapman was well prepared for his wait in weather much colder than he was accustomed to. He had on two pairs of long underwear, a jacket, an overcoat, and a hat.

Chapman had apparently been building a fantasy life for several years centered on John Lennon. He married a woman of Japanese descent (Lennon's wife was Japanese). He collected Beatles albums and played in a rock band.

An explanation for his motive may be found in the testimony of a psychiatrist during his trial: the more that Chapman imitated Lennon, the more he came to believe he was John Lennon. He eventually began to view Lennon as a phony. The fusion of his identity with Lennon became so engulfing that Chapman decided he too would become a phony if he did not stop the process in Lennon.

Outcome

Chapman withdrew an original plea of not guilty by reason of insanity and pleaded guilty to the murder of John Lennon. On August 24, 1981, he was sentenced to 20 years to life, with a recommendation that he receive psychiatric treatment. Chapman has five times been denied parole since he became eligible for release in 2000. He is currently locked up in the Attica Correctional Facility. When he was given the opportunity to offer a few words in his defense, Chapman read a passage from *The Catcher in the Rye*. A year later, when he was visited in prison by a reporter, he still had the book in hand.

122: Domestic Homicide

Domestic murder occurs when a family or household member kills another member of the household. This definition includes common-law relationships. More than one person may be killed when one family member is targeted. One example is the O. J. Simpson case that includes victims Nicole Brown Simpson (ex-wife of Simpson) and Ron Goldman (unrelated to the Simpsons). During the civil case against O. J. Simpson the attorney for the families, Daniel Petrocelli, requested pro bono assistance from one of the authors (JED). While he was in LA on another matter, the case materials were provided for analysis. The crime indicated and reflected two different distinct looks regarding how each victim was murdered. In reconstructing the case for Petrocelli, he was advised that Nicole was the primary target, with Ron Goldman being in the wrong place at the wrong time. They were murdered in different ways. Nicole was in all probability struck first in the head and rendered unconscious lying on the front steps of the condo where she lived. Ron Goldman was trapped inside a small front patio wall. There was no way out but to fight back. The unknown subject (UNSUB) stabbed and slashed at Goldman with one of the fatal stab wounds slicing his femoral artery. The blood from Ron Goldman from that knife is dripped back to Nicole where the UNSUB slices her throat from behind and nearly decapitating her.

There was no sexual assault and nothing belonging to the victims was taken. A bloody glove worn by the UNSUB was left behind. This was a premeditated crime with elements of both organization and disorganization. The killer went to the address with a plan, but what was not planned was to find Ron Goldman standing and talking to Nicole. Goldman's fight for his life and that of Nicole's caused the suspect to momentarily lose control and as a result potential evidence was left behind by the UNSUB and thus the appearance of disorganization. This was a personal cause domestic homicide. O. J. Simpson would be found guilty in the civil case.

There are two subcategories for this type of homicide: spontaneous domestic homicide and staged domestic homicide.

122.01: Spontaneous Domestic Homicide

A spontaneous domestic homicide is unstaged and is triggered by either a recent stressful event or a cumulative buildup of stress.

Defining Characteristics

VICTIMOLOGY

The victim has a familial or common-law relationship with the offender. In addition, there is a history of prior abuse or conflict with the offender.

CRIME SCENE INDICATORS FREQUENTLY NOTED

Usually, only one crime scene is involved in spontaneous domestic murder, and it is commonly the victim or offender's residence. The crime scene reflects disorder and the impetuous nature of the killing. The weapon will be one of opportunity, often obtained and left at the scene. There is no forced entry and no sign of theft. The crime scene may also reflect an escalation of violence—for example, the confrontation starts as an argument, intensifies into hitting or throwing things, and culminates in the victim's death.

There are often indicators of undoing. This is the killer's way of expressing remorse or the desire to undo the murder. Undoing is demonstrated by the offender's washing of the victim and the weapon. The body may be covered up, but it is not for concealment purposes. Washing or redressing the body, moving the body from the death scene, and positioning it on a sofa or bed with the head on a pillow are all expressions of undoing.

The attitude and emotional state of the family members present at the crime scene can offer insight into the victim–offender relationship. The offender is often at the scene when law enforcement or emergency medical personnel arrive and often makes incriminating statements.

STAGING

A spontaneous domestic murder will not involve staging. Personation in the form of undoing is possible but is for the benefit of the offender and is not intended to mislead law enforcement.

COMMON FORENSIC FINDINGS

Alcohol or drugs may be involved. Fingerprints are often present on the murder weapon. There usually are forensic findings consistent with a personal type of assault.

Depersonalization, evidenced by facial battery, overkill, blunt-force trauma, and a focused area of injury, is evidence of a personal assault. Manual or ligature strangulation is a common cause of death with domestic homicide. Gunshot wounds are also a forensic finding of this type of killing. The victim may show signs of being washed up or having wounds cleaned.

Investigative Considerations

If the crime occurs in the victim's residence, domestic murder should be considered. When other family members are contacted, they often describe a history of domestic violence involving the victim and offender. This is often supported by police reports. A history of conflict due to external sources (financial, vocational, or alcohol, for example) is a common element of domestic homicide. The offender may have delayed reporting the murder, often in order to change clothing and establish a legitimate alibi. Routinely, a third party discovers the body. The offender may have demonstrated personalized aggression in the past, as well as a change in attitude after the triggering event.

Search Warrant Suggestions

Although most of the evidence will be left at the crime scene, financial and medical records to verify the spontaneity of the crime should be requested.

Case Study: 122.01: Spontaneous Domestic Homicide

Background

On May 5, 1990, Martha Ann Johnson was convicted of first-degree murder for the smothering deaths of three of her four children. In a videotaped confession, Johnson, who weighs close to 300 pounds, admitted smothering Jenny Ann Wright and James Taylor by rolling on top of them as they slept. Martha said her motive was to bring her estranged husband home. Each of the homicides, which occurred between 1977 and 1982, was committed within 10 days of having an argument with her former husband, Earl Bowen. She received the death penalty in 1990 and remains on death row.

The first victim was James William Taylor, 23 months old. On September 23, 1977, Johnson states that she went in to wake up James from his nap. When she was unable to rouse him, she called for emergency medical personnel, and the child was rushed to the hospital. Attempts to resuscitate James were unsuccessful, and he was pronounced dead at 9:15 a.m. His death was attributed to sudden infant death syndrome (SIDS).

Three years later, on November 30, 1980, Johnson bathed, fed, and put three-month-old Tibitha Jenelle Bowen down for her nap. When she checked on the child later, she found the baby had turned blue. Rescue personnel were called and initiated resuscitative measures, which again proved futile. Tibitha was pronounced dead on arrival. Her death was also attributed to SIDS.

Earl Wayne Bowen was a 31-month-old child who had been in excellent health except for an occasional ear infection. On Friday afternoon, January 23, 1981, he was found with a package of rodent poison. Although he had some on his hands and mouth, it was not clear if he had ingested any. He was treated and released from the emergency room in satisfactory condition. However, according to his parents, he suffered seizures from that point on, lasting from a few minutes to hours. None of these seizures appeared to be witnessed by medical personnel. Despite the fact that the active ingredient in the poison did not cause seizures, the child was started on medication. While being taken to the hospital on February 12 during a seizure episode, he suffered a cardiopulmonary arrest. He was resuscitated after two hours and placed on life support. Subsequent therapy was ineffective; he was pronounced brain-dead, and life support was removed on February 15.

According to Johnson, her 11-year-old daughter, Jenny Ann Wright, was complaining of chest pains. She took Jenny to the doctor, who gave her Tylenol and a rib belt. On February 21, 1982, rescue personnel were again summoned to the Johnson residence. They found Jenny Ann face down on her mother's bed, with pink foam coming from her nose and mouth, and unresponsive to revival attempts.

Victimology

The victims were all children of Johnson by her three husbands, and all resided with her at the time of their death.

Crime Scene Indicators

In all cases, death was staged to appear from natural causes, the crime scene was in the residence, and the weapon was one of opportunity. Johnson weighs almost 300 pounds, and this certainly was a factor in the smothering death of 11-year-old Jenny.

Forensic Findings

Autopsy findings when smothering is the suspected cause of death are minimal. Petechial hemorrhages, one of the forensic indicators of asphyxia, are rarely seen in children, and practically never in infants. This proved to be the case with the three youngest victims. None had evidence of petechial hemorrhage; however, the autopsy of 11-year-old Jenny Ann revealed petechiae on the face around the eyes, face, and conjunctivae. There also were linear abrasions over both cheeks, another forensic indicator of asphyxial death. In three of the four cases, postmortem exams revealed congestion in the lungs or airways, or both, evidenced by frothy or foamy liquid coming from the mouth and nose, another finding common to asphyxiation. Earl did not exhibit this congestion because he had been on life support, which allowed for his airways to be suctioned.

Martha Ann Johnson demonstrated a consistent choice of "weapon" as listed in the planned domestic murder. It was a method that allowed her seven years of freedom before the cases were reopened after an *Atlanta Constitution* article in December 1989 questioned Johnson's family tragedies.

Investigation

The investigative consideration of greatest importance in this case is the cycle of domestic conflict that surrounded every incident. Every death was preceded 1 week to 10 days by marital problems that culminated in a separation, the child's death, and then reunion of Johnson and Earl Bowen, her spouse during the years of her children's deaths. Martha Ann Johnson was reported to have been battered by several of her four husbands, and she was completely dependent on her husband, Earl Bowen.

Martha Johnson was also highly influenced by her environment and had difficulty dealing with internal impulses, as evidenced by her weight. She sought life substance from her external environment through eating, her relationship with her children, and her husband. When this crucial crutch was removed from her life, she used her children to draw Earl Bowen back into an active relationship with her. Johnson experienced emotional crises due to her separation from Bowen. Her children's deaths served as a valve for the building internal tensions, which she was ill equipped to handle, in addition to providing the remedy: Bowen's return. It worked every time.

Outcome

Martha Ann Johnson was sentenced to death and remains on death row.

122.02: Staged Domestic Homicide

A staged domestic homicide is planned and may be due to the same stresses as in an unstaged domestic homicide. The major difference between the two homicides is seen in the crime scene.

Defining Characteristics

VICTIMOLOGY

The victimology for staged domestic homicide is the same as for spontaneous domestic homicide.

CRIME SCENE INDICATORS FREQUENTLY NOTED

The crime scene of the well-planned domestic murder reflects a controlled, organized crime. The weapon, fingerprints, and other evidentiary items often are removed. The body is usually not concealed. It will still often involve the victim's or offender's residence, but locations of crime scenes outside the home also are possible.

STAGING

Staging is frequently noted in the planned murder. Death may be staged to look accidental (a car malfunction or drowning, for example). Other deaths may appear due to secondary criminal activity, such as robbery or rape. The offender who stages a domestic rape–murder rarely leaves the victim nude; she is almost always partially clothed. Death may be staged to look like suicide, with a suicide note, guns rigged with string, or a drug overdose, for example. Natural causes—slow poisoning or overdose (insulin is a prime example of an overdose that can mimic natural death)—are also examples of staging.

COMMON FORENSIC FINDINGS

The forensic findings of a staged domestic homicide are similar to those for spontaneous domestic murder. The exception is when the suspect includes himself as an apparent victim. If the person posing the greatest threat (usually the male) to the alleged intruder receives no or nonlethal injuries while others are killed who pose less of a threat are killed, the investigator should become suspicious that the crime has been staged.

INVESTIGATIVE CONSIDERATIONS

In addition to the considerations listed for spontaneous domestic homicide, the offender will demonstrate a change in preoffense behavior toward the victim. Frequently, an improvement in the relationship is seen, and this apparent change of heart will be demonstrated in a highly visible manner to others. Postoffense interviews of close friends or family members often reveal that the victim had expressed concerns or fears regarding the victim's safety or even a sense of foreboding. The medical and psychiatric history of the victim becomes important if the investigator suspects the crime has been staged to appear to be a suicide or death by natural causes.

Case Study: 122.02: Staged Domestic Homicide

Background

Torran Meier was born in 1972 to 16-year-old Shirley Meier. Shirley's mother, Joyce, described her daughter's treatment of newborn Torran as "if he were a piece of property." Shirley did not want to hold her son, let alone give him the care and love he needed. Torran's father, Dennis, was driven away by Shirley's constant insults and belittlement. Dennis tried to maintain contact with his son, but Shirley forbade him to come near them. She told Torran his father was dead.

Throughout the years of mistreatment Torran was to endure, his grandparents tried to intervene on his behalf. Because Shirley became jealous if she saw Torran getting close to them, his grandparents were allowed to see him only on his birthdays between his fourth and seventh years. On his sixth birthday, when they showed up with gifts, Shirley flew into a rage and threatened to call the police if they did not leave. Torran's gifts were returned unopened a few days later because Shirley had decided he was not going to have a birthday party that year.

This incident was characteristic of Torran's life with Shirley. One of his first memories of his mother was climbing into a toy box during a game of hide-and-seek. Shirley sat on the toy box, ignoring his pleas to be let out, until the child had screamed and cried for half an hour.

Besides being the object of Shirley's cursing and screaming, Torran often suffered public humiliation when she ridiculed him in front of his friends. She would call him a faggot and tell him he would never be a real man. Torran never seemed to do anything that satisfied Shirley, from his playing high school football to the house cleaning and cooking she demanded of him.

Shirley's erratic and often violent behavior seemed to escalate as Torran became older. She also began to direct it toward her younger child, Rory. Torran was encouraged by his friends and grandparents to persist in his situation with Shirley until he graduated from high school, but the years of abuse had burdened him past his endurance. After 16 years of it, he finally retaliated.

Victimology

Shirley Meier had always been outgoing and lively by her parents' estimation. It was evident at a young age that she was a talented manipulator. She often fabricated elaborate stories for her parents and teachers in order to get her own way.

As an adult, Shirley went through three marriages, none lasting more than a few months because she abused her children. She became dependent on Valium, attempted suicide twice, and seems to have allowed her sense of propriety to slip away. She would often dress provocatively and go out to bars, leaving the two children home alone. On one occasion, she woke Torran up at 2:00 a.m. to pick her up at a bar 20 miles from their home. Torran was about 15 years old at the time and obviously troubled and unhappy.

Crime Scene Indicators

About 9:45 p.m. one evening in October 1985, Torran Meier set in motion a plan that he had been brooding over for months. Torran, a high school friend named Matt Jay, and a 23-year-old transient named Richard Parker whom Torran had befriended, finalized a murder scheme.

Torran rode home on his motorcycle, and the other two followed him in a car, which they parked down the street from his house. Torran entered the house alone and greeted his mother, who was sitting in the dining room. She began to yell at him for coming home so late. Torran offered the excuse of mechanical troubles with his motorcycle. He walked into the kitchen to get some dinner Shirley had left him and then went into his bedroom. He let Jay and Parker into the house through his window and left them hiding in his room with a noose he had made earlier.

Torran joined his mother, who began complaining about money. After he had finished his meal, he asked her to come into his room so he could show her something. She responded with her typical ire, stating that he was always interrupting her TV programs. Torran told her to wait for a commercial, at which time Shirley rose to follow him into his room.

Torran requested his mother to close her eyes or allow herself to be blindfolded before entering his room, both of which she refused, but she agreed to walk in backward. As she was backing through the door of Torran's room, she saw Jay coming at her from behind the door. Parker approached from the other direction and dropped the noose around her neck before she could react. Torran and Jay knocked her to the floor as Parker pulled on the noose.

The commotion caused by Shirley's kicking and screaming woke eight-year-old Rory and bought him to the doorway in time to witness his mother's death struggle. Torran intercepted Rory and led him to the family room, where he attempted to calm the crying child by watching TV. Over the next 20 minutes, Torran made a circuit between his room to help Jay and Parker and the family room to calm Rory.

When it was apparent that Shirley was finally dead, the three eased off her body. She was bleeding from the nose and mouth, so Jay held a rag under her face to prevent bloodstains on the carpet. After Torran closed the garage door to ensure privacy, Shirley's body was stuffed in the trunk of her five-year-old Thunderbird.

At this point, the three offenders discussed the fact that Rory knew what had happened. They concluded that the little boy would be too damaging a witness, so he would have to be killed.

The method of death they decided on was rat poison. Jay went to the store and purchased rat and snail poison. Torran laced a peanut butter sandwich and flavored milk with the poison, but Rory refused both after getting an initial bad taste. After a few minutes of thought, another course of action was decided on.

Ironically, Shirley had helped Torran decide how to stage her death. She had threatened her third husband many times that she was going to drive her car off a cliff someday. Torran had also heard this suicide threat and had made special note of it.

Malibu Canyon Highway contains some of the steepest canyon ledges in Southern California, which became the ideal setting to stage Shirley's suicide. The road twists along the face of a sheer rocky cliff. Because there are no guardrails, it is a common sight to see a tow truck hoisting a car up that went over the side.

After stopping to fill a gas can at a Shell station, Torran, Parker, and Rory (sleeping peacefully in the backseat) drove out to the canyon and chose a suitable spot. Next, they went back to the Meier's house and retrieved Shirley's purse. Once again they stopped at the Shell station and bought six dollars worth of gas. They proceeded to Jay's house, and he followed them in his father's vehicle.

When they arrived at the preselected spot in the canyon, Torran told Rory he had to be blindfolded and have his hands tied because he did not want Rory to know where Parker lived. Rory did not resist. At this point, Shirley's body was removed from the trunk and propped up in the driver's seat. With the engine running, a rag soaked with gasoline was stuffed in the gas tank opening. Parker then lit the rag while Torran and Jay aimed the car for the cliff and put it into gear. It rolled across the road, over an embankment, and down a hill. As flames spread through the car, it came to rest on a plateau halfway down the gorge. Torran, Jay, and Parker drove away, heading north.

Jay dropped Parker and Torran Meier off at the initial crime scene so any damning evidence could be removed. Signs of the struggle were cleaned up or removed. The poisons and the towels used to clean the blood from the carpet were dumped in a trash bin. The gas can was dumped, and Meier put the empty can back into the car. Satisfied that any traces of the murder had been removed, Torran Meier headed back to the gas station where he worked with Parker to pick up his bike.

Meanwhile, Rory had felt the car move, smelled the gasoline, and soon after saw the flames through his blindfold. He took off his blindfold and saw his mother's body leaning against the steering wheel with blood all over her face. He managed to free his hand, lower an electric window, and climb out. As the car was enveloped in flames, he climbed a hill crying for help. A young man driving by saw the flames and heard Rory's cry for help. He helped Rory up to the road and flagged down another car. The heat was too intense for anyone to get close to the car, and by the time the fire department and sheriff arrived, Shirley's body had already been burned beyond recognition.

Investigation

Rory told his story and gave a description of Torran's car to the sheriff. Meanwhile, Torran had suddenly felt like returning to the canyon. He and Parker had driven just far enough to pass the ambulance and sheriff car coming from the scene. Other sheriff units that had been dispatched to the scene recognized his car from Rory's description and pulled him over.

The extensive brutalization that Torran Meier suffered at the hands of his mother obviously fueled his decision to kill her. However, there seemed to be one incident that burdened him beyond his capacity to endure. It was in March 1985 when Shirley informed her mother that Torran no longer wanted to live at home and was not welcome there anymore. She had told Torran that going to live with his grandparents meant he could never return home.

Torran immediately moved in with his grandparents. The warmth and affection he experienced there made him feel hopeful that life could be free of the constant harassment and abuse he had known for most his life. Two weeks later, his hope was shattered when the police showed up at Shirley's request. She had sent them there to return her "runaway" son.

From this point on until the murder, everyone noticed the change in Torran's attitude. He began to miss school. His grandmother noticed he now had a blank look in his eyes. The statement that seemed to best describe Torran's state of mind was found on the side of a cup holder his grandmother saw him use: "Pardon me, but you've obviously mistaken me for someone who gives a damn."

Torran's conversation reflected his plans. He spoke to classmates and close friends about killing his mother and even showed one the noose that he had made. Torran's indiscretion concerning his crime is reflective of his immaturity. Most offenders do not leave quite as obvious a conspiratory trail.

Outcome

Torran made a complete confession and was found guilty of manslaughter and attempted manslaughter. He was subsequently sentenced to a maximum term of 12 years at the California Youth Authority in the psychiatric facility. He was reunited with his father during his trial. Both his grandparents and father vowed to support him through his trial and incarceration.

Richard Parker and Matthew Jay were found guilty of second-degree murder and sentenced to 15 years to life.

122.03: Neonaticide

Neonaticide, or murder of an infant within the first 24 hours of life, is the most common form of filicide, which is the killing of a child of any age by a parent. Research shows that 46% of infants killed die in their first hour of life. Compared to filicide, neonaticidal parents are younger, more often unmarried, and the pregnancy was more frequently unwanted.

Although the vast majority of neonaticides are committed by parents of the victim, overwhelmingly the mother, research has demonstrated no racial, cultural, or socioeconomic association with neonaticide. Premeditation of the crime is rare, with the more common scenario including a young, naive mother, with restrained communication about sexuality in the home and traditional and socially isolated homes with disciplining, harsh parents with whom she is close. Social isolation of a neonaticidal mother may be obvious, but it also may be subtle: she may be surrounded by friends and family, and yet no one really knows her.

It is common for neonaticidal mothers to remain in denial about the existence of the fetus during the pregnancy. Physical symptoms are ignored or explained away; weight gain is seen as a result of lack of exercise, and morning sickness becomes general nausea. Even if the pregnancy is confirmed by a physician, denial persists vehemently. Baby clothes and toys or pregnancy and name books are not purchased, and prenatal care is not sought out, for example. This denial often extends to those around her: family and friends are unaware of the pregnancy until discovery of the infant's body or the physical manifestations of birth make it known.

Denial can persist even through labor and delivery. Breaking water may be thought of as urination, and labor pain may be experienced as bowel movement or simple cramping, for which a hot bath may be sought for relief. Delivery is nearly always in secret or isolation, often occurring in the bathtub or on the toilet.

Some neonaticidal mothers experience dissociative symptoms during labor and after the birth; several neonaticidal mothers have reported amnesia about the events leading up to and surrounding the birth, the birth itself, or events immediately after the birth. Psychosis and depression, however, are relatively less frequent among neonaticidal mothers.

After the birth and disposal of the infant's body, the mother also may exhibit an unfazed or indifferent emotional stance, facilitated by her denial of the existence of the infant—reinforced with the neonaticide but dissolved with revelation of the crime.

Defining Characteristics

VICTIMOLOGY

The first hour of birth is particularly high risk for this type of victim. Male infants are more often killed than female infants on the day of birth, which is also the day children are most at risk of filicide. The typical neonaticide victim is born to a mother who has concealed his in-utero existence—from herself as well as others in her life.

There is no human connection to the developing fetus. Ultimately, the mother denies the neonate's victimhood.

CRIME SCENE INDICATORS FREQUENTLY NOTED

Typical methods of neonaticide are suffocation, strangulation, head trauma (usually from dropping into a toilet), and drowning (in the receptacle where the birth occurs). Use of weapons in neonaticide, such as knives, is more indicative of serious mental illness in the mother. At the same time, involvement of an accomplice supports the likelihood of organized, premeditated calculation in effecting the child's death and concealing it.

The crime scene may reflect evidence of only the birth, not the death. However, the scene of the birth may also reflect disorganized behavior, such as incomplete attempts to clean blood from the scene. Disorganized behavior may represent panic, particularly when birth and homicide transpire with a relative or other responsible party nearby who might discover the baby and intervene.

Disposal of the body, often in a trash receptacle, is not alone evidence of murder. Reconstruction of the infant's demise may be difficult under certain circumstances of method of homicide. Autopsy remains the most important means for identifying a murder.

STAGING

The events may be staged so as to falsely suggest that the baby was born dead or suffered accidental injuries during delivery. Forensic pathology evidence is helpful to resolve this question. One of the most common types of physiological evidence of live birth is the appearance of inflated lungs and an air bubble in the digestive tract. Unexpected death to the neonate in the context of evidence for denial of the pregnancy raises the likelihood of foul play.

Common Forensic Findings

The forensic findings of a neonaticide will include products of the birth such as the newborn, placenta blood, and umbilical cord. The location of the birth needs to be carefully investigated and samples of biological evidence taken for crime scene analysis. Clothing or bedding may contain forensics.

Investigative Considerations

A focal issue of investigation is whether the infant was born alive. The neonaticidal mother in denial often may repress or suppress her recollections of circumstances of the birth or simply may deny that she remembers and be withholding information. Physical evidence is often needed to prove that the infant was killed, despite the risk of stillbirth being remarkably low barring some congenital anomaly.

Many neonaticidal mothers exhibit a lack of emotion relating to the neonaticide. This response may reflect a detached, dehumanized relationship to the victim, or the "la belle indifference" of an unusual response to a significant life event. Denial and unconscious loss of memory are correlated with la belle indifference. Denial and intact memory are associated with a detached, dehumanized relatedness to the neonate.

While the overwhelming number of neonaticides are committed by the mother of the victim, there are cases in which the father is responsible or involved. When the father is involved or the mother has confided to him that she is pregnant, dissociation and denial are not part of the crime; premeditation is implicated. In this light, a mother who does not prepare for the arrival of a newborn may not be denying the pregnancy but planning to be without the newborn.

Fathers who commit neonaticide may fear that the presence of a baby might alter the romantic relationship or that presence of a baby out of wedlock may incur stigma. Other fathers may see the infant as a rival for the attention of the mother or may seek concealment of alternative paternity. Denial, however, is not associated with paternal neonaticide.

Case Study: 122.03: Neonaticide

Classification and Case Contributed by Michael Welner

Background

Violetta Raines was an 18-year-old Mexican immigrant who confessed to killing her newborn daughter.

Violetta lived in a small studio apartment with her father, Alfredo; her brother, Miguel, age 23; and her sister, Judith, age 21. She was afraid to tell her father of her pregnancy because she anticipated that he would ask her to leave the apartment and feared that he would disown her. She did not gain considerable weight and concealed her pregnancy with loose clothes. The child's father, Miguel Dilone, had returned to Mexico early in her pregnancy, never knowing he was going to be a father.

In early December 1997, her family and employer noticed no changes in Violetta's behavior or emotions. No one anticipated her childbirth.

Victimology

As the pregnancy went on, Violetta "tried to pretend it wasn't there," did not seek out prenatal care, and did not attend childbirth classes. Neither did she consider a name for the child or purchase baby clothes. She did not calculate a due date and did not consider giving the baby up for adoption.

Crime Scene Indicators

Late on the evening of December 3, 1997, Miguel opened the bathroom door, and his sister, holding a plastic bag and towels containing the deceased infant, hugged him in a manner that suggested she need help with her balance. As Violetta emerged from the bathroom, she told her sister and Miguel that she had experienced unusually heavy menstruation. They asked her if they should take her to the hospital, but she refused, saying, "I'll take care of it in the morning." Miguel helped her over to the bed. Violetta lay down to go to sleep with the plastic bag placed at the foot of the bed.

Alfredo then went to use the bathroom. Inside, he noticed a large amount of smeared blood on the black and white tiled floor and immediately suspected his daughter had given birth. He emerged from the bathroom and demanded that she show him the bag. She refused, saying, "It's going to give me too much pain." Alfredo snatched the bag from the foot of her bed and walked into the bathroom with it. As he did, Violetta burst into tears and cried out, "Please don't beat me."

Upon discovering the dead infant, Alfredo ordered the family to the hospital at once. There was no effort at that time to resuscitate the baby. He states that shortly after arriving at the hospital, his daughter dropped down on her knees and begged for forgiveness.

Forensic Findings

The report of the medical examiner indicated that the approximately 35-week-old gestational-age baby was born alive. Forensic evidence indicates that Violetta likely cut the umbilical cord.

The report noted no evidence for trauma from a crush injury. On the basis of abrasions across her face, cause of death was listed as suffocation. Although the baby was wrapped in towels in a bag and resuscitative efforts could have caused the same abrasions, evidence of hasty cleansing of the death scene, the defendant's lack of sophistication for basic cardiac life support, and the defendant's lack of motivation to resuscitate or seek help for the baby on discovery reflect that this was not a credible explanation.

Investigation

Violetta had concealed a four-month relationship from her father and brother for fear of disapproval and shame. She concealed her pregnancy for fear of eviction from home or alienation from her emotional support network.

The birth caught her completely by surprise, and before the night her child was born, she did not prepare for childbirth or a new arrival and did not acknowledge the physical effects of pregnancy until the night she delivered. Isolated in her privacy, responsive to the expectations of her family, and profoundly affected by shame, Violetta chose to try to forget she was pregnant.

On December 3, Violetta and her brother went to the movies, returning home in the late afternoon. Upon their return, Violetta began experiencing back pain and thought she might be coming down with the flu. She laid down to rest.

Violetta could not sleep and experienced continuous urinary urgency, ultimately returning to the bathroom around midnight. While in the bathroom, she rose from the toilet, was suddenly seized by excruciating pain, and fell to the floor. She avoided crying out for fear of waking her family and "giving her father a heart attack."

Lying on the floor, Violetta looked downward and saw her daughter's head emerging and decided to pull her out. She placed one hand across the face, covering the nose, and one hand behind the head. She then held her hand over the baby's nose and mouth, despite knowing that if she did so, the infant would stop breathing. When asked later why she did this, Violetta responded that she was frightened and did not "know what I was thinking."

Violetta stated that she fainted shortly after the birth, and upon waking, realized the baby was not breathing. Her father was knocking at the door, asking if she was all right. She cleaned up the blood, not wanting him to "be worried." An hour later, Miguel opened the bathroom door and founded his sister in her weakened postbirth state.

Outcome

Violetta pleaded guilty to manslaughter after the judge on the case made it clear that she did not want the defendant to serve considerable jail time. Violetta expressed a wish to become pregnant again in the future.

123: Argument/Conflict Murder

Argument/conflict murder is a death that results from a dispute between persons, excluding family or household members.

Defining Characteristics

Victimology

There is a high incidence of victims of this crime to be young adult, blue-collar or unemployed, and with a low education level. The offender is known to the victim. The victim commonly has a history of assaultive behavior and of using violence to resolve his problems.

An exception to this victimology is the person who has the misfortune to cross paths and ignite the volatile, impulsive offender who is predisposed to violent eruptions. The precipitating event is often a trivial incident, such as pulling in front of someone on the freeway.

CRIME SCENE INDICATORS FREQUENTLY NOTED

The crime scene of an argument/conflict murder is often spread out, demonstrating signs of offender and victim movement as well as signs of struggle. It is random and sloppy.

The weapon is bought to the scene due to the offender's predisposition to assaultive behavior. In this sense, it becomes a weapon of opportunity based on its ready availability. It may be left at the scene in addition to fingerprints, footprints, and other evidence. The victim is often unarmed. Generally, the body is also left at the scene and is not concealed.

STAGING

Staging is not present.

COMMON FORENSIC FINDINGS

Alcohol or drugs are often involved, and there is no evidence of sexual assault. The mode of death is usually based on the weapon availability: knife, blunt object, or firearm.

Investigative Considerations

The precipitating event of an argument or conflict is the cause of the dispute. The killing can be a spontaneous or delayed reaction to this event. The offender, like the victim, has a history of assaultive behavior and using violence to resolve problems. Due to the spontaneous nature of the attack, there are usually witnesses, however reluctant or inconspicuous. A point to consider is that the suspect lives in the vicinity of the attack or victim, or both. Witnesses may know the place of employment, hangouts, or residence of offender.

Search Warrant Suggestions

The investigator should search for articles in the location because the crime erupted quickly. A search should also be made for receipts of firearm sales, and the Alcohol, Tobacco, and Firearms registry should be checked.

123.01: Argument Murder

In an argument murder, death is precipitated by a verbal dispute. The defining characteristics, investigative considerations, and search warrant suggestions are discussed in classification 123.

Case Study: 123.01: Argument Murder

Background

On a hot July night in 1989, the police of a small East Coast city received a "shots fired" call. As they arrived at the scene of the incident, they observed a young White male sprawled out in the middle of the street. He had been shot in the chest and was dead. The officers learned from several witnesses that the victim had started arguing with another man over some money the offender owed the victim. The dispute soon escalated, with the victim punching the offender. The fight spilled out into the street and culminated with the offender's pulling a gun out and shooting the victim.

Victimology

The victim was a 22-year-old construction worker who had a history of being thrown out of bars for starting fights. He had a long history of assaultive behavior that included several arrests for aggravated battery and assault on a law enforcement officer. His reputation for solving problems with physical violence was well established at work and after hours, in the bars. The victim had had several confrontations with the offender before the night of his death. According to witnesses familiar with both men, they seemed to have a friendship of sorts that was periodically interrupted with brawls.

Crime Scene Indicators

The crime scene was in a tavern district that had a reputation for nightly brawls, especially during the hot summer months. The crime scene was spread out, with indicators of the struggle beginning in the bar. Bar stools and several tables were overturned. There were several blood spatter patterns indicating that both offender and victim had drawn each other's blood before the shooting.

The crime scene was random and sloppy, typical of this type of conflict. The body was left in the open, in the position that death had occurred. The weapon was brought to the scene and found farther down the street in a garbage can down an alley. There was an abundance of prints in the bar and a few on the murder weapon, although the offender had hurriedly wiped off the gun before discarding it.

Forensic Findings

The autopsy revealed that the victim had died from a single gunshot wound to the chest that penetrated the heart through the left ventricle, causing immediate death.

A .38-caliber bullet was recovered from the body. The victim's serum alcohol level was .21%, well over the .10% level of intoxication.

Investigation

Because of the abundance of witnesses and physical evidence, an arrest was made within hours of the shooting. The offender was arrested without incident at his home. His reputation mirrored that of the victim. He too had a history of assaultive behavior reflected by an arrest record.

The precipitating event of the dispute was some money that the offender had borrowed from the victim three weeks earlier. The offender had promised repayment several times but had failed to fulfill his promises. The offender was also very drunk when the victim began yelling at him and declaring his unreliability to the other bar patrons. The exchange became physical and culminated with the shooting.

Outcome

The offender pleaded guilty to manslaughter and was sentenced to 15 years.

123.02: Conflict Murder

In a conflict murder, death results from personal conflict between the victim and offender. The defining characteristics, investigative considerations, and search warrant suggestions are discussed in classification 123.

Case Study: 123.02: Conflict Murder

Background

Life for Kristen Costas was satisfying and agreeable. The 15-year-old was a member of her high school swimming team, soccer team, and community swim team. She had been selected for the varsity cheerleading squad and belonged to an exclusive volunteer group called the Bobbies. She was very popular at school, having many friends. She seldom dated but was well liked by the male students of her suburban California high school. Words like *pretty* and *vibrant* were used when describing her. Her father was an executive who could afford to give his only daughter the trendy clothes, ski vacations, and cheerleading training camp trips important to a teenager trying to find acceptance from other upper-middle-class peers.

For Bernadette Protti, adolescent life was not so pleasant. She was embarrassed by the modest living imposed by her father's income as a retired public utilities supervisor. This discomfort was accentuated daily as she went to school, surrounded by the sons and daughters of executives like Costas's father. Spring 1984 had not done much to boost her faltering ego. She was cut from the cheerleading squad, rejected from membership in an exclusive club similar to the Bobbies, and denied a place on the yearbook staff. These setbacks probably would have been nothing more than passing disappointments to the typical teenager, but to Protti, they confirmed her sense of failure and lack of self-worth. One friend described Protti as never believing she was accepted by her peers, even though she apparently was. She depicted Protti as having an obsession with being liked.

On June 22, 1984, Costas was at cheerleading camp when her mother received a call from an unidentified female around 10:00 p.m. The caller told Mrs. Costas that Kristen would be picked up for a secret Bobbies initiation dinner the next night. On June 23, Mr. and Mrs. Costas and Kristen's 12-year-old brother were attending a baseball banquet. At 8:20 p.m., Mrs. Costas phoned Kristen to wish her a good time at the Bobbies' dinner. Soon after, Kristen was picked up by a White female in an beat-up orange Pinto. They drove to the Presbyterian church parking lot and parked. After about 30 minutes, Costas became alarmed at the driver's behavior and exited the car.

Costas rang the doorbell of nearby friends, the Arnolds. When Mrs. Arnold answered the door, Costas explained that she had been with a friend at church who had "gone weird." Mrs. Arnold described Kristen as being visibly upset but not terrified. She noticed a girl about 15 with light brown hair on the front sidewalk as she let Costas in to call her parents. When her parents did not answer, Mr. Arnold offered to give Costas a ride home, which she accepted. He noticed the Pinto was following them as he drove Costas home, but Kristen reassured him it was okay.

When Mr. Arnold arrived at the Costas home, Kristen noted that her parents were not in yet and told Mr. Arnold she was going to go next door. He offered to wait until she was safely inside the house and watched as Costas walked to the door.

As he prepared to leave, he saw a female figure pass by the right side of his vehicle and enter the porch where Costas stood. At first, Arnold thought he was witnessing a fistfight. The form struck at Costas, and she fell to the porch screaming. The assailant disappeared seconds later.

Costas staggered to her feet and ran across the street crying for help. A neighbor who had come outside when he heard the scream went to her aid. She collapsed in his arms still asking for help and then lost consciousness. He began cardio-pulmonary resuscitation while his wife called emergency medical personnel.

Meanwhile, Mr. Arnold had started to pursue the Pinto as it squealed away, but decided to return to see if Costas needed help. By this time, the paramedics and police had arrived and were loading Kristen into the ambulance. Mr. and Mrs. Costas arrived home from their son's banquet just in time to see their daughter lying in the ambulance. Kristen Costas was pronounced dead at a nearby hospital at 11:02 p.m.

Victimology

Kristen Costas's chances of becoming a victim of a violent crime were reduced by her warm family relationship, minimal use of alcohol, and self-imposed dating restrictions. Her lifestyle reinforced this low-risk status. She lived at home, and because of her age and parental control, her socialization was restricted to places that would be considered low-risk environments (the church parking lot, which was the local hangout, and friends' homes, for example) as opposed to bars and nightclubs. She had reportedly experimented once with cocaine and once with marijuana, but this isolated use was not a factor when considering the attack.

The fact that Costas was well liked and popular would normally have been additional reasons for considering her status low risk. But because of the nature of the conflict that arose between Protti and Costas, this element elevated her risk to be targeted for a violent crime.

Crime Scene Indicators

In front of the door where the attack took place were multidirectional blood-splatter patterns. A few feet to the left of this area, a trail of blood splatter began that went down the walkway, the driveway, across the street, the neighbor's driveway, sidewalk, and onto the porch.

A butter knife was found at the scene, but this was not the murder weapon. A few latent prints remained unidentified, and one set from the porch post next to the attack site had insufficient detail for evaluation. There was nothing else to aid the investigation from the crime scene.

Forensic Findings

Kristen Costas had been stabbed five times. There was a defensive wound to the right forearm. Two of the wounds were to the back, both 13 centimeters long and puncturing the right lung and diaphragm and lacerating the liver. Of the two wounds from a frontal assault, one was 15.5 centimeters long and penetrated the left upper arm, chest, and left lung. The other was 4 centimeters and did minor damage. Any one of the three deeper wounds would have caused death by itself. There was no evidence of any other type of assault, physical or sexual.

Investigation

Over six months, 750 yellow or orange Ford Pintos, including the killer's, were checked by police, but no evidence was found associated with Costas's murder. More than 1,000 leads were investigated, and over 300 people were interviewed, including 100 girls from Costas's high school. A list of suspects was narrowed down to several dozen people.

The investigators then submitted the victimology, crime scene information, pictures, and autopsy records to the FBI Investigative Support Unit in Quantico, Virginia, for a criminal personality profile. The FBI analysts came up with a profile and sent it back to the sheriff's department in late October. With this profile, the investigators were able to narrow the list to one suspect: Bernadette Protti.

Protti was called in for another extensive interview (she had been interviewed at least four times previously) and another polygraph exam. She failed parts of the polygraph, but other parts were inconclusive. Several days later, Protti returned with her father to the sheriff's department and requested to speak with the FBI agent who had questioned her previously. She then offered a full confession for the murder of Costas.

Protti stated she had killed Kristen because Costas had rebuffed Protti's attempts to make friends with her. Protti was afraid Costas would tell everyone at school that she was a "weirdo." It was this fear of rejection, Protti claimed, that drove her to kill Costas.

Outcome

Bernadette Protti was convicted of second-degree murder and sentenced to 9 years. She was denied parole twice before the state Youthful Offender Parole Board released her on June 10, 1992, in a two-to-one decision.

124: Authority Murder

An authority murder involves an offender who kills persons who have an authority relationship or symbolic authority relationship by which the killer perceives he has been wronged. The target of the assault may be a person or a building, structure, or institution symbolizing the authority. Random victims are often wounded or killed during the assault as a result of their actual or perceived association with the authority figure or the institution being attacked.

Defining Characteristics

VICTIMOLOGY

The victimology of authority murder involves primary and secondary targets. The primary targets are the principal people whom the offender perceives as wronging him. The wrong may be actual, such as the offender's being fired, or may be imagined, based on a psychotic or paranoid delusion of a conspiracy. The secondary victims become random targets as a result of being in the wrong place at the wrong time because the offender generalizes their immediate presence to symbolize the authority.

CRIME SCENE INDICATORS FREQUENTLY NOTED

The offender is mission oriented: he is on the scene with his mission having ultimate priority. He has little or no intention to abort his plan and escape from the scene or from responsibility for the act. He may desire to die at the scene by suicide or by police bullets and thereby attain martyrdom for his actions and cause. There is always a direct and planned confrontation between the offender and victims.

Because of his obsession of being wronged over a period of time, the offender gathers and collects weapons and usually brings multiple weaponry to the scene of his confrontation. In addition, he often arms himself with an abundance of ammunition and other gear to sustain and support his attack. Weapons used are of optimal lethality (semiautomatic assault weapons, high power, scope sights), and as a result, the assault often develops into a mass or spree killing.

STAGING

Staging is not usually present.

COMMON FORENSIC FINDINGS

The forensic finding most prevalent in authority murder is the use of more than one firearm; often, the weapons selected are semiautomatic, selected for quick firing; they may be of more than one caliber. Therefore, various and numerous shell casings may be found at the scene, which will help establish the number of rounds fired. Wounds usually are severe and numerous. Multiple wounds on a victim may suggest the primary target, and the killing of the primary target may prompt the suicide of the offender. If the primary target is not taken, the offender may commit suicide or surrender when he runs out of ammunition.

Investigative Considerations

The offender will have a history of paranoid behavior and openly voicing dissatisfaction with general or specific circumstances in his life. There are usually long-term precipitation and predisposing factors in the development of this state, and a likely result is emotional or mental illness. The mental disorders commonly found among authority killers are depressive reactions, paranoia, or paranoid psychosis. Another result of this developmental situation is interpersonal failures and conflicts such as separation, divorce, job loss, failure in school, or other such personal life traumatic events that will precipitate the acting out against authority. Frustrations accompanied by the inability to handle or resolve such situations are often precipitating events. Suicide attempts are common.

Search Warrant Suggestions

Investigating officials should be aware of the offender's preparation period for the final event by looking for specific reading material, collections of weaponry, uniforms, paraphernalia, and other items of paramilitary interest. Statements made by the offender just prior to, during, and immediately after the assault should be carefully noted and documented by investigative personnel. The search should also look for diaries, scrapbooks, and computer logs and prescribed medications to link the suspect to psychiatric conditions.

Case Study: 124: Authority Murder

Background

Joseph T. Wesbecker, a twice-divorced 47-year-old White male, had asked for a transfer from his job as a pressman. He had complained that the job was too stressful, and as his emotional problems worsened during February 1989, his employers responded by placing him on disability leave. Wesbecker felt that his employers at Standard Gravure Corporation had inflicted a gross injustice on him despite the fact that his behavior had interfered with his duties and the duties of others in his workplace. Nearly every day for seven months, he brooded over how he would repay those in authority who were responsible for his alleged mistreatment.

On the morning of September 14, 1989, Wesbecker walked into the Standard Gravure Corporation plant, intent on seeking revenge on those who caused his problems. Using an AK-47 semiautomatic assault rifle and an assortment of other firearms, he killed or wounded over 20 people.

Victimology

Wesbecker's victims were all secondary targets since the primary targets of his aggression were the company's administrators, who were not in their offices at the time of the assault. His victims were fellow employees, yet on that particular day, Wesbecker considered them to be enemies because they symbolized the corporation's organizational structure.

Crime Scene Indicators

At 8:30 a.m. on September 14, Wesbecker arrived at the Standard Gravure plant carrying a duffel bag containing an AK-47 semiautomatic assault rifle, two MAC-11 semiautomatic pistols, a 9mm semiautomatic pistol, and a .38-caliber revolver. He carried hundreds of rounds of ammunition. When encountering a friend, John Tingle, who tried to persuade Wesbecker not to enter the plant, Wesbecker ordered Tingle to "get away," stating, "I told them that I'd be back."

After he gained entry to the plant, Wesbecker took the elevator to the third floor to the executive office complex. He opened fire as the elevator door parted, killing the receptionist and wounding several other office staff. He then proceeded down the hallway to the bindery, spraying the area with gunfire and killing and wounding more plant employees. He moved on to the Courier-Journal building, where he shot another employee.

Wesbecker proceeded to the Standard Gravure pressroom, into the basement, and back to the pressroom, firing his weapon all the way until he dropped his AK-47, raised his 9mm pistol under his chin, and killed himself. All events occurred in approximately nine minutes from the firing of the first shot. The police arrived on the scene and found Wesbecker dead. It was determined that he fired hundreds of shots during his random murder spree.

This crime is classified as a spree authority killing in that it was a confrontational type of assault spread throughout a large area (several buildings), leaving many dead and wounded in the wake of the assailant. Wesbecker had killed 7 people and wounded 12 others. He obviously intended to kill all who crossed his path and was intent on revenge, seeking out those in authority in the company where he worked. The offender came to the scene with multiple weapons and an abundance of ammunition. His shots were intended to be lethal, as demonstrated by the death toll and the fact that of the 12 surviving victims, 5 were critically wounded. Wesbecker was very mission oriented, with no escape plan.

Forensic Findings

Seven dead and 12 wounded people were found at the scene by police authorities. Another died three days later. Most of the victims died from massive blood loss due to gunshot wounds to the heart and chest area. Most of the 12 wounded workers were in serious to critical condition.

Investigation

The investigation of the shootings revealed that Wesbecker had a long history of mental and emotional problems. Two marriages had ended in divorce. He had been hospitalized on a voluntary basis at least three times between 1978 and 1987 for these problems. He was reported to be withdrawn and troublesome in his workplace and experienced job-related stress problems. He had once declined a promotion and a raise because he could not face the demands the job would place on him. He claimed that his exposure to an industrial chemical had caused memory loss, dizziness, and blackouts. He further attributed his exposure to the chemical for bouts of sleeplessness, racing thoughts, anxiety, anger, and confusion.

Wesbecker's feelings and acts of isolation, withdrawal, and depression are prominent preoffense behavior dynamics of the mass and spree authority killer. Furthermore, he was a single middle-aged White male who harbored a long-term grudge against the management of his employer and had accompanying emotional problems relating to his personal and work-related life. Wesbecker often spoke of his deep resentment toward his employer. Fellow employees recalled his conversations surrounding his fantasies of revenge against his company should he be mistreated.

Wesbecker had often articulated his feelings of worthlessness and had attempted suicide on three occasions: once through an overdose, another by breathing car exhaust fumes, and a third by hanging. He further articulated a desire to harm others in addition to his suicide attempts. The investigation failed to link Wesbecker to any of his victims to establish a personal cause or motive for shooting or killing any one or all of the individuals. Therefore, it must be assumed the shootings were random in nature rather than specific.

125: Revenge

Revenge killing involves the killing of another in retaliation for a perceived wrong, real or imagined, committed against the offender or a significant other.

Defining Characteristics

VICTIMOLOGY

When revenge is the motive for a homicide, the victim may or may not personally know the offender, but something in the victim's life—a significant event or interaction—is directly related to the actions of the offender. The revenge motive generated by this event may be unknown to the victim or the victim's family or friends. Multiple victims may be involved, depending on the nature of the event that triggered the act of revenge.

CRIME SCENE INDICATORS FREQUENTLY NOTED

There are often several locations involved with the offense. For example, the precipitating event may happen at one site at an earlier date, but the revenge is acted out later at another location.

An offender who has brooded over the victim's affront often demonstrates a less spontaneous crime that is reflected by the well-ordered crime scene. However, the mission-oriented offender may not be experienced at criminal activity. Some offenders are often in a highly charged emotional state from extensive fantasizing about the act of vengeance. The crime scene may reflect this inexperience, with a clear shift from an organized to a disorganized behavior. The offense is well planned up to the point of the killing. This may be manifested by a skillful approach to the crime scene (leaving no physical evidence) but a blitz style of attack, followed by a rapid exit, with the offender leaving an abundance of physical evidence. The weapon may be left at the scene. Since the act of vengeance was the priority and an end in itself, there may be no escape plan.

The weapon is most often a weapon of choice that the offender brings to the scene. It may be left there, too, especially with the type of offender described earlier.

The offense itself can be opportunistic and spontaneous. An example is the distraught friend or family member who brings a gun to court and shoots the alleged perpetrator of a crime committed against their loved one. A revenge killing committed in front of the victim's family is another example of the more impulsive form of this killing.

STAGING

Staging is not usually present.

COMMON FORENSIC FINDINGS

The weapon is one of choice, mostly likely a firearm or knife. The killing is close range and confrontational. The offender derives satisfaction of witnessing "justice" rendered before him or her. Contact wounds are prevalent. The presence of defensive wounds is possible and related in part to the degree of the offender's skill.

Investigative Considerations

Preoffense behavior by the offender will often follow a pattern in which he or she is at first very verbal about the incident that involves the victim's injustice. Interviews of those close to the offender often reveal that their conversations with the offender often pertained to this incident.

As the offender formulates a plan for vengeance, he or she may become preoccupied and less vocal in general. The offender will seek a weapon, if necessary, at this point.

After the offense, there is often a sense of relief on the part of the offender. The mission has been accomplished. He or she may even stay at the scene to savor this achievement and make no attempt to conceal his or her identity. The death of the victim is justified in the eyes of the offender; it is restitution. If the offender has this attitude, there are often witnesses to the offense.

The precipitating event that links the victim and offender is the key point of this investigation. However, this event may hold significance only to the offender and not be obvious to those associated with the offender or victim. It may not be obvious to the investigator, either. Also of importance is any significant person in either the offender's or the victim's life who may have direct or indirect involvement with the incident.

Search Warrant Suggestions

The offender may have kept the weapon and possibly bloodied clothing from the offense as mementos from which renewed satisfaction is derived that (his) justice has been served. There may be newspapers and other press relating to the significant or precipitating event. A record (written, audiotaped, or video-taped) of the fantasy and feelings leading to the offense may also be present at the offender's residence. There may be mail or other communications with the victim in the offender's possession.

Case Study: 125: Revenge

Background

On February 28, 2005, the husband of U.S. District Judge Joan Leftkow and the judge's mother were found shot twice at point-blank range in the forehead in the utility room of the Leftkow home.

Victimology

The intended target of the killer, Bart Ross, was Judge Leftkow herself, not her mother and husband.

Crime Scene Indicators

This offense involved the judge's husband and mother. The offender brought his weapon of choice, a .22-caliber gun, to the scene with him. Ross broke through a locked basement window and sat waiting for the judge to return home. Mr. Leftkow discovered Ross in the basement and he was shot; the mother heard the shot, and Ross said he had to shoot her as well. He followed each single shot with a second "to minimize suffering." Ross remained in the house and finally left because he decided killing "was not fun."

Forensic Findings

Shell casings were found at the crime scene. A fingerprint was found on the broken window in the utility room, and a bloody footprint was found in the house along with a mop used to clean up the blood spattered on the floor. Further evidence was found in the kitchen, including a cigarette butt in the sink and a soda can.

Investigation

Although there was considerable physical and forensic evidence left at the crime scene, suggesting a disorganized crime scene, no suspects were developed until a suicide note surfaced. On March 6, 2005, Ross killed himself and left a suicide note and letter with explanations for his actions. Blood and fingerprints matched the DNA samplings taken from the crime scene.

Outcome

The case was solved when Ross killed himself. In a four-page letter sent to NBC5 in Chicago, Ross outlined his grievance and desire for revenge. In 1992, he had had surgery for mouth cancer, which left him with a facial disfigurement. In 1995 he filed a medical malpractice suit, but the suit was dismissed because no violations had been noted in his medical records. Over the next seven years, Ross regularly filed appeals, becoming more and more frustrated by the system. He sent an angry letter to the governor and said he was unfairly represented by his lawyers. In 2004, he filed a civil rights case against the government, his lawyers, the doctors, and the hospital. Judge Leftkow dismissed the case due to lack of presentation of new evidence, and in October she denied a motion to reconsider.

126: Nonspecific Motive Murder

A nonspecific motive murder pertains to a homicide that appears irrational and is committed for an undetermined reason known only to the offender. It subsequently may be defined and categorized with more extensive investigation into the offender's background. It may involve a psychotic situation in which the offender is suffering from a severe mental illness and is killing because of that illness. This may include auditory and/or visual hallucinations and paranoid, grandiose, or bizarre delusions.

Defining Characteristics

VICTIMOLOGY

The victims of a nonspecific homicide are random, with no direct relationship between victim and offender. Victims can be male, female, adults, or children and demonstrate a variety of characteristics and lifestyle.

CRIME SCENE INDICATORS FREQUENTLY NOTED

The crime scene is usually a public place and poses a high risk to the offender. There is nothing missing from it, and it is disorganized, with no effort to conceal the victim. A firearm, the weapon of choice for this type of offender, is brought to the crime. This crime often becomes a massacre because it is the offender's goal to kill as many people as possible. This is reflected by the use of weapons that offer optimal lethality, multiple weapons, and an abundance of ammunition.

STAGING

Staging is not present.

COMMON FORENSIC FINDINGS

Because nothing is removed from the scene, an abundance of evidence is usually available, including shell casings, prints, and discarded weapons. High-powered, high-caliber, or high-capacity firearm use will be evident and enables the offender to accomplish his goal of mass killing. Wounds will be concentrated on vital areas: head, neck, and chest.

Investigative Considerations

This crime is almost exclusively committed during daylight in public places because the offender wants the highest death toll possible. Witnesses are often available to identify the offender because he is unconcerned with being identified. The offender has no escape plan and possibly intends to commit suicide or be shot by police. Through a broad neighborhood investigation, preoffense characteristics become evident: the offender usually has a disheveled appearance, is withdrawn, demonstrates an isolated affect, and possibly exhibits erratic behavior.

Search Warrant Suggestions

The home of the suspect should be searched for weapons, computers, and records.

Case Study 126: Nonspecific Motive Murder

Case Contributed by Colleen Maher

Victimology

On January 3, 1999, Kendra Webdale, a 32-year-old blonde aspiring writer, approached the platform of the Queens-bound N train at the 23rd Street station in New York City's Flatiron district. She worked as a receptionist at a recording company. In her free time, she enjoyed jogging in Central Park and researching ideas for a screenplay in the New York Public Library

Moments after Webdale arrived, 29-year-old Andrew Goldstein reached the station. He moved furiously around the platform, traversing from point to point and stumbling. Witnesses noted that he wore a beige trench coat, had bare feet, and mumbled incoherent words under his breath. His stumbling soon turned to pacing. In response to his frantic movement, a man asked him to stop, that he was making people nervous. Around 5:00 p.m., Goldstein walked up to a blonde woman on the platform. She asked what he wanted and he backed off. Next, he approached Kendra Webdale and asked her for the time. Undeterred by Goldstein's anxious behavior, she replied that it was shortly after 5:00 p.m.

Without warning, Goldstein picked Webdale into his arms and threw her onto the tracks just as a train pulled into the station. A witness of the event described her flying right under the train. She didn't have a chance to scream. She died instantly, crushed by the weight of the oncoming train.

Crime Scene Indicators

There was one crime scene, a crowded transit station in New York City.

Investigation

After the incident, Goldstein sat down on the platform. Twenty enraged onlookers crowded around him, berating him for his murderous action. One witness ran up to 23rd Street and Broadway to flag down police. Goldstein was heard to say that he was psychotic and needed to go to a hospital. Police arrived at the scene. Goldstein made no protest as he was frisked and handcuffed.

At the police station, Goldstein explained, "As I was standing on the platform there was a woman waiting for the train. . . . I got the urge to push, kick, or punch. . . . I feel like an aura, or a sensation, like you're losing control of your motor systems. And then, you lose control of your senses and everything. And then you feel like something's entering you. Like you're being inhabited. I don't know. But—and then, and then it's like an overwhelming urge to strike out or push or punch. . . .

This is like 10 times this has happened to me. Now this time, terrific, I mean bang zoom, you know it's right—right in front of a train. . . .

I shoved her, not knowing which direction I was going, coming or going, and then she fell onto the track and then I went into shock, horror. I saw the body go under and then I walked away.

After Goldstein gave his lengthy statement, the prosecutor, William Greenbaum, questioned him. His examination seemed to preempt Goldstein's use of an insanity defense. He inquired about Goldstein's subjective awareness of the wrongfulness of his act and his expectations for the resulting effect, essential elements of the insanity standard utilized by New York at the time. In *Insanity: Murder, Madness, and the Law*, Dr. Charles Patrick Ewing outlines the conversation as follows:

Prosecutor: You certainly agree that you knew what you were doing and you knew it was wrong.
Goldstein: Uh-huh. I got a cold. I don't know what the heck . . .
Prosecutor: That is, you pushed her onto the tracks, it was the cause of her death?
Goldstein: I see.
Prosecutor: No, tell me.
Goldstein: No, I'm sorry?
Prosecutor: Do you agree or disagree that you knew at the time you pushed her that it could cause her death?
Goldstein: Well, I wasn't thinking about anything about pushing her. When I—when it happens, I don't think. It just goes, push, you know? It's like a—like an attack of some kind. I pushed her. But I didn't push her thinking that she would wind up on the tracks. I didn't—didn't intend to push her in any direction. It just happened. It's like you break loose. I don't know.
Prosecutor: Well, did you expect that she would go off the platform?
Goldstein: No. No. No. No. I would never push anybody off the tracks.
Prosecutor: Because you know it's wrong.
Goldstein: Yeah.

Goldstein was subsequently charged with second-degree murder. After consultation with two court-appointed psychiatrists, Goldstein was declared fit to stand trial on February 10, 1999, despite his severe schizophrenia. As the prosecutor anticipated, Goldstein's attorneys formulated an insanity defense.

Psychiatric Evaluation

In the case of Andrew Goldstein, symptoms of paranoia and disorganized behavior were evident from early adulthood. Though he had been a successful student at Bronx High School of Science and once tested an IQ of 122, his transition to the State University of New York at Stony Brook was difficult. During his freshman year, Goldstein accused his mother of poisoning him and pushed her and as a result, he began receiving psychiatric treatment. Goldstein revealed that he heard voices and that he feared an organ was growing inside of him. He was diagnosed with paranoid schizophrenia. Over the next 10 years, he became a "revolving door" psychiatric patient, hospitalized more than a dozen times for his outbursts.

From 1992 until 1996, Goldstein was either hospitalized or living in the Leben Home for Adults, a supervised residence for the mentally ill. Mental health professionals documented his condition at the time using the following terms: *actively psychotic, highly delusional, in need or inpatient psychiatric admission,* and *schizoaffective.*

Goldstein began a pattern of assaultive behavior, attacking women who resembled his mother. In the next year, Goldstein was in and out of psychiatric facilities. On various occasions, he knocked a woman into a bookshelf at a bookstore, swung at women in a restaurant, shoved a woman on a subway train, and threw a book at the head of a female psychiatrist. Still, the only charge on his record was assault following the incident at the bookstore. In all incidents, he attributed his acts to an uncontrollable urge.

During a clinical interview in February 1998, Goldstein told a social worker that he feared he would hit someone upon being discharged. On December 14, 1998, Goldstein was discharged from the hospital with a referral for counseling and enough antipsychotic medication to last one week. Upon discharge, Goldstein promptly stopped taking his medication and failed to make contact with his referred mental health professional. After December 26, he received a letter informing him that if he had not contacted the clinic by January 6, 1999, his case would be closed.

Court Outcome

Defense psychiatrists diagnosed him as suffering from schizophrenia, with one testifying that Goldstein suffered from severe schizophrenia and one blamed the mental health system of New York for placing such a dangerous individual back on the streets.

An expert for the prosecution painted a different picture. Though she conceded that Goldstein was "probably schizophrenic," she denied that his condition necessarily supported an insanity defense. She testified that he knows he's charged with murder and he knows he could go to jail for a long time if he's convicted of murder. He'd rather go to a hospital.

A second psychiatrist for the prosecution diagnosed Goldstein with attention deficit disorder. During his cross-examination, defense counsel pressed the issue and the psychiatrist admitted that he had not read any of the 3,500-page psychiatric and medical history in which Goldstein was repeatedly diagnosed as schizophrenic. The prosecution fought the insanity defense with the theory that Goldstein's hatred of women, not his mental illness, served as motivation for the attacks. The prosecutor argued that Goldstein killed Webdale on his mother's birthday as a way to lash out against his mother's rejection. Near the conclusion of the trial, the judge refused to allow the defense to call a final witness who was prepared to testify that Goldstein was acting in a very confused way.

Despite the overwhelming evidence of serious mental illness, the jury could not reach a determination regarding the sanity of Andrew Goldstein. After five days of deliberation, the jury remained deadlocked. Though 10 jurors favored conviction, two jury members, a hospital worker and a former social worker, refused to issue a guilty verdict, and 10 months after the incident a mistrial was declared.

Before the second trial, Goldstein's counsel requested the ability to utilize a positron emission tomography (PET) scan, in the next trial, arguing that such evidence would counter any assertion from the prosecution that Goldstein was "malingering," or faking mental illness. Goldstein's counsel also argued that the extreme emotional disturbance suffered by the defendant made him ineligible for a murder conviction, instead making him eligible for a charge of manslaughter. Goldstein's counsel had him stop taking his antipsychotic medication two weeks before the second trial "in an effort to show the jury the debilitating effects of his mental illness." Unfortunately, this attempt was thwarted when a judge ordered Goldstein adhere to a strict medication regimen after he twice struck the court social worker.

In the second trial, the prosecution's expert, again conceded to the fact that Goldstein suffered from a disorder "in the schizophrenic spectrum." Still, she stated that it was a milder form that was substantially in remission at the time of the murder. She advanced a theory that Goldstein acted out of a long-standing hatred of women, not from an irresistible urge based in psychotic disorder. At the conclusion of this trial, the jury returned a verdict in less than two hours. Goldstein was convicted of second-degree murder and sentenced to spend 25 years to life in prison.

Goldstein's attorneys appealed his case over the course of the next five years. A timely holding by the United States Supreme Court in the case of *Crawford v. Washington* provided an opportunity for Goldstein's attorneys to specifically challenge the judge's decision to allow the prosecution expert to read hearsay statements into the record in the course of her testimony. Citing this precedent, the New York Court of Appeals held that Goldstein's "rights under the Confrontation Clause were violated when the psychiatrist was allowed to tell the jury what witnesses [the] defendant had no chance to cross-examine had said to her." Rather than pursue a third murder trial against Goldstein in the wake of this decision, the prosecution allowed him to plead guilty to manslaughter. His current sentence mandates that he be released from prison after no more than 23 years.

In addition to criminal proceedings, Webdale's family filed a civil suit. In June of 1999, Webdale's family sued seven hospitals and clinics that provided care for and discharged Goldstein prior to the murder. They filed for $20 million in pain, suffering, and death and for $50 million in punitive damages. The incident also served as a rallying point for legislators and advocates of changes to the mental health system. New York State Assemblyman James F. Brennan authorized a bill for $200 million to create an additional 2,500 hospital beds for chronically mentally ill patients. State Senator Thomas W. Libous introduced legislation for $5 million to provide aid for troubled former psychiatric patients. Governor George Pataki signed "Kendra's Law" into effect in August 1999, a law that allows courts to mandate treatment or institutionalization for mentally ill offenders. Caseworkers, family members, and roommates have the capacity to request a court order for an individual to adhere to treatment. This bill and other similar pieces of legislation provided additional funding for psychiatric treatment in New York.

Source: Ewing, C. P. (2008). *Insanity: Murder, madness, and the law.* New York, NY: Oxford University Press.

Case Study 126.01: Personal Cause Religion-Inspired Homicide

Classification and Case Contributed by Michael Welner

Background

Police were called to the small, quiet, and modest Brooklyn apartment building where Rose, an 81-year-old woman, was discovered dead by her building manager. When the decedent had failed to meet her niece at an outing scheduled earlier, the niece became concerned and visited the building.

When the niece was canvassing the building, she learned little from the neighbors; the niece sought out the building manager, who looked into Rose's apartment through a window accessible to the fire escape. There they saw her lying on the floor, dead.

Police investigating the building knocked on the door of an upstairs neighbor, Carmela Cintron. There was no answer when they knocked on Carmela's door; police then made their way up the fire escape to look into her apartment. When an officer looked into Carmela's back window, she ran into the bathroom, and he called to detectives in the front stairwell, who entered through an unlocked front door. Carmela subsequently confessed, in a rambling and disjointed statement, and was charged with Rose's killing.

Victimology

Rose lived alone for many years in the same apartment, a second-floor walkup. Carmela and Rose were initially friendly neighbors; Carmela would visit Rose's house frequently and sit and have coffee.

Earlier that year, Carmela had ransacked her own apartment during a fit of rage, and a relative told Rose about this. Subsequently Rose grew uncomfortable about having Carmela in her apartment and told her not to come around anymore. Despite this, Carmela would still occasionally walk downstairs to Rose's apartment when other guests were there. A friend recalled, "Carmela would ask her for money. . . . When Rose would say no, she would act weird. . . . Rose would let her come into the apartment, because she was a gentle woman . . . but she was scared of her." To another friend, Rose expressed her feelings that Carmela, "must think she had money because she had sold her apartment."

Crime Scene Indicators

There was no sign of forced entry, and indications were that the perpetrator had entered the apartment through the back window, using the fire escape. A number of potted plants lay smashed on the ground below.

Rose was found lying in a pool of what appeared to be blood, fully clothed. Strewn about Rose's body were a number of articles of food. In addition, coffee grounds were spread on and around Rose's body. Coffee grounds were streaked by the movement of the dying Rose's leg over food that had been thrown on the floor prior to her falling on it.

Blood spatter indicated that the door to the refrigerator was opened before she died. This demonstrates that the assailant was attacking Rose after she had already occupied herself in some way with the refrigerator. No weapon was identified at the scene.

While the location of her body, on the kitchen floor next to the refrigerator, was quite messy, there was no sign of activity elsewhere in the one-bedroom apartment and no evidence of robbery or items otherwise removed.

Forensic Findings

Rose suffered a variety of deep bruises and several rib fractures; the principal cause of death was listed as strangulation and a compound fracture of the related hyoid bone. The bruise pattern on the body reflects that only some of the blows came from Rose's own cane. The rest resembled punches or kicks or another blunt instrument. There was no sign of sexual trauma.

Investigation

Carmela, who worked as a nurse's aide in a Manhattan hospital, took leave in spring 1997 to undergo successive surgeries in the ensuing months. Also around this time, she was brought to Beth Israel Medical Center by ambulance after walking naked through her neighborhood.

Carmela had a history of destroying her own apartment, being "anxious," throwing things around her apartment, and episodes in which she hallucinated and spoke incoherently. She had no history of substance abuse.

Carmela had financial problems. She feared losing her disability benefits because she remained out on leave. She continued to remain deeply attached to an ex-husband, Luis, who was incarcerated. She provided Luis with many gifts, hoping he would return to her. Luis would also call Carmela collect, resulting in a several-hundred-dollar phone bill each time.

Carmela had a history of repeatedly assaulting her grandmother, particularly when her grandmother would not give her money for Luis. In the most serious attack, she broke five of her grandmother's ribs on one side and seven on another by stomping on her back.

Luis had remarried but nonetheless remained in contact with Carmela, writing her letters that suggested a romantic interest. When Carmela found out that the day after she had visited Luis in jail with a birthday gift that his wife had visited him for a conjugal visit, she was devastated.

In early August, her priest noted that Carmela was more ritualistic and more isolated during her prayer and attended mass more frequently.

The night before the killing, Carmela asked an acquaintance to assemble an exercise bike for her. As Carmela recalled, "I was upset, I wanted to take off weight. I was thinking about just being alone. . . . I was confused, and couldn't put all my thoughts together at one time. . . . I couldn't calm myself down." The teenager became frightened when Carmela climbed aboard the bike he had assembled and began pedaling it furiously. He ran all the way home, telling his mother that Carmela was "possessed."

The next morning, Carmela went out onto her fire escape and began dumping plants and soil to the ground below, then tossing the pots down as well. She made her way down from the third floor to the second floor on the fire escape.

She entered into Rose's apartment through the window leading into the kitchen. No one was there initially. After about 15 minutes, Rose entered her apartment and told Carmela, "You don't belong here . . . get out of the apartment."

Carmela, feeling rejected, grabbed Rose by the head and struck her on the corner of the wall, preventing her from exiting, and did not stop her assault until Rose was dead.

Closer examination of Carmela's apartment revealed icons, candles, and other symbols of devout practice of Brujeria. This Afro-Caribbean church was different from her own. Interviews with friends indicated that shortly before the killing, Carmela sought out a Bruja, or priest of the religion, to cast a spell on her behalf.

During the investigation, Carmela was very secretive about her Brujeria, not unlike many other practitioners of the faith. Likewise, she remained tight-lipped about her feelings for and reactions to Luis and what he would reveal to her in their telephone conversations. Only input from friends and close acquaintances revealed the extent of her engaging Brujeria to win Luis back.

When questioned about the dumped dirt, smashed pots, attack on Rose, and spreading of coffee on the floor, Carmela offered rational explanations and vehemently denied associations of any of these with Brujeria. Consultation with experts of this practice, however, revealed the spiritual significance of the coffee grounds and smashed pots.

Outcome

Carmela was diagnosed with borderline personality disorder and a brief psychotic episode in the context of separation. Because she was capable of appreciating the wrongfulness of her actions but was mentally impaired at the time of the crime, prosecutors offered her the opportunity to plead guilty to manslaughter, which she accepted.

Chapter 8

Sexual Homicide

130: Sexual homicide
131: Organized
132: Disorganized

133: Mixed
134: Sadistic
135: Elder female sexual homicide

130: Sexual Homicide

Sexual homicide involves a sexual element (activity) as the basis in the sequence of acts leading to death. Performance and meaning of this sexual element vary with offender. The act may range from actual rape involving penetration (either pre- or postmortem) to a symbolic sexual assault such as insertion of foreign objects into a victim's body orifices. A sexually based motivation is driven by the sexual needs/desires of the offender. There may or may not be overt sexual contact reflected in the crime scene.

131: Sexual Homicide, Organized

The term *organized* when used to describe a sexual homicide offender is based on assessment of the criminal act itself, comprehensive analysis of the victim, crime scene (including any staging present), and evaluation of forensic reports. These components combine to form traits common to an organized offender: one who appears to plan his murders, targets his victims, and displays control at the crime scene. A methodical and ordered approach is reflected through all phases of the crime.

Defining Characteristics

VICTIMOLOGY

The victim of a sexual homicide perpetrated by an organized offender is often an intraracial female. A single, employed person who is living alone is common

205

to this victimology. Adolescent males are also targeted, as demonstrated by the case of John Wayne Gacy.

The concept of victim risk is an important factor in assessing the victimology. Risk is a twofold factor. Victim risk is determined by age, lifestyle, occupation, and physical stature. Low-risk types include those whose daily lifestyle and occupation do not enhance their chances of being targeted as a victim. High-risk victims are ones who are targeted by a killer who knows where to find them, for example, prostitutes or hitchhikers. Low-resistance capabilities as found in the elderly and young elevate the level of victim risk. Risk can also be elevated by locations where the victim becomes more vulnerable, such as isolated areas. A victim's attitude toward safety is also a factor that can raise or lower his or her risk factor. A naive, overly trusting, or careless stance concerning personal safety can increase one's chance of being victimized.

The second facet of victim risk is in the level of gamble the offender takes to commit the crime. Generally, the victim is at a lower risk level if the crime scene is indoors and at a higher risk level if it is outdoors. The time of day that the crime occurs also contributes to the amount of risk the offender took: An abduction at noon would pose more hazard to the offender than at midnight.

The victim is typically not known to the offender but is often chosen because he or she meets the criteria. These criteria will especially be seen if multiple victims are involved: they will share common characteristics such as age, appearance, occupation, hairstyle, or lifestyle. The victim is targeted at the location where the killer is staked out; therefore, he or she becomes a victim of opportunity. Consequently, investigators may not observe similarities in the victim characteristics.

CRIME SCENE INDICATORS COMMONLY NOTED

There are often multiple crime scenes involved with the organized killing: the locale of initial contact or assault, the scene of death, and the body disposal site. If the victim is confronted indoors, the first crime scene (confrontation) is commonly the first or second floor of a building or a single-family dwelling. The offender may then transport the victim or body from the site of confrontation, necessitating the use of the offender's or victim's vehicle.

Weapons are generally brought to the crime scene but are removed by the offender after the completion of the crime. Use of restraints is often noted by the presence of tape, blindfolds, chains, ropes, clothing, handcuffs, gags, or chemicals. The use of restraints is reflected by the overall controlled, planned appearance of the crime scene. It reflects a methodical approach with a semblance of order existing prior to, during, and after the offense. If the offender has time, evidence, such as fingerprints or footprints, will be removed.

Also missing from the crime scene may be trophies or souvenirs, which include pictures, jewelry, clothing, or the victim's driver's license. These items do not necessarily have much extrinsic value, but to the offender they commemorate the successful endeavor and offer proof of his skill. They also serve as a means to fuel the fantasy of the act by serving as a remembrance.

Finally, if the offender has time, the victim's corpse will be concealed. The location for disposal is generally an area familiar to the offender.

STAGING

Staging may be present at the crime scene. The subject may stage the crime to appear careless and disorganized to distract or mislead the police. He may stage secondary criminal activity to cloud the basis for the primary motive of rape–murder, for example, a robbery or kidnapping.

COMMON FORENSIC FINDINGS

The forensic findings of an organized sexual homicide may be bite marks and saliva recovery on the body, semen in body orifices or on body pubic hair, and bruising or cutting of the sex organs. Aggressive acts as well as sexual acts will usually take place prior to death. Evidence of restraint devices may also be present.

The act of killing may be eroticized, meaning that death comes in a slow, deliberate manner. An asphyxial modality is often noted. An example is the deliberate tightening and loosening of a rope around the victim's neck as she slips in and out of a conscious state. Perimortem sexual activity may also be found in which sexual acts are performed in conjunction with the act of killing.

Investigative Considerations

Since the offender is usually socially adept, he often uses verbal means (the con) to capture the victim. He may strike up a conversation or a pseudo-relationship as a prelude to the attack. He may impersonate another role, such as a police officer or security guard, to gain victim confidence. To gain further access to the victim, the subject will typically be dressed neatly in business or casual attire.

The methodical approach common to this offender is incorporated into victim selection after staking out an area. When neighbors are questioned, particular attention should be paid to any strangers noted lingering around the neighborhood or anyone whose actions or appearance are as described above.

The organized sexual murderer often returns for surveillance of any or all of the crime scenes involved (point of abduction, assault, grave site). He may go so far as to interject himself into the investigation in an overly cooperative way or to offer bogus information. This serves the dual purpose of checking on the status of the investigation or reliving the crime.

A possible suspect may have a history of prior offenses of lesser notice, escalating to the homicide being investigated. His background should be checked for precipitating situational stress such as financial, employment, or marital or other relationship problems. He may have a history of recent residence or employment change. He may have even left town after the murder. If property is missing, local areas should be checked for burglaries.

Search Warrant Suggestions

Items that should be kept in mind when preparing a search warrant for a suspect are diaries, calendars, or newspaper clippings that commemorate the murder. Recordings may be found, either audio or audiovisual. Photographs of victims are another possible finding. The souvenirs or trophies should be kept in mind when formulating a search warrant. Any police or related paraphernalia as well as emails should also be looked for.

Case Study A: 131: Sexual Homicide, Organized

Background

Until his double life came to light with his arrest in February 2011, Canadian Air Force officer Russell Williams had a brilliant future, was a man entrusted with flying prime ministers and Queen Elizabeth II, and was the commander of Canada's largest Air Force base.

Victimology

Williams targeted girls and women in their teens and 20s and often photographed himself in their underwear, which he then stole. The first murder victim was Corporal Marie-France Comeau, an Air Force flight attendant from Colonel Williams's base.

Jessica Lloyd, the second murder victim, had been spotted by the colonel as he drove on a road near a cottage he owned. Williams had targeted the corporal after meeting her as she worked on a military flight.

Crime Scene Indicators

Two crime scenes were in the home of the victim and the home of Williams. And he made tapes of his sex assault of Lloyd after kidnapping her, taking her to his cottage, and raping and then killing her January 28.

Forensics

Authorities said Williams carefully catalogued the photos of himself with time and date stamps on hard drives in his Ottawa home. Some of the photos were panoramic shots of the victims' bedrooms. He kept the underwear in bags and boxes in his home and would sometimes burn them if he ran out of space.

After hours of repeatedly being raped and beaten in the head with a large flashlight, Comeau was suffocated by duct tape covering her mouth and nose.

The colonel was identified as a suspect after police stopped motorists at a roadblock, trying to match tires to a track print they had from outside Lloyd's home.

Investigation

Williams, a 23-year military veteran, had never been in combat but has been stationed across Canada and internationally, including a stint in 2006 as commanding officer of Camp Mirage, the secretive Canadian Forces base widely reported to be near Dubai. Williams had been a rising star in the Canadian Air Force and was in charge of Base Trenton in Ontario, the country's busiest Air Force hub.

After Corporal Comeau's body was discovered, Colonel Williams sent her father a letter of condolence in his capacity as base commander.

Colonel David Russell Williams, unmasked as a thief and killer, videotaped his extended, brutal assaults on the two women he murdered.

Williams burgled at least 47 homes, starting in 2007. Many of the targeted homes were in the same street as Williams's cottage in Tweed, Ontario. A further tranche of targeted homes were in the vicinity of Williams's main home in Orleans, outside Ottawa.

During one killing, he brought extra lamps into a room to improve its lighting.

Outcome

Williams pleaded guilty to the two murders, two other sexual assaults, and 82 break-ins. A 21-year-old single mother, said she was tied up, blindfolded, stripped, and held captive for more than two hours while he forced her into sexual acts and photographed her.

The disturbing accounts of the crimes were drawn from Colonel Williams's own meticulous records and videotapes of his two-year rampage, which began with home break-ins to steal girls' and women's underwear for his sexual arousal, and culminated in the murders. Williams took pictures of himself wearing the stolen underwear while masturbating or aroused.

Williams was given a life sentence with no chance of parole for 25 years for two murders and sexual assaults.

Case Study B: 131: Sexual Homicide, Organized

Background

The local police department of Columbia, South Carolina, received a worried call from the parents of a 17-year-old girl. Their daughter had taken her bike to the end of their driveway to get the mail and had never returned. When the parents went looking for her, they found her bike by the mailbox and alongside the curb.

After the abduction, the offender made several phone calls to the family and conversed primarily with the victim's older sister. He used an electronic device to disguise his voice because, he indicated, he was known to the family. These calls continued after the victim's death. The offender would make references to a letter—the victim's last will and testament he had sent to them. Although the victim died shortly after her abduction, he led the family to believe the victim was still alive until they found the body, a week later.

Victimology

The first victim was abducted from the end of her driveway. A nine-year-old White female, the next victim, was abducted from her yard a week following the discovery of the first victim's body. The offender contacted the first victim's sister and told her of the abduction and killing of the little girl, as well as the location of the body. During the last telephone conversation, the offender advised the first victim's sister that she would be the next to die.

Investigation revealed that both girls were low-risk victims. However, the fact that they were not likely to have the physical strength to fight or resist a strong male assailant increased their risk factor slightly. In the case of the first victim, it appeared the offender was taking pictures of her on her bike as she arrived at the mailbox. She became a victim of opportunity because she crossed the offender's path when he was staked out in search of a victim. The nine-year-old child was taken from her play area. This time the offender may have been looking for a victim, or he may have just happened on her and decided to act. This abduction was less sophisticated, so it probably was more of an opportunistic incident.

Crime Scene Indicators

The offender communicated by telephone with the victim's parents two days after the abduction and then with the victim's sister. With his voice disguised, the offender asked for forgiveness and expressed remorse. He gave the impression the victim was still alive. He told the victim's family he had taken her to a house where she was tied to the bed. Twelve hours later, the offender gave her a choice as to the method of her death: strangulation, suffocation, or drowning. The victim chose suffocation, at which time the offender placed duct tape over her nose and mouth.

The subject appeared to be following a written script. For example, when interrupted by family members of the victim, he would become upset. This suggested his obsessive–compulsive need to rigidly articulate details to the family. He gave directions to the crime scene that were so detailed that it was obvious that the offender had gone back to the crime scene to measure distances. The victim's body was placed in an area where she was well concealed.

Indicators from the body disposal site suggested that the subject was familiar with the area. There were three locations involved with each crime: the abduction site, the death scene, and the gravesite. The offender interacted with victims, so he had to have a place where he could comfortably spend an extended period of time with them. This location, also the murder scene, was discovered to be where the offender was housesitting. The gravesites were also locations he was familiar with.

Forensic Findings

The forensic findings indicated both victims had been bound with ligatures and duct tape. All bindings had been removed from the bodies before disposal. Duct tape residue was found on both victims' faces. The subject claimed the victims had been smothered. The bodies were far too decomposed to determine if they had been sexually assaulted. Both victims were fully clothed when their bodies were discovered.

Investigation

The crime was organized in terms of the abduction, murder, and disposal. A reconstruction of the crime and death scene indicated some offender sophistication with the telephone calls to the victims' families, his fantasy, and his degree of planning. He made the first victim write her last will and testament on a legal pad. The will was actually a letter to her family stating that she was ready to die and that she loved them. The offender mailed the letter to the family.

This letter was sent to the state laboratory for analysis, which revealed indented writing not visible to the naked eye. The writing was identified as a telephone number with one digit obliterated. By a process of elimination, people with similar telephone numbers were interviewed until a list of possible suspects was developed. One number belonged to a house in the abduction locale. When police contacted this person, he told them his parents were not at home but had someone house-sitting for them. His parents had given the house sitter their son's number in case of any problems. The man's name was Larry Gene Bell.

While this investigation was going on, criminal investigative analysts from the National Center for the Analysis of Violent Crime Investigative Support Unit (ISU) had been consulted. They had generated an offender profile and some investigative techniques for the local police department. When the offender was identified, he matched almost every offender characteristic listed. Larry Gene Bell was a 36-year-old White male who worked doing electrical house wiring. At the time of the murders, he was living with his mother and father. He had been married for a short time and had lived away from home.

The ISU agents provided an interrogation strategy that would offer a "face-saving" explanation for Bell. Bell confessed, claiming the "bad Larry Gene Bell did it."

Outcome

Larry Gene Bell was given two death sentences for the murders of the two girls. He was executed on October 4, 1996.

132: Sexual Homicide, Disorganized

The term *disorganized* when used in reference to a sexual homicide is based on the same factors that defined organized: victim and crime scene analysis, forensic evaluation, and assessment of the act itself. The unplanned, spontaneous nature of the disorganized perpetrator's crime is reflected in each of these factors. This "disorganization" may be the result of youthfulness of the offender, lack of criminal sophistication, use of drugs and alcohol, or mental deficiency.

Defining Characteristics

VICTIMOLOGY

The victim of a disorganized offender may be known to the offender since he often selects a victim of opportunity near his residence or employment. The victim is often from his own geographical area because this offender acts impulsively under stress and also because he derives confidence from familiar surroundings to bolster his feelings of social inadequacy.

If there are multiple victims of a disorganized offender, the age, sex, and other characteristics will show greater variance due to the more random nature of his selection process.

The risk factor of a disorganized sexual homicide victim is situational in the sense that by crossing the path of the offender, her risk is greatly elevated. The victim essentially becomes a casualty because he or she was in the wrong place at the wrong time. The other considerations when assessing victim and offender risk are as detailed in classification 131.

CRIME SCENE INDICATORS FREQUENTLY NOTED

The crime scene of a disorganized sexual homicide reflects the spontaneous, and in some cases symbolic, quality of the killing. It is random and sloppy with great disarray. The death scene and the crime scene are often the same.

The victim location is known since it usually is where he or she was going about usual daily activities when suddenly attacked by surprise. There is evidence of sudden violence to the victim, a blitz style of attack. Depersonalization may be present, as evidenced by the face being covered by a pillow or towels or in a more subtle way, as with the body rolled on the stomach.

There is no set plan of action deterring detection. The weapon is one of opportunity, obtained at the scene and left there. There is little or no effort to remove evidence, such as fingerprints from the scene. The body is left at the death scene, often in the position in which the victim was killed. There is no attempt or minimal attempt to conceal the body.

STAGING

Secondary criminal activity may be present, but usually it is more indicative of less sophisticated offender (disorganized offenders are often below average intelligence) than staging to confuse law enforcement.

The body may be positioned or deposited in a way that has special significance to the offender based on his sexually violent fantasies. It may be intended to make a statement or to obscure certain facts about the crime, for example, to disguise postmortem mutilation he is uncomfortable with. This should not be confused with staging, since the offender is generating a personal expression (personation) rather than deliberating trying to confuse the police.

Another example of the disorganized offender's personation of his ritualized sexual fantasies is the excessive mutilation of the breasts, genitals, or other areas of sexual association, such as the thighs, abdomen, buttocks, and neck. This overkill is the enactment of his fantasy.

COMMON FORENSIC FINDINGS

The disorganized offender is often socially inept and has strong feelings of inadequacy. These feelings of deficiency will compel him to assault the victim in an ambush, blitz style, that will immediately incapacitate her or him. Injury effected in a disorganized sexual homicide is usually done when the offender feels the least intimidated and the most comfortable with the victim. This will be when the victim is unconscious, dying, or postmortem. In addition, sexual assault will probably occur at this time for the same reasons.

There may be depersonalization, which entails mutilation to the face and overkill (excessive amount or severity of wounds or injury) to specific body parts. The face, genitals, and breasts are most often targeted for overkill. Body parts may be missing from the scene.

The blitz style of attack common to this homicide is often manifested by focused blunt trauma to the head and face and lack of defensive wounds. There is a prevalence of attack from behind. Since death is immediate to establish control over the victim, there is minimal use of restraints.

Sexual acts are postmortem and often involve insertion of foreign objects into body orifices (insertional necrophilia). This is often combined with acts of mutilation—for example, slashing, stabbing, and biting of the buttocks and breasts. Since these acts often do not coincide with completed acts of sexual penetration, evidence of semen may be found in the victim's clothing or (less frequently) wounds.

Most frequently death results from asphyxia, strangulation, blunt force, or the use of a pointed, sharp instrument.

Investigative Considerations

The disorganized offender usually lives alone or with a parental figure. He lives or works within close proximity to the crime scene. He has a history of inconsistent or poor work performance. He also has a past that demonstrates a lack of interpersonal skills, which may be manifested by involvement in relationships with a partner much younger or much older than he.

Preoffense circumstances demonstrate minimal situational stress and change in lifestyle. He will be considered odd by those who know him. This offender usually is sloppy and disheveled, with nocturnal habits such as walking aimlessly around his neighborhood.

Postoffense behavior exhibited may be a change in eating habits and drinking habits (more alcohol consumption) and nervousness. He may also have an inappropriate interest in the crime, for example, by frequently engaging in conversation about it.

Disorganized behavior may be evident in victim selection, crime scene, and forensics due to youthfulness, drug or alcohol impairment, external stressors (e.g., fear of discovery), or lack of criminal sophistication.

Search Warrant Suggestions

The disorganized offender does not concern himself with concealment of bloody clothing, shoes, or other evidentiary items such as victim belongings taken from the crime scene. In addition, souvenirs that serve as remembrances of the event and fuel the fantasy of the act may be found among offender possessions and in his computer files.

Case Study: 132: Sexual Homicide, Disorganized

Victimology

Jennifer Sidal, age 12, and her sister, Elaine, age 14, had decided to quit looking for Jenny's bicycle, which had been stolen a few hours earlier. It was eight o'clock and already quite dark out, so the two headed for home, Jenny on foot and Elaine on her bike. As Elaine rounded the corner of an electrical supply store, she glanced back and saw Jenny walking slowly, still a block away. Jenny had a physical problem that often caused her to lag behind the other children. Mentally, Jenny was very bright, with straight A's in school. Even though she was somewhat of a loner, she was considered friendly and was always quick to help others. Jenny lived with her mother and sister. Her parents had divorced 12 years previous, and although her father lived about 12 blocks away, she had not seen him for a year and a half.

Elaine arrived home a little after 8:00 p.m. Jenny never made it home. Her risk for being targeted as a victim of violent crime was minimal due to her lifestyle, social habits, and residence in a low-crime neighborhood. However, her young age and physical limitations elevated this risk factor. Because she was slower than other children, it was easier for an offender to single her out and separate her from a group. Her trusting attitude also may have been a factor elevating her risk level.

Jenny fit the victimology common to the disorganized sexual offender. She was a victim of opportunity, preyed on because her physical disability made her vulnerable and easy to get alone. This factor, plus her age, made her less of a threat to the inadequate type of person the disorganized offender usually is. This type of offender does not want a victim who will jeopardize his control of the situation. Her risk was situational: it was elevated because she crossed the path of the offender, giving him the opportunity to satisfy his need to rape and kill.

Crime Scene Indicators

The next day, Jenny's body was discovered by her uncle who was searching the area along with police and neighbors. The body was approximately halfway down a steep creek bank behind the electrical store. The creek had dense, high weeds and trees lining both banks. Although it was fenced off, there was a hole in the fence near the electrical supply store that neighborhood youths used when traveling to the adjacent residential area from local businesses.

The body was found approximately 10 feet down the creek bank path from the fence opening and 10 feet down the embankment. A small tree had prevented it from falling completely down the embankment. The embankment was quite steep, almost 90 degrees, and approximately 30 feet from path to creek. Jenny's shirt and bra were in place, but the body was nude from the waist down except for the socks. Some of the clothing was scattered along the creek bank, and her blue jeans and panties were found in the creek. The blue jeans were slit by a sharp instrument from the bottom cuff to just above both knees.

This crime scene was typical of the disorganized offender. The assault site, death scene, and body recovery site were all the same location. The weapon was one of opportunity: his fists to initially gain control and his arm to strangle the victim. The attack was a blitz style in which the offender struck Jenny with enough force to render her unconscious immediately. The body was left at the scene with little or no effort to conceal it. The crime scene portrayed the randomness and sloppiness characteristic of a disorganized offender. There was a high probability that foot-prints and other physical evidence had been left, but much of it was probably obliterated by a heavy rainfall before the body was discovered.

Forensic Findings

The autopsy revealed Jenny had died of strangulation. It was initially thought to be ligature strangulation by something large, for example, her blue jeans. The offender later described using his arm from behind to strangle her.

The focused blunt-force trauma, or depersonalization, often exhibited by disorganized offenders was present in this case. Jenny's face had been badly beaten with numerous cuts, abrasions, and contusions about the mouth and cheekbone areas. There was a lack of defensive wounds, another common forensic finding of this type of offense, since the victim is most often blitzed, with little chance to fight back. Restraints were not used, as is typical of the disorganized offender, for the same reasons defensive wounds are usually absent. A large amount of semen was found within the vaginal cavity; no semen was found elsewhere.

A more bizarre forensic finding noted with this case (yet routinely observed with the disorganized sexual killer) was the presence of deep postmortem cuts on the victim's wrists and forearms. There were also several "hesitation" cuts to these same areas—cuts that were almost exploratory in nature reflecting the offender's curiosity. They were not part of the sexual assault.

Investigation

As a result of numerous interviews by the local police, a sketch was prepared and placed on local television and newspapers. In conjunction with this, the FBI Investigative Support Unit (ISU) at Quantico, Virginia, provided an offender profile for the police to narrow the growing list of suspects. The offender was profiled as living in the same area as the victim. He would be known as a troublemaker who liked knives and had previous contact with the police, although not necessarily any arrests.

Several neighbors of the victim (and suspect) called police to report that a person who closely resembled the sketch lived in their neighborhood. Further investigation revealed this subject exactly matched the profile. The police again consulted the ISU for interrogation techniques to be used with this subject. As a result, 17-year-old Joseph Rogers confessed and then reenacted the crime for investigators. It was discovered he had previous contacts with Jenny, talking to her several nights before the attack. He was living a few blocks away from her, with a 16-year-old girlfriend. He had left home to make it on his own. He had drifted around, was unemployed, and a high school dropout. Roger pleaded guilty.

133: Sexual Homicide, Mixed

A crime scene may reflect aspects of both organized and disorganized characteristics for the following reasons:

- More than one offender may be involved; therefore, differing behavioral patterns will be manifested.
- The attack may begin as a well-ordered, planned assault, but it deteriorates as unanticipated events occur, for example, an inability to control the victim.
- The primary motive for the attack may be solely rape, but victim resistance or the offender's emotional state of mind leads to an escalation. This is especially seen with the hostile or retaliatory type of rapist. The victim selection may reflect an organized offender who carefully selects and stalks the victim. But then the body is not concealed or is poorly

concealed. The weapon is one of opportunity (e.g., a rock) that is left at the scene, and the crime scene would show great disarray. Forensic findings would show a blitz style of attack, overkill, blunt-force trauma, and often personal weapon use (hands and feet).

- Inconsistencies in offender behavior manifested during the offense may exhibit varying degrees of organized or disorganized behavior. The youthfulness of the offender and alcohol or drug involvement also contribute to a mixed crime scene.

- External stressors may alter the behavior of an offender. Precipitating factors that cause a buildup of tension may lead to an explosive, impetuous assault by a person who would normally approach the crime with planning and control. Ted Bundy is an example of this degeneration of an organized killer into a disorganized one due to external stressors. With all of his abduction–rape–murders previous to the Chi Omega murders, he carefully selected, stalked, and abducted his victims and used meticulous body concealment. His discomfort with the fugitive lifestyle, among other things, led to the explosive homicidal spree in which he bludgeoned random victims of opportunity (although coeds, they were random compared to his usual careful selection). Bundy used a weapon of opportunity obtained at the crime scene and left near another. He left their bodies openly displayed at the death scene, a marked departure from his usual attempts of body disposal. All of these later actions describe the typical behavior of the disorganized killer.

Case Study: 133: Sexual Homicide, Mixed

Victimology

Donna Lynn Vetter was raised in a rural environment that did not seem to equip her for life in San Antonio.

She used fresh air through open windows and doors instead of the air conditioner in order to save electricity: in her mind, frugality was more of an issue where she had lived than rape or murder. It was this naive and unsuspecting attitude that became a contributing factor to her death.

Vetter worked as a stenographer for the FBI in San Antonio. She had left home for the first time seven months earlier to move closer to her job. She was described as a quiet and hardworking introvert who rarely initiated conversation with fellow employees. She would usually stand quietly on the periphery and listen to the office chatter, almost never contributing her own thoughts or ideas.

When considering the list of characteristics that identify a victim's risk level, Donna Vetter would have been considered one less likely to be targeted as a victim, especially when compared to the other end of the spectrum (e.g., prostitutes). Her employment as an FBI stenographer; conservative dress and lifestyle (she did not go to bars or nightclubs); total lack of alcohol or drug use and criminal history; a modest income; and a quiet, withdrawn personality all contributed to this low-risk status. In addition, her age and physical state (no handicaps) did not increase her vulnerability as in some cases (elderly, children).

Nevertheless, two factors elevated her risk factor. One was the location of her apartment: an industrialized and commercial area of a lower-income blue-collar neighborhood. The second component was her trusting attitude and lack of concern for personal safety. She came from an environment in which rape and murder were distant concerns compared to the electric bill. Donna cooled her apartment using fresh air from open windows and doors just as she had done all her life in the country. She would simply smile at the concerns that her fellow employees or apartment security would voice over her lack of safety precautions.

On September 4, 1986, at approximately 9:10 p.m., Donna was observed watching television and doing leg exercises by a neighbor walking by her window (open as usual). At 10:30 p.m. as several other neighbors passed by her apartment, one noticed that the front window screen had been pulled out and notified security. Apartment security responded at 10:35 p.m. and found the front door ajar. Upon entering the apartment, they discovered Donna's nude body lying on the floor covered with blood.

Crime Scene Indicators

Donna was lying on her back on the living room floor. The fatal assault site appeared to be the kitchen, where the greatest concentration of blood was found in several large pools. A kitchen knife, a weapon of opportunity, was responsible for her wounds. It was found stuck between chair cushions. She had been dragged from the kitchen through the dining room, leaving a pronounced trail of blood. In the kitchen were her shorts, shirt, and underwear, apparently cut and torn off her. Her glasses were under the dining room table. Her car keys were on the table. There were no indications of ransacking in the apartment, and nothing appeared missing. The point of entry had been the front window: the screen was pulled out and a plant overturned just inside. There were footprints and palm prints on the murder weapon and living room end table.

The primary motive for this attack was rape, but when Vetter offered resistance, the offender responded with violence. Fighting back only heightened the anger and need for retaliation that he usually vented through raping. His inflamed emotional state made the line between rape and murder an easy one to cross.

Initial contact between Donna and the offender was a blitz style of attack. She was coming out of the bathroom when he hit her in the face, knocking her to the floor unconscious. Apparently Donna recovered enough to make it to the kitchen and grab a knife. This final act of resistance was enough to push the offender to the point of total retaliation. He grabbed the knife and repeatedly stabbed Vetter, dragged her to living room, and sexually assaulted her as she lay dying.

The death scene and crime scene were the same, with no attempt to conceal the body. Palm prints, fingerprints, and footprints were left at the scene, all components indicative of the offender's disregard of physical evidence due to the frenzied, unexpected escalation of violence.

Thus, elements of both organization and disorganization were apparent with this offense because of the volatile nature of an anger retaliatory rapist and the response of a conservative, naive girl. His inability to establish control over Vetter resulted in a deterioration of events that resulted in a more disorganized crime scene.

Forensic Findings

Donna had sustained blunt-force trauma to the face. In addition, there were three stab wounds to the chest, with one wound penetrating the heart, and stab wounds to the right calf and left upper thigh. There were defensive wounds to three fingers of the left hand and evidence of sexual assault.

A blitz-style attack, common to the anger retaliatory rapist who wants control of the victim as quickly as possible, was evident with this murder. The facial injuries were evidence of the excessive level of force employed by this type of rapist, especially when confronted with a resisting victim.

Palm prints, fingerprints, and footprints were subsequently linked to a subject, who was arrested for rape less than a month after the murder.

Investigation

On September 24, 1986, the San Antonio Police Department arrested 22-year-old Karl Hammond for the rape of a 30-year-old San Antonio woman. He was later linked to Donna Vetter's death when palm prints on the outside living room window and living room end table, fingerprints on the murder weapon, and footprints in the apartment proved to be his.

Hammond was a repeat offender; he had been convicted for the rape of a 17-year-old girl five years earlier. He had struck her in the face when she refused him sex and then raped her. He also was arrested for burglary three days after his release on bond for the rape charge. After serving four years, Hammond was released from the state prison in August 23, 1985, under provisions of the mandatory release program. At the time of his arrest, he was suspected of as many as 15 other Northeast Side rapes.

Outcome

Shackled and gagged due to numerous outbursts, Hammond appeared before a judge in March 1986. The jury found him guilty of capital murder. Before his sentencing, he escaped through an unlocked door in the jail but was recaptured within 48 hours in downtown San Antonio.

The case received a great amount of criticism, most notably from appeal lawyer Jordan Steiker, who felt Hammond had not received a fair trial: he was not allowed to testify, pertinent family background information was not introduced (specifically, he witnessed his own father being murdered by his brother), and he suffered audio and visual hallucinations. Denied clemency, Karl Hammond was put to death by injection on June 22, 1995, when he was thirty years old. When asked for a final statement, Hammond responded, "I know it's hard for people to lose someone they loved so much. . . . It's best for me to just say nothing at all."

134: Sexual Homicide, Sadistic

A sexual sadist is one who has established an enduring pattern of sexual arousal in response to sadistic imagery. Sexual gratification is obtained from torture involving excessive mental and physical means. The offender derives the greatest satisfaction from the victim's response to torture. Sexually sadistic fantasies in which sexual acts are paired with domination, degradation, and violence are translated into criminal action that results in death.

Defining Characteristics

Sadistic murder victimology has some similarities to the victimology described in classification 131.

Sexual sadists focus on victims who are White, female adults who are strangers. The victimology of this crime may include males, and multiple offenders have been known to prey on both women and men and may also target children, but exclusive victimization of children is less frequent. Blacks are preyed on to a much lesser extent.

There is an occasional indication of resemblance between a victim and someone of significance in the offender's life.

The victims are chosen through systematic stalking and surveillance. They are approached under a pretext such as requesting or offering assistance, asking directions, or impersonation of a police officer. A ruse may be employed: posing as a talent scout looking for perspective models or actresses and promising them jobs, for example.

There are also documented cases of sexually sadistic torture and the death of two victims involving the same event.

CRIME SCENE INDICATORS FREQUENTLY NOTED

There are often multiple crime scenes involved with this type of sexual homicide: place of initial encounter, torture and death scene, and body disposal site. The very nature of this crime, sadism expressed through torture, necessitates a secluded or solitary place for the prolonged period of time the offender spends with the victim. This captivity may range from a few hours to as long as six weeks. The offender's residence may be used if it can provide the required seclusion. The offender's vehicle will be altered for use in abduction and torture, disabling windows and doors, soundproofing, and installing police accessories.

Gloves are often worn to avoid fingerprints. Secluded sites are selected well in advance. The offender undertakes his crime with methodical preparation, and the crime scene reflects this. Torture racks or specially equipped torture rooms are constructed. Weapons and torture implements of choice are bought to the scene and removed if it is outside.

Restraints are usually present at the crime scene since they are common to this homicide. Sexual bondage, which is the elaborate and excessive use of binding material, unnecessarily neat and symmetrical binding, or binding that enables positioning the victim in a variety of positions that enhance the offender's sexual arousal is also noted.

The use of customized modes of torture may be evident, especially at the scene of torture and death, which include electrical appliances, vise grips, pliers, foreign objects used for insertion, and whips. Sexual arousal occurs most often with the victim's expression of pain and is evidenced by sexual fluids or possibly defecation at the scene.

The body is routinely concealed especially with the more organized offender, who is prepared with shovels, lime, and remote burial sites. Bodies have been burned also. Sometimes inconsistencies are noted, however, as victims have been left where they will be seen by intimates, can be easily found, or disposed of carelessly. Occasionally, the body may be transported to a location that increases the chance of discovery because the offender wants the excitement derived from the publicity that the body's discovery generates.

STAGING

It is possible that there are implications of overkill or depersonalization for pragmatic reasons, for example, to obscure the victim's identity. The offender may also tamper with the crime scene by staging secondary criminal activity (e.g., rape–murder, robbery) to veil the primary motive of sadistic murder.

COMMON FORENSIC FINDINGS

The offender engages in sex prior to death. "The Sexually Sadistic Criminal and His Offenses" (Dietz, Hazelwood, & Warren, 1990) lists the most prevalent sexual acts forced on victims: anal rape, forced fellatio, vaginal rape, and foreign object penetration (in decreasing order). A majority of offenders forced their victims to engage in more than three of these activities. The attack is antemortem since the primary source of pleasure for the sadistic killer is in the pain caused the victim as opposed to the actual sexual act.

The focus of battery is to the sex organs, genitals, and breasts. Sexually sadistic acts may include biting or overkill to areas with sexual association: thighs, buttocks, neck, and abdomen, in addition to the breasts and genitals. However, injury can be anywhere that causes suffering, for example, the elbow.

There is insertion of foreign objects into vaginal or anal cavities often combined with the act of slashing, cutting, or biting the breasts and buttocks. Evidence of sexual fluids is usually found in the body orifices and around the body. If partners are involved, this may be evidenced by differing sexual fluids and pubic hairs. Offenders may also urinate on the victim.

Ligature marks are common since restraints are frequently used, along with blindfolds and gags. Sexual bondage is prevalent.

The fact that the offender usually spends a long time with the victim is evidenced by varying wound and injury ages or varying stages of healing present in injuries inflicted by the offender. Blunt-force trauma from beatings; injuries from painful insertion, biting, whipping, and twisting breasts; and burn marks from heat sources and electrical devices are all possible forensic findings.

There are cases where victims were forced to drink or eat feces. Stomach contents reveal this, as well as any variations of it.

The act of killing is often eroticized; death comes in a slow, deliberate manner that the offender savors. But since an unconscious or dead victim does not afford the offender the gratification he seeks, great care is taken not to prematurely end her or his life. This caution is demonstrated by several cases in which subjects not only took special measures to keep their victim's conscious but actually revived near-dead victims in order to cause additional suffering.

The most common cause of death is by an asphyxial modality in the form of ligature strangulation, manual strangulation, hanging, and suffocation. Gunshot wounds, cutting and stabbing wounds, and blunt-force trauma are less frequent forensic findings as to cause of death.

Investigative Considerations

The perpetrators of sexually sadistic homicides are predominantly White males. Sometimes a partner is involved, either male or female. The subjects can be married while committing these offense, as shown by the research data of "The Sexually Sadistic Criminal and His Offenses" (Dietz et al., 1990); 43% are married, and 50% have children.

The offender is often involved with an occupation that brings him into contact with the public. He engages in antisocial behavior that may be manifested in arrest records (not necessarily sex-related offenses) and a history of drug abuse other than alcohol. He is often a police buff who possesses paraphernalia, literature, and weapon collections. The offender is likely to have a well-maintained vehicle since excessive driving is also characteristic of the sexual sadist.

The offender may return to the scene to determine if the body has been discovered or to check on the progress of the investigation.

Search Warrant Suggestions

The following are items common to sadistic offenders that should be included in a search warrant:

- Collection of items related to sexual or violent themes or both: pornographic literature, videos, bondage paraphernalia, detective magazines, sexual devices, and women's undergarments.
- Gun collections, police uniforms, badges, counterfeit ID, and books detailing law enforcement procedures.
- Vehicle modification to resemble police car; black-wall tires; two-way radios; a Bearcat scanner; whip antenna; flashing red lights; sirens for abduction or torture; disabled door handles and windows; soundproofing; restraining devices; shovels, lime, and other burial equipment; water and food; and extra fuel.
- Torture devices, cameras, recording equipment, and personal computers.
- Dealing with offenses: written records; manuscripts, diaries, threatening letters, calendars, sketches, drawings, audiotapes, videotapes, and photographs; personal items belonging to victims: undergarments, shoes, jewelry, wallet, driver's license, other victim ID.

Case Study: 134: Sexual Homicide, Sadistic
The Tool Box Killers

Background

During the last year of his incarceration at California Men's Colony at San Luis Obispo, Roy Lewis Norris met Lawrence Sigmund Bittaker. Both inmates had an extensive history with the law that involved a substantial amount of violent criminal activity. As the relationship developed, the two discovered several topics of mutual interest: dominating, torturing, and raping women. They also shared the attitude that with any future sexual assaults on women, they would leave no witnesses.

Bittaker was released in November 1978 and Norris in January 1979. After their reunion, the duo decided to fulfill their prison ambitions. The first thing they needed was the proper vehicle to ensure uncomplicated abductions. Bittaker found a 1977 silver GMC cargo van with a sliding door and no windows on the side, perfect for pulling up close and grabbing their victims.

Bittaker and Norris felt well prepared after spending the first half of 1979 outfitting the van with a twin-size mattress supported by wood and plywood, tools, clothes, and a cooler. They had carefully selected a remote area in the San Gabriel Mountains above the city of Glendora. It was a gated fire road that Bittaker secured with his own lock, added insurance that they would be left undisturbed. In addition, they had picked up more than 20 hitchhikers, not attacking any of them, but simply rehearsing for the right day.

The "right" day came on June 24, 1979, and at least four other times between June and October 31, 1979, during which Bittaker and Norris were responsible for at least five murders.

Victimology

Lucinda Schaeffer, age 16, lived with her grandmother in Torrance, California. She was an attractive girl who was active with her church, including the senior high fellowship group. On June 24, 1979, she attended a fellowship meeting at St. Andrew's Presbyterian Church in Redondo Beach. She had decided to leave early and walked home along Pacific Coast Highway instead of calling her grandmother for a ride.

Bittaker spotted her, making the comment, "There's a cute little blonde." The van pulled alongside her, and Norris asked her if she wanted to go for a ride and smoke some grass. She refused and kept on walking, with Norris and Bittaker following at a distance. Bittaker pulled up ahead of her and Norris waited on the sidewalk as Cindy approached. When she had reached him, the two exchanged a few words. Norris then grabbed her and dragged her to the van, threw her inside, and slammed the door. The van squealed out, and Bittaker turned the radio up to mask Cindy's screams. Norris taped her mouth and bound her hands and feet as they drove to the fire road.

Once they arrived, Bittaker and Norris smoked some pot while asking Cindy questions about her family and boyfriend in Wisconsin. After they grew bored, Bittaker and Norris took turns raping her. Next, Norris attempted to strangle Cindy but lost his nerve when he saw the anguished look in her eyes. Bittaker took over until Cindy collapsed to the ground, convulsing and attempting to breathe. Bittaker remarked that it took more to strangle someone than television showed, and Norris agreed. The two then tightened a coat hanger around her neck with a pair of vise-grip pliers until she was finally still. They wrapped her body with a blue shower curtain so the blood from the hanger cutting into her neck would not get on the van's carpet and dumped her body over the side of a deep canyon.

On July 8, Bittaker and Norris were again stalking victims on the Pacific Coast Highway when they spotted Andrea Joy Hall, age 18, hitchhiking. She was picked up by Bittaker and, at his urging, Andrea obtained a drink from the cooler in the back of the van, at which point Norris made his move to subdue her. Andrea's assault was much like Cindy's, with the exception that she was photographed, providing souvenirs for her killers to recall the look of terror on her face. At this point, Bittaker and Norris were becoming comfortable enough with their crime to experiment with torturing their victims, verbally and then physically. Andrea had an ice pick jabbed into her brain, first through one ear then the other. She was then strangled and thrown over the cliff.

The next two victims were Jackie Doris Gilliam, age 15, and Jacqueline Leah Lamp, age 13. The girls had been walking and hitchhiking casually along the road and had stopped for a rest at a bus stop bench when the van pulled up beside them. They entered the van voluntarily but became uneasy when the van turned away from the beach and headed for the mountains. As Leah attempted to open the van door, Norris struck her over the head with a bat. Bittaker stopped to help Norris subdue the two girls and then headed to the San Dimas.

Gilliam and Lamp were held for nearly 48 hours before they were tortured and murdered. Norris took approximately 24 instant pictures of Gilliam and Bittaker engaged in various sexual acts. She was then stabbed through the ear with an ice pick, manually strangled, and finally struck on the head with a sledgehammer.

Norris claims that Lamp was not sexually assaulted. Before he savagely battered her head with the sledgehammer, Bittaker remarked, "You wanted to stay a virgin; now you can die a virgin." With this torture session, as well with the next one, Bittaker and Norris decided to preserve their exploits by using a tape recorder.

Shirley Lynette Ledford was last seen hitchhiking on October 31, 1979, in Sun Valley. After Bittaker and Norris picked her up hitchhiking, they enacted the assault differently; instead of heading for their spot in the mountains, they opted to drive around the streets of San Fernando Valley. She was struck on the elbows repeatedly with a three-pound sledgehammer. Bittaker decided Ledford was not screaming loud enough to suit him, so he retrieved a pair of pliers and vise grips from his toolbox and pinched her nipples and vagina with them. Ledford's nude body was dumped on the front lawn of a Sunland residence, to see "what kind of press they would get."

Review of the victimology in this case illustrates several points that are common to sadistic murder committed by organized offenders. The victims were targeted because they suited the preferences of Bittaker and Norris: all of the victims were White females, within a narrow age range, unknown to the offenders, and considered high-risk victims because they were hitchhiking. (Schaeffer was not hitchhiking, but walking along the highway elevated her risk as a victim.)

Crime Scene Indicators

Bittaker and Norris's crime scenes typified organized sadistic murder. They were carefully planned offenses that reflected overall control in conversation and of the victims themselves by the use of restraints. Bittaker derived enjoyment from engaging victims in conversation that he governed. He used the conversation as a means of torture in itself; making victims plead for their lives substantiated his sense of domination.

Their abductions were well planned, beginning with the customizing they did on the van. The weapons, the tools of their assault, were never an issue until capture since the actual crime scene was within the van. At the abduction sites, the only evidence left behind was Schaeffer's shoe.

Bittaker and Norris transported the victims to remote sites that posed little to no risk of interruption or discovery. This ensured the lengthy contact with the victims that was required to fulfill the fantasies and drives that fueled their acts of sadistic murder. Several bodies were transported to a different disposal site from the death scene. With Norris's help, the broken skeletal remains of Gilliam and Lamp were found scattered over an area hundreds of feet along the canyon floor. No traces of Schaeffer or Hall's body were found due to the well-selected disposal sites. All of these indicators common to Bittaker and Norris crime scenes are evidence of controlled, organized offenders.

The setting of Ledford's death and assault was still within the realm of the organized, controlled scene, despite the body being left in view with no effort to conceal it. Bittaker's craving for some press time, recognition of his crime, was his incentive for this change in modus operandi (MO).

Forensic Findings

Lucinda Schaeffer and Andrea Hall's remains were never found. Partial remains of Gilliam and Lamp, including their battered skulls, were found in the Glendora Mountains. Gilliam still had the ice pick inserted in her right ear.

Shirley Ledford's autopsy revealed that death was due to strangulation with a wire ligature around the neck. There was evidence of multiple blunt-force trauma to the face, head, and breasts. Her rectum, the lining inside her rectum, and her vagina had been torn from being stretched too far, in part due to the insertion of a pair of pliers by Bittaker. There were bruises on her left elbow, a cut to the right index finger, and a puncture wound to the left hand. The wrists and ankles had ligature marks as well.

Ledford's autopsy report presented similar indicators of an organized sadistic murder as mentioned in possible forensic findings: focused blunt-force attack to the genital regions and the breasts, traumatic insertion by foreign objects, sodomy, and evidence of torture (hammer and pliers). There were sexual and aggressive acts prior to death, and restraints were used. In addition, Norris and Bittaker spent extended periods of time with the victims.

Investigation

Bittaker and Norris engaged in other crimes during this time beside sadistic murder. There were at least three separate incidents: an attempted rape, rape–kidnapping, and an assault with mace. Photos were also found after Bittaker and Norris's arrest that are indicative of another victim, an unknown White female, who remains missing.

One of the victims who was raped and released identified Bittaker and Norris as her assailants. They were arrested for charges other than the rape–murder charges in hope that one or both would fold under interrogation and confess. Norris eventually did, shifting the blame to Bittaker in an attempt to save himself.

The motive for Bittaker and Norris's brutal murders is perhaps best explained by Ronald Markman, a forensic psychiatrist who examined the offenders. He describes them as sociopaths who knew right from wrong but simply did not care (Markman & Bosco, 1989).

Outcome

On March 18, 1980, Norris pleaded guilty on five counts of murder, turning state's evidence against his friend. In return for his cooperation, he received a sentence of 45 years to life, with parole possible after 30 years. Bittaker denied everything. At his trial on February 5, 1981, he testified that Norris first informed him of the murders after their arrest in 1979. A jury chose to disbelieve him, returning a guilty verdict on February 17. On March 24, in accordance with the jury's recommendation, Bittaker was sentenced to death. The judge imposed an alternate sentence of 199 years 4 months, to take effect in the event that Bittaker's death sentence is ever commuted to life imprisonment. Bittaker is still on death row at San Quentin Prison, while Norris still sits at Pelican Bay Prison in California.

135: Elder Female Sexual Homicide*

This classification is used to refer to the homicide of a woman 60 years of age or older where the primary motive of the offender is identified through the sexual behavior at the crime scene. With the majority of these offenders, there is often some form of sexual intercourse. Despite the sexual interaction, there is often the absence of semen. In addition, many of these offenders engage in other sexual acts to include foreign object insertion and oral copulation (the offender both performing and receiving oral copulation on and from the victim, respectively). The offender may use his mouth on other sexualized areas of the victim, insert his fingers into her, and engage in other types of physical contact that focus on the sexual areas of the body. Despite the fact that the offenders in these cases are diverse in age and split relatively evenly between Black and White offenders (with a less significant contribution by Hispanic offenders), many collective demographic, lifestyle, and behavioral characteristics are found to be strikingly similar. These observations are consistent with the experience of investigators who have anecdotally described violent offenders of the elderly as younger offenders, assaulting the victims at or close to the victims' residences, living within close proximity to the crime scene, and generally unknown to the victim.

Defining Characteristics

VICTIMOLOGY

Elderly women are inherently more vulnerable to crime than younger women. First, they are more likely to live alone. Nearly 80% of elderly persons who live alone are female due in large part to an increased risk of widowhood and longer life expectancy (Taeuber & Allen, 1990). Second, for the elder female, vulnerability is related to physical size and strength. They are less capable of fleeing or resisting a physical attack than a younger person (Nelson & Huff-Corzine, 1998). As women age, they experience skeletal, neuromuscular, and other systemic changes that restrict mobility and reduce their abilities to escape or defend themselves. Elderly women, perhaps because of widowhood, are more likely than younger females to lack the guardianship common to children and younger women and thus are more likely to be perceived by motivated offenders as suitable targets. This vulnerability concept revealed that some rapists select elderly victims because of their vulnerability. Safarik and Jarvis (2005) noted that the sexual assault of the elder female is often an exceptionally violent crime

---

*Classification contributed by Mark Safarik.

that is motivated by the offender's desire to punish, dominate, and control his victim rather than the often assumed motive of sexual attraction or desire.

Safarik, Jarvis, and Nussbaum (2000), in a focused study of this type of sexual homicide, found that the mean age was seventy-seven. The victims were disproportionately White (86%). Blacks (9%) and Hispanics (4%) were also victimized, but Asian victims were rare. Ninety-four percent were killed in their own residences. Although elder females are the predominant residents of nursing homes and long-term care facilities and the victims of sexual assault in those facilities, sexual homicides in that setting are rare. The overwhelming majority of these women had lived in their residences for at least ten years, and many had lived there substantially longer. Unfortunately, this longevity may have produced unrecognized risk to the victim. White victims of Black and Hispanic offenders lived in neighborhoods characterized as transitional. These transitional neighborhoods were thought to have undergone a socioeconomic change from middle to lower class. Often accompanying such a change are other demographic transformations that result in social disorganization and increased criminal activity.

Contributing to their vulnerability, the majority of these victims had no home security beyond standard door and window locks. When examining the cause of death, strangulation was found to be the most frequently identified cause of death followed by blunt-force trauma. Death by a firearm was the least frequent.

Although the elderly in general are considered to be at low risk for becoming crime victims, elderly White females, particularly those living alone, are at an elevated risk in this type of homicide. Because they live alone, their risk level is situationally elevated, and they are thus perceived to be vulnerable by their offenders. The offender also perceives his risk to be lower. Once inside the residence, he is able to interact with the victim without interruption. The fact that she is elderly significantly reduces her ability to resist, protect herself, and escape. The majority of these women are injured more rather than less severely.

OFFENDERS

Offender populations are represented evenly between White and Black offenders, with a much smaller contribution by Hispanic offenders. Black males, though, are overrepresented when compared to U.S. population demographics. Black males cross the racial barrier and offend against both Black and White victims, as do Hispanic offenders. Recognizing the intraracial nature of these crimes appears to be applicable only if the victim is Black. If the victim is White, the intraracial aspect of violent offending does not appear to be as germane. White offenders rarely offend interracially. The proximity of the offender's residence to the crime scene is significantly influenced by the racial homogeneity of the neighborhood. Interracial offending of Blacks against Whites occurs more in heterogeneous communities. White against Black offending was found to be virtually nonexistent in heterogeneous communities. Nearly 60% of offenders live within six blocks of the victim, and with juveniles, half live on the same block. Most travel to and depart the scene on foot.

Despite their age or race, the offenders were found to have many similar attributes. For instance, 90% have criminal records, with burglary (59%) making up the highest proportion. Property and violent offenses were found to be nearly equally represented among those with criminal histories. Only a fifth of the offenders had a criminal history involving sexual offenses. This is important to remember because investigators confronted with investigating these crimes often spend precious initial time compiling lists of registered sex offenders. It is recommended that consideration be given to the fact that the overwhelming majority will not have such a criminal history. Most are unskilled and unemployed and have less than a high school education. Nearly all had a history of substance abuse, with alcohol, marijuana, and cocaine as the drugs most often abused. Finally, nearly half of the offenders confessed to the crime subsequent to their arrest, while another 19% made some kind of an admission relative to the crime yet continued to deny responsibility for the homicide. In terms of racial differences, Whites were observed to have confessed nearly twice as often as Blacks.

CRIME SCENE INDICATORS FREQUENTLY NOTED

Multiple crime scenes are rare. The initial encounter, assault, homicide, and subsequent postmortem activity usually occur at one location. Weapons are rarely brought to the scene. If the offender uses a weapon, he usually obtains it from the scene. Ligatures used to strangle, blunt-force objects, and knives are often found near the victim and subsequently left at the scene. Most offenders gain access to the victims through unlocked doors and windows or by using a ruse or con. The balance use force to gain access.

The approach used by most of the offenders was a blitz attack: the immediate and overwhelming use of injurious force to incapacitate the victim. Because offenders use the blitz approach, the use of restraints is rarely noted. Safarik and Jarvis (2005) developed the Homicide Injury Scale as a metric to assess the level of injury and provide quantitative evidence to support the differentiation of levels of homicidal injury. The severity of injury inflicted by the offender has been found to be predictive of both age and how close that offender lives to his victim. With respect to age, it is an inverse relationship: The more injury related to the victim's cause of death, the younger the offender. When assessing where the offender lives in relationship to the victim, empirical evidence supports the observation that the more severe the injuries are, the closer the offender lives to the victim.

Nearly three-fourths of the offenders killed their victims between 8:00 p.m. and 4:00 a.m., with most of those occurring after midnight. Offenders were found to have sexually assaulted their victims both vaginally and anally, with vaginal assault occurring three to four times as often. Overall, the offenders inserted foreign objects into the victim's body 22% of the time, with White offenders responsible for more than half of those cases. In addition, offenders younger than 24 years of age were responsible for more than half of all foreign object insertion. Semen was identified in fewer than half of the cases, with no differences noted for race or age. Sexual activity without the presence of semen was noted in the remaining cases. This sexual activity included fondling the sexual areas of the body, foreign object insertion, and posing the victim to expose the sexual areas of the body. Torture, more commonly found in organized offenders, is rarely seen with these offenders. Since the majority of offenders use a blitz approach, the sexual assault and interaction with the victim often occur during or subsequent to the victim's death.

Offenders are neither acquaintances nor complete strangers to their victims, but instead fall somewhere in between. This does not imply that a prior relationship existed between the offender and victim but rather that the offender was aware of where the victim lived prior to the crime and perceived her to be alone and vulnerable. These offenders generally have simple fantasies and can be described as concrete thinkers, rarely planning their crimes but instead acting impulsively. Although the majority remove property from the scene, the motive for their removal is financial gain. These offenders are not removing items described by law enforcement as trophies or souvenirs. They typically take cash and small items such as jewelry. These items are generally taken from the immediate vicinity of the victim or are located on the pathway out of the scene.

COMMON FORENSIC FINDINGS

These offenders are not evidence conscious and inadvertently tend to leave significant forensic evidence at their crime scenes. Semen may be identified vaginally, anally, and orally, as well as on the body and on clothing items near the body. The breasts should be swabbed for saliva. Fingerprints and trace evidence, including hairs and fibers, are commonly found on and around the victim. A number of offenders leave personal items at the scene—for example, hats, bandannas, underwear, and personal identification. Most activity engaged in by the offender, including the sexual interaction, occurs postmortem. Strangulation either as a single cause of death or in combination with blunt-force trauma or stabbing is the most prevalent cause of death. The level of injury noted in these cases is excessive and is an attribute believed to be distinct from other violent crimes.

Investigative Considerations

Hazelwood and Douglas's work (1980), which offers a categorization of sexual murderers on a continuum from organized to disorganized, may have significance. Applying this typology, these offenders are found to be overwhelmingly consistent with the disorganized typology. With that typology as a base of personality and behavioral characteristics and the empirical data revealing how close many of these offenders live to their victims, the neighborhood investigation becomes the key to identifying the perpetrators. Despite age and race considerations, the offenders are a homogeneous group from a lifestyle and behavioral perspective. The neighborhood investigation should be thorough and focus on persons in the area who evidence many of the personality, lifestyle, and behavioral characteristics highlighted here.

Overall, they can be described as socially inadequate, undereducated, and unemployed, or if employed it is in unskilled physical labor. Most have a criminal history, with burglary the most commonly observed. Their criminal activities are populated by misdemeanor-type offenses rather than serious felonies, including sexual offenses. This indicates that the offender is less likely to reside in a registered sex offender database. The majority are drug users and abusers. Because the majority are unemployed, they typically reside with someone on whom they are financially dependent. Nearly three-quarters are unmarried, and nearly half live with family members. Their average age is 27.

Most take cash, jewelry, or other small items of value. The theft of these items is for financial gain and is not taken to serve as mementos of the event for later fantasy enhancement.

Studies have shown that as the degree of injury severity increases, the offender age generally decreases, and he is likely to live closer to rather than farther from the victim. Juvenile offenders are more likely to be violent, live closer, engage in postmortem mutilation and foreign object insertion, and target women 75 years of age and older. They are less likely to leave semen.

Interviewing arrested offenders should focus on the financial gain aspect of the crime and avoid (at least initially) the sexual assault component. The interviews should be one-on-one, avoiding multiple interviewers. The interviewer should take a soft and empathetic approach despite the heinous nature of the homicide.

Search Warrant Considerations

See search warrant considerations under 130.

Case Study: 135: Elder Female Sexual Homicide

Case Contributed by Kevin Faherty

Between June 14, 1962, and January 4, 1964, thirteen single women in the Boston area were victims of a brutal death by strangulation. The question lingers today as to whether it was the work of one serial killer or several killers. At the time, it was determined that at least 11 of the homicides were the work of one man. All of the women were killed in their apartment, had been sexually assaulted, and were strangled with an article of their own clothing. In each instance, there were no signs of forced entry, meaning the perpetrator was either known to them or let in voluntarily. In 1965, Albert DeSalvo confessed to all of the eleven Boston Strangler murders, in addition to two more deaths. At the time, people who knew him contended he could not be responsible for such crimes, and the argument for his innocence can still be made today.

Victimology

Six of the 11 were between the ages of 55 and 75, and the other five ranged in age from 19 to 23. The other two possibilities were aged 69 and 85. On June 14, 1962, 55-year-old Back Bay resident Anna Slesers was found by her son at about 7:00 p.m. She was lying nude on her bathroom floor, face up, with her legs spread apart and the cord from her bathrobe tied around her neck. She had been sexually assaulted by an unknown object. Her apartment had been ransacked, with objects and drawers everywhere in attempt to make it look like a burglary, but nothing was missing.

Two weeks later Nina Nichols, age 68, of Brighton, was found with her legs spread and her housecoat and slip pulled up to her waist. She had been strangled by her two nylon stockings, which had been tied in a bow around her neck. She too had been sexually abused, and her vagina and anus were lacerated. Again her apartment was a mess, but nothing was missing.

That same day in Lynn, 65-year-old Helen Blake was killed at about 8:00 a.m. She was found face down and nude on her bed with her legs spread. She too had been strangled by a nylon, and there was also a brassiere tied around her neck in a bow. Two diamond rings were removed from her fingers, the first instance of robbery.

The police commissioner notified women to lock their doors and be wary of all strangers. The police began to investigate sex offenders and violent former mental patients. They were on the lookout for a man who sought older women in order to take out his hatred for his mother.

In mid-August of that year, Ida Irga, age 75, of Boston's West End was found on her back, nightdress torn, exposing her body. In a grotesque parody of an obstetrical position, her legs were spread about five feet, each raised on a separate chair, with a pillow under her buttocks, and the pillowcase knotted tightly around her neck. She was facing the front door, so that her body would be seen immediately when someone entered. The next day, Jane Sullivan, a 67-year-old Dorchester resident, was found after being dead for 10 days. She was found face down, nude in her bathtub, with her head under the faucet and her feet draped over the other end of the tub. She had been strangled by her nylons in the kitchen or hallway, where her blood was found. There may have been sexual assault, but her body had decomposed too much to tell. This killing was followed by a three-month break, where all detectives could do was rule out possible suspects.

In December, again in the Back Bay, 21-year-old African American Sophie Clark was found by her roommates on the living room floor, legs spread, with nylons and her slip tied around her neck. There was evidence of assault, and for the first time, semen was found on the rug. This was the first younger woman to be killed by the Strangler. Another woman in the building had seen a strange man there to check her paint, and when he complimented her on her figure, she silenced him, which enraged him, but he left hurriedly when she said her husband was sleeping in the next room. This took place about 10 minutes before Clark's death, and she was able to describe him as a 25 to 30-year-old man of average height and light hair, with dark pants and jacket.

Later that month, 23-year-old Patricia Bissette was found in her Back Bay apartment, with several stockings interwoven with a blouse strangling her. She lay under her covers up to her chin this time, she had signs of recent intercourse, and there was damage to her rectum. In early March, Mary Brown, age 68, was found in Lawrence beaten to death, strangled, and raped. Two months later, Beverly Samans, age 23, was found on her couch, hands tied behind her back, legs spread, with nylons and a handkerchief around her neck, and a cloth gagging her. She had died from four stab wounds to the neck and had an additional 18 stab wounds in the shape of a bull's eye on her left breast.

After a quiet summer, 58-year-old Evelyn Corbin was found strangled in Salem with two nylons and underpants in her mouth as a gag. Tissues with lipstick and semen on them were scattered about the bed, and sperm was found in her mouth. In November 1963, Joann Graf was found strangled with two stockings in an elaborate bow. Teeth marks were found on her breast, and the outside of her vagina was bloody from lacerations. A neighbor had been asked earlier if "Joan" Graf lived in the apartment building. The witness said he was a 27-year-old man wearing dark clothes and was let into her apartment. The last victim was found on January 4, 1964, and was the most brutal and grotesque. She was strangled with a stocking with two colorful scarves tied over it in bows. She was sitting with her back against her bed headboard, a thick semen-like liquid dripping from her mouth to her bare breasts. A broom handle had been inserted three and a half inches into her vagina, and at her feet was a bright Happy New Year card from the Boston Strangler.

Investigation

Attorney General Edward Brooke took over the investigation and instituted the Strangler Bureau to work nonstop and make it the city's highest priority. Although forensic mental experts claimed that the killings were likely the work of multiple killers due to the age differentials and slight inconsistencies of the crime scene, the Boston Police were on the hunt for one man.

A couple of years before the murders, Cambridge had had a string of strange sexual offenses with a man known as the "Measurement Man," who told women he had been referred to them for a modeling career and needed to take some measurements. Albert DeSalvo was arrested for breaking and entering an apartment and confessed to being the offender. He was a 29-year-old man with a wife and two children. He had a history of breaking and entering, assault and battery, as well as sexual offenses. In November 1964, a woman was tied spread-eagle and was fondled by a man whose description matched that of the "Measurement Man," and DeSalvo was again arrested. At the same time, Connecticut police were looking for the "Green Man," a sexual assailant who was aptly named for his tendency to wear green trousers. Again, it turned out to be DeSalvo, who claimed to have assaulted hundreds of women in four states, which may not be legitimate because of his braggart character. After being committed to the Bridgewater State Hospital, he became friends with another inmate, George Nassar, a manipulative genius. Together, they realized that the financial rewards for being the Boston Strangler would be great through books and the reward for his capture. DeSalvo figured he would be locked up for life anyway, so he would try to stay in a hospital and make money for his family.

Nassar's attorney, F. Lee Bailey, contacted DeSalvo, and he confessed to all 13 murders. He was able to go into great depth regarding the manner in which he killed his victims, the apartments' layouts, and small details regarding the placement and appearance of small items and evidence in each case. But there were also arguments against his claims: the financial motivation, no physical evidence at all against him, no witness descriptions matching his unique facial characteristics, and although Salem cigarettes were found at multiple scenes, DeSalvo was not a smoker.

Psychiatrist Ames Robey, after examining DeSalvo, noticed two things about him. One was that he had an incredible photographic memory. His ability to remember word for word and every detail was astounding. Second, because he always wanted to be a story, to be big, he wanted to have the notoriety attached with the Boston Strangler to be his own. Finally, two witnesses went to the hospital to identify DeSalvo; both agreed that DeSalvo did not look like the man they saw. But they were both reminded of the Boston Strangler when they saw his friend, the manipulator, George Nassar.

Outcome

The debate goes on today regarding the mystery of the Boston Strangler. It could have been Albert DeSalvo; it could have been his confidant in the hospital, George Nassar; or it could have been a combination of multiple killers all copying each other. Regardless of who was to blame or for how many of the deaths, it was Albert DeSalvo who was sentenced to life in prison and was killed there in 1973.

References

Dietz, P. E., Hazelwood, R. R., & Warren, J. (1990). The sexually sadistic criminal and his offenses. Bulletin of the American Academy of Psychiatry and the Law, *18*(2), 163–178.

Hazelwood, R. R., & Douglas, J. E. (1980). The lust murderer. FBI Law Enforcement Bulletin, *49*(3), 18–22.

Markman, D., & Bosco, D. (1989). Alone with the devil: And other famous cases of a courtroom psychiatrist. New York, NY: Doubleday.

Nelson, C., & Huff-Corzine, L. (1998). Strangers in the night: An application of the lifestyle routine activities approach to elderly homicide victimization. Homicide Studies, 2(2), 130–159.

Safarik, M. E., & Jarvis, J. P. (2005). Examining attributes of homicides: Toward quantifying qualitative values of injury severity. Journal of Homicide Studies, 9(3), 183–203.

Safarik, M. E., Jarvis, J. P., & Nussbaum, K. E. (2000). Sexual homicide of elderly females: Linking offender characteristics to victim and crime scene attributes. Journal of Interpersonal Violence, 17, 500–525.

Taeuber, C. M., & Allen, J. (1990). Women in our aging society: The demographic outlook. In J. Allen & A. J. Pifer (Eds.), Women on the front lines: Meeting the challenge of an aging America (pp. 11–46). Washington DC: Urban Institute.

Chapter 9

Extremist and Medical Homicide

127: Individual extremist homicide   128: Medical murders
   127.01: Political   128.01: Pseudo-mercy homicide
   127.02: Religious   128.02: Pseudo-hero homicide
   127.03: Socioeconomic

127: Individual Extremist Homicide

The crime classifications in the 127–128 section include individual extremist homicides and medical murders.

Ideology is a motivation to commit murders in order to further the goals and ideas of a specific individual or group. Examples of these include terrorist groups or an individual(s) who attacks a specific racial, gender, or ethnic group. Extremist homicide is committed on behalf of a body of ideas based on a particular political, economic, religious, or social system. Although the offender's beliefs may be associated with a particular group, the group does not sanction the actions of the offender. Murders may also fall into the category of hate crimes. This classification is for individual cause extremists in contract to group cause extremists.

Extremist Typologies

Classifying an extremist murder poses difficulty whether it is motivated by personal cause or group cause. Although this category deals with a lone offender (someone not acting on behalf of the group), an extremist murder motivated by personal cause often involves the same blending of multiple motives as a group cause killing.

The blending of political belief with religious dogma is found frequently in the motivation of the extremist murder. Religious and socioeconomic doctrines may also fuse and become a catalyst for extremist murder. The following typologies offer a general outline for the motives of an extremist murder.

POLITICAL

This type of killing is motivated by doctrines or philosophies in opposition to a current position of a government or its representatives. Assassinations such as Robert Kennedy's are included in this group. Political extremist homicides are classified as 127.01.

RELIGIOUS

This homicide is prompted by a fervent devotion to a cause, principle, or system of beliefs based on supernatural or supernormal agencies. Religious extremist homicides are classified as 127.02.

SOCIOECONOMIC / HATE CRIME

This offender kills due to an intense hostility and aversion toward another individual or group that represents a certain ethnic, social, or religious group. Socioeconomic extremist homicide is classified as 127.03.

Defining Characteristics

VICTIMOLOGY

The victim of an extremist murder usually represents the antithesis of the offender's system of beliefs; therefore, victimology depends heavily on the offender doctrine. This doctrine is not always readily apparent, so the victim's history becomes an essential step in discerning the motive. This history should include any social, political, or religious activities of the victim, as well as a complete lifestyle description.

Although victimology often will direct the investigator toward possible motives, extremist killings may involve secondary targets. These people become victims through association with the primary target. They may have had no political, social, or religious similarities with the primary target. Determining who the primary target was will usually help prevent confusion as to the offender's motive.

CRIME SCENE INDICATORS FREQUENTLY NOTED

The crime scene of an extremist murder usually occurs in a public place. The location of victim will often offer an indication as to the motive—for example, a body left near a gay bar or in a Black neighborhood.

The crime scene often will help the investigator determine if the offender is acting on his own or on behalf of a group. Group symbols or signs of the offender's attachment to the group left at the scene do not always mean the group is involved. The offender may have demonstrated a knowledge of group modus operandi (MO), but there are usually idiosyncrasies.

The usual signs of multiple offenders, such as numerous fibers, footprints, and fingerprints, will be absent. The crime scene of a lone offender tends to be less organized than one involving a group effort. The lone offender will usually have more difficulty than multiple offenders controlling the victim. A scene that spread beyond the site of confrontation, blood splatter patterns, or defensive wounds on the victim are all indicators of the lone offender having difficulty controlling the victim.

This offender often chooses an ambush or blitz style of attack because of the possibility of a problem with victim control. He may choose a long-range attack as a sniper (long-range attacks may also mean there is a conspiracy involved).

STAGING

Staging is not usually present.

COMMON FORENSIC FINDINGS

The victims of an extremist attack often suffer multiple wounds. The weapon of choice is usually a firearm or knife. However, an offender who adopts the MO of a particular group will also adopt its methods of attack. This might mean the offender uses blunt-force trauma or an explosive to kill, methods modeled on the group he identifies with.

Investigative Considerations

Preoffense behavior of the extremist killer often entails surveillance and stalking of the victim. His preoffense conversation will often reflect a preoccupation with the intended target. He may generalize, for example, making derogatory statements about all Blacks or all gays. Or he may have already selected an individual who represents the group he despises. Generally, when those associated with him are interviewed, they will especially remember him for this frequently verbalized animosity.

Postoffense conversation may reflect an interest in the homicide. The offender may even express satisfaction, such as, "He got what he deserved." The offender will often follow media reports and even collect newspapers clippings about the incident.

If the investigator receives any communiqués claiming responsibility, especially from an alleged group, the communiqué should undergo a threat assessment examination to determine authenticity. In some cases, the group identified may make disclaimers.

Search Warrant Suggestions

The most prevalent sign of an extremist attitude is literature. The investigator should look for reading materials such as pamphlets, recordings, or books pertaining to the offender's belief system. Other items to look for include:

- Physical trappings of the group or belief system, such as uniforms, paramilitary paraphernalia, or jewelry such as rings or necklaces containing symbols of the group.
- Diaries, logs, diagrams, sketches, recordings, or newspaper clippings concerning the homicide.
- Travel records, motel receipts, or rental agreements.
- Records of any firearm purchases.

Case Study: 127.01: Extremist Homicide, Political

Background

Abuse and neglect during his childhood had conditioned Joseph Paul Franklin to a life of failure and feelings of inadequacy. This inadequacy was reinforced by an accident during early childhood that robbed his left eye of sight. These early years of ridicule, punishment, and criticism shaped him into a disruptive and delinquent teenager who never finished high school despite being average to above average in intelligence.

Franklin initially found direction and acceptance with the Klu Klux Klan, the American Nazi party, and, finally, the fascist National State Rights party. Soon, however, he formed a purpose for his life that was not sufficiently serviced by these organizations. He felt they lacked the professionalism and commitment required of his mission.

The first expression of hatred he harbored toward Blacks was in 1976 when he wrote a threatening letter to President Jimmy Carter about Blacks and assaulted a racially mixed couple with mace. This targeting of Black men accompanied by White women became a characteristic of the victimology for later, more lethal attacks of which Franklin was suspected.

Victimology

On October 7, 1977, Alphonse Manning and Toni Schwenn, both 23 years old, had finished an afternoon of shopping at a Madison, Wisconsin, mall. They were just pulling out of the parking lot when their car was rammed from behind. The driver of the dark green car then jumped out of his car and began firing a handgun at Manning and Schwenn. Manning was struck twice; Schwenn, four times. Both died as a result of their wounds. Manning was Black; Schwenn was White.

On July 22, 1979, in Doraville, Georgia, Harold McGiver, age 29, had finished work at the Taco Bell restaurant he managed. As he walked from the front door of the restaurant toward his car, two shots were fired from a wooded area 150 feet away. McGiver was fatally wounded by the sniper.

On August 8, 1979, at the Falls Church, Virginia, Burger King, 28-year-old Raymond Taylor was sitting at a table, eating his dinner. At 9:50 p.m., the sound of breaking glass was heard as a high-velocity rifle bullet passed through a large plate glass window on the east side of the building. Taylor was pronounced dead at the Arlington County Hospital.

On October 21, 1979, Jesse Taylor and his common-law wife, Marian Bresette, were on the way home from a family outing with their three children when they decided to stop by the supermarket for a few groceries. The children stayed in the car while their parents went inside. A short time later, the couple emerged from the store and walked across the parking lot toward their car. As Taylor reached the car, a shot was fired from a clump of shrubbery, approximately 195 feet away. Taylor slumped against the car, moaning, "No, no, no." Two more shots struck him, driving him to the ground. Bresette, who knelt screaming over her dead husband, was then struck once in the chest by the same sniper, dying instantly.

On January 12, 1980, Lawrence Reese, age 22, had just finished eating his meal at Church's Fried Chicken in Indianapolis. It was 11:10 p.m., and he was standing with his back to the front window, waiting for the last customers of the day to leave. Reese was a regular customer at the restaurant, usually coming there before closing to eat chicken in exchange for sweeping up the place. Suddenly, the window behind him was shattered. Reese staggered four or five steps forward and collapsed. He was dead from a sniper's single bullet.

Two days later, around 10:50 p.m., Leo Watkins, age 19, and his father had just arrived at the Qwic Pic Market in a small shopping plaza in Indianapolis. Watkins often assisted his father, who worked as an independent exterminator. Watkins stood facing into the street by the front window while his father mixed the chemicals they would be using that night. They were waiting for the last customers to leave before starting. Watkins had been standing there about five minutes when he was suddenly struck in the dead center of the chest by a shot that exited his upper right back. The mortally wounded man ran about 30 feet along the front of the store and into an aisle before he fell.

On May 29, 1980, in Fort Wayne, Indiana, Vernon Jordan, the president of the National Urban League, participated in an Urban League meeting at the Marriott Hotel. The day's activities were completed, and Jordan spent the evening with one of the attendees, Martha Coleman. It was around 2:10 a.m. when Coleman brought Jordan back to the hotel. As Jordan exited Coleman's vehicle, he was struck once by a bullet fired from a grassy area approximately 143 feet away. Jordan was one of the few who survived the offender's attack.

Dante Brown, age 13, and Darrell Lane, age 14, of Cincinnati, were not as lucky. On June 6, 1980, the two boys decided to walk to a local convenience market. When they were about 50 feet from a railroad overpass, four shots were fired from the overpass. Each boy was struck twice. Darrell died instantly; Dante lived a few hours longer.

On June 15, 1980, Kathleen Mikula, age 16, and Arthur Smothers, age 22, were out for a walk. At 12:14 p.m., they were crossing a bridge on the outskirts of Johnstown, Ohio, when Smothers was struck down by three shots. Mikula was hit twice by the same sniper from wooded hillside 152 feet away. Both died from their wounds.

David Martin, age 18, had just graduated from his Salt Lake City high school at the beginning of the summer of 1980. He had worked full time during the summer in building maintenance for Northwest Pipeline. Despite his plans to begin studies at the University of Utah in several weeks, his employer had offered him continuing employment. It would be part time to accommodate his school schedule, a concession readily made because he had proven to be such an dependable employee.

Martin had a history of being a hard-working, responsible young man, giving up high school baseball for an after-school job. His friend, Ted Fields, age 20, also a Northwest Pipeline employee, had the same reputation of being an excellent employee. He had started as a mailroom clerk after high school graduation in 1978 and had already advanced to the position of data operations clerk. The future looked bright for both these young men.

On August 20, they decided to go for an evening jog through Liberty Park with two young women. At about 10:15 p.m., the joggers emerged from the west side of the park and were crossing the intersection of Fifth East and Ninth South. As they approached the center of the intersection, they heard a loud noise. Fields seemed to stumble and fell to the ground, calling out that he was hit. The rest of the group thought he was joking and told him to quit fooling around. Two more shots hit Fields as Martin and one of the women tried to drag him across the street. They were almost at the curb when Martin was hit. Martin yelled to the two women to get help, that he had been hit, too. A man driving through the intersection at this time thought the gunfire was coming from the east side of street and pulled his car around to try to block further attempts by the sniper. More gunfire drove him back into his car as he attempted to come to the aid of Fields and Martin. He observed several more rounds hitting the men as they were lying in the street. Fields and Martin were both dead on arrival at the hospital. One of the young women was struck on the elbow but not seriously injured. Fields was hit three times, Martin five.

All the male victims of Franklin were Black and predominantly young adults. All the female victims were White and in the company of a Black man. Vernon Jordan, the only victim with known involvement with civil rights activity, was, ironically, the only one who survived his injuries.

Each one of these victims became a target because of his or her race or apparent interracial affiliations. The offender had a definite criterion in mind, as demonstrated by victim similarities of age, race, and companionship. But the victims were victims of opportunity—the person closest to the window or the one who first crossed the scope of the sniper. Franklin chose areas that offered an abundance of targets, Black neighborhoods, and businesses that were frequented by Blacks.

Crime Scene Indicators

Several crime scene correlations were noted in most of the homicides. Six of the 10 shootings clustered between the two-hour span of 9:50 p.m. and 11:30 p.m. The other two episodes were between 6:40 p.m. and 7:00 p.m., and one was 2:10 a.m. The evening hours played an important role, allowing the sniper, a White man, to slip nearly unnoticed into predominantly Black neighborhoods and position himself at a vantage point that allowed him to kill with one shot, often from 100 to 150 yards. These vantage points were hills, woods, knolls, and alleys that were often dark in contrast to where the victim was. The shootings were all long distance except for one (the first one). They ranged from 100 feet to 150 yards, with one mid-distance killing of 40 feet.

The shootings all involved public places that increased offender risk, but this was negated by the distance of the shooting, the lack of pedestrian traffic, and the darkness provided by evening hours and poor lighting. Most of the victims were outside in a parking lot or street. The three victims who were killed inside were sitting or standing next to large windows in well-lit interiors.

The scarcity of physical evidence (one tire track, one foot print, and a handful of cartridge casings out of ten crime scenes) was indicative of offender sophistication. The lack of witnesses despite the public settings of the homicides also indicated the offender's composure and planning.

The general location of each incident near a major interstate, which allowed a quick, easy escape from the crime scene, reflected the methodical approach of an organized offender. Not only did this plan allow him to put distance quickly between himself and the homicide, but it allowed him to fade into the busy traffic of a major highway.

Forensic Findings

The choice of murder weapon served a dual purpose: it allowed the offender to distance himself from the victim, and it also provided optimized lethality with minimal shots. The two murders that did not involve a .30-caliber or .30–06-caliber bullet were the close and midrange murders. In this case, a choice of large-caliber weapon, .357-caliber Magnum and .44-caliber Magnum, inflicted equally fatal injuries.

Most of the injuries were chest wounds that damaged the heart, lungs, liver, and large thoracic blood vessels. Several of the victims were killed with one shot. This precise targeting of the vital organs (which in some cases, necessitated the use of scope) was another factor that revealed a proficient and experienced offender. There were a few cases of multiple wounds, especially when racially mixed victims were involved; Franklin kept shooting until they did not move. The accuracy was faultless; 32 bullets were fired at these victims without one miss.

Investigation

On September 25, 1980, a police officer was investigating a service station robbery in Florence, Kentucky. He was walking by a brown Camaro parked at the Scottish Inn Motel when he noticed a handgun on the front seat. A license check revealed that a warrant had been issued by Salt Lake City, Utah, for the owner of the vehicle, Joseph Paul Franklin. His car had been placed by witnesses near the vacant lot in which the shells were found from the Fields and Martin shootings.

Shortly after being taken into custody for questioning, Franklin escaped through a window. He left behind a car full of weapons and paraphernalia that tagged him as a suspect not only of the Utah murders but the series of sniper attacks that had left fourteen dead and two injured. In addition, he was suspected of as many as one dozen bank robberies.

Franklin fled first to Cincinnati but ended up being apprehended at a blood bank in Lakeland, Florida. (He frequented blood banks as a means to obtain money.) Franklin was interviewed by an FBI agent during the extradition trip back to Utah. He never admitted to his guilt during this interview, but within 24 hours admitted his guilt to his wife and a cellmate for all the shootings except Vernon Jordan.

Franklin was connected to many of the cities within the time period that the murders occurred by hotel receipts under aliases in his handwriting, weapons being bought or sold, appearances of a car similar to his near the crime scenes, or descriptions that fit him. In addition, he linked himself circumstantially to several of the offenses through his own admission of familiarity with the actual crime scenes.

The bigotry that gnawed at Franklin was evident during his teen years in a photograph that showed him proudly giving the Nazi salute wearing a swastika armband. His sister recalled that Franklin had always been a believer in Nazism and separation of the races.

Franklin decided that as an adult, he would not be deprived of the need to belong and to be special that his childhood had denied him. This lack of attention and the feelings of insignificance it produced required that he take special measures to give his life value and communicate the central theme of his life: "cleaning up America." Franklin decided his message would be taken seriously if it was spelled in blood.

Outcome

Joseph Paul Franklin was convicted of four counts of violating the civil rights of the victims and two counts of murder. He was sentenced to four life terms.

On August 21, 1990, Franklin was being interviewed by a Salt Lake City radio station. An hour into the interview, after refusing to comment about his guilt, he was asked again if had committed the murders. He sighed and answered yes. When prodded by the broadcaster, he responded, "The answer is yes. I won't discuss it any further other than to say yes."

127.02: Religion-Inspired Homicide

Religious beliefs may inspire homicide. While most discussion on such homicides centers on killings publicized as driven by identification with Satan, others may commit murder in the practice of their personal religion.

Because spiritual practice is so personal, adherents of even widely recognized religions may make homicidal choices. The more removed from the mainstream such practices are, the more likely the killing is to be associated with mental illness.

A number of major mental illnesses are associated with hyperreligiosity. Native to schizophrenia is a peculiarity of thinking; for the religiously preoccupied schizophrenic, spirituality may drive violence. Command hallucinations can compel one to homicide. Those experiencing manic episodes, when their grandiosity is religious, may express themselves violently.

In religions that encourage homicide, from violent cults to intolerant sects of Islam, proscription for homicide can be found in writings or preaching of spiritual leaders the assailant identifies with.

While religious ritual homicide is fueled by ideology, part of motivation may have nothing to do with religion, but with conflicts in the assailant's life.

Defining Characteristics

VICTIMOLOGY

Victims of religious ritual may be strangers or acquaintances of the offender. The more likely a victim is included in a delusion, the more likely that victim is closer to the assailant.

One early basis for suspicion of religion as a motive is an absence of conflict between the victim and the assailant, even when the two are acquainted. Given the relative spontaneity of many religious killings, victims are most frequently opportunistic targets.

CRIME SCENE INDICATORS FREQUENTLY NOTED

Religious influence on a crime is reflected in religious symbols and messages at the crime scene. These may include artifacts left behind, religious references in notes, even corpse defacement. Other ritualistic features may be present, from the use of the victim's blood to the presence of other material unrelated to and unnecessary for the commission of the crime.

Signs of ritual at a crime scene are often linked to sexual homicide. Sexual homicide is more common, and therefore warrants first consideration when the crime scene appearance conveys a sense that the killing was carried out in a particular way. However, sexual homicides also commonly feature the presence of ejaculate or distinct placement of a body in a manner that visually registers for later masturbatory fantasy. Or postmortem examination in a sexual homicide may reveal some activity involving the sex organs.

Sexual homicides may inspire the killer to remove keepsakes from the scene as trophies or may occur in a setting of a concurrent robbery. By contrast, a religion-inspired killer adds his or her own sense of holiness to the scene rather than removing items from it. When a killing appears to have a ritualized quality without a sexualized aspect, religion motive needs to be considered.

Weapons need not be of religious significance. However, weapon choice is an important weapon consideration, to the end that part of a religious ritual may mandate a specific weapon. Use of uncommon weapons, such as swords, warrant special consideration as to their relationship to religious symbolism.

The investigator must be careful not to confuse a hate crime with a crime in the name of religion, although both may be present. When the crime scene is of spiritual significance, the crime is more likely a hate crime targeting the religion represented there.

STAGING

Religion-driven homicide aims in part to act in the name of a deity and to communicate with that deity. Those who carry out religion-inspired crimes concern themselves more with their deity than misleading law enforcement. Therefore, while homicides may be staged to look like religion-inspired crime, religion-inspired crimes are not staged to appear like something else.

Investigative Considerations

The disorganization of the crime scene reflects on the spontaneity of the crime and the distress or the disorganization of the perpetrator. Evidence for religious motive, and especially for mental illness, guides the search for the perpetrator to closer in the neighborhood.

Investigators are helped by recognizing features of the crime and to what religions they relate, and how. The perpetrator may not be outwardly devout; however, evidence for traditional observance in the suspect's home, particularly of ritual and of the use of symbols, is consistent with a perpetrator who expresses religious practice though killing. These include writings, tapes, and other messages studied, which the perpetrator may collect at home.

Suspects under consideration may have experienced recent loss or loss of self-esteem due to a rejection. Actions in the name of "God" are dramatic ways to restore a sense of significance to those who have difficulty coping with such experiences of marginalization. The victim may or may not relate to that sense of marginalization. For some religion killers, the rejection comes romantically, anger is displaced through a vehicle of religion, and another victim is selected.

Search Warrant Suggestions

See search warrant suggestions under 127.

Case Study: 127.01: Individual Domestic Terrorism, Political-Inspired

Background

Jared Lee Loughner traveled by taxi to a town hall meeting at a Safeway store on January 8, 2011, in Tucson, Arizona held by Congresswoman Gabrielle Giffords. He shot and critically wounded Giffords, and killed six people, including a federal judge and a nine-year-old girl, and injured 13 others.

Victimology

Among the six people killed were U.S. District Judge John M. Roll; Giffords's aide, Gabe Zimmerman; and nine-year-old Christina-Taylor Green. Except for Congresswoman Giffords, the other victims just happened to be at the Town Hall meeting. They were not specifically targeted by Loughner.

Crime Scene Indicators

There was one crime scene, the parking lot in front of the Safeway store. Loughner was taken down by two men and arrested at the crime scene. His weapon was found on him.

Forensics

Loughner was armed with a Glock 9mm semiautomatic pistol loaded with 33 rounds of ammunition.

Investigation

Loughner admitted to the judge that he walked up to Congresswoman Giffords, drew his pistol, and shot her in the head at close range, intending to kill her, and then fired at the others, intending to kill them as well.

Jared Loughner was an only child of Randy and Amy Loughner. Until he turned 16, he described as average with no notable behaviors. He started showing symptoms of depression, and friends noticed behavior changes and described him as "odd and eccentric." For example, he would yell things out in the classroom and once went up to the chalkboard and started writing nonsensical things.

Friends began to avoid him, and he became isolated. His mental condition was worsening. He talked of killing himself and others. He made videos. He had a few jobs but was fired from two of them with one employer noting that he didn't seem to understand what the supervisor was telling him. He had two charges made against him—drug possession and defacing a street sign. Friends thought Loughner's life began to unravel when his high school girlfriend broke up with him and he began to abuse alcohol and drugs. He was rejected from military service as he admitted to marijuana use on numerous occasions during the application process.

In 2010, while a student at Pima Community College, he caused classroom disruptions. Campus police found a YouTube video where he made negative comments about the college. This resulted in his suspension from the school. A classmate commented that she thought he might commit a school shooting. Loughner spent a great deal of time online, had a strong interest in conspiracy theories, posted a video on his site titled, "America: Your Last Memory in a Terrorist," and raged against illiteracy in Arizona and calling actions by the U.S. Department of Education "unconstitutional."

Analysis of Loughner's writings suggested a distrust of the government. A friend indicated that Loughner had expressed a long-standing dislike for Gabrielle Giffords. An official close to the investigation said the suspect researched famous assassins, the death penalty and solitary confinement on the Internet before the shootings. Evidence seized from Mr. Loughner's home indicated that he had planned to kill Ms. Giffords, whom he had met at a similar event in 2007. In addition to his written statements, investigators have retrieved a cache of video recordings in which he expounded on a variety of topics and mentioned assassination.

Mr. Loughner had become increasingly erratic in the months before the attack, so much so that others around him began to worry. He had posted on his MySpace page at some point a photograph of a U.S. history textbook, on top of which he had placed a handgun. He prepared a series of Internet videos filled with rambling statements on topics including the gold standard, mind control, and SWAT teams. And he had started to act oddly during his classes at Pima Community College, causing unease among other students.

An analysis of Mr. Loughner's Web searches from computers showed that he was conducting Internet research days before the shooting and until just hours before he took a taxi to Ms. Giffords's gathering. The court documents indicated that the suspect had previous contact with the congresswoman. Also found in the safe at Mr. Loughner's home was a letter from Ms. Giffords thanking him for attending a 2007 "Congress on Your Corner" event, like the one she was holding when she was shot.

Loughner told his court-appointed psychiatrist that he could not believe Giffords was alive. He interpreted her survival from a close-range shot to her head was another example of his many failures in life.

Outcome

On August 7, 2012, Loughner pleaded guilty to 19 of the 49 grand jury indictment counts against him—the murders of six people and the attempted murders of 13. The plea was after a mental health official and a federal judge concluded that— because he's been taking his medications—he understood he was personally responsible for opening fire during a congressional constituent meeting in 2011. Mental health experts concluded that Loughner suffered from schizophrenia and had forcibly medicated him in jail with psychotropic drugs for more than a year.

Case Study: 127.02: Individual Domestic Terrorism, Religion-Inspired

On August 15, 2012, a man later identified as Floyd Lee Corkins II, entered the lobby of the Family Research Council building in downtown Washington, D.C., at 10:45 a.m., claiming he came to interview for an internship. He then said, "I don't like your politics," pulled out a gun and shot a guard, Leo Johnson, 46, who was able to wrestle the gun away and restrain the shooter. Corkins, who was heard to say, "Don't shoot me, it was not about you, it was what this place stands for," was then taken into custody.

Corkins, 28, was found to be carrying a backpack with two additional magazines loaded with 50 rounds of ammunition plus 15 Chick-fil-A sandwiches. Corkins had recently had been volunteering at a D.C. community center for lesbian, gay, bisexual, and transgender people.

Corkins lived with his parents in Herndon, Virginia. He was charged with assault with intent to kill and bringing firearms across state. Corkins legally purchased the handgun he used in the shooting—a Sig Sauer 9mm pistol—in Virginia the first week in August. He told the judge he had $300 in his account and was appointed a public defender.

The Family Research Council is a conservative group that stands for biblical values, including traditional marriage. In the past, the FRC has been listed on the Southern Poverty Law Center's list of "hate groups."

The organization strongly opposes gay marriage and abortion and says it advocates "faith, family and freedom in public policy and public opinion." The conservative group maintains a powerful lobbying presence, testifying before Congress and reviewing legislation.

The Family Research Council has steadfastly supported the president of Chick-fil-A and his staunch opposition to same-sex marriage, a stance that has placed the fast-food chain at the center of a hot-button national cultural debate.

Though the shooting was condemned by groups across the ideological spectrum, it tapped into divisions over cultural issues like same-sex marriage and drew finger-pointing about whether inflamed rhetoric on either side was to blame.

The Southern Poverty Law Center, an Alabama-based civil rights organization that tracks and litigates hate groups, labeled the FRC as a hate group in 2010 for what it called the group's anti-gay stance.

The Federal Bureau of Investigation was reported to have called the shooting an act of domestic terrorism.

Case Study: 127.03: Individual Domestic Terrorism, Socioeconomic Inspired

Background

James Eagan Holmes, 24, purchased a ticket to a sold-out midnight premier of the new Batman movie *The Dark Knight Rises* in Aurora, Colorado, on June 23, 2012.

Witnesses say he got up during the movie, went out a back exit door, returned through the same door, and fired on the crowd of more than 400 people.

Victimology

The highly anticipated third installment of the Batman trilogy opened to packed auditoriums around the country at midnight showings on Friday morning, and features a villain named Bane who wears a bulletproof vest and gas mask. Trailers for the movie show explosions at public events, including a football game. Many moviegoers were described as having dressed in costume to attend the opening night screening.

Bullets from the shooter tore through the theater and into adjoining theaters, where at least one other person was struck and injured. Ten members of the movie audience were killed in the theater, while four others died later at area hospitals. There were 58 injured and taken to local hospitals.

The number of casualties (70) made the incident the largest mass shooting in U.S. history.

Crime Scene Indicators

There were two crime scenes: the movie theater and the shooter's apartment. Holmes, a graduate student at a nearby college, entered the movie auditorium. He detonated multiple smoke bombs, and then began firing at movie viewers.

Forensics

Police and bomb squads found a large number of explosive devices and trip wires at Holmes's apartment as well as flammable and explosive materials that could have blown up not only Holmes's apartment but those near it. Bomb experts were able to defuse the devises.

- Holmes purchased his first weapon, a Glock 22 pistol on May 22, 2012.
- On May 28, he purchased a Remington Model 870.
- On June 7, just hours after failing his oral exam, he purchased a Smith & Wesson M&P15 semiautomatic rifle.
- On June 25, he mailed an application to join a gun club.
- He purchased a second Glock pistol on July 6.
- He bought 3,000 rounds of ammunition for the pistols, 3,000 rounds for the M&P15, and 350 shells for the shotgun over the Internet.
- On July 2, he placed an order for a Blackhawk Urban Assault Vest, two magazine holders, and a knife at an online retailer.

Investigation Considerations

Holmes was apprehended within minutes of the 12:39 a.m. shooting at his car behind the theater, where police found him in full riot gear wearing a ballistics helmet, bulletproof vest, bulletproof leggings, gas mask, and gloves. He was carrying three weapons, including a AR-15 assault rifle, which can hold upwards of 100 rounds, a Remington 12-gauge shotgun, and a Glock 22 handgun. A fourth weapon was found in the vehicle. Agents from the federal Bureau of Alcohol, Tobacco, and Firearms are tracing the weapons.

According to police sources, Holmes told the officers arresting him that he was "The Joker," referring to the villain in the second installment of the Batman movie trilogy, *The Dark Knight*. He also warned police that he had booby-trapped his apartment, leading officers to evacuate the Aurora apartment building.

One witness said she saw Holmes throw tear gas in the air, and as the tear gas exploded he started shooting. It was very hard to breathe and then flashes and screaming began. There was chaos and people began running.

Another witness said that about 20 or 30 minutes into the movie he smelled smoke. Everybody thought it was fireworks and then people started dropping and the gunshots became constant. He heard at least 20 to 30 rounds within that minute or two. Another witness saw Holmes slowly making his way up the stairs and just firing at people, just picking random people, and people trying to get away.

Unsealed court documents referred to by the district attorney stated that evidence indicated that "the defendant had conversations with a classmate about wanting to kill people in March 2012, and that he would do so when his life was over."

The document begins to construct a possible motive by citing existing evidence: that Holmes failed his graduate school oral boards in June and made threats to a professor at the school, and that after he was denied access to the university's Denver-Anschutz campus "he began a detailed and complex plan to obtain firearms and other equipment deployed in the theater rampage."

Source: Sandell, Dolak & Curry, 2012; Sangosti, 2012.

128: Medical Murders

Much of what we know about murderers who kill multiple victims, suggests Emeritus Professor of Humanities Philip Jenkins, depends on the victims whom we can identify. We also know that some categories are vastly more likely to be acknowledged and identified as such victims than others, that is, that everything depends on the methods used by the killer. If a female prostitute is found with her throat cut, the police will immediately be open to the possibility of murder. If 20 hospital patients die over a period of months, it may be a long time—if ever—before police become alert to the possibility of a medical serial killer, allowing very lengthy careers of crime. Successful medical killers—doctors, nurses, caregivers to the elderly—can claim victim lists far, far larger than most of the serial killers.

In Britain, the superstar medical murderer was Dr. Harold Shipman, with over 200 known victims. About 80% of his victims were women, with his youngest victim a 41-year-old man. Much of Britain's legal structure concerning health care and medicine was reviewed and modified as a direct and indirect result of Shipman's crimes, especially after the findings of the Shipman Inquiry that lasted almost two years. The coroner, John Pollard, who knew and worked with Shipman, has his own theory about the doctor's motives. He was quoted in the BBC News (2004):, "The only valid possible explanation for it is that he simply enjoyed viewing the process of dying and enjoyed the feeling of control over life and death, literally over life and death." One other observation made was that Shipman was 17 when his 43-year-old mother died of lung cancer. He saw the influence of doctors—administering drugs like morphine to alleviate pain—in the last days of a life. This experience preceded his own addiction to the morphine-like drug pethidine as a young doctor and his conviction, fine and firing from a practice for making out drug prescriptions to himself (BBC, 2004). On January 31, 2000, a jury found Shipman guilty of 15 murders. He was given a life sentence. He hung himself in prison in 2004.

Medical homicides usually are committed on victims who are critically ill. The motive of pseudo-mercy and pseudo-hero are used to suggest the rationalization of the offender. For example, the pseudo-mercy homicide offender believes inducing death is relieving the victim's suffering. The pseudo-hero homicide offender believes he is unsuccessful in attempts to save the victim from death.

Defining Characteristics

VICTIMOLOGY

The victims of pseudo-mercy/pseudo-hero killers are similar. The pseudo-mercy killer targets most often the critically ill, elderly, or infirm. They are usually patients in a hospital, nursing home, or other institutional setting. The victim is engaged in a client–caregiver relationship with the offender. The victim is rarely a random victim but is known to the offender. The victim's environment and lifestyle are low risk, but his or her dependency or state of health elevates risk. Offender risk varies with institutional setting, depending on amount of autonomy or supervision, shift, and quantity of staff. The victims of the pseudo-hero killer may include the critically ill patient since a medical emergency, such as a cardiac arrest, would not appear suspicious. Infants are also included as likely victims of the pseudo-hero murderer because of their mute vulnerability. When the crime scene is an institutional setting, the victim is one of opportunity with an increased risk factor due to the vulnerability that illness or age imposes. Outside the institutional setting, the pseudo-hero killer's victim is a random target who has become a victim of opportunity by being in the building the arsonist torches or in the zone where the emergency medical technician works.

CRIME SCENE INDICATORS

For the pseudo-mercy killer, the instrument of death is one of opportunity, often common to the institutional setting (drugs, syringes for air injection, or toxic substances, for example). Signs of struggle are minimal or absent. In an institutional setting, the pseudo-hero killer creates the crisis, usually with drugs. Syringes, medicine vials, and similar items should be collected for analysis of medications or substances peculiar to that patient's case or condition. In cases involving an emergency, the pseudo-hero killer is conveniently present. If the suspicious death involves a fire, elements of arson may be found.

STAGING

In a sense, staging is the central element of this homicide. The pseudo-mercy killer arranges the body to represent a peaceful, natural death. The death is most often staged to look like a natural death, but it is possible that accidental or suicidal death is staged. For the pseudo-hero killer, it is a miscarried attempt to stage a scenario, a life-threatening crisis, in which the offender has the starring role as the pseudo-hero. The fireman or arsonist sets the fire, only to rush back for the rescue. The nurse or emergency medical technician makes a timely response to the person after inducing the state of crisis. The target is made to look like a victim of a natural calamity (e.g., a cardiac arrest), an accident (faulty wiring that starts the fire), or perhaps criminal activity (hit and run, mugging, arson).

COMMON FORENSIC FINDINGS

Since the case may not have been reported as suspicious, detailed investigation is mandated. Exhumation may be required with analytical toxicology. Many times an autopsy is not performed if the death appears natural, but later scrutiny reveals poisoning, broken ribs, or other signs of suspicious death.

Liver biopsy, thorough blood-chemistry analysis, complete drug screen of blood and urine, and hair analysis for arsenic and drugs (especially digoxin, lidocaine, and smooth muscle–paralyzing drugs) should be performed. Asphyxiation should be checked for by petechial hemorrhage, taking an X-ray for broken ribs, and so on. In the case of the pseudo-hero killer, the postmortem examination should look for toxic levels of injectable drugs such as digoxin, lidocaine, and potassium hydrochloride.

Investigative Considerations

Suspected pseudo-mercy murders can be indicated by a rise in the number of deaths, especially if at all suspicious. Suspicious deaths should be checked for correlation between the suspect's shift and patient assignments. In nine cases of pseudo-mercy killers cited in an article in the *American Journal of Nursing*, the correlation between suspect presence and a high number of suspicious deaths was deemed sufficient to establish probable cause and to bring indictments by grand juries.

In the medical realm, an unusually high rate of successful cardiopulmonary resuscitation in conjunction with the unusually high death rate should be examined. Multiple cardiac or respiratory arrests in the same patient also should raise suspicion. Most unwitnessed cardiopulmonary arrests or patients who have multiple arrests do not respond to resuscitative measures. This could indicate that a pseudo-hero killer happens to be among the first to the scene as well as knowing the exact measures to remedy the problem.

Inspection of a suspect's employment history is important: the investigator should look for frequent job changes, with a corresponding increase of mortality associated with the suspect's employment. Other consideration include a significant rise in cardiopulmonary arrests or deaths in a particular patient population, cardiopulmonary arrests or deaths inconsistent with the patient's condition, cardiopulmonary deaths localized to a particular shift, or postmortem examinations revealing toxic levels of an injectable substance.

For the pseudo-hero killer, interviews of coworkers may reveal that the offender demonstrates an unusually high level of excitement or exhilaration while participating in the rescue or resuscitation efforts. Conversations may often involve the rescue or resuscitation incidents.

Search Warrant Suggestions

Vials of medications at the residence of the offender and literature concerning drugs beyond the scope of offender's practice (e.g., the *Physician's Desk Reference*) are among search warrant suggestions. Other suggestions include diaries, journals, and pictures. The pseudo-mercy killer may keep obituaries of victims. For the pseudo-hero killer, search warrants should include newspaper articles commemorating previous rescue efforts and implements of arson. The investigator should scrutinize the literature found, checking each page for underlining and modification.

128.01: Pseudo-Mercy Homicide

Death at the hand of a pseudo-mercy killer results from the offender's claim or perception of victim suffering and his or her duty to relieve it. Most often, the real motivation for pseudo-mercy killing has little to do with the offender's feelings of compassion and pity for the victim. The sense of power and control the offender derives from killing is usually the real motive. Case studies show that these offenders frequently commit serial murder.

Case Study: 128.01: Pseudo-Mercy Homicide

Background

In early 1987 a Cincinnati medical examiner was performing an autopsy on the victim of a motorcycle crash. As he was examining the stomach cavity, he detected an odor that smelled like almonds. After further testing, the pathologist concluded the victim had been poisoned with cyanide.

The ensuing investigation led to a 35-year-old nurse's aide, Donald Harvey. After his arrest, Harvey began confessing to numerous other murders, or "mercy" killings as he described them. Harvey enjoyed the limelight so much that he continued to add to the list of victims. The toll reached as high as 100 at one point, but Harvey could not supply details to many of the alleged killings. The actual number of victims is still uncertain, and Harvey's later confessions have been held suspect.

Victimology

Harvey claimed his first killings began in the early 1970s in Marymount Hospital, London, Kentucky. He confessed to murdering 15 patients between 1970 and 1971. He then moved on to Cincinnati and worked in a factory for several years before returning to hospital work.

From 1975 to 1985, Harvey worked in the Cincinnati Veterans Administration (VA) Medical Center. He claimed responsibility for at least 15 deaths at the VA hospital. He next moved on to Drake Memorial Hospital in Cincinnati in 1986, where he continued working as a nurse's aide. Harvey killed at least 21 patients at Drake Hospital. He was employed there until his arrest in August 1987.

Harvey preyed on the elderly, infirm, or chronically ill, most of them involved in a caregiver–client relationship with him. Most of the confirmed deaths took place in an institutional setting, which would have been considered a low-risk environment for the victims. However, the victims' debilitated condition that necessitated total dependence on a caregiver elevated their risk of becoming the victim of a violent crime. A few of Harvey's victims were outside the institutional setting, but he targeted them for revenge, not pseudo-mercy killing.

Crime Scene Indicators

Most of the crime scenes involved with the pseudo-mercy killings were in the hospital. There were no signs of struggle or violent death with most of the murders, which was one reason that Harvey was able to kill year after year without being caught. He usually used weapons to kill found in the institutional setting where the offenses occurred. He would use plastic bags and pillows, oxygen tubing, and syringes full of air. When he decided to poison patients, he brought arsenic and cyanide to work and mixed it with their food.

Forensic Findings

Harvey's victims died from a variety of causes. He smothered some by putting a plastic bag over the victim's face and then using a pillow. He killed several patients by cutting their oxygen supply off. One patient died of peritonitis after Harvey punctured his abdomen. Another patient was placed face down on his pillow by Harvey. The patient was unable to move, so he suffocated.

The rest of the victims died of arsenic or cyanide poisoning. The poisoning cases were supported through exhumation, but most of the other cases would have been difficult to prove without Harvey's confession. He was able to give details on these cases that corroborated his claims.

Investigation

During the initial stages of the investigation, Harvey claimed that he was putting people out of their misery. He described many of the patients as on their deathbed. Many never had any visitors, either because their families had forgotten them or because they had no family. He felt he was releasing these patients from a lonely, pain-filled existence. He hoped someone would do the same for him if he were sick and full of tubes. "I felt I was doing right."

But after the trial and his convictions, interviews with Harvey began to reveal the true motive for his pseudo-mercy killings. A picture of Harvey very different from the compassionate angel of mercy began to emerge. He began to describe the satisfaction he derived from fooling doctors, who assumed their patients had died of natural causes. He found murder to be a satisfying outlet for the tensions that built up from personal problems, relationships ending, and living alone. Sometimes he stated that he would kill just to relieve the boredom of his job.

Harvey, a homosexual, claims that the killing started two weeks after he was raped by a man from whom he was renting a room. He retaliated by preying on a totally helpless patient who was restrained to his bed because he was disoriented. He took a coat hanger, straightened it out, and rammed it through the man's abdomen, puncturing his intestines. The man lived for two days before dying of peritonitis.

Psychologists described Harvey as a compulsive murderer who killed because it gave him a feeling of power. Yet, Harvey claims, "I've been portrayed as a cold-blooded murder, but I do not see myself that way. I think I am a very warm and loving person."

Harvey was a sadist who studied and practiced the art of killing without, he hoped, ever being identified. No remorse was displayed. In fact, he enjoyed getting away with murder.

Outcome

Donald Harvey pleaded guilty to 26 counts of aggravated murder. His confession was part of a plea bargain that brought him three consecutive life sentences instead of the death penalty. Part of the plea bargain was the agreement that he would cooperate with the Kentucky authorities in exchange for a jail term that would run concurrent with his Ohio terms.

128.02: Pseudo-Hero Homicide

In pseudo-hero homicide, the offender creates a life-threatening condition for the victim and then unsuccessfully attempts to rescue or resuscitate the victim to appear valorous. Death is not intentional, but the bulk of cases reviewed have demonstrated that failures do not avert the offender from recidivism.

Case Study: 128.02: Pseudo-Hero Homicide

Background

On September 21, 1981, two licensed nursing attendants, Susan Maldonado and Pat Alberti, reported to work for their usual 11 p.m. to 7 a.m. shift at San Antonio Medical Center's Pediatric Intensive Care Unit (PICU). When they were greeted with the news that two of the unit's four young patients had died that evening, it strengthened a growing suspicion that Maldonado and Alberti had recently been trying to deny.

During their break, the two nurses sat down with the PICU logbook that kept track of each patient's name, age, admission diagnosis, admission date, doctor, discharge status, and assigned nurse. The correlation they found between the children who had died in the PICU during the prior months and the one person whose presence was documented during virtually every one of these codes (cardiac and/or respiratory arrest) presented the two nurses with an appalling reality: Either the nurse who had been on duty had incredibly bad luck, or she was deliberately killing babies.

The nurse, Genene Jones, had been considered the backbone of her shift at the medical center. She was experienced, cool-headed, and seemingly dedicated to her patients. She was more comfortable with pediatric medicine than many physicians. Her nursing skills were superior when caring for the critically ill babies, but it was during a crisis that she seemed to really shine.

Jones was a controversial figure. Her supporters described her as level-headed, quick, knowledgeable, and extremely competent in a code situation. She was so devoted to her patients that she insisted on carrying the tiny bodies to the morgue herself after unsuccessful resuscitation attempts. It was reported that Jones would often cry and sing to the dead infants as she tenderly cradled them. When the question was raised about the number of babies who seemed to be dying under her care, the response was that she always took care of most critically ill patients, so naturally she would have a lower recovery rate.

Jones's critics offered quite a different perspective. They said she bullied her way into any crisis in PICU, becoming argumentative with even the physicians who did not bow to her insistent recommendations. She threw temper tantrums if her authority was challenged and publicly berated physicians in front of staff and patient families. Jones seemed to crave and relish the pinnacles of emotion that a PICU nurse could experience, working in a place where the stakes were so high. But the theatrics she indulged in were an extreme and unprofessional emotionalism.

When Jones's associates started noticing the rising death toll in PICU and her connection with the dying babies, it did not take much to convince them she was the perpetrator. But when Alberti and Maldonado brought their discovery to the attention of several administrators, including the head nurse, they were told to stop backbiting and spreading rumors.

Victimology

The infants who died at the medical center while under the care of Genene Jones ranged between the ages of three weeks and two years. The one exception was a 10-year-old child who was mentally retarded and had the developmental age of an infant. At the clinic in Kerrville, Texas, where Jones worked after leaving San Antonio, all of the children who experienced a life-threatening crisis in her presence were under age two, with the exception of a seven-year-old severely retarded child. All of these children were involved in a client–caregiver relationship with Jones, either directly, with her as their assigned nurse, or indirectly, with her responding to the code or present at the time of death.

A general criterion for victim selection was the inability to talk and physical limitations due to age or developmental disability. Excepting this, these children would have been considered victims of opportunity. Their chances of becoming a mortality statistic increased significantly if Jones had the opportunity to care for them, however briefly.

Crime Scenes Indicators

The crime scenes involved two locations; the PICU and a pediatric clinic in Kerrville, Texas, where Jones went after the policy was instituted at Medical Center that licensed nursing attendants could no longer staff the PICU. One case finally bought Jones to justice.

Chelsea McClellan was a bright, healthy child of 14 months when she was brought to Dr. Kathleen Holland's office in Kerrville on August 24, 1982. Chelsea was the second child to be seen in the new clinic. She was there because of Petti McClellan's concern over the sniffles her daughter had developed.

While pregnant with Chelsea, Petti McClellan had required an early caesarean section. Chelsea had experienced respiratory problems due to this premature birth. Other than one bout of pneumonia at six months from which she fully recovered, Chelsea had been in excellent health.

While Petti was talking with Dr. Holland, her office nurse, Genene Jones, took Chelsea from Petti. Chelsea was becoming impatient with sitting still, so Jones offered to entertain her. Within five minutes, Jones was calling with urgency in her voice for Holland to come into the examining room where she and Chelsea were. When Holland entered the room, she was confronted with the shocking sight of the previously energetic, laughing child now draped limply over the treatment table.

Jones claimed that Chelsea had suddenly begun convulsing and stopped breathing. Once Dr. Holland provided Chelsea with oxygen, her blue coloring started to fade. She was transported to the hospital nearby, where she seemed to slowly respond, but her coordination was gone. Her arms would just flop around when she tried to reach for her face and remove her oxygen mask.

Within 30 minutes of admission to the intensive care unit, Chelsea was standing up in her crib, laughing and holding her arms out to the nurses who passed by. She was subjected to exhaustive testing, which revealed no abnormalities that may have caused the seizure episode. She was discharged from the hospital on September 2. While hospitalized, Chelsea had someone at her bedside constantly. Nothing besides the normal movements of a sleeping child was noted by the family and friends who kept the 10-day vigil. Chelsea had had no previous history of any seizure activity or apnea (cessation of breathing) before her visit to the Kerrville clinic where Jones worked.

On September 17, Petti McClellan brought Chelsea back to the clinic with her brother, Cameron, who had the flu. While Dr. Holland was looking at Cameron, Jones was to give Chelsea two routine infant immunizations. Jones tried to get Petti to leave while she inoculated the child, but Petti insisted it did not bother her to watch the children get shots. In addition, Chelsea started acting upset when Jones reached for her.

Petti recalls that Jones became irritated but acquiesced. As Petti held her daughter, Jones dabbed at her thigh with an alcohol swab and injected the first needle into the child's upper left thigh. Within seconds, Petti observed that Chelsea was not acting right. Petti became extremely alarmed at this point and pleaded with Jones to do something. Jones insisted nothing was wrong, that Chelsea was just angry about getting the shots.

Despite Petti's telling Jones to stop, that Chelsea was having another seizure, Jones was intent on giving the child the other injection. As soon as she injected the second shot, Chelsea quit breathing altogether, and her pink cheeks began to turn blue. Petti recalled that Chelsea appeared to try to say "mama" and soon after went completely limp.

Again, Jones summoned Dr. Holland, and the scene repeated just as it had less than a month ago. The ambulance responded at 10:58 a.m., speeding the child, with Jones and an emergency medical technician administering aid, to the hospital. Dr. Holland followed behind in her car. In the emergency room, within 25 minutes, Chelsea was again thrashing and upset at having the tube in her throat that provided oxygen directly into her lungs.

Dr. Holland decided Chelsea needed to be transferred to San Antonio, where a neurologist could find out what was causing these episodes. Thirty-five minutes later, Chelsea was wheeled from the emergency room to a waiting ambulance. She was resting quietly, breathing with some assistance, and very pink. Dr. Holland reassured the frightened McClellans that the emergency had passed.

Jones climbed in the back of the ambulance with Chelsea for the ride to San Antonio. Dr. Holland followed in one car and Chelsea's parents in another. Less than 10 minutes out of Kerrville, the heart monitor attached to Chelsea began to alarm. Jones yelled to the driver to pull over; Chelsea was suffering a cardiac arrest. She pulled syringes out of her black bag and began administering drugs to stimulate the little girl's heart. By this time Dr. Holland was in the ambulance and gave orders for the driver to get to the closest hospital.

Thirty-five minutes later, in the Comfort Community Hospital Emergency Room, Chelsea McClellan was pronounced dead. All attempts to restart her heart had failed, and she was beginning to show the inevitable signs of brain damage.

Dr. Holland stated on the death certificate that death was caused by cardio-pulmonary arrest due to seizures of undetermined origin.

After taking the dead child back from her stunned, weeping mother, Jones carried the child back to Sid Peterson Hospital in Kerrville. After arrival, she sobbed as she carried the body to hospital morgue.

Counting the two emergency situations that involved Chelsea, there were six respiratory arrests during the Kerrville clinic's approximately one month of operation. The same day Chelsea died, five-month-old Jacob Evans was brought to the clinic for an earache. He also experienced a respiratory arrest as a result of seizure activity reported by Jones. He was hospitalized and released six days later, never demonstrating any sign of a seizure disorder. A neurologist in San Antonio failed to uncover any possible source for the seizures after extensively testing Jacob.

The recurrence of life-threatening crises had finally attracted attention from the medical community. Dr. Holland began to entertain suspicions after Jones mentioned some missing succinylcholine had been found. Holland had never used this drug and wondered why it would even be out of its storage place in the refrigerator. The next day she checked the two bottles of succinylcholine in the refrigerator and discovered one had its plastic seal removed and had two distinctive needle holes in the vial's rubber stopper. It also had a slight difference in volume compared to the sealed vial.

When Holland confronted Jones, she first explained it as being done during one of the seizure episodes by another nurse who happened to be there when the emergency occurred. This nurse denied puncturing the stopper when questioned. Jones suggested that Holland just throw it away and forget the incident.

Dr. Holland responded that disposing of the vial was legally, medically, and ethically unacceptable to her. That afternoon, she submitted the vial to the Department of Public Safety for analysis after meeting with several doctors and the hospital administrator. While this was unfolding, Jones took a drug overdose and was briefly hospitalized.

Jones had staged all of these incidents to appear as medical emergencies arising from the natural course of a physical illness or disorder. If each of the 29 San Antonio PICU deaths that had been linked to Jones's presence were analyzed, this type of staging would emerge. It would also be evident in the six Kerrville emergencies.

Forensic Findings

It was determined the rubber stopper of the capless vial had two puncture sites that had been used multiple times. When the contents were analyzed, it was discovered the succinylcholine was 80% dilute, probably with saline.

On May 7, 1983, Chelsea McClellan's body was exhumed, and tissue samples were removed for toxicology studies. Seven days later, the prosecuting attorney received the call that succinylcholine had been found in the gallbladder, urinary bladder, the kidneys, the liver, and both thighs.

Investigation

The correlation between infant mortality and Jones's presence is best illustrated by the PICU logbook. This also demonstrates the localization of deaths to a particular shift. Jones was often present at the moment of cardiac arrest or among the first to respond.

Several witnesses to arrest situations involving Jones described her obvious state of excitement as beyond the usual level at a code situation. One went so far as to depict it as orgasmic.

In a number of cardiac arrest situations that involved Jones, the patients had died. In addition to the high number of codes, there were many patients who experienced multiple cardiopulmonary arrests (among survivors of the PICU epidemic as well as fatalities). A significant number of arrests and multiple arrests correlating to offender presence is a characteristic particular to the pseudo-hero killer. These factors provide the setting that enables the offender to enact the role of rescuer, while being the center of attention.

From November 9, 1981, until December 7, Jones was out of work on sick leave for minor surgery. The PICU chart reveals that during most of November and the first week of December, not a single baby died. In fact, there was not a single code during the 36-day period surrounding Jones's absence.

Isolating some of the deaths into singular incidents allowed reasonable medical explanations for the course of events. But many of the deaths posed enigmas: excessive bleeding of unknown etiology, disruptions of the heart rhythm, seizures in children with no previous history of any seizure activity, and sudden respiratory arrests. The administration of San Antonio Medical Center never recognized this compilation of facts as worthy of criminal investigation. The medical examiner was never notified for any of these deaths, even when physicians began sharing the suspicion that nursing misadventure was involved. So Jones moved on to Kerrville, to Chelsea McClellan, with the hospital's recommendation.

Evidence presented at the trial showed that Jones had ordered three more bottles of succinylcholine from the Kerrville Pharmacy and had signed Dr. Holland's name to receipts. In addition, Chelsea's babysitter testified that she observed Jones injecting something into the intravenous line as the child was being loaded into the ambulance for the trip to San Antonio. When she questioned Jones about it, Jones replied it was simply something to relax Chelsea. This struck the babysitter as odd, since Chelsea was already resting quietly. This alleged relaxant had not been ordered by either Dr. Holland or the emergency department physician.

Outcome

Genene Jones was found guilty of first-degree murder and sentenced to 99 years on February 15, 1984. On October 23, 1984, she was convicted of felony injury to a child for an incident involving an overdose of heparin (a blood thinner) she had given an infant in the PICU. Despite massive bleeding and several cardiac arrests, that child was one of the few who survived the fatal touch of Genene Jones.

References

BBC News. (2004). *Harold Shipman: The killer doctor*. Retrieved August 22, 2012, from http://news
.bbc.co.uk/2/hi/uk_news/3391897.stm

Sandell, C., Dolak, K., & Curry, C. (2012). Colorado movie theater shooting. *Good Morning America*.
Retrieved August 2, 2012, from http://gma.yahoo.com/colorado-batman-movie-shooting-
suspect-phd-student-085940589–abc-news-topstories.html

Sangosti, R. J. (2012, August 24). Court document: Aurora shooting suspect James Holmes discussed
"killing people" with classmate. *US News*. Retrieved August 25, 2012, from http://news
.mobile.msn.com/en-us/article_us.aspx?aid=13460395&afid=20

Chapter 10

Group Cause Homicide

140: Group cause homicide
141: Cult
142: Extremist homicide

142.01: Political
142.02: Religious
143: Group excitement

140: Group Cause Homicide

Group cause homicide pertains to two or more people with a common ideology that sanctions an act, committed by one or more of its members, that result in death. This category is divided into cult murder, extremist murder (paramilitary extremist murder and hostage extremist murder), and group excitement homicide such as a gang attack, fed by its own momentum and peer reinforcement, that escalates into murder.

141: Group Cause Homicide, Cult

A body of adherents with excessive devotion or dedication to ideas, objects, or persons, regarded as unorthodox or spurious and whose primary objectives of sex, power, or money are unknown to the general membership, is known as a *cult*. A cult murder pertains to the death of an individual committed by two or more members of the cult.

Defining Characteristics

VICTIMOLOGY

Occasionally, cult murder is the result of members preying on a random victim, but the prevailing casualty of this type of murder tends to be one who is a member of the cult or on the fringe of membership. Generally, multiple victims are involved.

CRIME SCENE INDICATORS FREQUENTLY NOTED

The crime scene may contain items that are symbolic, in the form of unexplained artifacts or imagery.

The status of the body is dependent on the purpose of the killing. If it is intended to be a widespread message, there generally will be little to no attempt to conceal the body. A death that is intended to intimidate within the smaller circle of the cult is often concealed through burial. A more organized group usually demonstrates more elaborate body disposal or concealment. There is a prevalence of mass gravesites on the grounds where a cult is based, for example, a farm or rural residence.

The crime scene usually exhibits evidence of multiple offenders as well as multiple victims by either a mass or spree killing.

COMMON FORENSIC FINDINGS

The forensic findings most common to this type of homicide involve wounds from firearms, blunt-force trauma, and sharp, pointed objects. There may be mutilation of the body as well. Multiple weapons may be seen with a single event.

Investigative Considerations

The leaders of destructive cults are often involved with scams and may have a criminal history. However, this may not be the case if the cult is a splinter group of a mainstream, conventional religion. In either case, the leadership displays a masterful ability to attract and manipulate people, exploiting their vulnerability.

The murder may not have any apparent religious overtones and ritualistic qualities. There may be a message after the killing, especially if it is intended for the public.

The motive is often presented to the general assembly of the cult as part of the group belief. The leader's motivation, however, will be a controlling factor: "a macho way" to justify the homicide, tighten his control of the group, or eliminate troublemakers or less devoted followers who threatened his authority.

Case Study: 141: Group Cause Homicide, Cult

Background

On January 3, 1990, investigators acted on an anonymous tip they had received and began to dig under a muddy barn floor on a farm 25 miles east of Cleveland. The property once had been occupied by a religious cult. Over the next two days, they unearthed five bodies; two appeared to be adult, two were medium size, and one was a child.

The former tenants were known as the Lundgren cult after their leader, Jeffrey Lundgren. Lundgren, his wife, son, and 10 members of his group were subsequently charged and arrested over the next few days for the slayings of the family of five.

Victimology

The victims were later found to be Dennis Avery, age 49; his wife, Cheryl, age 42; and their three daughters, Trina, age 15; Rebecca, age 13; and Karen, age 7. They had moved to Kirtland around 1987 from Independence, Missouri. Dennis Avery was described as working at various low-paying part-time jobs. "If it was not for some people, they would not have had food on their plates," said one Kirtland neighbor. The Averys were described as a quiet, shy family that kept to themselves. They attended services a few times at the local Reorganized Church of Jesus Christ of Latter Day Saints before joining the radical splinter group of Lundgren's followers.

Once the Averys joined Lundgren's cult, they were further isolated, typical of cult practice. Before their disappearance in April, they moved from Kirtland to a Madison Township home because they were behind in rent. It is possible the Averys were attempting to recede from the Lundgren cult, which contributed to their being targeted as the victims for a cult sacrifice. A neighbor described the sudden disappearance of the Averys as well as the rest of the commune as if "the earth opened up and swallowed them."

Crime Scene Indicators

The gravesite was an eight-foot-square area underneath the barn of the 15-acre farm. The barn itself was filled with trash piled four feet high. Police had to force their way through the rear of the barn because the only ground-level entrance was blocked by trash as well as a 1978 Volvo. Lake County Auto Title Bureau records showed a 1978 Volvo registered to Dennis and Cheryl Avery.

On top of the gravesite, as detailed from the informant's diagram, were several photos of the Avery family. The bodies were found in a common grave four feet deep. They had been sprinkled with lime and covered with dirt, rocks, and clay. Dennis Avery's body was in a plastic bag. All the bodies were found fully clothed. All the victims were bound hand and foot with duct tape. Their eyes and mouths were also covered with duct tape.

Forensic Findings

All the victims had been killed by gunshot wounds to the chest. Rebecca Avery had also been shot in the head. The murder weapon was a .45-caliber Colt semiautomatic handgun.

Investigation

The Avery family was killed by an execution-style method. This is evidenced by the use of duct tape to bind their hands and feet and cover their eyes and mouth. The number of victims also illustrates the investigative consideration that cult homicides are often a spree or mass killing. The photographs of the Avery family left on their grave most likely had a ritualistic significance to Jeffrey Lundgren's twisted interpretation of Mormon doctrine.

To understand the motive for the Avery family murders requires a closer look at the dynamics of the Lundgren cult, and especially its leader.

Jeffrey Lundgren was born in Independence, Missouri. He was a member of the Slover Park Reorganized Church until officials transferred him to Kirtland to serve as a guide at the Kirtland Temple. He married Alice Keehler in 1970 and lived for a while in a rented home in Macks Creek, Missouri. The beginnings of his deviation from the Reorganized Church doctrines began to emerge at this time. After Lundgren moved out, the landlord found an entire bedroom floor and closet littered with "heavy-duty" pornographic magazines.

It was also during this period (1986–1987) that Lundgren began to use his position as tour guide for the Kirtland Temple to proclaim his interpretation of church doctrine and recruit his followers. Lundgren's supervisor began to hear complaints from temple visitors that Lundgren was misrepresenting teachings of the Reorganized Church. In addition to ethical improprieties at the visitors' center, Lundgren was suspected of stealing money. In 1987, he was removed as a tour guide. In January 1988, he was defrocked as a lay minister because his teachings deviated from church doctrine and were considered apostate. Lundgren resigned from the church and had to move from his rent-free home provided by the church. He relocated to the farm four miles away.

Lundgren continued to make recruiting trips to Independence, Missouri, persuading members of the Reorganized Church, including Dennis Avery, to join his "Family." Lundgren became the personable "Father" and "Prophet" to emotionally troubled men and women made vulnerable by divorce, financial problems, or personal crises. He supported them, provided spiritual guidance, and took them in, giving them a place to belong. He became the guru who led his group to believe that he was the spokesman for God.

It was not long before Lundgren's zeal and manipulations allowed him absolute spiritual authority over the group. He matched couples in the commune based on visions he claimed came from God. Paychecks were signed over to him, phone calls were monitored, and when visitors came, he sat in on their conversations.

As group members became accustomed to Lundgren's control, the cult began to evolve into something more ominous than a religious sect. Rumors of paramilitary activity—shots being fired, use of code names such as Eagle-2 and Talon-2, fatigues, and marching—began to reach the ears of area officials. An informant told Kirtland police that Lundgren was planning an assault on the Kirtland Temple that included killing Reorganized Church leaders and hundreds of people who lived near the church. He felt that the massacre would cleanse the church and pave the way for the second coming of Christ. Several appointed dates for the attack came and went because Lundgren had a vision the time was not right.

Lundgren remained under the observation of the FBI and local police for several years. Finally, on April 18, 1989, almost 20 FBI agents interviewed Lundgren and eight followers for about three hours because agents learned some of the group wanted to leave the cult. But no one left and no arrests were made since a crime had not been committed. No one in the group even had a police record.

That night, or early the next morning, Lundgren and his followers left Kirtland. The police were getting too close to the grisly events of the preceding day, April 17.

A cult member who lived with Lundgren until April 1988 made the observation that the Averys were different from the others on the farm. They did not live there but visited a lot. They really were not "in"—half believing and half not. "They were weak in mind and strength. Everybody was doing 100 or so push-ups and Dennis could only do 5 or 10."

Surely, this lack of commitment on Dennis Avery's part was an affront to the image of "divine prophet" Lundgren ascribed to himself. Lundgren's choice of the Avery family as a cult sacrifice stems from this threat to his dictatorship. The precipitating factor for the murders arises from the tradition contained in the Book of Mormon concerning the search for the Sword of Laban. Lundgren was planning to lead his followers into the wilderness in search for this sword, but first there had to be a cleansing sacrifice. Dennis Avery and his family were that sacrifice. Lundgren probably used the story of Laban, who was killed by his own sword, to justify killing the Averys. Avery had bought a .45 for Lundgren two days before he was killed by a .45-caliber handgun. Since the Averys were about to abandon the cult, their death was justified by the Mormon "Doctrine of Blood Atonement" that teaches the penalty for abandoning the faith is the shedding of the sinner's blood. Lundgren could simultaneously satisfy his doctrinal beliefs, soothe his offended authority, and intimidate any other group members who may have been slipping from his control.

On April 17, the Lundgren "Family," including the Averys, gathered together at the Chardon Road farm for a "last" meal. When supper had ended, the men excused themselves with the exception of Dennis Avery. While the women entertained the rest of the Avery family, several men asked Dennis to follow them outside to the barn. As Avery entered the barn, he was hit with a stun gun. He promised his cooperation, probably still unaware of Lundgren's plans for him and his family. His hands, mouth, and eyes were then taped with duct tape, and he was led to the waiting grave. Once Avery was standing inside the hole, Jeffrey Lundgren passed judgment on him for allowing Cheryl to control their family and declared his heart impure. Lundgren then provided his remedy for this sin by shooting Avery in the chest with the .45 point-blank. Then Cheryl Avery was led to the barn, bound with duct tape, and also shot in chest as she knelt next to her husband's corpse. One by one the children were carried to the open grave after being bound by the tape and shot in the chest, with the exception of Rebecca, who was also shot in the head.

Two days later, the group packed up and left. They traveled from West Virginia to Missouri before finally splitting up around Thanksgiving.

On January 7, 1990, Jeffrey Lundgren, his wife, and his son were arrested outside a motel in National City, California. It is believed they were attempting to place their younger children with relatives in order to flee across the border to Mexico. Of the 13 charged in the cult slayings, 2, Danny Kraft and Kathy Johnson, remained at large for a short time but were arrested on January 10, 1990.

Outcome

Jeffrey Lundgren was sentenced to death on five counts of aggravated murder and kidnapping. Damon Lundgren, his son, was found guilty of four counts of aggravated murder and is on Ohio's death row. Alice Lundgren received five consecutive life sentences for conspiracy, complicity, and kidnapping convictions. Nine of their followers are in prisons scattered across the state.

142: Extremist Homicide

Extremist homicide is killing motivated by ideas based on a particular political, economic, religious, or social system. This category of homicide includes both the lone offender whose actions are endorsed by the group and the offense involving multiple offenders.

It is difficult to classify a homicide involving an extremist group into a single category. Group causes can rarely be isolated to a single typology. There is often a blending of one or more of the motivations described in this section. One example, Hezbollah, has political objectives that serve to further the Islamic religion. Hezbollah, whose name means "party of God," was founded in 1982 in response to the Israeli invasion of Lebanon. It is a Lebanese umbrella organization of radical Islamic Shiite groups and organizations that opposes the West, seeks to create a Muslim fundamentalist state modeled on Iran, and is a bitter foe of Israel. A terrorist group, it is believed responsible for nearly 200 attacks since 1982 that have killed more than 800 people. Experts say Hezbollah is also a significant force in Lebanon's politics and a major provider of social services, operating schools, hospitals, and agricultural services for thousands of Lebanese Shiites. It operates the al-Manar satellite television channel and broadcast station.

Right-wing groups like the Covenant, Sword, and Arm of the Lord combine religious concepts with elements of extreme racism. Fatal attacks on Blacks, Hispanics, and Jews are justified by these hate groups' interpretation of biblical passages, which differ significantly from those of mainstream religious groups.

Extremist Groups Using the Internet

The Internet has assisted extremist groups in carrying out their destructive plans. The shootings that occurred April 21, 1999, at Columbine High School in Littleton Colorado, illustrated how the Net aided two teenage boys. Eric Harris and Dylan Klebold were members of the Trench Coat Mafia, a group that consisted of a small clique of Columbine students. Harris had his own Web site that described his plans to take down Columbine High School, along with two others whose names were coded. In addition, the site contained information about their experiments with making and detonating pipe bombs. It is believed that the two boys learned how to make these pipe bombs from information they found on the Net.

Extremists commit their crimes on behalf of a body of ideas that they strongly believe in, although the group to which they belong does not sanction the actions of the offenders. The acts of September 11, 2001, show how Muslim extremists used the Net to help accomplish their plans.

In September 2001 the use of the Internet to create much larger crimes became shockingly apparent. International terrorists flew planes into the twin towers of New York City's World Trade Center and drove another commercial aircraft plane into the Pentagon in Washington, D.C., killing thousands of people. A third plane crashed in a field in Pennsylvania, killing all on board. Investigators soon discovered that the terrorists had left footprints in cyberspace, communicating with one another through the Internet and writing cryptic messages behind pictures that had been posted online. The attackers had employed the ancient Greek practice known as steganography—a method of placing secrets on the back of images. Following the deadliest attack ever on America, FBI agents secured records from Yahoo! and America Online, and confiscated computers that the terrorists had allegedly used in Florida and Virginia. In response, the Bush administration created a high-level, high-tech office to fight cyberterror.

After the events of September 11, criminal opportunists used the tragedy and the Internet to scam innocent people. These opportunists would go online and set up phony "charitable" Web sites. Thousands of dollars were given by citizens wanting to provide financial aid, only to discover later that the money went into the pockets of con men.

Extremist groups fall into these typologies:

- *Political.* This type of homicide is motivated by doctrines or philosophies that oppose a current position of government or its representatives.
- *Religious.* This is homicide prompted by a fervent devotion or a system of beliefs based on orthodox religious conventions. This type of offense does not include cult killings. Some examples of the mainstream religious groups included in this category are the Islamic, Jewish, and Christian religions.
- *Socioeconomic.* This murder results from an intense hostility and aversion toward another individual or group who represents a certain ethnic, social, economic, or religious group. This category includes hate groups such as the neo-Nazi skinheads, the Ku Klux Klan, and groups that prey on gays and lesbians.

Extremist group murder can rarely be isolated to a single typology. Classification is based on the predominant motive.

Defining Characteristics

VICTIMOLOGY

There are several types of victims targeted by extremist murder. Predominantly, the victim represents the antithesis of the offenders' system of beliefs; therefore, victimology depends on this doctrine. If multiple victims are involved, there will be similarities of race, religion, political beliefs, or social or economic status. Selectivity is apparent in varying degrees. The victim may be a victim of opportunity or a random target who just happened across the path of the offender at the wrong time. Conversely, a victim may be targeted and die as the result of a premeditated, well-planned attack.

Extremist murder victimology also includes the victims who come into conflict with the group's objectives. This type of fatality consists of the informant, the straying member, or any other member who poses a threat to either the leader's control or group integrity.

A third type of victim is the one who is killed due to association with targets of the group. An example is the 1988 stabbing death of 24-year-old Scott Vollmer by a skinhead, Michael Elrod. Vollmer had brought a Black friend to a party when Elrod began shouting racial slurs. Elrod, 19 years old, whose driver's license lists "Skin" as his middle name, stabbed Vollmer as he tried to intercede on behalf of his Black friend.

CRIME SCENE INDICATORS FREQUENTLY NOTED

This type of offense often includes multiple crime scenes: confrontation site, death scene, and body disposal or burial locale.

Crime scene indicators depend on the number of offenders: a lone offender acting on behalf of the group or multiple offenders. Generally, multiple offenders present the obvious crime scene indicators. There may be evidence of different weapons and ammunition. The victim usually is well controlled. An example of this at the crime scene would be minimal signs of victim escape attempts: widespread blood splatter patterns and trails, overturned furniture, and other signs of struggle. A significant number of victims may offer indication of multiple offenders as well.

If there are multiple offenders, the location of the crime scene may be one that is convenient and low risk for the killers. Offender risk is lowered by preplanning and surveillance for both the assault and abduction and escape. A group effort allows a more organized, methodical approach to the killing, especially with an abduction and murder. Body disposal will often be more elaborate and low risk when a group effort is involved. As in many of the individual homicides described in this manual, the crime scene is best represented by a continuum, from the disorganized, sloppy offense to the highly professional, well-organized one. The amount of physical evidence left at the scene and the ease of assault, abduction, and escape depend on the sophistication of the group.

A lone offender may also demonstrate control and organization at the crime scene, depending on his or her level of professionalism. However, the number of victims will most likely be limited, and the overall offense usually is not committed with the ease of one involving multiple offenders.

The calling card of the group, such as symbols or communiqués, may be left at the scene.

STAGING

Staging is not present because the homicide is intended to communicate some message on behalf of the group.

COMMON FORENSIC FINDINGS

The physical evidence of multiple offenders (fibers, hairs, prints, shoe impressions) may be evident at the crime scene depending on the level of group organization. There may be evidence of different weaponry, for example, different caliber firearms or combinations of weapons such as firearms and knives.

The forensics often demonstrate the calling card or signature aspect of the group. For example, the preferred method of attack for Yahwehs is dismemberment, especially decapitation; for the Irish Republican Army, bombing; for many left-wing groups, firearms; and for skinheads, blunt-force trauma from personal weapons such as hands and feet. Multiple wounds or excessive trauma are other indicators of possible group involvement. The lone offender will mostly likely lack the signs evident of multiple offenders.

Investigative Considerations

Preoffense behavior may be evident in the planning, surveillance, and selection of the victim. In addition, the ease of escape will often demonstrate this preplanning. An example is with bombings that use a transmitting device: one person will trigger the bomb from a car, while the other is driving them away from the scene, thus allowing for an escape masked by the confusion of the explosion.

Postincident analysis of any claims or communiqués is important to determine authenticity. An investigator should not conclude that the communicating party is the offender without careful examination through psycholinguistics and other avenues.

A postoffense protection conspiracy by the group should be expected. Great caution should always be used when approaching any group meeting places or compounds. The use of booby traps is not an uncommon practice of many extremist groups.

Search Warrant Suggestions

Search warrant suggestions include documentation of offense preplanning and execution stages, such as computers, diaries, journals, recordings (audiovisual or audio), maps, and photos of victim. Also useful are media materials pertaining to group beliefs and activities and to the victim, especially if the murder is a political assassination. Firearms, explosive devices related to group signature, and evidence of stalking (travel tickets or receipts or photos) should be considered.

142.01: Extremist Homicide, Political

Extremist groups often adopt a paramilitary organizational structure and method of operation. Characteristics of a paramilitary extremist group include the wearing of uniforms, the use of training compounds, a hierarchy of leadership based on rank, and an internal code of discipline and conduct. They are highly organized groups and often have an abundance of written materials pertaining to their beliefs and structure.

Defining Characteristics

CRIME SCENE INDICATORS FREQUENTLY NOTED

The crime scene of a paramilitary extremist group is usually highly organized. The use of military tactics and modus operandi (MO) will be demonstrated. Knowledge of the group's MO will be important in examining not only the crime scene but also all elements of the offense. There will be no staging because the intent of the killing is to convey a message.

COMMON FORENSIC FINDINGS

The forensics of a paramilitary attack generally do not demonstrate overkill. The assault is usually a clean kill, exhibiting a military style of operation. Firearms and explosives are most frequently the weapons of choice.

INVESTIGATION

The offense will involve selection, surveillance, and even rehearsal. Suspects involved in paramilitary operations often have criminal records. Booby traps are especially a danger when approaching this type of extremist group operation.

Case Study: 142.01: Extremist Homicide, Political

On November 6, 1973, Marcus Foster, a highly respected Black superintendent of the Oakland, California, school system, was leaving an education committee meeting with his deputy, Robert Blackburn. As they exited the building, two gunmen ambushed them, killing Foster and wounding Blackburn. The autopsy on Foster revealed the killers had used bullets filled with cyanide crystals.

A letter sent to a local radio station stated that the Symbionese Liberation Army (SLA) was responsible for the ambush. The letter said that Foster and his deputy had been found guilty by a court of the people for "crimes against the children and life of the people." Some of these "crimes" included the proposal to form a school police unit, identity cards for students, and an effort to coordinate teachers, probation officers, and police to help reduce juvenile crime.

The SLA was founded by a Black escaped convict, Donald DeFreeze. Its roots sprang from the Black prison population in California. The most famous incident involving the SLA was the kidnapping of heiress Patty Hearst, who later joined the organization and assisted in a bank robbery perpetrated by the SLA.

On January 10, 1974, police arrested Russell Jack Little, age 24, and Michael Remiro, age 27, near Concord, California. A ballistics report linked a gun in Remiro's possession to Foster's murder. Shortly afterward, a nearby house belonging to another SLA member was set on fire. Police responding to the call found a cache of guns, ammunition, explosives, cyanide, and SLA pamphlets. They also discovered a list of officials marked for kidnapping and execution.

Outcome

On May 17, 1974, six members of the SLA were killed in a shootout with the police. The FBI arrested Patty Hearst after 16 months as a fugitive on September 18, 1975. Little and Remiro, both admitting their membership to the SLA, were sentenced to life imprisonment for the murder of Marcus Foster and the attempted murder of deputy Blackburn.

Case Study: 142.02: Extremist Homicide, Religious

Background

On January 11, 1983, Memphis Police officer R. S. "Bob" Hester, along with two other patrolmen, responded to a bogus tip about a shoplifting warrant for Lindberg

Sanders, who resided at 2239 Shannon Street. Upon entering the residence, a group of individuals later described as religious fanatics attacked the three officers in an apparent attempt to capture them. One officer was shot in the face but managed to escape. The second officer was severely beaten about the face and head but also managed to escape.

At 3:15 a.m. on January 13, members of the Memphis Police Department TACT team swept into the house through a back door and found Officer Hester dead. The seven offenders who had held him hostage were subsequently killed when they engaged police in a gun battle.

Victimology

Patrolman Hester, age 34, was one month shy of his 10-year anniversary as a Memphis police officer when he was taken hostage. He had worked the North Precinct most of his career. He was hurt once in the line of duty in 1977 when he was attacked by a man in a pool hall.

Officer Hester had the reputation for making a great deal of quality felony arrests. He had received several commendations as well. He also was active with the police department athletics.

Crime Scene Indicators

The crime scene combined the last known hostage location and place of confrontation with police: both usually contain indicators crucial to any hostage-murder. The incident involving Officer Hester never left the confines of the Shannon Street house.

Forensic Findings

The autopsy report of Officer Hester stated he had suffered numerous injuries caused by blunt-force trauma. Most of the injury was focused on his face and head. His skull was fractured in at least one place along the hairline. There were numerous scrapes and lacerations on Hester's head and face in addition to bruises on his upper thigh and abdomen near the groin. There were lacerations behind the elbows and below both knees. A blunt instrument had produced two puncture wounds on his right leg. Cause of death was summarized as "beaten to death." Hester's time of death was estimated to be around 12 to 14 hours before the house was stormed.

Investigation

Lindberg Sanders, the leader of the "Shannon Street Seven," was described by friends as once being an easy-going, dependable craftsman. He began to undergo a change in 1973 when he was hospitalized for psychiatric problems. After several more hospitalizations and outpatient treatment, Lindberg was diagnosed as a schizophrenic with religious delusions. He quit working altogether in 1975 and devoted his time to reading the Bible and holding meetings at his Shannon Street home. From these meetings, a small group of followers emerged who adopted Sander's beliefs and routinely gathered with him to fast, smoke marijuana, and read the Bible. Lindberg believed that pork and scavenger fish should not be eaten, and water could be drunk only if it was colored. His followers would put mustard, Kool-Aid, or ketchup in their water so it was not clear.

At some point, Lindberg's doctrine began to take an ominous direction, dictating that police were agents of the devil, antireligious, and anti-Christian. The precipitating factor of the Shannon Street siege may have been that Sanders believed the world was due to end that week. His group had congregated four days before the incident and began to fast and pray in preparation for the end. Lindberg had expressed his belief that he was gifted with a special immortality, so he expected to survive the end of the world as well as a bullet from a policeman's gun.

The incident actually started with an earlier call on January 11 when police were told a suspect wanted in a purse snatching was at the Sanders residence. The police talked to Sanders and those gathered with him at his home. The members of the group were very upset that the world had not ended Monday, as Sanders had predicted. The responding officers left without incident since there was nothing that could to lead to an arrest.

At 9:00 p.m. the call was placed for them to return. This is the one that Patrolman Hester responded to. He and the other two officers were met with a barrage of gunfire. The two other officers escaped, although both were wounded. Negotiators tried for the next 24 hours to reason with Sanders, without success. On January 12 at 11:11 p.m., all of the lights in the house were turned out by its occupants. After a 30-hour siege, the police stormed the house with automatic weapons and tear gas, killing Sanders and the six other men. Hester had been beaten to death several hours earlier, the police said.

143: Group Excitement

A death that results from group excitement—a group's aggression escalates in proportion to the actions committed to the victim—can be structured or unstructured, with a contagious component.

Defining Characteristics

VICTIMOLOGY

The victim can start as a targeted individual and as the chaos and excitement escalate, more random persons become involved. Another variation of this is that the group chooses a victim randomly. There are often multiple victims and possible surviving victims of the attack.

CRIME SCENE INDICATORS FREQUENTLY NOTED

There are often witnesses to this type of attack, although they may be hesitant to come forward. The attack usually occurs in an open, public place. The weapons used are typically those of opportunity, especially personal weapons such as the hands and feet. The crime scene is disorganized with no cover-up; the body is left in the open with minimal to no effort to conceal it. There are usually signs of the multiple offenders involved: fingerprints, footprints, fibers, semen, and others.

COMMON FORENSIC FINDINGS

There is usually overkill due to bludgeoning and generalized blunt-force trauma. The victim shows multiple wounds from a frenzied assault. There may sexual assault or insertion.

Investigative Considerations

Drugs and alcohol are often involved with the offenders. The attack is of short duration, and there are often witnesses due to the openness of the crime. Since a loosely structured group with no main leader is involved, the weakness of the group may be exploited.

Search Warrant Suggestions

Search warrant suggestions include documentation of offense preplanning and execution stages, personal computers of the suspects, their diaries, journals, recordings (audiovisual or audio), maps, and photos of victim. Also useful are media materials found in their apartments pertaining to group beliefs and activities.

Chapter 11

Arson/Bombing

*200: Vandalism-motivated arson
201: Willful and malicious mischief
    201.01: Experimentation with
        fire/explosives
    201.02: Reporting/causing
        false alarms
    201.03: Hoax devices
202: Peer/group pressure
209: Other
*210: Excitement-motivated arson
211: Thrill seeker
212: Attention seeker
213: Recognition (hero)
214: Sexual perversion
219: Other
*220: Revenge-motivated arson
221: Personal revenge
    221.01: Spite
    221.02: Jealousy
222: Institutional retaliation
223: Intimidation
229: Other
*230: Crime concealment
231: Murder
232: Suicide

233: Breaking and entering
234: Embezzlement
235: Larceny
236: Destroying records
239: Other
*240: Profit-motivated arson
241: Fraud
    241.01: Insurance
    241.02: Liquidate property
    241.03: Dissolve business
    241.04: Inventory
242: Employment
243: Parcel clearance
244: Competition
249: Other
*250: Extremist-motivated arson
*251: Terrorism
252: Discrimination
253: Riots/civil disturbance
259: Other
*260: Serial arson
261: Spree arson
262: Mass arson
*270: Serial bombing

Arson is the crime of setting a fire with intent to cause damage. A fire investigation is an unenviable task. The devastation, charred debris, collapsed structures, and water-soaked ashes, together with the smoke and stench, make

---

*While there is no explicit case example given, this classification denotes the motive as described in the text.

Table 11.1 Arson Rate per 100,000 Inhabitants (FBI, 2012)

2002	2003	2004	2005	2006	2007	2008	2009	2010
32.4	30.4	28.2	26.9	26.8	24.7	24.1	21.3	19.6

the task uninviting and difficult. See Table 11.1 for Arson Rate per 100,000 Inhabitants.

Statistics from the FBI's Uniform Crime Report–2010 note the following (FBI, 2010):

- In 2010, 15,475 law enforcement agencies provided 1 to 12 months of arson data and reported 56,825 arsons.
- Arsons involving structures (e.g., residential, storage, public, etc.) accounted for 45.5% of the total number of arson offenses. Mobile property was involved in 26.0% of arsons, and other types of property (such as crops, timber, fences, etc.) accounted for 28.5% of reported arsons.
- The average dollar loss due to arson was $17,612.
- Arsons of industrial/manufacturing structures resulted in the highest average dollar losses (an average of $133,717 per arson).
- Arson offenses decreased 7.6% in 2010 when compared with arson data reported in 2009.
- Nationwide, there were 19.6 arson offenses for every 100,000 inhabitants.
- In 2010, there were 8,806 arrests for arson (a rate of 3.7 per 100,000 inhabitants).
  - 3,132 of those detained were under 18 years of age, 4,382 were over 18 years of age (FBI, 2010).
  - 6,237 were male, 1,277 were female (FBI, 2010).
  - 6,592 were identified as White, 1,978 as Black, 100 as Native Indian, 96 as Asian or Pacific Islander (FBI, 2010).

The best arson investigation uses a team of trained personnel. It begins with fire brigade staff. Police and insurance investigators are added for their skills in determining motive and opportunities. An electrical engineer or electrician is required to investigate electrical systems. Scientists have a valuable role to play. They should be able to arrive at a fire scene without any predetermined ideas. An analytical approach, using patient, thorough, and systematic technique should reveal critical and vital information.

The basic role of an investigator at a fire scene is twofold: to determine the origin of the fire (the site where the fire began) and then to examine the site of origin closely to try to determine what caused a fire to start at or near that location. An examination typically begins by trying to gain an overall impression of the site and the fire damage; this could be done at ground level or from an elevated position. From this the investigator might proceed to an examination of the materials present, the fuel load, and the state of the debris at various places. The search for the fire's origin should be based on elementary rules:

- Fire tends to burn upward and outward, so investigators should look for V patterns along walls.
- The presence of combustible materials will increase the intensity and extent of the fire, and the fire will rise faster as it gets hotter. Investigators therefore look for different temperature conditions.
- The fire needs fuel and oxygen to continue.
- A fire's spread will be influenced by factors such as air currents, walls, and stairways. Falling burning debris and the effectiveness of firefighters will also have an influence.

If a fire is not the result of an accident, it must be arson. The motives to commit arson include vandalism, fraud, revenge, sabotage, and pyromania. A major objective in any suspected case of arson is to locate, sample, and analyze residual accelerants.

It is a primary mission of the National Center for the Analysis of Violent Crime (NCAVC) to conduct arson offender research in order to provide investigative assistance to police and fire agencies in unsolved arson cases. Through this research, the NCAVC has recognized that identifying the offender's motive is a key element in crime analysis. It then uses this method of analysis to determine the recognizable personal traits and characteristics exhibited by an unknown offender. Motive can be defined as an inner drive or impulse that is the cause, reason, or incentive that induces or prompts a specific behavior (Rider, 1980). The following motive classifications consistently appear and have proven most effective in identifying offender characteristics:

- Revenge
- Excitement
- Vandalism
- Profit
- Crime concealment

Arson: General Characteristics

Defining Characteristics

Victimology: Targeted Property

- The essential factor that often determines the motive.
- Random, opportunistic versus specific.

CRIME SCENE INDICATORS FREQUENTLY NOTED

- Organized arsonist:
  - Elaborate incendiary devices (e.g., electronic timing mechanisms, initiators).
  - Less physical evidence; if forced entry, more skillful (e.g., footprints, fingerprints).
  - Methodical approach (e.g., trailers, multiple sets, excessive accelerant use).
- Disorganized arsonist:
  - Materials on hand.
  - Matches, cigarettes, more common accelerants (lighter fluid, gasoline).
  - More physical evidence left (handwriting, footprints, fingerprints).

COMMON FORENSIC FINDINGS

- Incendiary devices: Components (initiators, timing devices, candles, electronic timers, tape, wires).
- Accelerants: Gasoline, lighter fluid, mixtures (gasoline/kerosene).
- More sophisticated accelerants: Diesel/kerosene, water soluble (alcohol).
- Molotov cocktail: Glass fragments for fingerprints, cloth for fiber match.

Search Warrant Suggestions

- Evidence of incendiary devices: Packing, components, fireworks, fire-crackers, tape for matching with crime scene evidence, how-to books.

200: Vandalism-Motivated Arson

Vandalism-motivated arson is due to malicious and mischievous motivation that results in destruction or damage. The types of vandalism-motivated arson in this category are willful and malicious mischief (201), peer/group pressure (202), and other (209).

DEFINING CHARACTERISTICS

VICTIMOLOGY

Educational facilities are a common target for arson motivated by vandalism. Other properties targeted by the vandal arsonist are residential areas and vegetation (which includes grass, brush, woodland, and timber).

CRIME SCENE INDICATORS FREQUENTLY NOTED

Arson by vandalism frequently involves multiple offenders who act spontaneously and impulsively. If multiple offenders are involved, one personality tends to be the leader or instigator of the group. The typical crime scene reflects the spontaneous nature of the offense and is representative of a disorganized crime. The offenders tend to use materials present at the site and leave physical evidence at the scene such as footprints and fingerprints. Occasionally, flammable liquids are used. The offenders may gain entrance to a secured structure through windows. Evidence will show a mechanical breaking of the glass as opposed to heat breakage. Matchbooks, cigarettes, and spray-paint cans (used for graffiti) often are present. Other signs suggesting vandalism may be present, including writing on chalkboards, materials missing from the scene, and general destruction of property.

COMMON FORENSIC FINDINGS

Analysis of any flammable liquid used is the main forensic finding. The occasional use of firecrackers or fireworks provides additional evidence for forensic analysis. If the offenders entered the property by breaking a window, glass particles may be present in the clothing of the identified suspects.

Investigative Considerations

The typical offender is a juvenile male who has seven to nine years of formal education. He tends to have a record of poor school performance and does not work. He is single and lives with either one or both parents. Alcohol and drug use generally are not associated with the fire setting. The offender may be already known to the police and may have an arrest record. It also is probable that at least one of the offenders is known to school authorities as being disruptive and having a problem dealing with authority.

The majority of these offenders live less than one mile from the crime scene. Most flee immediately from the scene and do not return. If they do return, they view the fire from a safe and distant vantage point.

To narrow the scope of the investigation and limit the number of suspects, the investigator should solicit the help of school, fire service, and police officials. These officials would be the most likely to come into contact with previous vandalism-motivated activities of the juvenile offender.

Search Warrant Suggestions

- Spray-paint cans.
- Items from the scene, especially if a school was the target.

- Explosive devices; fireworks, firecrackers, packaging, or cartons.
- Flammable liquids.
- Clothing; evidence of flammable liquid; glass shards, for witness identification.
- Shoes: Footprints, flammable liquid traces.

Case Study: 201: Willful and Malicious Mischief

Background

At 10:37 p.m. on a clear, cool Saturday night in the fall of 1990, a fire was discovered at a junior high school. The fire caused in excess of $250,000 damage to the school's library and an adjacent all-purpose room. As insurance costs were extremely high in the low-income area this school served, coverage was minimal and included large deductibles. The financially strapped school district was unable to repair all the structural damage, let alone replace the books lost in the fire.

Victimology

The school, built in 1972 to serve grades 6 through 9, had a history of fires over the years, but none were as large as this one. As with many other schools, vandalism was a problem. There were occasional false fire alarms and bomb threats, and graffiti was evident in many areas of the building. Periodically, shop equipment and windows were broken deliberately with rocks. There was also some theft.

Crime Scene Indicators

After interviewing firefighters, investigators examining the crime scene determined that a library window facing an interior courtyard had been broken. Glass had been removed from the lower edge of the frame, and a sweatshirt was placed over the sill, apparently so that the burglars would not cut themselves. Inside the building, investigators found the origin of the fire in a wastebasket against a wall, beside a photocopier. Hundreds of books had been pulled from the shelves and lay in the aisles where they had fallen. By noting the protected floor areas beneath the books, firefighters confirmed that the books were in that position before the fire began. Smoke damage and fire damage were too extensive to determine if other acts of vandalism took place. The fire was ruled to be arson.

Forensic Findings

No evidence of flammable liquid was found at the scene. It appeared that an open flame was applied to the available material in and around the wastebasket. No footprints were found that could have belonged to the suspects, and if there were any, they were obliterated during the firefighting efforts. A fragment of basalt block was found on the floor inside the library, opposite the broken window. The sweatshirt found was of medium size, dark blue in color, and had no lettering.

After the sweatshirt was dried and examined carefully (it was soaking wet due to the firefighting efforts), black hairs were found inside it.

Investigation

Because of the type of target, the manner of attack, and the evidence found at the scene, investigators suspected that students might have been responsible for setting the fire. They approached school authorities and asked a vice principal for a list of students she thought capable of the crime. After consulting student counselors, she supplied 23 names. Several days later, as investigators were nearly through interviewing those listed, they received a call from the mother of one of the students. She reported that her son had told her that another student had boasted that he and another youth had set the fire. These two students, whose names were on the list provided by school authorities, were interviewed and separately confessed to the crime.

Outcome

The boys, both 14 years old, were turned over to juvenile authorities. Both had been in previous trouble involving minor violations, and one was suspected of involvement in burglaries. They were adjudicated delinquent and remanded to the state youth facility. Their parents could have been liable for fire damage; however, neither had insurance or was able to pay.

210: Excitement-Motivated Arson

The excitement-motivated arsonist is prompted to set fires because he craves excitement that is satisfied by fire setting. This offender rarely intends the fire to harm people. The types of arsonists included in this category are thrill seeker (211), attention seeker (212), recognition (hero) (213), sexual perversion (214), and other (219).

DEFINING CHARACTERISTICS

VICTIMOLOGY

The type of property targeted will help determine the motive. Dumpsters, vegetation (grass, brush, woodland, and timber), lumber stacks, construction sites, and residential property are common targets of the excitement fire setter. The offender may select a location that offers a good vantage point from which to safely observe the fire suppression and investigation. In some cases where fires occur inside unoccupied structures, volunteer firefighters and fire buffs should not be eliminated as possible suspects. Both lone and multiple offenders are common to this type of arson.

CRIME SCENE INDICATORS FREQUENTLY NOTED

The targeted properties are often adjacent to outdoor areas that have a reputation as a hangout or place of frequent parties. The offender often will use materials on hand. If incendiary devices are used, they usually have a time-delay mechanism. Offenders in the 18- to 30 -age group are more prone to use accelerants. Matches and cigarettes are frequently used to ignite vegetation fires.

A small percentage of excitement fires are motivated by sexual perversion. At these crime scenes, the investigator may find ejaculate, fecal deposits, or pornographic material (magazines or pictures). In most cases, this fire setter uses available material and starts small fires.

COMMON FORENSIC FINDINGS

In addition to the standard examination of fingerprints, vehicle and bicycle tire tracks, and so on, the forensic analysis that is performed should look for the possible remnants of the components of incendiary devices. If the arsonist is motivated by sexual perversion, ejaculate or fecal material may offer forensic information of value.

Investigative Considerations

The typical excitement arsonist is a juvenile or young adult male with 10 or more years of formal education. This offender is generally unemployed, single, and living with one or both parents. His family tends to be from the middle-class to lower-middle-class bracket. In general, this offender is socially inadequate, particularly in heterosexual relationships. Serial offenders are common to this category of fire setters.

The use of drugs or alcohol usually is not found with the youngest offenders but does occur with older ones. A history of police contact for nuisance offenses is prevalent with the excitement-motivated offender. The older the offender is, the longer the record.

The distance that the offender lives from the crime scene can be frequently determined by an analysis of the targets he or she burned. Through target and cluster analysis, the investigator can determine if the offender is mobile.

Some excitement-motivated arsonists do not leave once the fire has started. They prefer to mingle with the crowds who have gathered to watch the fire. The offenders who do leave the scene usually return later and observe the damage and activity of their handiwork.

Search Warrant Suggestions

Vehicle

- Material similar to incendiary devices used: Fireworks, containers that components were shipped in, packaging, wires.
- Floor mats, trunk padding, carpeting: Residue from accelerants (not conclusive evidence but indicative).
- Beer cans, matchbooks, cigarettes: To match any brands found at the scene.

House

- Material similar to incendiary devices used: Fireworks, containers that components were shipped in, packaging, wires.
- Clothing, shoes: Accelerant and soil samples if vegetation fire.
- Beer cans, matchbooks, cigarettes: To match any brands found at the scene.
- Cigarette lighter, especially if subject does not smoke.
- Diaries, computers, journals, notes, logs, recordings, and maps documenting fire.
- Newspaper articles reporting fires.
- Souvenirs from the crime scene.

Case Study: 212: Attention Seeker

Background

During the summer months, several junior volunteer firefighters sat in the fire station of a small city, complaining that no one, least of all their chief, took them seriously. These 16- and 17-year-olds were thrilled at the chance to ride on the fire engines they had always admired. Yet they often were stung by the chief's criticism of their performance. As the bored youths sat and talked, they had an idea: if they could set a fire in a vacant house, they would have a chance to show the chief how well they worked. Although some of the young volunteers were reluctant, none of them challenged the idea.

Victimology

Over the span of one year, 10 houses were set on fire. The houses were vacant and had been deemed uninhabitable before the fires occurred. Few of these houses were insured.

Crime Scene Indicators

Fire investigators noticed a pattern: all of the fires occurred in a jurisdiction served by the volunteer fire department, were in vacant houses, and were set during nighttime hours. All the houses had electricity and other utilities disconnected.

Forensic Findings

The fires were set with available material: paper products found at the scene, such as newspapers, cardboard, and kindling of all sorts. These materials were gathered, piled somewhere within the building, and then set on fire with a match or cigarette lighter. No traces of flammable liquid were found. Any footprints or tire tracks were obliterated when the youths returned with the fire-suppression equipment. Forcible entry was rarely necessary and was not apparent at the crime scenes.

Investigation

With so many youthful co-conspirators, the truth eventually reached the authorities conducting the investigation. A search conducted during the course of the investigation produced a diary in which one of the volunteers detailed the times and locations of a few of the fires. The author of the diary implicated himself and other volunteers, who in turn provided investigators with additional names. Subsequently, 11 of the volunteer firefighters were charged with arson. One defendant was quoted as saying, "It isn't like we wanted to go out and burn down houses to hurt people. The firehouse was like our second home."

Outcome

Since the defendants had no prior criminal records, they ultimately received sentences ranging from probation to juvenile detention time, depending on the extent of their involvement.

220: Revenge-Motivated Arson

A revenge-motivated fire is set in retaliation for some injustice, real or imagined, perceived by the offender. This offense may be a well-planned, one-time event compared with the other categories of arson, or the offender may be a serial arsonist taking revenge against society, with little or no preplanning. Many arson motivations have an element of revenge in addition to the main motive. The types of revenge-motivated arson included in this category are personal retaliation (221), societal retaliation (222), institutional retaliation (e.g., against the government) (222), group retaliation (e.g., against gangs) (222), intimidation (223), and other (229).

Defining Characteristics

Victimology

As with most of the other arson categories, victimology becomes the key factor in determining the motive. This is especially true with the revenge category. The victim of a revenge fire generally has a history of interpersonal or professional conflict with the offender. Examples are conflicts developing from a lover's triangle, a landlord–tenant relationship, or an employer–employee association. Revenge-motivated arson also tends to be an intraracial offense.

The targeted property often varies with the sex of the offender. Female subjects usually target something of significance to the victim, such as a vehicle or personal effects. The ex-lover revenge arsonist frequently burns clothing, bedding, or other personal effects. For the revenge arsonist in general, residential property and vehicles are the prime targets. Arsonists who seek revenge against society may exhibit displaced aggression by choosing targets at random. Other offenders retaliate against institutions such as churches, government facilities, and universities or corporations.

CRIME SCENE INDICATORS FREQUENTLY NOTED

The female offender usually burns an area of personal significance, such as the living room sofa or the bedroom. She often starts the fire by using the victim's clothing or other personal effects. If she targets the victim's vehicle, she usually sets fire to the interior passenger compartment.

The male arsonist also may begin with an area of personal significance, but his fire-setting episode is more wide ranging and destructive. He may use an excessive amount of accelerant and sometimes Molotov cocktails.

COMMON FORENSIC FINDINGS

The female arsonist's accelerant of choice tends to be flammables that are readily accessible, such as lighter fluid. The male in this category is inclined to use excessive amounts of accelerants such as gasoline. If he uses a Molotov cocktail, cloth for fiber comparisons, glass for possible fingerprints, and accelerant residue are important forensic evidence.

Investigative Considerations

The revenge fire setter is predominantly an adult male with 10 or more years of formal education. If employed, this offender usually is a blue-collar worker of lower socioeconomic status. A revenge arsonist typically resides in rental property. Although this offender tends not to be a loner and has close relationships, the relationships generally are not stable or long term. An exception is the revenge-motivated serial arsonist, who is often a loner.

The revenge arsonist often has some type of prior law enforcement contact for crimes such as burglary, theft, or vandalism. The use of alcohol with this offense is common. The offender also may use drugs during the crime, but alcohol use is more prevalent. The offender is rarely accompanied to the crime scene and seldom returns once the fire is set. In fact, he wants as much distance between himself and the fire as possible and concentrates on establishing an alibi. The offender usually lives within the affected community. Mobility is a factor with him, so he often uses a vehicle to get to and from the crime scene. This is in contrast to the revenge-motivated serial arsonist, who frequently walks to the scene. After the fire, the offender may increase alcohol consumption. He expresses a short-lived sense of relief and satisfaction and an uncaring attitude toward the victim.

Since the revenge fire is a focused attack, the investigator needs to determine who has suffered the most from this fire. Does the victim have a history of conflict with someone? If the victim is a landlord, has he evicted anyone recently? If the victim did have an evolving conflict with someone, was an escalation of violence apparent?

The investigator is cautioned that documented studies show the events that precipitate the revenge-motivated arson may take place months or even years prior to the fire, a factor that is commonly overlooked. An investigator should be prepared to expand the search if no suspects or viable leads are apparent from the beginning.

Search Warrant Suggestions

- If accelerants are used: Shoes, socks, clothing, glass particles in clothing (if there was a break-in).
- Discarded, concealed clothing.
- Bottles, flammable liquids, matchbooks.
- Cloth (fiber comparison), tape (if an explosive device was used).
- Objects taken from the scene.
- Clothing, shoes if a liquid accelerant was used (or a homicide victim's blood; glass fragments if windows were broken during burglary attempt).

Case Study: 221: Personal Revenge

Background

A private residence located in a metropolitan suburb was the scene of personal-revenge arson. The owner, a male who lived alone in the house, had been away for a few days. When he returned, he found the interior of his house on fire. In trying to extinguish it himself, he discovered that two fires had been set.

Victimology

One fire was set in the bedroom and another on the living room couch. A closed bedroom door prevented the two fires from burning together. The living room television set was missing.

The owner of the house often had male visitors, and recently before the fire had a male friend living with him.

Crime Scene Indicators

The fire was suspicious to investigators from the outset. It was obvious that two separate fires had occurred, with the closed bedroom door preventing the fires from communicating. Investigators eliminated all possible accidental causes of the fire, leaving arson as the only possibility. In the bedroom, a large bed was completely consumed by fire, and the wall behind it was damaged. In the living room, a couch had burned completely through the floor to the ground below. Smoke damage was extreme throughout the home.

Forensic Findings

There was no evidence of forced entry. Doors to the house were locked when the owner returned. The fires were accelerated by lighter fluid applied to both the bed and the couch. An open flame, such as a match or cigarette lighter, was used to ignite the flammable materials. The concentration of fire destroyed both items of furniture. On closer examination of the surrounding areas, the bed and couch were determined to be the points of origin.

Investigation

When the victim noticed his television set was missing, he mentioned to police that a 21-year-old male acquaintance who had recently moved out of the house wanted that television set and previously had stolen other property from him. The former roommate was located and, when interviewed, confessed to setting the fires.

The offender stated he had lived in the victim's home for a few months and moved out about one month before the fire. He complained that visitors went through his belongings and spoke negatively about him to others. Furthermore, on one occasion when all of the guests were drinking, one of them took sexual advantage of him. Intent on revenge, the offender returned to the house when he knew the owner was away and gained entry with a key he had kept. While he was removing the television, he thought about the unpleasant sexual incident and became angrier. He obtained some lighter fluid from a nearby convenience store, returned, and set the fires. He had set the couch on fire because that was where the sexual episode had taken place.

Outcome

The offender was convicted and sentenced to prison for an eight-year term.

230: Crime Concealment Arson

In this category, arson is a secondary or collateral criminal activity, perpetrated for the purpose of covering up a primary criminal activity of some nature. The types of crime concealment–motivated arson in this category are murder (231), suicide (232), breaking and entering (233), embezzlement (234), larceny (235), destroying records (236), and other (239).

DEFINING CHARACTERISTICS

VICTIMOLOGY

The targeted property is dependent on the nature of the concealment. The target may be a business, a residence, or a vehicle.

CRIME SCENE INDICATORS FREQUENTLY NOTED

- *Murder concealment.* The fire is an attempt to obliterate the fact that a homicide has been committed, destroy forensic evidence of potential lead value, or conceal the victim's identity. The investigator should observe the position and location of the victim to determine whether the victim was alive when the fire started, and if so, why the victim could not escape. Victims grouped together should lead one to suspect murder.

    The offender commonly uses liquid accelerant. Although the origin of the fire is usually on or near the victims, many of these fires are not adequate to totally consume the body or the evidence. The offender tends to act toward the disorganized end of the spectrum. Correspondingly, the investigator should expect to find more physical evidence than with other arsons. An attack that appears be personalized suggests a lone offender. There is also the "DNA torch," an offender who, concerned about the detection of unique genetic markers contained in anatomical fluids, uses fire to conceal a homicide that involves a sexual assault.

- *Burglary concealment.* With an unsophisticated or less experienced burglar, the crime scene often reflects the use of available materials to start the fire and the presence of multiple offenders.

- *Auto theft concealment.* In the case of auto theft concealment, the offender will use or strip and burn the vehicle to eliminate prints. The crime frequently involves multiple offenders.

- *Destruction of records.* When arson is used to destroy records, the fire is set in the area where they are contained. In arson-for-profit cases, records are commonly one of several points of fire origin.

COMMON FORENSIC FINDINGS

With the use of forensics, one should determine if the victim was alive when the fire began and why he or she did not escape. If the victim sustained injuries, it should be determined whether they were result of the fire or from a deliberate injury, which could have been sufficient to have prevented escape. The victim of a DNA torch will demonstrate a concentrated area of burns around the genitals. In this case, the investigator should suspect that a sexual assault has occurred.

Investigative Considerations

Alcohol and recreational drug use is common to the crime concealment–motivated arsonist. The offender can be expected to have a history of police or fire department contacts or arrests.

The offender is most likely a young adult who lives within the surrounding community and is highly mobile—especially someone involved in auto theft. The offender who uses arson to conceal burglary or auto theft is routinely accompanied to the scene by co-conspirators. Almost all offenders in this category leave the crime scene immediately and do not return. Postoffense behavior may include an increase in alcohol or drug consumption.

Murder concealment is usually a one-time event and does not involve serial arson. The investigator inquiring into an arson set to destroy records should discover who would benefit from their concealment.

Search Warrant Suggestions

- Refer to the classification dealing with the primary motive.
- Gasoline containers.
- Clothing, shoes if liquid accelerant was used (or if there was a homicide victim).
- Glass fragments if windows were broken during a burglary attempt.
- Burned paper documents.

Case Study: 231: Crime Concealment, Murder

Background

During the early morning hours, a fire department responded to a fire involving a 70-year-old two-story residence. The fire soon became a three-alarm blaze requiring over an hour and a half to suppress. As firefighters sifted through the debris, they discovered a badly burned body in what appeared to be a sitting position on a sofa in the living room. They noted a hole approximately two inches in diameter in the left frontal area of the skull. Suspecting foul play, they notified the police department's homicide team.

Victimology

The victim was identified as an 86-year-old woman who had lived alone at the residence for 35 years. According to one of her three sisters, she had not allowed anyone into her home for six or seven years preceding her death. One sister, who lived nearby, delivered the victim's meals to her but never was allowed farther than the front door.

The victim kept large amounts of money hidden away in the many boxes she had stacked around the house. Her reputation of being a miser was common knowledge in her neighborhood. Her sisters told investigators that the victim was afraid of fire and consequently never cooked or used candles, did not smoke, and had the heat turned off.

The victim was a feisty woman who had confronted an intruder in the house just two days before her death. She told her sister that during the night, she had awakened to see the intruder and threatened to "poke him full of holes" if he did not leave. She then struck him with a broom handle. She never reported the burglary attempt to the police.

Crime Scene Indicators

The fire investigators quickly determined that arson was the cause of the fire. Common combustibles and furniture upholstery had been ignited with an open flame in the living room. The use of available materials to start a fire is a typical crime scene indicator of the less sophisticated arsonist. The origin of the fire was on or near the sofa, where the victim's body had been found.

Most murder concealment fires are not adequate to destroy the corpse. Even in this instance, in which the fire was aided by the large amount of combustible materials in the house (cardboard boxes full of books, magazines, clothing, and other items piled three to four feet deep in some rooms), investigators found an intact body.

Several pieces of fabric and paper with red stains similar to blood were found in the vicinity of the body. In addition, forcible entry had been made through the rear door.

Forensic Findings

The autopsy revealed a concentration of burns around the victim's head. Although the corpse was badly burned, pathologists were able to locate and accurately identify the multiple trauma injuries, unrelated to the fire, that had caused her death. The trauma consisted of an irregularly edged hole in the frontal temporal area of the skull and more than 100 stab wounds over the entire body. Two of these wounds were gaping holes approximately four inches by three inches. It was obvious the fire began postmortem and was intended to conceal the corpse.

Investigation

The police received several telephone calls that provided direction to the investigation. In addition, immediately after the fire, a paperboy came forward and told police he had seen two males counting money on a stairway during the morning after the discovery of the fire. As he approached the men, he was warned to keep walking and forget what he had seen. The boy had observed dried blood on the back of one of the suspect's hands.

Subsequently the police arrested three juvenile males. A female was discovered to have picked them up at the scene in her car, but she was not directly involved with the break-in and murder. The suspects were single males living with family members within the surrounding community of the victim. Each had lengthy histories of disruptive behavior at school and police records for arrests (including burglary). All three admitted to heavy alcohol and drug use, with a marked postoffense increase in consumption. They did not return to the scene after the fire was set.

Outcome

After the suspects were arrested and interviewed, each admitted his role as a participant in the crime but shifted the major responsibility of the homicide to one of the others. All three were found guilty of first-degree felony murder and arson and were sentenced to a maximum of 26 years in prison.

240: Profit-Motivated Arson

Arson for profit is a fire set for the purpose of achieving material gain, either directly or indirectly. It is a commercial crime and exhibits the least passion of any of the motivations that generate the crime of arson. The types of profit-motivated arson found in this category are fraud (241)—including fraud to collect insurance (241.01), fraud to liquidate property (241.02), fraud to dissolve business (241.03), and fraud to conceal loss or liquidate inventory (241.04)—employment (242), parcel clearance (243), competition (244), and other (249).

Defining Characteristics

VICTIMOLOGY

The property targeted by arson for profit includes residential property, businesses, and modes of transportation such as vehicles and boats.

CRIME SCENE INDICATORS FREQUENTLY NOTED

This type of arson usually involves a well-planned and methodical approach. The crime scene demonstrates a more organized style by containing less physical evidence that would identify the offender and more sophisticated incendiary devices. When a large business is burned, multiple offenders may be involved.

Because the complete destruction of the target is intended, an excessive use of accelerant and multiple sets are evident. Accelerant trailers may also be found at the crime scene.

A lack of forced entry is not infrequent in arson-for-profit cases. Use of incendiary devices is more prevalent than the use of available materials. Such devices are often elaborate—for example, constructed with timing devices, electrical timers, initiators, and candles. The remnants of these devices usually can be found at the crime scene.

Items of value are often removed, especially if a residence is the target. For example, the removal of expensive paintings before the fire may be evidenced by the presence of studs to hold the paintings but no residue of frames present after the fire. Investigators may observe substitution of lower-quality furniture and clothing and lack of personal effects, such as family pictures and photo albums. A suggestion for the investigator is to count the clothes hangers, especially in the woman's closet, to see if the subject's claims of lost belongings match what appears at the crime scene. The torching of select areas not consistent with the pattern of an accidental fire should also raise suspicion.

The point of origin of the fire can be a determining factor. Because the intent of the offender is usually to totally destroy the target of arson, the selected point of origin is that which is most efficient to establish the desired loss—for example, in a structure fire, probable multiple points of origin, and in an inventory fire, centered on or restricted to that portion of the inventory affected.

COMMON FORENSIC FINDINGS

A common forensic finding with arson for profit is the use of sophisticated accelerants (water-soluble accelerants such as alcohol) or mixtures (such as gasoline with diesel fuel or kerosene). Because the use of incendiary devices is common with this arson, components of these devices, such as initiators, electrical timers, timing devices, and candles, are additional findings that may assist the investigator.

Investigative Considerations

The typical primary offender in this category is an adult male with 10 or more years of formal education; this may vary, however. A secondary offender is the "torch for hire," who most frequently is a male, 25 to 40 years of age, and usually unemployed. The torch operates as an agent for the primary offender, who contracts for the torch's services and is the dominant personality in the total offense.

The typical primary offender for commercial fires may have no police record. The torch for hire will likely have a prior arrest record for offenses such as burglary, assault, public intoxication, and possibly even a previous arson.

The offender generally lives more than one mile from the crime scene. Many arsonists for profit are accompanied to the crime scene, and most leave the scene and do not return.

The offender's preoffense conversations with others may offer indications of premeditation; for example, a subject planning to burn his business might tell workers to remove their personal effects the day before the fire breaks out. A recent change of ownership or increase in insurance policy should raise suspicion. The investigator should look for any of the following indicators of financial difficulties if arson for profit is suspected:

Business

- Decreasing revenue.
- Increasing production costs.
- New technology making current processes or equipment inadequate.
- Costly lease or rental agreements.
- Unprofitable contracts, loss of key customer.
- Failure to record depreciation.
- Personal expenses paid with corporate funds.
- Bounced checks.
- Hypothetical assets, liens on assets, overinsured assets.
- Inventory levels: Removal prior to fire, overstocking caused by over-production, exaggeration of loss.
- Litigation against business or owners.
- Bankruptcy proceedings.
- Two sets of books maintained.
- Prior-year losses.
- Prior insurance claims.
- Duplicate sales invoices.
- Alleged renovations.
- Frequent change of ownership preceding fire.
- Use of photocopies instead of original source documents.

Personal

- Bounced checks.
- Costly lease or rental agreements.
- Large number of overdue bills.

- Inability to pay current bills (such as utilities or telephone).
- Credit limits imposed by lenders.
- Payment of bills by cashier's check or money order.
- Alleged renovations.
- Sales between related parties.
- Negative cash flow but with appearance of continued financial health.

Search Warrant Suggestions

- Check financial records: worksheets, loan records, credit history, accountant's books, bank records, income tax forms, bank deposit tickets, canceled checks, check stubs.
- If evidence of fuel or air explosion (gasoline vapor and ambient air mixture at sufficient temperature) at the scene, check emergency rooms for patients with burn injuries (this type of explosion does not occur in accidental fires).
- Determine condition of utilities (gas, electric) as soon as possible (eliminate gas, the common accidental cause of fires).

Case Study: 241.01: Insurance Fraud

Background

Early one summer morning, the owner of a rural residence drove to a neighbor's home and asked that the fire department be called. He told neighbors that he had discovered a fire in his house, but his telephone was out of service, so he could not report it himself. He then drove back to his burning home.

Witnesses to the fire noticed that the owner was fully dressed at such an early hour and that he appeared very calm, even after the fire had completely destroyed his home. By the time fire units arrived, the fire had totally destroyed his house; all that was left standing was the fireplace chimney.

Victimology

Although the property had been purchased only nine months before the fire, there were four trust deeds. The total purchase price was $271,000. The buyer had made a $5,000 cash down payment to the previous owner but never made any further payments. The buyer had obtained a policy insuring the dwelling for $171,000, the contents for $85,000, and $24,000 for additional living expenses in case of fire.

Crime Scene Indicators

When examining the fire scene, arson investigators found burn patterns that indicated a flammable liquid had been used to accelerate the fire throughout the house, patterns that were inconsistent with an accidental fire.

Forensic Findings

The carpeting that had been located under the washer and dryer was burned in a manner indicating that flammable liquid had flowed underneath the machines. Furthermore, the investigators found burned studs showing that the fire had been hottest near the floor. They concluded that flammable liquid had been distributed in the kitchen, the living room, the two bedrooms, and the den.

Investigation

Shortly after the fire, the owner of the home submitted a claim to the insurance company. The insurance company subsequently paid the owner $12,000 in advance claims, over $51,000 to the mortgage holders, and nearly $7,000 to clean up the site.

Several of the items listed on the formal sworn claim submitted to the insurance company by the owner were subsequently found in two storage lockers. In one of the storage lockers, deputies found an expensive automobile that had been reported stolen.

Outcome

The owner was arrested, convicted, and sentenced to eight years in state prison. He was found to have an extensive criminal record, which included previous arson-for-profit schemes, as well as mail fraud and a host of minor offenses stretching throughout his adult life.

250: Extremist-Motivated Arson

Extremist-motivated arson is committed to further a social, political, or religious cause. The types of arson in this category are terrorism (251), discrimination (252), riots/civil disturbance (253), and other (259).

Defining Characteristics

VICTIMOLOGY

Analysis of the targeted property is essential in the determination of the specific motive for extremist arson. The target usually represents the antithesis of the offender's belief. Examples of targets are research laboratories, slaughterhouses, and fur stores burned by animal rights groups; abortion clinics targeted by extremist right-to-life groups; businesses targeted by unions; religious institutions targeted by individuals holding contrasting beliefs; and groups or individuals targeted by political extremist organizations who seek to intimidate or eradicate racial, religious, political, or sexual-oriented opponents.

CRIME SCENE INDICATORS FREQUENTLY NOTED

The crime scene reflects an organized and focused attack by the offender. Multiple offenders are common to this arson. These offenders frequently employ incendiary devices, such as Molotov cocktails, which offer both offender and forensic information. Offenders may leave some form of message (e.g., spray-painted symbols or slogans or literature supporting their cause) at the crime scene. Symbolic messages often indicate younger offenders. Communiqués are sometimes delivered orally or in writing to the media claiming responsibility or attempting to justify the violent act.

When confronted with obvious overkill in setting the fire, investigators should be aware of the possibility of extreme concentrations of flammable or combustible materials used to set the fires. Unexploded incendiary devices may be found at the scene.

COMMON FORENSIC FINDINGS

The general arson outline at the beginning of this chapter details more common forensic findings. Extremist arsonists often are more sophisticated offenders and may use incendiary devices.

Investigative Considerations

The extremist offender is frequently readily identified with the cause or group in question when friends, family, and other associates are interviewed. The offender may have previous police contact or an arrest record for violations such as trespassing, criminal mischief, or civil rights violations. Postoffense claims should undergo threat assessment examination to determine authenticity.

Search Warrant Suggestions

- Literature, writings, paraphernalia pertaining to a group or cause; manuals and diagrams if an incendiary device was used (how-to books).
- Incendiary device components, travel records, sales receipts, credit card statements, bank records indicating purchases.
- Flammable materials, liquids, and containers used to transport the accelerants to the scene.

251: Extremist-Motivated Arson, Terrorism

The terrorist bomber is a criminal intent on frightening a community. This class of crime is new to the 21st century and a result of the terrorist attacks in the United States on September 11, 2001. The case discussed, however, is a classic from the 1950s, when Americans were not living with terroristic threats.

Domestic terrorism is extremist activity within the borders of the United States by an American. Other domestic terrorists in the United States have been Timothy McVeigh, who was responsible for bombing a federal building in Oklahoma City in 1995; Eric Rudolph, who was responsible for bombing abortion clinics and the Olympics in Atlanta; Ted Kaczynski, the Unabomber; and those responsible for various school shootings at the end of the 20th century. Terror activity can be motivated by political, religious, or economic ideas. It can be carried out by a lone offender or multiple offenders.

Case Study: 251: Extremist-Motivated Arson, Terrorism

Case Contributed by Kristen Moore

Background

George Metesky, a mild-mannered toolmaker, was dubbed the Mad Bomber after terrorizing the citizens of New York City for 16 years between 1940 and 1956. During that time, he assembled, planted, and detonated 31 pipe bombs in the city. He claimed that his motive was revenge against the Consolidated Edison Company (Con Edison), the major energy provider to the area. He claimed it was liable for a plant accident that occurred in 1931, causing him to be disabled and a sufferer of tuberculosis. This could never be proven, so his disability claim was denied.

Victimology

Metesky never killed anyone with his bombs, a fact that he referred to as "by the hand of God." However, he seriously injured 15 people. An investigation into the analysis of the crime scenes discloses how his bombings were linked and how he was eventually brought to justice. One way this was accomplished was through his modus operandi (MO), the actions necessary to carry out the offense. Although he planted bombs months or even years apart, he always used a homemade pipe bomb that was created from untraceable items. As time passed, he began perfecting his MO by creating bombs of greater sophistication.

Crime Scene Indicators

Included in the crime scene analysis, the investigators focused on the signature aspect, or the calling card of the bomber. This consisted of unusual behavior beyond what was necessary to commit the crime. In letters placed on various bombs and those that Metesky sent to the police and media, the letters "F.P.," later disclosed to represent "Fair Play," were signed at the bottom. In addition, his signature became the way in which he constructed the bombs, allowing investigators to link them.

Another indicator was the presence of staging, that is, purposeful altering of the crime scene prior to the arrival of the police. This was usually done to redirect the investigation away from the most logical suspect or to protect the victim. In these bombing incidents, there were no signs of staging; in fact, the offender wanted to be known to the victim. Not only did he make it obvious that he was a disgruntled ex-employee of Con Edison, but he later disclosed to investigators the exact date and nature of his injury. For years, the New York City Police Department searched to locate the Mad Bomber.

The Mad Bomber planted his first bomb at the Con Edison building on West Sixty-Fourth Street on November 16, 1940. He left it in a wooden toolbox on a windowsill in the building. Although this bomb never exploded, it did bring a message to the management of the company. The bomb boasted an ominous note: "Con Edison crooks, this is for you." Ironically, this note would have been destroyed if the bomb had detonated. After a brief investigation, both the company and the police disregarded the incident. Then, the following September, a second home-made device was located a few blocks from Con Edison offices. Focusing on the offender's MO and signature, they were able to link the incidents. Once again, the incident was widely ignored by the media.

The United States entered World War II three months later. An unusually patriotic and uncharacteristic letter was sent from this domestic terrorist to police headquarters. It read: "I will make no more bomb units for the duration of the war—my patriotic feelings have made me think this. Later I will bring the Con Edison to justice—they will pay for their dastardly deeds." Indeed, the Mad Bomber did not plant any bombs during the next nine years. His presence was still felt, however, in the dozens of threatening letters he sent to Con Edison, the police, movie theaters, and private individuals.

On March 29, 1950, a third unexploded bomb was discovered, this one in Grand Central Station, a hub for New York travelers. Once again investigators quickly linked the construction of this bomb to the others found near Con Edison. Not long after, a bomb exploded in a telephone booth inside the New York Public Library and then one at Grand Central Station. It seemed that the Mad Bomber used his nine-year hiatus to perfect his bomb-making skills and his MO.

Investigation

The attack that ultimately led to Metesky's arrest occurred on December 2, 1956, in the Paramount Movie Theatre in Brooklyn. At 7:55 that evening, a bomb ripped through the theater, seriously injuring three people. Metesky had slashed open the underside of a seat and inserted the bomb there before slipping out of the theater unnoticed. After this attack, the police department decided to try a new means of finding the perpetrator.

A psychiatrist from the New York Department of Mental Health, James A. Brussel, was brought on to the case to create a criminal profile of the bomber. His job was to decipher what kind of person would do this and what motivated him to commit such acts. Brussel developed the modern science of criminal profiling, making its use widespread in modern criminal investigations.

Brussel created the following profile for the Mad Bomber: a neat, meticulous, skilled, middle-aged male, holding a grudge against Con Edison. From his letters, it was determined that he was most likely a former employee who believed that he was permanently injured by the company and was seeking revenge. Brussel determined that he suffered from the mental disorder of paranoia. Sufferers of this disorder believe themselves to be perfect beings. They believe that they do not make mistakes, they are not crazy, and if something goes wrong, there must be an external force causing the error. The bomber's letters also revealed other character-istics of paranoia, such as a sense of persecution, tenacity to hold a grudge, intense resentment of criticism, and a feeling of superiority. From the nature of these notes, Brussel determined he was Slav, thereby most likely Roman Catholic, and lived in Connecticut. Based on the Freudian theory, Brussel determined that the bomber suffered from Oedipus complex, meaning he was probably unmarried and lived with single female relatives other than his mother. Brussel's final conclusion about the bomber was that "when you catch him, and I have no doubt you will, he'll be wearing a double-breasted suit. And it will be buttoned."

Once this profile was spread by the media, people stepped forward claiming to be the bomber. Even citizens with only the highest intentions in mind were incriminating friends and neighbors who fit the description. During this part of the investigation, the bomber increased the frequency of his attacks and wrote more letters to the media, wanting to make sure he got credit for his work. In one incident, his arrogance almost got the best of him: he telephoned and threatened Brussel at his home. During this time, an old employee file was found on George Metesky, a man who fit the criminal profile created by Brussel perfectly.

Outcome

George Metesky was 53 years old when he was caught, living in Waterbury, Connecticut, with two unmarried elderly sisters. Neighbors said he was a strange man who kept to himself and did not seem to have a job. They often wondered what he did on his frequent trips to New York City and what he was making in his workshop at night. On the night of January 22, 1957, he was finally arrested and quietly confessed to being the bomber, although adding, "One thing I can't understand is why the newspapers labeled me the Mad Bomber. That was unkind." The police asked him to change from his night robe before he was taken in. Surprisingly, he walked out of the house wearing a double-breasted suit, buttoned. He admitted that his motive was revenge against Con Edison. When asked if he was sorry, he laughed and said, "Yes. I'm sorry I injured people, but I'm glad I did it."

During his trial and subsequent conviction, testimony and expert witnesses were not necessary because Metesky confessed to the crime when he was arrested. Toward a harsher sentence, the judge could consider that Metesky had been terrorizing the public. In addition, he was exploding bombs that seriously injured innocent people to get the attention of and seek revenge on a major corporation in the city. Nevertheless, he did take a nine-year hiatus from his terrorist activities as an act of patriotism and never killed anyone in his attacks. He never showed any remorse for his actions.

Metesky was found insane on April 18, 1957, and committed to the Matteawan State Hospital for the criminally insane. Stemming from his acute paranoia, he was unresponsive to treatment and truly believed that his psychiatrists were conspiring against him. At times he was confused as to why he was there and was quick to point out that he had purposely constructed the bombs not to kill anyone. He was released in 1973.

260: Serial Arson

Arsonists who set fires repeatedly are referred to as serial fire setters. The National Center for the Analysis of Violent Crime classifies compulsive fire setting as mass, spree, or serial.

The serial arsonist is involved in three or more separate fire-setting episodes, with a characteristic emotional cooling-off period between fires. This period may last days, weeks, or even years. Serial arson is the most serious type of arson due to the apparent random selection of victims and unpredictable gaps between incidents. Furthermore, a serial arsonist may commit a spree of arson during each fire-setting episode. Serial arson is not a separate or distinct motive for setting fires; rather, it is a pattern of fire setting frequently encountered in revenge-, excitement-, or extremist-motivated arsons.

Serial arsonists often create a climate of fear in entire communities. Community leaders tend to compound the problem by pressuring law enforcement agencies to identify and quickly apprehend the fire setter. Often, the arsonist evades apprehension for months as investigators become increasingly frustrated by a lack of experience in handling these baffling cases.

Serial Arsonist and MO

Just as the serial killer or rapist develops an MO, so does the serial arsonist. An arsonist's MO may involve targeting structures of a certain type that offer easy access and escape. The use of certain accelerants and incendiary devices is a component of the MO, as is the selection of a specific site to set the fire, for example, inside, outside, in a toolshed, or near a furnace.

The signature aspects of an arsonist may include evidence of bizarre behavior at the crime scene. He may take certain items from the crime scene, like women's undergarments or cheap costume jewelry—items that are not valuable monetarily but are meaningful to him. He may leave something at the crime scene. One fire setter would draw pictures on the walls before setting fires. He may defecate or urinate at the scene. In addition, specific incendiary mixtures and accelerants, such as the unusual combination of kerosene and gasoline, may be indicative of a signature.

An investigator should apply the same principles used in detecting the signature aspect of a sexual assault or homicide to arson. The crime scene must be analyzed for any offender activity that appears unusual or unnecessary for the successful perpetration of the arson.

Defining Characteristics

VICTIMOLOGY

This arsonist usually selects vulnerable targets such as unoccupied or abandoned property, during nighttime hours. The choice of targets is often specific.

CRIME SCENE INDICATORS FREQUENTLY NOTED

This type of arson usually involves an organized crime scene with little, if any, physical evidence left at the scene. The arsonist is intelligent and not easy to apprehend. He uses sophisticated devices.

COMMON FORENSIC FINDINGS

Forensic findings of materials found at the crime scene may correspond to the underlying motivation. For example, a large quantity of flammable liquid may indicate a revenge fire or arson for profit. Spray-paint samples from an aerosol can might point to vandalism as a motive. A lack of forensic evidence may be indicative of the serial arsonist who uses available material to kindle his fires. Conversely, many wild-land serial arsonists use cigarette and match devices.

Investigative Considerations

The typical offender in this category is usually male. He is generally older than the single-event arsonist. He tends to be educated and an achiever. He generally has good interpersonal relationships and is socially adequate. Often, he is employed and skilled. Serial arsonists often have a history of substance abuse and a history of police contact or arrests for minor nuisance offenses.

The offender walks to the scene of the fire and generally lives within one mile of the crime scenes. He is very likely to be familiar with the crime scenes and can justify his presence in the area.

It is important to analyze the cluster centers of fire activity. The tighter the cluster is, the closer to the area of significance to the offender, such as his residence or place of employment.

Case Study: 260: Serial Arson

Background

During the summer and fall months, a series of arsons targeting unoccupied dwellings plagued a medium-sized midwestern community. The arsonist's fires became increasingly destructive and life threatening, alarming local residents and overtaxing the resources of law enforcement and fire officials. Based on a request by local law enforcement for assistance, the NCAVC participated in the case.

Victimology

The targeted property consisted at first of abandoned dwellings in an area marked for an urban renewal project. The arsonist escalated his fire setting over time to include occupied dwellings when the owners were away. In one later case, a fire was set to a house when the family was sleeping inside.

Crime Scene Indicators

The fires were set to the inside of the abandoned buildings using whatever material was at hand to kindle the fire. Available materials were also used to set fire to the outside porches of occupied dwellings. In more than one case, kerosene or another flammable liquid was used when found at the scene by the offender. On several occasions, footprints were found. With other fires, where little damage was done, matches were found at the origin. Due to the fairly limited geographical area in which the fires occurred, it was apparent the arsonist walked to the scene of the fires, which all took place between 11:00 p.m. and 3:00 a.m.

Forensic Findings

Available material, particularly paper goods such as newsprint or cardboard that survived fires that did little damage, was examined for identifying information. Partial prints were recovered but may not have been those of the offender. Photographs and plaster casts were made of footprints suspected of belonging to the arsonist.

Investigation

Local investigators interviewed scores of potential witnesses and failed to develop any good suspects. Unable to break the case, the police turned to the NCAVC for assistance.

Arson specialists from the NCAVC examined all the case material submitted, which included a spot map, reports, and photographs. The analysis consisted of a target, temporal, and geographical study of the incidents. The conclusions of the analysis suggested the offender was a White male between the ages of 19 and 25, an unemployed loner with an alcohol problem. His apparent undetected movements to and from the crime scenes suggested a familiarity with the neighborhood. The geographical cluster analysis indicated the location of the "centroid" predicting the area in which this offender lived. Psychologically, the arsonist was predicted to be an underachiever who did poorly in school and was raised in a dysfunctional home in which he still lived with one parent. It was predicted he would have an arrest record with a variety of minor offenses. The police were directed to look for an individual who was unkempt in appearance and behaved in a disorganized fashion. The police were able to develop a suspect based on the NCAVC report and investigative suggestions.

Outcome

The suspected arsonist confessed to the police during an initial interview and was convicted of 12 of the 23 counts of arson. He was sentenced to 30 years in prison.

270: Serial Bombing

Serial bombing involves planning to launch bomb attacks usually in public places like rail stations, bus stations, different key point installations, as well as government offices at district levels in a geographic locale or country. Eric Rudolph pleaded guilty to the bombing of the 1996 Summer Olympics and other bombings, citing a hatred of abortion, gay rights, and the government as his motive. On April 7, 2005, he entered the guilty pleas in a plea agreement that gave him four life sentences and avoided the death penalty.

Case Study: 270: Ted Kaczynski, the Unabomber: Serial Bomber

In May 1998, Theodore J. "Ted" Kaczynski was found guilty and sentenced to life in prison for a series of 16 bombings that claimed three lives and injured 23 other people, two of them seriously. Kaczynski either mailed or hand-placed all of the bombs between May 1978 and April 1995. He initially targeted individuals associated with universities and the airline industry—thus, the FBI code "Unabom" and, later, "Unabomber."

The Unabomber case is an excellent example of an MO that evolves with repeated offenses and increased skill. Most of the earliest bombs were pipe bombs constructed with such untraceable common materials as match heads and batteries. The third bomb, which was planted in a package in the cargo hold of American Airlines flight 444, featured a detonator controlled by an altimeter. Despite the fact that the bomb only caught fire and failed to explode, this detonation system indicated a new level of complexity in the Unabomber's MO. The sixth bomb, sent to Vanderbilt University, contained smokeless powder. The eighth bomb, left in a computer lab at the University of California–Berkeley, was the most powerful yet. It contained ammonium nitrate and aluminum powder. On December 11, 1985, the Unabomber planted a bomb outside a computer store in Sacramento, California. This bomb, the eleventh, had a gravity trigger and a backup system, and it was filled with nails to make the blast more harmful. It exploded as soon as it was touched and caused his first fatal bombing.

Kaczynski had a distinctive signature. From the beginning of the bombings, he showed a fascination with wood. One of his victims, president of United Airlines at the time, was named Percy A. Wood. Wood received the bomb hidden inside a book published by Arbor House. Another intended victim was named LeRoy Wood Bearnson. Perhaps most intriguing, in June 1995, Kaczynski sent a letter to the *San Francisco Chronicle* bearing the return address of Frederick Benjamin Isaac (which, interestingly, would be abbreviated FBI) Wood of 549 Wood Street in Woodlake, California. His final target was the headquarters of the California Forestry Association.

His obsessions carried over into the ritualistic details found in the handiwork of his bombs. He built many of the electrical and switching mechanisms in them from scratch, even though these components are available at most hardware stores for relatively little cost. He constructed elaborate wooden housings for many of the bombs. By the time Kaczynski was apprehended on April 3, 1996, it was estimated that more than 100 hours of work would have gone into the construction of one of his bombs. It was evidently a point of pride for him; in a letter to the *Washington Post*, Kaczynski boasted about the precision and care with which he assembled his bombs. Some of his correspondence, which he signed as a member of the "Freedom Club," points to another (literally) signature element of his crimes: the letters "F.C." were found on the remnants of several of the bombs.

When investigators and prosecutors face a situation as convoluted and confusing as the Unabomber case, the recognition of the offender's signature is of paramount importance. Broad geographical range and initially baffling victim selection can make it very difficult to establish motive. In such an information vacuum, the various facets of the signature become increasingly important in linking an offender to his crimes.

References

Federal Bureau of Investigation. (2010). *Uniform crime reports: Crime in the United States 2010.* Retrieved March 15, 2012, from www.fbi.gov/about-us/cjis/ucr/crime-in-the-u.s/2010/crime-in-the-u.s.-2010/property-crime/arsonmain

Federal Bureau of Investigation. (2012). *Uniform crime reports.* Retrieved March 15, 2012, from www.fbi.gov/about-us/cjis/ucr/ucr

Rider, A. O., (1980). The firesetter: A psychological profile. *FBI Law Enforcement Bulletin,* 49, 6–8.

Chapter 12

Rape and Sexual Assault

*300: Criminal enterprise rape
*301: Felony rape
   *301.01: Primary felony rape
   *301.02: Secondary felony rape
*310: Personal cause sexual assault
*311: Indirect offenses
   *311.01: Isolated/opportunistic
   offense
   *311.02: Preferential offense
   *311.03: Transition offense
   *311.04: Preliminary offense
*312: Domestic sexual assault
   *312.01: Adult domestic sexual
   assault
   *312.02: Child domestic sexual
   abuse
   312.03: Elder sexual assault
*313: Opportunistic rape
   *313.01: Social acquaintance
   rape
   313.01.01: Adult
   313.01.02: Adolescent
   313.01.03: Child
   313.01.04: Elder
   *313.02: Authority rape
   313.02.01: Adult
   313.02.02: Adolescent
   *313.02.03: Child
   313.02.04: Elder

*313.03: Power–reassurance rape
   313.03.01: Adult
   *313.03.02: Adolescent
   313.03.03: Child
   313.03.04: Elder
*313.04: Exploitative rape
   313.04.01: Adult
   313.04.02: Adolescent
   313.04.03: Child
   313.04.04: Elder
*314: Anger rape
   *314.01: Gender
   *314.02: Age
      *314.02.01: Elderly victim
      *314.02.02: Child victim
   *314.03: Racial
   *314.04: Global
*315: Sadistic rape
   *315.01: Adult
   *315.02: Adolescent
   315.03: Child
   *315.04: Elder
*319: Abduction rape
   319.01: Adult
   319.02: Adolescent
   319.03: Child
   319.04: Elder
*330: Group-cause sexual assault
*331: Formal gang sexual assault

---

*While there is no explicit case example given, this classification denotes the motive as described in the text.

331.01: Single victim
331.02: Multiple victims
*332: Informal gang sexual assault
332.01: Single victim
332.02: Multiple victims

*333: Military sexual trauma
*333.01: Sexual harassment
*333.02: Rape/sexual assault
*390: Sexual assault not classified
elsewhere

One of the most common predatory crimes with which law enforcement personnel have to deal is rape. There is an ongoing debate within and among the law enforcement community, the health care community, and the women's movement about whether rape should be classified as a crime of sex or violence, and this will not abate any time in the foreseeable future. From our own experience and knowledge of the subject, we can say that whatever the definition, control, dominance, and anger are key components. Former prosecutor Linda Fairstein argues that rape is a crime of violence in which sex is the weapon. She further explains, "There is a sexual element to this that isn't part of any other crime, and that can't be denied. It's very much the piece of the crime that the victim doesn't want to happen or is afraid of. And so to me, it was about the one weapon that this type of offender had that other offenders don't use and victims don't want used against them" (Fairstein, 1993).

Rape and sexual assault leaves its victims, their partners, friends, and loved ones devastated. But we do a grave disservice to all victims and potential victims if we do not invest the time and effort to distinguish between types of rape and rapists. It may seem more sympathetic and caring to proclaim, for instance, that date rape is the same as stranger rape, but it is not true. So much depends on the circumstances of the assault. To assert that a date rape that does not involve a weapon and does not cause the victim to fear for her life is the same as a stranger abduction–rape at knife- or gunpoint in which the victim is brutally beaten dangerously oversimplifies the situation and hinders our ability to defend against both crimes and their different types of perpetrators. There are certain elements that all sexual assaults share. But what they do not share is, in some ways, even more important if we are to learn prevention strategies from them and help victims recover from their individual traumas. Many things are required of the diligent, sensitive emergency staff when dealing with a victim of sexual assault. After excellent medical care, by far the most important of these are caring and empathy.

Statistics from the FBI's Uniform Crime Report (UCR) note the following (FBI, 2009):

- In 2009, the number of forcible rapes was estimated at 88,097. By comparison, the estimated volume of rapes for 2009 was 2.6% lower than the 2008 estimate, 6.6% lower than the 2005 number, and 2.3% below the 2000 level. The rate of forcible rapes in 2009 was estimated at 56.6 per 100,000 female inhabitants, a 3.4% decrease when compared with the 2008 estimated rate of 58.6.

- Rapes by force comprised 93.0% of reported rape offenses in 2009, and attempts or assaults to commit rape accounted for 7.0% of reported rapes.

Statistics from the Bureau of Justice Statistics' National Crime Victims Survey (NCVS) note the following (Truman & Rand, 2010):

- 125,910 victimizations with a victimization rate of 0.5 per 1,000 persons age 12 or older.
- The rate of rape or sexual assault remained generally stable from 2000 to 2007 before declining between 2007 and 2009.
- Female victims of rape/sexual assault were victimized by a stranger 21% of the time; intimate partner 41% of the time; friend or acquaintance 39% of the time.

See Table 12.1 Bureau of Justice Statistics NCVS 2005: Rape/Sexual Assault Statistics.

Table 12.1 Bureau of Justice Statistics NCVS 2005: Rape/Sexual Assault Statistics

Age of Offenders	15–17 years old: 11%
	18–20 years old: 15%
	21–29 years old: 26%
	30 and over: 45%
	Other/unknown: 3%
Location of Offense	At victim's home: 36%
	Near home: 1%
	Friend/relative/neighbor's home: 24%
	Other commercial building: 1%
	On school property: 8%
	Common yard, park, field, playground: 3%
	On street other than near home: 9%
	Other: 18%
Rape/Sexual Assault Reported to Police	Overall only 38% reported
	Age 12–19 reported 33% of the time
	Age 20–34 reported 30% of the time
	Age 35–49 reported 62% of the time
	Age 50–64 reported 37% of the time
Activity of Victims at Time of Incident	Working or on duty: 11%
	Going to or from work: 1%
	Going to or from school: 3%
	Going to or from other place: 4%
	At school: 5%
	Leisure activity away from home: 29%
	Sleeping: 20%
	Other activity at home: 25%
	Other: 2%

Rape and sexual assault include criminal offenses in which victims are forced or coerced to participate in sexual activity. Physical violence may or may not be involved. In many offenses involving children, the offender may gain the cooperation of the victim using little or no force. This "seduction" of child victims has no comparable offense when committed against adults. The terms *rape* and *sexual assault* are used interchangeably in this manual and are not to be construed as a legal definition. Each jurisdiction applies its own legal definition to an offense.

Victims of rape and sexual assaults are generally divided into four categories:

- *Adults,* defined as individuals at least 18 years of age who are almost always pubescent and usually considered capable of consent under laws proscribing sexual conduct. Some exceptions may include persons who are mentally retarded, brain impaired, or psychotic.
- *Adolescents,* defined as individuals 13 to 17 years of age who are usually pubescent but whose legal status under laws proscribing sexual conduct varies from state to state and even statute to statute within the same jurisdiction.
- *Children,* defined as individuals 12 years of age or younger who are usually prepubescent and are considered minors incapable of consent under almost all laws proscribing sexual conduct.
- *Elders* are usually defined as age 60 or older.

Every attempt should be made to evaluate whether a rape was committed for situational or preferential sexual motives. Situationally motivated sexual assaults are those committed to fulfill sexual and other needs without the elements of the offense being necessary for arousal or gratification (such as raping a woman because she is available and vulnerable). Preferentially motivated sexual assaults are those committed to fulfill sexual and other needs with some elements of the offense being necessary for arousal or gratification (e.g., raping a woman because the offender cannot feel aroused or gratified without an unwilling partner).

Preferentially motivated sexual offenses usually involve strong patterns of behavior or sexual rituals that are difficult for the offender to change. Sexual ritual involves repeatedly engaging in an act or series of acts in a certain manner because of a sexual need. In other words, in order for a person to become sexually aroused or gratified, he or she must engage in the act in a certain way. This sexual ritualism can include the physical characteristics, age, or gender of the victim; the particular sequence of acts; the bringing or taking of specific objects; or the use of certain words or phrases.

Sexual ritual is more than the concept of method of operation, or modus operandi (MO), known to most law enforcement officers. MO is something done by an offender because it works. Sexual ritual is something done by an offender because of a need. Therefore, it is much harder for an offender to change, vary, or adjust the ritual than his MO. Both preferential and situational sex offenders may have an MO, but the preferential offender is more likely to have a sexual ritual.

Attempting to identify both patterns of behavior (MO and ritual) and distinguishing between them is a difficult but worthwhile investigative effort. From an investigative view, the preferential offense often has clear evidence that the offender thought about, planned, and went searching for a particular victim. In the situational offense, there is evidence of impulsive, opportunistic, predatory behavior, such as the victim being present or a spur-of-the-moment decision to offend.

It is especially important in child victim rape and sexual assaults to attempt to determine if the child was the victim for preferential or situational reasons. The corroborating evidence, whether there are additional child victims, how to interview a suspect, and so on depend on the type of child molester. Situational child molesters do not have a true sexual preference for children but engage in sex with children for varied and sometimes complex reasons, ranging from child availability to offender inadequacy.

The preferential child molesters have a definite sexual preference for children. Their sexual fantasies and erotic imagery focus on children. Preferential child molesters almost always have access to children, molest multiple victims, and collect child pornography or child erotica.

A preferential child molester (pedophile) might have other psychosexual disorders, personality disorders, or psychosis or may be involved in other types of criminal activity. A pedophile's sexual interest in children might be combined with other sexual deviations (paraphilias), which include indecent exposure (exhibitionism), obscene phone calls (scatophilia), exploitation of animals (zoophilia), urination (urophilia), defecation (coprophilia), binding (bondage), baby role playing (infantilism), infliction of pain (sadism, masochism), real or simulated death (necrophilia), and others. The preferential child molester is interested in sex with children that might, in some cases, involve other sexual deviations. A preferential sex offender who is involved in a variety of specific sexual deviations might become a situational child molester by selecting a child victim who is available or vulnerable. The preferential child molester must have high amount of victim contact and high level of fixation.

Victim Contact

A preemptory distinction is made between offenders who have spent a substantial amount of their time in close proximity to victims (high contact) and offenders who have spent little or no time with victims outside of rape and sexual assaults (low contact). Amount of contact is a behavioral measure of the time spent with victims. It includes both sexual and nonsexual situations but excludes the contact that results from parental responsibilities. The contact distinction must be distinguished from the fixation decision, which attempts to assess the strength of an individual's pedophilic interest.

Evidence for high contact includes structured and nonstructured involvement with a victim through an occupation or through recreation—for example, schoolteacher, bus driver, carnival worker, riding stable attendant, newspaper delivery person, scout leader, sports coach, youth group volunteer, minister, priest, or babysitter. These occupational criteria are intended only to help identify the level of contact for those already determined to be child molesters. Other evidence for high contact may include regular visits by the victim to the offender's home or the offender acting as an adopted father or big brother. In addition, we assume that repeated sexual (nonincestual) encounters with a victim imply the development of a relationship that goes beyond sexual involvement. For that reason, when there are three or more sexual encounters with the same victim, the offender is coded as having high contact.

Fixation

The level of fixation decision attempts to access the strength of an offender's pedophilic interest.

An offender is considered highly fixated if any of the following are present:

- There is evidence of three or more sexual encounters with a victim, and the time period between the first and third encounter was greater than six months. These encounters may be with a single victim over many incidents and should not be limited to charged offenses.
- There is evidence that the offender has had enduring relationships with the victim (excluding parental contact). This includes sexual and nonsexual contact and professional and nonprofessional contact.
- The offender has initiated contact with children in numerous situations over his lifetime.

General Forensic Evidence Collections

There are many physical evidence recovery methods and procedures that can be used in investigating rape and sexual assault. These methods and procedures usually depend on the age and sex of the person on whom they are used, as well as whether the individual is a victim or suspect. The following is essentially a general description of forensic evidence. More detailed information can be found in Hazelwood (2009).

Most of the evidence will come from the victim and falls into the following categories: clothing, bed linens, human hair (head and pubic), swabbing (vaginal, penile, oral, and anal), vaginal aspirate, oral rinse, nasal mucus, fingernail scrapings, blood, saliva, and miscellaneous debris. Each item must be packaged separately to avoid transfer of evidence from one item to another. Sections of manila-type wrapping paper or sturdy paper bags can be supplied for packaging purposes. Unstained control samples of all the gathering mediums are retained and packaged separately. Rape and sexual assault evidence kits that contain the necessary equipment usually are used by hospital examining staff.

All bed linens and clothing worn by the victim should be obtained and packaged in a sealed, secure condition. The head hair region of the victim is combed or brushed for evidence substances. This requires the use of an uncontaminated comb or brush specifically for the head area. The comb or brush and adhering materials are packaged and sealed. An appropriate amount of hair to represent color, length, and area variation is obtained. Hairs should be pulled whenever possible. Known hairs should be acquired after the head hair combing and brushing procedure is completed.

The pubic region of the victim is combed or brushed for evidence materials. An appropriate amount of hair to represent color, length, and area variation is obtained. Hairs should be searched for whenever possible. Known pubic hairs should be acquired after the pubic hair combing and brushing procedure is completed.

In the event an individual is observed to have excessive body hair, a separate, uncontaminated comb or brush and appropriate packaging material can be used to collect trace evidence, such as fibers from clothing that may be present.

The vaginal, oral, and anal cavities are swabbed to detect the presence of spermatozoa or seminal fluid. In addition to vaginal swabbing, aspiration of the vaginal region is accomplished by irrigation with saline solution. Spermatozoa not located through the swabbing procedure may be recovered in this manner. The mouth of the person examined can be rinsed in order to remove spermatozoa not collected using the swabbing procedure. The rinse is expectorated into a tube or vial. A control sample of rinse is retained and packaged separately. Control samples of the irrigation and rinse fluids also are retained and packaged separately.

For male victims, the penis is swabbed to detect the presence of blood or other evidence.

Nasal mucus samples can be of use. Nasal mucus is acquired by having the individual being examined blow his or her nose on cloth. The mucus may contain spermatozoa that were deposited in the mouth or facial area. An unstained portion of the cloth can function as a control sample.

Using appropriate materials, the area underneath the fingernails is scraped for significant debris, such as hairs, fibers, blood, or tissue. The gathering implement is retained. It is suggested that each hand be scraped individually and the resulting debris packaged separately.

Blood is drawn into a sterile test tube for forensic testing purposes. A minimum of 5 milliliters is recommended, preferably without the inclusion of a chemical anticoagulant or preservative.

Evidence materials that fall into the category of miscellaneous debris are substances not included in the previous categories and can often be observed during the forensic examination. These also should be collected and packaged separately. A section of paper or cloth on which the person can stand while undressing can be supplied. In addition, a separate piece of paper or cloth can be used to cover the examining table to collect any evidence that is dislodged during the examination.

300: Criminal Enterprise Rape

Criminal enterprise rape involves sexual coercion, abuse, or assault that is committed for material gain.

301: Felony Rape

Rape committed during the commission of a felony such as breaking and entering or robbery is considered felony rape. The classification is made specific as to whether the rape was primary or secondary in intent.

301.01: Primary Felony Rape

The intent of primary felony rape is a nonsexual felony such as robbery or breaking and entering. The victim is at the scene of the primary felony and is sexually assaulted as a second offense. If the victim were not present, the felony would still occur.

Defining Characteristics

VICTIMOLOGY

The victim is usually an adult female. Either the victim is employed at the crime scene or the felony occurred in the victim's residence.

Evidence of a breaking and entering, burglary, or robbery, such as missing property, is noted in a primary felony rape.

COMMON FORENSIC FINDINGS

See the general forensic evidence collection for sexual assault as described at the start of this chapter.

Investigative Considerations

Investigators should look for similar felonies in the area of the crime. These felonies usually have reported similar items stolen and a similar MO. The sexual offense is situationally motivated.

Search Warrant Suggestions

Warrants should be requested for the suspect's residence and car. Suggested items should include but not be limited to clothing to test for blood, hair and fibers, ligatures, newspaper articles related to similar crimes, and any of the victim's possessions reported stolen.

Case Study: 301.01: Primary Felony Rape

Case Contributed by Leonard I. Morgenbesser

Background

Robert Griffin, an African American, was born on November 19, 1972. He had two prior commitments to New York State's prison system before standing trial for three sex crimes against victims who were 4, 10, and 67 years of age.

Victimology

Griffin's first crime, on July 31, 1997, was the abduction and sexual assault of a 4-year-old girl taken from her home and found several hours later in a driveway in another town. The mother noted her daughter was in bed asleep. She watched television and fell asleep on the couch. When she was awakened by her husband at about 1:10 a.m., they realized the child was missing and searched the house unsuccessfully for her. They called police after seeing an open rear window with the screen removed.

A doughnut deliveryman found the 4-year-old at about 1:30 a.m. wearing only a nightshirt and clutching her underwear in her hands. He thought perhaps she was sleepwalking. He observed, "She was hiding. She was scared that somebody was going to come and get her. That's how I knew something was wrong." The young victim told police that the man who took her smelled like a skunk, wore dark clothing, and had dirty white skin.

Griffin's second rape victim, age 10, told police, "I heard a doorbell and a lot of walking around. This man told me I had to go with him because my mother was in trouble." The man pushed her away from the telephone, pulled off her pants, and sodomized and raped her, before striking her in the head with a five-pound dumbbell. She said, "I was yelling a lot and he told me to be quiet. He put a knife to my throat." She called 911 when he left.

On September 1, 1999, Griffin's third victim, age 67, was putting groceries in her car in the parking lot of the same community in which he had earlier sexually assaulted the 4-year-old girl. She told police, "Some person walked behind me and proceeded to grab my throat and held my mouth closed. I was knocked to the ground and molested."

At the time Griffin raped the 10-year-old girl, he was in prison, sentenced of attempted burglary, second degree, a felony. However, due to rules in effect at that time, he was on work release from the prison system and was program eligible since he was a nonviolent offender and had no history of violent crime (the system did not know at the time of his work release of his abduction and sexual assault on July 31, 1997, before he began his prison sentence for burglary).

Forensic Findings

Forensics cleared this case. In 2000, Griffin was returned to state prison while on parole from his original 1998 attempted burglary sentence. While in custody, he was arrested after evidence taken from the victims in the three sex crimes was allegedly matched with his DNA in the New York State DNA database of convicted felons. This match, which occurred as part of a regular comparison of felon DNA with DNA left at the scenes of crimes, constituted the first cold DNA match in Monroe County since the state database was vastly expanded during 1999.

Investigation

With the forensic evidence, police then went back to review the cases and statements from victims.

Eventually, Griffin told police that he had entered the home of his first victim intending to burglarize it but was alarmed when he heard a barking dog. He took the 4-year-old girl from her bed because "I did not want to leave empty-handed." He placed her in sheets, put her into his car, touched and sodomized her after she awoke in the car, and then masturbated before leaving her at a stranger's house. Regarding his second victim, Griffin told police he smoked cocaine before tossing a rock through the window, assaulted the 10-year-old girl, and then struck her in the head with the dumbbell "so she wouldn't remember what I looked like." He chose the home because it was not well lighted. For his third victim, Griffin told police he raped the woman "with the intention of robbing her for drugs" but that drugs made his desire for sex reach "from the bottom of my feet to the crown of my head."

Outcome

Griffin was sentenced to 4 to 8 years for grand larceny and criminal possession of stolen property. He reportedly rejected an offer of 38 years in state prison in exchange for a guilty plea prior to his triple-sex trial.

301.02: Secondary Felony Rape

The primary intent of the offender in secondary felony rape is rape with a second felony also planned. The nonsexual assault felony would still occur if an adult female were not present.

Defining Characteristics

VICTIMOLOGY

The victim is usually an adult female.

CRIME SCENE INDICATORS FREQUENTLY NOTED

Evidence of breaking and entering or robbery is present.

COMMON FORENSIC FINDINGS

In addition to the general forensic evidence, the forensic report indicates that the offender's primary focus while at the crime scene was the rape, not the robbery. The secondary felony was planned and committed knowing the victim would be present and was carried out after the rape.

Investigative Considerations

In secondary felony rape, the offender targets the victim and crime scene and has been in the area before. There will be a history of robberies and rapes in the area. In addition, the sexual offense is preferentially motivated.

Search Warrant Suggestions

Warrants should be requested for the suspect's residence and car. Suggested items should include but not be limited to clothing to test for blood, hair, and fibers, ligatures, newspaper articles related to similar crimes, and any of the victim's possessions reported stolen.

Case Study: 301.02: Secondary Felony Rape

Victimology

A masked offender confronted a 21-year-old White, single female in her residence at 5:30 a.m. He had entered her apartment through an open bathroom window. He put a razor to the victim's throat, forcing her to the ground and threatening her with the razor. He took off her pants and underwear and told her he would cut her if she did not comply. He removed a tampon and threw it in her face. He forced oral sex and then raped her. He robbed the victim and fled the scene.

Offender Characteristics

The offender is a 35-year-old, single, Black male who states he lives in a racist White society. Although charged with multiple offenses, he feels he did not commit the offenses and believes that the five women he was accused of raping worked for him as prostitutes because he was their pimp.

He is the third oldest of seven children born to parents who divorced when he was eight years old. His father is an engineer; his mother is a registered pharmacist and dietitian; his siblings hold responsible jobs. The offender has an eleventh-grade education and served one and one-half years in the army.

The offender could also be classified as an anger rapist. His victims included White and Black women who were social acquaintances, as well as strangers. His assaults were violent, had a high level of aggression, and were preferentially motivated.

Outcome

The offender was sentenced to 15 to 20 years for assault with intent to rape, with concurrent sentences for five counts of rape and for armed robbery, assault and battery, assault with intent to murder, and indecent assault and battery.

310: Personal Cause Sexual Assault

Rape and sexual assault motivated by personal cause is an act ensuing from interpersonal aggression that results in sexual victimization to persons who may or may not be known to the offender. These assaults are not primarily motivated by material gain and are not sanctioned by a group. Rather, an underlying emotional conflict or psychological issue propels the offender to commit rape and sexual assault. Although the case may be legally defined as rape, the term *sexual assault* is used in this classification to encompass a wide range of forced and pressured sexual activities.

311: Indirect Offenses

There are four categories for this group of indirect offenses that occurs for sexual gratification. The defining characteristic is that the offense involves no physical contact between victim and offender. Police need to investigate and deal with these offenses given the amount of time and priority they have available.

There are no unique crime scene indicators. Forensic evidence is not available because there is no physical contact between the offender and victim. Search warrants are not useful until a suspect has been identified.

Offenders in these four categories may be viewed as undesirable individuals, but when they are interviewed with empathy and understanding, the police officer may find that the individuals already have committed serious contact sexual offenses. Spending time with these offenders may have an important payoff in solving other rape and sexual assault crimes.

One question to consider regarding these offenders is whether they are dangerous. It is important to evaluate two points: focus and escalation.

Do these crimes have a focus? Is there a pattern occurring over and over? Anything that indicates a pattern, such as the offender calling the same number repeatedly or exposing himself at the same location, should be evaluated carefully. The most important aspect of focus to evaluate is victim focus. Are victims being selected at random, or is a specific individual being targeted?

Is there escalation? Has this individual escalated his behavior from peeping outside to burglarizing an indoor location? Is he progressing to more serious invasive activity over time?

It is important to investigate the background of the nuisance offender. What did the individual do as a teenager? Is this a 60-year-old man who has been doing this for years? What else is happening in the individual's life? Does he have a stable life? Did he go to school? Is he working? Is he functioning? Such interview areas help to evaluate the offender.

311.01: Isolated/Opportunistic Offense

Isolated/opportunistic offenses are isolated incidents of individuals who take an opportunity or something presents itself; for example, they call someone on the phone and get a wrong number and blurt out an obscenity, or when in a public place after having had too much to drink, they urinate as a woman walks by and turn and expose themselves. Another example is an offender who walks down a street and takes advantage of an opportunity to look into a window at something sexually stimulating.

311.02: Preferential Offense

Preferential offenses relate to the psychiatric diagnoses termed the *paraphilias*. The acts are the individual's preferred sexual act; examples are the true voyeur and the exhibitionist. Sexual gratification is intended from the act. These are the individuals for whom this has been a long-term pattern of compulsive behavior. The individual may have regular routes for window peeping or elaborate procedures covering such behavior, such as walking a dog. In some cases, the offender carries a video camera to record his sexual interest.

The key to this type of case is having the time to discover the evidence, as it is a highly solvable case. What makes this type of case easy to solve are these rigid, ritual patterns of behavior. The offenders return to specific areas over and over for peeping, or they expose themselves in certain places. They repeatedly make obscene phone calls, which makes it easy to trace them. Thus, although the preferential pattern is highly solvable, the demand for solving contact sex offenses often takes a higher priority for police departments.

311.03: Transition Offense

The transition offender may be caught in a peeping act, but he is trying to find out if the act is capable of producing sexual gratification. He is exploring his arousal patterns, building confidence, and improving his ability to commit crime. This offender is often a younger individual, such as a teenager who is exploring his sexuality and starts out with peeping. However, this is just an early step in his criminal sexual development. In one case, a serial rapist described this type of early sexual interest. No one had stopped or encountered him at this early point. Although not all nuisance sex offenders progress to more serious offenses, some do.

311.04: Preliminary Offense

A preliminary offender is an individual whose nuisance offense is a preliminary aspect to contact sexual offenses. He may be a fetish burglar who cases a home prior to returning to commit a rape and sexual assault. This noncontact offense is a prelude to other serious sex offenses. For example, the rapist may be a window peeper. The police officer encounters him window peeping prior to his intended future rape at that location. The important point is that any nuisance offense may be a prelude to a contact offense and needs to be evaluated as such.

312: Domestic Sexual Assault

Domestic sexual assault occurs when a family member, household member, or former household member sexually assaults another member of the household. This definition includes common-law relationships. The rape and sexual assault may be spontaneous and situational and is triggered by a recent stressful event, real or imagined, perceived by the offender as an injustice. It also may be the result of a cumulative buildup of stress over time.

312.01: Adult Domestic Sexual Assault

Domestic sexual assault of an adult includes assault of a spouse and sexual assault on a nonmarital companion with whom the offender is living if it appears that he has been in a long-term relationship with the victim.

Defining Characteristics

VICTIMOLOGY

The victim has a familial or common-law relationship with the offender. There is usually a history of prior abuse or conflict with the offender.

CRIME SCENE INDICATORS FREQUENTLY NOTED

Usually, only one crime scene is involved, and it is commonly the victim's or offender's residence. The crime scene reflects disorder and the impetuous nature of the assault. It may also reflect the escalation of violence; for example, the confrontation starts as an argument, intensifies into hitting or throwing things, and culminates in the rape and sexual assault.

COMMON FORENSIC FINDINGS

Alcohol or drugs may be involved. If the rape and sexual assault is preceded by violence, trauma to the face and body may be seen on the victim.

Investigative Considerations

If the crime occurred in the residence, domestic rape and sexual assault should be a consideration. When other family members are contacted, they often describe a history of domestic conflict involving the victim and offender.

A history of conflict due to external sources (financial, vocational, or alcohol, for example) is a common element of domestic rape and sexual assault. The offense is usually situational. The offender may have demonstrated aggression in the past, as well as a change in attitude after the triggering event.

Search Warrant Suggestions

A search warrant is used to collect clothing or weapon at the offender's residence if different from the victim's. Computers are also taken for information regarding other possible victims.

Case Study: 312.01: Domestic Sexual Abuse

Case Contributed by Dante Orlando

Background

Anthony Sims, 23, was arrested in April 2009 in Terre Haute, Indiana, after he was accused of raping a relative. He was charged with rape and incest.

Victimology

The victim was the biological sister of Anthony Sims. She was 18 at the time. Both Sims and his sister shared the same mother and father and both lived in their mother's home with others.

Crime Scene Indicators

The crime occurred in one room. The perpetrator had entered his sister's bedroom late one night. The crime lasted over an hour. Sims told police that he and the alleged victim often flirted, and he said he was "messed up on marijuana" when he began rubbing the victim's stomach while she lay sleeping on a mattress at her mother's home. That touching continued to sexual intercourse, which the victim reported to police after she was taken to Regional Hospital for treatment a short time later by her older brother's girlfriend.

Forensics

DNA evidence from Indiana State Police crime lab technicians proved that victim and perpetrator's blood relationship and the occurrence of rape.

Investigative Considerations

In a taped recording released in court, Anthony Sims told police he did have sex with his sister but it was not rape. He also told police he knew it was incest but did not know it was illegal. Sims also said he had "joked around" about having sex with his sister before.

The victim, however, said she was scared when she realized that Sims was with her in bed, and that she told him "no" three or four times before the incident ended.

Sims claimed that the sexual intercourse had been consensual and that no rape was perpetrated.

Sims had a criminal record that included 16 juvenile cases and 7 cases as an adult. He was on probation for burglary at the time of the rape and was not in compliance with his probation.

Outcome

While the defense attempted to call into doubt whether Sims and the victim shared the same father, he was found guilty of both incest and rape by a jury composed of eight women and four men. He was sentenced to serve 5 years for incest and 16 years for rape. The judge also recommended that Sims receive counseling for anger management and sex crimes during his prison stay, and ordered Sims to register as a sex offender.

312.02: Child Domestic Sexual Abuse

This classification refers to rape and sexual assault on any household member under the age of majority in the state where the crime is committed.

Defining Characteristics

VICTIMOLOGY

The child victim has a familial relationship with the offender. There is often a history of prior abuse or conflict with the offender. Other children or adolescents in the family may also be sexually or physically abused.

CRIME SCENE INDICATORS FREQUENTLY NOTED

Usually, only one crime scene is involved, and it is commonly the victim's or offender's residence.

COMMON FORENSIC FINDINGS

If the rape and sexual assault take place over a period of time, there may be evidence of vaginal or anal scarring. However, lack of medical corroboration does not mean the child was not victimized.

Investigative Considerations

Prior abuse of the victim or other members of the household may have previously been reported by other family members or third parties.

Search Warrant Suggestions

A search warrant is indicated for clothing and bed linens, especially if the family member is in the residence with the child.

313: Opportunistic Rape

The motive of the offender is important to determine for both the investigation of a case and treatment of the offender and victim. There is one classification system for rapists that has been empirically tested: the Massachusetts Treatment Center: Rapist3 (MTC:R3; Knight & Prentky, 1990).

Opportunistic motive refers to an impulsive rapist type who shows little planning or preparation. He usually has a history of unsocialized behavior, and the rape serves as an example of the degree to which he lacks interpersonal awareness. These rapists show no concern for the welfare or comfort of their victims. The rape is for immediate sexual gratification rather than the enactment of a highly developed fantasy or sexualized ritual. The rape is in the service of dominance and power.

Four age brackets are identified under each group: adult, adolescent, child, and elder. One of each group will be described with a case study. Classification of sexual assault and rape as opportunistic, sexualization (power–reassurance or entitlement), pervasive anger, or sadistic uses, as the determining criterion, the amount of aggression involved. Evidence for high expressive aggression used to determine the correct classification includes any combination of the following:

- Injuries greater than minor cuts, scratches, and abrasions.
- Force in excess of that needed to attain victim compliance, such as slapping, punching, or kicking when there is no evidence of victim resistance.
- Specific acts in the offense, for example, mutilation, burning, stabbing, choking to unconsciousness, biting, kicking, anal penetration, or insertion of foreign objects.
- Desire or attempts to humiliate a victim through derogatory, demeaning remarks, any use of feces or urine, any forcing a male to observe, or evidence of forced fellatio after sodomy.

The MTC:R3 classification of motivation follows.

Sexualization Motive

Sexualization motive is a component of all rape because the assault occurs within a sexual situation. However, some sexual assaults have a higher degree of sexualization than others. It essentially refers to a high degree of preoccupation with gratifying one's sexual needs. Sexual preoccupation is typically evidenced by highly intrusive, recurrent sexual and rape fantasies, frequent use of pornography, reports of frequent uncontrollable sexual urges, use of a variety of alternative outlets for gratifying sexual needs (e.g., massage parlors, X-rated movies, sex clubs, strip bars), and engaging in other deviant sexual behaviors (paraphilias), such as voyeurism, exhibitionism, or fetishism. The sexual assaults of these offenders are often well planned, as evidenced by a clear, scripted sequence of events; possession of assault-related paraphernalia; and an apparent plan to procure the victim and elude apprehension after the assault.

Four rapist types are hypothesized to possess a high degree of sexual preoccupation. All four types have in common the presence of protracted sexual and rape fantasies that motivate their sexual assaults and influence the way in which their offenses occur. In MTC:R3, there are two major subgroups based on the presence or absence of sadistic fantasies or behaviors: the sadistic and nonsadistic groups. The sadistic group includes two subtypes (overt sadist and muted sadist), and the nonsadistic group includes two subtypes (power–reassurance and entitlement). Thus, these four types are differentiated primarily by the content of the fantasies and the ways in which the fantasies are expressed through behavior.

Sadistic Types

Both of the sadistic types show evidence of poor differentiation between sexual and aggressive drives and a frequent co-occurrence of sexual and aggressive thoughts and fantasies. For the overt sadistic type, the aggression is manifested directly in physically injurious behavior in sexual assaults. For the muted sadistic type, the aggression is expressed either symbolically or through covert fantasy that is not acted out behaviorally.

An offender's behavior must reflect his intention to inflict fear or pain on the victim and to manifest a high level of aggression if he is to be classified as an overt sadistic rapist. Moreover, since a feature of sadism is the synergistic relationship between sexual arousal and feelings of anger, there must be some evidence that the aggression either contributed to sexual arousal or at least did not inhibit such arousal. Since the two feelings (sexual arousal and anger) have equal ability to enhance or increase the other, the sexual acts may precede aggression, or the aggression may precede the sexual acts. The cardinal feature in either case is the intertwining or fusing of the two feelings such that increases in one lead to increases in the other. As a group, overt sadistic rapists appear to be angry, belligerent people who, except for their sadism and the greater planning of their sexual assaults, look very similar to the pervasively angry rapists.

To be classified as a muted sadistic rapist, there must be evidence that the victim's fear or discomfort, or the fantasy of violence, contributed to the offender's sexual arousal (or did not inhibit such arousal) and that the amount of physical force in the sexual assault did not exceed what was necessary to gain victim compliance. Symbolic expressions of sadistic fantasy characterize these offenders, who may employ various forms of bondage or restraints, non-injurious insertion of foreign objects, and other sexual aids, such as Vaseline or shaving cream. What is absent is the high level of expressive aggression that is clearly manifest in overt sadism. As noted, the higher social competence of muted sadistic offenders may explain the difference in aggression, with the greater social sophistication of muted sadistic rapists attenuating or muting the aggression. In general, muted sadistic offenders, except for their sadistic fantasies and their slightly higher lifestyle impulsivity, resemble the high social competence, nonsadistic rapist.

Nonsadistic Types

For the nonsadistic sexualized rapists, the thoughts and fantasies that are associated with their sexual assaults are devoid of the synergistic relation of sex and aggression that characterizes the sadistic types. Indeed, these two rapist types are hypothesized to manifest less aggression than any of the other rapist types. If confronted with victim resistance, these offenders may flee rather than force the victim to comply. Their fantasies and behaviors are hypothesized to reflect an amalgam of sexual arousal, distorted male cognitions about women and sexuality, feelings of social and sexual inadequacy, and masculine self-image concerns. Compared to the other rapist types, these offenders have relatively few problems with impulse control in domains outside sexual aggression.

Vindictive Motivation

The core feature and primary driving force for the vindictive type is anger at women. Unlike the pervasively angry rapist, women are the central and exclusive focus of the vindictive rapist's anger. Their sexual assaults are marked by behaviors that are physically injurious and appear to be intended to degrade, demean, and humiliate their victims. The misogynistic anger evident in these assaults runs the gamut from verbal abuse to brutal murder. As noted, these offenders differ from pervasively angry rapists in that they show little or no evidence of anger at men (e.g., by instigating fights with or assaulting men).

Although there is a sexual component in their assaults, there is no evidence that their aggression is eroticized as it is for the sadistic types and no evidence that they are preoccupied with sadistic fantasies. Indeed, the aggression in the sexual assault is often instrumental in achieving the primary aim of demeaning or humiliating the victim (e.g., forcing the victim to fellate the offender). Vindictive rapists also differ from both the pervasively angry and overt sadistic offenders in their relatively lower level of lifestyle impulsivity (they have relatively fewer problems with impulse control in other areas of their lives).

313.01: Social Acquaintance Rape

Subcategories of social acquaintance rape are adult, adolescent, child, and elder. In this offense, there is a prior knowledge of or relationship between the victim and offender. Often, the relationship is social, and for adults and adolescents, the assault usually occurs on a date. Other relationships include student–teacher, athlete–coach, or priest–altar boy affiliations. For child cases, the relationship might include a neighbor or family friend. For elder cases, the relationship might include caregiver in the home.

Defining Characteristics

VICTIMOLOGY

This type of offense involves low expressive aggression and no severe physical injuries to the victim. It begins with a consenting interpersonal encounter.

OFFENDER CHARACTERISTICS

It is likely that this offender has good social skills and has not been involved in serious criminal activities. The offense is usually situational for adult and elder victims and preferential for child victims.

CRIME SCENE INDICATORS FREQUENTLY NOTED

The crime scene is usually the victim or offender's residence.

COMMON FORENSIC FINDINGS

See the section on general forensic evidence collection at the start of the chapter if the victim reports the rape shortly after it occurred.

Investigative Considerations

Prior abuse of the victim or other members of the household may have previously been reported by other family members or third parties.

Search Warrant Suggestions

If the rape is reported immediately after it occurred, a search warrant should be requested to obtain offender clothing to test for blood, hair, and fibers. If there is a long delay between the rape and reporting, search warrants will provide access to little evidence.

Case Study: 313.01: Social Acquaintance Rape

Background and Victimology

Rose had a brief, romantic involvement with Frank approximately two years before the sexual assault, which occurred in 1979, but she had not seen him in the interim. Then, one evening while en route to a friend's house for dinner, she found herself driving by Frank's home and impulsively decided to stop to say hello. Frank, who greeted Rose in his bathrobe at the downstairs back door, sent Rose to a nearby liquor store to purchase liquor for him. They had a drink together, and Frank continued to drink after Rose had finished. At first, they talked and reminisced about old times. At some point, Frank rolled and smoked a cigarette he made from substance that he kept in a jar.

As Frank became increasingly intoxicated, he started to become physically and sexually suggestive. Eventually, he grabbed at Rose, threatened her with an ornamental knife, and burned her with his cigarette, according to Rose's testimony. Frank became even more aggressive, and at various times, he slapped, kicked, punched, and pulled Rose into the bedroom, where he raped her three times, both vaginally and orally.

Eventually, Frank fell asleep, and Rose managed to leave the apartment and get to her car, only to discover she had left some of her belongings inside the apartment. When she reentered the apartment, Frank was on the telephone with his girlfriend, with whom he had a date later that evening. The girlfriend hung up, and an enraged Frank became angry and shouted at Rose. As Rose headed toward the back stairs to leave, Frank kicked or pushed her down the stairs, causing her to fall into the window in the door at the bottom of the stairs, where the broken glass cut her deeply.

After some delay, Frank drove Rose to the hospital because she was almost blinded by the blood in her eyes, but only after she promised not to reveal how she was injured. At the hospital, she told the hospital personnel that she had fallen down the stairs. After she was treated, Frank drove her back to his apartment, where she stayed and slept until the next morning, when she drove herself home.

It was not until two days later, under the prodding questions of close relatives, that Rose revealed the true source of her injuries and the fact that Frank had raped her. She returned to the hospital, where she was examined for rape trauma.

Outcome

Rose pressed criminal charges against Frank immediately, and her attorney filed a civil action within a few weeks of the incident in order to obtain a real estate attachment against the defendant's holdings, as there was a possibility that he would transfer his property to a relative.

Frank was acquitted of all criminal charges in March 1980. In the civil suit, the trial court directed a verdict in favor of the third-party defendant, Frank's homeowner's insurer. An appeals court overturned the directed verdict in favor of Rose, the plaintiff.

313.02: Authority Rape

The subcategories of authority rape are adult, adolescent, child, and elder. The relationship between the victim of authority rape and the offender is one of subordination and status imbalance. One person has power over another by employment, education, or age. The offender uses this authority relationship to take advantage of the victim.

Defining Characteristics

VICTIMOLOGY

The victim is known to the offender. The offender must be in some authoritative relationship to the victim (teacher, supervisor, manager or employer, parole officer, therapist, or physician, for example). Typically, there is low expressive aggression, with no severe physical injuries to the victim.

OFFENDER CHARACTERISTICS

The offender uses familiarity to gain access to or trust of the victim. This is often a preferential offense.

COMMON FORENSIC FINDINGS

The victim should be referred for a sexual assault examination.

Investigation

The investigator should seek out other subordinates of the offender for possible victimization and check current and past affiliations of the offender.

Search Warrant Considerations

If the rape is reported immediately after it occurs, a search warrant should be requested to obtain offender clothing to test for blood, hair, and fibers. If there is a long delay between the rape and reporting, search warrants will provide access to little evidence.

Case Study: 313.02.01: Authority Rape, Adult

Background and Victimology

Five patients, ranging in age from 22 to 78, accused their physician of sexual assault and rape between fall 1983 and fall 1984. The 22-year-old victim described how the physician who was treating her for what she believed was a cyst on her ovary questioned her about her sex life and molested her with an ungloved hand during a pelvic examination. He asked her if she had an orgasm when having sex and that, if not, he could show her how. The doctor then leaned against her and rubbed his pelvis against her while examining her breasts. When asked why she waited four months before telling a fellow worker about the assault, the woman testified, "I thought it was in my head that he was doing something wrong."

Another woman, age 23, testified that during three visits to the doctor for stomach pain, the doctor asked her each time "how often I had sex with my boyfriend, if I pleased my boyfriend." On the last visit, the doctor told her to get up from a chair, pressed his pelvis against her stomach, and asked "if I could please him."

A 38-year-old deaf woman being treated by the doctor for severe stomach pain testified that during one visit, the doctor examined her with ungloved hands and asked if she enjoyed oral sex, how often she had sex, and what positions she used. Then he asked, "Could we go somewhere where nobody knew either of us and let it go from there?"

A 79-year-old woman, weeping and in a wheelchair, testified that the doctor wanted to look at a rash on her back and lifted her onto an examining table where he raped her. Her 84-year-old husband testified that his wife appeared very shaky and upset when she returned home and that he noted blood stains on her underclothes. Charges were entered against the doctor after receiving the complaint from victims.

Offender Characteristics

This offender targeted a wide age range of victims.

Crime Scene Indicators

There was a subordinate patient–doctor relationship between the victim and offender and an offender-controlled environment. He committed an offense only when a nurse was not present and would be guaranteed of not being interrupted.

Forensic Findings

There was too great a time period between the rape and the reporting of the rape for meaningful forensic evidence.

Investigation

When the offender's picture was carried by the local media, additional victims came forward. A search warrant was used for the victim's medical records and other records for use during the trial.

Outcome

The physician was convicted on all charged counts of sexual assault. His appeal of the convictions was denied, and he was sentenced to prison for 7 to 10 years.

313.02.03: Authority Rape, Child

The primary aim of an offender in this category is to have sex with a child. Sexual activity with children may range from a few acts to a lifelong pattern. These offenders tend to be self-centered, with little or no concern about the comfort or welfare of the child. The sexual acts are typically phallic (the goal is penetration and achieving orgasm, with the child used as a masturbatory object), and the victims are usually strangers. The offenses are usually impulsive, with little or no planning; physical injury is absent or minimal. These offenders are usually promiscuous, with many different victims of varying ages. Vulnerable individuals include the sick, the disabled, and the handicapped as well as healthy children in day care settings.

Defining Characteristics

VICTIMOLOGY

The victim is under the state's age of majority. The child can be either male or female.

CRIME SCENE INDICATORS FREQUENTLY NOTED

There is low expressive aggression (i.e., no more aggression than necessary to secure victim compliance). There is no evidence that aggression or victim fear is an important part of the offense or that it is needed to enhance sexual arousal. There is no attempt to relate to the child or to engage the child in nonsexual activities. These offenders tend to be predatory and exploitive. The offense is usually preferential.

Case Study: 313.02.03: Authority Rape of a Child

Gerald A. Sandusky played football for 4 years at Penn State and was a defensive coordinator for 23 years for its Division 1 football program. In 1977, he started Second Mile, a group foster home dedicated to helping troubled boys from absent or dysfunctional families. Sandusky had the means, motive, and opportunity to sexually abuse boys over an extended time period. He selected his boys from Second Mile. He would invite them to football games, to spend time with his family, and attend activities at Penn State. The victims were quickly drawn into Sandusky's world of big-time college football: gifts, trips, sporting events, and hanging out with a guy who seemed to be loved by everyone.

Sandusky was accused of molesting eight boys over a 15-year period. A key allegation against the 67-year-old former coach was that he was seen raping a 10-year-old boy in the Penn State athletic building shower in 2002. Sandusky claimed he was a surrogate father to the boys he developed close relationships with through his Second Mile charity for at-risk youth. He said he was just roughhousing with the kids.

His primary pattern would be to maneuver the boy into close contact and then hug or rub the body followed by a shower where he would then have sexual contact.

The Sandusky Grand Jury Report (2011) listed eight boys that were sexually abused by Gerald Sandusky. Table 12.2 outlines the patterns of the sexual abuse. These were preferential offenses, and Sandusky was an authority offender.

The Freeh Report

Former FBI Director Louis Freeh released the results of a seven-month investigation into the Penn State child sex abuse scandal in July 2012. The major finding was the "consistent disregard of the Penn State most senior leaders for the safety and welfare of Sandusky's child victims." These men, the report continues, concealed Sandusky's victims from the Board of Trustees, the University community and authorities for over a decade and they showed a striking lack of empathy for the child victims, failed to determine the identity of the child, and exposed this child to further harm by alerting Sandusky. The cover-up of the child sexual abuse was in the service of a "culture of reverence for the football program that was ingrained at all levels of the campus community."

Perjury and failure-to-report charges were filed against former Penn State athletic director Tim Curley and resigned vice president of business and finance Gary Schultz. Prosecutors alleged the administrators ignored a 2002 report from a graduate assistant that he saw Sandusky having sex with a young boy in a shower.

Table 12.2 Grand Jury Report of Sandusky's Victims of Sexual Abuse

Victim/Age	Opportunity	Motive	Disclosure	Outcome	Outcome	Outcome
#1, 11/12; started '05/06 until 2008	Second Mile Taken to restaurants, sports events, bought gifts, slept over in Sandusky's basement	Kiss, fondle, oral, 61 phone calls, hand on leg, cracking his back	Witnessed by coach as wrestling; mother calls school	Reported to school authorities	Ban Sandusky from Penn State locker rooms	
#2, 3/1/02			Grad student witnessed Sandusky in shower sodomizing young boy	Reported to Paterno next morning; week later reports it to Curley and Schultz; told it was reported to Second Mile	Ban Sandusky from locker rooms	
				Never heard anything more until called to testify at GJ in 2010	Had been a 1998 investigation by PA Child Welfare department	
					Sandusky given emeritus standing in 1999 with office, access to sport facilities	
#3, 12/13 in 2000	Second Mile, invited to his home, then gym, slept in basement	Contact in shower, rub shoulders, bear hugs, fondle		Never reported		
#4, 12/13 in 1996–1997	Second Mile, invited with family picnic, fixture with family	Contact while swimming, soap battles, oral/anal penetration, bought him marijuana, cigarettes	Never disclosed			

(continued)

Table 12.2 (*Continued*)

Victim/Age	Opportunity	Motive	Disclosure	Outcome	Outcome
#5, 7/8 in 1996	Second Mile, invited to football games	Hand on knee while driving, showers, rubbing him, resisted	Not invited to games or out after resisting; never disclosed		
#6, 7/8 in 1995 or 1996	Second Mile, invited to picnic with Sandusky family after football games	Played "Polish soccer" and then wrestle and shower; bear hug from behind	Mother saw son's wet hair, he told of showering with Sandusky; mother called University Police who investigated but nothing happened Second boy not subpoenaed because in military outside United States	Detectives interviewed Sandusky, who admitted being in shower with kids naked; mother confronted him also Was told not to shower again with boys	
#7, 10 in 1994	Invited to Penn games, stay overnight at Sandusky home; knew several of the boys in Sandusky's "circle"	Bear hugs, crack his back, hands in waistbands, blurry memory of the showers	Had phone calls from Sandusky and his wife before testifying but did not return the calls		

The NCAA fined Pennsylvania State University $60 million for its handling of the Sandusky child sex-abuse case. The school also was stripped of all its wins from 1998 through 2011, barred from postseason games for four years, and lost 20 total scholarships annually for four seasons, according to a release from the NCAA.

Source: www.boston.com/sports/blogs/thebuzz/2012/07/penn_state_to_l.html

313.03: Power–Reassurance Rape

The subcategories of power–reassurance rape are adult, adolescent, child, and elder. The rape usually occurs as a blitz or sudden, unexpected assault. It is usually a situational assault unless the victim has been targeted. The classification of power–reassurance implies the dynamics of the offender. Most often, this offender is committing the rape as a test of his competence and manhood. The rape is compensatory for his feelings of sexual inadequacy. Fueling the behavior is a fantasy that the woman will like the "sex" and therefore want more. The reality, of course, is that the behavior is forced penetration, without consent, and by threat—all elements of rape.

Defining Characteristics

Victimology

The victim is usually unknown to the offender. If known, the victim will be a casual acquaintance, such as someone living in the same neighborhood or working in the same building. There is usually low expressive aggression, with no severe physical injuries to the victim.

Victims of choice are generally about the same age as or younger than the perpetrator, and usually of the same race. If he dates at all, the women he dates will be younger and less sophisticated than he; this is the only way he can feel equal. Because of his feelings of inadequacy, he gains control by surprise; he doesn't have the self-confidence or skills to con his way into a victim's apartment smoothly and is more likely to break in the middle of the night, for example.

Offender Characteristics

The offender often makes some attempt to relate to the victim and assure the victim that he does not intend to injure him or her. The offender generally has had problems as an adolescent or adult. The offense often is planned, at least to the extent of the offender's having thought about the assault (such as a rehearsed fantasy). These offenders may have other signs of sexual preoccupation and sexually deviant behavior. This type of offender has been descriptively termed a *compensatory rapist*.

The *power–reassurance rapist* feels himself to be inadequate, not the type with whom women would voluntarily become involved. He compensates for these feelings of male inadequacy by forcing women to have sex with him. All the while, as the designation suggests, he is looking for reassurance of his own power and potency. This type has sometimes been referred to as the "gentleman rapist," or even classified as an "unselfish" rapist, in large part because his offenses, while traumatic, are usually less physically damaging to his victim than those of other types of sex offenders. Such a rapist may even apologize during the assault or ask the victim if he is hurting her—a question that serves his own need for reassurance more than it expresses a genuine concern for the victim. Therefore, the terms *gentleman* and *unselfish* are applicable only within the context of the full spectrum of rapist types (Hazelwood, 2009, pp. 97–109).

This type tends to be a loner who fantasizes that his victim actually enjoys the experience and might even fall in love with him. He may go so far as to contact the victim after the assault and ask her to go out with him. Of course, the reality of rape cannot live up to his fantasies: Instead of winning over a reluctant lover, he has terrorized, hurt, and angered an innocent person. Most rapists of the power–reassurance variety will admit later that they did not enjoy the sex with their victims. The experience did not satisfy the underlying obsession and, therefore, he will have to try again with another woman.

When we delve into this type of perpetrator's past, we generally see a history of unusual or bizarre masturbatory fantasies, often voyeurism, exhibitionism, cross-dressing, and/or obscene phone calls. He frequents adult bookstores or movies and collects pornography. If he has a specific sexual dysfunction, it is likely to involve premature ejaculation, which would be exhibited in consensual relationships he may have and which he would report as a problem (from his point of view only) in his rapes.

He will tend to prefer the night and operate in his own residential or work area—in other words, within a very prescribed comfort zone—and will usually travel to the crime scene on foot. If he is a serial offender, this is particularly true of his first offenses. He uses a weapon of opportunity, often something he found at the crime scene. His patterns of crime are generally consistent, and the entire act, from the time he overpowers his victim until the time he leaves, is relatively brief, sometimes as little as 5 or 10 minutes. He will not use profanity or try to demean or humiliate his victim to the extent that the other rapist types will, but may require her to recite a "script" in which she praises his lovemaking or expresses desire for him. He might cover the victim's eyes or mask his own features, both for the self-preservation motive of preventing identification and the possibility that he knows he should be ashamed of his actions. He is timid and will do whatever the victim allows him to. Rather than tear off her clothes or force her to strip, he may only expose the parts of the victim's body he intends to assault.

He is apt to keep a journal, news clippings, or some other record of his assaults to reassure himself of his potency. For the same reason, he may take souvenirs, such as pieces of the victim's underwear. Afterward, he may feel guilty or remorseful. But unless he is a first-timer who tries it, doesn't like it, and decides never to do it again, he *will* do it again. He will keep raping until he is caught or stopped in some other way, such as being arrested and incarcerated, or killed or seriously injured in another crime or other unrelated incident. He tends to live alone or with parents or in some other type of dependent relationship. His mother probably was—or is—very domineering. He is employed below his ability level in a job that does not require a lot of contact with the public. While this is the least physically dangerous type of rapist, if he is successful over a series of attacks, his confidence can be boosted and he may become more physically aggressive.

Numerically, this is the most common type of rapist.

Case Study: 313.03.01: Power–Reassurance Rape, Adult

Background and Victimology

Eugene's sexual offense history began in his early 20s (during the time he was married) with exhibitionism. Four years after he began exposing himself, he assaulted two young women. When he grabbed one woman, with his genitals exposed, the other woman slapped him in the face. He released his hold, and the two women ran away.

Two years later, he committed his first rape. While walking along a riverbank, he observed a jogger running toward him. He stopped her by asking a question. After they had conversed for a while, he grabbed her, fondled her breasts, and forced her to remove her clothes. He placed her clothes on the ground and told her to lie on them. While raping her, he repeatedly asked her sexual questions. After achieving orgasm, he left.

A second rape occurred about one year later. This offense was similar to the first: he picked up a pedestrian, drove her to a park, and raped her, again asking the victim for assurance that the assault was a pleasurable experience.

Offender Characteristics

Eugene is a 30-year-old divorced male who came from a relatively large, intact family. His father worked many hours away from home and returned to the house only on weekends. When he was at home, he spent most of his time drinking; however, there is no evidence that he was abusive toward members of the family. Because his mother also worked and consequently was gone much of the time, caretaking and child-rearing responsibilities were assumed by the immigrant paternal grandmother, who spoke almost no English.

Eugene got along poorly with his five brothers and sisters. He stated that he was the black sheep. His school-related difficulties began as early as the third grade; his earliest memories are of skipping school and vandalizing deserted buildings. Although clearly of average or above-average intelligence, he repeated several grades and eventually dropped out of school before finishing the tenth grade.

He enlisted in the Army and remained in the service for several years, with a record marked by disciplinary hearings. Shortly after discharge from the service, he married.

The marriage lasted two years and produced one child, who died at birth. Although the child allegedly died of natural causes, his wife and in-laws blamed him for the death.

His employment history was as erratic as his school and military history. He worked as a truck driver in construction, in warehouses, as a security guard, for moving companies, and as a mechanic, quitting all jobs he held, typically within two months.

Eugene's childhood, juvenile, and young adult history of instability, low frustration tolerance, acting out, and delinquent behavior underscores his impulsive lifestyle. The compensatory nature of his offenses is amply illustrated by his exhibitionism, his attempts to confirm his sexual adequacy, and his attempts to reassure the victim as well as himself.

Outcome

Eugene was convicted of two rape charges.

313.03.02: Power–Reassurance Rape, Adolescent

The primary aim of the offender in this rape is to develop a relationship with an adolescent. The sexual activities are secondary to the interpersonal intent. The victim is seen as an appropriate social and sexual companion; the offender perceives that the relationship is mutually satisfying and that it benefits the adolescent in some way. The sexual acts usually are limited to fondling, caressing, kissing, frottage, or oral sex performed on the victim. The victim may be known to the offender, and the relationship between the victim and the offender is usually long term or there have been multiple encounters with the victim. The offenses are usually planned and are not characterized as impulsive. The offenses are not violent, and rarely is there any physical injury to the victim.

Case Study: 313.03.02: Power–Reassurance Rape, Adolescent

Background and Victimology

Jim's criminal record started in 1973 at the age of 23. His first offense was an attempted rape of an 18-year-old woman. The same year, he committed a second, similar offense against a 17-year-old woman. In neither case was there physical force, and in neither case did the assault eventuate in rape. In 1974 he raped a 19-year-old woman, in 1975 a 23-year-old woman, and in 1976 a 15-year-old girl.

This last rape was the offense for which he was committed. In every case, his MO was more or less the same: picking up a hitchhiker, brandishing a knife, and threatening harm, but never applying more force than needed to gain submission. In fact, in the first two assaults, the victims talked him out of the rape.

The scripted or ritualized aspect of the pattern assaults suggests Jim's compensatory nature. The offender had no long-term history of conduct disorder. The acts themselves had an element of premeditation in that he set out to locate victims on the occasions of the crimes. On several occasions he expressed interest in dating the victims and was apprehended after the last rape when he met his victim for a date the next evening. Jim represents the pure compensatory rapist.

Offender Characteristics

Jim was the first of three sons. His early years were described as reasonably happy ones. However, after being laid off from his job as a machine operator, his father started drinking heavily and became destructive during fits of rage. Jim graduated from high school and worked as a general laborer before joining the military. After a full term in the military, he was again employed as a laborer. At the time of the last rape, he was working as a security guard. He met his wife while in the military, and they were married a short time later. They were divorced after about three years, and Jim was given custody of their three-year-old child.

Investigation

Police investigated each victim report. On several occasions, Jim had expressed interest in dating the victims and was apprehended after the last rape when he met his victim for a date the next evening. The police were waiting for him after working with the victim to set up the pseudo-date.

Outcome

Jim was sent to the Massachusetts Treatment Center, Bridgewater, Massachusetts, for sex offender treatment in 1978 after having been convicted of kidnapping and rape.

313.04: Exploitative Rape

The subcategories of exploitative rape are adult, adolescent, child, and elder. In exploitative rape, expressed aggression is generally low and does not exceed what was necessary to force victim compliance. Callous indifference to the victim is evident.

Defining Characteristics

VICTIMOLOGY

The victim may be an adult, adolescent, child, or elder. The victim, either female or male, is usually unknown to the offender.

Victims of preference will tend to be around his age. He is on the prowl for a victim of opportunity, and this activity could take place in a bar or neighborhood he has targeted. Once he has a woman under his control, his only concern is getting her to submit sexually to him. That is the real thrill for him—the sex act is satisfying as an act of domination and control rather than for providing what we think of as sexual gratification. Once he has forced submission, as far as he is concerned, the experience is over. But during that encounter, he can be expected to inflict multiple assaults on the victim. Anal assaults are common. Masks or attempts at disguise or hiding his face are uncommon. With this type of offender, there will often be an interval between rapes—a day, a month, six months—until he once again goes on the hunt; however, unlike the power–reassurance rapist, he will not try to maintain any contact with or come back to a victim once he has left her, although he often threatens to return if she reports the assault to police.

OFFENDER CHARACTERISTICS

The offender usually has limited formal schooling; a poor job record; and short-term, unstable relationships. He is usually impulsive and has a long record of serious behavioral problems or of arrests for criminal offenses, starting in adolescence and throughout most of his adult life.

The *exploitative rapist's* crimes result from seizing an opportunity that presents itself rather than by fantasizing about the act ahead of time. He might approach a potential victim with a ruse or con, or it could be a direct, overpowering, blitz-style attack. Unlike the power–reassurance rapist, this type will not appear in any way concerned with the victim's welfare. He is selfish—verbally, physically, and sexually. He may suffer from some form of sexual dysfunction, and if he does, it will be just as apparent with his wife, girlfriend, or any other consenting partner as it will be with a victim of force. Such sexual dysfunction often has to do with retarded ejaculation or difficulty in reaching climax.

This type of rapist will be very body-conscious. He will want a macho reputation, to be known as a man's man, and therefore is likely to have some physically oriented employment. He is interested in sports. His vehicle will reflect that image, too. In some regions of the country, it would be a Corvette or other muscle car; in others, it might be a pickup truck, well equipped for hunting. He does not take well to criticism or authority. He probably did not do well in high school or go to college. If married, he will have a history of cheating on his wife and paying scant attention to his children. When we look into the background of offenders like this, we very often find that his father treated his mother in the same way the offender treats women.

Next to the power–reassurance rapist, this is the most common type of rapist.

Case Study: 313.04.01: Exploitative Rape, Adult

Background and Victimology

Richard is a 32-year-old single male. His first rape was a 25-year-old woman. He grabbed her around the throat and placed a knife to her neck, forcing her to the basement of a building. The victim was held prisoner and repeatedly raped and sodomized. The offender stole a small amount of money from her purse before allowing her to leave. His second victim, 27 years old, was seized on the street and forced into a vacant house, where she was raped and change removed from her purse. The third victim, 25 years old, was seized at knifepoint on the street, forced to her apartment, and repeatedly raped and sodomized. The victims were blindfolded, and the last one was bound with a rope. None of the victims were injured by weapons.

Offender Characteristics

Richard was the third of four brothers. His father was a cab driver who both worked and drank regularly. He was described as a womanizer and was abusive when intoxicated. His mother was a waitress and a maid. She attended church regularly and appeared to have been devoted to her family. Shortly after the death of a younger sister (age six months), Richard (then two years old) began wandering away from home. By the age of three, he was killing kittens by locking them in a refrigerator, and by age four, he was removed from a day nursery for fighting. By age six, he was pulling up girls' dresses and exposing himself. He was placed in a home the same year and remained in penal institutions, juvenile detention centers, and foster homes throughout his life. He remained in the fourth grade until his 16th birthday. He eventually earned his general equivalence diploma while in prison. Richard had a long juvenile and adult criminal record that included numerous instances of larceny, statutory burglary, breaking and entering, motor vehicle offenses, armed robbery, assault and battery, and rape.

Richard's profile is typical of an exploitative, high-impulse rapist. The assaults were all impulsive, predatory acts. Although there was little gratuitous aggression (compared with the expressive rapist), there was no concern for the victims' fear or discomfort (compared with the compensatory rapist). There is a long history of behavioral management problems going back to early childhood, resulting in a low level of adult social, professional, and interpersonal competence. It is this extensive history or acting out concomitant with a low level of social competence that distinguishes this individual from the power–reassurance rapist (see Case Study 313.03.01).

Investigation

Richard was well known to the police. After the victims reported the rapes, the detective reviewed his files and developed a suspect list. Richard's name was high on the list. He had no alibi for the evenings in question. Moreover, items taken from the victims were traced to him after a search warrant was secured.

Outcome

Richard was sent to the Massachusetts Treatment Center in Bridgewater for sex offender treatment in 1975 after having been convicted of rape, sodomy, armed robbery, breaking and entering, and assault and battery.

314: Anger Rape

Sexual assault in the category of anger rape is characterized by high expressive aggression; unprovoked physical and verbal aggression or physical force in excess of that necessary to gain victim compliance must be present. The primary motive for the offense is anger, not sexual gratification. These offenses are predominantly impulse driven (e.g., opportunity alone, possibly coupled with impaired judgment due to drugs or alcohol). The degree of force used in this type of assault is excessive and gratuitous. The violence is an integrated component of the behavior even when the victim is compliant. Resistance from the victim is likely to increase the aggression, and serious injury or death may occur. The rage is not sexualized, suggesting that the assault is not fantasy driven.

Defining Characteristics

VICTIMOLOGY

When the offender knows the victim, the assault on that victim appears to be the result of the offender's easy access to that victim. The victim is usually a woman and high expressive aggression must be present. In addition, there must be clear evidence from the offender's behaviors or verbalizations that the primary intent of the rape is to hurt, demean, humiliate, or punish the victim (e.g., by calling the victim names or forcing the victim to engage in acts that are seen by the offender as demeaning or humiliating, such as fellatio).

For this type of anger rapist, the victim represents a person—or group of people—the offender hates. This could be a mother, wife, or girlfriend, even women in general. But his anger and resentment need not be rooted in an actual or legitimate wrong ever perpetrated against him.

It would not be unusual for this type to be involved in an ongoing relationship with a woman. Because he is driven by rage, the consequences of the anger rapist's attack can be anything from verbal abuse, to severe beating, to murder, though the fact that his conscious or subconscious intention is to get the anger out of his system means that this type usually will not kill. His attacks will be episodic, not at predictable intervals, triggered by precipitating stressors involving the woman or women to whom his rage is actually directed.

In almost all cases, the displacement means that he will not attack that person. He may attack someone else he knows, using weapons of opportunity such as kitchen knives or even his own fists if he is strong enough. Because he wants not just to overpower but to humiliate his target, there could be anal sex followed by oral sex and a great deal of profanity, and the context of his behavior will be an intention to degrade, such as by ejaculating on the victim's face or clothing.

Therefore, it is important for the examiner to realize that crucial DNA and other evidence can be found on many parts of the victim's body and her clothes. Whenever this is a possibility, a delicate but thorough line of questioning on this topic is indicated, with the twin goals of preserving the chain of evidence while ensuring the victim's emotional well-being.

OFFENDER CHARACTERISTICS

Rage is evident in this offender. He may have manifested behaviors listed for sadistic sexual assault, but these must appear to be punishing actions done in anger, not to increase sexual arousal.

The violence is a lifestyle characteristic that is directed toward males and females alike. The rape is but one feature in a history of unsocialized aggressive behavior noted across various social settings.

This type is far less common than either of the previous two, possibly as little as 5% of rapists.

314.01: Anger Rape, Gender

The category of gender anger rape is reserved for offenders who hate women and express their rage through rape.

Case Study: 314.01: Anger Rape, Gender

Background and Victimology

A 26-year-old woman was awakened at 2:00 a.m. when the offender, Randy, put his fist through the glass door of her apartment building. He reached in and unlocked the door as the victim came out into the hallway. He grabbed her around the neck, put a knife to her throat, and dragged her into his car. When in the car, he warned her that if she moved, he would "chop her up" with the knife. When they arrived at an abandoned building, he forced her to undress, dance in the nude, and utter obscenities about women while dancing. He grabbed her breasts and buttocks and grabbed her hair and slapped her face, all while ordering her to repeat more obscenities about women over and over again. He then sodomized her, performed cunnilingus, forced her to perform fellatio, and finally had intercourse with her.

Throughout the assault, he told her to keep swearing, saying he liked to hear it. Eventually, he got back into his car and drove off, leaving the victim to walk five miles to the nearest house.

Offender Characteristics

Randy's father died in a car accident when he was two years old. His mother was a cocktail waitress and heavy drinker who died of pneumonia at the age of 30. After his father died, Randy was raised by foster parents. He reports not seeing his mother more than six times a year after that. His relationship with his foster parents was apparently a good one. His foster father died when Randy was 13. His foster mother alone was unable to provide the supervision and guidance he needed, and before long he was getting into trouble with the law.

At the age of 17, Randy left home and moved in with a male companion. He never married, although at the time of arrest he was engaged. He attended six different primary and secondary schools, eventually dropping out in the 11th grade at age 17. In the five years between leaving high school and his arrest, he held many different jobs, primarily as dishwasher, busboy, cook, and clerk. He had been drinking heavily since he was 16 and also used amphetamines, cocaine, and marijuana.

Although this was his first sexual offense, Randy had a long history of delinquent behavior, including 10 prior court appearances for motor vehicle violations, larceny, writing bad checks, and drugs.

This is a typical case of a high-impulse, anger rapist. The primary aim of the rape was the expression of rage through physically assaulting, degrading, and humiliating the victim. A pattern of chronic acting out began in the offender's early adolescence, reflecting an impulsive lifestyle. Comments from his psychiatric report suggested that his behavior was frequently unplanned and guided by whim and that there was an exaggerated craving for excitement. Although Randy's impulsiveness did not appear until adolescence, some offenders express an impulsive style as early as childhood.

Investigation

After reporting the rape to the police, the victim took them back to the area where she had been raped. The abandoned building was found, as well as evidence that eventually tied Randy to the crime scene.

Outcome

Randy was a 22-year-old single male when sent for sex offender treatment to the Massachusetts Treatment Center, Bridgewater, in 1977. He was convicted of rape, kidnapping, armed robbery, assault with a dangerous weapon, and unnatural acts.

314.02: Anger Rape, Age

The motive of the offender in age anger is to seek out victims of a specific age group, usually elderly or young.

314.02.01: Anger Rape, Elderly Victim

The victim must be a woman 60 years of age or older. High expressive aggression must be evident and the choice of an elderly victim must be intentional on the part of the offender (i.e., not strictly a victim of opportunity).

Case Study: 314.02.01: Anger Rape, Elderly Victim

Background and Victimology

A 65-year-old widow returning from church entered her bedroom and noted that several bureau drawers were open and that jewelry and money were missing. Walking into the den, she was struck by a closed fist to her face. A man grabbed her by the throat and threw her onto a couch. The intruder tore off her clothing, tried to strangle her, and said, "Die, damn you, die." He then sexually assaulted the woman.

Offender Characteristics

Dan, age 25, came from a broken home and lived until age 6 with a foster family. His natural mother abandoned the family when Dan was 3. When his father remarried, Dan went to live with his father and stepmother. The stepmother was a severe disciplinarian who burned Dan's fingers with a cigarette lighter when she caught him smoking.

Dan ran away from home as often as he could. There were frequent family arguments and beatings because he was a slow learner in school. Dan attended four grammar schools and four high schools. Part of his high school experience was at a boys' training center, where he was labeled an unruly child. At ages 14 and 15, he admitted to being obsessed with thoughts of murdering his stepmother, and he continually thought of ways to carry out the killing.

Dan enlisted in the Army at age 19 and served six years. He reports receiving approximately 20 reprimands for misconduct during this time. He claims to have become addicted to alcohol and drugs while in the service.

Dan married a woman whose husband had been killed in Vietnam, and the agreement to marry was for the purpose of splitting the extra pay he would receive if they married. They never lived together and were divorced 10 months later. Dan claimed to be tripping on LSD during his rape offense.

Investigation

After reporting the rape to police, the victim's apartment was examined for crime scene evidence. Dan's fingerprints were found, and he subsequently confessed to the rape.

Outcome

Dan pleaded guilty to the crime of rape and was sentenced to a five-year term.

314.02.02: Anger Rape, Child Victim

This category of anger rape is reserved for offenders who express extreme anger at children, with no evidence that the aggression is eroticized (not sadistic); the aggression is rooted in rage or anger at the victim as a child, the world, people in general, or some specific individual. Any physical injury to the child results by accident: due to the clumsiness or ineptness on the part of the offender or because the victim may have been pushed in a struggle and accidentally hit his or her head.

Case Study: 314.02.02: Anger Rape, Child Victim

Background and Victimology

The victim, a 9-year-old boy, lived at a church-operated home for boys. According to Bruce, the 16-year-old offender, the two met, talked a bit, and decided to hunt for snakes and fish at a nearby reservoir. As they sat on a dock fishing, Bruce started fondling the boy, becoming sexually aroused. He undid the boy's pants and performed fellatio. He then began to try to take the boy's pants off. The boy resisted as Bruce turned him over on his stomach, preparing to sodomize him. They fell into the water, and a struggle ensued. The boy slipped on a rock and hit his head, which rendered him unconscious. Bruce tried to lift the boy but slipped, dropping the boy into the water. "He was not dead the first time he hit his head, but I'm sure he was dead the second time," said Bruce.

Offender Characteristics

Bruce has a brother two years older than he is. His parents divorced when he was a few months old. The brother, according to Bruce, beat him up daily from the time he was 3 until he was 10 or 11. When he was 5, the mother and two boys moved to live with his maternal grandfather. This was an important relationship for Bruce; however, the grandfather died four years later. Bruce reports that soon after he turned 11, he was fishing one day when an 18-year-old youth approached him and told him about a good fishing spot in the woods. As they proceeded into the forest, the youth forced fellatio and sodomy on Bruce. He claimed he yelled, but that it did no good. He felt helpless, and the act was painful.

Upon entering the seventh grade, Bruce tested in the high intelligence range and was advanced two grades. He was socially immature and found it too lonely to be with the older adolescents. He became rebellious and hostile and spent most of the years between ages 12 and 16 on his own, in youth detention centers or psychiatric facilities. His juvenile criminal involvement included 16 court appearances on 43 charges, including shoplifting, assault and battery, use of a dangerous weapon, motor vehicle violations, and four charges of sexual abuse of juveniles under 14. He maintained that the victims were willing partners around his own age.

Bruce began homosexual activities in early adolescence and moved in with a male partner. However, six months later, this adolescent was killed in a car accident, and Bruce attempted suicide by consuming an overdose of aspirin. The assault of the boy at the reservoir happened on the anniversary of his friend's death.

Crime Scene Indicators

The victim's body was found floating in the reservoir. The body wore no trousers. A search of the area revealed shorts with the victim's initials sewn inside.

Forensic Findings

The coroner's examination revealed a laceration one and a half inches in length and a half-inch in width on the forehead, as well as multiple blows to the head. The victim weighed 45 pounds. Asphyxiation by drowning was noted as possible cause of death.

Investigation

Crime scene evidence was found on the victim. When detectives began interviewing persons at the boy's home, they developed investigative leads linking Bruce to the victim. Several people had seen him leave with the victim.

Outcome

Bruce was sentenced to 18 to 20 years for manslaughter and 18 to 20 years concurrent for rape. He was committed to the Treatment Center at Bridgewater, Massachusetts, under Massachusetts law as a sexually dangerous person.

314.03: Anger Rape, Racial

This category is reserved for what appears to be racially motivated rape.

Defining Characteristics

VICTIMOLOGY

Victims are of a different race from the offender.

Case Study: 314.03: Anger Rape, Racial

Background and Victimology

Joe is a 28-year-old Black man with two index offenses: one against a 22-year-old White female and the other against a 27-year-old White female. Both offenses occurred in the presence of the victim's boyfriend. In one instance, the offender approached a couple as they were about to enter their apartment. He came up behind them and forced his way into the apartment after them. He made the boyfriend stand in the corner of the room facing the wall while he raped the woman. The second offense had a similar MO. During the rape, Joe made degrading racial comments to both the victims and their boyfriends.

Offender Characteristics

Joe, bright and charming, had a long history of nonsexual crimes including breaking and entering, larcenies, and motor vehicle offenses. He grew up in the inner city. The rapes occurred in the suburbs and in the vicinity where he worked. His work was low-skilled industrial park work. He dropped out of high school in the 10th grade. He was never married but had a variety of consenting sexual companions.

Investigation

Crime scene evidence was developed from the locations of the offenses. Detectives took a careful history from both the victim and her boyfriend. Fingerprints were obtained, and Joe became the lead suspect. A photo lineup was used to identify Joe.

Outcome

The offender was convicted of all charges of rape and committed to the Treatment Center at Bridgewater, Massachusetts, under the Massachusetts Sexually Dangerous Predator Act. After serving a 15-year sentence, Joe would remain at the treatment center until psychologists determined he was no longer sexually dangerous.

314.04: Anger Rape, Global

This category is reserved for offenders who appear to be globally angry at the world. This is a high-expressive-aggression assault with no evidence of sadism and no evidence that the offender is focally angry with women.

Defining Characteristics

VICTIMOLOGY

Typically, the victim is unknown to the offender. Usually, there is moderate to severe physical aggression and injury to victim.

OFFENDER CHARACTERISTICS

This offender is impulsive and has had behavioral problems and encounters with the law beginning in adolescence and into his adult life. Typically, the offender has few social skills. Often, he has a history of verbal and physical assaults on both males and females. Usually, the offenses are not planned.

Case Study: 314.04: Anger Rape, Global

Background and Victimology

A 17-year-old woman was walking along a city road as the offender, Steven, drove by. He stopped his car beside her, stepped out, and asked her where she was going. He did not hear her answer and asked again in an angry manner. She turned to walk away, which made Steven feel as though she was rejecting him and trying to make a fool of him. He punched her in the stomach, grabbed her under her chin, pulled her into his car, and drove away to a secluded area. After he parked the car, he told her to get into the back seat. When she refused, he climbed into the back and dragged her over the seat beside him. He undressed her and violently penetrated her. He states that he then withdrew, without having an orgasm, and let her out of the car, threatening to kill her if she made mention of the attack. When he was arrested shortly after, he immediately admitted his guilt.

Offender Characteristics

Steven came from a relatively normal, seemingly unremarkable family. He had an older sister and a younger brother, both of whom appeared to be living normal lives. His father was a strict disciplinarian. His mother was a passive, quiet, religious woman who rarely questioned her emotionally detached husband. His father was a 25-year veteran mechanic. Family life was described as stable and uneventful. Steven remained in school through the eighth grade, held a few part-time, unskilled jobs, and joined the military. He received an honorable discharge after less than one year of service.

During the diagnostic interviews subsequent to his trial, he discussed the incident, describing himself as enraged at the time, not sexually excited. He had gone to visit his girlfriend, whom he had been seeing off and on since early adolescence with no sexual activity throughout the courtship. He found her necking on the porch with another man and drove from her house in a blind rage. He was partially aware as he drove away that he was going to look for somebody to attack sexually. His anger was global.

Steven had an active sexual life, but only with women whom he considered to be "bad." These relationships were short-lived, ending when he was directly confronted with their promiscuity. Terminating the relationship always occurred with violence, either in assaults on the women or on the boyfriends who replaced him.

His late adolescence was marked by the repetitiveness of these experiences. Over and over again, he became involved with promiscuous women who would then prove to be unfaithful. On the one hand, he could permit himself to have intercourse only with women he knew to be sexually indiscriminate. On the other hand, he maintained the fantasy that they would be faithful to him.

This is an exemplary case of a pervasively angry, low-impulse rapist. As one diagnostic report stated, Steven's attitude toward women was "tremendously hostile and bordering on rage." His pattern was to jockey for a position in a relationship with a woman where he would feel ashamed, foolish, and hurt. He would respond aggressively, at times explosively, typically at the woman. He created an effective outlet for discharging—and displacing—his rage. There was never any indication that this aggression was eroticized. Finally, there was no evidence of the developmental turbulence, the behavioral management problems, and the poor social and interpersonal competence characteristic of high impulsivity.

Investigation

The victim made an immediate report to police, who returned to the crime scene and were able to develop leads as to the offender. Joe was arrested shortly after the rape and immediately admitted his guilt.

Outcome

Steven at age 24 was committed to the Treatment Center in Bridgewater, Massachusetts, in 1965 for sex offender treatment. He was convicted of rape. Other than the commitment offense, he had no criminal history. He was released after 18 years when psychologists determined he was no longer sexually dangerous.

315: Sadistic Rape

The level of violence in a sadistic offender's rape must clearly exceed what is necessary to force victim compliance; the offender's sexual arousal is a function of the victim's pain, fear, or discomfort. Behavioral evidence may include sham sadism (such as whipping, bondage), violence focused on the erogenous parts of the victim's body (such as burning, cutting, or otherwise mutilating the breasts, anus, buttocks, or genitals); insertion of foreign objects in the vagina or anus; intercourse after the victim is unconscious; and the use of feces or urine within the offense.

The *sadistic rapist* is in many ways the most dangerous sexual predator of all. The purpose of his attack is to live out his sadistic sexual fantasies on the unwilling victim. With this type, sexual fantasy and aggression merge, which is why he is also referred to as an anger–excitation rapist. Aggression and sadistic fantasy feed on each other, so as the level of aggression rises, his level of arousal rises accordingly. His aggression is not anger-based, as it is with the previous category. In fact, he can be quite charming and seductive as he lures intended prey into his web. He is completely self-centered. The only thing he cares about is his own pleasure and satisfaction. And he derives satisfaction from hurting people, of having them in his power (Hazelwood, Dietz, & Warren, 2009). Therefore, with this type, we expect to see various forms of mental and physical torture, and the physical torture may be directed particularly at sexually significant parts of the body such as mouth, breasts, genitals, buttocks, and rectum. His weapon of choice is frequently a knife, because it is so intimidating and causes mental anguish on the part of the victim. He often cuts or tears off his victim's clothing because he figures she will not need it after he has finished with her. Depending on his preferences, there may be much sexual activity, probably highly perverse in nature, or even none. He could, for example, prefer to penetrate with a sharp object rather than with his penis. His language will be commanding and degrading, but impersonal. The victim is merely there as an actress in his self-scripted drama, and her role is to show fear and respond to pain. Thus, there is often a victim of preference, symbolic to him in some way, be she old or young, White, Black, or Asian, slim or full-figured, black-haired or blonde, redhead or brunette.

The sadistic rapist anticipates his crime and has perfected his MO over the course of his criminal career. As his fantasy evolves and he gains more experience with different victims, he will take more time planning ahead for successive crimes. He brings his weapon(s) with him and may have a torture kit made up in advance, including pliers or other sharp instruments, whips, manacles, needles, or whatever he needs to fulfill his fantasy. Since his assault unfolds over a long period of time, he will have a place to which he can take his victim where he knows they will not be disturbed. This might be an obscure cabin in the woods, or a specially outfitted and soundproofed van. He may tell the victim that if she does what he tells her he will not hurt her further or will let her go, but this is only a ruse to control her and get her to cooperate. Because his satisfaction lies in the act of tormenting and dominating his victim, he may take photographs or record the scene as it unfolds on either audio- or videotape. For the same reason, he may also take souvenirs to help him relive the experience and demonstrate to himself that he "owns" the victim. These souvenirs might include jewelry, items of clothing or underwear, or even body parts.

The attack itself will tend to be highly symbolic. There will be no remorse because the rapist has totally depersonalized his victim; he does not even think of her as a human being. This is the type of rape that most often ends in murder. In fact, killing the victim may be an integral part of the sadistic fantasy scenario. He may even continue to engage in activity with the body after death. It is generally impossible for the victim to play on his sympathy because he has none. He wants her to suffer. The only instance in which he might relent is if the victim can somehow break through the depersonalization and get him to regard her as an individual. This occurred, for example, in one instance in which a victim stated that her husband had cancer. It happened that the rapist's brother was battling cancer, and he let her go. Another time, a sadistic rapist revealed in a prison interview that one of his victims reminded him of his mother so he released her. Unfortunately, this is a very uncommon scenario with the sexual sadist.

The sadistic type is usually White, with above-normal intelligence, and may be college-educated with a good middle-class job. He has a dominant personality and likes to collect bondage and sadomasochistic pornography. He may also collect related items, such as knives, guns, or Nazi memorabilia, and read military, law enforcement, or survivalist literature. He may have a large attack-type dog, such as a German shepherd, Doberman, or Rottweiler. Because of his intelligence and planning, he will be difficult to apprehend.

This is the least common type of rapist.

Comparison of Rapist Types

As we all know, human nature is not exact, and not every rapist fits neatly into one of these four rapist categories described here. There is often a mixed presentation, with elements of one classification grafting onto the general description of another, which is why it is so difficult to give specific advice to potential victims as to how to react to a sexual criminal, particularly under the acute stress of the attack itself. But in the great majority of cases, one category will dominate, and our reaction should be molded around the understanding of what motivates that specific type of rapist and what he is after (Douglas & Olshaker, 1998).

In any discussion of criminal personality, the cautions and cautionary tales hold equal importance with the conclusions. This only serves to underscore why we say it is so difficult to give ironclad advice. Montie Rissell was in some ways an unusual rapist–murderer. He attacked and murdered five women near his home in Alexandria, Virginia, while still in his teens, later blaming his criminal behavior on having to live with his mother rather than his father after his parents' troubled marriage broke up when he was age seven. By the time he was in high school, he had a rap sheet detailing driving without a license, burglary, car theft, and rape.

Rissell's first killing was savagely instructive of the dangers of misinterpreting offender behavior. Still in high school, on probation, and receiving psychiatric counseling as a provision of that probation, he heard from his girlfriend—a year ahead of him and then away at college—that their relationship was over. A trigger emotional event of this nature is generally the precursor to a serial sex crime. Rissell promptly drove to the college, where he spotted the young woman with her new boyfriend. Rather than express his rage on the person he felt hurt by, he drove back home, fortified himself with beer and marijuana, and spent hours sitting in his car in the parking lot of his apartment complex. Several hours later, another vehicle appeared, driven by a single woman. On the spur of the moment, Rissell decided to get back what he had just lost. He approached the other car, pulled a handgun on the woman, and forced her to go with him to a secluded area nearby.

As it happened, Rissell's victim was a prostitute, which is significant for two reasons: She would not have the same fear having sex with a stranger that someone outside the profession would; and, though frightened, she would probably draw on a strong and well-developed survival instinct. Her behavior, according to the prison interview with Rissell, reflected this. When she was alone and defenseless and it was clear that her attacker intended to rape her at gunpoint, she attempted to diffuse the situation by hiking up her skirt, asking him how he liked it and in what position he wanted her.

Rather than making him gentler or more sensitive to her, this behavior enraged him. As an anger (or anger–retaliatory) rapist, Rissell was set off by what he perceived as his victim's attempt to *control* the situation. In fact, when she subsequently feigned orgasm in an attempt to gratify him, he became greatly upset that she was "enjoying" the experience. This reinforced in him the notion that all women are whores. He was able to depersonalize her and it was easy for him to think about killing her, an idea that was solidified in his mind when she attempted to run away, thereby further "controlling" the situation (Douglas & Olshaker, 1995).

Had the attacker been a power–reassurance rapist, resistance or struggle might have prevented the attack, and acquiescence might have mitigated its severity. However, in the case of this anger–retaliatory rapist, the opposite was true. And once this type has killed, found the act satisfying, and realized he can get away with it, his escalation to serial rapist–murderer takes place. He will not stop until something stops him.

In light of these and other considerations, the only nearly absolute advice we feel comfortable imparting to victims relates to a few key behavioral indicators on the part of the rapist or potential rapist. If an offender wears a mask or otherwise attempts to disguise his identity, that is a "good" sign. In most cases, it signifies that he intends to get away with the crime, leaving his victim alive but unable to identify him. If he does not attempt to prevent identification, this could signify at least two scenarios, neither of them good. The first is that he is disorganized, "making it up as he goes along," which means that his actions may be unpredictable even to himself. The second, even more dire, is that while he plans to get away with his crime, to ensure this outcome he does not intend to leave a victim alive to identify him. That being the case, resistance of whatever kind the victim can muster would be indicated. Unfortunately, this does not mean she might not be hurt, just that the consequences of not resisting are even riskier. Likewise, another indication to resist by any means possible would be if an offender orders his victim into a car, intending to take her away from the abduction point, because once in the vehicle she loses all control, all possibility of alerting others, and therefore all possibility of intervention (Douglas & Olshaker, 1998).

315.01: Sadistic Rape, Adult

Most often, there is high expressive aggression with moderate to severe injury to the victim. Frequently, the offender uses items to inflict pain or injury, such as cigarettes, knives, sticks, or bottles. In some cases of "sham" or muted sadism, there is clear evidence of eroticized aggression (insertion of foreign objects, bondage, and whipping, for example) without extensive physical injury.

Defining Characteristics

VICTIMOLOGY

Typically the victim is unknown to the offender; however, the victim may be an acquaintance.

OFFENDER CHARACTERISTICS

Typically, the offender has had behavioral problems, sometimes beginning in adolescence, that often worsen in adulthood. As described by Dietz, Hazelwood, and Warren (1990), a sexual sadist is one who has established "an enduring pattern of sexual arousal in response to sadistic imagery." Sexual gratification is obtained from torture involving excessive mental and physical means. Sexually sadistic fantasies, in which sexual acts are paired with domination, degradation, and violence, are transmitted into criminal action that results in rape. Usually, the offense is at least partially planned, sometimes in detail.

Case Study: 315.01: Sadistic Rape, Adult

Background and Victimology

On the occasion of the first rape, Martin, the offender, was at an after-school party and assaulted a 14-year-old. When she refused his advances, he choked her in and out of consciousness. He became aroused by her cries for help. When she regained consciousness, he was still lying beside her. The commitment offense occurred one year later when Martin, age 19, sadistically killed a 30-year-old woman by manual strangulation. According to Martin, he had met the victim in a bar, and they left together to go to a secluded area to engage in sex. He described binding the victim and choking her until she did not respond. He left the woman and returned home.

Offender Characteristics

Martin was the sixth oldest of nine siblings. He described his family life as "horrible, with emotional and physical abuse." He portrayed his father as the ruler of the household, who made sure that "orders were carried out"; otherwise, frequent physical abuse resulted. His mother was described as passive and obedient and often colluded in the beatings by reporting incidents or punishable behavior to her husband. At age 13, Martin was sent away to a training school for being a habitual school offender. His early schooling continued to be sporadic, and he was eventually expelled in the 10th grade. All employment had been of a menial nature.

Martin did not have a long history of violent crime. Most of his transgressions involved truancy, lying, or cheating, and disruptiveness in school. His criminal record contained mostly alcohol- and automobile-related offenses. He had committed two violent crimes: the initial rape attempt, which was reduced to assault and battery, and murder.

Investigation

The victim's body was found and the crime scene secured and examined for evidence. Fingerprints and other evidence were found and linked to Martin. This victim was then linked to the first victim and confirmed by Martin's confession.

Outcome

Martin was a 25-year-old single male committed to the Treatment Center at Bridgewater, Massachusetts, for mandatory sex offender treatment. He was convicted of second-degree murder. In both offenses the motive was clearly primarily aggressive and sadistic. He was indiscriminate in terms of the victim's age. The first victim was a child and the second an adult woman. It did not appear, however, that sex was used as a vehicle for venting anger, but rather that the aggression was antecedent to or concurrent with sexual arousal. His lifestyle throughout adolescence was characterized by impulsive acting out; indeed, none of his serious crimes had any semblance of premeditation, compulsiveness, or ritualism.

315.02: Sadistic Rape, Adolescent

The offender is sexually aroused or otherwise derives pleasure from placing the victim in pain or fear; sadistic acts may include aggressive sodomy, insertion of foreign objects; and violence focused on the breasts, genitals, or anus. The sexual acts often occur during or after the violence and aggression.

Case Study: 315.02: Sadistic Rape, Adolescent

Background and Victimology

Terry had no juvenile criminal record. His first offense occurred two years after discharge from the service. The victim was a 17-year-old male whom Terry picked up while "cruising." Terry smacked, punched, and kicked the victim for 20 minutes before forcing the victim to engage in fellatio. When the victim refused to engage in intercourse, Terry pulled a knife out and began stabbing him in the abdomen. Just prior to the stabbing, Terry demanded that the victim masturbate while cutting himself with the knife. Following the assault, Terry called an ambulance and the police. Terry claimed the acts were consensual, and no charges were made against him. The commitment offense took place about one year later.

Terry picked up a 16-year-old male hustler and drove toward his home. Before reaching his house, they got into an argument. Apparently, Terry had paid the victim in advance for services that the victim decided he did not wish to provide. Terry stabbed the victim 15 times, penetrating the thorax, heart, and aorta. He then mutilated the body by amputation of the penis at the most proximal point. The penis was never found, and there is some suggestion that it may have been ingested.

Offender Characteristics

Terry came from an upper-middle-class, professional home. He did not, however, experience a normal childhood. From early childhood into adolescence, he was plagued by night terrors, nightmares, and sleep talking and sleepwalking. He bit his fingernails and sucked his thumb until age 16. He had few, if any, friends and was convinced that peers did not like him. His pathological shyness kept him in his room through much of his childhood.

His mother felt "very badly" that he was so lonely. When she failed to coax him from his room, she resorted to purchasing expensive toys for him to play with. Terry was sickly much of the time, often febrile, and described as "glassy-eyed." Although the parents described their sons as "very good boys . . . always obedient," Terry felt particularly alienated and withdrawn as he became more and more aware of homosexual feelings. Upon graduating from high school, he enlisted in the Air Force. He spent four years in the service, compiling an excellent record that included five commendations for meritorious action. During this time, he also attended college and earned a degree. After discharge from the service, he began the first of a series of jobs in sales. He proved to be a highly successful salesman ("well spoken, polite, quiet but firm") and was said to be earning in excess of $6,000 a month at the time of his arrest. Terry has a long psychiatric history, with depression and alcoholism presenting as primary features.

Investigation

Witnesses heard the two men quarreling, and a description of Terry led to his interrogation.

Outcome

Terry was 25 years old and single when he was committed to the Treatment Center at Bridgewater, Massachusetts, declared a sexually dangerous person after having been convicted of second-degree murder and rape. As an adult, Terry had led an exemplary life. He had good interpersonal skills and acquired a fair degree of academic and professional competence. He was described as "pleasant" and "charming" by coworkers. He certainly did not lead what could be called an impulsive lifestyle. He had no criminal record up to the point of his first offense. His two assaults were ritualized, compulsive, and highly sadistic, much along the lines of the classic Jack the Ripper case.

315.04: Sadistic Rape, Elder

People are often surprised when we group children, prostitutes, and the elderly together as victims. But it is a fact that these three groups are uniquely linked because of their vulnerability. A given predator may view children (boys, girls, or either), or prostitutes, or elderly women as his preferential victim. But he may also use any of these three groups as a "warm-up," a practice before moving on to more challenging victims. A young (probably teenaged) beginning rapist, for example, may target an elderly woman because, at this point, such a victim is all he can handle. Once he learns what to do, he will then go after his true victim of preference.

An elderly woman is particularly vulnerable, not only because of physical weakness or infirmities, but also because of her dependence on others for maintenance and repairs around the house, running errands and doing chores, providing transportation, and the like. Often, the individual providing such service is not well known to her. A stranger let into the house or apartment to deliver something or make a repair can gather valuable intelligence information for a future assault, burglary, or scam. Since it is often difficult for senior citizens to get to a bank regularly, they may keep relatively large amounts of cash at home—an attractive target to a young, unsophisticated offender.

An early case in which one of the authors (JED) was called to consult involved the 1977 murder of an elderly woman, Anna Berliner, in her home in Oregon. Local police had also sought help from a clinical psychologist about the type of offender they were dealing with in this crime. Among the victim's injuries were four deep pencil wounds in the chest. The psychologist had conducted interviews with approximately 50 men charged with or convicted of homicide. Most of these examinations had been done in prison. Based on his experience, he predicted that the offender would be someone who had spent a fair amount of time in prison, probably a drug dealer, because only in prison is a sharpened pencil widely considered a deadly weapon.

The author disagreed, believing that the age and vulnerability of the victim, the overkill, and the facts that it was a daytime crime and nothing of great value was missing suggested an inexperienced juvenile offender. The pencil was there—a weapon of opportunity requiring no great analysis or skills to employ.

The killer turned out to be an inexperienced 16-year-old who had gone to the victim's house scheming to get a contribution to a walk-a-thon in which he was not actually participating.

The key feature of this crime scene was that all behavioral evidence suggested an offender who was unsure of himself. An experienced felon attacking an elderly woman in her home would be very sure of himself. Merely picking up on a single piece of evidence does not give the entire picture. This is something we must keep in mind throughout our evaluations of offenders in crimes against the elderly (Douglas & Olshaker, 1995).

319: Abduction Rape

In this offense, a person is forcibly moved from one location to another. The rape occurs at the second location.

Abduction by nonfamily members is defined in the National Incidence Studies of Missing, Abducted, Runaway, and Thrown-Away Children (1989) as the coerced and unauthorized taking of a child into a building, a vehicle, or a distance of more than 20 feet; the detention of a child for a period of more than one hour; or the luring of a child for the purpose of committing a crime. Included in this category is stereotypical kidnapping, which requires that the child be missing overnight, be killed, be transported a distance of 50 miles or more, be ransomed, or that the perpetrator evidences an intent to keep the child permanently.

Case Study: 319.03: Abduction Rape, Child
Case Contributed by Jackie Tagliamonte

Victimology

On June 10, 1991, at age 11, Jaycee Dugard was kidnapped on her way to the school bus stop by as her stepfather watched from his driveway two blocks away. Searches began immediately after the kidnapping, but no reliable leads were generated. She remained missing for more than 18 years until she was discovered at the age of 29.

Crime Scene Indicators

The gray car that Jaycee's stepfather saw drive up to Jaycee was one of the only crime scene indicators. The stepfather reported seeing a male and a female in the gray car. Those were the only crime scene indicators that were documented.

Forensic Findings

There were no forensic findings from the abduction site. She was able to hide a butterfly-shaped ring that she kept with her for the next 18 years.

Investigative Considerations

Jaycee Dugard was kept hidden in a small, concealed area behind the home of Phillip and Nancy Garrido in Antioch, California, for 18 years. On August 26, 2009, she was discovered in the course of another investigation. The day earlier, convicted sex offender Phillip Craig Garrido visited the campus of UC Berkeley accompanied by two young girls. Their unusual behavior there sparked an investigation involving the police and his parole officer. It was later revealed that the girls were the children of the long missing Jaycee Dugard.

Outcome (Offender) and Legal Issues Involved in Court Proceedings

Garrido and Nancy, a married couple who had a criminal history, kidnapped Jaycee and held her hostage 168 miles away. Phillip and Nancy Garrido were charged with abduction, rape, and forcible confinement. At the trial, Dugard and stated a stun gun was used to incapacitate her when Garrido forced her into his car. At the Garridos' home, Jaycee was placed inside a small soundproofed bolted shed, handcuffed, left naked, and threatened that dogs were trained to attack her if she tried to escape. During her confinement, she was forced to have sex frequently with Garrido and threatened with a stun gun if she did not comply. It was further revealed that Nancy Garrido was fully involved with the kidnapping and confinement of Jaycee. Jaycee's testimony stated that she and Nancy would watch television and have dinner together, and that Nancy would at times offer to have sex with Garrido to spare Jaycee. During her time in captivity, Jaycee Dugard bore two daughters, who were aged 11 and 15 at the time of her reappearance in 2009. She testified that she never tried to escape due to fear about what would happen to her. On June 2, 2011, Phillip Garrido was sentenced to 431 years; his wife received 36 years to life in prison.

In 2010, the State of California approved a $20 million settlement for Jaycee Dugard for the lapses of the Department of Correction made in failing to properly supervise Garrido.

Case Study: 319.04: Abduction Rape, Adolescent

In the early morning of June 5, 2002, Elizabeth Smart was suddenly woken with a hand on her chest and the sensation of a cold sharp object to her throat, hearing the whispered threat not to make a sound, to come with him or her family would be killed. For nine months, Elizabeth Smart was held captive in the mountainous area behind her house. She was held captive, forcibly raped, and transported across state lines to California.

Victimology

Elizabeth Smart, 14, at the time of her abduction was one of six children and raised in the Latter Day Saints church. A witness to the abduction was her 9-year-old sister, Katherine, who told her parents that a man came with a knife and took Elizabeth.

Crime Scene Indicators

The initial crime scene was Elizabeth's bedroom. Additional crime scenes were the wooded area where Elizabeth was kept captive and raped.

Forensics

There were no DNA evidence or fingerprints found at the scene of the abduction. The doors had been locked that night, but the security system was not turned on.

Investigation

The case relied almost solely on the eyewitness testimony of the 9-year-old sister. Her first report was mixed. She said the abductor had dark hair on his head and arms, was wearing light-colored clothing, and that her sister was taken at gunpoint, all of which was inconsistent.

Four months later, Mary Katherine identified Elizabeth's abductor as "Immanuel," a homeless man who had worked about five hours for the family. His name was learned to be Brian David Mitchell. The sister would later say that Mitchell was wearing a black sweat suit and sneakers and Elizabeth was taken at knife point.

Mitchell had previously seen Elizabeth in November 2001 when he did some work on the family home. He became fixated on her and monitored her for months later. He was systematic in his approach, being careful not to leave evidence wearing dark clothing, a stocking cap, and gloves.

Mitchell was a fundamentalist excommunicated member of the Church of Jesus Christ of Latter Day Saints. Mitchell reported that he was told by God that he should take Elizabeth as his second wife. Mitchell forced Elizabeth into a pseudo marriage ceremony.

Mitchell spent seven years in a psychiatric facility with a series of failed competency hearings before he was found competent to stand trial. While the defense used this as evidence of his insanity at the time he committed the crimes against Smart, the prosecution indicated Mitchell was cunning and devious and able to trick the courts into deeming him incompetent to stand trial to avoid incarceration in federal prison.

Various psychiatric diagnoses and theories of motivation were given at trial.

Richart DeMier, a court appointed forensic psychiatrist said Mitchell was not making rational decisions about his criminal defense, specifically that he believed God would deliver him from prison in two years' time. He concluded that Mitchell was a paranoid schizophrenic who was incompetent partly due to Mitchell's belief that he was ordained to fulfill a special role in the world and putting himself on par with Jesus or God. Forensic psychologist Stephen Golding concluded that Mitchell had a delusional disorder with deviant sexual behavior and paranoia. Jennifer Skeem, a psychology professor found Mitchell incompetent to stand trial and that he had a rare delusional disorder. Forensic psychiatrist Michael Welner found Mitchell competent to stand trial, finding that he suffered from a range of disorders, including pedophilia and antisocial and narcissistic personality disorders, but that he was not psychotic or delusional. Dr. Welner researched the level of acceptance and the roles played by revelations, prophets, and prophesies in religions of the Latter Day Saints movements that Mitchell was a part of. His conclusions included the fact that Mitchell can control situations and that "lust trumped religion" for Mitchell. He also noted that Mitchell is used to operating in a parallel world of concealment and obfuscation just as most polygamist breakaway groups from the modern LDS church do. In his conclusions, he also compared Mitchell's behavior to that of pedophile Catholic priests who "routinely and dramatically distort their relationship with God" to justify their sexual acts (Egan, 2003).

330: Group-Cause Sexual Assault

This category is used for multiple (three or more) offenders. When there are two offenders, each should be classified under personal cause. Although there clearly are group dynamics (contagion effects, defusing of responsibility) and social dynamics (highly developed gang cultures in particular communities or cities) that foster gang rape, the factors that motivate each of the offenders may well be different.

331: Formal Gang Sexual Assault

A formal gang is characterized by some internal organizational structure, a name and other identifying features (e.g., colors, insignias, or pattern of dress), and some evidence of group cohesiveness (e.g., members owe some allegiance to the gang and gather to participate in a variety of activities). In sum, the gang must have some mission or purpose other than assault.

Case Study: 331.01: Formal Gang Sexual Assault, Single Victim

Victimology

In 1981, four teenagers went to a rock concert held at a large amphitheater. During intermission, a group of 12 men wearing shirts labeled "The Black Disciples" entered. The teenagers became frightened of the accumulating noise and decided to leave. As they were exiting to the center aisle, several of the men grabbed one of the couples and threw them to the aisle. The young woman's clothes were ripped off her. Five of the men circled her, pulled her up by the hair, and forced oral sex on her. A sixth man then threw her back on the floor and inserted a tire iron into her vagina. Several security guards stopped the assault. The young woman was taken to a nearby hospital.

Offender Characteristics

The offenders were part of a group well known in the city. The six men were arrested and charged with various counts of assault and rape.

Outcome

The six men plea-bargained to the offenses as charged. Nine years later, the young woman was awarded a substantial settlement.

332: Informal Gang Sexual Assault

An informal gang is a loosely structured group that congregates, typically on the spur of the moment, with a common purpose of marauding or otherwise engaging in antisocial activity. Although the group may have one or more leaders, there is no formal organizational structure. This category also includes all other instances of multiple offender assault in which there is no evidence that the group constitutes a formal gang.

Case Study: 332.01: Informal Gang Sexual Assault, Single Victim

Victimology

Damon and three companions were driving around when one of them suggested that they "grab a girl and have some fun." They picked up a hitchhiker, and while driving, took turns raping her. When it was Damon's turn, he engaged in frottage but did not actually rape her. The victim was raped repeatedly over a period of two hours while in the car. Eventually, they arrived at an abandoned house, where all four men, including Damon, raped the victim throughout the night, occasionally waving revolvers in her face to subdue her. The following day, they drove back to the victim's home and dropped her off.

Offender Characteristics

Damon was a 21-year-old single male. His father was a self-educated engineer who was gainfully employed until his premature death from heart failure. Damon described his father as a chronic, heavy drinker who suffered from bouts of deep depression and crying spells that lasted off and on for days. Damon reported that his father was never abusive to anyone in the family. His mother was a college-educated schoolteacher who was "strict, puritanical, very religious, and a teetotaler." Damon's early years seemed to be stable and reasonably happy. While in elementary school, he was an above-average student with an above-average IQ. His academic performance drifted into the average or satisfactory range during the last two years of high school, coinciding with the death of his father when Damon was 15.

After the death, the family seemed to fall apart. His mother became seriously ill and eventually bedridden. His older brother was incarcerated for assault and battery. Damon dropped out of school in his senior year and enlisted in the service. He was honorably discharged after six months at the discretion of the military. The primary difficulty was Damon's intractable behavior. Damon's employment history after the service can best be described as "good—when he was in the mood." He was perceived by his employers as apathetic, unreliable, and diffident. Overall, Damon's educational, military, and professional track record reflects an evolving picture of social maladjustment, poor interpersonal skills, and a particular disaffection with authority.

Two months after leaving the service, he was arrested for stealing hubcaps; the charges were later dropped. This was the only known criminal offense other than the rape, for which he was committed to the Treatment Center at Bridgewater, Massachusetts, for sex offender treatment. The commitment offense occurred exactly two years after discharge from the service.

In this case, the offense was clearly exploitive. In fact, the expressed intention "to grab a girl and have some fun" could not be stated in a more predatory, exploitive way.

Outcome

Damon was committed to the Treatment Center in Bridgewater, Massachusetts, in 1967 for sex offender treatment after having been convicted of rape, kidnapping, and assault with a dangerous weapon. The remaining defendants were convicted on charges of rape.

333: Military Sexual Trauma

Military sexual trauma (MST) is not a diagnosis but is the term used by the Department of Veteran Affairs (DVA) to include sexual harassment, sexual assault, rape, and other acts of violence.

Military sexual trauma has its own statistics and history. The military first pledged to crack down on sexual assault and harassment in 1992, in the wake of a scandal that surfaced at the Navy fliers' annual Tailhook Association convention in Las Vegas, where some 90 victims were allegedly assaulted by as many as 175 officers. A year and a half later, a Pentagon report found that Tailhook was not an isolated incident, but the culmination of a "long-term failure of leadership." But just four years later, there was another scandal at Maryland's Aberdeen Proving Grounds, where assault charges were brought against a dozen male officers for sexual assault on female trainees. Then, in 2003, the U.S. Air Force Academy was also accused of systemically ignoring an ongoing sexual assault problem on its premises. Most recently in 2010–2011, at Lackland Air Force Base in Texas, four male instructors were charged with having sex with, and in one case raping, female trainees. One Air Force instructor was convicted of 20 counts of rape and aggravated sexual assault and sentenced to 20 years in prison.

A 2012 Pentagon report found that, in 2011, 3,192 incidents of sexual assault were reported within the U.S. military—up 1% from 2010. According to the Defense Department's own estimate, just 15% of actual incidents are reported, putting the real number at some 19,000 assaults each year. Under current policy, reports of sexual assault are handled directly within the military's chain of command. There's little incentive to investigate accusations, and as a result, cases are rarely prosecuted. According to the report, nearly 70% of substantiated, "actionable" cases did not go to trial because of lower-level command discretion.

333.01: Military Sexual Harassment

The DVA defines sexual harassment as repeated, unsolicited, verbal or physical contact of a sexual nature, which is threatening in nature.

333.02: Military Sexual Assault/Rape

Case Study: 333.02: Lackland Air Force Base Scandal

Background

The scandal came to light in June 2011, when a young female trainee came forward and accused her male instructor, Staff Sergeant Luis Walker, of assaulting her. Subsequently, 12 of Lackland Air Force Base's 475 instructors were accused of sexual impropriety with 31 different female recruits. Nine of the men accused were in the same squadron.

Victimology

Four women testified that as new Air Force recruits in 2009, Walker sexually harassed and assaulted them.

Crime Scene Indicators

The women told jurors that Walker gained their trust to get them alone in his office or an empty dormitory and forced them into kissing, touching, and sex.

The first victim who testified told jurors that before assaulting her in his office, Walker had made sexually suggestive comments to her and hugged and kissed her in a stairwell.

Another female airman testified that Walker pushed her against a wall one time in his office and put his hand down her pants. She testified that Walker told her if she told anyone about it, she would get kicked out with a dishonorable discharge.

Forensics

There was no DNA evidence in the cases because of the long delay in reporting. Although there is surveillance video in many of the Lackland training buildings, prosecutor argued that Walker knew to pick areas where there were no cameras and that surveillance footage typically gets erased every 20 days.

Investigation

The young women recounted how they were ordered to go to darkened supply rooms and empty dorms, where they were subjected to unwanted advances by instructors who wielded near-absolute power over them.

Prosecutor claim Staff Sergeant Luis Walker was a serial predator who routinely targeted recruits. The 28 counts leveled against him included 1 rape, allegations of sexual harassment and sexual misconduct with 9 other women, 4 of whom he had sex with and 5 of whom he allegedly coerced into performing sexual favors for him by threatening their careers.

Testimony

Airman 5 testified that Sergeant Walker tried to win her confidence by sympathizing with her after she had been upset by bad news from home. He later began sending suggestive texts to her cell phone before cornering her in a supply closet and forcing her to have sex with him. The woman said she did not report the episode out of fear that Sergeant Walker would "recycle" her in punishment, meaning force her to redo basic training. "I was scared and miserable and hurt," the woman testified. Her version was corroborated in court by a friend.

Another witness, identified as Airman 8, said Sergeant Walker called her into his office and pressured her to show her breasts. She mentioned the episode to other recruits, and word got back to Sergeant Walker. She testified that he then called her back into his office and warned her: "If you had a problem with it, then you should have come to me, instead of running your mouth. Remember, I'm staff sergeant, you're a trainee." "I went numb," the woman testified. "I was scared. What if he punished me or ruined my career?"

Outcome

Staff Sergeant Luis Walker was found guilty on 28 counts, including adultery, violating regulations, and committing sexual crimes against female trainees. He was sentenced to 20 years in prison (Dao, 2012).

390: Sexual Assault Not Classified Elsewhere

This category is reserved for assaults that cannot be classified elsewhere.

References

Dao, J. (2012). Lackland Air Force Base Instructor guilty of sexual assault. *New York Times*. Retrieved August 26, 2012, from www.nytimes.com/2012/07/21/us/lackland-air-force-base-instructor-guilty-of-sex-assaults.html?_r=1&pagewanted=all

Dietz, P. E., Hazelwood, R. R., & Warren, J. (1990). The sexually sadistic criminal and his offenses. *Bulletin of the American Academy of Psychiatry and the Law, 18*(2), 163–178.

Douglas, J., & Olshaker, M. (1995). *Mindhunter: Inside the FBI's elite serial crime unit* (pp. 137–142, 349–350). New York, NY: Scribner.

Douglas, J., & Olshaker, M. (1998). *Obsession* (pp. 358–363). New York, NY: Scribner.

Egan, T. (2003, March 14). In plain sight, a kidnapped girl behind a veil. *New York Times*. Retrieved August 2, 2012, from www.rickross.com/reference/smart/smart11.html

Fairstein, L. (1993). *Sexual violence* (pp. 13–18). New York, NY: William Morrow.

Hammer, Heather, Andrea J. Sedlak, and David Finkelhor. National Incidence Study of Missing, Abducted, Runaway, and Thrown-Away Children. (NISMART), 1999. 2007. ICPSR04566-v1. Ann Arbor, MI: Inter-university Consortium for Political and Social Research [producer and distributor], 2007-07-19. doi:10.3886/ICPSR04566.v1. Retrieved February 21, 2013 from http://www.icpsr.umich.edu/icpsrweb/ICPSR/studies/04566

Hazelwood, R. R. (2009). Analyzing the rape and profiling the offender. In R. Hazelwood & A. Burgess (eds.), *Practical aspects of rape investigation: A multidisciplinary approach* (4th ed., pp. 97–122). Boca Raton, FL: CRC Press.

Hazelwood, R. R., Dietz, P. E., & Warren, J. I. (2009). The criminal sexual sadist. In R. Hazelwood & A. Burgess (eds.), *Practical aspects of rape investigation: A multidisciplinary approach* (4th ed., pp. 463–473). Boca Raton, FL: CRC Press.

Knight, R. A., & Prentky, R. A., (1990). Classifying sexual offenders: The development and collaboration of taxonomic models. In. Marshall, W. L., Laws D. R., and Barbaree, H. E. (Eds.), Handbook of Sexual Assault: Issues, Theories and Treatment of the offenders (p. 23–52) New York: Plenum Press.

Laws, D. R., & H. E. Barbaree (Eds.), *Handbook of sexual assault*. New York, NY: Plenum.

Sandusky Grand Jury Report (2011). CBS Chicago. Retrieved August 14, 2012, from http://cbschicago.files.wordpress.com/2011/11/sandusky-grand-jury-presentment.pdf

Truman, J. L., & Rand, M. R. (2010). *National Crime Victimization Survey.*, Washington, DC: Department of Justice, Bureau of Justice Statistics.

U.S. Department of Justice, Federal Bureau of Investigation (2009). Crime in the United States. Washington, D.C. Retrieved February 21, 2009 from http://www2.fbi.gov/ucr/cius2009/offenses/violent_crime/forcible_rape.html

Chapter 13

Nonlethal Crimes

400: Nonlethal crimes
401: Communication threats
    401.01: Direct threats
    401.02: Indirect threats
    401.03: Conditional threats
    401.04: Nonspecific threats
402: Threat delivery
    402.01: Visual communication
    402.02: Verbal communication
    402.03: Written communication
        402.03.01: Letter
        402.03.02: Symbolic

402.04: Physical
    communication threats
410: Stalking crimes
411: Domestic stalker
412: Nondomestic stalker
413: Erotomania stalker
420: Robbery
421: Bank robbery
422: Home invasion robbery
430: Burglary
440: Assault
450: Battery/abuse

400: Nonlethal Crimes

There are criminal acts that begin as, and sometimes remain, nonlethal crimes. In some of the crimes, such as burglary, threats, and stalking, there may be no physical contact, and the victim is not physically injured. However, the psychological trauma may be great and put the victim in fear for his or her life. These nonlethal acts may precede direct physical acts and serious physical injury and may escalate to a lethal crime. These nonlethal acts need to be addressed for prevention of escalation to lethal acts as well as investigated for legal charges. This chapter classifies the following crimes: threats, stalking, robbery, burglary, assault, and battery/abuse crimes that involve children, handicapped adults, domestic partners, and elders.

401: Communication Threats

A communication threat is defined as an attempt to inflict harm by a threat subject. Communication threats do not involve physical contact. However, the threat subject may escalate to physical contact, and such action would be classified as assault.

Threat analysis seeks to assess the genuineness, viability, and potential impending danger of the threat. As with all other investigations, the forensic analyst has priorities that are followed in concert with law enforcement as well as institutional goals and objectives. Threat analysis has the following goals:

- To save lives by evaluating the level of danger for physical assault or harm.
- To evaluate threat potential (hoax versus nonhoax) in order to reduce unnecessary panic and to better use security resources.
- To develop investigative techniques and strategies by advising on how to communicate with the offender or how to cause him or her to surface during the investigation.
- To help identify and apprehend the offender by attempting to provide general characteristics of the person or persons issuing the threat and his other motive in order to focus the investigation.
- To recover money or property if a ransom has been paid prior to police involvement.

Terrorist threats are when a person threatens to commit any offense involving violence to any person or property with the intent to place a person in fear of imminent serious bodily injury.

Defining Characteristics

VICTIMOLOGY

Threats may be targeted to terrorize a particular person, a building, a business, or an institution. The motivation for a threat might also include a desire on the part of the subject to force an action, as when inmates threaten a specific violent act if their demands for better conditions within a correctional facility are not met.

The most critical classification is the level of victim risk. Risk level can be categorized as low, moderate, high, or imminent danger. Assessment of the threat is made as to whether the person making the threat has the knowledge, ability, motivation, and access to weapons that would give him the opportunity to carry out the violent act.

CRIME SCENE INDICATORS FREQUENTLY NOTED

Although there is usually no specific crime scene involved in threats, the reason for the threat, or motive, is critical to analyze. Threats are made for a variety of reasons and are driven by an assortment of often complex motives. Some of the reasons that individuals threaten include these:

- To warn: "If you don't stop what you are doing, you will regret it."
- Harass: "You'll never escape me."
- Intimidate: "If you don't do what I say, you'll be sorry."
- Manipulate: "If you don't do what I say, your child will be hurt."
- Frighten: "You're a dead man."
- Alarm: A heavy-breathing phone call late at night.

The motives that underlie various forms of threats are similar to other types of criminal acts. The motivations may be conflict, sex, love, hate, vengeance, or guilt. In addition, the need for excitement, recognition, or attention or a wish to inflict punishment on another may be underlying motives. Another obvious and more frequent motive might be an offender whose primary motive is criminal enterprise. This offender's aim is for financial gain through illegal means, such as extortion or kidnapping.

STAGING

Staging is not usually noted.

INVESTIGATIVE CONSIDERATIONS

The intent of the threat is critical to analyze. Threats cover a wide variety of criminal behavior. Ten categories have been developed for purposes of assessing the intent of the threat communication.

1. *Threats to physically assault or harm.* These threats are directed toward elected or appointed officials, judges, movie and rock stars, spouses, ex-spouses, police officers, former employers, or hospital staff (e.g., to gain admission or certain prescription medication). For example, a mental health patient arrived at an institution to see the on-call psychiatrist. The patient was seeking admission and apparently believed that the small axe he brought with him would ensure the psychiatrist's compliance with his demand for admission.
2. *Threats to extort money.* These are often directed toward chief executive officers, bank officials, prominent or wealthy individuals, or members of the entertainment industry. In hospitals, threats may be directed toward staff, visitors, or patients to extort money for food, transportation, or illicit substances.

3. *Threats to kidnap.* These are directed to elected or appointed officials, members of their families, dignitaries, prominent individuals, and corporate officials.

4. *Threats to bomb.* These are directed toward individuals at all levels, schools, churches and synagogues, abortion clinics, courthouses, government buildings, nuclear facilities, military bases, and casinos, among others.

5. *Threats to deface or damage property.* These are directed toward schools, churches and synagogues, abortion clinics, animal research facilities, utility plants, military bases, and nuclear facilities, among others.

6. *Threats to disrupt events.* These are made to disrupt municipal functions, political rallies, parades, marches, ceremonies, public events, rock shows, civil rights rallies, and others.

7. *Threats to taunt, harass, and intimidate.* These are made by agitated or terminated employees, disgruntled consumers, competitors, ex-lovers, ex-spouses, unfriendly neighbors, unknown enemies, substance abusers and mentally unstable persons, or individuals intent on expressing unsolicited attention or affection.

8. *Threats to product tamper.* These are related to poisoning or contamination of foods, medicines, cosmetics, water or blood supplies, and hygienic products; tampering with sensitive manufacturing equipment; and others.

9. *Threats to sabotage.* These are directed at military bases, ammunition manufacturers and shippers, aircraft plants, nuclear facilities, manufacturers of scientific equipment, research and development centers, product technologies, and marketing strategies, among others.

10. *Hoaxes.* These are a fabricated threat created by pseudo-victims alleging the receipt of obscene phone calls, or letters from nonexistent offenders.

Threats must be examined for both content and style. Content analysis includes an examination of words, syntax, semantics, structure, symbols, phrases, essential meanings, and the overall substance of the threatening message. Stylistic analysis includes an examination of the writing instrument, paper type, envelope, writing style, margins, indentations, spacing, punctuation, and overall grammatical ability.

The manner of expression also must be examined, such as the implied emotional tone, the construction and design of the message, the way words are used to express thoughts, and the author's overall artistic expression. For example, the verbal threat, "I'm going to get you back," implies a prior event, anger, and revenge.

Search Warrant Suggestions

Search warrants need to be obtained to search the residence, car, and other areas for copies of written threats, photographs, diaries, and written materials.

Threats, actual or perceived, may be subdivided into types based in part on the verbiage or content contained within the threat. The types are direct, indirect, conditional, or nonspecific threat.

DUTY TO WARN

Another consideration involves the threat issue of "duty to warn." Health care providers need to sort out what, if any, duties they owe to warn third parties when threats of violence have been made by their patients toward specific individuals. This issue developed as a result of the landmark decision in *Tarasoff v. Regents of University of California* (1976) in which the California Supreme Court held that psychotherapists could be held liable for failing to exercise reasonable care to protect a third party when the therapists know or should know that their patient presents a serious danger of violence to another.

In the Colorado shooting case, the psychiatrist treating accused Aurora theater gunman James Holmes was so concerned about his behavior that she notified other members of the University of Colorado Behavioral Evaluation and Threat Assessment, or BETA, team that he could potentially be a danger to others. The alert came more than a month before the Colorado shootings that left 12 dead.

Holmes was charged with murdering 12 people and shooting 58 others on July 20, 2012, in an Aurora movie theater during the midnight showing of the new Batman movie.

However, because Holmes suddenly dropped out of school, the committee never acted, nor did it alert authorities of their concerns.

The threat assessment team held a formal meeting about Holmes, but never had a chance to intervene. The group reportedly believed that it had no control over Holmes after he dropped out of school. But could the threat assessment team have legally done anything to prevent the shootings? The reported answer was that it depends. Psychiatrists and patients generally have a doctor–client privilege. The patient holds the privilege and the doctor usually cannot reveal anything that is said during consultations.

However, there may be exceptions to the rule when a specific threat or crime is discussed. So if the psychiatrist knew of a concrete plan to commit a crime, she may be obligated to divulge the information.

While Dr. Lynne Fenton may have been concerned enough about James Holmes to alert the threat assessment team, she may not have had enough to alert the police.

401.01: Direct Threats

Direct threats leave no room for misinterpretation on the part of the recipient. The threats are aimed at a specific target (person or institution). Direct threats offer no conditions, exemptions, or options. Often the wording is blunt, straightforward, candid, and explicit. For example, on July 26, 1996, an Atlanta 911 operator received a call saying, "There will be a bomb in Centennial Park. You have 30 minutes." This telephonic threat to a crowded public setting, which preceded by 18 minutes a terrorist act of bombing, triggered great fear for millions of Americans.

Offenders have taught that fear is a power tactic. They know that if they can generate fear in some form of a threat, they can manipulate and achieve whatever they want. Threat analysis is one strategy to identify and intervene with a threat subject and counter terrorist fear.

401.02: Indirect Threats

Indirect threats are either spoken or written in a vague manner. They usually contain wordy language that is not forthright or candid. The message or intended theme is often circuitous and may be buried within oblique wording or symbolic passages.

In cases of threats against a hospital, for example, the motive can be an angry family member or a disgruntled former employee. The person issuing the threat is either an ex-employee or a former patient. In a case where a father died following surgery, two brothers wrote a letter saying, "Your butchers killed him and we will get you." An investigation revealed that both brothers had criminal records for assault and battery.

401.03: Conditional Threats

A threat that insists on the acquiescence of the targeted victim to the terms being dictated is a conditional threat. Conditional threats imply that they are contingent, tentative, restrictive, or provisional depending on the victim's response to the demands being made. The threat generally outlines a set of prescribed behaviors that must be met in order for the victim to avoid possible harm. It often includes words or phraseology such as "if you want to avoid . . . " or "unless you follow my instructions . . . " For example, a walk-in patient demanded of the on-call psychiatrist, "If you don't give me a prescription for Xanax, I'm going to tear this office apart."

401.04: Nonspecific Threats

Nonspecific threats are aimed at a larger collective group or institution; that is, they do not name a particular individual. Targets of nonspecific threats included members of the federal judiciary, members of the medical profession, members of the U.S. Congress, and the White House.

402: Threat Delivery

Valuable information can be derived about the person issuing the threat and his and her motives by a consideration of how the threatening message was delivered. This classification is by visual, verbal, written, symbolic, or physical mode.

402.01: Threat Delivery, Visual Communication

A visual threat may be a drawing, a gesture, or a body movement. One example involved a nurse being greeted in the following manner by a known "behavior management problem" patient each time he saw her: He made eye contact with her and then pretended to shoot her with a hand motion imitating the firing of a pistol; he never spoke a word to her.

402.02: Threat Delivery, Verbal Communication

Verbal threats made during personal encounters with targeted individuals often involve offenders who are suffering from some degree of mental illness or emotional instability. In these types of cases, the offender's identity is known, and certain intervention strategies are recommended in conjunction with a dangerousness assessment in order to prevent a potential violent confrontation.

Often, a verbal threat is delivered by telephone. The threat may be a short, succinct message or a long, complex scheme. Occasionally, the caller may disguise his or her voice and demand to speak with only the targeted victim. Some offenders use prerecorded tape messages over the telephone, and the calls may be made locally, long distance, or collect. Other investigative considerations include possible background noises, foreign accents, local dialects, and a consideration of specific calling patterns.

The verbal threat may be tape-recorded. Tape-recorded threats may be short and succinct or involve long, complex schemes. The other important considerations include determining if the caller attempts to disguise his or her voice, whether background noises are detectable, and whether the tape was mailed or played over the telephone. Tape-recorded messages often reflect extensive criminal sophistication, especially in elaborate extortion, kidnapping, or product tampering cases.

402.03: Threat Delivery, Written Communication

Written threats are usually delivered by letter or e-mail. The great majority of threat cases that are analyzed by a threat analyst are those in which the identity of the subject is unknown. In seeking to identify the unknown perpetrator, the method of delivery must be carefully assessed.

One woman wrote to a hospital that bad medicine she received as a patient caused her to get sicker at home. The hospital wrote back denying her claim. When she retaliated by writing to a U.S. senator, he responded by siding with the hospital. She then wrote to the U.S. attorney general's office, charging there was a conspiracy between the hospital and the senator. In another example, a patient wrote letters threatening to kill his wife, the mayor, his doctor, and the president of the United States.

Threats to deface or damage property may be directed toward building walls and grounds. In one case, the person who issued the threat wrote sexual graffiti on the walls adjacent to his former partner's office. In another case, an employee's name was written on a wall with the notation that she was a drug dealer.

402.03.01: Letter Threat

Letter threats are often handwritten and may be in block print or an otherwise disguised format; they also may be prepared on a computer. In some instances, they are fabricated using the cut-and-paste method, and on rare occasions may be printed by use of a template or constructed with an embossing tool. In all instances, they must be evaluated for both content and stylistic characteristics. An advantage of a letter threat is that it provides law enforcement with valuable documentary evidence for further comparison to other letters and for other forensic tests customarily conducted in the crime lab. The Mad Bomber case (Chapter 7) and the Unabomber case (Chapter 1) are illustrative of this type of threat.

402.03.02: Symbolic Threat

Symbolic threats involve an item with a frightening connotation often positioned clearly in the threat subjects view. One example of a symbolic threat involved an employee who reported arriving at his desk each morning for a week to find a broken pencil placed visibly on his appointment book. In another case, a patient sent his therapist of two years flowers, gifts, and cards. He called her on several occasions and left messages using a pseudonym on her answering machine. When she did not respond, he sent her a bunch of dead flowers.

402.04: Physical Communication Threats

A physical threat may involve the person's using his or her hand or a weapon. One example involved an angry patient who was denied a weekend pass. He broke a glass and held it to a staff member's throat, demanding his pass.

Physical threat delivery can compound when there is direct confrontation. A 49-year-old patient and two elderly women were waiting for a bus at a hospital bus stop when they were threatened by a robber. The patient said to the robber, "You are not going to ask for money?" The robber said he was and opened his jacket to display a large knife in his pocket. The patient became agitated and struck the robber, breaking his nose. The perpetrator pressed charges; the patient was successful in arguing it was self-defense.

As an example, the Philadelphia district attorney's office charged National Basketball Association star Allen Iverson with multiple crimes, including two counts of making "terrorist threats." Under Pennsylvania law, there are two kinds of terrorist threats. One is similar to mass-scale terrorism: it is essentially any threat made to force the evacuation of a movie theater, apartment complex, or other public building. So any phoned bomb threat is a terrorist threat, and threatening just one person with bodily harm is also considered a terrorist threat. This is what Iverson was charged with. According to press accounts, he forced his way into an apartment, brandished a gun, and threatened the occupants. Iverson was apparently searching for his wife.

410: Stalking Crimes

Threats indicate anger and aggression toward a subject and are often visible acts. In contrast, stalking tends to be more clandestine and secretive until a subject acts toward his or her victim.

Stalking is the act of following, viewing, communicating with, or moving threateningly or menacingly toward another person. It may in result in threats to injure, actual injuries, or homicide. Stalker crimes are primarily motivated by interpersonal aggression rather than by material gain or sex. The purpose of stalking resides in the mind of stalkers, who are compulsive individuals with a misperceived fixation. Stalking is the result of an underlying emotional conflict that propels the offender to stalk or harass a target. Targets of stalkers often feel trapped in an environment filled with anxiety, stress, and fear, which often results in their having to make drastic adjustments in how they live.

Stalking can be viewed as occurring on a continuum from nondelusional to delusional behavior. Delusional behavior indicates the presence of a mental disorder (psychosis). Nondelusional behavior, although reflecting a gross disturbance in a particular relationship, does not necessarily indicate a detachment from reality. This distinction is significant because of the potential legal implications. What most readily distinguishes the behavior of this spectrum is the type and nature of the relationship an offender has had with his target.

On the extreme delusional end of this spectrum, there is usually no actual relationship; the relationship exists only in the mind of the offender. On the nondelusional end of the spectrum is usually a historical relationship between the offender and victim. These tend to be multidimensional relationships such as marriage or a common law relationship, replete with a history of close interpersonal involvement. In between these two poles are relationships of varied dimensions and stalkers who exhibit a mix of behavior. The offender may have dated his target once, twice, or not at all. The target may only have smiled and said hello in passing or may in some way be socially or vocationally acquainted.

For the purpose of classification, we divide this spectrum of stalking behavior into three general types: domestic (nondelusional), nondomestic (a mix of nondelusional and delusional behavior), and erotomania (delusional). Of note, the terms target and victim are not necessarily interchangeable. The term target is used to describe the primary recipient of the stalker's attention. However, in many cases, those people around a stalker's target become victims of the stalker's behavior.

Defining Characteristics

VICTIMOLOGY

A stalking victim feels reasonable fear of bodily injury or death to self or to a family or household member or damage to property. Stalking can be perpetrated by the stalker or by someone acting on her or his behalf. It can take the form of verbal threats or threats conveyed by the stalker's conduct, threatening mail, property damage, surveillance of the victim, or following the victim.

CRIME SCENE INDICATORS FREQUENTLY NOTED

The stalker may do some or all of the following: follow the victim or victim's family or household members; vandalize the victim's property; inflict damage to property—perhaps by vandalizing the car, harming a pet, or breaking windows at the victim's home; make threatening calls or send threatening mail; or drive by or park near the victim's home, office, or other places familiar to the victim.

Common Forensic Findings

The stalker believes or knows that his or her actions will instill fear of death or bodily injury to the victim or a member of the victim's family or household. Threats can be explicit (e.g., stating that he is going to kill the victim) or implied (e.g., veiled threats or hurting the family pet). Threats have to be aimed at a specific person; they cannot be general. Threats may be conveyed by the stalker or by someone acting on behalf of the stalker.

Staging

Staging is not usually used in stalking crimes.

Investigative Considerations

A stalker tries to control the victim through behavior or threats intended to intimidate and terrify. A stalker can be an unknown person, an acquaintance, or a former intimate partner. A stalker's state of mind can range from obsessive love to obsessive hatred. A stalker may follow a victim off and on for days, weeks, or even years. The stalker may even have had contact with the victim on more than one occasion.

This conduct has to occur on more than one occasion and be directed toward the victim or the victim's family or household members. More than one police report is not required. The acts may include threatening contact by mail or by phone or damaging the victim's property.

Search Warrant Suggestions

Warrants to search should include the stalker's residence, car, and other known areas.

411: Domestic Stalker

Domestic stalking occurs when a former boyfriend or girlfriend, family member, or household member threatens or harasses another member of the household. This definition includes common law relationships as well as long-term acquaintance relationships. The domestic stalker is initially motivated by a desire to continue or reestablish a relationship, which can evolve into an attitude of, "If I can't have her, no one can."

Defining Characteristics

VICTIMOLOGY

The target knows the stalker as an acquaintance or may have a familial or common law relationship that the target has attempted to terminate. The target is aware of the stalking and may have requested a restraining order or assistance from law enforcement on prior occasions. In addition, there is a history of prior abuse or conflict with the stalker. The target may report a sense of being smothered in the prior relationship.

CRIME SCENE INDICATORS FREQUENTLY NOTED

The domestic stalking case often culminates in a violent attack directed at the target. Usually the scene of this attack involves only one crime scene, and it is commonly the target or stalker's residence or place of employment. The crime scene reflects disorder and the impetuous nature of the stalker. A weapon is usually brought to the scene. There could be signs of little or no forced entry and no sign of theft. The crime scene may also reflect an escalation of violence; for example, the confrontation starts as an argument, intensifies into hitting or throwing things, and could culminate in the target's death and would then be classified as domestic homicide (see classification 122). Others, such as family members and boyfriends or girlfriends, may be involved in an assault. If the target has taken steps to keep the stalker away (changed phone number, changed residence, or a restraining order, for example), the only access the stalker may have is at the target's place of employment. In such cases, coworkers, security personnel, customers, or others in the area may become victims. In some instances, the stalker will abduct his target in an attempt to convince her to stay with him.

The stalker may be at the scene when law enforcement or emergency medical personnel arrive or may commit suicide. The stalker may make incriminating statements.

COMMON FORENSIC FINDINGS

Alcohol or drugs may be involved. There usually are forensic findings consistent with a personal type of assault. Depersonalization, evidenced by facial battery and a focused area of injury indicative of anger, is an example of a personal assault.

Investigative Considerations

If the crime occurs in the target's residence, domestic stalking should be considered. When other family members are contacted, they often describe a history of domestic violence involving the target and stalker. This is often supported by police reports. A history of conflict due to external stressors (financial, vocational, or alcohol, for example) is a common element of domestic stalking. The stalker may have demonstrated personalized aggression in the past, as well as a change in attitude after the triggering event.

Search Warrant Suggestions

Although most of the evidence will be left at the crime scene, the investigator should request diaries and financial and medical records to verify any premeditation of the crime.

Case Study: 411: Domestic Stalker

A 43-year-old woman who recently separated from her 50-year-old husband worked at the same casino as he did. About a month after she began dating another man, she became aware that her husband was following her into the parking garage and then, by car, to her home. Several weeks later, after work one evening, the woman was forced at gunpoint into her car by her husband and forced to drive to his house, where he raped and beat her. She reported the domestic abuse to the police, was given a protective order, and changed the hours she worked at the casino after telling her employer the situation. A month later, her husband again abducted her from the garage, forced her to drive to his house, and once inside raped and threatened to kill her and then himself. During the beatings, the woman received a serious cut to her forehead from the knife he held on her. She managed to convince him to take her to the emergency department, where after seeing that she had been admitted, he left. The woman told the staff of the murder–suicide attempt, and the police were notified. When they arrived at the man's house, he refused to come out. Gunshots were heard, and when the police entered the house, they found the husband had committed suicide by a gunshot wound to the head.

412: Nondomestic Stalker

The nondomestic stalker targets an individual and interacts with that target through hang-up, obscene, or harassing telephone calls; unsigned letters; and other anonymous communications or continuous physical appearance at the target's residence, place of employment, shopping mall, or school campus. The stalker is often unknown to the target. It is unlikely the target will become aware of being stalked until the stalker's activity is well under way. Only after the stalker has chosen to make personal or written contact will the target realize the problem.

Defining Characteristics

VICTIMOLOGY

The target, usually a female, has often crossed paths with the stalker, most likely without notice by the target. She will therefore have no knowledge of the stalker's identity. The relationship between the stalker and target is one-way. The target will eventually become aware of the physically present nuisance stalker.

Other potential victims are spouses, boyfriends or girlfriends, or anyone viewed as an obstacle coming between the stalker and his target.

CRIME SCENE INDICATORS FREQUENTLY NOTED

Stalking is an ongoing, usually long-term crime without a traditional crime scene. The stalking occurs at the target's residence, place of employment, shopping mall, school campus, or other public place. There will be a number of aborted or obscene phone calls or anonymous letters addressed to the target professing love or knowledge of the target's movements. Written communications are often left on vehicle windows or placed in mailboxes or under doors by the stalker. The tone of communications may progress from protestations of adoration, to love, to annoyance at not being able to make personal contact, to eventually threatening and menacing.

The stalker may place himself or herself in a position to make casual contact with the target, at which time verbal communication may occur. A description of this contact may be used in a later communication to terrorize or impress on the target that the stalker is capable of carrying out any threats.

Investigative Considerations

The investigator should trace telephone calls and perform threat analysis of the written or phone communications. Careful analysis of early communications may provide leads for identifying the stalker. He or she as well should observe the target's places of employment, residence, mall, or campus for stalker. Since communications are often left on or in the target's vehicle, observation of vehicles can often lead to the identity of the stalker. The target should be interviewed about any suspicious seemingly accidental contacts she may have had in the recent past, such as being bumped into while shopping, door-to-door salesmen, telephone solicitations, or a stranger asking to use the telephone or asking for directions.

Search Warrant Suggestions

The primary items to search for are photographs, literature (newspaper articles, books, magazine articles), and recordings concerning the target. Diaries, journals, calendars, or surveillance logs detailing the stalker's preoccupation and fantasy life with the target may also be found. Recordings of telephone calls to targets are often made and retained.

Other items to look for are evidence of contact or attempted contact with the target: telephone records or returned letters, for example. Credit card records, ticket stubs, and hotel receipts are often kept as souvenirs and may be helpful in documenting travel in pursuit of a target. Computer equipment should not be overlooked as a repository for information.

Case Study: 412: Nondomestic Stalker

Victimology

A man who stalked a woman was arrested outside her house carrying weapons, a stocking mask, and other items. The woman told police she recently found her bathing suit taped to the windshield of her car. On one other occasion, she found some of her undergarments draped on the car's mirror. Police sources revealed that one week prior, the victim had found cartridge casings from a handgun taped to the car's window.

Investigation

On the night of the arrest of the stalker, the victim saw a man outside her apartment and called the police. Minutes later, the police arrested the stalker, who months prior to this incident had been acquitted of burglarizing the woman's home.

The stalker was found sitting in his vehicle less than a hundred yards from the victim's apartment. Officers searched the stalker and found a knife and a key to the victim's residence. In his vehicle they found a .22-caliber pistol and ammunition, a stun gun, mace, a camera and film, two sets of binoculars, two tape recorders, two flashlights, pictures of the victim's residence and car, rubber gloves, cotton gloves, a stocking mask, a large nylon bag and a bag with a change of clothes, several condoms, a book of nude pictures, a gun cleaning kit, and a cooler filled with ice and beer.

Outcome

The offender was arrested and pleaded guilty to stalking. He was sentenced to 2 years.

413: Erotomania Stalker

Erotomania-related stalking is motivated by an offender–target relationship based on the stalker's fixation. This fantasy is commonly expressed in such forms as fusion (the stalker blends his personality into his target's) or erotomania (a fantasy-based idealized romantic love or spiritual union of a person rather than sexual attraction). The stalker can be motivated by religious fantasies or voices directing him to target a particular individual. This preoccupation with the target becomes consuming and ultimately could lead to the target's death.

The drive to stalk arises from a variety of motives, ranging from rebuffed advances to internal conflicts stemming from the stalker's fusion of identity with the target. In addition to a person with high media visibility, other victims include superiors at work or even complete strangers. The target almost always is perceived by the stalker as someone of higher status. Targets often include political figures, entertainers, and high-media-visibility individuals but do not have to be public figures. Sometimes the victim becomes someone who is perceived by the stalker as an obstruction.

When erotomania is involved and the target is a highly visible media personality (usually someone unattainable to the stalker), the target becomes the imagined lover of the stalker through hidden messages known only to the stalker. The stalker builds an elaborate fantasy revolving around this imagined love. Male erotomaniacs tend to act out this fantasy with greater force than do female.

Defining Characteristics

VICTIMOLOGY

The target is aware of the stalker through many prior encounters or communications (letters or phone calls). The target often has high media visibility. Many times the initial contact with a public figure will be in the form of fan mail.

CRIME SCENE INDICATORS FREQUENTLY NOTED

As with other classifications of stalking, the activity of the erotomania stalker is often long term, with written and telephonic communications, surveillance, and attempts to approach the target. With the passage of time, the activity becomes more intense, with the stalker's attitude shifting to one of, "If I can't have her, no one can."

The majority of erotomania-motivated attacks are close range and confrontational. The stalker may even remain at the scene. These encounters tend to be spontaneous, as reflected by a haphazard approach to the target: evidence is left, and there are likely to be witnesses. This does not mean the stalker did not fantasize, premeditate, and plan the stalking; all of these elements characterize this crime. Rather, the actual act is usually an opportunistic one. The stalker takes advantage of an opportunity to interact with the target as it is presented to him.

COMMON FORENSIC FINDING

Firearms are the most common weapon carried by stalkers, especially with a distance stalking. Occasionally, they use a sharp-edged weapon such as a knife. The sophistication and type of weapon will help establish the degree of stalker sophistication. If the target of the stalker is killed, the vital organs, especially the head and chest, are most frequently targeted.

Investigative Considerations

The stalker almost always surveys or stalks the target preceding the encounter with the target. Therefore, the availability of the target's itinerary and who may have access to it is one investigative consideration. There is a likelihood of preoffense attempts by the stalker to contact the target through telephone calls, letters, gifts, or visits to the target's home or workplace. There may even be an incident involving law enforcement or security officers having to remove the stalker from the target's residence or workplace.

The stalker's conversation often will reflect this preoccupation or fantasy life with the target. When those associated with the stalker are interviewed, they typically recall that much of the stalker's conversation focused on the target. He or she may have claimed to have had a relationship with the target and may have invented stories to support this encounter.

Assistance should be requested from FBI's Investigative Support Unit or mental health professionals experienced with these complicated cases.

Search Warrant Suggestions

The primary items to search for are photographs, literature (newspaper articles, books, magazine articles), maps, letters from a celebrity target to a stalker, surveillance photos of the target, and recordings concerning the target. Diaries and journals detailing the stalker's preoccupation or fantasy life with the target may be found.

Other items to look for are evidence of contact or attempted contacts with the target: telephone records, returned letters or gifts, motel receipts, gas bills, rental agreements, or airline, bus, or train tickets implying travel to locations where the target has been. Credit card records also may be helpful in this regard.

Case Study: 413: Erotomania Stalker

Background

On the morning of March 15, 1982, Arthur Richard Jackson, age 47, was waiting near Theresa Saldana's West Hollywood apartment house. As Saldana rushed out to a music class at Los Angeles City College, Jackson approached. When Saldana paused to unlock her car, Jackson asked, "Excuse me. Are you Theresa Saldana?" Saldana replied, "Yes."

Her identity confirmed, Jackson began stabbing Saldana with a hunting knife. He stabbed and slashed her so hard and so often that the knife bent. Hearing Saldana's screams, a delivery man rushed to her aid and wrested the weapon away from Jackson.

The intervention of the delivery man, heart-lung surgery, and 26 pints of blood saved Saldana's life.

Victimology

Theresa Saldana was a 27-year-old actress Jackson had identified with through watching movies.

The Offender

Arthur Jackson was born in Aberdeen, Scotland, in 1935 to an alcoholic father and a mother whom investigators believe may have been schizophrenic. He was an odd and fanatical child who often became lost in fantasy. In an 89-page autobiographical letter addressed to Saldana written in 1982 shortly after his arrest, Jackson wrote that at age 10, he became fixated on a neighbor girl called Fiona. He also described a sexual encounter with an older boy at age 13.

It was also in this letter to Saldana that he expressed his "torturous love sickness in my soul to you combined with a desperate desire to escape into a beautiful world I have always dreamed of (the palaces of gardens of sweet paradise), whereby the plan was for you, Theresa, to go ahead first, then I would join you in a few months. . . . I swear on the ashes of my dead mother and on the scars of Theresa Saldana that neither God nor I will rest in peace until this special request and my solemn petition has been granted."

At 17, he suffered his first nervous breakdown. It took a full year before Jackson was released from the Scottish psychiatric hospital where he sought treatment. After his release, he began a trip across two continents, working in London as a kitchen porter, in Toronto as a zoo helper, and in New York as a jack-of-all-menial-trades.

In 1955 he joined the U.S. Army. While in the Army, he fell in love with a fellow soldier and suffered another nervous breakdown. He was sent to Walter Reed Hospital in Washington, D.C., for psychiatric treatment. While in the hospital, he was given a weekend pass in honor of his 21st birthday in 1956. Jackson spent his birthday by going to New York, where he attempted suicide with an overdose of sleeping pills.

Discharged from the Army, he continued to wander across the United States. In 1961, the U.S. Secret Service arrested Jackson for threatening President

John F. Kennedy. Later that year, he was deported to Scotland, where he occasionally lived with his widowed mother. During this period, he was a vagrant on the dole and seldom stayed in one place for more than a few months.

In 1966, Jackson reentered the United States through Miami and was given a six-month visitor's visa. He was deported when he overstayed the six months.

He first became aware of Saldana in 1979, when he sat in an Aberdeen theater and watched *I Want to Hold Your Hand*, a film about Beatlemania. Movies were Jackson's only reality. Jackson conceived mad passions for women in movies whom he thought of as stars.

Two years later he saw Saldana in *Defiance*, a movie in which she plays a girl trying to make a life for herself in a crime-ridden slum. When costar Jan-Michael Vincent was attacked in the movie by a street gang, the scene provoked vivid memories of his own 1956 suicide attempt. Focusing his excitement on Theresa, Jackson convinced himself he could win the actress by "sending her into eternity."

Investigation

Jackson began stalking Saldana in early 1982, the year he illegally returned to the United States. He took several cross-country bus trips in this single-minded quest.

He initially went to New York City, where he tried to contact Saldana's relatives and business associates, pretending to be an agent with a script for her. He was unable to locate Saldana. A trip to Los Angeles also yielded nothing. Only after he returned to New York from California did he manage to trick one of Saldana's relatives into telling him the actress lived in Hollywood.

While he stalked Saldana, he tried to purchase a gun in many different states but was prevented by state laws requiring a minimum of a driver's license for identification. The only weapon available to Jackson was a hunting knife.

After returning to Hollywood, he hired a private detective, who provided Saldana's address. During questioning by the police, he was asked why he had tried to kill Saldana. Jackson replied, "Read my diary. It's all in there." Jackson had kept a dairy of his quest in his knapsack.

Outcome

Jackson, convicted of attempted murder and inflicting great bodily injury, was given the maximum sentence of twelve years in prison. While in custody, he also confessed to the murder of two people during a robbery of a London bank in 1962. Jackson continued to write to Saldana in prison as well as reporters about his quest for Saldana.

420: Robbery

Robbery is a crime of seizing property through violence or intimidation. Because violence is an ingredient of most robberies, they sometimes result in the harm or murder of their victims. Robbery is generally an urban crime.

In common with most legal terms, the precise definition of robbery varies by jurisdiction.

The element of force differentiates robbery from embezzlement, larceny, and other types of theft. Armed robbery involves the use of a weapon. Highway robbery takes place outside and in a public place. Carjacking is the act of stealing a car from a victim, usually at gunpoint. Bank robbery is the robbing of banks and financial institutions.

Defining Characteristics

VICTIMOLOGY

The victim of a robbery can be an individual or a group of people. It can also be a home, bank, a store, and other places with cash or items to be stolen. The goal is generally cash.

The victim's risk is situational. It is the robber's perception of the victim that puts the victim at risk. The risk for the robber is dependent on his relationship with the victim and his or her expertise in the crime.

CRIME SCENE INDICATORS FREQUENTLY NOTED

The robber usually spends a minimum amount of time at the scene. Typically, he brings a weapon or a threat of having one, such as a bomb. Sometimes the communication between the robber and the victim is written or verbal. Communication is minimal.

STAGING

Staging is not typical.

COMMON FORENSIC FINDINGS

In bank robberies, there is often a note left for analysis. If the victim has been bound, there will be restraints available.

Investigative Considerations

Robberies are usually planned. Surveillance tapes should be secured for both prior casing of the building and the robbery itself. Careful interviewing of witnesses will assist in developing a sketch of the robber for media distribution or photos from the security cameras.

Search Warrant Suggestions .

There should be a search for the stolen items. In bank robberies, there will be marking dye on clothes and the surroundings.

421: Bank Robbery

Bank robbery is usually accomplished by a solitary criminal who brandishes a firearm at a teller and demands money, either orally or through a written note. The most dangerous type of bank robbery is a takeover robbery in which several heavily armed (and armored) gang members threaten the lives of everyone in the bank.

The first bank robbery in the United States took place on March 19, 1831, and was committed by Edward Smith, who stole $245,000 from the City Bank on Wall Street in New York City. He was caught, convicted, and sentenced to five years in Sing Sing prison.

Due to modern security measures like security cameras, well-armed security guards, silent alarms, exploding dye packs, and special weapons and tactics (SWAT) teams, bank robberies are now rarely successful. Few criminals are able to make a successful living out of bank robbery over the long run, since each attempt increases the probability of being identified and caught. Today most organized crime groups tend to make their money by other means, such as drug trafficking, identity theft, or online scamming and phishing. However, bank robberies are still fairly common and are sometimes successful, although eventually most robbers are found and arrested. An FBI report states that the rate of clearance by arrest for bank robbery in 2001 was second only to that of murder.

Case Study: 421: Bank Robbery

Background

This study is an atypical bank robbery because it was committed by more than one person and is a well-known case. Campbell Hearst, better known as Patty Hearst (born February 20, 1954), now as Patricia Hearst Shaw, is an American newspaper heiress and socialite. She is the granddaughter of William Randolph Hearst and was the victim of a 1974 kidnapping, but soon afterward became a criminal herself: She robbed a bank and spent time in prison (although she later received a presidential pardon).

Hearst was born in San Mateo, California, the third of five daughters of Randolph Apperson Hearst. She grew up primarily in the wealthy San Francisco suburb of Hillsborough, California, and attended Crystal Springs Uplands School

She was kidnapped on February 4, 1974, shortly before her 20th birthday, from the Berkeley, California, apartment that she shared with her fiancé, Steven Weed, by an urban guerrilla terrorist group called the Symbionese Liberation Army (SLA). When the attempt to prisoner-swap Hearst for jailed SLA members failed, the SLA made ransom demands that resulted in the donation by the Hearst family of $6 million worth of food to the poor of the Bay Area. After the distribution of food, Hearst was still not released.

Victimology

The victim was the Sunset branch of the Hibernia Bank.

Crime Scene Indicators

On April 15, 1974, Patty Hearst was photographed wielding an assault rifle while robbing the Sunset branch of the Hibernia Bank. Later communications from her were issued under the pseudonym Tania and revealed that she was committed to the goals of the SLA. A warrant was issued for her arrest, and in September 1975, she was arrested in an apartment with other SLA members.

Forensic Findings

In her trial, which started on January 15, 1976, Hearst claimed she had been locked blindfolded in a closet and physically and sexually abused, which caused her to join the SLA. Her defense was largely based around the claim that her actions could be attributed to a severe case of Stockholm syndrome, in which captives become sympathetic with their captors. Hearst further argued she was coerced or intimidated into her part in the bank robbery.

Outcome

Attorney F. Lee Bailey defended Patty Hearst, who was nevertheless convicted of bank robbery on March 20. Her sentence was eventually commuted by President Jimmy Carter, and Hearst was released from prison on February 1, 1979. She was granted a full pardon by President Bill Clinton on January 20, 2001, the final day of his presidency.

After her release from prison, Hearst married her former bodyguard, Bernard Shaw. Currently, she lives with her husband and two daughters in Connecticut.

422: Home Invasion Robbery

Home invasion may be viewed as the residential form of an automobile carjacking. Like the crime of carjacking, most police agencies don't track home invasions as a separate crime. The crime will be recorded as a residential burglary (if no one as home) or a robbery if homeowners were present. Home invasion crimes may begin as nonlethal and then take a drastic turn to assault or homicide as in the Petit case discussed later in this chapter.

Criminal Profile

Residential burglars work mostly during the day and when a residence is more likely to be unoccupied. Most burglars work alone and tend to probe a neighborhood looking for the right residence and the right opportunity. Burglars will try to avoid a confrontation and will usually flee when approached. Most burglaries do not result in violence unless the criminal is cornered and uses force to escape.

Home invasion robbers, in contrast, work more often at night and on weekends when homes are more likely to be occupied. The home invader will sometimes target the resident as well as the dwelling. The selection process may include a woman living alone, a wealthy senior citizen or a known drug dealer, for example. It is not unheard of for a robber to follow someone home based on the value of the car or the jewelry observed. Some home invaders might have been a delivery person, installer, or repair vendor to the individual's home. Home robbers rarely work alone and rely on an overwhelming physical confrontation to gain initial control and instill fear in the homeowner. The greatest violence usually occurs during the initial sixty seconds of the confrontation and home invaders often come prepared with handcuffs, rope, duct tape, and firearms. Some in-home robbers appear to enjoy the intimidation, domination, and violence and some even claim to experience a rush of adrenaline (McGoey, 2012).

Dangerous Trends

The act of committing a home invasion is escalating much like carjacking. The reason for the increase seems to follow a similar pattern. Much like automobiles, the traditional commercial targets for robbers like convenience stores and fast-food restaurants have hardened themselves against criminal attack and have reduced available cash. Technology has allowed commercial establishments to install affordable video surveillance systems, silent alarms, and other crime-deterrent devices. A residence, by comparison, is now a more attractive choice.

Home invaders know that they won't have to overcome alarm systems when the home is occupied or be worried about video cameras and silent alarms. Unlike robbing a retail store, home invaders expect privacy once inside a home. Once the offenders take control of a residence, they can force the occupants to open safes, locate hidden valuables, supply keys to the family car, and PIN numbers to their ATM cards. Home invaders will try to increase their escape time by disabling the phones and sometimes will leave their victims bound or incapacitated. It is not unheard of for robbers to load up the victim's car with valuables and drive away without anyone in the neighborhood taking notice (McGoey, 2012).

Method of Operation

The most common point of attack is through the front door or garage. Sometimes the home invader will simply kick open the door and confront everyone inside. More common is when the home invaders knock on the door first or ring the bell. The home invader hopes that the occupant will simply open the door, without question, in response to their knock.

Home invaders will sometimes use a ruse or impersonation to get a person to open the door. They have been known to pretend to be delivering a package or flowers, or lie about an accident like hitting a parked car. Once the door is opened for them, the home invaders will use an explosive amount of force and scream out threats to gain control of the home and produce fear in the victims. Once the occupants are under control the robbers will begin to collect the valuables (McGoey, 2012).

Some home robbers have been known to spend hours ransacking a residence while the homeowners are bound nearby watching in terror. Some robbers have been known to eat meals, watch TV, or even take a nap. A major fear is that the robbers might commit more violence like sexual assault or even murder. Some robbers have kidnapped and forced a victim to withdraw cash from their ATM machine or take them to their small business to rob it as well (McGoey, 2010).

Case Study: 422: The Petit Triple Homicide

In the late afternoon of July 22, 2007, Mrs. Petit and her daughter went to a local grocery store for groceries. They were unaware that two men had targeted them and followed them home planning a home invasion for the next day.

However, in their early morning arrival, they found Dr. Petit sleeping on a couch on the porch. One offender hit him over the head with a bat and restrained him in the cellar at gunpoint. The children and their mother were each bound and locked in their respective rooms. Dissatisfied with the lack of cash available, a bank book was found indicating more cash. Mrs. Petit, forced to leave her daughters with the assailants, drove to the bank. The bank surveillance cameras captured the transaction as she informed the teller of her situation. The teller then called 911 and reported the details to police. Dr. Petit had been able to free himself and call to a neighbor for help but not before his wife and daughters had been raped, murdered, and the house set on fire. Police apprehended Steven Hayes and Joshua Komisarjevsky as they tried to flee in the Petit's car.

Both Hayes and Komisarjevsky were found guilty and the jury recommended the death penalty. The Connecticut state judicial branch, for the first time in state history, offered posttraumatic stress assistance to jurors who served in the triple-murder trial. Because the jurors were required to look at disturbing images and hear grisly testimony, during the two-month trial, their service necessitated these actions.

430: Burglary

Burglary is a nonconfrontational property crime that occurs when no one is at home. Becoming a burglary victim can leave a family feeling vulnerable and violated.

Defining Characteristics

VICTIMOLOGY

The victim is the property. The majority of home and apartment burglaries occur during the daytime when most people are at work or school. The summer months of July and August have the most burglaries, with February having the fewest crimes.

CRIME SCENE INDICATORS FREQUENTLY NOTED

Burglaries are committed most often by young males under 25 years of age looking for items that are small and expensive and can easily be converted to cash. Favorite items are cash, jewelry, guns, watches, laptop computers, VCRs, video players, CDs, and other small electronic devices. Quick cash is needed for living expenses and drugs.

COMMON FORENSIC FINDINGS

Seventy percent of burglars use some force to enter a dwelling, but their preference is to gain easy access through an open door or window. Ordinary household tools like screwdrivers, channel-lock pliers, small pry bars, and small hammers are most often used. Burglars continue to flourish because police can clear only about 13% of all reported burglaries and rarely catch the thief in the act.

Use of state DNA databases involving samples from felons convicted of certain crimes has yielded some data on fetish burglars who go on to commit sexual offenses. Any body fluids found should be subjected to analysis and the Combined DNA Index System (CODIS).

Investigation Considerations

Although home burglaries may seem random in occurrence, they actually involve a selection process. The burglar's selection process is simple: choose an unoccupied home with the easiest access, the greatest amount of cover, and the best escape routes.

Burglars enter residences illegally to steal merchandise or property that someone else owns; however, motives may vary among thieves. For example, the motive of a criminal enterprise burglar is profit, whereas the motive of a fetish burglar is sexual. Sometimes both motives are operating. It is important not to dismiss panty thieves as nuisance offenders when their intent is not a nuisance but represents a serious intention or motivation to harm someone sexually. Fetish burglars' motive consists of the sexually provocative images that the stolen items (such as lingerie or leather) convey and the physiological arousal they may experience committing such an act. The motive of the fetish burglar is secret and has to do with the content or theme of a specific (perhaps sexual) fantasy. Because of the sexual motive, a fetish burglar (similar to sex offenders in general) is not likely to stop without intervention by law enforcement. An arrest is necessary to interrupt the pattern. Recognizing motivation is a key component to understanding the crime and the criminal and to evaluating the danger to society.

Search Warrant Suggestions

There should be a search for the stolen items, including fetish items.

440: Assault

Aggravated assault is usually differentiated from simple assault by the offender's intent (to murder or to rape, for example), the extent of the injury to the victim, or the use of a deadly weapon, although legal definitions vary by jurisdiction. Sentences for aggravated assault are generally more severe, reflecting the greater degree of harm or malice intended by the perpetrator.

Defining Characteristics

VICTIMOLOGY

The victim can be a person, child, adult, or elder. There has been an attempt by the offender to cause bodily injury. The offender causes such injury purposely, knowingly, or recklessly in circumstances and shows callous indifference to the victim.

CRIME SCENE INDICATORS FREQUENTLY NOTED

The offender may cause bodily injury by use of a deadly weapon.

COMMON FORENSIC FINDINGS

Aggravated assault offenders used personal weapons (such as hands, fists, and feet) in 26.9% of offenses, firearms in 19.1% of offenses, and knives or cutting instruments in 18.2% of offenses. Other types of weapons were used in 35.9% of aggravated assaults.

STAGING

Staging may be involved to make the assault look like an accident, for example, stating a child fell when he was actually shaken.

Investigative Considerations

Careful interviewing of multiple witnesses is important to check for consistency in statements. Assault and abuse cases by family members or caregivers will need to be reviewed carefully.

Search Warrant Suggestions

A search warrant would help to identify patterned marks of assault on a victim if the weapon can be found—for example, a rope or belt used to bind a victim or a belt used to strike a victim. The suspect's home and car could be searched for a specific weapon.

450: Battery/Abuse

The crime of battery involves an injury or other contact on the person of another in a manner likely to cause bodily harm. It is often broken down into gradations for the purposes of determining the severity of punishment—for example:

- Simple battery may include any form of nonconsensual, harmful, or insulting contact, regardless of the injury caused.
- Sexual battery may be defined as nonconsensual touching of the intimate parts of another.
- Family violence battery may be limited in its scope between persons within a certain degree of relationship. Statutes with respect to this offense have been enacted in response to an increasing awareness of the problem of domestic violence.

- Aggravated battery is generally regarded as a serious offense of felony grade, involving the loss of the victim's limb or some other type of permanent disfigurement of the victim. As successor to the common-law crime of mayhem, this is sometimes subsumed in the definition of aggravated assault.

In some jurisdictions, battery has recently been constructed to include directing bodily secretions at another person without their permission. In some jurisdictions, this automatically is considered aggravated battery.

As a first approximation to the distinction between battery and assault, the overt behavior of an assault might be A advancing on B by chasing after him and swinging a fist at his head, while that of an act of battery might be A actually striking B.

Within U.S. law in most jurisdictions, the charge of criminal battery requires evidence of a mental state (mens rea).

Case Study: 450: Battery/Abuse

Background

Caleb's father told the doctor that he and his wife, Crystal (Caleb's mother), had been separated for the past eight months and that since the separation, Caleb had been with his father 90% of the time. He said Caleb's mother was now pregnant with a baby by a different father and had recently wanted to see more of Caleb. The evening before, Caleb had been with his mother. His father dropped him off at the mother's around 6:00 p.m. and picked him up that morning at 5:30 a.m. Caleb's mother resides with her mother, although her mother is gone a lot. When he dropped off Caleb, the mother's new boyfriend was there, but he was not seen in the morning when the father picked up Caleb.

Victimology

Caleb was 16 months old when he was brought to an emergency room by his father for evaluation of alleged physical abuse.

Crime Scene Indicators

When the father picked up Caleb, he noted red spots on the child's left cheek. He thought it was food and tried to rub it off. Caleb's mother said that Caleb had an allergic reaction to the carpet. Caleb's father took him to day care and at that time noticed the marking on the face looked like a handprint. The father called the pediatrician, who told him to bring the child to the hospital. At the hospital, the father told the doctor that Caleb was walking and falling a lot, but he had never noticed him to have bruises in the past.

Forensic Findings

An examination revealed an area of petechiae, 5 by 10 centimeters, with several red linear marks. The impression was physical abuse from a handprint. X-rays of the entire body did not reveal any other injury. Child Protective Services (CPS) was notified, and a report was sent to law enforcement.

Investigation

The CPS social worker made many telephone attempts to contact Caleb's parents in an effort to determine who had abused Caleb. The social worker was unsuccessful for four months. She gathered the parents and maternal grandmother for a meeting in July. All parties said they did not believe his mother had hit him, but they had no other explanation. Her report stated that his mother was involved with a boyfriend and that both parents were responsible for the child's care when Caleb was with them. The referral of child abuse was substantiated, and the referral was closed.

On December 27, Caleb's mother's boyfriend called 911 and said that Caleb was not breathing. The emergency medical technicians responded, but Caleb could not be resuscitated. The boyfriend was charged with the homicide.

Outcome

Police interviews during the investigation revealed the following:

- Caleb's mother was being abused by her boyfriend. She identified four separate times he had shoved her around. The boyfriend admitted he had roughed her up several times and that he had an anger problem.
- The boyfriend was a registered sex offender. He had failed to report his address in November of that year and was put on probation. This information was reported in the newspaper article on Caleb's murder.
- The newspaper also reported the boyfriend's criminal history of corruption of a minor, receiving stolen property, grand theft, preparation of cocaine for sale, and forgery. He also was stopped for driving with a license plate that was not properly displayed.
- Caleb's mother admitted that Caleb had seemed depressed for months before his death. X-rays and autopsy indicated that Caleb had an old head injury estimated to have occurred 7 to 10 days prior to his death.
- Caleb's mother permitted her boyfriend to stay with her because he said he had no other place to live. She also said he was lazy and was not working.
- The police were asked to search the home for an L-shaped weapon to match the pattern of injury on Caleb's skull. They found a loaded gun belonging to the boyfriend.

This was a case that fell through the cracks. If there had been better coordination and sharing of information between CPS and law enforcement, the domestic abuse and child abuse would have been the basis for charging the boyfriend and possibly preventing the fatal injury to Caleb.

Case Study: 450: Battery/Abuse

Background

The defendant was a 50-year-old Black male who was the registered domestic partner of the victim, a 39-year-old White woman. There was a history of abuse dating back to the birth of their daughter, 10 years prior. The mother never called the police or made reports of the abuse to authorities. She was a schoolteacher. On at least two occasions, she missed work because of visible injuries sustained at the hands of her partner. Her work associates, including her supervisor, were suspicious of the bruises but never made any report.

Victimology

Ms. J was seriously attacked in July 2004 but did not go to the hospital until five days later, primarily because the partner accused her of faking it and also threatened it would "open Pandora's box" because of his criminal record. The defendant had a criminal record, which included at least one prior domestic violence case (in which the victim was his "wife" and his prostitute). The victim in that case had a daughter, not believed to be the defendant's. That case went to trial, but the defendant was convicted only of a misdemeanor, not the numerous felonies he was indicted on.

Crime Scene Indicators

Testimony of Ms. J from a videotape made while she was hospitalized from the assault provided the following information. Mr. B was verbally abusive, said she messed up things, would hit her on the back of the head, berate her, order her to stand still and keep her arms down, punch her in the stomach, order her to lie down, spread her legs, hit her with an extension cord on her legs and pubic area, and state he wanted to kill her. He said she would lose her job when the school found out she was incompetent.

One time that he hit her in the face, she received two black eyes and swollen gums. She lied to school authorities that she was visiting her grandmother for two weeks. She was hit for the way she cooked the rice, for not washing his shirts well enough, and for "speaking like a wimp." Ms. J did tell her doctor about the bruises. He advised her to leave the partner, saying, "They never change."

Ms. J rationalized her partner's behavior and believed that he would change. She did not want to "mess up his dream" of being successful. She was staying with him because of the daughter and did not want the daughter to know of the abuse.

The assaultive event in July started because she had not washed fruit particles sufficiently out of a container that was to be used to hold water for their daughter. Mr. B hit his partner, saying she should have learned how to clean a container by this time. He kicked her in the stomach as she lay on the floor and slammed her head against the tiles. She went back to cleaning the container but felt a great deal of physical pain, saw flashes, and felt very hot. She went to the bathroom and vomited green liquid several times. He made her get up, but she could not stand straight. He forced her to eat the next day, and she kept vomiting. This continued for several days, to which Mr. B said she was "milking this for attention." He kept very close watch on her and refused to let her leave the apartment. On the fifth day, he said he was taking the daughter out. Ms. J wrote him a check and after he left, she managed to get herself to the emergency room. She was in such critical condition that the doctor called her mother in another state to say he did not think she would live.

Forensic Findings

Diagnoses at the hospital included pancreatic traumatic injury and peritonitis. Her pancreas had been severed in half, and the necrotic part of it was removed. Her spleen was removed. She was treated for postsurgical hypoinsulinemia and postoperative infection. Over her two-week hospital stay, she told staff of the domestic violence.

Investigation

Child Protective Services had the daughter examined for possible child abuse. No bruising or injuries were detected. Mr. B was arrested on attempted murder charges. In the hospital, Ms. J agreed to press charges. Once home, however, she hired a lawyer for her partner and one for herself and refused to talk with the prosecutor.

Outcome

A Sirois hearing was held on the basis of an "unavailable witness" and to determine if expert testimony could be provided to explain aspects of domestic violence. To allow testimony at trial, the judge needed to have verified that there was an adequate research basis to the theories and dynamics of domestic violence. At trial, Ms. J minimized her injuries and stated she did not want to be a party to sending Mr. B to prison. Mr. B nevertheless was convicted and sentenced to 10 years in prison.

Case Study: 450: Battery/Abuse

Case Contributed by Leonard Morgenbesser

Victimology

A 73-year-old woman awoke in the early morning of July 10, 2004, to the sound of breaking glass. When she opened her door, a man charged inside, grabbed her, muffled her mouth, and made her promise not to call the police.

Crime Scene Indicators

The assailant spoke only Spanish, but the victim knew him from his landscaping her yard in April. After the man calmed down, the victim showed him family pictures, shared stories, and offered him something to eat.

Forensic Findings

He ate a banana, drank some milk, and fell asleep. He awoke, used the bathroom, got undressed, and exposed himself to the victim but fell back asleep. Swabs of the milk glass were taken as well as fingerprints on broken glass and his clothing.

Investigation

The victim barricaded herself in the bathroom with a telephone, which she used to call her daughter, who called the police. The police arrived to find the assailant's clothes strewn around the house; he was wearing sweat pants and had a condom in the pocket. He told police he intended to steal jewelry.

Outcome

The 25-year-old intruder, Vasquez-Garcia, was found guilty of two counts of residential burglary, one count of false imprisonment of an elder, and one count of elder abuse. One of the two burglary charges arose from another woman, a 78 year old, who contacted investigators after learning of the other incident. She testified at trial that when he was landscaping her yard in April 2004, he had used her bathroom and exposed himself to her.

The jury's foreman said the jury's main challenge came when deciding the count of elder abuse. The jury had to decide whether the intruder reasonably should have known the age of the victim. The defendant faced up to even years and four months in prison.

Reference

McGoey, C. E. (2012). *Home invasion robbery: Protecting your family with a security plan.* Retrieved August 12, 2012, from www.crimedoctor.com/homeinvasion.htm

Tarasoff v. Regents of University of California, 551 P.2d 334 (Cal. 1976).

Chapter 14

Computer Crimes

Allen G. Burgess

500: Computer crimes
510: Computers as the target
511: Malignant software
512: Computer data as the target
513: Denial of service
520: The computer user as the target
521: Identity theft
522: Invasion of privacy
523: Cyberstalking
524: Crimes against children
    524.1: Internet solicitation of children
    524.2: Child pornography
        524.2.1: Online solicitation of children
        524.2.2: Distribution of child pornography

524.2.3: Production of child pornography
530: Criminal enterprise
531: Money laundering
532: Child pornography (has been moved under 524)
533: Internet fraud
    533.01: Bank fraud
    533.02: Fraudulent Internet transactions
540: Internet-initiated crimes
541: Threats via the Internet
542: Internet-initiated homicide
543: Cybergang crime

500: Computer Crimes

Crimes involving the computer have emerged as a new class of crimes. The U.S. Attorney's Office's Computer Hacking and Intellectual Property Section (CHIPS) was created to prosecute high-technology and intellectual property offenses, including computer intrusions, denial of service attacks, virus and worm proliferation, Internet fraud, and telecommunications fraud.

The computer can be the target of the crime, the user of the computer can be the victim of the crime, information in the computer can be the target. In addition, criminal enterprises are using the computer, and computers are used by criminals incidental to the crime.

Computer crimes are divided into four major classifications: the computer as the target of the crime (510), the computer user as the target (520), criminal enterprise (530), and threats via the Internet (540). Criminal enterprise is where the computer is used as a weapon of the crime or the computer is incidental to the crime. Threats via the Internet include stalking as well as extortion.

510: Computers as the Target

A computer as the target of the crime occurs when the computer itself is the "victim" of the crime. The computer can also be a target when it or its components (hard drives, monitor, software) are stolen, but these types of crimes are classified under larceny or theft and are not included in the 510 classification. Included in this classification are crimes that target the user of the computer, the data stored on the computer, the software on the computer, or the intellectual property or trade secrets on the computer. Software programs have been developed to target computers. These programs go under many names: virus, worms, Trojan horse, spyware, and malware, to name a few. These types of programs fall under the heading of malignant software. Offenders who create and proliferate viruses, worms, and Trojan horses are known as hackers.

511: Malignant Software

Defining Characteristics

Malignant software such as viruses, worms, and Trojan horses targets the computer or the software on the computer with the intent to do harm to the computer.

Viruses are malicious code embedded in programs or e-mails that damage the computer hardware or software.

The worm is code that can damage computer files and programs or slow computer performance; it is delivered by another program or application, usually via e-mail. Viruses and worms were originally delivered by removable media but now can be found in e-mails, e-mail attachments, and free programs available over the Internet. Viruses and worms have also been found embedded in pictures.

Trojan horses are programs placed on a computer to capture and send information to a third party unbeknown to the computer user. They have been used in cases of identity theft (see classification 521). Another type of Trojan horse captures the user's keystroke information and searches for personal and financial information. This type of program is called a *key logger*. The key logger can be used to exploit a user's financial accounts by posing as the user. Another type of Trojan horse is a program that turns the user system into a spam generator. When spam is sent to the infected computer, it forwards that spam to all the addresses contained in the address books resident on the computer.

Another harmful program is the logic bomb, a program that destroys data or crashes systems when a certain event occurs. An early example was the one labeled Cookie Monster. Cookie Monster would appear on the screen and say, "Cookie! Cookie! Cookie! Cookie!" If the user could not type the word cookie into the keyboard fast enough, it would destroy or "eat" a file or files on the computer system. Another example of a logic bomb is a program that was written to search for a programmer's Social Security number; if it was not found, all payroll records would be destroyed on the computer.

VICTIMOLOGY

The victims are all computers, especially personal computers, attached to the Internet. Malignant software can be transmitted over the Internet, computer disks, CD-ROMs, flash cards, and any other form of computer storage.

COMMON FORENSIC FINDINGS

Targeted computers have missing files, slow response and processing speeds, an inability to access antivirus software, or fail to start. The offender's computer will have malignant software creation tools and copies of the software program. A Trojan horse offender's computer will also have the addresses of successful implants. The offender's computer data will be encrypted.

Investigative Considerations

The targeted computer should be serviced by another computer or Internet service to scan for malignant software. The offender's computer should be unplugged (not turned on and not closed down if it is on) and taken to a qualified facility where the hard drive will be removed and scanned with special software using another computer. This special software reads the patterns of ones and zeros from the disk without executing programs on the disk. Offenders typically build in programs during the boot cycle (computer start-up) that require a special password or procedure. If the password or procedure is not followed, the program will erase all files associated with the creation of the malignant software.

Search Warrant Suggestions

The cybercrime scene includes the victim's computer and the potential suspect's computer. Evidence collection is exclusively court order based, where forms must be submitted to a judge who approves the collection of evidence from an Internet service provider (ISP). The basis of a search warrant is for the purpose of obtaining documents that connect the victim to the perpetrator. The success of the discovery process is dependent on the particular ISP's record keeping, which includes how long it keeps individual customers' records. Information about the crime takes the form of bits and bytes found on the involved parties' computers. However, sophisticated cybercriminals can learn how to manipulate the bits and bytes, making it harder for law enforcement to trace.

The search warrant for the offender's location should list all computers and all forms of computer storage: disks, data CD-ROMs, DVDs, magnetic tapes, external hard drives, mini-drives (sometimes called memory sticks), flash memory modules, programming documentation, e-mail addresses (possible sources of malignant software creation programs), the computer and all its peripherals, and all program CD-ROMs. The search warrant should also include the offender's Internet accounts.

512: Computer Data as the Target

Crimes with the computer data as the target are changing data, replacing data, or creating new data on the computer. Data such as payroll information, credit history, and stock information are typical targets for this crime. This changing, replacing, or creating fraudulent data such as corporate information for stock fraud or false tax returns is usually associated with securities fraud or wire transfers. These types of computer crimes can also be considered under the criminal enterprise classification (530). Other crimes within this classification are software piracy and the theft of intellectual property from the computer. Software piracy or theft of intellectual property not on the computer but on electronic media falls into the theft or larceny classification or under criminal enterprise (530).

Defining Characteristics

VICTIMOLOGY

The victims are computers and the data they contain, especially personal computers, attached to the Internet. Malignant software can be transmitted using the Internet, e-mail and spam, computer disks, CD-ROMs, flash cards, and any other form of computer storage.

COMMON FORENSIC FINDINGS

Changes in computer data can be detected if the data were backed up, that is, copies of the data were stored on another computer, CD-ROM, computer disk, or magnetic tape. If backups are available, a computer program can be used to compare files to determine which data were changed. The changes in data could provide clues to the offender.

Investigative Considerations

The targeted computer should have its hard drive removed and analyzed by special computer software to determine not only the changed data but search for possible Trojan horse software that tests for data checks and then destroys the corrupted data before they can be analyzed.

Search Warrant Suggestions

Research has revealed that offenders often like to keep some type of memento reminding them of their crimes. With regard to cybercrime, there is virtually no difference: offenders still want to keep information about their crime for personal documentation. These items might include photographs, Web sites, e-mails, storage disks, software, and folders. The documentation could contain a list of the victims the perpetrator has assaulted and may have coded descriptions of what was done to each of the victims. Most likely this information is encrypted. Investigators need to take this information to a specialist who can break the code.

The search warrant for the offender's location should list all computers and all forms of computer storage: disks, data CD-ROMs, DVDs, magnetic tapes, external hard drives, mini-drives (sometimes called memory sticks), flash memory modules, programming documentation, e-mail addresses (possible sources of malignant software creation programs), the computer and all its peripherals, and all program CD-ROMs. The search warrant should also include the offender's Internet accounts.

Case Study: 512: Computer Data as the Target

Background and Victimology

Oleg Zezev was accused of trying to steal confidential information belonging to Bloomberg L.P. and its customers. Bloomberg L.P. is a multinational financial data company that provides its customers in the international financial community with timely financial information and trading data through a computer network. Zezev then used that information to threaten Bloomberg's founder, Michael Bloomberg, that if he did not pay him $200,000, he would disclose this information to Bloomberg's customers and the media in an effort to harm Bloomberg's reputation. Zezev was the chief information technology officer at Kazkommerts Securities (Kazkommerts) located in Almaty, Kazakhstan.

Forensic Findings

The e-mail came from an e-mail account at a company called Hotmail that Zezev had registered under a false name. The e-mail was traced back to Kazkommerts Securities, where Zezev worked. After receiving the first e-mail, Bloomberg computer specialists were able to piece together how Zezev had broken in and rewrote the software on the Bloomberg system to prevent him from accessing the system again.

Investigation

In the spring of 1999, Bloomberg provided database services to Kazkommerts. As a result, Kazkommerts was provided with Bloomberg's software to gain access to Bloomberg's services over the Internet. Bloomberg canceled those services in 1999 because Kazkommerts did not pay its bill.

In March 2000, Zezev manipulated Bloomberg's software to bypass Bloomberg's security system in order to gain unauthorized access to Bloomberg's computer system so that he could pose as different legitimate Bloomberg customers and employees. On 11 separate occasions during March 2000, Zezev illegally entered Bloomberg's computer system and accessed various accounts, including Michael Bloomberg's personal account as well as accounts for other Bloomberg employees and customers. Zezev copied information from these accounts, including e-mail inbox screens, Michael Bloomberg's credit card numbers, and screens relating to internal functions of Bloomberg. He also copied internal information from Bloomberg that was accessible only by Bloomberg employees.

According to the evidence at trial on March 24, 2000, Zezev sent Michael Bloomberg an e-mail from Kazakhstan using the alias "Alex," attaching various screens he had copied from Bloomberg's computer system demonstrating his ability to enter the system as any user. He then asked for payment and threatened: "There a lot [sic] of clever but mean heads in the world who will use their chance to destroy your system to the detriment of your worldwide reputation."

Zezev sent an e-mail on April 17 to Bloomberg threatening that if he did not send Zezev $200,000, he would disclose to the media and Bloomberg's customers that he was able to gain unauthorized access to Bloomberg's computer system.

Michael Bloomberg, acting in conjunction with FBI agents, sent Zezev e-mails saying that if Zezev wanted the money, he would have to meet with him and some of Bloomberg's computer specialists in London and explain to them how he was able to break into Bloomberg's computer system.

Zezev traveled from London to meet with Bloomberg. On August 10, 2000, Michael Bloomberg, Tom Secunda, the head of technology at Bloomberg, and a British undercover agent posing as Bloomberg's bodyguard met with Zezev and Yarimaka, an associate of Zezev, in London. The meeting was recorded by undercover videotape. At the meeting, Zezev introduced himself as "Alex." Michael Bloomberg told Zezev that he was extorting his company. Zezev was arrested after the meeting and subsequently extradited from England to the United States to face the charges in the indictment.

Outcome

On February 26, 2003, Zezev was convicted, after a three-and-a half-week jury trial in U.S. District Court, on all counts of a four-count indictment charging him with crimes arising from his scheme to hack into Bloomberg L.P.'s computer system: conspiracy to commit extortion, attempted extortion, sending extortionate threats, and computer intrusion. Zezev was sentenced in Manhattan federal court to over four years in prison.

513: Denial of Service

This crime occurs when a computer service is the target of the offender. Overwhelming an Internet site with many phony requests for service is an example of this type of crime.

Defining Characteristics

VICTIMOLOGY

The victims of this type of crime are the computers used by Internet service providers (ISP) (Google, Yahoo, MSN, and others) and online retail services (such as Wal-Mart and eBay).

COMMON FORENSIC FINDINGS

Service denial is indicated when the targeted site is unable to respond to normal service requests. Computer logs will show many erroneous or trivial requests occurring at the same time from many sites. The offender will have placed Trojan horse software on many computers and triggered an attack at some specific time in the future. The sites chosen for the Trojan horse software typically are college and university computers, which have many users and can be easily hacked because some legitimate users failed to use hard-to-break passwords. Additional service request sites could be personal computers attached to the Internet that have been compromised.

Investigative Considerations

The targeted computers' logs should be analyzed in an attempt to determine the Internet protocol (IP) addresses of the sending computers.

Search Warrant Suggestions

The search warrant for the offender's location should list all computers and all forms of computer storage: disks, data CD-ROMs, DVDs, magnetic tapes, external hard drives, mini-drives (sometimes called memory sticks), flash memory modules, programming documentation, e-mail addresses (possible sources of malignant software creation programs), the computer and all its peripherals, and all program CD-ROMs. The search warrant should also include the offender's Internet accounts.

Case Study: 513: Denial of Service

Background

The offender, Allan Eric Carlson, was a disgruntled Phillies fan (the Phillies were losing games) and took revenge by hacking into computers around the country, hijacking or "spoofing" the return addresses of e-mail accounts of reporters at the *Philadelphia Inquirer* and the *Philadelphia Daily News* and e-mail accounts at the Philadelphia Phillies baseball team, and launching spam e-mail attacks. The indictment charges that when launching the spam e-mails, Carlson's list of addressees included numerous bad addresses. When those e-mails arrived at their destinations, the indictment charges that they were "returned" or "bounced" back to the person who purportedly sent them: the persons whose e-mail addresses had been "spoofed" or hijacked. This caused floods of thousands of e-mails into these accounts in a very short period of time.

Victimology

The victims included reporters at the *Philadelphia Inquirer* and *Philadelphia Daily News* and e-mail accounts at the Philadelphia Phillies baseball team.

Investigation

Using the e-mail addresses of the *Inquirer*, *Daily News*, and the Phillies, the FBI was able to enlist its offices throughout the nation and conduct a thorough investigation. It used trace programs to determine the sources of the denial of service messages to locate the true sender of the spoofed computers. Carlson was charged with 79 counts of computer fraud and identity theft (classification 521) for illegally using the e-mail addresses of the reporters.

Outcome

Carlson was convicted of the 79 counts of computer fraud and identity fraud and was sentenced to four years' imprisonment.

520: The Computer User as the Target

The user can be a target of identity theft, fraud, or stalking. In the first two crimes, the offender is seeking financial gain, and in stalking (sometimes called cyberstalking), the offender is harassing the computer user using the Internet (by e-mail, chat rooms, and instant messaging, for example).

Case Study: 520: The Computer User as the Target

Background and Victimology

Jerome T. Heckenkamp, age 24, of Los Angeles gained unauthorized access to eBay computers during February and March 1999. Using this unauthorized access, he defaced an eBay Web page using the name "MagicFX," and installed a Trojan horse computer program (program containing malicious code masked inside apparently harmless programs) on the eBay computers. He then secretly captured user names and passwords that he later used to gain unauthorized access into other eBay computers.

Heckenkamp had gained unauthorized access to Qualcomm computers in San Diego in late 1999 using a computer from his dorm room at the University of Wisconsin–Madison. Once he gained this unauthorized access, he installed multiple Trojan horse programs that captured user names and passwords that he later used to gain unauthorized access into more Qualcomm computers.

Outcome

Heckenkamp pleaded guilty in federal court to gaining unauthorized access and recklessly damaging computer systems of several high-technology companies. His guilty pleas resulted from felony charges filed against him in both the Northern and Southern Districts of California. On March 13, 2002, a grand jury in the Northern District of California returned a 16-count indictment charging him with computer intrusions, unlawful interception of electronic communications, and witness tampering. On September 5, a grand jury in the Southern District of California returned a 10-count indictment charging him with computer intrusions and unlawful interception of electronic communications. The cases were consolidated in the U.S. District Court for the Northern District of California in March 2003. Under the terms of a plea agreement joined by the U.S. Attorney's Offices for both districts, Heckenkamp pleaded guilty to one count from each of those indictments, each charging unauthorized access into a computer and recklessly causing damage. Heckenkamp also agreed that the court could consider losses from other indicted counts in determining his sentence, including unauthorized access to computer systems of Exodus Communications, Juniper Networks, Lycos, and Cygnus Solutions.

Heckenkamp was sentenced to eight months in prison and eight months of electronic monitoring and home confinement; was ordered to pay restitution to the victim companies in the amount of $268,291; and was ordered to serve a three-year term of supervised release, during which time he would be prohibited from using a computer with Internet access absent approval from a probation officer.

521: Identity Theft

This classification covers crimes where the information needed to accomplish identity theft, such as social security number, credit card, and bank PINs, is obtained from a user's computer using the Internet. This classification does not include identity theft when the personal data are obtained by other means, such as trash or loss of wallet and credit cards.

It is estimated that 25% of state, county, and city Web sites contain Social Security numbers of property owners, government employees, taxpayers, and others. At one time the Pentagon Web site contained the Social Security numbers of high-ranking military officers. This practice was stopped when many of these top-ranking military officers became victims of credit card fraud.

A new type of identity theft by means of the computer is now referred to as phishing. It is the stealing of personal information such as credit cards and bank data from the Internet. This is done by sending an e-mail to a person requesting his or her Social Security number, credit card, or bank account information under the guise of being a legitimate vendor used by this computer user. A good example is the use of bank logos and Web site layout to appear to be a legitimate bank site requesting information to update its online account. The request usually makes it appear to be an urgent matter by stating that if the user does not update the information, his or her online account will be canceled. The typical user responds by quickly providing the information requested. It is estimated that in 2004, some 57 million people were targets of phishing. In June 2004 alone, there were 1,422 phishing attacks. The number of attacks in 2004 increased over those in 2003 by an estimated 1,126%. About 19% of recipients open the e-mail and click the link. About 3 to 5% of recipients divulge the personal financial information.

Defining Characteristics

VICTIMOLOGY

The victims of this type of crime are those who use the computer for online activities such as shopping, banking, and paying bills.

COMMON FORENSIC FINDINGS

Common findings are unauthorized credit card charges, credit card accounts unknown to the victim, unauthorized bank account withdrawals, and addresses on the illegal accounts different from the victim's address.

Investigative Considerations

The victim should register with all credit services to report the possible identity theft. The investigator should trace addresses and the location of erroneous credit card charges and look for possible travel patterns of the offender.

Search Warrant Suggestions

The search warrant for the offender's location should list all computers and all forms of computer storage: disks, data CD-ROMs, DVDs, magnetic tapes, external hard drives, mini-drives (sometimes called memory sticks), flash memory modules, programming documentation, e-mail addresses (possible sources of malignant software creation programs), the computer and all its peripherals, and all program CD-ROMs. The search warrant should also include the offender's Internet accounts.

Case study: 521: Identity Theft

Background and Victimology

From June 18 through June 27, 2003, Van T. Dinh purchased approximately 9,120 put option contracts for the common stock of Cisco Systems at the strike price of $15 per share through his online trading account at Cybertrader.com. Each put contract Dinh purchased gave him the right to sell 100 shares of Cisco common stock at $15 per share, if the share value fell to that price or below, until the contract's expiration, which was set for July 19, 2003. Dinh paid $10 per contract, for a total purchase price of approximately $91,200. If the value of Cisco shares had fallen relatively precipitously during the short period of the life of the contracts, Dinh would have stood to make a large profit—a highly speculative but potentially lucrative gamble.

On July 7, 2003, a member of Stockcharts.com's stock-charting forum, who lived in Westborough, Massachusetts, received a message from an individual named "Stanley Hirsch," who turned out to be Dinh. He responded to the e-mail, thus providing his personal e-mail address to Dinh. On July 8, he received an e-mail sent to his personal e-mail address inviting him to participate in a so-called beta test of a new stock-charting tool. The sender, identified as Tony T. Riechert, provided a link in the e-mail message to enable this potential investor to download a computer program that purported to be the stock-charting application. Tony Riechert was another name that Dinh used in connection with this scheme.

The purported application sent to the potential investor was actually a disguised Trojan horse that contained a series of keystroke-logging programs that enable one Internet user to remotely monitor the keystrokes of another user.

Once the investor had installed the program on his computer, Dinh was able to use the intrusion programs to identify this investor's online TD Waterhouse account and to extract password and log-in information for that account.

By July 10, nine days before the expiration date of Dinh's Cisco options, Cisco's stock was trading at approximately $19 per share, making it likely that Dinh's $15 Cisco put options would be worthless at the time they expired and he would stand to lose the entire $91,200 he had paid to purchase the options. On July 11, Dinh used the password and log-in information for the investor's online account to place a series of buy orders for the Cisco options, depleting almost all of the account's available cash—approximately $46,986. The buy orders for the investor's account were filled with 7,200 Cisco put options sold from Dinh's account. As a result of the execution of these buy orders, Dinh avoided at least $37,000 of losses (some of the $46,986 in funds taken from the investor's account went to commission costs).

Dinh had placed additional purchase orders from the investor's account, which went unfilled only because the investor's account had already been depleted of funds by Dinh.

Outcome

Van T. Dinh pleaded guilty on February 9, 2004, to an eight-count indictment charging him with causing damage in connection with unauthorized access to a protected computer, committing mail and wire fraud, and knowingly executing a scheme and artifice to defraud the investor and others in connection with a security and to obtain by means of false and fraudulent pretenses, money and property in connection with the purchase and sale of a security. He was sentenced to one year and one month in prison, to be followed by three years of supervised release and a $3,000 fine for the unauthorized access to a protected computer and other crimes in connection with his unlawfully accessing a computer belonging to the investor, and using information gained through that intrusion to make unlawful trades with funds in the investor's online brokerage account. In addition, an $800 special assessment was imposed. Prior to sentencing, Dinh paid full restitution to the victim investor in the amount of $46,986, which represented the entire amount of money taken from the investor's account.

522: Invasion of Privacy

This crime involves sending spam or unsolicited sexually explicit material by computer user via the Internet.

Defining Characteristics

VICTIMOLOGY

The victims of this type of crime are the users of the Internet. Pornographic spam is sent to a large number of sites in an attempt to recruit new customers.

COMMON FORENSIC FINDINGS

Pornographic material will be found on the user's computer as well as the address of the sender. In most cases, this address will not be real.

Investigative Considerations

The investigator should try to trace the path through the Internet or sign up for the service and do an online trace.

Search Warrant Suggestions

The investigator can obtain a warrant to the Internet service provider (ISP) to trace the path of the sender of pornographic data. When the location of the sender is determined, the investigator should obtain a search warrant for the offender's location. This search warrant should list all forms of computer storage: disks, data CD-ROMs, DVDs, magnetic tapes, external hard drives, mini-drives (sometimes called memory sticks), flash memory modules, programming documentation, e-mail addresses (possible sources of malignant software creation programs), the computer and all its peripherals, and all program CD-ROMs. The search should look for the pornographic data as well as addresses of customers. Pornographic material at the offender's site should be compared with the pornographic material at the victim's site.

523: Cyberstalking

Cyberstalking is the use of the computer to follow a target of the stalker. Cyberstalking is an extension from the physical form of stalking. Electronic media such as the Internet are used to pursue, harass, or contact another person in an unsolicited fashion. In certain instances, this pursuit can transform into the physical world, where interpersonal violence occurs.

Defining Characteristics

VICTIMOLOGY

Cyberstalking is similar to physical stalking except contact with the victim is with the Internet using e-mail, chat rooms, and instant messaging. The victim is typically female.

COMMON FORENSIC FINDINGS

The victim's computer will have copies of the transmitted messages as well as the address of the sender. The address of the offender may not be his or her real address, and the investigator will have to do online tracing when and if the offender sends additional messages.

Investigative Considerations

The investigator can try to hold the sender online to trace the sender's location.

Search Warrant Suggestions

The investigator can obtain a warrant to trace the path of the sender of the stalking messages. This warrant will be to the ISP. When the location of the sender is determined, the investigator should obtain a search warrant for the offender's location.

The search warrant should list all computers at the offender's location and all forms of computer storage: disks, data CD-ROMs, DVDs, magnetic tapes, external hard drives, mini-drives (sometimes called memory sticks), flash memory modules, programming documentation, e-mail addresses (possible sources of malignant software creation programs), the computer and all its peripherals, and all program CD-ROMs. The search warrant should also include the search for copies of the messages sent previously to the victim.

524: Crimes

The Office of Juvenile Justice and Delinquency Prevention in 1998 began to label online sexual crimes directed toward children as Internet Crimes Against Children (ICAC). ICAC were defined as any computer-facilitated sexual exploitation of children, including online solicitation, 524.1 and child pornography, 524.2 (Office for Victims of Crime, 2001). The terms that law enforcement uses to describe Internet child sex offenders are traders and travelers. Traders are child sex offenders who trade or collect child pornography online (Armagh, Battaglia, & Lanning, 2000; McLaughlin, 2000). Travelers are sex offenders who engage in discussion with children online and use their skills at manipulation and coercion to meet a child in person for sexual purposes (McLaughlin, 2000; Office for Victims of Crime, 2001).

524.1: Online Solicitation of Children

A new dynamic is introduced into the crime when the offender seeks to meet the child in person. At that point, the classification changes to that of a traveler. Traveler cases involve offenders with a wide range of sexual interests. Cases can involve a male adult seeking a male youth. In one case, Anthony Gray, age 31, an Oxford University scholar, was found guilty of two counts of sexual assault (McAuliffe, 2001b). The charges involved a 14-year-old boy he had met in a gay Internet chat room. The jury heard how the theology graduate chatted with the schoolboy on Gay.com more than 20 times after lying about his age. Gray then traveled to meet the 14-year-old and persuaded the boy to spend the night with him at a hotel. The judge ordered that Gray's name be placed on the sex offenders register immediately. The jury took just over two hours to find him guilty. Gray was sentenced to five years in jail for assaulting the boy (Roberts, 2001).

Women too may be travelers. Adriane Ione Smith, age 30, was charged with a third-degree sexual offense and second-degree assault (Kalfrin, 1999a). Police said that Smith met a youth in an Internet chat room and later drove to meet the 15-year-old for a liaison at a hotel. The boy's mother, believing him missing, notified authorities after discovering e-mail messages on her child's computer from Adriane. The mother thought that the e-mail was from another teenager. At the bottom of the message was a phone number, which she called. When a man answered and she asked to speak to his daughter, Adriane, the man replied, "That's not my daughter; that's my wife" (Kalfrin, 1999a, para. 8).

International travelers are very much a part of this crime and will involve the FBI. In one case, a Scottish university lecturer was sentenced to seven years on child sex charges after an FBI sting operation caught him traveling to the United States to have sex with a boy he met over the Internet (McAuliffe, 2001a). David Steinheimer, age 38, used sexually explicit e-mails and pornographic images of himself to coerce a 13-year-old boy into meeting him for the purposes of having sex. He pleaded guilty to six separate charges, including using the Internet to entice an individual under age 18 into sexual activity. In the United States, federal law permits FBI agents to enter chat rooms posing as children in order to identify and arrest pedophiles before any physical assault has taken place. However, to prevent police from entrapping an innocent bystander, officers must prove that the suspect initiated the encounter. In the United Kingdom, "the Police and Criminal Evidence Act prevents sting operations, stating that such methods make police 'agents provocateurs' and evidence gathered in this way is inadmissible" (McAuliffe, 2001a, para. 7).

Intervention may fail. In an international case, Franz Konstantin Baehring, age 35, lured a 14-year-old girl to Greece from her home in Florida (Spencer, 2002). Baehring and the girl spoke on the telephone, sent letters in the mail, and e-mailed each other, even after the girl's mother expressly forbade communication and pleaded with Baehring to stop communicating with her. One day the mother arrived home from work to find that her daughter had disappeared. The mother shared her concerns and intuition with law enforcement, who initially doubted a 14-year-old girl could travel without a passport. Officers found the girl by tracing her messenger screen name to Thessoloniki, Greece. The girl was discovered in Greece and reunited with her mother. Baehring was taken into custody.

Baehring had managed to enlist the help of a cell phone employee by duping her into believing that the girl was a victim who had to be rescued from emotional, physical, and sexual abuse. He also conned the employee into taking the girl to the airport. By enlisting the aid of Robert Arnder, a fellow child sexual predator whom Baehring had met online, he arranged to have the appearance of the 14-year-old girl altered; she could then use a passport belonging to Arnder's 18-year-old daughter, which facilitated her travel to Greece. U.S. authorities found e-mails between the 14-year-old girl and Arnder's daughter on the young girl's computer and called Ohio police. When police arrived, the girl had already traveled to Greece; however, Arnder was arrested after police found child pornography, some relating to the missing girl, from Kon Baehring on his computer. Arnder was later sent to prison for 85 years for child rape in another case. It was found that his daughter had also been a victim of abuse.

Baehring claimed that he helped abused children and that any suggestion that he traded in child pornography was obscene (Spencer, 2002). He also claimed to be a member of sixty-eight organizations that fight child pornography, but a check of some of the groups he named revealed that none of those organizations knew of Baehring. Initially, the 14-year-old girl's mother went to Greece to testify against Baehring; however, the court ruled there could be no trial without the primary witness. Months later, the mother returned to Greece with her daughter to testify during a three-day trial. The girl explained in detail how Baehring sexually abused her, asking that he go to jail for what he did; however, she also said that she still loved him. In his defense, Baehring claimed that the mother had drugged and brainwashed the girl into testifying against him. Baehring was found guilty, but received a sentence of only eight years. Given parole and time off for good behavior, he could be released from prison in three years.

524.2: Child Pornography

In decades past, the dark world of pornography and child pornography could be found underground or in the seedier parts of town at adult bookstores, bordellos, and other outlets. That era is gone. The Internet brings the most taboo sexual subjects into the privacy of one's home or workplace computer. Everything from erotic photos of youngsters to sadomasochistic Web sites to videos of rape and other forms of sexual violence are now only a keystroke away.

There are pictures available of children five or six years old who are naked, with their hands tied in front of or behind them or with belts tied around their ankles and hanging upside down from the ceiling, with adults doing unspeakable things to these children in still photos and in online videos. By the mid-1990s, the Internet had an estimated 5,000 worldwide child porn sites. Those who create and transmit these images are clever in their ability to hide where the pictures originated and how they were being sent to individuals around the world. A digital photo being e-mailed from, say, Detroit to Los Angeles can be routed through Sweden, Japan, and Turkey before reaching California. Those who know their way around the Internet can make this kind of trafficking in child pornography almost impossible to track.

The Internet has created other problems as well. In the past, pedophilia was viewed as perhaps the greatest taboo in modern society. People engaged in it usually had to pursue this activity alone and had to keep it extremely secret. The Net now offers support groups for those interested in molesting children. These sites not only encourage such predators but also advise them on how to lure children away from parents and on the best techniques to seduce children without getting caught. An entirely new criminal realm has exploded across the face of the globe and with no boundaries.

Inevitably scandals began to erupt. In 1996 in Belgium, several children connected to a pornographic ring were murdered. The next year, another scandal was uncovered in Spain, and that same year 250 people were arrested in France for selling or possessing videotapes of small children being raped and tortured. In 1998, the Dutch police found a group of child pornographers in Zandvoort who were selling images of children on the Internet to buyers in Europe, Great Britain, Russia, Israel, and the United States. These images shocked even the most hardened investigators of child pornography.

The federal legal definition of child pornography, found at 18 U.S.C. § 2256 (8), has been updated numerous times and now includes images of real children engaging in sexually explicit conduct and computer-generated depictions indistinguishable from real children engaging in such acts. Indistinguishable was further defined as that which an ordinary person viewing the image would conclude is a real child engaging in sexually explicit acts (Office of the Law Revision Counsel, 2009).

Child pornography crimes fall into three subcategories, possession, distribution, and production. Offenders may be charged with possession of child pornography, or distribution of child pornography, or production of child pornography or any combination of the three categories.

524.2.1: Possession of Child Pornography

Definition: Possessing material involving the sexual exploitation of a minor with intent to traffic; possessing material involving the sexual exploitation of a minor.

Defining Characteristics

VICTIMOLOGY

The victims are the children in the photos and when these children are identified by the National Center for Missing and Exploited Children their victim statements are used in sentencing the offender.

Common Forensic Findings

Pornography will be found on all or a combination of the offenders computer(s), CD-ROMs, DVDs, backup hard drives, and all other forms of digital media.

Investigative Considerations

When the search warrant is executed use standard procedures for seizing the computer. Do not turn it off or on, unplug desktops, and remove batteries from laptops. Remove all other parts from the computer in the laboratory.

Case Study: 524.2.1: Possession of Child Pornography

The case of Patrick Daniels, a 34-year-old psychologist who worked almost exclusively with children, was believed to be the first person in Canada to go to trial on charges of importing and possessing child pornography acquired through the Internet. He was found guilty after an intensive investigation that began in the spring of 1995 and involved Canadian, U.S., and Mexican authorities. He was sentenced to 30 days of house arrest because the judge said he presented no danger to the public.

524.2.2: Distribution of Child Pornography

Definition: Trafficking material involving the sexual exploitation of a minor; receiving, transporting, shipping, soliciting, or advertising material involving the sexual exploitation of a minor.

Defining Characteristics

Victimology

As with possessions, the victims are the children in the photos, and when these children are identified by the National Center for Missing and Exploited Children, their victim statements are used in sentencing the offender.

Common Forensic Findings

Pornography will be found on all or a combination of the offenders computer(s), CD-ROMs, DVDs, backup hard drives, and all other forms of digital media. Search of the offender's computer should yield a list of customers and sources for child pornography.

Investigative Considerations

Same as possession of 524.1 Child Pornography.

Case Study: 524.2.2: Distribution of Child Pornography

Nathaniel Levy, age 21, a psychology major who wanted to be a kindergarten teacher, was arrested at his dorm for promoting sexual performance of a child, a felony punishable by seven years in prison. The student transmitted 35 sexually explicit photos of children, some of them as young as 18 months, over the Internet. Levy was caught after undercover investigators asked him via the Internet to send them photos in exchange for a videotape. Once investigators received the photos, they agreed to meet Levy at his dorm room, where he was arrested. Levy, whose computer name was "NateTSnake," pleaded guilty to charges of possessing child pornography and was sentenced to five years ("Child Porn Seeker," 1997).

524.2.3: Production of Child Pornography

Definition: Sexually exploiting a minor by production of sexually explicit visual or printed material; custodian permitting minor to engage in sexually explicit conduct; advertisement for minors to engage in production.

Defining Characteristics

VICTIMOLOGY

The children used in the productions produced by the offender. These children may even be the children of the offender. These offenders will be also charged with other offenses against children.

COMMON FORENSIC FINDINGS

The studio used to produce the pornography will contain the staging material used in the pornography. There should be the master used to create copies for distribution. Pornography will be found on all or a combination of the offenders computer(s), CD-ROMs, DVDs, backup hard drives, and all other forms of digital media. Search of the offender's computer should yield a list of customers and sources for child pornography.

Investigative Considerations

In addition to the investigative considerations for possession of child pornography the investigator need to seek out the identity of the children used in production.

Case Study: 524.2.2: Production of Child Pornography

Heidi Wischniwsky, age 32, a technical writer for an information technology company, was charged with possessing and making child pornography (Bell, 1997). It is believed that she was the first woman in Canada to be charged in connection with child pornography on the Internet. Wischniwsky was fired from her place of employment after a coworker discovered pornographic material on an office computer. The company reported the incident to the police, who confiscated the computer and numerous files stored on floppy disks. The investigator in charge confirmed that some of the pictures featured children as young as three or four years old.

530: Criminal Enterprise

Criminal enterprise is now performing white-collar crime, money laundering with a computer, wire fraud, child pornography, and other types of fraud using a computer.

White-Collar Crime

Check-kiting scams have been growing on the Internet. A popular one throughout the Midwest involved people going through the Yellow Pages and scanning logos from well-known corporations. Then they added that logo to a phony check they had created through the Net. Next, they wrote a payroll check to themselves and cashed it at a local convenience store. A group of con artists would do this quickly in one major city, cashing a lot of checks at different locations, before leaving town. In one day, the criminals could easily cash $10,000 worth of checks. The method worked well because most convenience store employees would not think of refusing to cash a check with a logo from a Fortune 500 company.

Not all of the financial action on the Net was confined to local scams and small players. In the spring of 2000, the U.S. Attorney's Office in New York City filed charges against 120 persons, including several prominent members of organized-crime families, who were charged with allegedly swindling stock market investors out of more than $50 million. Among those named were Anthony Stropoli and Frank Persico, reputed associates of the Columbo crime family, and Robert Lino, an alleged capo in the Bonanno crime family. According to the authorities, the suspects used phony press releases to falsely hype certain stocks over the Internet in order to boost the price of securities that they already owned. As soon as the stocks inflated, the people generating the false information sold their securities and left other investors with shares that were basically worthless.

Case Study: 530: Criminal Enterprise

Background

Alexey V. Ivanov, of Chelyabinsk, Russia, was indicted with eight counts of wire fraud, two counts of extortion, four counts of unauthorized computer intrusions, and one count of possessing user names and passwords for an online bank. The charges stemmed from the activities of Ivanov, age 23, and others who operated from Russia and hacked into dozens of computers throughout the United States, stealing user names, passwords, credit card information, and other financial data and then extorting the victims with the threat of deleting their data and destroying their computer systems.

Investigation

All of the victim companies fully cooperated with the FBI during the investigation. Ivanov and his partner, 25-year-old Vasili Gorchkov, were arrested in Seattle after traveling to the United States during an investigation by the FBI. Ivanov and Gorchkov, who is awaiting trial on similar charges in Seattle, came to the United States for what he thought was a job interview with Seattle-based computer security company called Invita. In fact, Invita was an undercover FBI company that allowed investigators to obtain the evidence needed to charge the two Russians.

Outcome

Ivanov was sentenced to a term of imprisonment of 48 months, to be followed by three years of supervised release. He had previously pleaded guilty and admitted to numerous charges of conspiracy, computer intrusion, computer fraud, credit card fraud, wire fraud, and extortion. In sentencing Ivanov, the district judge described his participation as a "manager or supervisor" in an "unprecedented, wide-ranging, organized criminal enterprise" that "engaged in numerous acts of fraud, extortion, and intentional damage to the property of others, involving the sophisticated manipulation of computer data, financial information, and credit card numbers." The district judge found that Ivanov was responsible for an aggregate loss of approximately $25 million.

531: Money Laundering

Money laundering is a crime used to make illegal funds appear to be legal. An example was a programmer who was paid to modify code in banking programs to ignore banking regulations to alert the FBI for transactions in excess of ten thousand dollars for organized crime accounts. Another money-laundering scheme was creating programs to generate false revenues for crime-controlled businesses.

Defining Characteristics

VICTIMOLOGY

The victims are public and government tax agencies.

COMMON FORENSIC FINDINGS

In money laundering, false revenue will be generated by computer programs or user entry. The actual revenue will also be on the computer because the offenders need to know how much money was laundered.

Investigative Considerations

The investigator needs to determine the amount of legitimate revenue; the excess is laundered money. In one case where a restaurant was used to launder money, the real revenue was determined by counting the linen napkins to determine the number of meals served. This was then compared to the number of computer-generated meals.

Search Warrant Suggestions

The search warrant should include all computers, computer-related storage, computer programs, and Internet accounts. The computers should be searched for multiple sets of financial transactions, which will be encrypted. Printed copies of the transactions should also be requested.

532: Child Pornography

Now found under 524, Crimes Against Children.

533: Internet Fraud

Criminals use the computer to create credit card fraud, bank account fraud, and even counterfeit passports.

Case Study: 533: Internet Fraud

Background and Victimology

The offenders attempted to steal more than $10 million in computer equipment from Ingram Micro, a large electronics distributor in Santa Ana, California.

Forensic Findings

The offenders were a group of six men led by Calin Mateias who was located in Romania; the others were located in the United States. Mateias began hacking into Ingram Micro's online ordering system in 1999. Using information obtained from his illegal hacking activity, Mateias bypassed Ingram's online security safeguards, posed as a legitimate customer, and ordered computer equipment to be sent to Romania. When Ingram Micro blocked all shipments to Romania in early 1999, Mateias recruited Olufemi Tinubu, Valeriu Crisovan, Jeremy Long, and Warren Bailey from Internet chat rooms to provide him with U.S. addresses to use as mail drops for the fraudulently ordered equipment. Crisovan, Tinubu, Finley, and Long recruited others, including high school students, to provide additional addresses and to accept the stolen merchandise. The defendants in the United States would either sell the equipment and send the proceeds to Mateias, or they would repackage the equipment and send it to Romania.

Mateias and his co-conspirators allegedly fraudulently ordered more than $10 million in computer equipment from Ingram Micro. However, Ingram Micro was successful in intercepting nearly half the orders before the items were shipped.

Investigation

Ingram Micro became suspicious of orders from clients that were not consistent with their previous orders. The FBI, working with Romanian law enforcement, was able to trace the fraudulent orders to Mateias.

Outcome

All six defendants were charged with conspiring to commit mail fraud by causing Ingram Micro to ship computer equipment based on the false pretenses that the equipment was ordered by legitimate customers. In addition, Mateias, Tinubu, Finley, Crisovan, and Long were charged with mail fraud.

Case Study: 533: Internet Fraud

Background

Juju Jiang, operating from his home in Flushing, New York, and using a computer program designed to record computer passwords and user names, attempted to gain access to the computer accounts of approximately 15 subscribers of GoToMyPC, a company that offers individuals the ability to remotely access their personal computers from any computer connected to the Internet. Jiang obtained these users' passwords and user names by installing computer software for this purpose at a Kinko's in Manhattan. He then used these passwords and user names in attempts to gain access to those subscribers' personal computers in order to obtain credit card and other information stored on those computers.

Victimology

Jiang's alleged fraud came to the light after a subscriber of GoToMyPC, who was at home, heard his personal computer turn on without any action on the subscriber's part and then observed the cursor of the PC move around the screen and files on the PC being accessed and opened as if by remote control. Afterward, he observed his computer access a Web site known as www.neteller.com, an online payment transfer service, and observed an account in his name being opened at Neteller, without his authorization.

A short time later, the victim observed his computer accessing the Web site for the American Express Corporate card and, using information stored on his computer, saw his computer attempt to access his card account file. The victim then manually regained control of his PC, terminated the computer session, and contacted officials of Neteller in order to direct them to close the unauthorized Neteller account that had been opened in his name.

Investigation

Federal authorities, with logs of GoToMyPC used on the victim's computer, traced the attacking computer by its IP address, first to the company providing it cable modem service and then to a specific Queens address. With GoToMyPC's help, federal agents found that at least nine other customer accounts had been used by the same suspicious computer.

The agents obtained a search warrant and went to Jiang's home. Four desktops and a laptop whirred in his bedroom, and according to court documents, telltale signs of digital subterfuge were scattered about the room: sticky notes containing bank account numbers, Kinko's credit card receipts, and books and manuals on hacking.

Outcome

Jiang was arrested on charges of computer fraud for attempting to gain access to the accounts of numerous subscribers of GoToMyPC.com. He was sentenced to 27 months' imprisonment, 3 years of supervised release, and $201,620 in restitution.

533.01: Bank Fraud

This crime occurs when money is illegally obtained from one bank account and transferred electronically to another account that is usually in another bank and typically another country. Access to the targeted bank is via the Internet. Wireless connections to the Internet are used to commit crimes, where it is difficult to identify the user.

Investigative Considerations

The targeted computer should have its hard drive removed and analyzed by special computer software not only to determine the changed data but to search for possible Trojan horse software that tests for data checks and then destroys the corrupted data before they can be analyzed. All computer logs should be analyzed for suspicious activities, and all Internet activity should be searched for illegal access and messages.

Search Warrant Suggestions

The search warrant for the offender's location should list all computers and all forms of computer storage: disks, data CD-ROMs, DVDs, magnetic tapes, external hard drives, mini-drives (sometimes called memory sticks), flash memory modules, programming documentation, e-mail addresses (possible sources of malignant software creation programs), the computer and all its peripherals, and all program CD-ROMs. The search warrant should also include the offender's Internet accounts.

533.02: Fraudulent Internet Transactions

This crime occurs when a buyer purchases goods at an Internet auction and sends money but never receives the goods purchased.

Another type of fraudulent Internet transaction is Web site fraud, also called shopping cart fraud. This crime involves the creation of a URL similar to a legitimate site, and the unsuspecting user is apprised of large savings on the purchase of hard-to-obtain products. Accessing any one of the erroneous Web sites can lead to fraud.

Cybercriminals are not confined by state borders. Equipped with just a computer, a cybercriminal can use the Internet to commit a variety of crimes, from violent crimes to crimes against e-commerce.

540: Threats via the Internet

Defining Characteristics

This crime occurs when a computer user is threatened over the Internet. Threats can be delivered by e-mail, instant messaging, and spam.

VICTIMOLOGY

The computer user can be threatened with bodily harm, family and friends can be threatened with bodily harm, or the user's business can be threatened with destruction.

Common Forensic Findings

The computer of the targeted user will have logs and copies of the threatening messages. The offender's computer should also have copies of the threats, as well as the user's computer addresses, e-mail, and IP.

Investigative Considerations

The targeted computers' logs should be analyzed in an attempt to determine the IP addresses of the sending computers.

Search Warrant Suggestions

The search warrant for the offender's location should list all computers and all forms of computer storage: disks, data CD-ROMs, DVDs, magnetic tapes, external hard drives, mini-drives (sometimes called memory sticks), flash memory modules, programming documentation, e-mail addresses (possible sources of malignant software creation programs), the computer and all its peripherals, and all program CD-ROMs. The search warrant should also include the offender's Internet accounts.

Case Study: 540: Threats via the Internet

Background

A Massachusetts juvenile committed a series of hacking incidents into Internet and telephone service providers; the theft of an individual's personal information and the posting of it on the Internet; and making bomb threats to high schools in Florida and Massachusetts. All took place over a 15-month period.

Victimology

The victims were a Florida school, a major telephone service provider, a school in Massachusetts, and local emergency services, requiring the response of several emergency response units to the school. The victims suffered approximately $1 million in damages.

Investigation

The offender's criminal conduct began in March 2004 when he sent a bomb threat to a Florida school. As a result of this threat, the school was closed for two days, while a bomb squad, a canine team, the fire department, and emergency medical services were called in.

In August, he logged into the Internet computer system of a major Internet service provider (ISP) using a program he had installed on an employee's computer. This program allowed the juvenile to use the employee's computer remotely to access other computers on the internal network of the ISP and gain access to portions of the ISP's operational information.

In January 2005, the juvenile gained access to the internal computer system of a major telephone service provider that allowed him to look up account information of the provider's customers. He used this system to discover key information about an individual who had an account with the telephone service. He accessed the information stored on this individual's mobile telephone and posted the information on the Internet. During this same period, the juvenile used his access to the telephone company's computer system to set up numerous telephone accounts for himself and his friends, without having to pay for the accounts.

Also in January 2005, an associate of the juvenile set up accounts for the juvenile at a company that stores identity information concerning millions of individuals, allowing the juvenile to look at the identity information for numerous individuals, some of which he used for the purpose of looking up the account information for the victim whose personal information he posted on the Internet.

In the spring of 2005, the juvenile, using a portable wireless Internet access device, arranged with one or more associates to place a bomb threat to a school in Massachusetts and local emergency services, requiring the response of several emergency response units to the school on two occasions and the school's evacuation on one.

In June 2005, the juvenile called a second major telephone service provider because a phone that a friend had fraudulently activated had been shut off. In a recorded telephone call, he threatened that if the provider did not provide him access to its computer system, he would cause its Web service to collapse through a denial-of-service attack—that is, an attack designed to ensure that a Web site is so flooded with requests for information that legitimate users cannot access it. The provider refused to provide the requested access. Approximately 10 minutes after the threat was made, the juvenile and others initiated a denial of service attack (classification 513) that succeeded in shutting down a significant portion of the telephone service provider's Web operations.

Investigation

The targeted computers' logs were analyzed, and the IP addresses of the sending computers were identified. Once the real Internet address was determined, agents went to the offender's home, arrested him, and executed the search warrant.

Outcome

In a sealed court proceeding, the Massachusetts teenager pleaded guilty in U.S. District Court to an indictment charging him with nine counts of juvenile delinquency. The court imposed a sentence of 11 months' detention in a juvenile facility, to be followed by 2 years of supervised release. During his periods of detention and supervised release, the juvenile was barred from possessing or using any computer, cell phone, or other electronic equipment capable of accessing the Internet.

541: Internet-Initiated Homicide

The Internet has become a new place for criminals to find unsuspecting victims. It has made the search easier than ever before. With just a touch of a key, subjects can enter a special-interest chat room, for example, a sadomasochistic chat room, and have potential victims at their disposal. Most often subjects have used the Internet to convince and lure individuals to meet them in person. Those who step over from the imaginary world of the Internet into the real world are putting themselves in a highly risky situation. An August 2002 *Washington Times* article reports how one jewelry dealer, Rick Chance, met a woman online and planned a meeting at a hotel where he would present her and an interested friend an estimated $1 million worth of jewelry. He was found dead the next day with a bullet in his chest and the jewelry and woman gone. In this case, the woman not only used violence, but also there was a criminal enterprise aspect with regard to the jewelry that was taken and the murder.

Unsuspecting victims may advertise on various Web sites. For example, Wikipedia notes that Craigslist Killer is a name given by the media to individuals who were accused of murdering their victims after meeting the victims through Craigslist, a popular classified advertising Web site. The name has been applied to:

- Michael John Anderson, former resident of Savage, Minnesota, who was convicted in 2009 of having murdered Katherine Ann Olson in October 2007.
- Philip Markoff (1986–2010), American medical student who was charged with the murder of Julissa Brisman in Boston, Massachusetts, in 2009.
- Long Island Serial Killer (*Craigslist Ripper*), an unidentified serial killer suspected of using Craigslist to find and murder at least four prostitutes in Long Island, New York.
- John Katehis murdered ABC radio news reporter George Weber in Brooklyn. The two had met via Craigslist; Weber was found bound and stabbed 50 times.

One of the cases, Philip Markoff, is the case study.

Case Study: 542: Internet-initiated Homicide

Case Contributed by Michelle Gaglia

Background

Philip Markoff was a second son raised with his brother by his mother and stepfather. He graduated from high school in 2004 where he had been elected into the National Honor Society and was a member of the history club, the Youth Court and played on the school bowling and golf teams. He graduated from SUNY-Albany in 2007 as a premedical student and was in his second year at Boston University School of Medicine at the time of his arrest on April 20, 2009. He was engaged to a premedical student, and they planned to be married August 14, 2009.

Victimology

Trisha Leffler, Markoff's first victim, was a 29-year-old traveling escort from Las Vegas, Nevada. After finding her listing in the "exotic services" section of Craigslist, he agreed to meet her for $200 per hour.

Julissa Brisman, Markoff's second victim, was a 25-year-old aspiring model from New York City. She advertised her massage services in the "exotic services" section of Craigslist. Julissa had been described as a former "party girl" who was successfully cleaning up her image and quitting drinking. In an attempt to make money, she began offering "sensual/exotic massages."

Corinne Stout, Markoff's third and last victim, was a stripper from Las Vegas who advertised private lap dances on the "exotic services" section of Craigslist.

Crime Scene Indicators

On Friday April 10, 2009, Markoff met Leffler at the Westin Coply Place Hotel in Boston. He drew a gun on her, forced her to the ground, put on black leather gloves, and restrained her with zip ties. He removed his phone number from her cell phone and stole her credit cards, debit cards, and $800 in cash. He cut phone lines in the hotel room, tied Leffler to the bathroom doorknob, and taped her mouth. Before leaving, he took a pair of Leffler's underwear and put them in his pocket.

On Tuesday, April 14, 2009, Markoff met Brisman at the Copley Marriott in Boston. After attempting to defend herself, Brisman was struck in the head with the gun and shot three times in the chest. Markoff had succeeded in getting one zip tie on her before shooting her. Brisman was pronounced dead at Boston Medical Center.

On Thursday, April 16, 2009, Markoff met Stout at a Holiday Inn Express in Warwick, Rhode Island. Markoff attempted to rob Stout at gunpoint. Using the same kind of zip ties as in the previous two incidents, he restrained her and left her lying on the floor. When Stout's husband returned to the hotel room, Markoff fled.

Forensic Findings

Although Markoff put leather gloves on when restraining Leffler, he removed them to delete her phone number from her cell phone, leaving fingerprints. He also failed to wear gloves when placing tape over Leffler's mouth. Additionally, several hotel surveillance cameras were able to capture his image. Leffler was able to provide a positive identification of Philip Markoff. A friend of Brisman was also able to find an e-mail from Markoff arranging to meet with Brisman. Using the IP address, police were able to trace the e-mail to Markoff's apartment in Quinsey, Massachusetts.

In February, Markoff had used a fake ID to buy a gun in New Hampshire. After searching Markoff's apartment, police found a stash of underwear taken from his victims and a gun hidden inside a hollowed-out *Grey's Anatomy*. There was a match between the gun found and the bullets used to kill Julissa Brisman.

Investigation

Markoff presented himself in the image of a perfect member of society. He was bright, attractive, and a medical school student. He was engaged to a young woman he had been dating since college.

After searching his laptop, investigators learned that Markoff had been interested in "sexually adventurous" Web sites and had expressed himself as interested in experimenting with transvestites and serving as a submissive partner. He listed chains, collars, and leashes as his interests. This suggests Markoff was leading a double life. Online, he was one thing—SexAddict5385—trolling for anonymous encounters. Offline, he was Philip Markoff, slightly awkward, nerdy med school student, engaged to be married to Megan McAllister. For some people, the ability to apparently disappear into the online world, take on another identity altogether, is merely intriguing. But Philip's was a textbook case of the double life. Dr. Jekyll, medical man, interested in saving lives meet Hyde, the lurking killer. Oscar Wilde described the peculiar allure of a secret life as feasting with tigers. The danger is part of its appeal (Petri, 2011).

Outcome

Philip Markoff committed suicide on August 15, 2010, in Boston's Nashua Street jail one day after what would have been his one-year wedding anniversary. He had made three prior suicide attempts. This successful attempt was by self-inflicted wounds using a sharp blade to slash his wrists and cut the femoral artery in his leg. He then wrapped a garbage bag over his head and stuffed toilet paper in his throat. Before dying, he surrounded himself with pictures of McAllister and wrote "Megan" and "Pocket" in his own blood above the door of his jail cell. Cause of death was suffocation.

Markoff had been indicted for the first-degree murder of Brisman and kidnapping and armed robbery of Leffler. Although Markoff pleaded not guilty, it is theorized that he committed suicide to spare his ex-fiancee the shame of testifying at his trial.

543: Cybergangs

The Internet has organized cybergangs that roam the darkest recesses of the Internet. The gangs are so technically proficient that they can reach into another's computer and swipe his or her password, home address, and telephone number. They can steal financial records and sabotage the files on anyone's hard drive, destroying everything that has been created and stored. As soon as these gangs were found to be operating in the online world, software companies began building firewalls to keep them out. Each time one of these firewalls—which shut down the computer portals that allow new information—are cracked by a hacker, new barriers are generated to become more impenetrable. It is a game of one set of technology masters taking on the other, with the side of prevention sometimes winning and sometimes taking a loss. Everything about the Internet is a competition to expand the boundaries of what is possible.

The more advanced cybercrime organizations give smaller, more isolated tasks to separate groups of people spread around the world and the Internet. Thus, a particular group only performs one function and likely only knows information about its own role in the crime activity. This type of cybergang crime is different from the hit-and-run fraud perpetrated by earlier identity thieves, in which the same person or group would typically be responsible for the fraud process from beginning to end.

Case Study: 543: Cybergang Banking Heist

A coordinated cybercriminal network pulled off one of the largest and most complex banking heists ever, withdrawing $13 million in one day from ATMs in six countries. The massive breach hit Fidelity National Information Services Inc. (FIS), a Jacksonville, Florida–based firm that processes prepaid debit cards discovered the breach on May 5, 2011 (Liebowitz, 2011).

The attackers first broke into FIS's network and gained unauthorized access to the company's database, where each debit card customer's balances are stored. FIS prepaid debit cards include a fraud protection policy that limits the amount cardholders can withdraw from an ATM with a 24-hour period. Furthermore, once the balance on the cards is reached, the cards cannot be used until their owners put more money back onto the cards.

The criminals obtained 22 legitimate cards, eliminated each card's withdrawal limit, and cloned them, sending copies to conspirators in Greece, Russia, Spain, Sweden, Ukraine, and the United Kingdom. When the prepaid limit on each card got too low, the hackers simply reloaded the fraudulent cards remotely. At the close of the business day on Saturday, March 5, the criminals began taking out money from ATMs. By Sunday evening, the scam was over, and the attackers had stolen $13 million.

References

Armagh, D. S., Battaglia, N. L., & Lanning, K. V. (2000). *Use of computers in the sexual exploitation of children* (Portable Guide No. NCJ 170021). Washington, DC: U.S. Department of Justice.

Bell, M. (1997, February). *Local woman charged in child pornography case.* Retrieved June 15, 1999, from http://www.monitor.ca/monitor/issues/vol4iss7/fidocop.html#7

"Child Porn Seeker," The Buffalo News (Buffalo, NY) July 2, 1997.

Kalfrin, V. (1999a, January 1). Adult woman arrested for sex with boy: Relationship began on Internet. Retrieved August 30, 1999, from http://www.apbnews.com/newscenter/breakingnews/1999/01/01/kidsex0101_01.html

Kalfrin, V. (1999b, February 12). Molester accused of seeking sex via library computer: Ex-con went online in search of underage victims, cops say. Retrieved August 30, 1999, from http://www.apbnews.com

Liebowitz, M. (2011). How a cyber crime gang steals $13 million in one day. *Security News Daily*. Retrieved August 24, 2012, from www.msnbc.msn.com/id/44291945/ns/technology_and_science-security/t/how-cyber-crime-gang-stole-million-day/

McAuliffe, W. (2001a, March 12). FBI nets Scottish Web paedophile. Retrieved October 3, 2002, from http://news.zdnet.co.uk

McAuliffe, W. (2001b, February 21). Oxford scholar used Net to lure schoolboy. Retrieved October 3, 2002, from http://news.zdnet.co.uk

McLaughlin, J. F. (2000). *Cyber child sex offender typology*. Retrieved August 8, 2000, from http://www.ci.keene.nh.us/police/Typology.html

Office of the Law Revision Counsel. (2009). *Child pornography*. Retrieved March 8, 2010, from http://uscode.house.gov/uscode-cgi/fastweb.exe?getdoc+uscview+t17t20+1029+39++%28child%20pornography%29%20%20%20%20%20%20%20%20%20%20%20

Office for Victims of Crime. (2001). OVC bulletin: Internet crimes against children. Washington, DC: U.S. Department of Justice, Office of Justice Programs.

Petri, A. (2011). *Why the Craigslist killer matters*. ComPost. Retrieved August 24, 2012, from http://voices.washingtonpost.com/compost/2011/01/why_the_craigslist_killer_matt.html www.ojp.usdoj.gov/ovc/publications/

Roberts, P. (2001, April 6). "Chatroom sex" controls urged. Retrieved October 22, 2002, from http://news.bbc.co.uk/1/hi/uk/wales/1262298.stm

Spencer, S. (2002). Web of seduction. CBS 48 Hours. Retrieved on February 21, 2013, from http://www.cbsnews.com/8301-18559_162-625934.html

Chapter 15

Increased Globalization of Crime

Stefan R. Treffers

600: Global crimes
601: Illegal migration
  601.01: Autonomous migrant
    entries
  601.01: Human trafficking &
    smuggling
    601.01.01: Trafficking
      migrants
    601.01.02: Human
      smuggling
  601.02: Visa overstayer
602: Cross-border organized crime
  602.01: Cigarette smuggling
  602.02: Cross-border smuggling
    of weapons

602.03: Trafficking of narcotics
603: Biological attacks and
  bioterrorism
  603.01: Biological attacks
604: Chemical attacks and
  terrorism
  604.01: Chemical attacks
605: Hostage taking
606: Bombings and explosive
  attacks and terrorism
  606.01: Explosive attacks and
    terrorism
607: Aerial hijackings

600: Global Crimes

Globalization has played an important role in the advancement of technology and the global expansion of trade, which has been facilitated by reduction in costs of transportation and communication. Increasing global connectivity has allowed for the unabated transfer of goods, services, and knowledge with a communal goal of prosperity (Viano, 2010). However, global capitalism has created shifts in labor opportunities leaving some groups economically vulnerable in the midst of increasing inequalities and levels of deprivation that deny individuals of basic necessities. In attempt to establish a new life, these marginalized populations seek migration to developed countries that, at the

431

same time, have implemented increasingly limiting migration and settlement policies (Aas, 2007). Migrants are forced to engage in illegal migration through clandestine crossings, smuggling services, or even trafficking groups.

Mechanisms of globalization have also allowed groups involved in illegal activities to enjoy the benefits of technological innovations, advances in telecommunication, and increased mobility. Organized crime groups have been able to emulate market mechanisms by forming alliances and networks, laundering capital, investing into research and development, adopting modern accounting systems, using global information networks, and protecting themselves against risk (Mittelman & Johnston, 1999). These groups have also taken advantage of trends towards deterritorialization where borders are contested and law enforcement agencies overlap in jurisdiction. Furthermore, increased trade under agreements such as the North American Free Trade Agreement (NAFTA) have allowed for the movement of concealed drugs, weapons, and other licit and illicit products to cross borders uninspected.

Globalization has expanded international travel, increasing the country's vulnerability to terrorist attacks. Increased communications have allowed terrorists to develop large networks, which facilitate recruitment and funding. The development of new technologies has provided terrorists with an arsenal of different weapons, explosive devices, surveillance equipment, and chemical and biological warfare agents. Globalization has also played a political relevance in issues of terrorism. Nassar (2009) claims that, "The World Trade Center buildings symbolized global capitalism under American leadership" and "The Pentagon symbolized American power and its global reach." Counter-terrorism strategies have also become globalized where nations have increased cooperation and knowledge sharing in combating terrorist activity.

601: Illegal Migration

601.01: Autonomous Migrant Entries

Mexican clandestine crossings in the South Texas Corridor during 2000 to 2003 give a good representation of the sociodemographic profile of migrants who choose to cross the border without the use of coyotes or other smuggling services. These crossings usually occur between legal entry points where migrants can avoid border patrol. According to the Enceusta sobre Migracion en la Frontera Norte de Mexico (EMIF), 95% of crossers were men who were married and were the heads of their household in Mexico; 90% were under the age of 40 and a large majority had dropped out of the Mexican equivalent of U.S. high school (Spener, 2009). Motivated by economic opportunities in the United States, it appears that many border-crossers were employed in low-paying, manual occupations such as agriculture or construction. Migrants returning from the United States revealed that the same type of work in Texas earned them up to six times the income they earned in Mexico (Spener, 2009).

Although, this form of border crossing may be underestimated for women, other data sources confirm that during this time period, most clandestine crossings were undertaken by men. Spener (2009) suggests that men and women have different migratory patterns where women are more likely than men to enter the United States legally or to use fake or rented documents to enter legal entry points. In addition, he suggests that women are more likely to make "one-time-only" moves to the United States (Spener, 2009).

Migrants crossing the border commonly traveled in small groups led by an older, more experienced migrant who had previously travelled specific paths across the border. Migrants gathered supplies such as food, minimal clothing, light blankets, and plastic tarps for sleeping. Crossing the border to South Texas involved the crossing of the Rio Grande where many migrants drowned; emphasizing the inherent danger in clandestine crossings by land. To cross the river, migrants looked for either a shallow crossing, used a boat, or swam across the river at night using inner tubes of tires and stashing clothes in plastic bags to keep them dry. Upon crossing the river, the more difficult task of evading and passing immigration checkpoints involved crossing the desert-like Texan brush lands. These checkpoints were located within the United States interior beyond the legal point of entries. Some migrants relied on relatives, friends, or paid acquaintances to pick them up and drive them out of the border region; a task which put the driver in danger of apprehension and severe consequences. With the implementation of Operation Rio Grande, which increased enforcement in the area surrounding the river, the task of crossing through the region became increasingly difficult. In addition, the Illegal Immigration Reform and Immigrant Responsibility Act instituted harsher penalties, intensified surveillance, and increased tools to battle clandestine crossings along the entire U.S.–Mexican border creating an increased reliance on coyotes to aid in illegal entries into the United States from Mexico (Spener, 2009).

601.01: Human Trafficking

The success of developed industrial economies has historically relied on large movements of migrant labor forces. The demand for migrant labor has remained strong in developed countries like the United States acting as a "pull" factor for migration (Aas, 2007). In addition, many migrants from third world countries dream of a better life and the opportunity to participate in a consumer lifestyle glamorized by Western media and culture. However many of these developed countries have recently placed limits on migration and settlement resulting in increased illegal immigration. Furthermore, border controls of the developed world have intensified forcing third world migrants to choose more dangerous routes. These routes frequently involve trafficking networks, which often deceive and exploit those desperate enough to invest their money and trust in hopes of starting a new life in another country. An important distinction must be made between *human smuggling* and *human trafficking*, terms that are often believed to be synonymous. Human smuggling "refers to cases where migrants enter a transaction with full consent and are free to leave at the end of the process" (Aas, 2007). Whereas human trafficking may involve the use of threats, force, abduction, fraud, or deception, or other forms of abuse and coercion for the purpose of exploitation. Due to the hidden nature of trafficking, law enforcement agencies continue to face difficulties in finding and apprehending groups responsible. Even when trafficking operations are discovered, conviction rates are relatively low (Aas, 2007). Aas (2007) attributes low conviction rates of trafficking to the difficulty of distinguishing between smuggling and trafficking, a low prioritization by a male-dominated police culture, and reluctance on the part of victims to cooperate with police out of fear and mistrust of the police themselves.

Exploitation

Exploitation of migrants includes, but is not limited to, "work in deviant markets such as drug pushing, begging, prostitution, and illegal or untaxed labour" (Di Nicola, 2005, p. 182). According to the UN, "Exploitation shall include, at a minimum, the exploitation of the prostitution of others or other forms of sexual exploitation, forced labour or services, slavery or practices similar to slavery, servitude or the removal of organs" (Di Nicola, 2005, p. 183). Although research and media tends to reveal human trafficking stories that involve the movement of people from developing to developed countries, it is important to note that such stories are not always the case. Trafficking has been known to occur between developing countries such as women and children who are trafficked from Burma, Cambodia, and Vietnam to India, Malaysia, Pakistan, and Thailand for sexual exploitation. According to Di Nicola (2005), this occurs for two possible reasons. The first is a well-being differential where one country may be more attractive relative to the other. The second reason is that the demand in the destination countries for migrants is fueled by a strong sex tourism industry (e.g., Thailand) (Di Nicola, 2005). It is also important to note that people can be trafficked within a country, as human trafficking does not require a transnational element (Logan, Walker, & Hunt, 2009).

Women and girls form the majority of victims who are exploited for the purpose of involuntary domestic servitude. This type of labor is hard to detect and even when victims escape, they are offered little protection as many countries do not consider involuntary domestic servitude a form of human trafficking (Cullen-DuPont, 2009). Many cases of forced labor within countries such as Mauritania, Pakistan, or regions in West Africa commonly derive from people who are born into debt-bondage originating from their families' debts. People are also trafficked across nations for forced labor and experience various types of harms and deprivations as well as life-threatening work. Trafficking for human organs has also become popular as economies based on "transplant tourism" have developed in some countries. Wealthier people may offer certain basic needs to those who don't have the option to refuse it in return for organs such as kidneys. In some extreme cases, the harvesting of human organs has been known to be involuntary and facilitated by threats or nonconsented removal during surgery (Cullen-DuPont, 2009).

Types of Trafficking Operations

Individual entrepreneurs or amateur smugglers are individuals who traffic persons on a very small scale; usually one or two persons at a time. They are mainly responsible for transportation purposes, undoubtedly the riskiest part of the smuggling process. Their work may either be classified as "spontaneous, illegal, non-organized, and unsophisticated trafficking and smuggling" or may be hired by criminal organizations and are easily replaced. Examples include *passeurs* in Italy or *coyotes* who smuggle Mexican migrants into the United States via land routes (Di Nicola, 2005).

More advanced than amateur smugglers are small enterprises which range in levels of organization and usually have established and tested routes for the transport of migrants. These groups may have small affiliations with other groups and may only practice their trade in a small number of countries (one or two). According to Di Nicola (2005), these groups may act as regional subcontractors with associates in other countries. An example of these groups is small gangs which travel through Europe selling women to prostitution markets where they are repeatedly sold to other gangs (Di Nicola, 2005).

Medium and large enterprises are much more sophisticated and are able to operate in a larger geographical area spanning over more than two countries. These groups may participate in various criminal endeavors with high levels of expertise. An example of this type of group is a Slovenian criminal group that trafficked women from Russia, Moldova, and Ukraine, through Hungary, the Republic of Serbia and Montenegro, Croatia, and Slovenia to Italy. They also participated in subcontracted work from Asian criminal associates and transported people from China to Bangladesh using the same route (Di Nicola, 2005).

Multinational enterprises are groups which have the capacity to transport persons over thousands of miles. They have established headquarters in the different regions in which they operate. Examples of these groups are the Chinese Triads and the Japanese Yakuza (Di Nicola, 2005).

Di Nicola (2005) has identified some important trends with regards to both smuggling and trafficking of migrants. She argues that the greater the distance to travel and the more countries to travel through, the more sophisticated and more organized are the groups that facilitate the movement. In comparison to human smuggling, trafficking of migrants for purposes of labor exploitation require a higher level of expertise and consequently are usually undertaken by more sophisticated groups who develop large criminal networks and associations with other groups. Smuggling enterprises further distinguish themselves from trafficking groups in that they are usually specialized and nonopportunistic. They are unlike traffickers who may "shift from one illicit activity to another, diversifying their operational sectors on the basis of mere opportunism alone" (Di Nicola, 2005).

Process of Trafficking Migrants

The first stage of the process of trafficking involves the recruitment of migrants in the country of origin. Traffickers may actively seek people who desire to work abroad and may disguise themselves as travel, employment, or talent agencies advertising their services in newspapers or on the Internet. Some traffickers who specialize in the exploitation of women may focus their search for prostitutes working in local nightclubs or may advertise in newspapers offering work for women as dancers, models, housemaids, waitresses, or air hostesses. Some criminals may promise marriage or, in rare cases, participate in kidnappings (Di Nicola, 2005). False promises of work and the opportunity to earn relatively higher wages seem attractive given the victim's circumstances. Those who have experienced poverty, deprivation, conflict, or oppression are particularly vulnerable to these offers and are persuaded by traffickers pursue a new and better life in another country (Di Nicola, 2005). Once the victim agrees to the process, the trafficker will ensure that the victim's cooperation is binding and makes it difficult, if not possible, for the victim to back out. Bales and Lize (2005) explain that, "If the victim is socially and culturally isolated and without any money at the time of recruitment the victim feels she or he had little choice but to go along" (Bales & Lize, 2005). To establish further control and dependence, the trafficker will take away the victim's identity and travel documents (Bales & Lize, 2005).

Transporting persons may involve long and complex travels across a number of countries before reaching the final destination. Travel may be facilitated by the use of various means including planes, cars, trains, boats, or motorboats. In some cases, trafficked or smuggled persons may end up staying in intermediate countries for some time before moving on to their destination (Di Nicola, 2005). Victims may be locked up in safe houses where they may be subject to poor living conditions as well as harsh treatment in the form of harm and physical restraint. This period of confinement is characterized by the trafficker's aim to "disorient the victim, to increase his or her dependence, to establish fear and obedience, to gain control" (Bales & Lize, 2005).

Routes traveled usually are already tested, have less risky borders and protection, and may vary depending new opportunities that may present themselves. The use of false documents for disguising migrants is common however a legal work permit can also be obtained by having fake work contracts produced beforehand. Other methods include obtaining a tourist visa or claiming political asylum at the borders (Di Nicola, 2005). Corruption of governments in developing countries may facilitate recruitment as well as uninhibited operation of trafficking activities due to the lack of punishment and accountability of traffickers (Logan et al., 2009). The cooperation of corrupt officials, including police, ensures further safeties allowing traffickers to operate in a low-risk environment.

Trafficked victims who reach the destination country will face, or have already faced, exploitation in the form of forced labor, prostitution, or begging. They are informed of the debts they have incurred from their transportation and other associated costs and are expected to do whatever it takes to pay them off. The enforcement of false debts provides traffickers with a rationale to use violence if the victim refuses to work (Bales & Lize, 2005). Bales and Lize (2005) argue that there is a psychological aspect of manipulation involved in having the disoriented victim take responsibility and assume their own debt. Logan and colleagues refer to psychological confinement that can be created through the lack of transparency of how much debt is diminishing, the addition of exorbitant charges, and the implementation of interest rates which all make the debt almost impossible to pay off. Furthermore, paying off one's debt has been described as an insurmountable task due to the costs of food, rent, medicine, and condoms that are added everyday (Cullen-DuPont, 2009). Their exploitation may also be facilitated by the use of violence and threats against victims' families; threats made to seem real by traffickers' claims of ties to people or organizations who can bring harm in origin countries. Psychological abuse and degradation are also common tactics employed by traffickers who threaten victims about exposing their circumstances to their family or the public (Logan et al., 2009). In addition, victims are often told that local police will arrest or brutalize them and immigration officers will deport them if found (Bales & Lize, 2005). Even when faced with the opportunity to escape, a victim may believe that the risks of running into law enforcement or immigration officers outweigh the continued experience of abuse. Other forms of entrapment may include the use of drugs or alcohol, purposeful isolation from the public, and the confiscation of legal papers that clarify the identity of the victim (Logan et al., 2009). Victims who lack knowledge of alternative options may not be aware of services that could help them. Victims who are unaware that what is happening to them is a crime may remain entrapped and dependent on the trafficker (Logan et al., 2009). This may be exacerbated by victims' poor language skills, which further isolate them.

601.01.01: Trafficking Migrants

Defining Characteristics

VICTIMOLOGY

Trafficking victims are most often those who have experienced some level of deprivation and poverty. Although not necessarily from the poorest backgrounds, these victims have a desire for a better life, which makes them vulnerable to traffickers who claim fulfill such a desire. The level of education of victims varies; however it was found that least educated victims were easily manipulated while those with a desire for further education put them at risk for being trafficked. People who experienced discrimination on account of their group status or social category were also more likely to seek the services of traffickers to escape oppression and attempt to make a new start in a new country (Bales & Lize, 2005). The Logan report listed the following characteristics which increase vulnerability to trafficking: lack of knowledge about legal rights or how to get help, cultural factors that facilitate trafficking conditions, or even acceptance of human trafficking as part of the culture. Being young, strong, and healthy was considered to increase vulnerability as well (Logan et al., 2005). According to the United Nations Office on Drugs and Crime (UNODC), women are the most frequent victims of trafficking. Some are offered jobs abroad such as housekeeping, restaurants, or modeling positions, while other times, traffickers pose as boyfriends who've fallen in love with the victim. Traffickers take these women on vacation or have runaway marriages only to later hand her over to other traffickers or use various methods of coercion to force her into prostitution. It is common for this type of deception to be used on younger women where traffickers use emotional coercion to play upon the desires of girls who want to believe they are loved (Cullen-DuPont, 2009).

Children are also a commodity for traffickers and are either abducted for prostitution or placed into prostitution by their families. Many families who experience a high level of poverty may be persuaded by traffickers to send their children abroad for what they believe are entry-level employment opportunities, apprenticeships, or even formal education. In some cases, such as in Thailand, parents have knowledge and give consent to have their daughters participate in the sex industry and send some of the earnings back home. In addition, boys and girls may be victims of child sex tourism where people from around the world engage in acts with children with "the promise or illusion of anonymity" (Cullen-DuPont, 2009).

There are also characteristics that make victims more attractive to traffickers. Traffickers may look for victims who need work and are able to move in search of work. In addition, those who are socially isolated may have weak links in their own community and, as a result, are more likely to accept working in another country. Traffickers look for victims who have particular traits that are fitting to the type of labor they will perform. Bales and Lize (2005) explain that, with respect to sexual exploitation, concepts of sexual attractiveness differ between cultures and "certain attributes of ethnicity and appearance are known to be worth more to buyers in receiving countries, thus narrowing the trafficker's choice of victims" (Bales & Lize, 2005, p. 21).

Di Nicola (2005) offers three main types of trafficking victims who become involved in the sex industry. Exploited victims are women who have previously worked in the sex industry and are tricked into working in another country under conditions similar to slavery. Deceived victims are tricked into believing that they will be employed in another country in the service or entertainment sector, and instead are forced into prostitution (Di Nicola, 2005). Kidnapped victims are uncommon because traffickers attain compliance easier by exploiting the desires and aspirations of their victims (Bales & Lize, 2005).

CRIME SCENE INDICATORS FREQUENTLY NOTED

Safe houses used for the purpose of trafficking humans are often the site at which passports are taken away and replaced by false ones. Safe houses are commonly above or connected to legitimate business workplaces. To minimize costs, these living quarters are often poorly maintained. In addition, safe houses fulfill various other functions such as sites for financial transactions, preparation of passport photos, money laundering, and transfer points for other trafficking victims (Leman & Janssens, 2007).

STAGING

Not applicable.

COMMON FORENSIC FINDINGS

Important signs to lookout for are cuts, bruises, broken bones, signs of depression, posttraumatic stress, malnutrition, substance abuse, and other long-term health problems (Cavanaugh, 2011).

Investigative Considerations

One of the initial tasks of the investigation should be corroborating victims' statements from testimonies of other victims and witnesses or from physical evidence. Identifying additional and previous victims will help build a strong case against the trafficker. Moossey (2009) explains that "even if one victim's testimony seems less convincing . . . the cumulative testimony of several women, each describing the trafficker's use of coercion and fraud, can be persuasive to judges and juries" (Moossey, 2009, p. 7).

Officers should use covert methods to acquire as much evidence as possible before raiding and terminating a trafficking enterprise. Valuable information can be obtained about the scope of the trafficking operation, locations of activity, and other victims involved. However, evidence of immediate or ongoing harm or the exploitation of children may require immediate intervention allowing for only a small window of time to use these methods (Moossey, 2009).

Research from case studies has revealed that adequate training is necessary for law enforcement agencies involved in trafficking cases. Agencies must have the capacity for their officers to recognize signs of human trafficking, to be sensitized to deal effectively with trafficking victims and to have adequate language skills to facilitate interviews with victims (Bales & Lize, 2005).

When interviewing victims, agencies must be aware of a victim's reluctance to share information with law enforcement. In many cases, traffickers mislead victims into believing that police will arrest or hurt them if they are found. Traffickers also threaten to bring harm to victims or their families if they reveal any information to the police. This may lead victims to deceive police early in the interviewing process. Moossey (2009) suggests that agencies should anticipate this and find a way to gain a victim's trust (Moossey, 2009). He explains that instead of attempting to secure admission to already know facts, agencies should establish rapport with the victim and initially focus on less sensitive information before inquiring about traumatic aspects of one's victimization (Moossey, 2009).

Some victims may have been empowered by their trafficker to watch over other victims (monitors or enforcers). It is important to house and interview victims separately as well as observe their interactions with each other (Moossey, 2009).

Witnesses and clients may provide important evidence that can corroborate victims' statements. It is important to take a broad view of leads and locate persons who were in contact with victims (Moossey, 2009). Investigations which successfully resulted in prosecutions were ones which involved prosecutors who were willing to follow up on every lead to corroborate evidence (Bales & Lize, 2005).

Due to the lengthy nature of investigations and prosecutions, it is important to keep track and keep in touch with victims so that they can testify at trial (Moossey, 2009).

Support and care services should be provided to victims who may have experienced severe physical, psychological, or sexual harms. Investigators should inform victims of the services available to them and pass on contact information for the agencies that provide these services (Bales & Lize, 2005).

Search Warrant Suggestions

With regard to sex trafficking cases, places in which victims lived or engaged in commercial sex typically contain the most significant corroborating evidence. Items such as debt and income ledgers, tally sheets, phone number lists, bank records, victims' diaries, provocative clothing, digital evidence on phones and laptops, and sex-related items may serve as important pieces of evidence. Addresses or phone numbers may help identify specific locations where victims engaged in commercial sex and agents are advised to obtain rollover warrants to search these locations (Moossey, 2009).

Moossey (2009) also suggests that photographs and film of locations where victims are housed may, in some cases, provide compelling evidence to prove that victims were not there willingly, especially when living quarters appear small, crowded, unsanitary and contain restraints and posted rules.

Human Smuggling

Human smuggling differs from human trafficking in a few aspects. Most importantly, both processes involve the movement of persons for profit, however the absence of exploitation makes smuggling, for the most part, a consenting process where the relationship between the transporter and the smuggled individual ends once the agreed upon destination is reached (Bales & Lize, 2005; Logan et al., 2009). In contrast, human trafficking victims may encounter debt bondage and subsequent labor exploitation upon arrival. Another importance distinction between the two terms is the transnational element of smuggling, which, by definition, requires some method of illegal border crossing or entry (Bilger, Hofmann, & Jandl, 2006). This is not necessarily the case with human trafficking where people can be trafficked in their own country (Logan et al., 2009). Finally, smuggling has been conceptualized as a service industry characterized by networks of independent contractors rather than a criminal organization with a hierarchal structure, which characterizes most upper-level trafficking groups (Bilger et al., 2006).

COYOTE-ASSISTED BORDER CROSSING

Although it is evident that the United States has witnessed numerous cases of migrant smuggling undertaken by a myriad of different individuals and groups, no other smuggling group has been more pervasive or prevalent than the Mexican coyotes who facilitate the illegal movement of Mexican migrants into the United States. Coyotes take on a number of different roles and may operate as individuals or as commercial transport enterprises. It must be noted, however, contrary to media depictions of large organized smuggling "rings," coyotes develop networks of independent contractors who carry out particular parts of the operation. Spener (2009) points out those commercial transport enterprises could operate with as few as five people. Smaller-scale coyotes may offer exclusive services such as those dedicated to providing river-crossing services using rafts, paddleboats, or inner tubes to migrants or other coyotes. Some coyotes may earn a living by selling or renting border crossing documents including passports, residence cards, or plastic-embossed laser visas. For those who can afford it, documents can be provided to migrants that they can present to U.S. consular officials to qualify for nonimmigrant visas (international traveler's visa). On one hand, these individuals can avoid the daunting trek across the border via land routes, however they may face a higher level of punishment if caught: possible misdemeanor, illegal entry and felonious impersonation charges. Coyotes will bring migrants with false documents to legal entry points at peak times when traffic is heavy and the borders are busy (Spener, 2009). There have also been noted cases of U.S. officials who have collaborated with coyotes and have facilitated illegal crossings. Some examples include immigration officers who allowed migrants to pass through border control without inspection for a fee and visa sales at U.S. consulates in Mexico (Spener, 2009).

More organized networks may accumulate migrants in border towns and transport them using tractor-trailer rigs through immigration checkpoints. To avoid inspection dogs, coyotes order migrants to bathe and put on new clothes. Gamma ray machines used at borders are not always used, especially during times of heavy traffic. Even if migrants are found, most coyotes will promise another attempt at crossing the border when they are returned to Mexico encouraging migrants not to be cooperative with officials. Other methods of entry into the United States include land routes around legal points of entry. Migrants are then driven to a nearby town where they can be delivered to family or friends who will pay the smuggling fee. Alternatively, migrants may be driven to a safe house where individuals who are responsible for payment can be contacted (Spener, 2009).

CHINESE HUMAN SMUGGLING GROUPS IN THE UNITED STATES

By analyzing the structure and organization of Mexican coyotes, it has become clear that media-propagated conceptions about organized criminal groups do not accurately portray the types of smuggling groups that facilitate the entry of migrants into the United States. On that note, Chinese smuggling organizations have been observed to operate in a similar nature of Mexican coyotes and "deviate significantly from those of traditional triad societies" (Zhang & Chin, 2002, p. 738). Zhang and Chin (2002) revealed that Chinese smugglers or "snakeheads" are, for the most part, individuals who see a financially reward-ing opportunity in transporting Chinese nationals through the use of personal networks. Big snakeheads are individuals who have the ability to travel in and out of China, have connections with government agencies, have established contacts in transit countries, and generally invest more into their business with intentions of maintaining continuous, large-scale operations. Small snake-heads, however, are limited in their ability to travel and usually reside in or near sending communities (Zhang & Chin, 2002). Smuggling networks observed by Zhang and Chin (2002) generally took the form of three or four members allied through a business relationship based on a commitment towards eventual profits. There are numerous roles and responsibilities that can be either undertaken by members of the smuggling group, associates in a smuggler's network, or hired persons. These include recruiters, coordinators, transporters, document vendors, guides, enforcers, debt-collectors, and coop-erative public officials. Together, these individuals use three major strategies of entry: (a) entering Mexico or Canada and crossing the borders into the United States, (b) using air routes to enter the United States, or (c) the use of fishing freighters to enter American ports (Zhang & Chin, 2002).

601.01.02: Human Smuggling

Defining Characteristics

VICTIMOLOGY

Many researchers have conceptualized smuggling as a transnational service indus-try rather than a form of organized crime. Under such market-like conditions, migrants who use the services are generally referred to as customers or clients. Clients become victims when smugglers employ violence, deception, or other forms of abuse. However, it is important to realize that such cases are relatively uncommon as "systematic maltreatment of clients would seriously harm the smugglers' reputation on which their business crucially depends" (Bilger et al., 2006, p. 80).

Spener (2009) revealed that a majority of clients who used the services of coyotes to cross the border into Texas were young, working class Mexicans with little formal education.

Border management organizations in Central and Eastern Europe demon-strate that the most apprehended migrants in 2004 were single male individ-uals, between the ages of 20 and 40. One-fifth of apprehended migrants were female (Jandl, 2007).

CRIME SCENE INDICATORS FREQUENTLY NOTED

Migrants experiences reveal that making contact with smuggling services was an easy task carried either at a location of known reputation or immediate surroundings. Intermediaries or recruiters either were completely unknown to migrants, acquaintances, or individuals in refugee communities who have collaborated with smuggling professionals (Bilger et al., 2006).

Small-scale or self-employed smugglers usually offer short-distance smuggling services on an occasional basis and carry out the whole operation themselves. Larger smuggling networks, however, are structured having different positions with different responsibilities. Organizers act as managers of the whole smuggling operation and usually have minimal or no contact with clients. Intermediaries act as mediators between the organizer and clients and are responsible for the implementation of the smuggling operation. In some cases, the intermediary took on the role of the recruiter as well, however in other cases the recruiter was portrayed as an independent responsibility carried out by migrants who were looking to make some money. Guides are usually knowledgeable of the local environment and are responsible for accompanying clients and carrying out border crossings. Consequently, they face the highest risk of being apprehended. Other positions include spotters, drivers, or messengers who perform occasional jobs as well as external agents such as cooperating officials, border police, and private house owners who aid in the success of the operation (Bilger et al., 2006).

Method of payments may vary; however, arrangements can be made to involve partial payments or step-by-step release payments as certain parts of the journey are completed. In contrast to the deception involved in trafficking, smuggling operations resemble a relatively trustworthy operation equipped with insurances and guarantees of arrival. Of course, trafficking organizations may aim to mimic these characteristics and methods of gaining trust of potential victims. Good reputation communicated through word of mouth between migrant networks may play as the single most important factor in advertising reliability and trustworthiness of smuggling services. Smugglers have strong incentives to meet their promises in a highly competitive smuggling market, which allows for migrants to easily select or change service providers (Bilger et al., 2006).

Relationships between smugglers and their clients may take on different forms. Van Liempt and Doomernik (2006) identified three basic types of interaction. One type gives full control to the migrant who chooses the destination and the smuggler simply acts as a facilitator. In another form, the smuggler is the decision-maker and determines the final destination. The last type of interaction involves a negotiation of prices and preferences of destination countries (Van Liempt & Doomernik, 2006).

Safe houses are commonly rented places accompanied by smugglers who supervise inmates. It is common for smugglers to permanently reside or live in a safe house. Migrants may be housed in safe houses until their debt is paid off (Leman & Janssens, 2007). In most cases, an arrangement has been made to have relatives send money to the smugglers upon arrival, and it is not until the money is received that the migrant will be able to leave the safe house (Spener, 2009).

Border authorities in central and eastern Europe have noticed an increase in the use of false documents produced by increasingly sophisticated equipment. Most common is the use of another person's passport with an exchanged photo. Other ways of falsifying passports include correcting the expiry date, forging visa stamps, or chemically removing border-crossing stamps (Jandl, 2007).

For transport across land routes, smugglers often use rented vehicles such as cars, taxis, vans, minibuses, trucks, refrigerator semi trailers, and so on. When using official road borders for illegal crossings, smugglers often use trucks and cargo spaces for concealing migrants. Busy border traffic in addition to transport during dawn or foggy days may inhibit effective inspections, which use thermo-visual and carbon dioxide detecting equipment (Jandl, 2007).

Preferred smuggling destinations may be characterized by relaxed border controls, easily accessible, low penalties for smuggling, and ease of asylum claims (Van Liempt & Doomernik, 2006).

Dougherty (2004) describes parts of the border where there are foot trails and tire tracks along stretches of the desert where coyotes and illegal immigrants frequently cross. Fences are cut or destroyed and large amounts of waste define areas that are used as rally points; places where illegal immigrants meet before they travel to coyote pickup spots (Dougherty, 2004).

STAGING

Migrants are known to come into contact with people who pose as coyotes and lead victims to an isolated area where they assault and rob them (Spener, 2009).

COMMON FORENSIC FINDINGS

According to Jandl (2007), the most common method of falsifying traveling documents has been the use of another individual's passport and the replacement of the identification photo by temporarily removing the protective film. Other methods involve altering expiry dates, forging visa stamps, or chemically removing border-crossing stamps (Jandl, 2007).

Investigative Considerations

According to Spener (2004), apprehended migrants are unlikely to cooperate with police and law enforcement, especially if they have not been mistreated by their smugglers. This sometimes makes the identification and arrest of smugglers a difficult task. However, one of the most common ways that the INS apprehends smugglers is when family or friends express their worries in a call to police. This is commonly the case when smugglers hold migrants in safe houses until relatives are able to pay the full expenses of the smuggling trip (Spener, 2004).

Search Warrant Suggestions

Although Spener (2004) noted that in cases where firearms were recovered, smugglers were typically not known to wield or use the weapons. They were more likely to control the movement of migrants through fear and threatening migrants that if they left the safe house, they would be discovered by law enforcement.

There have been documented cases where migrants have died of dehydration, hypothermia and suffocation in tractor-trailers and railcars emphasizing the importance of inspection and acquisition of search warrants for suspected holding cells (The Victoria Advocate, 2003).

601.02: Visa Overstayer

The Department of Homeland Security (DHS) has taken a considerable interest in identifying and taking enforcement action against people who stay within the United States past the expiry of their visas. Their concerns lie especially with overstays that have been associated with terrorist-related activity such as 5 out of the 19 hijackers of the September 11 attacks who were identified as visa overstayers (Government Accountability Office [GAO], 2011). Other agencies and programs such as the U.S. Customs and Border Protection (CBP), the U.S. Immigration and Customs Enforcement (ICE), and the U.S. Visitor and Immigrant Status Indicator Technology Program (US-VISIT) also deal with screening and overstay enforcement. Nonimmigrant visas may be issued for business travel, pleasure, tourism, medical treatment, and student exchange programs. Upon arrival, non-immigrants are inspected by CBP where biographic as well as biometric data is collected and admissibility for entry is determined. Legal consequences for overstaying are 3 to 10 years of inadmissibility for entry based on the length of the overstay. Due to the enormous volume of cases of visa overstayers, the Counterterrorism and Criminal Exploitation Unit (CTCEU) prioritizes investigations to leads that pose a high perceived risk to national security and public safety (GAO, 2011).

602: Cross-Border Organized Crime

602.01: Cigarette Smuggling

Historically, cigarette smuggling activities have been most prominent in regions located on the border of Canada and the United States. During the 1990s, taxes imposed on cigarettes and tobacco were significantly higher in Canada creating a large price differential and a profit margin comparable to that of drug trafficking. As a result, smuggling operations spread across Canada implementing sophisticated distribution networks and developing partnerships with criminal groups. In fact, police revealed evidence that aboriginal criminals in Ontario were facilitating the development of distribution and smuggling operations in aboriginal communities in Western Canada (Beare, 2002).

Today, cigarettes remain the most widely smuggled legal consumer product in the world. Over one third of legally exported cigarettes end up being smuggled in what some estimate to be a multibillion-dollar-per-year illegal enterprise with links to transnational organized crime and international terrorism (Madsen, 2009). Parallel markets have also sprung up to produce counterfeit cigarettes, equipped with repackaging facilities and new sources of tobacco. The European Anti-Fraud Office has suggested that approximately 65% of all smuggled cigarettes are counterfeit and more than half are produced in China (Madsen, 2009). At the same time, tobacco companies have been alleged to knowingly export extraordinarily large amounts of cigarettes that would later be smuggled back into Canada, amassing significant profits of their own (Beare, 2002).

Main Modes of Cigarette Smuggling

Canadian manufactured cigarettes are exported tax-free to the United States and are also sold within Canada in duty-free stores and embassies. Cigarettes that reach American wholesalers are then smuggled back into Canada either through the French owned islands of St. Pierre and Miquelon off the coast of Newfoundland or in native reserves along the border Canadian–U.S. border in Ontario, Quebec, and New York (Beare, 2002). Cigarettes are then distributed for sale through organized networks to wholesalers, retail shops, and street vendors. American manufactured cigarettes are also smuggled through the same conduit. Tax-exempt cigarettes available to status natives on reserves are also purchased and transported to major cities in Canada. However these purchases are limited under a quota system and are subject to federal excise duty (Luk, Cohen, & Ferrence, 2007). Domestically produced cigarettes usually are produced by either small plants run by organized crime groups or large industrial plants located in First Nation communities. They are commonly wrapped in clear, resealable plastic bags and distributed primarily on reserves through "smoke shacks" (Luk et al., 2007).

Consequences of Cigarette Smuggling

In addition to losses in potential tax revenue, cigarette smuggling has created a financial burden for government and law enforcement agencies designated for interdiction efforts to disrupt organized smuggling operations. Not only are such efforts costly, law enforcement officials have stated that they have only been successful in apprehending vulnerable, inexperienced, and unsophisticated individuals and groups. Most worrisome is the increasing involvement of criminal organizations and families who take up cigarette smuggling as an extension of other illegal activities. Their involvement may foster a higher degree of competition and violence, some of which has already been documented by police investigations (Beare, 2002). In light of large profit potential and relatively low penalties for cigarette smuggling, it is not surprising that what was once dominated by an opportunistic network of autonomous entrepreneurs is now composed of more sophisticated and organized groups of criminals. Furthermore, large profit margins have allowed smugglers to invest in technology enabling them to better evade law enforcement agencies. Beare (2002) claims that illicit profits initiate a cycle where smuggling profits go into the purchase of weapons, casino operations for laundering purposes, and political lobbying activities.

Case Study: Cross-Border Crime in the Akwesasne Community

The Mohawk community of Akwesasne located on the Canadian–U.S. border on the St. Lawrence Seaway introduces an interesting case of organized criminality that has established a cross-border conduit for the smuggling of contraband, illegal goods and persons (Jamieson, 1999). Given its convenient location, there has been a history of profit-making activities that have benefited from price differentials between the United States and Canada. In the 1970s, cheaper gasoline sold on Akwesasne reservations attracted residents of upstate New York (Jamieson, 1999). In the mid-1990s, the Canadian government became increasingly concerned with illicit trading involving the smuggling of alcohol and cigarettes in the region. It was believed that Canadian produced tobacco products were exported tax-free to American wholesalers and smuggled back into Canada returning large profits (Jamieson, 1999). The financial incentive to participate in such activities was a result of increasing levels of excise taxes on tobacco products implemented by the Federal government of Canada in an ongoing public health campaign which aimed to discourage smoking (Jamieson, South, & Taylor, 1998).

However, many of the activities identified by law enforcement agencies as "smuggling" are conversely perceived by the Mohawks of Akwesasne as part of a routine and legitimate form of domestic trade involving the right of all First Nations people to travel freely across borders established by non-Aboriginal societies (Jamieson, 1999). A majority of the Mohawk community of Akwesasne share a consensus of sovereignty over their own territory as well as border-crossing rights which they claim are recognized under various treaties such as the Treaty of Utrecht (1713) and Article III of the Jay Treaty (1794). They also believe that "all cross-border rights emerge from their status as a nation with enduring sovereignty which has never been conquered by any colonial power, nor ceded any of its rights"

(Dickson-Gilmore, 2002, p. 15). Further complicating the matter is the fact that within the community, political and legal jurisdictions are ambiguous and even contested causing problematic coordination of law enforcement to combat illicit smuggling activities (Jamieson, 1999). Dickson-Gilmore (2002) points out that the Akwesasne community is "subject to a remarkable array of provincial, state, Canadian and U.S. federal laws and policed by at least seven different law enforcement agencies" (Dickson-Gilmore, 2002, p. 13).

It appears that illicit cross-border activities pose as a lucrative source of prosperity in an otherwise limited environment of legitimate opportunities (Dickson-Gilmore, 2002). This is especially troublesome considering that movement of firearms and illicit drugs are also facilitated through the same hub, luring outsider organized crime groups to become involved. In fact, what started as a relatively small "butlegging" operation has expanded to include liaisons with the Hell's Angels, ethnic-based drug groups, and Asian organized crime groups involving smuggling of alcohol, drugs, and migrants (Dickson-Gilmore, 2002).

In 1994, the federal government of Canada announced its intention to reduce excise taxes for cigarettes in an attempt to reduce the large price differential under what the government called the National Action Plan on Smuggling. Part of this plan included the Anti-Smuggling Initiative, which increased extra manpower to Canada Customs for stronger interdiction efforts as well as funding for new surveillance technologies laid out in a span of five years. Cigarette manufacturers also experienced increased surveillance, which ensured cigarettes bound for out of the country wholesalers were shipped to their respected destinations (Jamieson et al., 1998). However, Schneider suggests that although program evaluations revealed a substantial decrease in contraband tobacco after the implementation of this initiative, "evidence suggests that reductions in Canadian cigarette taxes made during the same period were the most powerful policy tool in influencing cigarette smuggling" (Schneider, 2000, p. 3). Schneider (2000) also concludes that operations and increased enforcement geared towards dismantling smuggling groups has not been a strong deterrent to well-organized crime groups. Rather, the initiative has displaced smuggling groups to other areas, forcing them to adopt new methods of smuggling and concealment, establish new routes, and become more cautious in their activities (Schneider, 2000). More recently, amendments have been made to Canadian legislation to target organized crime groups by introducing new criminal organization offenses, simplifying the definition of criminal organization, and expanding seizure and forfeiture provisions (Department of Justice Canada, Evaluation Division, 2004).

602.02: Cross-Border Smuggling of Weapons

In consideration of stricter regulations concerning the sales and ownership of weapons in both Mexico and Canada, the United States offers a relatively low-cost source for weapons both because of weak regulations and a great number of guns already in the hands of American citizens (Cook, Cukier, & Krause, 2009). Available trace data has revealed that a large majority of weapons used in crime in Canada and Mexico originate from the United States. These illegal weapons are primarily used by criminal groups that vary in levels of organization and power. Most notable are the stories of violence between Mexican drug cartels who compete for control over smuggling routes into the United States (Miller, 2010). There is no doubt that such violence has been elevated by easy access to smuggled weapons of all types and sizes. These weapons have empowered drug cartels to subvert state authority; illustrated by conflicts where cartels are better armed than the police (Cook et al., 2009). In Canada, although overall levels of homicide have been decreasing, gang-related homicides have been on the rise with a majority involving guns (Cook et al., 2009).

Weapons can be obtained in the United States through a few different methods. The highest level of regulated sales occur through federally licensed dealers (FFLs) who are required to keep records of sales, run a NICS check prior to completing a sale, and perform background checks on customers who purchase a gun (Ex-convicts, illegal aliens, hospitalized mental patients, and minors are prohibited from purchasing weapons). The activities of licensed dealers are also regulated by the Bureau of Alcohol, Tobacco, Firearms and Explosives (ATF). Licensed and unlicensed dealers forgo all of these requirements when selling guns from their own private collection making it difficult to trace the last purchaser of weapons used in crimes. Unlicensed sellers may seldom know if a customer is prohibited from purchasing weapons, especially if they are not required to perform background checks (Miller, 2010). In some cases, both licensed and unlicensed sellers may be willfully blind when selling guns to prohibited persons or making sales intended for smuggling purposes. Guns can also be purchased by "straw purchasers," who act as a middleman and knowingly purchase weapons for prohibited persons. Gun shows across the United States remain a major source for weapons that are smuggled into Mexico. It is estimated that between 30 and 40% of all gun transactions take place at gun shows through unlicensed sellers (Cook et al., 2009). Smugglers who purchase guns will often use cash to avoid leaving any trails or evidence of purchase while fulfilling money-laundering objectives (Miller, 2010). Another alternative to obtaining large amounts of guns in a short span of time is by committing theft or robbery. Licensed dealers, domestic distributors, manufacturing plants, legal exports, and army surplus depots are also potential targets (Cook et al., 2009).

Once weapons are acquired in the United States, there a few different ways by which they can be trafficked to another country. False declaration, false documentation, and concealment have been used to commercially ship weapons from the United States to Canada (Cook et al., 2009). Cook et al. (2009) uses the example of Chinese-made AK-47 rifles mislabeled as hunting rifles that were discovered en route to Canada. Many shipments cross the border into Canada unchecked in cargo trucks and NAFTA-sanctioned railways (Miller, 2010). Smuggling operations to Mexico are characterized by what some refer to as *tráfico hormiga,* or trail of ants—small batches of weapons that cross land borders. Researchers have indicated that weapon sources are concentrated and appear to be organized by gangs rather than small transactions in the informal market. Their movement across the border is facilitated by corrupt customs officials and police and transported through routes already developed for the smuggling of other illicit goods (Cook et al., 2009). Although a majority of weapons entering Mexico originate from the United States, other sources in Central America are known to provide weapons previously imported during the civil wars in El Salvador, Nicarauga, and Guatemala (Cook et al., 2009).

In an effort to reduce the prevalence of gun smuggling into Mexico, the ATF has increased regulatory inspections of licensed dealers and gun shows to reduce illegal gun transactions. The ATF has also introduced Project Gun Runner, which increases the number of personnel dedicated to preventing weapons from falling in the hands of organized crime and reducing gun-related violence in Mexico. The project also provides training for Mexican law enforcement agents to use inspection equipment and to better identify firearm traffickers. Finally, the ATF has introduced the use of a system which can trace firearms to where they were legally purchased which may help identify patterns of smuggling into Mexico (Cook et al., 2009).

Despite improvements made by the ATF, it is likely that gun smuggling will continue to exacerbate border violence in Mexico without appropriate changes in legislation with respect to the purchase and selling of weapons in the United States. Laws which enable individuals to sell weapons without paperwork make it difficult to obtain evidence and secure convictions for illegal transactions (Miller, 2010). It is crucial that a multifaceted approach must be utilized to impair gun smuggling operations including strong legislation regulating weapon sales and preventing illegal transactions at the point of purchase (Miller, 2010).

602.03: Trafficking of Narcotics

Although the availability of weapons from the United States has appeared to escalate violence at Mexican border, it is the insatiable demand for drugs that has established fierce competition over routes into the United States. The violence extends to the Mexican government and police as they attempt to wage a drug war against the cartels by hiring more personnel and using the latest technology to intercept the movement of illicit drugs. However, the cartels have proven to be adaptable and become more efficient, more technologically mobile, and better consolidated in their smuggling operations (Payan, 2006).

The majority of drugs that enter the United States from Mexico are smuggled by members of the drug cartels that have monopolized certain regions of Mexican border cities. However, small-time smugglers are known to cross the border through points of entry with concealed drugs in their body or clothing. Most of these border-crossers are novices or are hired by small-time drug dealers who focus their activities on transporting marijuana. The risk of being apprehended makes transporting other drugs such as cocaine and methamphetamines not worth the risk as marijuana is relatively cheap (Payan, 2006). Larger smuggling operations usually use vehicles such as cars, vans, and pickup trucks to conceal larger amounts of drugs. Common compartments used for hiding drugs are the gas tank, behind the dashboard, in the spare tire, and in the body of the car. They are also wrapped in tinfoil, Saran wrap, or other packaging and covered in substances such as gasoline, oil, or perfume to disguise any detectable smells (Payan, 2006).

Vehicles carrying concealed drugs arrive at the border with a few different strategies. Sometimes, smugglers rely on chance and select certain times of the day where crossings are most congested or they select weather conditions that would make certain forms of detection more difficult (Spener, 2009). Sometimes groups of vehicles loaded with drugs are sent to the border along with an easily detectable member who, upon being discovered, distracts border agents and allows the other members to pass through with less thorough inspection. In collaboration with spotters disguised as vendors, smugglers can identify patterns of border inspection or look for distracted officers and send vehicles their way. The most effective strategy involves the cooperation of border officials posted at points of entry either through bribes or familial ties. Payments anywhere from $10,000 to $20,000 can be an attractive supplement to one's salary for allowing just one vehicle to pass through without inspection (Payan, 2006). Payan suggests that the most common method among today's cartels is the use of cargo trucks under the guise of the NAFTA formal economy. Out of the millions of trucks that pass through the U.S.–Mexico border, only a small portion of them are thoroughly inspected (Payan, 2006).

Campaigns to increase security on the border and interdict smuggling operations have only been successful in apprehending smaller, less sophisticated drug entrepreneurs while large cartels have become flexible to respond to law enforcement tactics (Payan, 2006). It is evident that pervasive corruption has undermined the entire efforts of border agencies and homeland security to effectively battle this form of organized crime.

603: Biological Attacks and Bioterrorism

Biological attacks are carried out by the dissemination of bacteria, biological toxins, or viruses that can be spread through the air, food and water, and/or through direct contact. Attacks can go undetected for long periods of time and may only become evident once unusual patterns of illness are identified (Homeland Security Office of Intelligence and Analysis and FBI, 2008).

Contagious bacterial infections can be spread to others by direct or indirect contact. These bacteria will cause damage to host tissues by producing harmful toxins and causing a range of diseases. Centers for Disease Control and Prevention identified the *Yersinia pestis* (plague) as a high-priority agent that could cause a threat to national security. Viruses are also a potential cause for contagious disease that can cause damage to living tissue by invading host cells, using the DNA from those cells to replicate, and destroying host cells once replication is complete. Possible agents that can be used in terrorist attacks include the *Variola* virus and *Ebola* virus (Homeland Security Office of Intelligence and Analysis and FBI, 2008).

Noncontagious biological weapons can also be used such as *Bacillus anthracis* (causative agent of Anthrax), botulinum toxins, bubonic plague (can cause contagious, pneumonic form), and tularemia. The dispersal of such agents has been recorded in history such as the letters containing anthrax that were mailed to various locations in the United States in 2001 causing five deaths or the release of plague-infested fleas and plague-saturated rice on the Chinese population of Chekiang Province by the Japanese Army which killed thousands from 1939 to 1940 (Homeland Security Office of Intelligence and Analysis and FBI, 2008). Toxins such as *Tricothecene mycotoxin* (T2), *Aflatoxin*, and botulinum have also been identified as threats that can be delivered using rockets, aerial bombs, and spray tanks.

The globalized food and agricultural systems may facilitate the spread of pathogens that can infect livestock and crops. The loss in profits associated with such attacks may be the preferred goal in what is called *agroterrorism*. Known pathogens have been identified to cause diseases such as the avian influenza, foot and mouth disease in animals and wilt disease in crops causing millions of dollars in damage. Zoonotic pathogens which are transmissible from animals to humans such as the avian influenza are also of concern as exampled by the 57 countries that were affected in 2007 (Homeland Security Office of Intelligence and Analysis and FBI, 2008). *Bacillus anthracis*, *Clostridium botulinum* toxin, *Cryptosporidium parvum*, and *Salmonella typhimurium* are all potential biological agents that can contaminate food and water systems.

603.01: Biological Attacks

Defining Characteristics

VICTIMOLOGY

Large population centers are likely targets for the release of biological agents. Victims may range in characteristics; however, children and older adults may be the most vulnerable victims.

CRIME SCENE INDICATORS FREQUENTLY NOTED

Health care professionals would likely be the first to identify patterns of illness that would be associated with biological terrorist attacks. Early warning systems that monitor for airborne pathogens may help indicate such attacks. Key components of the ability to conduct biological attacks include the possession of a pathogenic bacteria or virus which could cause communicable disease. These agents may be acquired through theft from laboratories or isolated from sources in nature. Another component is a vector or mechanism of dissemination. These agents may be released in an enclosed space through a cloud or vapor that is protected from humidity, wind, and ultraviolet radiation. Ventilation, air conditioning, and heating systems are potential locations where agents can be released. Agents can also be introduced to an individual or animal, which may transmit the disease to other people either directly or indirectly through contact with inanimate objects (Homeland Security Office of Intelligence and Analysis and FBI, 2008).

STAGING

Agents can be released to emulate a natural outbreak by using vectors that are native to a specific area.

COMMON FORENSIC FINDINGS

Packages, weapons, vectors, associated materials, or traditional forensic evidence (hair, fibers, fingerprints) are analyzed. Covert attacks, which are more difficult to discover, may have limited evidence and investigators may rely on medical histories, diagnoses, and isolates extracted from victims. Microbial forensic scientists will analyze evidence using various methods to identify characteristics and possible sources of pathogens (Budowle et al., 2007).

Investigative Considerations

Although individual states may have varying responses to a bioterrorist event, the collaboration of law enforcement and public health agencies is crucial in identifying the source of the outbreak and reducing the harm caused by the attack. In the event of such attacks, the FBI, Department of Justice takes lead responsibility for investigation of domestic bioterrorism in the United States. The initial immediate response is the assessment of potential threat of the attack and is carried out with the consultations of other experts from agencies such as the Department of Health and Human Services, Centers for Disease Control and Prevention, the U.S. Department of

Agriculture, and experts from academic or industry backgrounds. The use of microbial forensics to analyze evident would help identify the source of the bio-agent and possibly provide a crime scene reconstruction (Budowle et al., 2007). Health professionals and epidemiological experts will partake in an outbreak investigation that will involve the following steps (Dembek, Pavlin, & Kortepeter, 2007):

1. Preparing the necessary response elements (personnel, equipment, laboratory).
2. Verifying the diagnosis and confirming the existence of the outbreak.
3. Defining the outbreak and seeking a definitive diagnosis based on information collected from historical, clinical, epidemiological, or laboratory sources.
4. Developing a case definition including the common features of illness as well as counting cases.
5. Developing exposure data including information on persons, places, and times.
6. Implementing control measures with continual evaluation.
7. Developing hypothesis of how the disease occurred, how it is spreading, and potential risk to the uninfected.
8. Evaluating the hypothesis analytical studies and refining the hypothesis if necessary.
9. Formulating a conclusion about the nature of the disease and the exposure route.
10. Communicating the findings to the appropriate agencies.

Law enforcement will conduct interviews with affected populations and facilitate collection of biological or clinical samples of evidence.

Search Warrant Suggestions

In accordance to the search warrants issued during the 2001 anthrax attacks, physical search and forensic swabbing for the following items should be conducted (FBI, 2008):

- Assembled or unassembled biological threat agent or weapon.
- Laboratory equipment used to in the production or replication of biological threat agents.
- Personal protective equipment.
- Items used in the delivery of biological weapons.

- Documents including those related to planning of the attack, blueprints, receipts for purchases, instructional publications, maps, and archived communication.
- Bank documents pertaining to the expenditure of funds for activities.
- Phone records.
- Keys and documentation related to storage facilities.
- Real and false identification documents.

For a comprehensive list, refer to www.fbi.gov/about-us/history/famous-cases/anthrax-amerithrax/08-429SWAffAttach07524.pdf

Case Study: The 1995 Sarin Attack

The Japanese cult, Aum Shinrikyo also known as Aum and Aleph, was founded in 1984 by Shoko Asahara. As of 2009, its membership was estimated to be around 1,650 people in Japan, but was as large as 40,000 members worldwide. The group's belief system consists of a combination of tenets from Buddhism, Hinduism, Christianity, and a strong obsession with the apocalypse. In the early 1990s, the group made attempts to carry out at least nine biological assaults. One plan was to spray botulinum toxin, a lethal bacterial-based poison, from buildings and modified delivery vans. The cult also experimented with other biological toxins such as anthrax, cholera, and Q fever, many of these experiments taking place in public spaces including buildings in Japan, residential areas, and areas surrounding U.S. military bases. However, Aum took a new focus on chemical warfare after many biological attacks had failed. In 1995, the group members carried out a chemical attack on the Tokyo subway system by releasing a nerve agent sarin onto train cars in what would be known as the deadliest domestic act of terrorism in Japan's history. The attack was part of a larger plot to overthrow the Japanese government and start a world war. On the rush hour morning of March 20, 1995, Aum coordinated the release of a liquid form of sarin onto five train cars on three separate subway lines. The perpetrators punctured sarin packages with the tips of umbrellas causing the sarin to evaporate into fumes. Witnesses reported commuters who lay on the ground with blood gushing from their noses and mouths. In the aftermath, twelve victims were killed and an estimated six thousand people required medical attention. It was later discovered that Aum was capable of producing thousands of kilograms of sarin a year and had acquired military helicopters that could be used to distribute the gas. Twelve members of Aum, including Aum founder Shoko Asahara, were sentenced to death for the subway attack. Japan's longest running manhunt finally ended on June 15, 2012, with the arrest of Katsuya Takahashi, Asahara's former bodyguard. He was tracked down following the arrests of two other fugitives associated with the attack, officially bringing closure to the case.

Source: Fletcher, H. (2012). *Aum Shinrikyo. Japan, cultists, Aleph, Aum Supreme Truth.* Retrieved July 8, 2012, from www.cfr.org/japan/aum-shinrikyo/p9238

604: Chemical Attacks and Terrorism

Chemical attacks commonly include the use of toxic commercial and industrial chemicals as well as warfare agents with intention to cause mass morbidity and casualties. These chemicals range in toxicity and may be dispersed in several forms such as liquids, gases, or solids. Terrorists may obtain chemical agents through theft, purchase, or production depending on the desired chemical agent and its availability. In Iraq, stolen chlorine was used with vehicle-borne improvised explosive devices in insurgent attacks. The diffusion of chemical agents is affected by various conditions such as humidity, temperature, and wind; factors which are mitigated when chemicals are released in enclosed spaces. In fact, heating, ventilation, and air conditioning systems are likely targets as high airflow can disperse chemicals quickly (Homeland Security Office of Intelligence and Analysis and FBI, 2008).

604.01: Chemical Attacks

Defining Characteristics

VICTIMOLOGY

Victims of chemical attacks range in characteristics as terrorists may target specific areas rather than specific groups of people. Enclosed areas that house large populations or allow large populations to flow through are potential targets for such attacks. Historically, the sarin gas attack in the Tokyo subway in 1995 was a targeted attack on trains passing through stations that were home to the Japanese government. Locations where large amounts of chemicals are produced and stored also can cause devastating effects if sabotaged. The GAO identified chemical facilities as potentially attractive targets which could pose a threat to surrounding populations. One hundred twenty-three chemical facilities were shown to have worst-case scenarios that would involve millions of people exposed to toxic gases (Lippin et al., 2006).

CRIME SCENE INDICATORS FREQUENTLY NOTED

Chemical agents that could potentially be used in terrorist attacks include nerve agents, vesicants or blistering agents (e.g., mustard gas), pulmonary agents (e.g., chlorine and phosgene), and cyanide toxins (Henretig, Cieslak, & Eitzen, 2002). Chemicals such as arsenic, benzene, cyanide, dioxin, lead, mercury, pesticides, and thallium are potential agents which can be used to contaminate food or water systems (Homeland Security Office of Intelligence and Analysis and FBI, 2008).

Agents can be dispersed using weaponized packages such as envelopes, bomblets, or exploding containers. Aerosol spray cans and vacuum sealed plastic bags are also common dispersal systems (Nance, 2008).

STAGING

Not applicable.

COMMON FORENSIC FINDINGS

Analysis of blood samples of victims can identify exposure to certain chemicals. For example, decrease in blood cholinesterase is a good indicator of nerve gas exposure. Sarin gas left on leaves after attempted murder of local court judges in Japan were analyzed and revealed the production of hydrofluoric acid from hydrolysis (Seto, 2001). In general, supporting evidence of a chemical attack may be obtained from the analysis of biological markers of exposure such as urinary metabolites and chemical bonds between DNA and the chemical itself. Analysis of environmental samples and degradation products of chemical agents may offer strong evidence of a chemical attack. The use of some agents such as sulfur mustard gas is easy to confirm because they persist in the environment for long periods of time (Black & Read, 2007). However, sarin nerve gases evaporate quickly and decompose easily in the environment and the body (Seto, 2001). Mass analysis will determine the concentration of chemicals in a given sample (Black & Read, 2007).

Investigative Considerations

Important factors to note include the types of samples collected, the time at which they were collected, eye witness accounts of the events that have unfolded, and accurate reporting of medical symptoms and casualties (Black & Read, 2007). In the event of the use of chemical agents such as sarin, samples must be collected very soon after the event, as nerve agents are less persistent in the environment.

Search Warrant Suggestions

Items found in safe houses may include protective suits, decontamination kits, gas masks, toxic gas detectors, containers for chemicals, animals used for testing agents, preservation systems, chemical dispersal systems, and so on (Nance, 2008).

605: Hostage Taking

Hostage taking involves the detainment of a person accompanied by a threat to injure, kill, or further detain that person in order to guarantee that certain actions or promises will or will not be carried out. According to Brandt and Sandler (2009), hostage events account for 15% of all terrorist events from 1968 to 2005. Hostage taking is used to achieve ideological, monetary, and political goals and may involve demands made to the government such as the release of prisoners and troop withdrawal like that of the 32 Chechen terrorists who stormed a school in Beslan, Russia, in 2004 (McDaniel & Ellis, 2009). Hostage taking missions are among some of the most dangerous and risky activities, but can result in significant publicity; sometimes the primary goal of terrorists (Brandt & Sandler, 2009). In some cases, such as the hostage taking in Beslan, terrorists may be martyrs willing to sacrifice themselves for a certain goal. It is possible, in these cases, that terrorists may not expect their demands to be met, but have deeper intentions to create the maximum psychological effect on the international community (McDaniel & Ellis, 2009).

Like the United States, many other countries have adopted a no-concession policy towards hostage taking. Many believe that meeting the demands of hostage takers will encourage future incidents of hostage taking. Although the policy of no-concession has not been extensively tested, some argue that one country's concession or their abandonment of a no-concession stance may influence terrorists to believe that the authorities of another country might behave similarly (Brandt & Sandler, 2009). Hostage situations can be resolved in three ways: (a) the hostage taker gives up, more likely in situations involving an opportunistic hostage taking (attrition); (b) by force; or (c) by agreement (Wilder, 1981).

Defining Characteristics

VICTIMOLOGY

Victims vary. Diplomats, international business executives, members of the judiciary, and other individuals of political importance may be likely targets.

CRIME SCENE INDICATORS FREQUENTLY NOTED

Hostage takers who are involved in barricade siege situations tend to be armed and often have or threaten the use of explosives.

STAGING

Not applicable.

COMMON FORENSIC FINDINGS

Forensics may play an important role not so much in the analysis of physical evidence, but more so, in the assessment of a hostage taker and the use of forensic psychologists and other mental health professionals by crisis/negotiation teams. It is estimated that between 30 and 58% of agencies with a crisis/negotiation team use a mental health consultant as either a consultant, an integrated team member, a primary negotiator, or a primary controller/operational commander. As an advisor (most common role), the psychologist may profile and assess the suspect in his/her motivation, agenda, and vulnerabilities in order to suggest sequences of dialogue designed to defuse the situation (Hatcher, Mohandie, Turner, & Gelles, 1998).

Investigative Considerations

Investigative teams must be (MacWillson, 1992):

- Capable of recalling all events that took place.
- Establish identity and motivation of hostage takers.
- Assist and advise officers on course of action.
- Setup an incident-based information system to record all pertinent information, initially focused on people involved.
- Interview and interrogate all individuals involved.
- Preserve evidence.
- Prepare a report with concluding statements.

Search Warrant Suggestions

The requirement of a warrant is eliminated in cases that meet the "exigent circumstances" requirement outlined by the Supreme Court. Officers "who have established probable cause that evidence is likely to be at a certain place and do not have the time go get a search warrant" may conduct a search without a warrant and are authorized to use force to enter a dwelling if police are denied entry or there is no one present to allow entry. This pertains to situations that "include danger of physical harm to an officer or others, danger of destruction of evidence, driving while intoxicated, hot-pursuit situations and individuals requiring rescuing" (Harr & Hess, 2006).

Case Study: The Beslan School Hostage Crisis

Over a span of three days during September 2004, over 1,100 people were taken hostage (including 777 children) in Beslan, North Ossetia, Russia. The group responsible consisted of mostly heavily armed Ingush and Chechen Islamic militants who demanded an end to the Second Chechen War and Russian withdrawl from Chechnya. The majority of the hostages spent 52 hours in a gymnasium measuring 10 meters wide and 25 meters long deprived of food, water, and medicine while militants refused the removal of dead bodies. Russian security forces stormed the building on the third day of the standoff, using tanks, incendiary rockets and other heavy weapons. Explosions set off fires that engulfed the building followed by a gun battle between the hostage takers and Russian security forces. It was estimated that 334 hostages were killed, including 186 children; hundreds more were injured and many were reported missing. In the aftermath, many of the injured died in the only hospital in Beslan, which experienced a shortage of beds, medicine, and surgery equipment. A terrorist hunt by the government ensued resulting in the detaining of more than 10,000 people without proper documentation. Laws on terrorism and powers of law enforcement agencies were enhanced. Power was consolidated in the Kremlin, reforms were made to the electoral system, and powers of the President of Russia were expanded in what was perceived by some as numerous repeals of democratic reforms.

606: Bombings and Explosive Attacks and Terrorism

606.01: Explosive Attacks and Terrorism

Defining Characteristics

VICTIMOLOGY

Explosive terrorism remains a real and dangerous threat as explosive devices and materials have been used over 70% of the time in terrorist incidents. Bombing targets are hard to predict. Military and government agencies such as embassies are prime targets; however restaurants, office buildings, and highly populated areas may also be targeted. Many cases of domestic terrorism have involved bombings, arson, and other attacks on abortion clinics (Burke, 2007).

According to Burke (2007), bombing incidents are preceded by threats approximately 33% of the time.

Crime Scene Indicators Frequently Noted

Explosions can be defined as either physical where high-pressure gas released is produced by mechanical means or as chemical explosives that generate pressure through chemical reactions that take place within the fuel or explosive material. For an explosion to occur there must be oxygen usually in the form of a chemical oxidizer, fuel or combustible substance, ignition, and confinement of fuel and the oxidizer. Some explosives are electrically ignited to initiate a secondary explosive in what is usually referred to as an explosive train (nitroglycerine, TNT). Other explosives are detonated by heat or shock, which creates a detonating wave, sudden production of gases, and instantaneous decomposition of explosive material (mercury fulminate). Detonations involving high-yield explosive material will cause shock waves, blast pressures, shrapnel, and fragments to travel away from the blast in all directions. The reaction will occur at speeds faster than sound exampled by the fact that one will see the explosion and feel the shockwave before they can hear it. Low-yield explosives consist of auto combustion at speeds slower than sound, but may also produce a detonation such as the low-yield explosive materials that were used in the World Trade Center bombing (Burke, 2007).

Vehicles can be used to house explosive materials connected to timed or remote triggering devices as exampled by both the World Trade Center bombing and Oklahoma City bombing (Burke, 2007). The vehicle used to conceal explosives in the World Trade center bombing was packed with 1,200 to 1,500 pounds of homemade urea nitrate and containers of compressed hydrogen gas (Nance, 2008). Pipe bombs are commonly used by terrorists because they are easy to make and their required precursors can be obtained from hardware stores. Flashlights have been identified as potential housing units for pipe bombs. They can be filled with either gunpowder or plastic explosives and easily concealed in backpacks. Ammonium nitrate, which is available in the form of fertilizer, can be used as a chemical oxidizer and mixed with fuel to create an explosive mixture. Black powder is another substance that can be used in explosives and is one of the most common fillers for pipe bombs. Dynamite is made of nitroglycerine which is a severe explosion risk and highly sensitive to heat and shock. Homemade bombs can be made with the help of step-by-step instructions readily available on the Internet, in books, and in videotapes. These instructions may also enable someone to produce potassium nitrate, a common ingredient of black powder. These types of bombs may be difficult to detect as they can be disguised and incorporated into almost any object. Explosive devices may be used together with chemical, biological, nuclear, or incendiary materials to increase damage inflicted on structures and people (Burke, 2007).

STAGING

Not applicable.

COMMON FORENSIC FINDINGS

The al-Qaeda safe house located in New Jersey and used for preparations in the bombing of the World Trade Center in 1993 provided useful evidence during the investigation. Detectives found the house full of acids and other chemicals used to assemble explosives. Traces of nitroglycerine and urea nitrate were found on the carpet and ceiling. Other materials such as hobby fuse, one-gallon containers holding nitric acid and sodium cyanide as well as containers of nitroglycerine (Nance, 2008).

Investigative Considerations

The Department of Defense has outlined some situations that should be reported to law enforcement agencies and illicit subsequent investigation (as quoted in Burke, 2007):

- Anonymous tips, phone calls, or notes of a threatening nature that might identify groups or carry extremist messages.
- Surveillance by suspicious persons of federal offices or federal employees performing official duties.
- Unidentified or unattended packages, cans, or other containers left in or near government offices.
- Unattended and unoccupied vehicles parked in unauthorized or inappropriate locations, particularly those in close proximity to buildings or other structures.
- Requests for plans, blueprints, or engineering specifications for federal buildings or commercially owned buildings that house government offices, by those who have no official reason to have them.
- Unauthorized access even to unsecured areas by unknown or unidentified persons who have no apparent reason for being there.
- Packages or heavy envelopes that arrive in the mail from unknown senders or which have a peculiar odor or appearance—often without a clear return address.
- Confrontation with angry, aggressively belligerent, or threatening persons by federal officials in the performance of their official duties.

- Extremely threatening or violent behavior by coworkers who indicate that they may resort to revenge against a group, company, or government agency.

Search Warrant Suggestions

Search warrants for locations such as safe houses may allow law enforcement to gather important evidence and prevent further activities. Discrepancies between who pays rent and who actually lives there may reveal links to financial sources. The presence of weapons, unusual quantity of military grade ammunition, manufactured and purchased chemicals, ammonium nitrate fertilizer, high octane racing fuel or fuel oil, or books on chemical bomb formulas may indicate premeditated bombings (Burke, 2007).

Case Study: Oklahoma City Bombing

On April 19, 1995, a bomb ripped through the Alfred P. Murrah Federal Building in Oklahoma City at 9:02 in the morning killing 168 and wounding more than 500 including 21 children under the age of five. Timothy McVeigh, age 27, drove a rented truck carrying a bomb that consisted of about 5,000 pounds (2,300 kg) of ammonium nitrate and nitromethane, a motor-racing fuel. He was convicted, sentenced to death, and executed for the bombing. [The following analysis is reprinted with permission from Douglas & Olshaker (1999), pp. 261–269.]

We begin any investigation into bombing by considering three essentials: the motivation of the bomber, his traits and characteristics, and the crime analysis. Power, as it is for the arsonist, is one of the primary motives. There are the strictly mission-oriented people who are thrilled by the act of constructing and placing the bomb and come up with an overarching cause as an excuse. There is the technician, whose gratification comes from the elegance of the design. There is the criminal enterprise, involving the extortionist or profit-oriented bomber. There are bombs set in political, racial, religious, or labor disputes, just as is seen in fire setting. There are those who set bombs for revenge. And there are those who use bombs as dramatic means of suicide. There can be mixed motives, too. Timothy McVeigh could easily fit into the power, mission-oriented, political, and revenge classification. Essentially, it is important to know *why* the bomb was made, set, and exploded.

The bomber's personal traits and characteristics have to be inferred. But from our research study and interviews, we start out with some basic assumptions. The bomber tends to be a White male of average or above average IQ. He is an underachiever but a meticulous plotter and planner. He's cowardly (even more so than the assassin) and nonconfrontational, nonathletic, a loner with self-perceived inadequate personality or social skills. This profile fits McVeigh pretty well; especially as he moved closer to his actual bomb making, he conformed more and more the profile.

The final key investigative consideration is crime analysis and this includes the critical evaluation of the explosive devise itself. What level of expertise or training does it suggest? Are there any unique components, workmanship, or design elements? Was it a time-set, remote-controlled, or booby-trap explosive? When we correlate the devise with the crime, does it appear that the bomb builder and the bomb setter are one in the same, or more than one?

What about victimology? Is the victim (or victims) accidental, or targeted? Random or predictable? What was the risk factor for the victim being in his particular place at this particular time? And how big a risk is the offender taking by constructing or placing this bomb?

Is the physical property that was targeted easily accessible, or remote? Is it individually owned, corporately owned, or government owned? Was the bomb set off at a time of day when it would be reasonable to expect that there would (or would not) be victims on the premises? Is this a single incident or part of a series?

All these questions help determine who. And why. Timothy McVeigh was strong on motive—strong on hatred and resentment, strong enough to set a bomb he had to know would kill and maim many people. He was weak on technique—basic criminal sophistication. He was arrested an hour and a half after the bombing, about 75 miles away when a state trooper stopped him because his battered car had no license plate. Looking in the car, the trooper noticed a gun and arrested him, then took him to jail.

There was significance to the date of the bombing. It was Patriot's Day (the anniversary of the Revolutionary War Battle of Concord, a commemoration the militia movement holds dear) and the second anniversary of the fiery end of the branch Davidian siege at Waco, Texas. Meanwhile, the FBI recovered the vehicle registration number from the wreckage of the truck used to deliver the bomb and traced it to where it had been rented. The clerks there gave them a description of the renter and had FBI artists transform a sketch that was circulated throughout the area. A motel owner recognized the sketched face and gave agents McVeigh's name. They ran it through the National Crime Information computer and learned that he was being held in a jail in Perry, Oklahoma, and about to be released. When McVeigh's clothing was examined, traces of residue from the detonation could be found on his shirt.

607: Aerial Hijackings

Hijackings can occur in various different forms. Most common are hijackings of aircrafts and ships. Historically, many successful aviation hijackings, or "skyjackings," involved escapes to Cuba during the 1960s. Political terrorism during the late 1960s was characterized by the hijackings of aircraft for the purpose of exchanging hostages for prisoners housed in Israel by the Popular Front for the Liberation of Palestine (PFLP) (Minor, 1975). The famous case of D. B. Cooper in 1971 demonstrated the use of skyjacking as a means of extortion. His success and escape with the ransom money created an epidemic of 19 skyjackings of a similar nature in the following year (Gladwell, 2001). Enhanced security during that time has displaced skyjackings to be undertaken by more sophisticated individuals and those who are willing to die for their cause. As evidenced by the events of September 11, airliners have become weapons used to destroy specific targets rather than leverage for negotiations and demands. Hijackings can take many forms and have various motivations. Hijacking for retention involves the seizure of passengers on board a plane and a threat to their lives forcing compliance to the terrorists' conditions or demands. Usually, their aims are political in nature and they may intend to impose a psychological effect to the public of government agencies. Hijacking for movement facilitates the transport of terrorists to or from a region that they are restricted from exiting or entering while holding passengers hostage as guarantees. Hijacking for destruction is the use of an aircraft as a weapon for destroying a specific target and maximizing the overall damage by ensuring the deaths of the passengers on board. Direct actions against the aircraft are characterized by actions to destroy the aircraft in the air using improvised explosive devices or weapons outside of the aircraft such as rocket-propelled grenade launchers, antitank guided missiles, or heavy machine guns (Arasly, 2005).

Defining Characteristics

VICTIMOLOGY

Passengers may be victims who play a political significance to the goals of terrorists who hijack an airliner. Flight 219 originating in Tel Aviv carried a majority of Israeli passengers and was hijacked by terrorists of the Popular Front for the Liberation of Palestine (PFLP) in an attempt to hold them ransom for the exchange of political prisoners. Diplomatic buildings may also be targets for the use of airliners as human operated cruise missiles with intentions for large-scale destruction. Other high-profile targets may include buildings that have a large human capacity or buildings that have a symbolic meaning such as the World Trade Center, which is symbolic of the center of global financial power.

CRIME SCENE INDICATORS FREQUENTLY NOTED

Aircrafts used to destroy certain targets may include cargo aircraft, gliders, helicopters, commercial passenger aircraft, and privately owned aircraft. Terrorists may seek creative ways to smuggle weapons or explosives on board and use them to take control over the aircraft (Homeland Security Office of Intelligence and Analysis and FBI, 2008).

Many in-flight bombings such as the Pan Am Flight 103 over Lockerbie revealed passengers who checked in bags and never boarded the flight (Nance, 2008).

STAGING

Not applicable.

COMMON FORENSIC FINDINGS

Investigation of debris may reveal traces of explosives used such as in the Lockerbie bombing where forensic investigators were able to conclude the use of Semtex. Forensic examination of clothing that was damaged by the explosion revealed the maker and origin of clothing that were in close proximity with the IED. The make of a particular pair of trousers were traced to a privately owned retail outlet in Malta where further inquiry led to descriptions of the individual who purchased the trousers (Ushynskyia, 2010).

Structural damage of the aircraft may indicate exact locations of the bomb such as the small holes caused by explosive hot gases apparent in the fuselage of aircraft that exploded over Lockerbie. Identifying the location of the bomb can help determine at which airport the bomb boarded the plane.

Gas chromatograph technology was used to analyze the chemical composition of pieces of debris and revealed high concentrations of bomb residue on some items.

Investigative Considerations

Forensic investigation may first focus on identifying victims through dental and genetic material. Later forensic investigation may include the analysis of flight data recorders, debris analysis, structural damage, and hijacker identification through surveillance records. Following the Lockerbie bombing, investigators ordered the reconstruction of the aircraft and forensic analysis of suitcases, which exhibited explosive damage. Traces of Semtex, a plastic explosive, were revealed. Fragments of a circuit board and the container of the bomb were also recovered and analyzed (Marquise, 2006).

Search Warrant Suggestions

The critical point of detection of aerial hijackers is the rush and congestion of the airport. The hijacker takes advantage of pressures on airport security to sift through thousands of passengers and attempts to blend into the crowd. In the case of *U.S. vs. Moreno,* the judges acknowledged the gravity of the air piracy problem in the United States and suggested that the airport is a critical zone where fourth amendment exceptions should apply for warrantless searches.

In addition, they believe that airport security officials should always perform a "pat down" when there is appropriate basis for a search (*Moreno v. United States*, 1973). Furthermore it has been established that "once a passenger enters the secured area of an airport, the constitutionality of a screening search does not depend on consent. That legal conclusion rests firmly on Supreme Court precedent and on the government's interest in ensuring the safety of passengers, airline personnel, and the general public" (*Aukai v. United States*, 2007). This applies to general searches prior to boarding and it is emphasized that when a person consents to a search within the airport, they do not have the right to revoke their consent as traditionally granted in public spaces outside the airport (Reid, 2010).

References

Aas, K. F. (2007). *Globalization & crime*. London, England: Sage.

Arasly, J. (2005). Terrorism and civil aviation security: Problems and trends. *Connections: The Quarterly Journal*, 4(1), 75–89.

Aukai v. United States, 04-10226 (2007).

Bales, K., & Lize, S. (2005). *Trafficking in persons in the United States, final report to the national institute of justice*. Retrieved on August 2, 2012, from www.ncjrs.gov/pdffiles1/nij/grants/211980.pdf

Beare, M. (2002). Organized corporate criminality: Tobacco smuggling between Canada and the U.S. *Crime, Law & Social Change*, 37(1), 225–243.

Bilger, V., Hofmann, M., & Jandl, M. (2006). Human smuggling as a transnational service industry: Evidence from Austria. *International Migration*, 44(4), 59–93.

Black, R. M., & Read, R. W. (2007). Environmental and biomedical sample analysis in support of allegations of use of chemical warfare agents. *Toxin Reviews*, 26(1), 275–298.

Brandt, P. T., & Sandler, T. (2009). Hostage taking: Understanding terrorism event dynamics. *Journal of Policy Modeling*, 31(1), 758–778.

Budowle, B., Beaudry, J. A., Barnaby, N. G., Giusti, A. M., Bannan, J. D., & Keim, P. (2007). Role of law enforcement response and microbial forensics in investigation of bioterrorism. *Croation Medical Journal*, 48(1), 437–449.

Burke, R. (2007). *Counter-terrorism for emergency responders* (2nd ed.). Boca Raton, FL: Taylor & Francis Group.

Cavanaugh, S. (2011). On the lookout for human trafficking. *Canadian Nurse*, 107(2), 24–25.

Cook, P. J., Cukier, W., & Krause, K. (2009). The illicit firearms trade in North America. *Criminology & Criminal Justice*, 9(3), 265–286.

Cullen-DuPont, K. (2009). *Global issues: Human trafficking*. New York, NY: Infobase.

Dembek, Z. F., Pavlin, J. A., & Kortepeter, M. G. (2007). Epidemiology of biowarfare and bioterrorism. In Z. F. Dembek (ed.), *Textbooks of military medicine: Medical aspects of biological warfare*. Washington, DC: Borden Institute.

Department of Justice Canada, Evaluation Division. (2004). *Measures to combat organized crime: Mid-term evaluation*. Policy Integration and Coordination Section.

Di Nicola, A. (2005). Trafficking in human beings and smuggling of migrants. In P. Reichel (ed.), *Handbook of transnational crime and justice*. Thousand Oaks, CA: Sage.

Dickson-Gilmore, E. J. (2002). *Communities, contraband and conflict: Considering restorative responses to repairing the harms implicit in smuggling in the Akwesasne Mohawk Nation*. Retrieved on August 9, 2012, from www.rcmp-grc.gc.ca/pubs/abo-aut/contraband-contrebande-eng.pdf

Dougherty, J. (2004). *Illegals: The imminent threat posed by our unsecured U.S.-Mexico order*. Nashville, TN: WND Books.

Douglas, J., & Olshaker, M. (1999). *The anatomy of motive*. New York, NY: Scribner.

Federal Bureau of Investigation. (2008). *Amerithrax investigation: Release of affidavits/search warrant*. Retrieved August 10, 2012, from www.fbi.gov/about-us/history/famous-cases/anthrax-amerithrax/08-429SWAffAttach07524.pdf

Government Accountability Office (GAO). (2011). *Overstay enforcement: Additional mechanisms for collecting, assessing, and sharing data could strengthen DHS's efforts but would have costs*. Report to the Committee of Homeland Security and Governmental Affairs, U.S. Senate.

Gladwell, M. (2001). *Safety in the skies: How far can airline security go?* Retrieved on August 9, 2012, from www.gladwell.com/pdf/safetysky.pdf

Harr, J. S., & Hess, K. M. (2006). *Constitutional law and the criminal justice system*. Belmont, CA: Wadsworth.

Hatcher, C., Mohandie, K., Turner, J., & Gelles, M. G. (1998). The role of the psychologist in crisis/hostage negotiations. *Behavioral Sciences and the Law, 15*, 455–472.

Henretig, F. M., Cieslak, T. J., & Eitzen E. M. Jr. (2002). Biological and chemical terrorism. *Journal of Pediatrics, 141*(3), 311–326.

Homeland Security Office of Intelligence and Analysis and Federal Bureau of Investigation. (2008). *Potential terrorist attack methods: Joint special assessment*. Retrieved on August 9, 2012, from www.gwu.edu/~nsarchiv/nukevault/ebb388/docs/EBB015.pdf

Jamieson, R. (1999). Contested jurisdiction communities and cross-border crime: The case of Akwesasne. *Crime, Law & Social Change, 30*(1), 259–272.

Jamieson, R., South, N., & Taylor, I. (1998). Economic liberalization and cross-border Crime: The North American Free Trade Area and Canada's border with the U.S. Part I. *International Journal of Sociology of Law, 26*(1), 245–272.

Jandl, M. (2007). Irregular migration, human smuggling, and the eastern enlargement of the European Union. *International Centre for Migration Policy Development, 41*(2), 291–315.

Leman, J., & Janssens, S. (2007). The various "Safe"-house profiles in East-European human smuggling and trafficking. *Journal of Ethnic and Migration Studies, 33*(8), 1377–1388.

Lippin, T. M., McQuiston, T. H., Bradley-Bull, K., Burns-Johnson, T., Cook, L., & Gill, M. L. (2006). Chemical plants remain vulnerable to terrorists: A call to action. *Environmental Health Perspectives, 114*(9), 1307–1311.

Logan, T. K., Walker, R., & Hunt, G. (2009). Understanding Human Trafficking in the United States. *Trauma, Violence, & Abuse, 10*(1), 3–30.

Luk, R., Cohen, J. E., & Ferrence, R. (2007). *Contraband cigarettes in ontario*. Toronto: Ontario Tobacco Research Unit, Special Report Series.

MacWillson, A. C. (1992). *Hostage-taking terrorism: Incident-response strategy*. New York, NY: St. Martin's Press.

Madsen, F. G. (2009). *Global institutions: Transnational organized crime*. New York, NY: Routledge.

McDaniel, M. C., & Ellis, C. M. (2009). The Beslan hostage crisis: A case study for emergency responders. *Journal of Applied Security Research, 4*(1), 21–35.

Marquise, R. A. (2006). *Scotbom: Evidence and the Lockerbie investigation*. New York, NY: Algora.

Miller, B. J. (2010). Fueling violence along the southwest border: What more can be done to protect the citizens of the United States and Mexico from firearms trafficking. *Houston Journal of International Law, 32*(1), 163–199.

Minor, W. (1975). Skyjacking crime control methods. *Journal of Criminal Law and Criminology, 66*(1), 94–105.

Mittelman, J. H., & Johnston, R. (1999). The globalization of organized crime, the courtesan state, and the corruption of civil society. *Global Governance, 5*(1), 103–126.

Moossey, R. (2009). Sex trafficking: Identifying cases and victims. *National Institute of Justice Journal, 262*, 2–11.

Moreno v. the United States, 475 F.2d 44 No. 72-2484 (1973).

Nance, M. W. (2008). *Terrorist recognition handbook: A practitioner's manual for predicting and identifying terrorist activities* (2nd ed.). Boca Raton, FL: Taylor & Francis Group.

Nassar, J. R. (2009). *Globalization & terrorism: The migration of dreams and nightmares* (2nd ed.). Lanham, MD: Rowman & Littlefield.

Payan, T. (2006). The drug war and the U.S.—Mexico Border: The state of affairs. *South Atlantic Quarterly, 105*(4), 864–880.

Reid, P. (2010). *U.S. airports a "Constitutional Twilight Zone."* CBS News. Retrieved on August 10, 2012, from www.cbsnews.com/2100-201_162-7082555.html

Schneider, S. (2000). Organized contraband smuggling and its enforcement in Canada: An assessment of the anti-smuggling initiative. *Trends in Organized Crime, 6*(2), 1–31.

Seto, Y. (2001). *The sarin gas attack in Japan and the related forensic investigation.* Organisation for the Prohibition of Chemical Weapons. Retrieved on August 9, 2012, from www.opcw.org/news/article/the-sarin-gas-attack-in-japan-and-the-related-forensic-investigation/

Spener, D. (2004). Mexican migrant-smuggling: A cross-border cottage industry. *Journal of International Migration & Integration, 5*(3), 295–320.

Spener, D. (2009). *Clandestine crossings: Migrants and coyotes on the Texas—Mexico border.* Ithaca, NY: Cornell University Press.

Ushynskyia, S. (2010). Pan Am Flight 103 investigation and lessons learned. *Aviation, 13*(3), 78–86.

Van Liempt, I., & Doomernik, J. (2006). Migrant's agency in the smuggling process: The perspectives of smuggled migrants in the Netherlands. *Institute for Migration and Ethnic Studies, 44*(4), 165–189.

Viano, E. (2010). Globalization, transnational crime and state power: The need for a new criminology. *Rivista di Criminologia, Vittimologia e Sicurezza, 3–4*(1), 63–85.

The Victoria Advocate. (2003, August 28). *Safehouses in immigrant smuggling chain identified.* Retrieved on August 2, 2012, from http://news.google.com/newspapers?nid=861&dat=20030828&id=CXpTAAAAIBAJ&sjid=pYUDAAAAIBAJ&pg=6883,7169874

Wilder, S. H. (1981). International terrorism and hostage-taking: An overview. *Manitoba Law Journal, 4*(1), 367–376.

Zhang, S., & Chin, K. (2002). Enter the dragon: Inside Chinese human smuggling organizations. *Criminology, 40*(4), 737–768.

Chapter 16

Mass and Serial Homicide

Multiple-victim homicides can be classified under the existing structure without having their own unique group of codes. For example, in 1994 in Newark Valley, New York, a 47-year-old woman, Waneta Hoyt, was convicted of murdering her five infant children between January 26, 1965 and July 28, 1971 (Gudjonsson, 2003, p. 542). Waneta Hoyt's crime is classified under 122.02: Staged domestic homicide and serial murder. Domestic homicide implies a familial relationship between victims and offender. All five murders were staged so that the deaths appeared accidental and as a result of sudden infant death syndrome (SIDS). Her first and third children were found dead in their cribs, as if they suddenly died due to unknown reasons. Her second child was staged to have died from choking on rice cereal, and her last two children as a result of prolonged apnea and eventually SIDS late at night (Gudjonnson, 2003, p. 542). Furthermore, Waneta Hoyt's murders are placed under the category of serial murder, which is the killing of two or more victims over an extended time period and at various locations.

This chapter contains cases of multiple motive homicides with multiple victims of mass murder and serial murders. In many of these cases, there can be spillover between the types of murders described. Mass murder is defined as the killing of four or more victims at one location or crime scene. The serial murderer kills more than two victims and involves more than one location or crime scene. It is also important to consider the differences between serial and mass killers in terms of state of mind, motivation and mode of apprehension.

Mass Murder

A mass murderer kills his victims in one place with one crime scene. The location of the murders may be on the open street, inside a home or building, or at a school, theater, church, or post office.

There are psychological and criminological discrepancies between the two type of murder. Regarding mass murderers, with the exception of materially motivated and attention seeking offenders, there is usually no attempt to avoid capture whatsoever. They might enter a gunfight with the police, but ultimately they know they are going to be outnumbered and lose. A much larger representation of mass murderers also choose to commit suicide or "death by cop" when cornered. Mass murders are chiefly act-focused crimes involving guns, fire, or explosives. Paraphilias and deviant sexual acts are comparatively rare. Victims are more frequently family members than in serial murder cases.

On March 26, 2006, Aaron Kyle Huff, age 28, walked in on a house party carrying two guns, more than 300 rounds of ammunition, a baseball bat, and a black machete. He began shooting and killed six people between the ages of 14 and 32. He told guests as he blazed away, "There's plenty for everyone." Police said the victims, many of them dressed up as zombies in black with white face paint, had met Huff earlier in the night at a rave called Better Off Undead and invited him to a party at their rented home. Huff left the party at about 7:00 a.m. and returned wearing bandoliers of ammunition and carrying a twelve-gauge pistol-grip shotgun and a handgun. He fired on the 30 young partygoers gathered in the house before walking out. Huff committed suicide when confronted by an officer outside the house early Saturday.

Mass murder can be combined with a spree-type murder when the murderer goes to more than one location to find and kill his victims. The case study is about mass murderer Charles Whitman, who killed his wife at one location and his mother at another. The next morning he went to a third location, the University of Texas Tower, where he killed multiple people. Whitman can be classified as both serial, spree, and a mass murderer. He used multiple methods of killing: he strangled his mother, used a knife to kill his wife, and used a rifle to kill people from the University of Texas Tower.

Case Study: Charles Whitman

Case Contributed by Kathryn A. Reboul

In 1966, Charles Whitman did not feel respected. He felt that despite all his hard work, he was not achieving success in almost all areas of his life. In July, Whitman heard of the Speck killings: Richard Speck had killed eight nurses in their Chicago school dormitory and had gotten a huge amount of publicity. The notoriety Speck received from his murders may have seemed appealing to Whitman. In fact, the same week as the publicity of the Speck killings, he visited the Tower.

It would not have been hard for him to figure out how to get that attention for himself. He had already spoken of shooting people from the tower at the University of Texas, and given his military training he knew how to use the tower as a fortress from which to kill other people. He was trained and certified as a sharpshooter in the U.S. Marines. Using guns was something he had mastered since childhood and it had brought him accolades while in the military.

Timeline to the Shootings

Months before the shooting, Whitman commented to friends about going up to the tower to shoot people. But no one took him seriously and no one seemed to think that this statement might be an indication that they needed to reach out to him.

On his own Whitman requested psychiatric help. On March 29, 1966, he met with Maurice D. Heatly, a University of Texas psychiatrist. Whitman told Dr. Heatly of his parents' separation was upsetting him greatly and he was overwhelmed. He also complained of "irrational thoughts" and that "something was happening to him and he didn't seem to be himself." He mentioned that he had twice assaulted his wife and that she was afraid of him. He had also indicated to Heatly that he had been a marine and had been court-martialed for fighting. Heatly stated in his report about Whitman's meeting with him that Whitman "readily admits having overwhelming periods of hostility with a very minimum of provocation." During their meeting, Whitman spoke sometimes with great hostility and then quickly could become weepy. He also made "vivid reference" to "thinking about going up on the tower with a deer rifle and start shooting people."

Whitman had made a specific threat of violence that, given his military background, he would have had the expertise to carry out. He had a problem with hostility and irrational thoughts and mentioned that he had committed violent acts in the past.

The Crimes

The last week of July 1966 had been very hot. On Thursday, July 28, and Friday, July 29, many people noted that Whitman had appeared fine in his classes and work. People who saw him on the evening of July 31 said he was especially calm.

Whitman sat down on Friday night to write a letter to the world to explain his actions. He wrote the letter as if he had already killed his wife and mother, when in fact he had not yet killed either. He was interrupted by a knock on the door by friends. Charlie was unusually calm. He talked quite normally about a number of topics, and at one point the three of them went out for ice cream. After they left, he probably put his note where Kathy would not see it and then went to pick up his wife from work.

There was nothing notable about the evening. Kathy had a conversation with a friend, and Kathy and Charlie called her parents to talk. All seemed normal. During a visit at a friend's home, Margaret, Charlie's mother, called him to let him know where she was. Charlie asked if he and Kathy could come over for a while to cool off before bed. Margaret rushed home. Kathy may have been sleeping when her husband left.

Victimology

Whitman arrived at his mother's a few minutes after midnight. Although no autopsy was done, it is believed that he strangled her with a hose and then gave her a fatal blow to the back of the head. After he killed her, he engaged in undoing behavior: he placed her in bed and covered her up. When she was found, she looked almost as if she were sleeping. He then wrote a note in which he spoke of relieving her of "suffering here on earth" and then went on a venomous tirade about his father.

Crime Scene Indicators

After the murder, Whitman returned home and quietly entered his bedroom. He pulled back the covers to expose his wife's body and stabbed her five times in the chest. She died instantly, probably without waking up. He pulled the sheets up to cover her body.

Before he left, he placed the note by her body and used rugs to cover the blood on the floor. In a move that displayed premeditation of his upcoming crimes, he left a note on her door that he wrote (but appeared to be from her) asking the housekeeper not to disturb her in the morning. He was buying himself more time.

In the lobby he asked the night watchman to let him back into his mother's apartment to get a prescription bottle. The night watchman let him in. Charlie reappeared in a moment with a pill bottle, then left the apartment and headed home.

He retrieved the note he had been writing earlier in the evening when friends had stopped by. He wrote, "friends interrupted 8–1–66 Mon 3:00 a.m. Both Dead," and then continued with ramblings. He also wrote a note to each of his brothers and to his father. (To this day Whitman's letter to his father has not been made public.) The notes to his brothers were short and seemed to be an attempt to explain their mother's feelings to them.

Whitman began to fill a large trunk with supplies. It took the Austin Police five pages to inventory all the items. It was clear from the food, foot powder, water, and various items that he thought he might be up in the tower for some time. And it was clear from the guns, knives, and massive amounts of ammunition that he was prepared to kill a lot of people.

He called Kathy's supervisor and told her that Kathy was sick and would not be coming to work that day. Once again, he was indicating he wanted to have the time to follow through on his plan to commit mass murder.

The trunk was heavy, so he rented a dolly for $2.04. He also cashed two checks and bought more ammunition and another rifle at a hardware store. He left and then soon came back to return a bent clip of ammunition. This last act almost seems to indicate that to his very last moment, he planned on being meticulous and that his plans of mass murder may have even calmed him and helped him to focus enough to commit a complex and horrific act.

He then went to a gun shop, bought more ammunition, cleaning solvent, and an automatic shotgun. And finally he called his mother's workplace so her absence would not be questioned.

When he finished packing everything, he had three rifles, an automatic shotgun, a revolver, and two pistols. The most accurate of these weapons was the Remington 6mm with 4X scope. With the scope he could have shot accurately at 800 feet. The automatic shotgun would have less accuracy for the 231 feet he was trying to cover than any of the rifles. (The height of the observation deck on the tower, where Whitman was shooting from, was 231 feet from the ground.) The revolver and pistols may have indicated he expected to be shooting at close range. And the amount of ammunition was staggering. An inventory of his ammunition after he had stopped shooting listed 9 full boxes of ammunition and 16 other types of ammunition or an estimated total of 700 rounds of ammunition.

To get to the top of the tower with a trunk on a dolly without appearing suspicious, he dressed like a workman and blended in. It was not until he reached the 28th floor that anyone questioned him. There, the receptionist probably questioned what he was doing with the dolly. He shot her. Two adults walked past the scene without noticing the murdered woman and went down the tower. Then a family of tourists came up to the 28th floor and tried to enter the door that he had blocked. He shot at them, killing two instantly. He then barricaded the door again.

Sniper Shootings

Soon, Whitman would begin to follow through on his plan. He began to shoot people from his fortress on the observation deck of the University of Texas Tower. His first victim was an unborn baby in its mother's womb. He killed the baby without killing the mother. And then he killed the baby's father. He continued his rampage until he had killed 13 people and wounded 31. Five days later, another individual died. Another death years later was also attributed to Whitman's actions.

Whitman never shot any victim more than once. He maintained cover by shooting through rainspouts so he was not an easy target, and he retreated quickly after he made a shot. The police did not have the same type of high-power long-range weapons and could not shoot accurately at such a distance. Ironically it was the citizens of Texas who had the best weapons. Many rushed to the campus with their own high-power weapons to kill the sniper whose identity was not yet known.

Whitman's rampage finally ended when he was killed by two police officers. He had held the campus hostage for 96 minutes. His murders finally ended approximately 12 hours from the time he had killed his mother.

Types of Victims

Whitman had three types of victim. First, his mother and his wife were victims of domestic violence. His second victims were third-party victims, killed because Whitman thought they would interfere with his plan of going up on the tower to start shooting people. These victims were the receptionist in the tower and a family going up the tower.

Not everyone that Whitman encountered became a target for shooting. Whitman let two people, Don Walden and Cheryl Botts, go past him to leave the tower. They were not stopping him from his goal of shooting people from the tower, so he may not have felt the need to shoot them. They also engaged in activities that reduced their likelihood of victimization. They were friendly, did not question Whitman's behavior or the environment, and quickly got out of Whitman's way. Their demeanor, behavior, and speed saved their lives in a situation where they were at high risk for being killed.

When they encountered Whitman, they smiled and said, "Hello." They did not comment on the two rifles he was holding and did not realize that a stain on the floor was blood. (It was on a dark floor so it would not have been obvious.) Cheryl warned Don not to step in the "stuff." They were not upset by a chair lying on its side. In these cases, acting innocent saved their lives. Or it may have been Whitman's disguise that saved their lives. Because he was wearing a janitor's uniform, the stain and overturned chair did not seem threatening. And because he was a clean-cut young man who appeared to have a reason for being there, they did not feel threatened by his guns. Don almost made a comment that Whitman "was going to shoot pigeons."

Whitman's third type of victim was the strangers he shot from the tower. Like his third-party victims, they were simply in the wrong place at the wrong time. There is nothing to indicate he knew any of the people he shot from the tower.

Risk Level of Victims

Of all the people killed on August 1, Kathy Whitman had the highest risk level of being killed by Whitman in a domestic violence homicide. She had disclosed to her parents that she was afraid that Charlie could kill her. She was living with a violent man with a history of assaulting her who had an arsenal of weapons that he was comfortable and skilled at using. His description of her as "My Most Precious Possession" was disturbing and indicated that he thought of her more as a possession than an individual in her own right. The fact that she left him and spoke of divorce may have increased her risk of violence from him. Whitman's mother's leaving her husband in March 1966 may have served as a reminder of Kathy's "betrayal" of him. Separation or threat of separation can increase a victim's risk of homicide in an abusive relationship.

Within Dr. Heatly's March 29 report were statements Whitman made about his wife's having less fear of him than in the past because he had made a more intense effort to avoid losing his temper with her. Today, this would be understood as a red flag where the abuser's behavior suddenly changes prior to his murder of her.

Margaret Whitman could be viewed as a moderate- to high-risk victim because her presence was adding stress to her overstressed, volatile, heavily armed son who was using an excessive amount of stimulants. Before she was murdered, she was also at risk from her husband, C. A. Whitman, because he had previously assaulted her.

In his final notes to the "world," Whitman reiterated his intense hatred of his father. Whitman was desperate to stop the calls from his father to help his mother to return to an abusive relationship. Of all the people he killed, he did not kill the one person he hated the most, suggesting great fear of his father or a desire for him to suffer by not having his wife return.

Whitman's third-party victims, the tower receptionist and the family of tourists, were at the wrong place at the wrong time. They did not die because they were in dangerous professions or engaged in dangerous behaviors. They would be considered low-risk victims.

The strangers whom Whitman killed and wounded were mostly low-risk victims engaged in low-risk behaviors. It was the middle of the day and on a college campus. The victims were primarily students, college staff, and teachers coming or going to class, lunch, or home. Most were in their teens, 20s, and 30s.

Some individuals did increase their risk by attempting to shoot Whitman or attempting to rescue the wounded. Billy Speed, a police officer, was in Whitman's line of fire because of his profession.

Whitman's Death

It is clear that Whitman anticipated his own death. There are some statements in notes he wrote before his death that sounded like a last will and testament. He requested an autopsy, asked to be cremated, and requested that his dog be given to his wife's parents.

He was settling his affairs. He asked to have his pictures developed. And he stated that he was explaining his actions so this type of thing could be avoided in the future. Everything indicated he did not expect to have the opportunity to explain later. He wrote numerous letters. He left a note by his mother's body explaining her death, and he left a note by his wife's body explaining his recent deterioration of his state of mind. He also wrote to his brother Patrick, his brother John, and his father. Whitman had an elaborate plan, but there was no indication that he had planned any escape route.

Whitman chose to engage in activity that he could reasonably assume would lead to his death. His actions indicated that he was suicidal. The fact that his cause of death was gunfire by one or two police officers does not change that he in effect set up his own death. Whitman's death could be termed *suicide by cop* or *suicide by proxy*, in which a suicidal person sets the stage to be killed by law enforcement.

Autopsies

The autopsy on Charles Whitman was compromised because he was embalmed before he was autopsied and no toxicology tests were done on his blood or urine. Whitman felt something physical was wrong in his head. To many people's surprise, he was right: Whitman had a brain tumor. During the autopsy, it was identified as approximately the size of a pecan and said to be located in the white matter below the gray center thalamus. There is some disagreement about the effect this tumor had. Some felt it could have caused extreme action. Others feel it would have no effect at all. And others felt that it would have caused a lot of pain that could be a partial explanation for his behavior and his headaches. It is also interesting to note that Whitman's skull was unusually thin, at 2 to 4 millimeters.

Many people in law enforcement state that Whitman is the reason special weapons and tactics (SWAT) teams were developed. It was clear that the police at this time did not have the type of weapon they needed to shoot Whitman from the ground. It is also clear that fewer people would have died if they had been able to get to him sooner. If the events of August 1, 1966, happened again today, the police would react more quickly, in a more organized fashion and with better weapons.

Spree Murder

Spree murder is a subcategory of serial murder. Spree murderers appear to select their victims at random and tend to do their damage within a short time span. They are like killing machines up to the point that they are caught or turn themselves in. The killer often commits suicide or goes for what is known as *suicide by cop:* putting himself in a position where police will have to kill him.

Spree killers select victims who will meet their personal needs at the time. In other words, they kill for money, sex, or simply because they are hungry. In cases involving spree killers, authorities usually know who they are looking for: they have the killer's identity. As a fugitive, he may go to an area where he feels comfortable, the way alleged railroad killer Angel Maturino Resendez, also known as Rafael Resendez-Ramirez, stuck to the tracks.

Some spree serial killers have a shorter time span between murders, perhaps days, and where the victims may not have a common thread. It is similar to an extension of a mass murder episode; however, the killer moves from one location to another during his killing spree rather than barricading himself in one location, as does the mass murderer. The duration of the spree can be brief as in the case of Wesbecker (nine minutes) or can be much longer as in the case of Charles Starkweather or Christopher Wilder (weeks and months). As a rule, the spree is of shorter duration. This type of offender is usually mission oriented and demonstrates no escape plan. He most often is killed by responding police or kills himself in a final act of desperation. Occasionally, he is captured to stand trial. When this occurs, the offender often admits his crimes by pleading guilty or pleads not guilty by reason of insanity.

Case Study: Andrew Cunanan

Case Contributed by Danielle Esposito

Andrew Cunanan reached headline news in 1997 after shooting the famous designer Gianni Versace on his doorstep in Florida in broad daylight. Before killing Versace, the FBI had Cunanan on their Top Ten Most Wanted list for four other murders over the previous two months across the country.

Victimology

Cunanan killed four men before he killed Versace. His first two murders were two men he knew personally: his friend Jeffrey Trail, on April 27, 1997, in Minneapolis, Minnesota; and his lover, architect David Madson, who was found outside Minneapolis on April 29, 1997, with gunshot wounds to the head. Police recognized a connection, as Trail's body had been found in Madson's Minneapolis loft apartment, and started an intensive manhunt.

After the two murders, Cunanan drove to Chicago and killed prominent real estate developer Lee Miglin, age 72, on May 4, 1997. Cunanan escaped in Miglin's car to Pennsville, New Jersey, at the Finn's Point National Cemetery, killing a caretaker named William Reese, age 45, on May 9, 1997. Cunanan killed him for his pickup truck.

While the manhunt resumed for Reese's truck, Cunanan remained in hiding in Miami Beach, Florida, for months between his fourth and fifth murders.

On July 15, 1997, at around 8:30 a.m., Andrew Cunanan followed Gianni Versace home from breakfast. He came up behind him while he was putting the keys in his front door and shot him in the back of the head, point-blank. After Versace fell to the ground, he shot him twice more.

Crime Scene Indicators

There were multiple inside and outdoor crime scenes. In shock, Madson rolled up the body with Cunanan, and the two of them headed out of Minneapolis in Madson's Jeep. Forty-five miles out of Minneapolis, he pulled over the Jeep and shot Madson three times in the head. It is still unknown as to why Miglin was targeted. Cunanan left his passport and a weapon used in killing Miglin in the Mercedes, again leaving evidence for the police to find.

Forensics

Trail was beaten with a claw hammer over 30 times. Cunanan bound and tortured Miglin by kicking him, driving a pair of pruning shears through his chest, and cutting his neck with a hacksaw. Afterward, he ran over Miglin's body with his own Mercedes.

Investigation

Cunanan's last murder appears to have been premeditated. After shooting Versace, Cunanan ran and was chased by a witness. Police found the truck in a nearby parking garage. In the truck, they found the clothes Cunanan had just been wearing, another passport, and newspaper clippings of his murders.

Cunanan was next sighted in a nearby Miami houseboat. The SWAT team found Cunanan inside on the bed clad in only his boxer shorts and shot through the mouth with the same gun he used to shoot all the other victims.

Outcome

Cunanan left no note to explain his murders. To try to understand his motive, a look at his background and personality provides some understanding of the killer and his motivation.

Andrew Philip Cunanan was born on August 31, 1969, to Modesto Cunanan and Mary Anne Shilacci. Filipino-born Modesto served for the Fleet Marines in Vietnam. While away from home, he came up with the idea that his wife was being unfaithful, to the point where he questioned the legitimacy of his children. By the time Andrew was born, Mary Anne had become so depressed she was unable to care properly for the infant leading Modesto to claim how he raised the children on his own.

Modesto and Mary Anne argued increasingly as the years went on. Cunanan saw his mother's fear of his father and grew up with a distorted view of families. But Cunanan tended to brag to his friends about his family's wealth until his stories were told so often and were so unbelievable he became known as a pathological liar.

At age 13, Cunanan had his first gay experience. He was often recalled as being self-absorbed, always wanting to be the center of attention, a trait often seen in people who become violently antisocial. Cunanan also began to come up with aliases for himself and would change his appearance, sometimes drastically. He also began dating older men whom he could live off and would buy him expensive things. Andrew Cunanan was good looking, intelligent, suave, smooth, flamboyant, and an extroverted imposter.

Two months before killing Versace, Cunanan checked into a Miami hotel under an alias and was active in the nightlife. He wore disguises, which he did from the beginning of his rampage, almost on instinct. He enjoyed altering his appearance often, and during his rampage, the FBI sent pictures of him in many different disguises. He made several risky appearances while in Miami, knowing that the police were looking for him, including loitering near Versace's home. He was believed to have looked for Versace in high-priced gay Miami bars.

No one knows Andrew Cunanan's motivation for all the killings. Cunanan had fallen in with the underground gay culture of San Francisco and was involved with drugs and well known as a popular sex slave. He appeared in many pornographic movies, got pleasure from sadomasochism, and truly enjoyed his status in the underground. Fantasy had played a role in Cunanan's life from early on as an escape from his parents, and grew to involve his imagined status with celebrities and the belief that the world revolved around him.

Cunanan's tendency toward jealousy seems to have played a large role in some of his murders as well. Trail and Madson had become everything he could not: they were professionals and still developing, while he was stagnant, and their families accepted their homosexuality, while his did not. This envy also plays a large role in Versace's murder. It is likely that Cunanan saw Versace as a kind of icon for the gay community. Versace was a symbol of everything Cunanan wanted to be—a successful homosexual and a rich celebrity—and he lashed out at him. These were all traits that Cunanan desperately wanted. There is also a possibility that he targeted Versace because he was seeking worldwide notoriety that he was not attaining from his previous murders. Cunanan seemed to be killing for one of two reasons: he either needed something from the person he killed (such as a truck) or he needed to be the person. Although his motivations may have revolved around necessity and jealousy, there was something deeper in his psyche building up to the killings.

The reports of Cunanan's personality show many of the behavioral features of a psychopath. He was described as being glib, superficial with a sense of superiority over the police and convinced the world revolved around him. He was a master of disguises and deception. He was a complete chameleon and described as an intelligent con man. He continually showed a lack of remorse or guilt in each of his murders and was unconcerned with others' feelings. People were expendable. He lived a parasitic lifestyle off the wealthy men he dated, never having an apartment of his own, never holding a steady job and lacking long-term goals. He was promiscuous from age 13, even gaining notoriety for it later on. He had no responsibility, and all his money came from his parents, his boyfriends, or prostitution. He tended to put on a mask to those he met. People recalled him as soft-spoken and unassuming, intellectual and worldly, or a flamboyant party boy. He deceived and eluded everyone, continually causing people to ask questions about him. He did this all the way to the end.

Type of Murderer: Spree or Serial?

Professionals speculated on the type of murderer he was. When he was on the run, no one knew where he would strike next. There seemed to be no pattern to whom he was killing and where. The signature and pattern were not prominent. His methods of murder included knives and guns.

Serial killers tend to go about their lives and murdering on the side, while spree killers act in passion and without the emotional cooling-off period. In this sense, Cunanan seemed to be more of a spree killer. He falls into this category because of the victims who seemed to be a target of opportunity, except for Versace, who appeared to be targeted.

Serial Murder

By definition a serial criminal is a successful criminal. The more times he is able to get away with a particular offense, the better able he will be to refine his modus operandi (MO) to continue getting away with the same crime. In any given case, this may be because the offender is above average in intelligence, despite his record of underachievement. Many serial offenders, particularly of the organized variety, are reasonably bright. But success at avoiding detection and capture can also be due to the obsessive amount of time and energy the offender puts into fantasizing, planning, and evaluating the crime. When one of the authors (JED) was a teenaged agricultural intern, he noted with amazement the uncanny ability of cows to wander out of seemingly secure enclosures. He finally concluded that if the cow had nothing else on its mind, it could devote all of its mental resources to the task of finding a way out, however long it took. The situation of the sexual predator who spends an inordinate amount of his time, intellect, and emotional resources on his crimes turns out to be a somewhat analogous situation.

Thus, armed with an understanding of the commonalities among criminal sexual predators, it is equally important to understand the differences. Because only then may we be equipped to evaluate the offender as an individual, to lend aid and support to his victims, to assist in his prosecution, and to make an attempt to predict his likelihood of future violence. The method and manner in which a crime is committed relates directly to the personality type of the criminal.

Sex and violence become intertwined at a very early age in the background of a serial killer and it evolves over a period of time. People don't wake up one morning and decide to go out and kill people. There is an evolutionary process.

A serial killer typically tries to evade being apprehended to the best of his or her ability—not by shooting it out with cops, but by avoiding falling on their radar altogether. Their crimes generally show greater evidence of paraphilias and deviant sexuality than mass murderers (female serial killers, obviously less so). They also tend to target strangers. A serial killer usually goes after strangers, but the victims tend to share similarities such as gender, age, or occupation. Although he prefers a certain look or background, it does not mean he will not substitute another victim if he cannot find his intended target.

At any given time, there are between 35 and 50 serial killers in the United States, and that is a conservative estimate. About a dozen serial killers are arrested each year.

Areas where there is prostitution, a drug culture, runaways, so-called throwaways, street people, and children gravitating to bus depots are fertile ground for serial killers. Compounding the problem, there are more than seventeen thousand police agencies in the United States, some with limited technology and the inability to share information. If there is an inability to link cases, agencies may not even know they have a serial killer on their hands. Throw into the mix the mobility of the offender—within a state or across state lines—and he can get away with murder.

Serial Murder Case: Green River Killer

Case Contributed by Michael Maddaleni

Background

For 20 years starting in the early 1980s, a serial killer terrorized the Seattle area of Washington State, leaving behind a trail of women's bodies. The first were discovered in 1982 in or near Washington State's Green River, and the killer was soon being referred to the Green River killer. The serial murder investigation was one of the longest and largest in United States history (Smith & Guillen, 1991).

In 2001, investigators eventually got their man. Gary Ridgway was arrested, and as part of a controversial deal that helped him avoid the death penalty, pled guilty to killing 48 women. He is now serving life imprisonment without parole at the state penitentiary in Walla-Walla, Washington (Prothero & Smith, 2006).

Victimology

On August 12, 1982, a young woman's body was found posed half in the Green River, half on the riverbank by a worker looking out over the river. Three days later a man rafting on the same river looked into the water and saw an African American woman staring back at him face up in the water. As he turned around, he saw another body in the water (Reichert, 2004). The three women were identified prostitutes that worked the "Strip" on Pacific Highway.

Over the next 20 years, the bodies of numerous other women were discovered around the same area in eight clumps. All of the bodies found were naked and left in degrading positions.

Crime Scene Indicators

There were several crime scenes to include the initial contact meeting of the victim, the river, and isolated dump sites. Most of the victims were young prostitutes or runaways who had been dumped in water, muddy areas, or woodlands in a 30-mile radius. A few were discovered in trash heaps and dumpsters by the Sea-Tac Airport.

Forensics

The medical examiner determined that the first three women found had been asphyxiated, probably strangled, and that semen was discovered in two of their bodies (Rule, 2004). In 1982 there was not any DNA technology or DNA databases available to help identify whom the semen belonged to. Two bodies had triangular shaped stones tightly inserted into their vaginas that required surgical removal (Reichert, 2004). The information about the triangular rocks was *not* public knowledge but suggested a signature to the police.

There were microscopic paint samples traced back to his truck-painting company to link him to several of the murders.

Investigation

The first body was lying facedown, unclothed, in three feet of water. She was weighted down with rocks that had been laid on her foot, knee, buttocks, and shoulder. The second body, submerged 10 feet farther upstream in water that was a little deeper, was lying face-up, and was nude except for a front-closure bra that had been opened. This body had been secured with rocks on her right leg and hip, left ankle, and shoulder (Reichert, 2004). There was a third body in the brush near the other bodies.

Police theorized that whoever killed these young women took great time to hide the victims and spent time at the crime scene weighing the bodies down with rocks. They profiled the man was strong to carry the three bodies from a vehicle and down the steep bank and its slippery grasses (Rule, 2004). The police began their investigation interviewing pimps as well as other prostitutes. When five bodies were found, a Green River Task Force Team was formed dedicated solely to the investigation and apprehension of the Green River Killer, or GRK. Investigator Bob Keppel provided a profile "signature" of a single serial killer as each of his victims had been asphyxiated, some with ligatures discovered on the scene and each one had been left in a sexually degrading position, naked and dirty. The rocks placed inside of the victims represented an exaggerated statement of the same sexual hostility (Reichert, 2004).

The criminal investigation to track this killer was extensive and exhausting. Numerous suspects were questioned, but women kept disappearing and more bodies in various degrees of composition kept being discovered. FBI serial killer profilers and criminal investigators were called in to aid the investigation. They were able to pinpoint that many of the victims had known one another, and most had a history of prostitution. From these observations, they figured they were looking for a man who most likely hated women and had a deep, fanatical religious sense.

One prostitute, Marie, that was working the "Strip" was watched and followed by her pimp who saw her get into a pickup truck that was dark colored with primer spots where repairs to the body had been made. When Marie did not return, her pimp reported her missing to the police.

The man's truck was spotted in front of a house and the man who answered the door identified himself as Gary Ridgway. He fit the description of the man who picked up Marie—White, medium build, mid–30s. Ridgway confirmed that the truck was his but added that he had no idea what the police were talking about. There was no woman in his house, and he hadn't picked one up on the "Strip" the night of April 30 (Reichert, 2004).

About a year had passed, and while new bodies were found, there weren't any astonishingly new developments in the case. On September 18, 1983, detectives were called to recover a skeleton lying face down in a boggy area off Star Lake Road (Reichert, 2004). A few weeks later, another skeleton was found, more than 25 highway miles away from the original Green River burial ground. Either these bodies weren't from the GRK, or he was moving farther and farther away. These sites were very well hidden, so it is almost impossible to think that he came upon these areas at random. One skeleton, which was found at an apple orchard, had a pyramid-shaped rock sitting in between her pelvic bones right where her vaginal canal would be. This strongly affirmed a GRK connection. By November 1, 1983, the total body count was up to a dozen (Reichert, 2004). Not only were 12 dead but there was at least 20 other girls on missing persons report. Even though so many bodies were found, there had been a surprisingly small amount of evidence actually found. There was great intensity to find a suspect. In the middle of March 1984, 400 people marched in downtown Seattle as part of a "Take Back the Night" demonstration (Reichert, 2004). This put all kinds of unnecessary extra pressure on the Green River Task Force, especially with the increasing body count. Over the next two months, 11 more bodies would be found in various dumpsites. In March, the remains of four more bodies showed up, near the airport in Seattle. Within a few days of that discovery, police had found another burial site along Star Lake Road. Near the third body found by Star Lake Road, there was a second skeleton lying right next to it, but this skeleton was not human. It was a fairly large dog, which had been placed head to head with the human remains (Reichert, 2004). This was an odd discovery and it was difficult to figure out the symbolism. In April, two more bodies were found and a bleached-out human skull, complete with teeth and jawbone, that had been perched on a stump (Reichert, 2004). This placement of the scene showed far more than merely a dump site. The killer was spending time here, he enjoyed being around these bodies. At this point, the body count was up to 23 victims.

In May of 1984, a known prostitute Rebecca came forward and said that she met a man who had offered her $20 for oral sex. When the man was unable to get an erection he accused Rebecca of biting his penis and grabbed her by the neck in a very strong chokehold. Rebecca was eventually able to get away. She told police the assailant left in his pickup truck, that she had seen the man's employee ID card and he worked for a truck manufacturing company and his name was Gary Ridgway.

The police enlisted the help of the last person that anyone would ever expect. They went to a Jacksonville max-security prison to interview one of the most infamous serial killers in the entire world who committed his crimes in Seattle. His name was Ted Bundy, and the police actually thought they could use his serial killer mind to get into the mind of the GRK. Most of what Bundy said was relatively useless, but he did offer some good insight. He said that the sexual lore of a dead body is just too much to resist. The police needed to leave some of the bodies alone and just stake out the area around the body and the killer would most likely fall into their hands. He also said that the unknown subject (UNSUB) most likely enjoyed violent pornography and the police should put on a film festival with these so called "snuff" movies. The police could record all of the license plates of the people that attended. This could be a good suspect pool because it would be nearly impossible for the GRK to resist this temptation. As crazy as it seemed, Ted Bundy gave the police some insight that they would not have thought of otherwise.

At this point (mid to late 1985), the case began to slow down a bit. The police didn't have very many leads and everything they did have seemed to bring them to a dead end. The newspaper headlines seemed to slow to a crawl and people were losing interest in the case, but two important things did happen in that time period. The police in Oregon had discovered a body in Oregon that would be tied to the GRK. This meant that the killer had crossed state lines and it was only time before the FBI had entered into the case. The second was a discovery of another dump site near Mountain View Cemetery which was near Star Lake Road. The recovered bones of one of the bodies showed legs spread so far apart that it appeared as though both hips were dislocated (Reichert, 2004). This showed some more insight into the killer in that he most likely came back and had sex with the dead bodies. The profile of this man continued to evolve but his identity was becoming more and more difficult to figure out. By the end of the summer in 1986, the death count was up to 36.

Officially, there were no longer any new disappearances in the Seattle area, and the public seemed to have grown bored with an investigation that apparently had no end and no answers (Rule, 2004). With so little interest in the case, it seemed only logical that there would be less manpower involved in the case. Even some members of the police department believed that the GRK had either moved away or died or something along those lines. Detective Dave Reichert knew that the GRK was out there but there wasn't much he could do to change the minds of the members of the police department. He would have to accept the facts: The Green River Team was going to have to take funding cuts as well as cuts in manpower.

Since the pool of new suspects was ever dwindling, the remaining team members decided to look deeper into some of the old suspects. One that stood out was Gary Ridgway, the Des Moines truck painter who had attacked a young prostitute (Reichert, 2004). A few pieces of evidence jumped off the page at them. The first was that Ridgway had been on strike for three weeks in 1983. According to the best estimates of the medical examiner and detectives, three of the victims had been killed during that period. At no other time had the Green River Killer been so active (Reichert, 2004). Another piece of evidence was that Ridgway had been pulled over by police with one of the victims in his car with him, but police didn't see anything wrong at the time of him being pulled over, so they let him drive away. For the next couple of years, the police would look heavily into Gary Ridgway. They would tail him and interview people that were close to him. Ex-wives told police that he was ex-military and was into rough kinds of sexual encounters. Eventually police were able to get a warrant and seize Ridgway's car. They also were able to bring him down to the police station, where Ridgway readily agreed to give hair samples as well as chew on a piece of gauze so that police might be able to discover his blood type (Reichert, 2004). The search of Ridgway's home came up empty and it appeared as though police were back to square one, but Detective Dave Reichert and his team were not so sure that Gary Ridgway was an innocent man.

There had been about eight more women that had gone missing in the mid 1980s that were thought to be possible Green River victims, but at this point no one really knew for sure. As early as 1989, it was clear to everyone that the big push to find the GRK was over (Reichert, 2004). Most of the members of the team were transferred to new assignments. The main detective, Dave Reichert, was reassigned to a new position as of April 2, 1990. He and the rest of his team realized that they needed to move on, but they had a great deal of trouble moving on because they knew that GRK was still out there.

A lot can happen in 10 years. People get older, retire, and move on with their lives. But when the century changed from the 20th to the 21st, the world of science saw a whole new world of techniques, most importantly DNA analysis. This would nail down the case and it would be the main reason for the conviction and discovery of the identity of the Green River Killer.

September 10, 2001, Tom Jensen, one of the policemen working closely with the GRK case, came into a meeting room with three envelopes in his hand. One of them was the semen found in one of the first victims, the second was from the semen found from another victim, and the third was the DNA from one of the suspects. When Jensen pulled each DNA profile out one by one, it became quite clear that they were exact matches. The third profile belonged to the most interesting suspect they had found, Gary Ridgway. Detectives had saved the DNA from the gauze he willingly chewed on and the semen from the victims was also saved. This was the link they needed. The killer of the first three victims was now known, and the cops could only hope that this was the killer responsible for the rest of the brutal murders.

Ridgway had no idea that the trap he had evaded for two decades was about to close on him. He went to work as usual on Friday morning, November 30, 2001 (Rule, 2004). This day would not be a regular day for Ridgway because as he left work that afternoon, he was met by two detectives. They approached Ridgway as he exited the building and they told him that he was under arrest for several murders of women in King County. Ridgway's only response was "okay." Although everyone believed he was the killer of all the women, they could only absolutely link him to three of them. It would take a confession to prove that he was responsible for the rest of the bodies found.

Norm Maleng was the prosecuting attorney in the case against Gary Ridgway and he said that he absolutely would not back down in seeking the death penalty for Ridgway. Unfortunately, when faced with these difficult decisions, Maleng found that he had to change his mind for the good of the public. The defending attorneys for Ridgway came to Maleng with a deal. Ridgway would admit to the murders and help police locate the rest of the bodies if they only pursued life in prison. Maleng was resistant at first, but he decided to think about the families of the remaining missing women and he agreed to the deal and would seek life in prison in exchange for some closure for the rest of the families.

Outcome

Questions were still unanswered. Who was Gary Ridgway? What happened to him that made him so evil? Why did he hate women so much? Where did his intense sexual drive come from?

As a part of his deal, Ridgway would accompany police to many of his burial sites to help police locate more victims, and they were called his "field trips." These field trips were important to Ridgway because they were really the only way he could see the outdoors, but the problem was, Ridgway was telling lies. He told police that he kept mementos (jewelry) from the women and kept it all in a hidden location. When police went looking for it, they searched for hours and found nothing. The same thing happened when Ridgway told police about a burial site. Police searched for hours and hours but they didn't find anything except for a skeleton of an opossum. It was clear that Ridgway was purposely lying to the police. It was suggested that Ridgway lied because he subconsciously wanted to be executed, to make himself appear like less of a monster, so that true-crime writers would portray him more positively, to build himself up, to make himself seem more powerful, to maintain control over the bodies of his victims (Reichert, 2004). At another point he said he killed simply because he wanted to (Rule, 2004).

Interviews with Ridgway revealed serious childhood issues, Ridgway was a chronic bed-wetter and his mother would march him into the bathroom and wash him down in a cold bath spending over 15 minutes soaping, washing, and drying his penis and testicles, even though he often became erect when she did that. She had appeared half naked in front of him, and he admitted that he had been sexually aroused (Rule, 2004). Some of the rituals, specifically, as they related to bathing behavior with his mother were rituals that he repeated with some of his prostitutes prior to engaging in sex with them as well as postdeath bathing them in the river.

Ridgway had necrophiliac interests. He recounted a story of his father who worked at a mortuary saying that he witnessed a man having sex with a corpse. He liked the idea of "having sex with someone that is dead, because you wouldn't get caught. No feelings. She wouldn't feel it (Reichert, 2004, p. 250).

Ridgway described his mother's parenting style was a blend of titillation, humiliation, and threats (Reichert, 2004). Even though he would continually think about having sex with her, he also had quite a bit of violence and rage pent up inside of him. After his mother threatened to place Ridgway in a school for the mentally retarded (because of academic struggles), he fantasized about slitting her throat with a kitchen knife to scar her. This violence would also become a reality in his youth. At a very young age, he was especially fond of killing birds that escalated into killing a family cat (Reichert, 2004). He said the act relieved his anger at the family. Ridgway also set fires to help ease his frustration. All of these events were red flags that something was very wrong with the young Gary Ridgway.

As a teenager, Ridgway lured a six-year-old boy deep into the woods, and then he stabbed him in the abdomen. As blood dripped down the little boy's stomach, Ridgway ran off saying that he wanted to know what it felt like to kill somebody (Reichert, 2004). The Task Force was able to find that young boy, now an adult man, to verify an example of how early on Gary began to obsess over sexual and violent fantasies and to acting on them at an early age.

Ridgeway can be typed as a serial killer and demonstrates many of the characteristics associated with psychopaths. He told authorities that he did not recall the names or even faces of many of his victims, but knew exactly where most of them were buried. He said that killing gave him a thrill, and the women he had chosen were all disposable, used only to satisfy his pleasure. He went out at night with the intent to kill, but did not pick the victim until he got to the scene. He also said that he picked prostitutes because they were easy targets because they were accessible and less likely to be reported missing. He demonstrated another behavior typical of serial killers in explaining that he liked to bury the bodies near one another so he could drive past the area, remember his crime, and relive the pleasure the experience gave him. One ex-wife said that Ridgway liked having sex outdoors and had had sex with her at one of the dump sites.

During his confession, Ridgway proved to be proud of his crimes. He told investigators that he considered killing prostitutes his "career" and the thing he was good at. He hated women because he felt that they always had power over him, and his actions were a compulsion to gain and maintain control. He viewed women as objects and lacked any kind of caring or compassion. Like many other psychopaths, Ridgway had an inability to demonstrate intimacy with anyone and had difficult performing sexually unless he was in a dominating position. Even in death, Ridgway needed to be in control. He confessed to necrophilia, sometimes up to several days after killing. His obsession with maintaining control even affected the way Ridgway viewed his dump sites. He admitted that every time victims' remains were discovered, he felt as though something was being taken away from him.

As an adult, Ridgway remained close to home, leaving only briefly for a tour in the Navy. He was married several times, had a son, and usually had a steady girlfriend. He worked at a paint store, went to church, and appeared to fit into the community. He believed that his first wife cheated on him while he was oversees, and he later said she became a "whore." His ex-lovers claimed that Ridgway was preoccupied with sex, demanding it two or three times a day, and he liked to have sex outdoors. He also demanded anal sex and bondage from his partners on several occasions.

Over the next few years, Ridgway continued his obsession with sex and bondage and frequently interacted with prostitutes. During his second marriage, it appears that Ridgway was either already killing or making preparations to begin. His ex-wife said that Ridgway was getting odder: He would practice walking noiselessly around the house and would jump out and put her in a chokehold. He carried tarps and blankets in the back of the cars and told her to stay away from the garage. During and after church services, he would often cry, and at night he would sit with an open Bible in front of him. Soon after their divorce, Ridgway's first known victim was discovered.

This lethal combination of sexual obsession mixed with rage and violence inevitably turned Ridgway into the adult he became. He began killing women in 1982. He would pick up the prostitutes because they were simply the easiest targets. When he first started killing, he realized he was disturbed by the victim's faces when they were dying, so he refined his technique. After the sexual encounter with the prostitute, he would approach them from behind and put them in a chokehold or use some sort of ligature to choke them to death, but the murder did not end here. These bodies were his *prizes*. He would then wrap the bodies up and take them to a chosen dump site. With many of his victims, Ridgway wasn't finished after they were dead and disposed of. He would go back to rape their bodies, brushing away maggots if necessary (Reichert, 2004). Even scarier was what he did with the women who fought back. One victim, Marie, struggled so hard that she gouged his arm. He was so enraged that he placed her body far, far away because she didn't deserve to be with the other bodies of women who didn't fight him off. This also shows that Ridgway viewed these bodies as his sexual property and wanted to continue to maintain full control over them even after they were dead.

Once Ridgway began killing, it consumed him. He claimed that at the height of his killing spree, he was sleeping only a few hours a night and then would go out "patrolling" for his victim. He picked younger women because they were the easiest to control, and he liked the way they tended to be more vocal in pleading for their lives. Once he solicited the prostitute, he would try to get her to come back with him to his house or to a wooded area where he would have sex with her, kill her, and then deposit the body. As the killings went on, his modus operandi became more advanced. He would offer to give rides to two women and establish their trust so that later, if he saw one alone, she would be more willing to come with him. Sometimes he even used a picture of his son to put the women at ease. He also told investigators that he needed to be in the right mood to hunt, which was calm and easy going.

The trial consisted of victim's families being allowed to address Ridgway in the courtroom one week before Christmas on December 18, 2003. Dozens of people took their turns addressing Ridgway primarily saying he was *trash*, an *animal*, a *terrorist*, a *coward*, and worse (Reichert, 2004). Two surprising things did happen that day at the sentencing. The first was Kathy Mills, the mother of victim Opal Mills saying that she forgave Gary Ridgway, which is an incredibly powerful thing to do considering what he had done. The other was a little more shocking. This statement, by Robert Rule, actually made Ridgway shake, cry, and turn away (Reichert, 2004). Robert Rule was the father of Linda Rule, who had disappeared in September of 1982 at age 16. Rule said to Gary Ridgway that there are people here that hate you. I'm not one of them. I forgive you for what you've done. You've made it difficult to live up to what I believe, and that is what God says to do, and that's to forgive, and He doesn't say to forgive just certain people. He says to forgive all. So you are forgiven, sir (Reichert, 2004).

The final statements of Gary Ridgway were as follows. "I know the horrible things my acts were. I have tried for a long time to get these things out of my mind. I've tried for a long time to keep from killing any ladies. I'm sorry that I put my wife, my son, my brothers, and my family through this hell. I hope they can find a way to forgive me. I'm very sorry for the ladies that were not found. May they rest in peace. They need a better place than where I gave them" (Reichert, 2004).

After Ridgway was finished speaking, the judge read the name of each one of his victims out loud and said that Ridgway would serve a life sentence for each one of them. Gary Ridgway was sentenced to 48 consecutive life sentences. Right before Ridgway was leaving the courthouse, the judge ordered Ridgway to turn around and look at the people in the hearing room. He then said, "As you spend the balance of your life in a cell in prison, I hope the last thought you have of your time in the free world is of their faces. If you have one bit of emotion, you will be haunted for the rest of your life" (Reichert, 2004). And with that, the 20-year search for one of the world's worst serial killers finally came to a close.

References

Gudjonsson, Gisli H. (2003). *The psychology of interrogations and confessions: A handbook*. West Sussex, England: Wiley.

Prothero, M., & Smith, C. (2006). *Defending Gary: Unraveling the mind of the Green River Killer*. San Francisco, CA: Jossey-Bass.

Reichert, D. (2004). *Chasing the devil: My twenty-year quest to capture the Green River Killer*. New York, NY: Little, Brown.

Rule, A. (2004). *Green River, running red: The real story of the Green River Killer, America's deadliest serial murderer*. New York, NY: Free Press.

Smith, C., & Guillen, T. (1991). *The search for the Green River Killer*. New York, NY: Onyx.

Chapter 17

Poison and Biological Agents as Weapons

Arthur E. Westveer, John P. Jarvis,
Carl J. Jensen, III, and Anne M. Berger

Poisoning[*]

Homicidal poisoning is an intriguing but poorly described phenomenon (Greene & Ferslew, 2009). Other than a few published reviews of some famous historical poisoning cases, little has been written on the characteristics of the poisoner and his or her victim (Westveer, Trestrail, & Pinizzotto, 1996). A further review of the international forensic literature does not reveal any previously published epidemiological studies dealing with criminal investigative analyses, or psychological profiles, of the homicidal poisoner.

The Uniform Crime Report (UCR) program has traditionally been used to look for fluctuations in the level of crime and to provide criminologists with statistics for research and planning. From these data, the Supplemental Homicidal Reports reveal much of what is known empirically about the nature and scope of homicidal behavior in the United States.

Of the 186,971 SHR reports in the United States for 1990 to 1999, 346 (0.19%), or 1.9 per 100,000 total homicides, were poisonings involving a single victim and a single offender, or a single victim and an unknown number of offenders. This compares with 292 similar homicidal poisonings reported during the 1980s. Therefore, the 1990s saw an increase of 18% in reported homicidal poisonings, which equates to a 35% increase in the rate of these cases coming to the attention of law enforcement during the 1990s. The effective investigation of homicides generally, and poisoning cases in particular, often depends on a number of factors, including such basic investigative data as victim demographics, possible offender characteristics, geographical and temporal features of the case, and any particular incident attributes that may assist law enforcement.

---

[*]This section on poisoning was written by Arthur E. Westveer, John P. Jarvis, and Carl J. Jensen III.

491

Westveer, Jarvis, and Jensen analyzed SHR data and concluded that the incidence of reported homicides due to poisoning was only a small portion of the SHR data for the decade. One can only wonder if more of these types of homicides remain undetected, as there are many holes in the investigative net through which homicidal poisoners can slip. It should also be highlighted that many of the demographics of poisoning offenders remain largely unknown, at least when compared to that of overall homicides during the decade. This would seem to indicate that homicide investigators may have been presented with a poisoned victim but were unable to identify the offender. An old and wise adage related to homicide detection is that "all deaths are homicides until facts prove otherwise." As evident from the cases identified at the outset of this research and the statistical analysis offered here, perhaps this adage could be more relevant to poisoning cases if it were rephrased as follows: "All deaths, with no visible signs of trauma, may be considered poisonings until facts prove otherwise."

What other factors may be important to the identification of a poisoning homicide offender? Among the many factors that need to be identified are the offender's socioeconomic level, IQ, level of education, professional training, personality (introversion/extroversion), ethnicity, prior criminal history, marital harmony, and psychological status. These factors of homicidal poisoners cannot be elucidated from the SHR reports. This information can be generated only by in-depth research into actual circumstances surrounding such poisoning cases.

Another study describes homicidal poisoning deaths in the United States during 1999 to 2005. Greene & Ferslew (2009) used a trend analysis of homicidal poisoning death with vital statistics data. The National Mortality Statistics database was queried using "homicide" as injury intent and "poisoning" as mechanism for the years 1999 through 2005. Counts and rates were obtained for subgrouping by using demographic data and ICD-10 codes. Findings indicated the overall homicidal poisoning death rate was low between 1999 and 2005. The most common type of poison used was medications. Substantially higher rates were observed in vulnerable populations at extremes of age, particularly infants, and among Blacks.

The research offered here, coupled with investigative experience, provides the basis for extending criminal investigative analysis. Such analyses may assist law enforcement personnel in their investigations by arming them with a clearer picture of the poisoner. Finally, while this work has focused on individual incidents of homicidal poisoning behavior, the importance of these patterns may be even more significant now. That is, the potential for toxic substances being used as a weapon of mass destruction may prove to be more of a substantial threat than in the past. In addition, the expanding elderly population may provide additional victims for those who wish to commit a homicide that appears to be death by natural causes. Understanding some of the attributes of homicidal poisoners as examined here may enhance the ability of the law enforcement and forensic communities when they are called on to assist in the prevention and investigation of homicides.

Homicidal poisonings remain one of the most difficult crimes to detect and prosecute. Because there are often few visible signs of a homicidal poisoning, all too often the victim's death may be certified as being due to a natural or unknown cause, and important evidence of the crime is often buried with the victim. Therefore, a great number of homicides by poisoning are detected only when specific toxicological analyses are carried out after the exhumation of the victim's remains.

Case Studies

The following cases, selected from FBI and police files, as well as public source court documents, identify incidents in which the nature of the initial poisoning was either not detected or was misdiagnosed by criminal or medical investigators. In most of these cases, the initial causes of death were thought to be accidental or due to natural causes, but were later determined (through considerable legal and investigative effort) to be deaths due to homicide where poison was the weapon of choice.

Case 1

In a small country town, a White male became suddenly very ill with what his family claimed was pneumonia. Upon admission to the local hospital, he was treated with antibiotics and painkillers. Ten days after the onset of his symptoms, he died from his illness. Unbeknown to the authorities, the victim's wife was involved in an adulterous affair and wished to marry her lover. When she returned some highly toxic herbicide to a fruit grower, he became suspicious and contacted the police. Investigation revealed that the victim's wife had collected on a $55,000 insurance policy and was pressuring her paramour into marriage. The police had the husband's body exhumed and discovered the highly toxic chemical paraquat in his body.

Disposition: As a result of these findings and other evidence, the wife was arrested and charged with the death of her husband. She was later convicted and sentenced to five years' imprisonment and treatment in a mental hospital.

Case 2

In 1999, officers were called to a residence at 3:30 a.m. to treat an eight-month-old baby who had been reported to have stopped breathing. The boy was transported to the local hospital and died later that morning. It was presumed that the infant had suffered from sudden infant death syndrome. Autopsy revealed the child to have had a blood ethanol level of 0.12 (120 mg/dL). Upon further investigation, the father was found to have given the child a toxic dose of peppermint schnapps.

Disposition: The father was arrested and charged with negligent homicide for the alcohol poisoning of his son.

Case 3

A 33-year-old woman was found dead in her waterbed. A black substance was discovered around her mouth and nose. The investigating officer, recalling similar evidence from a case 12 years earlier, suspected possible cyanide poisoning. During the autopsy, the distinctive bitter-almond-like odor common to cyanide poisonings was detected. Laboratory tests confirmed the presence of cyanide in the victim's blood but not in her stomach contents. Due to this finding, it was thought that the victim was somehow forced to inhale hydrogen cyanide gas. Police later discovered that her husband worked at an exterminating company where hydrogen cyanide was readily available.

Disposition: Investigators combined this information with evidence of both marital and financial problems and arrested the husband. Prosecutors have sought a first-degree murder conviction and a possible life sentence.

Case 4

Background

Dorothea Puente was born Dorothea Helen Grey on January 9, 1929, in California and led a tumultuous life that ended in a murder conviction in 1993 at age 64. Until her arrest in 1988, Puente had committed several crimes of various sorts and spent years running from probation.

Victimology

The seven victims, four female and three male, found in her yard were all at least 55 years old, and the oldest two were both 78. Several were discovered underneath cement slabs, and most were so severely deteriorated that the cause of death could not be discovered. Vera Faye Martin, age 64, wore a still-ticking watch when she was unearthed. Leona Carpenter, age 78, whose leg bone was mistaken for a tree root by detectives searching Puente's yard, was one of the three victims for whose murder Puente was convicted. Betty Palmer, also age 78, was buried under a statue of St. Francis of Assisi in the front yard; she was wearing a nightgown but missing her head, hands, and lower legs. Dorothy Miller, age 64, one of two known alcoholics among the seven victims, was buried with her arms duct-taped to her chest, and Benjamin Fink, age 55, also an alcoholic, was buried in his boxer shorts. The victims' attire led the court to believe most were killed at night and their murders were planned, although it also supported Puente's defense that all the deaths were the result of natural causes or suicide.

Puente was also associated with two other murders: those of Monroe and of her one-time boyfriend Everson Gillmouth, whom she wrote to while she was in prison serving a robbery sentence from 1982 to 1985. He picked her up from jail in a 1980 red pickup truck, which she gave to her handyman, Ismael Florez, in November 1985. She had hired him to help her around the house, completing tasks such as building a wooden box six feet three inches by two feet that she filled with "junk" and had him drop into the river. A box fitting the description was found less than three months later, in January 1986, by two fishermen; the remains of an elderly man inside were unidentifiable, so Puente could never be charged with his murder.

Crime Scene Indicators

There were multiple missing person reports. The main crime scene was the back yard of Mrs. Puente and where she had buried the bodies.

Forensics

When she found an opportunity, Puente would overdose her victims with the prescription-strength sleeping pill Dalmane, which was found in all seven bodies in her back yard. She let them die before burying them.

Toxicology, DNA, and dental records were important forensics for the cases.

Investigation

Puente committed what is believed to be her first murder in spring 1982 when a 61-year-old acquaintance, Ruth Munroe, died of a drug overdose just after moving into Puente's house in Sacramento at 1426 F Street. Munroe overdosed on Tylenol and codeine, leading the coroner to dismiss it as a suicide. Despite Puente's questionable record to date, no one considered her greed a strong enough motive to warrant murder. Within a few months, Puente was charged with drugging four elderly people and robbing them while they were sedated. She served only three years of a five-year sentence and was released with orders to stay away from the elderly and not to handle government checks of any sort. These instructions would lead to part of her murder defense years down the road. In just three years from her release, Puente managed to lure at least seven people into her home under the patronage of a halfway house, murder them, and steal their social security checks that they gave her permission to cash.

The crimes for which Puente is best known occurred in the house at 1426 F Street, which was used as a boarding house for the elderly, with her personal residence on the second floor. It was not until November 1988 when neighbors began complaining of a foul stench coming from her garden that she was discovered by two Sacramento detectives in search of a missing mentally retarded man, Alvaro "Bert" Montoya, who had been a tenant of Puente and was reported missing by his social worker.

Puente was calculating as she searched dive bars in the area for victims who had little or no family who would report them missing and investigated their social security benefits before offering them a room. She charged them $350 a month for two meals a day and a room, and so as not to ignite neighbors' suspicions, she always planted a story before they disappeared saying they did not feel well or were going away. Puente did not let the tenants go in the kitchen, make phone calls, or touch the mail, and she made all of them sign over rights to cash their social security checks so she could distribute the money after she siphoned some off for herself. Despite having a full bar to herself in her second-story residence, she did not allow tenants any alcohol.

Puente was even able to obtain unwilling help from friends and neighbors. She had a close acquaintance, 54-year-old Patty Casey, who drove a cab and later admitted to driving Puente to pick up fertilizer and cement, sometimes several times a week. Homer Meyers, a tenant who refused to sign over endorsement rights to Puente, was evicted but not until he unwittingly dug Montoya's grave after Puente asked him to dig a four-foot hole for a new apricot tree, which she planted over Montoya's body.

Outcome

Puente was convicted of five types of crimes: forgery, living in a brothel, vagrancy, robbery, and eventually murder. Her first criminal conviction was in 1948 when she stole checks from a friend to buy a few clothing items. After serving time, she violated her probation and left town. Twelve years later, she was convicted of residing in a brothel and spent 60 days in a Sacramento jail, only to be released and convicted on vagrancy charges that brought her another 60 days in jail. She managed to stay away from the law until 1978, when she was caught again forging thirty-four checks from tenants living at her halfway house in Sacramento.

Puente's Background

Puente survived a tumultuous childhood as the offspring of two alcoholics. She was the sixth child and lost her father to tuberculosis at age eight and her mother a year later to a motorcycle accident. By the age of 17, she had moved out on her own to Washington, where she began a life of pathological lying that led directly to crime. Puente constantly lied about her age and her background, confessing only to her cabby friend, Casey. She had an obsession with expensive items and clothes. She married several times, usually to much younger or much older men whom she could control, and at least one, her 14-year marriage to Axel Johnson, is known to have been a violence-filled relationship.

Crime Classification

Dorothy Puente was an organized killer, targeting her victims in bars and those who were close to death, which made their slip from unconsciousness to death simpler. She hid behind her "granny" image and fooled neighbors with lies to cover up missing individuals or the stench from her yard. She would claim there was a sewer problem and that she had dead rats in the basement. She covered up most of the murders by burying the bodies in solid earth so they would decay.

Puente was also a serial killer, and her motivation for the homicides was financial profit. Everyone who knew her attested to her obsession with expensive things. Puente collected about $5,000 from the seven tenants buried in her yard, and she was still collecting Gillmouth's pension well after his disappearance.

Puente's crimes would be classified as criminal enterprise homicide whereby the weapon was poison. Detectives found expensive bottles of perfume in Puente's room, as well as a huge closet filled with designer clothing. The crime scene was organized. Her home was familiar territory to her, and she had absolute control to protect the crime scene. She was a veteran criminal who was adept at talking her way into and out of things and had easily controlled her victims.

Could Puente have been stopped prior to the murders? Before her suspected first murder in 1982, Puente was in prison for nine years serving two separate forgery convictions, 180 days serving prostitution and vagrancy charges, and at the end of these was let go early from a five-year sentence for robbery after just three years in prison.

Biological Agents as Weapons*

The use of biological weapons in warfare is not new. It has been documented throughout history. Long before the nature of microorganisms was understood, an association between corpses and disease was made. Ancient Romans contaminated the wells of their enemies with dead animals. In the fourteenth century, the Tatar army hurled the remains of bubonic plague victims over the city walls of Kaffa (now Feodossia, Ukraine), a strategic seaport on the Crimean coast. In the fifteenth century, Pizarro gave clothing contaminated with the smallpox virus to South American natives, and during the French and Indian War (1754–1767), Lord Jeffrey Amherst gave blankets from smallpox hospitals to Native Americans who were loyal to the French (Lewis, 2002). In 1932, the Japanese began experimenting on human beings at Biological Weapons Unit 731 outside Harbin, Manchuria, China. At least eleven Chinese cities were attacked with anthrax, cholera, shigellosis, salmonella, and plague, and at least ten thousand died.

The mode of transmission has varied, but the intent has been the same: to deliberately disseminate disease-producing organisms among the enemy. While early perpetrators often took advantage of natural epidemics, scientific advances and the development of Internet technology have made access to biological pathogens relatively convenient for today's biowarriors. The World Health Association in 2001 concluded that the development of biological agents as weapons has kept pace with world advancements in the field of biotechnology. History proves that every major new technology of the past has come to be exploited intensively not only for peaceful purposes, but also for hostile ones. Once predominantly a concern of the military, the use of biological agents as weapons against civilians is now a reality.

The Centers for Disease Control and Prevention (CDC; 2001) defines bioterrorism as the intentional release of viruses, bacteria, fungi, or toxins from living organisms to produce death or disease in humans, animals, or plants. Biological weapons are devices that are intended to deliberately disseminate disease-producing organisms or toxins.

There are a number of reasons that biological agents are appealing as weapons. Frequently referred to as the poor man's atom bomb, they can be produced with an economic outlay that is significantly less than conventional weapons. There is the ability to cause large numbers of casualties with minimal logistical requirements. Since biological weapons are made up from living organisms, they are often considered more dangerous than chemical weapons because they are hard to control and it is difficult to predict how the organism will react, mutate, and spread. Hurlbert (1997) reported that biological toxins are among the most toxic agents known. For example, the quantity of

---

*The section on the use of biological agents as weapons was written by Anne M. Berger.

botulinum toxin contained in the dot of an "i," when delivered properly, is enough to kill ten people. With the exception of the smallpox virus, the microbial agents used to make some of the most lethal biological agents occur naturally and can be cultivated in unsophisticated labs by individuals with little scientific training.

Weaponizing the agents is a bit more of a challenge but not insurmountable. Technical expertise is required to produce high-quality, military-grade biological weapons and a reliable means of dissemination. Terrorist applications are less demanding. Easily concealed and silently released, perpetrators can work from a distance or escape before detection of the event. There is separation between the act and the outcome. In contrast to chemical agents that result in illness fairly quickly after being released, the effects of biological agents may not be seen for several days to weeks later because of the incubation period. Cases are more likely to be dispersed throughout multiple areas with individuals seeking medical care from different providers. Early recognition is likely to require a high index of suspicion.

When evaluating the numerous biological agents that could be used as weapons, the CDC (2000) used a risk matrix based on the possible public health impact, the delivery potential, the stability of the agent, the special preparation requirements, and the ability to generate fear. Category A agents are those that are of the most concern. This is because they can be easily disseminated or transmitted from person to person, can cause a high number of mortalities with the potential for major public health impact, can cause public panic and social disruption, and require special action for public health preparedness. This chapter discusses the top four Category A biological agents: anthrax, smallpox, botulism, and plague.

ANTHRAX

Anthrax may be one of the oldest known biological weapons. The name is derived from the Greek word for coal (anthrakis), because the disease causes black coal-like skin lesions. Gorner (2001) reported that anthrax was well known to the Greeks and Romans and widespread in Europe for thousands of years. The disease may have made its literary debut in the Old Testament (Exodus 9:1–7) as the fifth of 10 plagues. Moses took ashes from a fire and produced the symptoms of cutaneous anthrax among Pharaoh's soldiers and livestock. We know today that the incineration of livestock is not sufficient to kill anthrax spores. Cieslak and Eitzen (1999) identified anthrax as the single greatest biological warfare threat. Research on anthrax as a biological weapon began more than 80 years ago. Today, at least 17 nations are believed to have offensive biological weapons programs (Inglesby et al., 1999).

Anthrax is an acute infectious disease caused by *Bacillus anthracis*, a spore-forming bacterium. It is naturally occurring in the soil and is widely distributed on almost all continents, although it is more frequently seen in developing countries or those without veterinary public health programs. Anthrax is a zoonotic disease, which means that it can be passed from animals to humans. All mammals appear to be susceptible to anthrax, but it is more frequently seen in those that graze on grass, such as cattle, sheep, and goats. Because it is a spore, it can survive for many years in suboptimal conditions. It has been known to survive in the soil for up to sixty years. Areas with rich organic soil (pH below 6.0) and dramatic changes in climate such as prolonged drought or abundant rainfall appear to produce zones where the soil is more heavily contaminated with anthrax spores. In the United States, these zones closely parallel the cattle drive trails of the 1800s (Cieslak & Eitzen, 1999).

In humans, anthrax presents as three distinct clinical forms of the disease: cutaneous (skin), inhalation, and gastrointestinal. The symptoms of the disease vary depending on how it is contracted. Naturally occurring anthrax is usually acquired following contact with an infected animal or contaminated animal products such as hides, wool, bone, or meal. The most common route of infection is through the skin, but the most serious form is caused by inhalation of the spores. Historically it has been related to work in agriculture or industry. Once called woolsorter's disease, it was most frequently associated with tannery, wool, and goat hair mill workers. The largest recorded outbreak of inhalational anthrax in the United States during the twentieth century occurred in the late fall of 1957 among workers at the Arms Textile Mill in Manchester, New Hampshire. Over a 10-week period, five cases of inhalation anthrax and four cases of cutaneous anthrax developed among men working in different areas of the mill. Four of the individuals with inhalation anthrax died. Coincidentally, the anthrax vaccine was being tested at the mill at the same time. No one who received the vaccine developed the disease (Belluck, 2001). Naturally acquired anthrax is usually susceptible to antibiotic treatment. The mortality rate for occupationally acquired cases in the United States is 89%, but many of these cases occurred before the development of critical care units and, in some cases, antibiotics (Inglesby et al., 1999).

In the United States there were 224 cases of cutaneous anthrax reported between 1944 and 1994. It is estimated that there are approximately 2,000 cases reported globally each year (Inglesby et al., 1999). Once the anthrax spore enters the skin, it begins to germinate. Exposed areas of skin, such as the arms, hands, face, and neck, are the most frequently affected, particularly if there are abrasions or previous cuts present. After an incubation period of approximately seven days (the range is 1 to 12 days), an itchy red raised rash begins to appear. Initially it may resemble a spider bite or even acne (Altman, 2001). Within one to two days, it develops into a painless fluid-filled vesicle with swelling of the surrounding area. The fact that it is painless is important in differentiating between cutaneous anthrax and the bite of the brown recluse spider. On days five to seven, the vesicle dries and forms a depressed black scab that eventually falls off within a week or two. Fever, malaise, headache, swollen lymph nodes, and severe swelling may accompany the ulcers. It can take up to six weeks to fully recover, and there is usually no permanent scarring. Diagnosis is made by culture or smear. Without antibiotic treatment, the mortality rate for cutaneous anthrax can be as high as 20%. Although antibiotic therapy does not appear to change the course of the ulcer formation and healing, it decreases the chance of progression to a systemic infection (Inglesby et al., 1999).

Gastrointestinal anthrax is uncommon and generally follows the consumption of undercooked contaminated meat. Symptoms can occur from one to seven days after ingestion and result in two distinct patterns. If the spores are deposited in the upper gastrointestinal tract, ulcers may appear at the base of the tongue, along with a sore throat and swollen lymph nodes. If the spores are deposited in the lower intestinal tract, an individual may present with nausea, vomiting, and malaise, followed by bloody diarrhea. As with cutaneous anthrax, sepsis can follow advanced infection (Inglesby et al., 1999).

Inhalational anthrax is the most serious form of the disease. The mortality rate is 90 to 100% without antibiotic treatment and 75% with treatment. Until the 2001 cases, there had been only 18 cases of inhalational anthrax reported in the United States in the past 100 years. The onset of symptoms generally occurs 1 to 5 days after inhaling a sufficient number of aerosolized spores into the lungs. Some cases have been as long as 60 days after exposure. The immune system responds by destroying some spores, but others are carried to the lymph nodes in the chest and begin to multiply there. As the bacteria germinate, a toxin is produced and released into the bloodstream. The disease then progresses rapidly as the toxin causes fluid collection, hemorrhaging, and necrosis.

Smallpox

Smallpox is thought to have first appeared in northeastern Africa or the Indus Valley of south central Asia nearly 12,000 years ago. Throughout history, smallpox outbreaks occurred globally until it was eradicated through a worldwide vaccination program. It is a highly contagious disease caused by the variola virus and most commonly presents in two clinical forms: variola major and the milder variola minor. Because it is a virus, there is no specific treatment, and the only prevention is vaccination. This disease affected millions of people each year. Survivors often remained blinded or disfigured. The last case seen in the United States was in 1949 (CDC, 2001). The United States discontinued smallpox vaccinations in 1972 because the vaccine had potential risks, and the disease was no longer seen in the country.

More than 500 specimens of the smallpox virus were kept, mainly for research purposes, at the CDC in the United States and the Russian State Research Center of Virology and Biotechnology in Koltsovo, Novosibirsk. Due to dwindling financial support for laboratories in Russia, some bioterror experts are concerned that smallpox samples, as well as technical expertise, may have fallen into the wrong hands (Hagman, 2001).

The disease is spread from person to person or through contaminated clothing or bed linens. After a two-week incubation period, the prodromal symptoms appear, including a high fever, headache, and body aches and abdominal pain. This is followed by a rash of small, red spots, which appear first in the mouth and throat and the face and forearms, spreading to the trunk and legs. The spots develop into sores within the mouth, and the fever generally falls. Within a day or two, the rash becomes raised, and deeply embedded vesicles filled with thick opaque fluid appear. They have a characteristic depression in the center. Unlike the superficial chickenpox lesions, which appear in crops at various stages, these lesions are all at the same stage and also appear on the palms of the hands and the soles of the feet. Individuals are contagious from the time that the rash develops until the last scab disappears (Henderson et al., 1999). Historically, about one-third of those infected died. Vaccination can be done preventatively and as postexposure infection control. Antiviral research is ongoing.

BOTULISM

Botulinum toxin is the most poisonous substance known. Development of it as a possible biological weapon began more than 60 years ago. It is a spore-forming anaerobe that is naturally found in the soil and marine environments, although no cases of waterborne botulism have ever been reported (Arnon et al., 2001). There are seven distinct types of botulinum toxins that have been classified by the letters A through G. When absorbed into the body through the gastrointestinal system, inhalation, or a wound, the toxins block acetylcholine release and stop the conduction of stimulus across nerve synapses. All of the toxin types produce the same symptoms of bilateral descending flaccid paralysis. This includes cranial nerve palsies such as drooping eyelids, blurred or double vision, difficulty swallowing, and difficulty breathing. The onset of the symptoms is dose and route dependent.

Early recognition depends on a high index of suspicion. Confirmation is obtained by laboratory test that may take several days; therefore, clinical diagnosis is important. Administration of an equine antitoxin may minimize the severity of the disease (Arnon et al., 2001). The paralysis of botulism can persist for weeks, with the need for supportive therapies such as a ventilator and nutritional support.

PLAGUE

The plague has had a significant impact on world history. Multiple outbreaks have swept over the population, resulting in population losses of 50 to 60%

(Center for Civilian Biodefense Strategies, 2000). It is caused by the gram-negative bacterium *Yersinia pestis* and is transmitted by infected fleas or direct contact with animal tissue or droplet infection. Depending on the route of infection, it can present as bubonic (75 to 90% of cases), septicemic, or pneumonic. Plague is found in rodents and their fleas on every populated continent except Australia (Inglesby et al., 2000). In the United States, 390 cases of plague were reported from 1947 to 1996. Eighty-four percent of those cases were bubonic plague and were concentrated in California, New Mexico, Arizona, and Colorado. The last case of human transmission was in Los Angeles in 1924.

Naturally occurring plague is usually acquired through the bite of an infected flea. After a 2- to 10-day incubation period, painful regional lymph nodes swell (buboes) along with fever, chills, and weakness. This is called *bubonic plague*. It can progress to septicemia if untreated, with a mortality rate of 40 to 60%. A small number of individuals may develop primary septicemic plague without having had buboes when bacteria are deposited directly into the bloodstream. Petechiae and ecchymoses mimic meningococcemia.

If the bacteria are inhaled, pneumonic plague may develop. Two to three days after exposure, individuals may present with a fever, cough, severe chest pain, bronchospasm, cyanosis, and hemoptysis. Chest X-rays would show extensive, progressive consolidation. This is rarely seen in the United States. Early diagnosis and treatment are essential. Once again, a high index of suspicion is required.

The plague is one of three quarantinable diseases subject to international health regulations. The other two are cholera and yellow fever. It is a disease that must be reported to the World Health Organization. There are approximately 1,000 to 3,000 cases of the plague reported globally each year.

Moving Forward

In the light of the anthrax mailings, the World Health Organization rushed to revise its 1970 technical guidelines on the health aspects of biological and chemical weapons as a call for action for governments to be ready for possible biological and chemical terrorism. It also launched a global outbreak and response network: a cross-linked system of existing networks to continuously monitor reports and disease outbreaks worldwide. Glass and Schoch-Spana (2002) emphasized the importance of extending these networks and enlisting the general public as a capable partner when planning response strategies. Bioterrorism policy discussions and response planning efforts have tended to discount the capacity of the public to participate in the response to an act of bioterrorism. They pointed out that the general public is an interconnected matrix of networks and subnetworks organized around social institutions and relationships that should be enlisted as capable partners. Resources, communications, and leadership structures can be used to facilitate a better and more coordinated response. Resourceful, adaptive behavior should be the rule and not the exception. Providing information will be as important as providing medication.

Increased knowledge and awareness of biological agents and their potential use as weapons build a strong first line of defense in facing future challenges. Maintaining a high index of suspicion, understanding the risks, and providing accurate information can help to decrease fear and improve effective responses. Microbiology is currently discussing the emerging science of bioterrorism forensics: using molecular epidemiology techniques to establish a chain of evidence rather than identifying the source of the outbreak. It raises the question of what will be legally binding types of evidence (Evans, 2002).

References

Altman, L. K. (2001, December). *First challenge in anthrax case: Not missing it*. Retrieved January 2002, from http://www.ph.ucla.edu/epi/bioter/firstchallengeanthrax.html

Arnon, S. S., . . . Tonat, K. (2001). Botulinum Toxin as a Biological Weapon: Medical and Public Health Management, *JAMA 285*(8), pp. 1059–1070.

Belluck, P. (2001, October 21). The epidemic: Anthrax outbreak of '57 felled a mill but yielded answers. *New York Times*. Retrieved January 2001, from http://www.ph.ucla.edu/epi/bioterr/anthraxoutbreakNHmill.html

Center for Civilian Biodefense Strategies. (2000). *Plague*. Retrieved March 2002, from www.hopkinsbiodefense.org/pages/agents/agentplague.html

Centers for Disease Control and Prevention. (2000, April 21). *Biological and chemical terrorism: Strategic plan for preparedness and response*. Recommendations of the CDC strategic planning workgroup (RR-4). Retrieved January 2002, from www.cdc.gov/mmwr/PDF/RIMR4904.pdf

Centers for Disease Control and Prevention. (2001). *Smallpox overview*. Retrieved February 2002, from www.bt.cdc.gov/agent/smallpox/overview/disease-facts.asp

Cieslak, T. J., & Eitzen, E. M. (1999). *Clinical and epidemiological principles of anthrax*. Retrieved February 2002, from www.cdc.govinciod/EID/vol5no4/cieslak.htm

Evans, G. (2002, August). *Bioterrorism forensics: If the bug does not fit you must acquit*. Retrieved August 2002, from www.findarticles.com/cf0/mOKHU/4_9/84396010/print.jhtml

Glass, T. A., & Schoch-Spana, M. (2002). Bioterrorism and the people: How to vaccinate a city against panic. *Clinical Infectious Diseases, 34*, 217–223. Retrieved March 2002, from http://www.journals.uchicago.edu/CID/journal/issues/v34n2/011333/011333.text.html

Gorner, P. (2001, October 21). From the Bible to battlefield, anthrax has widespread past. *Chicago Tribune Online Edition*. Retrieved October 26, 2002, from www.chicagotribune.com/news/showcase/chi-0110210054oct21.story?coll=cials-hed

Greene, S., & Ferslew, B. (2009). Homicidal poisoning deaths in the United States 1999–2005. *Clinical Toxicology, 47*, 342–347.

Hagman, M. (2001). WHO helps countries prepare for bioterror attacks. *Bulletin of the World Health Organization, 79*(11), 1089.

Henderson, D. A., Inglesby, T. V., Bartlett, J. G., Eitzen, E., Jahrling, P. B., Layton, M., et al. (1999). Smallpox as a biological weapon: Medical and public health management. *Journal of the American Medical Association, 281*(22), 2127–2137.

Hurlbert, R. E. (1997). *Biological weapons: Malignant biology.* Retrieved August 2002, from www .slic2wsu.edu:82/hurlbert/micro101/101biologicalweapons.html

Inglesby, T. V., . . . Tonat, K. (2000). Plague as a Biological Weapon: Medical and Public Health Management, *JAMA 283*(17), pp. 2281–2290.

Inglesby, T. V., Henderson, D. A., Bartlett, J. G., Eitzen, E., Friedlander, A. M., Hauer, J., . . . Tonat, K. (1999). Anthrax as a biological weapon: Medical and public health management. *Journal of the American Medical Association, 281*(18), 1735–1744.

Lewis, S. K. (2002). *History of biowarfare.* Retrieved March 2002, from www.pbs.org/wgbh/nova/ bioterror/history.html

Westveer, Arthur E., Trestrail, John H., and Pinizzotto, Anthony J. (1996). Homicidal poisonings in the United States: An analysis of the Uniform Crime Reports (UCR) from 1980–1989. *American Journal of Forensic Medicine and Pathology, 17*(4), 282–288.

PART III

Legal Issues

Chapter 18

Interviewing, Interrogation, and Criminal Confessions

Gregory M. Cooper, Michael P. Napier, and Susan H. Adams

"The defendant's own confession is probably the most probative and damaging evidence that can be admitted against him."
Justice Byron White, *Bruton v. United States* (1968)

In determining and isolating the guilt of an offender, there is no evidence more incriminating, damning, and conclusive than a voluntary confession. Although the underlying thrust of an interrogation is to explore and resolve issues, the successful interview of a culpable offender culminates when the truth is surrendered in a confession.

All of the physical evidence and eyewitness testimony combined is never worth as much as the criminal's own self-incriminating words: "I did it." The admissible confession proves guilt independently. It requires no authentication, no chain of custody, no scientific examination, no opinion testimony, no inferences, and no interpretation.

The Prosecution's Arsenal

THE EYEWITNESS

Eyewitness testimony is undeniably vital to a successful prosecution; however, it is often characterized by weakness. The witness may have problems seeing or hearing and describing what occurred. In addition, the witness may have a subtle reason to maliciously misrepresent the facts or alter them by unintentional or even targeted prejudice. The witness may be afraid to get involved and consequently becomes reluctant. Inconveniently before trial, witnesses may alter their account or become forgetful, move out of the state, or even die.

It is well known that two eyewitness accounts of the same incident can differ significantly. Research has substantially illustrated this effect.

The data of experimental psychology now establishes quite securely that no two individuals observe any complex occurrence in quite the same manner; that the ability of different individuals to retain and recall observations differ; that the elements which are retained and recalled are influenced by past experience and attitudes; and that the ability of various individuals to express what they have observed, retained, and recall vary greatly. There is no wholly reliable witness since the observations of all witnesses are faulty in some degree and some situations (Loevinger, 1980).

Although an eyewitness account greatly authenticates an occurrence, it should not be overestimated. The effects of time, the limits of human perception, and recollection, bias, prejudice, greed, and all human emotions influence perception.

PHYSICAL EVIDENCE

Physical evidence is also imperfect. Questions can be raised about the method of collection, preservation, analysis, and introduction of evidence. All too often, strong cases have been jeopardized and lost due to evidentiary error. Still an integral part of the effective prosecution, the strength of physical evidence is enhanced when combined with the complete prosecutorial arsenal.

PLEA BARGAINING

In some cases, law enforcement officers may take offense even at the suggestion of associating an efficiency and value factor to the application of justice. Nevertheless, plea bargaining must be unconditionally accepted as a negotiable leverage, especially considering the monumental costs of the American justice system and effective use of tax dollars.

Plea bargaining a settlement between first- or second-degree homicide, for example, is an extremely difficult approach for the prosecution to accept. Even worse is a descent to manslaughter, especially when the investigation suggests a more serious charge. Some prosecutorial weakness effectively targeted by the defense may release the offender from being prosecuted to the full extent of the law; worse, he may escape any form of judicial justice whatsoever. Nevertheless, a plea-bargaining agreement can and should be sustained as an effective antidote when there is insufficient evidence to support the maximum charge and accompanying penalties.

THE CONFESSION: THE BEST WEAPON

Admissions of guilt are essential to society's compelling interest in finding, convicting, and punishing those who violate the laws (*Moran v. Burbine*, 1986).

Surpassing all other forms of evidence and reinforcing their support of the truth, the confession remains unique. Unquestionably, the confession will prompt immediate deliberation of both advantages and disadvantages of a trial or plea-bargaining alternative. If a trial is warranted, a voluntary, admissible confession is undeniably paramount in considering the totality of the evidentiary presentation. The admissible confession will strengthen the integrity of both the eyewitness account and the physical evidence while fueling the synergistic effect of the prosecutorial arsenal.

A legal description of a confession is contained in the following case proceedings: "An accused person knowingly makes an acknowledgement that he or she committed or participated in the commission of the criminal act. This acknowledgement must be broad enough to comprehend every essential element necessary to make a case against the defendant" (*James v. State*, 1952).

According to this legal description, a confession should consist of (a) an acknowledgment of the commission of or participation in a criminal act that (b) must be sufficiently comprehensive to include every element of the criminal act as defined by statute.

To fully understand and implement the confession as described earlier, a review of burden of proof and the criminal act requirements and their implications is warranted.

BURDEN OF PROOF

Criminal investigators assume the prosecution's responsibility to prove guilt beyond a reasonable doubt. This includes the requirement of proving each element of the offense for which the accused is charged. There is no prosecution without the presentation of proof. And the proof is initially discovered, organized, assessed, and finally presented to the prosecution by the investigator. A successful prosecution, which secures a conviction, is the fruit of a productive, meticulous, and intensive investigation. If the prosecution fails to prove all of the elements of a crime beyond a reasonable doubt, the verdict dictates the accused guilty of a lesser crime. Failure of the prosecution to gather and introduce sufficient evidence to meet this burden will result in an acquittal or, at least, the reduction of a more serious crime to a less serious one (Klotter, 1990).

CRIMINAL ACT REQUIREMENTS

There are several factors that need to be addressed to determine whether in fact what happened was a crime. These are termed criminal act requirements.

- *Actus reus.* Before a person may be convicted and punished for a crime, the prosecution must present evidence that the person (acting as a principal, accessory, or accomplice) committed a criminal act as defined by statute. Each element of the crime prescribed by law must be present in the offender's actions to duly constitute a criminal offense. This principle is referred to as *actus reus*. It is the first condition required to label an act a crime.

- *Mens rea.* The formula for committing a crime is incomplete without the evidence of criminal intent. The actus reus must be combined with the criminal state of mind (mens rea) to constitute a crime. If the defense can show that the defendant's mind was innocent, a crime has not been committed.

  Criminal intent must accompany the criminal act except as otherwise provided by statute. Criminal intent can also be satisfied if the act is accompanied by such negligent and reckless conduct as to be regarded by the law as the equivalent to criminal intent (Klotter, 1990).

  This concept may be expressed in the following formula:

  Criminal act (actus reus) + Criminal intent (mens rea) = Criminal conviction

- *Causation.* The criminal conviction formula incorporates through logically deductive reasoning the existence of a causal relationship between conduct and results. In other words, for "one to be guilty of a crime, his act or omission must have been the proximate cause thereof" (Klotter, 1990). There is usually little or no difficulty in showing causal relationship.

In summation, the prosecution must show the following:

- A specific party or parties participated.
- Criminal acts as constituted by law were committed.
- There was the presence of a criminal state of mind.
- The conduct was the proximate cause of the crime.

What does the criminal act requirement (actus reus, mens rea, and causation) have to do with the confession? What is the relationship between the confession and the prosecution's burden of proof responsibility?

Recall the previous legal description of the confession: that it requires acknowledgment and comprehensive culpability of each required element to constitute a crime.

Regretfully, interviews are concluded prematurely for many reasons, sometimes unknowingly. While devoting a concentrated effort to the first criterion (participation in the criminal act), the interviewer mistakenly overlooks the pivotal third criteria (criminal intent). Although the offender's acknowledgments may satisfy the actus reus and causation provisions of the criminal act requirements, the admission alone is insufficient to expose every essential element necessary to make a case against the defendant.

The offender's admission may reveal his participation in a criminal act (actus reus) and that his conduct was the direct cause of the crime (causation). The act, although interrelated, is only a reflection of his character. However, it does not fully reveal his character or criminal state of mind, and it is imperative that this be displayed. The interview provides the investigator a chance to extract and unravel his thought process, and reveal his criminal state of mind.

CRIMINAL INTENT

To comprehensively understand the act, the criminal mind must be unraveled. This issue is especially significant when a crime is classified by various degrees of seriousness depending on the defendant's state of mind. Not only must the confession reflect that the defendant did something "bad," but also it must show that he had a "bad" intent. This distinction is especially useful for the prosecution when it is essential to determine the level of seriousness of the crime and its associated degree of punishment. Moreover, it may also be considered when assessing the predictability of the defendant's propensity toward violence and potential for recidivism.

The confession provides the psychological environment for the offender to reenact the crime. It sets the stage for him to relive his behavioral role (actus reus) and display his psychological role (mens rea). The well-prepared interviewer can write the script for the final scene as the offender recounts each phase of the crime. The interviewer can preview the offense by allowing the offender to escort him through every scene until the full panorama of events is related. The interviewer assumes the role of a scribe while he urges the offender to mentally return to the crime and dictate his every act, precipitating thoughts, emotions, and feelings. The defendant's own explanation of his mens rea (state of mind) will uncover his criminal intent.

Criminal intent can effectively be articulated and demonstrated by building the mens rea portion of the confession from the foundation of three basic questions:

1. Did the offender premeditate?
2. Did the offender deliberate?
3. Did the offender harbor malice aforethought?

These three questions provide the framework to formulate queries that solicit the defendant's thoughts, behavior (including habits), and feelings he experienced before, during, and after the crime. The interviewer should not restrict his review of the defendant's history but should probe as far back as possible. Furthermore, if the content of the confession clearly illustrates the defendant's willful misconduct, it will reject an alleged impaired understanding of his criminal behavior. This renders the diminished capacity or insanity defense implausible.

There is no shortcut approach to producing an all-inclusive confession. But when considering the consequences of failing to solve a capital crime, expediency should never be an issue.

Preparing for the Prescriptive Interview

Prescriptive interviewing is a tool to supplement law enforcement efforts in achieving successful results during the interview. It will also serve to elevate the interviewer's awareness of steps that can be applied to increase interview effectiveness. Enhanced interview skills and techniques are especially fitting in the light of the Supreme Court's decision in the case *Minnick v. Mississippi* (1990), when it ruled six to two precluding law enforcement officials from reengaging a suspect after the suspect had requested an attorney. The Court stated that "when counsel is requested, interrogation must cease, and officials may not reinitiate interrogation without counsel present, whether or not the accused has consulted with his attorney." Consequently, it is best to assume that law enforcement has one opportunity to interview a defendant. Therefore, the interviewer will serve the public's best interest with an exhaustive preparation. If the interview does not terminate with the confession, neither will it be unresolved with a burden of regrets.

The vital link to a successful interview is preparation, which establishes the foundation to developing a successful approach in the interview setting. Preparation has four steps:

1. *Data collection.* Comprehensive and meticulous data collection system must be implemented to reconstruct each phase of a capital crime. Each criminal offense consists of fundamental elements that must be present to conform to specific criminal code requirements. Data collection is a principal factor in determining that those requirements have been met as prescribed by law.

2. *Assessment.* Assessing the relevancy of the data to the crime is required. It is necessary to objectively judge the value of the data collected to determine if they apply to the elements of the crime, that is, whether the information contributes to the criminal act requirements.

3. *Analysis.* Analysis of the data is imperative to complete the preparatory process. Law enforcement must do more than merely see that each criminal element is intact. Professionalism requires organizing and dissecting the information, thereby observing the complex web of interrelated components of the crime. For example, I may "see" a set

of stairs before me; however, I "observe" that there are exactly sixteen steps covered with a distinctive color and quality of carpet. In addition, the carpet is soiled and cluttered with specific toys and items of clothing, suggesting the presence of children of corresponding ages. The condition of the carpet and disarray of clothing and toys may also suggest the house-cleaning habits of the owners and even imply an economic and social stratum. It is during this phase of preparation that meaning and substance are assigned to the (criminal) act and the actor. Armed with this enhanced understanding, the fourth step is applied.

4. *Theorizing.* Theorizing assumes the challenges of identifying the motivation underlying the criminal thought process and reconstructing the crime. It attempts to mentally crystallize the interwoven thread or current of thought that the criminal mind uses to justify his crime and general behavior.

This sometimes laborious preparatory process will elevate the interviewer's ability to empathize with the offender's state of mind and prompt a better understanding of his thoughts and rationalization.

The preparatory phase of the interview is preeminent in conducting a successful interview. There is no substitute for this principle, and it should never be sacrificed for convenience or expediency. Granted, depending on the grievous nature of the crime, varying degrees of effort will be applied. However, especially with capital crimes, success will be tantamount to preparation.

CRIME CLASSIFICATION

Crime classification integrates all preparatory steps of the interview. It is the precursor to humanizing the offender and revealing his thought process. It includes the accumulation and assimilation of data compiled during the investigative phase for the purpose of conducting a criminal investigative analysis. To formulate a profile of the criminal personality, a criminal investigative analyst will review and analyze area photos, maps, sketches, crime scene photos, victimology, and all incident-related reports. The analyst also examines autopsy and forensic findings, initial and follow-up reports, and newspaper clippings. A microscopic examination of this information will begin to reveal behavioral characteristics of the offender, thereby exposing major personality traits.

The process applied by a criminal investigative analyst in developing an offender's personality characteristics is similar to a forensic pathologist. The forensic pathologist identifies the elements surrounding the cause and method of death by closely examining the physical evidence through an autopsy. The criminal investigative analyst examines all referred reports and documents and conducts a behavioral autopsy. This process may suggest the cause or motive of the crime and offer implications of the offender personality as suggested by the method selected to commit the crime. An assessment of the offender's behavioral patterns can unmask an undercurrent of emotional deficiencies and needs manifested by the offender. An improved understanding of or insight into these emotional deficiencies and needs can provide a solid foundation for the interviewer. This foundation will support the strategic construction of tailored approaches and appeals to prevail upon the offender.

Consider, for example, the advantage an interviewer would have when he has in his possession the following personality characteristics of the suspect extracted from a criminal analysis generated from the analysis of a disorganized lust murder:

- Of average intelligence and a high school or college dropout.
- Probably unemployed or blue-collar, unskilled occupation.
- Financially dependent on a domineering female.
- A previous criminal record of assault-related offense.
- Probable voyeuristic activities.
- Probable pornography interest and collection.
- Alcohol or drugs exhibited in his behavior.
- Keen sense of fantasy.
- Inability to carry out preplanned activities.
- Difficulty in maintaining personal relationships with a female for an extended time.
- A need to dominate and control relationships.
- Sexually inexperienced.
- Sexually inadequate.
- Never married or a brief, combative marital relationship.
- Sadistic tendencies.
- Controlled aggression but rage or hatred.
- Confused thought process.
- Feels justified in his behavior while feeling no remorse or guilt.
- Defiant of authority.
- Low self-esteem.
- Frustration from lack of direction of control of life.
- Combustive temper.
- Impulsive.
- Deep anxiety.

While considering these characteristics in concert with investigative activities confirming some of the biographical and descriptive information provided, an interviewer can begin to observe this offender. The interviewer may recognize and exploit certain personality characteristics and associated emotional deficiencies. In pondering the offender's behavior, thought processes, and aligned emotions, the interviewer is now better prepared to design various approaches to conform to the offender's personality.

Although traditional and canned approaches have worked in the past, they must not be overestimated. Abraham Maslow said, "He who is good with a hammer tends to think everything is a nail." Square pegs will not fit in round holes. This process assists the interviewer in stepping out of his world and into the foreign territory of his adversary. If the offender decides to cooperate, it will be because he can justify his decision from his perspective. There is only one frame of reference that is important in the offender decision-making process: his own. And if the interviewer successfully influences the offender to conform, it is because an alliance was forged in the offender territory. The offender must be able to visualize the personal advantage in complying. The interviewer must develop the ability to speak the same language to extract the best evidence: the confession.

The criminal investigative analysis process permits the diagnosis of offender emotional strengths and weakness and general behavioral characteristics. Having been briefed with this information, the interviewer is better prepared to prescribe effective interview approaches that are customized to the offender's perspective. Such prescriptions may indicate:

- Identifying who should conduct the interview.
- Where the interview should take place.
- What type of environment is best suited for the particular approach or approaches used.
- How the approach or appeal should be constructed.
- What emotional appeals are most likely to be effective.

Before a tracker begins a journey into unknown territory to apprehend an enemy, he enlists all possible resources to familiarize himself with the known terrain, climate, and environment. This permits him to identify the type of survival tools and skills needed to accomplish the task. Remember that the offender has been preparing his responses to conceal his guilt from the moment he committed the crime, and probably before. He will use every tactic available to counter and dismantle every offensive attack. To know your enemy is the best strategy. It takes time, commitment, and grueling effort.

Preceding the morning of his date of execution, the notorious serial killer Ted Bundy told FBI special agent Bill Hagmaier of the National Center for the Analysis of Violent Crime (NCAVC): "If you want to catch the big fish, you must be willing to go under and into the deep water to catch them." Bundy proceeded to tell Hagmaier that he would "take him under with him."

Although prescriptive interviewing is not a panacea for the challenges in obtaining confessions, it is still one more precision instrument to be used in swaying the balance of justice in society's favor. A prescriptive interview will enhance law enforcement's efforts to persuade serious capital offenders to escort us under the water into the caverns of their torrential minds, surrender their secrets, and expose their culpability. It is hoped that the successful use of this method will both promote the cause of justice and deter effects of recidivism.

Challenges to Confessions (FBI, 2002)

Some critics of law enforcement techniques have gained notoriety as well as some credibility. (The word *critics* is used throughout this chapter to denote a small number of social psychologists who have testified for the defense regarding the legal admissibility of some confessions.) Several criticisms earn merit by reminding investigators of practical procedures to safeguard the interviewers' most valued work product, the confession (Napier & Adams, 1998).

Critics use the term coercive to describe interview and interrogation tactics, claiming that they result in a coerced confession. The difficulty of identifying, with certainty, the number of confessions obtained through coercion hampers the critics' position (Cassell, 1997). Acquiring an accurate representation of false confessions obtained under police questioning remains imperative, and on-going research attempts to address this need (Jayne & Buckley, 1998). Even if each alleged false confession was indeed deceptive, the occurrence of alleged false confessions, when viewed in the framework of the millions of suspect interviews conducted annually, is statistically minuscule. Yet professional officers view a single false confession as one too many.

The challenges to law enforcement interview tactics can be grouped into five categories. The application of corresponding interview principles, which involve simple and appropriate adjustments in style and technique, can address the criticism of law enforcement interview tactics. The application of these principles will enhance the suspect interview processes and strengthen the admissibility of confessions. When used .regularly, these principles will illustrate the good-faith efforts of law enforcement in handling the investigative responsibilities of identifying suspects and obtaining constitutionally admissible confessions.

Category 1: Behavior

CHALLENGE: READING THE SUSPECT'S BEHAVIOR

One censure of police procedures involves observing the behavior of suspects in the interview room and selecting specific suspects for more intense investigative inquiry. Critics allege that an officer's ability to interpret behavior, such as the aversion of direct eye contact, is inadequate to protect the innocent from unreasonable investigative focus (Leo & Ofshe, 1997), which may cause an improper concentration of limited police resources on the wrong suspect, thereby allowing the guilty party to escape detection. Critics accuse the police of placing excessive reliance on hunches and on-the-spot reading of verbal and nonverbal characteristics, using methods that are neither scientifically valid nor reliable. Investigations may focus on the wrong person because techniques do not distinguish between stressful responses caused by deception and responses to stress caused simply by accusatory interviewing (Ofshe & Leo, 1997a). Behaviors improperly interpreted by investigators may take on the weight of perceived evidence and increase the intensity of the police focus.

INTERVIEW PRINCIPLE: FOLLOW THE FACTS

Some cases do not contain the gift of clear evidence to follow on the path to the case solution. Investigators therefore rely on investigative experience and anecdotal lessons to identify responses consistent with known deceivers or individuals with guilty knowledge. Law enforcement must place "gut instincts" in context, however, by comparing them with investigative and evidentiary facts, which take precedence over instincts. Thorough investigative techniques will avoid a narrow focus on specific individuals by investigating all viable leads capable of identifying additional suspects and eliminating wrongly identified suspects. If the investigative hunch or the supposition does not align with known facts, investigators always should follow the facts.

Category 2: Traits

CHALLENGE: IDENTIFYING PERSONAL VULNERABILITIES

Several critics point out that certain individuals possess traits that make them overly susceptible to police interrogation techniques, thereby leading to coerced confessions (Ofshe & Leo, 1997b). These impressionable traits include youthfulness, a low or borderline intelligent quotient (IQ), mental handicap, psychological inadequacy, recent bereavement, language barrier, alcohol or other drug withdrawal, illiteracy, fatigue, social isolation, or inexperience with the criminal justice system (Gudjonsson, 1992). These traits have sufficient strength to affect the suspect's decision-making process, mental alertness, and suggestibility.

Interview Principle: Know the Suspect

The most productive interviews are planned well in advance. Except in exigent circumstances, competent investigators have learned to invest time in the initial information-gathering process (Vessel, 1998).

Investigators can design the initial, low-key interview phase to obtain norming information about how suspects normally respond verbally and nonverbally. This also presents an opportunity to gather information from suspects about their education and language ability, difficulties in life, and the foundation for their successes in life. By learning details about all aspects of a suspect's life and lifestyle, investigators can avoid subsequent problems.

For example, if officers believe that particular suspects have low IQs, they should not only check school records but also determine social-functioning ability. Do these offenders have below-normal intelligence but a reputation for being street smart? To what language levels do they respond? What are their language difficulties or drug use patterns? How do they function in the real world? As noted by one interrogation expert, although suspects may have below-normal intelligence, they also may possess "a Ph.D. in social intelligence" or what police officers call street smarts (Holmes, 1995).

By examining varied aspects of suspects' lives and closely questioning each source of information, investigators can compile a witness list to later defend their choice of investigative techniques. Law enforcement should not accept assertions of mental or personality disability. They should ask for specific examples and exceptions from witnesses who know the suspects. Vulnerable qualities should not exclude suspects from being interviewed. Such vulnerabilities as reduced mental capabilities, the ability to withstand pressure, bereavement, mental illness, age, or other personal traits that may increase suggestibility require special care when using questioning techniques. Investigators should place the suspect's vulnerability in context, adapt the investigative approach, and fully document any adaptations. In addition, law enforcement officers should plan specific word use to determine if suspects understand questions at a particular language level or if the investigator's terminology needs an explanation. If suspects understand language typically used with other offenders, investigators should document that fact, thereby substantiating concern for not overwhelming suspects or taking advantage of any declared vulnerability.

Case Example

A 10-year-old girl suddenly disappeared from a public street while on an errand to a store. A 29-year-old man became a suspect, and through police investigation, he also became a suspect in a similar incident involving another prepubescent female 10 years earlier. Although the suspect was labeled intelligence handicapped at an early age, carefully gathered background information indicated his capability of dealing with life and living alone. Based on this knowledge, investigators felt that language adjustments were not necessary. Later testimony clearly indicated that the suspect understood each question and that he responded appropriately. Challenges to his multiple confessions were denied. The suspect now is on death row; his convictions for the two murders were based on confessions.

Category 3: Statements

CHALLENGE: CONTAMINATING CONFESSIONS

Some critics believe that police officers inadvertently contaminate confessions by relying on questions that contain crime scene data and investigative results (Gudjonsson, 1992). Using crime scene or investigative photos in the questioning process may amplify this flaw. Through these procedures, the police might in fact "educate" suspects (Zulawski & Wicklander, 1998) by providing knowledge that suspects simply repeat in an effort to escape intense interrogation pressure. As a result, suspects appear to offer a valid confession.

INTERVIEW PRINCIPLE: PRESERVE THE EVIDENCE

To avoid contaminating a suspect's subsequent admissions and unnecessarily revealing investigative knowledge, investigators should initiate the criminal involvement phase of questioning by using only open-ended questions, which avoid the pitfalls of leading or informing suspects. These questions begin with such phrases as, "Describe for me . . . ," "Tell me about . . . ," and "Explain how . . . " These questions force suspects to commit to a version of events instead of simply agreeing with the investigator; they also prevent disclosing investigative knowledge. Because suspects may provide a wealth of information in this free narrative form, open-ended questions make successful lying difficult (Gudjonsson, 1992). If, however, suspects decide to lie, open-ended questions provide a forum. This aspect of the open-ended question technique may help investigators because every lie forecloses avenues by which suspects may later try to defend themselves (Zulawski & Wicklander, 1998).

Investigators must receive answers to open-ended questions without any type of judgment, reaction, or interruption. By allowing suspects to tell their stories without interruption, investigators fulfill the basic purpose of an interview: to obtain information. In addition, they benefit from committing suspects to a particular position (Holmes, 1995), which may contain information that later becomes evidence of guilt or provides a connection to the crime, crime scene, or victim.

The questioning process does not become contaminated when investigators initiate the interview with open-ended questions. Investigators have not told suspects the details of the crime or subsequent investigation and thereby have preserved the evidence. After listening to the narrative responses to the open-ended question, skilled investigators will probe with additional open-ended questions and ask direct, closed questions later.

Displaying crime scene photos to suspects prior to obtaining admissions appears to have limited usefulness. By showing graphic details of the crime, suspects receive information that, when parroted back, gives substance to their confessions. Crime scene photos may include holdout information, which primarily serves to validate confessions. However, from a psychological perspective, few, if any, suspects will be shocked into confessing when they see reminders of their gruesome acts.

Case Example

A 13-year-old female was raped, murdered, and decapitated. A 16-year-old male was questioned as an alibi witness for the suspect. During his questioning, the police became suspicious of his personal involvement in the crime. Eventually, he provided a description of the crime and pointed out crime scene details indicative of his direct involvement in the murder and decapitation. Investigators remained persistent, and the youth later provided an explanation of how he knew incriminating details. He reported that while he was being questioned, an investigator sorted through crime scene pictures attempting to locate a specific picture. The suspect stated, "When he switched . . . the pictures real quick, I saw what was happening before them pictures [the pictures selected for the investigator's specific question]. . . . He says, where do you think the body was? But when he was switching them, I saw where the body was. . . . Then he says, where is the head part. . . . Anybody's going to know where a person's place is when they got the big, yellow thing [crime scene tape] around the water thing, the toilet. They had that caution thing all around there. I says, 'okay, right there' [indicating the exact location of the head]." Of special note, this youth had an IQ of about 70. Subsequently, the correct suspect was convicted of the crime and sentenced to life in prison. The charges against the alibi witness subsequently were dropped.

Category 4: Options

CHALLENGE: CREATING FALSE REALITY

Some critics allege that police use techniques that create a false reality for suspects by limiting their ability to reason and consider alternative options (Ofshe & Leo, 1997a). Some argue that the police intentionally present only one side of the evidence or options available to suspects, namely, only the ones that benefit the police. Once suspects accept a narrowed option, inferred benefits coerce them, such as avoidance of a premeditated murder charge in favor of describing the crime as an accident. The obvious benefit of accepting a suggested lesser alternative leads suspects to be coerced into a false confession out of fear of the police and possible prosecution.

INTERVIEW PRINCIPLE: ADJUST MORAL RESPONSIBILITY

The interviewer should question suspects, not provide legal counsel (Caplan, 1985). The investigator's purpose does not include providing options for guilty suspects to conceal their involvement.

Experienced investigators understand the following aspects of confessions (Holmes, 1995):

- Confessions are not readily given.
- Full confessions originate with small admissions.
- Guilty suspects seldom tell everything.
- Most offenders are not proud of their violence and recognize that it was wrong.
- Guilty suspects omit details that cast them in a harsh, critical light.
- Offenders usually confess to obtain a position they believe to be advantageous to them.

Astute interviewers use rationalization, projection, and minimization to remove barriers to obtaining confessions (Napier & Adams, 1998). These represent the same techniques that suspects use to justify and place their sometimes abhorrent behaviors in terms that assuage their conscience. Thus, these psychological techniques serve two purposes: they allow investigators to protect society by identifying guilty suspects and provide face-saving opportunities for suspects to make it easier for them to confess.

These techniques initially downplay the suspects' culpability by omitting their provocative behavior, blaming others, or minimizing their actual conduct. In certain circumstances, investigators might need to suggest that the suspects' criminality was an accident (Jayne & Buckley, 1998) or the result of an unexpected turn of events, which the victims might have provoked. Investigators attempt to obtain an admission or place the suspect near the scene or with the victim. From the original admission of guilt, experienced investigators refine their techniques by using all of the case facts to point out the flaws and insufficiency in the original admission and to obtain a fuller, more accurate description of the suspect's criminal behavior (Jayne & Buckley, 1998). Practiced interviewers use the initial admission as a wedge to open the door to additional incriminating statements.

The suggestion that investigators interrupt an admission of guilt in a homicide case to debate whether a suspect committed a premeditated or spontaneous murder is unrealistic. The final disclosure of case facts and laboratory results will provide details to reveal the most likely version of events. Seasoned interviewers know that the interview and interrogation phase constitutes only one portion of the entire investigation.

Category 5: Consequences

CHALLENGE: PROMISING COERCIVE END-OF-LINE BENEFITS

Investigators move into clearly coercive territory when giving clear and substantial identification of end-of-line benefits to confession. The coercive aspect comes from investigators' statements that remaining silent will lead to greater penalties but confessing to a minimized scenario will result in reward (Ofshe & Leo, 1997b). Investigators may openly suggest that suspects will receive the most serious charge possible without a consent to the offered lesser interpretation of their actions (Ofshe & Leo, 1997a). Many interviewers blatantly and precisely state the suspect's expected penalty in unmistakable terms, such as the death penalty versus life imprisonment or life imprisonment versus 20 years. Similarly, investigators may threaten harm through investigation or prosecution of a third party, such as a wife, brother, or child, if suspects reject the lessened scenario. Some critics accurately have identified these tactics as being coercive enough to make innocent people confess to a crime that they did not commit.

INTERVIEW PRINCIPLE: USE PSYCHOLOGY VERSUS COERCION

The interview and interrogation system generally recognized as the most widely used and adapted in the United States follows the limitations imposed by the ethical standards, as well as the dictates, of the courts (Inbau, Reid, Buckley, & Jayne, 2001). U.S. courts have allowed investigators the breadth of creativity in interviewing suspects, but any coercive investigative acts are offensive to the skilled professional. Successful interviewing does not hinge on coercive techniques because talented investigators have a ready reservoir of productive, acceptable, and psychologically effective methods. Blatant statements by investigators depicting the worst-case scenario facing a suspect who does not accept a lesser responsibility are coercive and unnecessary. In general, these statements follow the pattern of, "If you don't cooperate, I am personally going to prove your brother was up to his eyeballs in this murder. He will go down hard." Statements of this type are clearly coercive and less effective than the use of psychological techniques of rationalization, projection, and minimization.

Nevertheless, a distinction exists between blatant statements and subtle references offered for interpretation as the suspect chooses. Suspects engage in a self-imposed, personal decision-making process that incorporates their life experiences, familiarity with the criminal justice system, and their time-tested psychological processes of rationalization, projection, and minimization. They may explain reasons for the crime (rationalization), blame others (projection), or lessen their culpability and express remorse even if it is unfelt (minimization). Guilty suspects attempt to describe their criminal acts as understandable, in a manner that places them in a better position to obtain the desired lenient treatment. They eagerly listen for any opportunity to look good. Investigators are not responsible if suspects choose to offer an explanation of guilt that places them in what the suspects perceive as a favorable position. Investigators achieve part of their goal because the suspect must admit culpability to achieve this desired perceived position.

Investigators must accept the admission, return to the basics of the investigation, and obtain a statement that comports to the reality of the crime. Investigators too must go well beyond the "I did it" admission. They must press for minute details to tie suspects to the crime scene to disclose their active participation in the crime.

Corroboration anchors the most secure confession. Some suspects may not readily provide information to support their involvement in a crime for fear of exposing the true nature of their evil acts. However, a suspect's corroboration by providing details known to only a few individuals solidifies a confession. Evidence linking such details as the location of the body, the weapon, or the fruits of the crime provides a superior foundation for preventing the retraction of a confession or one otherwise successfully challenged in court.

Personal Dignity

A final principle that underpins the entire interview process involves the concept of dignity. All individuals are entitled to maintaining their personal dignity and self-worth. Convicted felons have explained that they more likely would confess to an investigator who treated them with respect and recognized their value as a person (Zulawski & Wicklander, 1998). Allowing suspects to maintain dignity, even in adverse circumstances, is professional and increases the likelihood of obtaining a confession. One experienced investigator provides advice for interviewing the suspect of a particularly serious crime: "Remember, he has to go on living with himself" (Holmes, 1995).

Many investigators now videotape their interviews to document the confession, which allows attorneys and the jury to view it. This also allows investigators to view their interviewing performance and thus learn from critiquing it. Videotaping can remind the investigator to treat the suspect with respect as a person, regardless of the nature of the crime.

Conclusion

Law enforcement agencies are governed, sometimes invisibly, by their organizations' value systems. Although organizations are built from the bottom up, their values flow in both directions. The concept of professionalism for the investigator begins with basic duties and carries through to a legal responsibility, providing sworn testimony in open court about ethically and legally obtained evidence.

The manner in which an investigator approaches interviewing and interrogation may symbolize the ultimate reflection of the professional values of a department. Casual values appear as a casual attitude, which translates into matching behavior. The appearance of casual values in the interview room may result in suppression of admissions or confessions, but it also may reflect a casual approach to law enforcement at all levels. All aspects of law enforcement must reflect vigilance to the highest policing values, but nowhere is this more important than in the interview room and in presenting the investigative product of the interview.

References

Bruton v. United States, 391 U.S. 123 (1968).

Caplan, G. M. (1985). Questioning Miranda. *Vanderbilt Law Review, 38*, 1417.

Cassell, P. G. (1997). Symposium on coercion: An interdisciplinary examination of coercion, exploitation, and the law, and coerced confessions: Balanced approaches to the false confession problem. A Brief Comment on Ofshe, Leo, and Alschuler. *Denver University Law Review, 74*, 1127.

Federal Bureau of Investigation. (2002). Challenges to confessions. Copyright © 2002 by ProQuest Information and Learning. All rights reserved. Copyright United States Federal Bureau of Investigation, Nov. 2002. Reprinted with permission.

Gudjonsson, G. (1992). *The psychology of interrogations, confessions, and testimony.* Hoboken, NJ: Wiley.

Holmes, W. D. (1995). Interrogation. *Polygraph, 24*(4), 241.

Inbau, F. E., Reid, J. E., Buckley, J. P., & Jayne, B. C. (2001). *Criminal interrogation and confessions* (4th ed.). Gaithersburg, MD: Aspen.

James v. State, 86 Georgia App. 282, 71, S.E.2d 568 (1952).

Jayne, B. C., & Buckley, J. P. (1998, Winter). Interrogation alert! Will your next confession be suppressed? *Investigator*, pp. 11, 12.

Klotter, J. C. (1990). *Criminal law.* New York, NY: Anderson.

Leo, R. A., & Ofshe, R. J. (1997, May 30). *The consequences of false confession: Deprivations of liberty and miscarriages of justice in the age of psychological interrogation.* Paper prepared for the Annual Meetings of the Law and Society Association, St. Louis, MO.

Loevinger, L. (1980). Preface. In J. Marshall (Ed.), *Law and psychology in conflict.* Indianapolis, IN: Bobbs-Merrill.

Minnick v. Mississippi, 111 S. Ct. 486 (1990).

Moran v. Burbine, 89 L. Ed. 2d 410 (1986).

Napier, M. R., & Adams, S. A. (1998, October). Magic words to obtain confessions. *FBI Law Enforcement Bulletin*, pp. 11–15.

Ofshe, R. J., & Leo, R. A. (1997a). The social psychology of police interrogation: The theory and classification of true and false confessions. *Studies in Law, Politics, and Society, 16*, 241.

Ofshe, R. J., & Leo, R. A. (1997b). Symposium on coercion: An interdisciplinary examination of coercion, exploitation, and the law and II. Coerced confessions: The decision to confess falsely: Rational choice and irrational action. *Denver University Law Review, 74*, 998.

Vessel, D. (1998, October). Conducting successful interrogations. *FBI Law Enforcement Bulletin*, 1–6.

Zulawski, D. E., & Wicklander, D. E. (1998, July). Special Report 1: Interrogations, interrogation: Understanding the process. *Law and Order*, p. 87.

Chapter 19

Wrongful Convictions
Causes, Solutions, and Case Studies

Peter Shellem

No study of violent crime would be complete without a look at the rising tide of proven false convictions that began in the late 1980s with the advent of advanced DNA testing and continues to this day. It should be of special concern to investigators, whose job is to determine the truth. Each time a convicted murderer or rapist is released from prison, exonerated by DNA or other evidence, it represents a breakdown of the system and a black eye to law enforcement. More important, in most cases, the real perpetrator escaped apprehension and prosecution and likely will never be brought to justice.

The exposure of these cases is having an impact throughout what most agree is the best justice system in the world. Juries are becoming more skeptical and want more solid evidence in serious criminal cases. Government and law enforcement agencies also are responding to the problem.

One of the most dramatic repercussions came in January 2003, when outgoing Illinois governor George Ryan cleared that state's death row of all 171 prisoners, commuting their terms to life in prison, while pardoning four death-sentenced inmates who were challenging their convictions. Ryan, once a staunch supporter of the death penalty, made the decision in the wake of 13 exonerations of death row prisoners. He said statistics showing more than half of the death sentences in his state were reversed on appeal also played a part in his decision to stop executions until reforms were made. On January 20, 2004, then governor Rod Blagojevich signed the final piece of major death penalty reform package. The new laws address serious flaws in Illinois' capital punishment system.

In 2004, Congress passed the Justice for All Act, which gives federal convicts access to DNA testing and provides for improved defense for capital defendants. It also increased the maximum compensation the federal government can be required to pay wrongfully convicted defendants from a flat fee of

$5,000 to $100,000 per year of imprisonment in capital cases and $50,000 per year in noncapital cases.[1] States across the country have or are in the process of enacting legislation to give convicts access to DNA testing if it can prove their innocence, which will likely lead to more exonerations. Multimillion-dollar lawsuits have led some states to enact reparations legislation to pay unjustly convicted inmates for the time they spent in prison.

Several states and countries have also created commissions to study the problem and cases that are being challenged. In 2002, the Supreme Court of North Carolina created an innocence commission in the wake of several highly publicized exonerations. A year later, Connecticut became the first state in the United States to create an innocence commission by statute. Leaders in other states are considering proposals for similar commissions. Meanwhile, more innocence projects are popping up at law schools and journalism schools across the country.

The holy grail for many death penalty opponents is an innocent defendant who has already been executed. They believe once that can be demonstrated, it will lead to the abolition of the death penalty. In 2005, that quest was focusing on Larry Griffin, who was executed by the state of Missouri on June 21, 1995, for killing a 19-year-old drug dealer in a drive-by shooting on June 26, 1980, in a crime-plagued neighborhood. The victim was widely believed to have murdered Griffin's brother about six months earlier. He had been charged but released because of a lack of evidence. A yearlong investigation by the National Association for the Advancement of Colored People found that a man injured in the same shooting, who was never called as a witness, says Griffin was not involved. The key witness in the case was a police informant with an extensive criminal history who later said police showed him a photo of Griffin and said they knew he did it.[2]

According to a study by Gross, Jacoby, Matheson, Montgomery, and Patel (2005) there were 340 exonerations nationally between when DNA testing became widely available in 1989 through 2003. The study found that half of the 327 men and 13 women spent 10 years or more in prison, and 80% had served at least five years. The study also showed that the number of exonerations was dramatically increasing from an average of twelve a year from 1989 through 1994 to an average of 42 a year since 2000. The highest yearly total in Gross et al study was forty-four in 2002 and again in 2003.[3]

Most innocence projects consider only murder or rape convictions with lengthy prison terms and will take cases only when biological evidence is available for testing. Experts agree that similar percentages of wrongful

[1] http://frwebgate.access.gpo.gov/cgi-bin/getdoc.cgi?dbname=108_cong_public_laws&docid=f:publ405.108.pdf

[2] www.stltoday.com/stltoday/news/special/srlinks.nsf/story/9270DD9B25C367FB8625703B007B8C70? OpenDocument

[3] www.law.umich.edu/NewsAndInfo/exonerations-in-us.pdf

convictions would likely be found among other populations of convicts. Furthermore, they consider only cases in which DNA cleared the defendant as exoneration. Under that standard, several of the cases cited in this chapter would not qualify, although the defendants were freed by courts. The Death Penalty Information Center, which lists only capital convictions in which the defendants were freed by courts, pardoned because of evidence of innocence or acquitted at retrial, counted 121 exonerations between 1973 and 2005.[4]

Ninety-six percent of the exonerations in Gross et al. study were in murder and rape cases. An earlier study by Gross found that eyewitness misidentification occurred twice as often in robbery cases as in rape cases, leading him to conclude that if there was a way to identify false convictions in robbery cases like DNA in rape cases, there would be more exonerations in robbery convictions than in rape cases.

There are some clear patterns in false convictions that have come to light. For murder, the leading cause of the false convictions is perjury—including perjury by police officers, by jailhouse snitches, by the real killers, and by supposed participants and eyewitnesses to the crime who knew the innocent defendants in advance. False confessions also played a large role in the murder convictions that led to exonerations, primarily among two particularly vulnerable groups of innocent defendants: juveniles, and those who are mentally retarded or mentally ill (Gross et al., 2005).

In the *Kinge case*, police had manufactured fingerprint evidence to get a conviction. The defendant, Shirley Kinge, was sentenced to twenty-two to sixty years in prison for what was believed to be her role in the brutal murder of an entire family in New York State.

Kinge spent two and a half years in prison and sued the state. David Harding, the officer who said he found Kinge's fingerprints on a gas can used in an arson after the murders, was sentenced to 4 to 12 years after admitting planting evidence in seven cases. The case against Harding, which eventually included the prosecution of his partner, supervisor, and three other troopers, revealed almost routine fabrication of evidence and showed they had planted fingerprints in forty cases involving murder, burglary, rape, and drugs. Prosecutors found out about the widespread corruption when Harding bragged about it while interviewing for a job at the CIA. In an ABC News interview, Harding blamed the intense pressure to solve violent crimes, but a special prosecutor in the case said it was "laziness, ego, and self-glorification."

Obviously, not all investigators turn to lying and fabricating evidence because of the recognized pressure of their jobs. Honest officers can be led down the wrong path by any number of factors, including poor witnesses, false confessions, reliance on corrupt informants, bad science, and tunnel vision or a

---

[4]www.deathpenaltyinfo.org/article.php?scid=6&did=110

combination of these factors. Overzealous prosecutors and inept defense attorneys can also contribute to wrongful convictions.

Steven Drizin, the legal director of the Center on Wrongful Convictions at Northwestern University School of Law,[5] said officers can unintentionally create scenarios where false convictions occur. "Most wrongful convictions are not cases where police officers try to frame innocent people," Drizin said. "They have a reason to believe that someone is a suspect in a crime and they view the entire investigation as confirming their belief that someone is guilty while ignoring or discounting evidence of innocence." He said investigators might make mistakes in investigations when they become afflicted with tunnel vision on one theory of the case and may ignore cautions about the procedures they use.

Stanley R. Gochenour, a former police officer who as a private detective has investigated more than 500 homicide cases, said the investigator provides the bottom line to a case: "What the system depends on to avoid the conviction of innocent citizens is the active pursuit of the truth at the investigation level. Detectives use their education, training and experience to objectively search out the truth. After determining the actual truth, they turn that truth over to professional advocates for the crafting of a prosecution. Prosecutors are advocates interested in winning. Detectives should be analysts interested in actual truth. The system relies on the independence of detectives as a guard against the problems associated with advocacy and ostensible truths."

The Innocence Project at the Benjamin N. Cardozo School of Law[6] has found that the most prevalent cause of wrongful convictions is mistaken identity. Of 157 people it has helped to exonerate nationwide, more than 75% were convicted based in whole or in part on eyewitness testimony.

The Innocence Institute of Point Park University in western Pennsylvania[7] concluded in a study in 2005 that most police departments in Pennsylvania were not following federal guidelines for conducting witness identifications and other lineups. The study also showed that other states plagued by unjust convictions had implemented scientifically tested techniques to prevent further false identifications.

Guidelines issued by the National Institute of Justice in 1999 recommend a double-blind method of presenting a photo array to witnesses using an officer not involved in the investigation so there is no possibility of influencing the response. They also say mug shots should be viewed one at a time and that investigators should warn witnesses that the suspect may not be in the array to reduce guessing.[8]

---

[5]www.law.northwestern.edu/wrongfulconvictions

[6]www.innocenceproject.org/about/index.php

[7]www.pointpark.edu/defaultaspx?id=1511

[8]www.ncjrs.org/pdffileslinij/178240.pdf. *Eyewitness Evidence: A Guide for Law Enforcement.*

Rodney Nicholson did not need an innocence project to get him out of jail for two robberies he did not commit. A convicted robber aided him. Nicholson was arrested in December 1998 when he showed up in a checkout line at a central Pennsylvania supermarket that had been robbed twice the month before. A store employee who had witnessed one of the holdups called police and identified Nicholson as the robber. Other employees supported the identification in one-on-one viewings. Police also looked at Nicholson's extensive criminal record in determining whether to arrest him. Nicholson was charged in both robberies, was convicted, and was awaiting sentencing when a convicted robber contacted his attorney. More than a year after Nicholson's arrest, Louis Greenley, who was serving a 20- to 50-year term for shooting an off-duty police officer during a robbery at a nearby pharmacy, took credit for the supermarket robberies. His claims of "wanting to do the right thing" were met with skepticism by prosecutors, who naturally suspected he had little to lose by adding a few more years to his lengthy sentence. However, he was able to support his claim with evidence that he had been involved in a traffic accident shortly after and near the scene of one of the robberies. After an investigation, prosecutors agreed to drop the charges and free Nicholson. Nicholson spent 15 months in prison before his release.

Care should be taken when interviewing children or other easily influenced witnesses. Numerous child care cases involving multiple accusations of sexual abuse arose in the early 1980s. Convictions in most of those cases were later overturned because of how the children were repeatedly and intensively questioned. Most started with one accuser, but led to mass allegations of widespread abuse. Some led to changes in the law. In the case of Margaret Kelly Michaels, the New Jersey Supreme Court set new standards for interviewing children in abuse cases. Michaels, a college senior from Pittsburgh who was hired by Wee Care Day Nursery in Maplewood, New Jersey, was convicted of more than one hundred counts of abuse for allegedly molesting dozens of children under her care for the seven months she worked there. She was sentenced to 47 years in prison and served almost 5 years before an appellate court freed her because of improper interviewing techniques that the prosecution had used. Investigators repeatedly questioned the children, asking them leading questions, ignoring negative responses while reinforcing positive ones, and going so far as giving the children badges and telling them they could be "little detectives" if they helped keep Michaels in jail, tapes of the interviews showed.

In response, the New Jersey Supreme Court ruled that once a defendant can show some evidence that interviews are biased, he or she is entitled to a hearing in which the burden shifts to the prosecution to show they were not. And while experts are not permitted to testify about a witness's credibility, the court allowed psychiatric professionals to comment on the interview techniques and their effect on the reliability of the children's statements. Prosecutors chose not to retry Michaels.

False Confessions

A confession is the most powerful evidence that can be presented against someone charged with a crime. Few people believe an innocent person would admit to a serious crime. Yet it happens with surprising frequency. The Center on Wrongful Convictions found that 59.5% of the 42 wrongful murder convictions it documented since 1970 relied in whole or in part on false confessions of either defendants or codefendants.

Project researchers have also identified more than one hundred cases where defendants or suspects falsely confessed, and they report a startling number of cases involving mentally retarded or impaired suspects. Two of those defendants spent years in prison and came within weeks of being put to death before they were exonerated.

In one of the most notorious false-confession cases, five New York City youths were convicted of the brutal rape and beating of an investment banker who was jogging in Central Park in 1989. Their videotaped confessions did not match the physical evidence in the case. The victim, who was left in a coma, was unable to identify her assailants. DNA evidence later corroborated the 2002 confession of a dangerous sex offender who was serving 33 years to life for murdering one woman and raping three others. By that time, most of the teens had already served their sentences.

Some false confessions come about because of police misconduct, while many involved suspects with mental infirmities that prevented them from holding up to pressure that normal people could withstand. Police promise leniency for a confession to a crime that would otherwise be met with harsh punishment. They tell suspects they have evidence against them that they do not. They question suspects for hours to wear them down. All of these techniques are valid but should be used with caution.

As of this writing, Victoria Banks remained in prison for a crime that most people who have reviewed the case say never happened. In May 1999, Banks, who has a reported IQ of 40, requested a furlough from the Choctaw County Jail in Butner, Alabama, claiming she was pregnant and about to give birth. A prison doctor who examined her did not believe she was pregnant, but another said he heard a fetal heartbeat, and she was freed on bond.

When she was taken back into custody in August, she did not have a baby. She initially said she had a miscarriage, but after intense questioning by authorities, Banks, her estranged husband, Medell, and her sister, Diane Bell Tucker, confessed and were charged with capital murder for the murder of the infant. Faced with the possible death penalty, all three pleaded guilty to manslaughter and were sentenced to 15 years in prison. What authorities did not know at the time was that Victoria Banks had a tubal ligation in 1995 and could not get pregnant. In 2001, Michael P. Steinkampf, director of Reproductive Endocrinology and Fertility at the University of Alabama School of Medicine in Birmingham, examined Victoria and concluded the tubal ligation was still intact and it was physically impossible for her to become pregnant.

In spite of the evidence, the prosecution in the case pursued vigorous appeals. Tucker was freed for time served on July 17, 2002, after agreeing not to appeal the case further. An appeals court found that a "manifest injustice" occurred in Medell Banks's case and sent it back to the lower court. On January 10, 2003, Medell Banks was freed at the outset of his second trial, when he agreed to plead guilty to tampering with evidence after tapes of his interrogation showed he repeatedly said he knew nothing about a baby, but admitted he heard a baby cry after hours of questioning. Victoria Banks did not appeal.[9]

While police interrogators are reluctant to record interrogations because of the methods used to break a suspect down, some states are requiring video- or audiotaping of custodial interviews in response to the problem. The supreme courts of Alaska and Minnesota have held that defendants are entitled to have their interrogations recorded. Illinois lawmakers passed legislation in 2003 requiring the electronic recording of suspects in homicide cases. Some police departments across the country have implemented recording policies on their own. Experts say videotaped confessions would carry more weight in court and would dissuade dishonest officers from corrupting the process. One of the key problems is police contaminating the suspect by providing crucial information about the crime that would be known only to the perpetrator.

A taped interview did not help William M. Kelly Jr. In 1990, Kelly, a 28-year-old borderline retarded man, confessed to the murder of a woman whose body was found at a landfill outside Harrisburg, Pennsylvania. Kelly repeatedly confessed to the crime and reportedly led investigators to the scene of the murder, describing how he bludgeoned Jeanette Thomas to death with a tree branch. He confessed to police and his attorney and pleaded guilty to third-degree murder. He was sentenced to 10 to 20 years in state prison.

It was not until two years later that investigators noted the similarities between Thomas's slaying and those committed by serial murderer Joseph D. Miller, who dumped two of his victims in the same landfill. The DNA from the Thomas crime scene matched Miller, who ultimately confessed to her murder. Kelly was freed. Investigators were led to Kelly by witnesses who said they had seen him in a bar with Thomas prior to the slaying.

Although he was much taller than Miller, Kelly vaguely resembled him and had a similar speech impediment. A psychiatrist who interviewed Kelly at length said the combination of alcohol blackouts and his mental condition made him susceptible to believing he had committed the crime when questioned by police. Kelly's confession was tape-recorded, but only after lengthy interviews that were not recorded.

---

[9]www.justicedenied.org/choctawthree.htm

Drizin said that is part of the problem: Police record only the confessions, not the interrogations that precede them. "If the interrogation which preceded the confession is not taped, there is no way of knowing whether police officers used deception, trickery, threats, promises of leniency, et cetera to induce the confession," Drizin said. "There is also no way of knowing whether the details, which only the true perpetrator would know, were suggested to the suspect or originated from the suspect."

While some questions arose about how Kelly could have led police to the crime scene, a much more insidious process produced a confession from Barry Laughman, another mildly retarded man who spent 16 years in prison for the rape and murder of an 85-year-old neighbor before DNA evidence set him free in 2004. Laughman, then 24 years old, was accused of the slaying of his distant relative, Edna Laughman, who was discovered by relatives in her home near Gettysburg, Pennsylvania, on the evening of August 13, 1987. She was found lying with her upper body on her bed and her feet on the floor, naked except for a bra pulled above her breasts and a dress thrown over her face. The victim had pills stuffed in her mouth and a pill bottle was in her right hand. Her belongings had been ransacked. A Marlboro cigarette had been extinguished on a chair next to the bed, and four more butts plus a Marlboro box lid were found throughout the home.

An autopsy showed she had been beaten and tried to defend herself. She was hit on the back of her head, and bruises covered her arms, legs, and nose. She had suffocated on the pills. Lacerations showed she had been raped, and semen remained on the body. The pathologist determined that sex had been performed during or after her death.

Despite being warned by Barry Laughman's family and coworkers that he was mentally disabled and would likely be so nervous during any police interview that he would seem suspicious, former Pennsylvania state trooper Jack Holtz zeroed in on Laughman as the prime suspect. At trial, Holtz, who was involved in other controversial cases in which the defendants went free, would say that he matched three bruises on Edna Laughman's arm with Barry Laughman's inability to use his pinky.

After telling Barry that a whorl fingerprint was found on the cigarette box lid and pointing out that Barry had whorl-type fingerprints (which make up 25 to 35% of all fingerprints), Holtz said he knew Barry did it and wanted him to tell the truth. He was joined by another trooper, who took notes while Holtz asked the questions. Barry admitted he had broken into Edna's house the night before her body was found. In his confession he said, "I stopped at Edna's house. I knew she was there and I wanted to have sex. I went inside her home through the front window. She was there, she heard me coming in. She had her bra on. She started to run toward the kitchen. I chased after her and hit her on the head with the flashlight. I knocked her down and dragged her back to her bed or pile of clothes. She had a bra on and I slipped it up. I was holding her around the arms. I asked her if I could have sex with her. She says no. Then I did it anyway. I had sex with her after I put pills in her mouth. She made a choking sound when I put the pills in her mouth. I dumped the whole bottle of pills in her mouth and was holding her nose. I then stroked her throat."

At trial, Holtz said Laughman offered up details that should have been known only to the killer. However, given the results of the DNA test 16 years later, that could not possibly have been the case. The troopers also ignored evidence that another man was seen lurking in the neighborhood and that Edna was seen alive the morning after Barry supposedly killed her.

Frank Donnelly, a cold case investigator with the Pennsylvania State Police whose work as a county detective helped lead to Laughman's release, said the most important thing in evaluating a confession is corroboration. "I view a confession like any other evidence: with a bit of skepticism," Donnelly said. "A lot of investigators think once they have a confession, they're done. Sometimes that's just the beginning." He draws an analogy to auto repair: "If you're fixing a car, if you have it right, the part should slide into place. A lot of time if you're jamming the parts in, you either have the wrong parts or you're putting them in wrong."

Despite evidence that contradicted his confession, Laughman's prosecution for capital murder proceeded. He became a victim of what has become known in legal circles as *junk science.*

Junk Science

Experts in the courtroom are given a privilege no other witnesses get: they are permitted to render their opinion on evidence. Their testimony can often make or break a case. Critics say junk science from forensic experts can lead to false convictions under a number of categories, including misinterpretation of test results, suppression of exculpatory evidence, exaggeration of statistics, an undue reliance on evidence that can only be said to be consistent, theories based on conjecture, and outright fabrication of testing results.

While some experts feel crime laboratories should be independent, the Innocence Project is recommending they at least be subject to the same oversight as private labs. Texas and New York now have forensic science commissions overseeing the labs. The Innocence Project recommends that they be subject to proficiency testing and accreditation. They also recommend that defense attorneys be given funds to conduct independent testing in cases where lab results are being used by the prosecution.

Ray Krone, of Dover township, York County, spent more than 10 years in Arizona prisons before DNA evidence cleared him of the 1991 murder of bartender Kim Ancona and led to a new suspect. Krone had been convicted twice, largely on the basis of expert testimony, which was later shown to be scientifically flawed, about a bite mark.

The prosecution hid the fact that a nationally renowned dental expert had rejected the theory that Krone's teeth matched a bite mark on the victim. Further analysis of the bite mark evidence showed that the orthodontist who claimed to be an expert in bite mark evidence had pressed a mold of Krone's unusual tooth pattern over the bite on Ancona's nipple, leaving a further impression that appeared to implicate Krone. Police were led to Krone because his telephone number was in Ancona's personal telephone book. A U.S. Postal Service employee and air force veteran, Krone had no criminal record before the homicide case. He was convicted and sentenced to death, but on retrial, the judge overrode the jury's sentencing recommendation and gave him life. DNA from saliva around the bite mark was fed into the Combined DNA Index System (CODIS), the National Criminal Offender Database, and led to Kenneth Phillips, a sex offender who lived a few hundred yards away from the bar where Ancona was killed. Phillips was serving time in the same prison as Krone. Krone was released in 2002 after spending 10 years in prison.

In Barry Laughman's case, evidence that should have cleared him before he went to trial was twisted and used against him. After his arrest, the troopers took blood samples to compare with semen found on Edna's body. The semen was from a person of type A blood who secretes his blood type into other bodily fluids. Barry also secretes his blood type, but he is type B.

At a trial where the prosecution was seeking the death penalty, Janice Roadcap, a chemist for the Pennsylvania State Police, explained the discrepancy with several different theories. She suggested that bacteria could have attacked the B antigens. She said Edna had type A blood, and that her vaginal secretions could have overridden Barry's blood type. She said that antibiotics Edna was taking for a urinary tract infection could have changed the blood type. In addition, Roadcap acknowledged at trial that she probably amended her notes after Laughman's blood type was verified as type B. She wrote in the margins of the report that the swabs were moist when placed in vials, and breakdown of B antigens could have occurred.

Serology experts said none of these explanations has any basis in science. They said Roadcap should have maintained the samples for further testing to try to prove her theories, but Roadcap returned them to a state police locker, where they deteriorated. That point was brought up by the judge in his charge to the jury on the death penalty. The jury opted for life in prison without the possibility of parole. Laughman sued Holtz, Roadcap, and the state police for civil rights violations. A federal civil rights lawsuit was settled in August 2007 for an undisclosed amount of money.

Laughman's is not the only murder case where Roadcap has come under fire. Steven Crawford spent 28 years in jail for the murder of his 13-year-old friend, John Eddie Mitchell, based primarily on Roadcap's testimony. That testimony was contradicted by her original lab notes, found years later, that were never turned over to Crawford's attorneys through three trials.

Crawford, who was 14 years old at the time of the murder, filed suit against Roadcap and a state police fingerprint expert who helped formulate the prosecution theory. The state refused to defend the pair, saying if Crawford's accusations were true, they were acting outside the scope of their employment.

Mitchell disappeared while making collections for his paper route on September 12, 1970. His body was found the next day in a garage behind Crawford's family home in Harrisburg, Pennsylvania, after a neighbor found a bloody hammer in an adjacent garage. Police searched the area and found Mitchell's body under a green 1952 Chevrolet in the Crawford family's boarded-up garage. A white 1957 Pontiac station wagon parked tightly next to it was splattered and smeared with his blood. An autopsy showed Mitchell had been struck on the back of the head at least three times with a blunt object that perforated his skull. He had a cut and a less severe fracture on his forehead, and two of his front teeth were knocked out. He also had been stabbed twice in the chest, with one of the wounds leaving a five-inch track to his backbone. The estimated time of death was 1:00 p.m. the day before. The $32 he had collected on his rounds was missing.

The crime went unsolved for four years. In the meantime, Crawford was sent to juvenile hall for car theft and burglary charges. Despite an alibi, police were convinced he had a role in the slaying because he had told an officer searching the garages that there was nothing in his family's garage but two old cars. The arrest came four years later when Crawford turned 18. Investigators said they had identified three palm prints on the station wagon as Crawford's. It took them more than two years to make the match, which was never challenged in court because Crawford frequently played in the garage.

At some point, John Balshy, a state police fingerprint examiner, said he noticed microscopic red flecks in the fingerprint powder. The prints were given to Roadcap, who performed a presumptive test for the presence of blood using a reagent that turns blue when it reacts with blood. Through three trials, Roadcap, Balshy, and a city detective testified that they observed the chemical reaction give a positive indication for blood on the ridges of the prints.

This later became the whole theory of the case: since the blood was only on the ridges of the prints and not in the valleys, it had to be on Crawford's hand when it touched the car, rather than blood randomly splashed across an existing print or a print left on top of blood.

At trial, the only documentation of this test turned over to Crawford's defense was a two-sentence typed report saying the test "indicates the presence of blood deposited by the donor of the print." Bolstered by expert testimony, this finding indicated the blood had to be on Crawford's hand when it touched the car.

Crawford was convicted in three trials in 1974, 1977, and 1978. The case languished for years until the fall of 2001, when a briefcase belonging to a deceased detective in the case was found by two youths in a neighboring community. The case contained Roadcap's original handwritten notes, which were done contemporaneously with the testing. They said, "Numerous particles in the valleys also gave a positive reaction." Crawford's attorneys argued that would have bolstered the defense theory that Crawford's prints were already on the car when blood splashed on it. That part of the report was blacked out in the original that was later pulled from state police archives.

While prosecutors said the notes did not clear Crawford, they conceded he never got a fair trial and dropped charges against him, saying it was unlikely they could obtain another conviction. On June 19, 2006, the state settled with Steven Crawford for an undisclosed sum.

Overzealous Prosecution

Prosecutors have a duty to seek justice, not just convictions. Sometimes, though, in the heat of battle, they become blinded by their belief that a defendant is guilty. This can lead to bending the rules of court to the point where their actions cause courts to free suspects whether they are guilty or innocent.

On September 18, 1992, the Pennsylvania Supreme Court, citing "egregious" conduct by prosecutors and state police, freed former high school principal Jay C. Smith from death row in the murders of English teacher Susan Reinert and her two young children. The notorious case had spawned two books and a television miniseries based on best-selling author and former police officer Joseph Wambaugh's *Echoes in the Darkness* (1987).

The court's ruling changed the double jeopardy law in Pennsylvania, determining a new trial was not a sufficient remedy when prosecutors act outrageously to obtain a conviction. The court based its holding on a deal with a prison informant that was hidden from the defense and on physical evidence that would have helped the defense but was not turned over during the trial.

"The record establishes the bad faith of the prosecution beyond any possibility of doubt; indeed it would be hard to imagine more egregious prosecutorial tactics," Justice John P. Flaherty wrote in the court's opinion. What was widely known at the time of the ruling, but not mentioned in the Court's opinion, was that Wambaugh had promised the lead investigator in the case, Trooper Jack Holtz, $50,000 for information on the investigation on the condition that Smith be arrested and tried. Evidence of that deal surfaced when a junk man removed trash from Jack Holtz's attic earlier that year. Other evidence, including a comb that was supposedly introduced as a trial exhibit and notes contradicting his testimony, was found in the trash removed from Holtz's home.

Smith was convicted of conspiring with William S. Bradfield Jr., another English teacher in Upper Merion School District, to kill Reinert, whose nude and battered body was found in the trunk of a car abandoned in the parking lot of suburban Harrisburg motel in motel in 1979. They also were found guilty of murdering her two children, whose bodies have never been found. While Bradfield, Reinert's fiancé, stood to gain $750,000 in life insurance proceeds from Reinert, Smith was being sent to jail on robbery charges in a Harrisburg courtroom the same day Reinert's body was found a few miles away. Bradfield told friends and colleagues that Smith planned to murder Reinert and set up an alibi for himself at the New Jersey shore.

Bradfield was arrested first and was tried separately in a trial where the prosecution contended he was trying to frame Smith. A comb bearing the insignia of Smith's army reserve unit was found under Reinert's nude and battered body. A pin found in his car months after he went to jail was identified as belonging to Susan Reinert's daughter. Smith was a likely fall guy. A retired U.S. Army reserve colonel and strict high school principal, he led a double life. He was involved in drug use and bizarre sex and had been convicted of dressing as a security guard to rob department stores. He also was suspected of killing his daughter and her husband, two heroin addicts who disappeared without a trace several years before Reinert's murder.

The court based part of its ruling freeing Smith on rubber lifters that contained several grains of sand. A retired state trooper testified at trial that he had used the hinge lifters to remove sand from the victim's toes. Since that testimony bolstered the defense theory that she had been killed at the Jersey shore by Bradfield, the prosecutor, Richard L. Guida, attacked the trooper's credibility in cross-examination and initiated a perjury investigation against him. The lifters, which were found in a state police evidence locker by another trooper, were turned over to Holtz in the last days of the trial but were not turned over to the defense for almost two years after the conviction. After an investigation, prosecutors dated the ink used to mark the lifters to the time of the 1979 autopsy, seven years before the trial. Nevertheless, they suggested a private detective working for the defense somehow planted them in a state police evidence locker.

The prosecution also steadfastly denied there was a deal with Raymond Matray, a cop turned burglar turned jailhouse informant, who testified Smith confessed to the slayings. Matray was released from jail a year before he was entitled to parole and to this day has never served the remainder of his sentence. Holtz retired from the force while under investigation. Several other convictions he obtained were later overturned, one at least in part on the basis of notes found by the junkman. By the time the court freed Smith, Guida was serving time in federal prison for distributing cocaine. Bradfield died in prison. Smith was freed after serving 6 years on death row. Many still believe he was involved in the murders.

The International Case of Amanda Knox Case

Meredith Kercher, a University of Leeds exchange student from Coulsdon, Surrey, was discovered with her throat slit November 2, 2007, in the hilltop town of Perugia, just two months after she arrived in Italy during her year abroad. She was last seen leaving a friend's house around 8:30 p.m. on the night of her murder. Two mobile phones, two credit cards, and 300 euros in cash were later discover to have been stolen.

Amanda Knox, 21, studying in Perugia and one of Kercher's roommates and her boyfriend, Raffaele Sollecito, 26, a computer engineering student, were unable to get into Meridith's room and called the Italian military police. The responders were not the carabinieri but the postal police who primarily investigated crimes like Internet fraud and stolen phones, not homicides. Kercher's door was forced open and inside was her body.

The police theorized her employer, Patrick Lumumba, was the one to kill Kercher. They had Knox sign a confession, written in Italian, that said Knox had accompanied Lumumba to the house where he stabbed Kercher.

Both Knox, Sollecito, and Lumumba were arrested. However when forensic tests came back, the DNA evidence and fingerprints at the crime scene did not match the suspects, but instead a fourth person, Rudy Guede.

On December 5, 2009, an Italian court sentenced Amanda Knox to 26 years in prison and Raffaele Sollecito to 25 years after they are found guilty of murdering Kercher during a drunken sex assault. The case was appealed.

Before the verdict in the appeal case, John Douglas gave an interview to Krista Errickson as to his analysis of the case as follows.

Amanda Knox and Raffaele Sollecito

An analysis requires access to all the case information. In the Amanda Knox case, there was crime scene evidence collection tapes to view. John Douglas provided the following interview/analysis of the Knox case to Krista Errickson, an American journalist (Squires, 2011).

From the profiles created, none of the behavioral or forensic evidence leads to Amanda and Raffaele. There's no history or experience related to violence or mental illness in their backgrounds. This is not a case of serial killers, cold-blooded murderers. They used marijuana, but that's not some hard-core drug that will change a normal personality.

Behavioral evidence implying guilt would be fleeing (which only Guede did). One would look for signs of nervousness, increased substance use, or increased rigidity in their personalities, behaviors along that line—Knox and Sollecito went out to buy underwear and were observed kissing—not signs of guilt.

For Amanda and Raffaele to commit a horrific crime and then hours later, be back at the crime scene, does not fit. These were two young people who couldn't fathom what had taken place. (It was so surreal) they thought they were going to stroll in and out of there and justice would prevail. But, it didn't happen that way. Justice did not prevail.

Number of Killers

The crime scene does not indicate the presence of three individuals in the room where Meredith was murdered, only one. What was done to the victim, the way in which the crime occurred, was not the result of three people. This can be concluded without a DNA test.

Behavior reflects personality. And that behavior fits only Rudy Guede. Guede has the history; he was an experienced criminal, he had the motive and all evidence points to him. It was a brutal, bloody homicide, and it's a reflection of his personality. And that behavior was exhibited at the crime scene. That's his "canvas"; the result is his "artwork" of the subject (victim).

You should be able to find other "canvases" of his like that—not necessarily homicide, but you should find a violent past in this person's background. It was known that he committed some robberies, but there are more likely more cases that he may have been involved which remain unsolved.

Motive

The primary motive was burglary. But we have an opportunistic offender here. And that opportunity was presented when Meredith came home, and she became the victim of the opportunity.

Some argue that covering Meredith's body with a duvet proves the murderer was female. There are different reasons why someone will cover a body. There's a certain sense of wanting to undo the crime. Guede didn't leave after the crime, but he did not want to look at her. It's not that he didn't feel good about what he has done. He's a sadistic individual with a violent past. He put the blanket over her because he was wandering around the apartment and didn't want to see her.

This was a very pedestrian murder. And that's not to diminish this beautiful woman's life, Meredith. It's not that complicated, crimes are not so complicated.

What Went Wrong?

The first investigators started off on the wrong track and did not know what they were handling. The collections and preservation of evidence was done incorrectly and led to contamination. The crime scene video notes all the mistakes that were done.

The media was interested and involved in this case from the beginning but damaged the investigation. The media can shape people's opinion. A single photograph seen out of context, can affect us. The investigators can also be responsible for leaking information to manipulate the media and thus, public opinion.

First, there were too many people in those rooms. They should have removed Amanda, Raffaele and anyone who was not part of the investigation team, and roped it off.

From the video, the investigators can be seen passing evidence, dropping it on the ground, using the same tweezers, not changing gloves, no protective caps to cover hair. Any insider can recognize these errors. What the investigators have done may seem right on the "outside," they had their protective clothing, boots, but cross-contamination of the evidence was more than evident.

Cross-contamination means that evidence from anyone who came and went in those rooms had the potential to leave their DNA, prints, etc. and run the risk of being transferred microscopically.

DNA of Sollecito's was said to have been found on Meredith's bra clasp. DNA of Amanda Knox's is said to be on the murder weapon; on the knife's handle and Meredith's on the blade.

The knife was not the murder weapon. It hasn't been found and probably never will. It doesn't fit with the imprint made on the bed sheet, or the wounds found on Meredith. The evidence collection video from December 18 shows a knife, randomly chosen, from Sollecito's apartment and transported to the lab.

The video taken on November 2 shows the bra clasp, very clearly on the floor of the crime scene. On December 18, after returning to the scene more than 16 times, the video shows the bra clasp, still there. It had already been kicked and shuffled around on the floor for six weeks! Second, the amount of DNA, supposedly, that was Sollecito's, is highly suspect.

The evidence was two tiny pieces of DNA out of the plethora that should have been collected and analyzed.

Amanda's Confession During the Interrogation

She was interrogated from 10 p.m. until 6 a.m. These are not sophisticated young people—it would not take a dozen interrogators to break them. No one could hold up, especially over five days.

Amanda's Accusation of Patrick Lumumba

The police knew they had negroid hairs at the crime scene. Amanda exchanged texts the night before with Patrick Lumumba, who is of African descent, like Guede. Lumumba owned the bar where Amanda worked as a waitress. He told her she wasn't needed for work that night. Because the DNA evidence had not come back yet, they jumped to the conclusion the hairs belonged to Lumumba. They interrogated her accordingly. The tactics used was to have Amanda say what the police wanted. People confess under severe psychological pressure.

The prosecution had a theory from the beginning and continued with it, despite the facts. They discounted evidence that didn't support their theory. Their theory was a threesome murder and they allowed theory to rule over evidence. (The prosecutor created "sex game" before he ever knew about Guede's being there). As long as they heard it somewhere . . . well, it must be true then.

The lead prosecutor recently said that "there is a huge, powerful, and unbreakable picture of circumstantial evidence which points against both of them."

Circumstantial evidence is the weakest evidence of all. Witnesses can be bought off, or bargain for favors, recollections that can't be counted on . . . it's fine to start with, in fact, so are hunches, so are theories, but that all has to go out the window if the hard evidence, and in this case, there's an overwhelming amount of it, points in another direction.

The motivation of some prosecutors is to win, no matter what it takes, even if truth doesn't fit into their facts and figures.

This is not exclusive only to Italy. For instance, during the West Memphis Three case, the prosecution team created a grand, theatrical scene in the courtroom. They viciously stabbed a grapefruit with a knife in the attempt to prove it was the type of a weapon that created wounds on the victims. They did this to influence the jury and win the case. Only later, during the appeal, it was discovered that the wounds on the bodies of the boys had not been inflicted by a knife at all, but by an alligator snapping turtle! (The children's bodies were thrown into a river).

They did begin to panic when the evidence returned and did not match up to the other two; it was all going to Guede. Instead, they returned, over and over to the crime scene, even six weeks later—what was it? Why do you have to go back? Did you miss something? Did you get some new lead? Did you develop something in the lab, and now you have to find it? No. They had to go back because they were looking for something, anything, to fit their theory.

Following theory over evidence can be a strong part of a prosecutor's behavior. A jury convicts but it is the *way* the evidence was presented to the jurors. There was no evidence; there is no evidence.

Two people were convicted that should have never been convicted. The media pictured Amanda as a cold-blooded murderer. Frankly, I was surprised that they were charged. I was surprised by the conviction. The appeal is wrong. It's wrong because of the lack of concrete evidence. No forensic evidence, no behavioral evidence. Nothing points to their guilt. They've got nothing. The police have the person who killed their daughter! It is Guede. Only Guede.

There were three victims here. It's horribly unfortunate that Meredith lost her life that night, but Amanda Knox and Raffaele Sollecito almost lost theirs, too. At least the judge and jury who acquitted came to their senses, and Amanda Knox and Raffaele Sollecito only lost four years each.

The convictions of Knox and Sollecito were overturned on appeal in October 2011 by a panel of six jurors and two judges. In an official statement of their grounds for overturning the convictions the judges wrote there was a "material non-existence" of evidence to support the guilty verdicts at the trial. The appeal judges further stated that the prosecution's theory of an association between Sollecito, Knox, and Guede was "not corroborated by any evidence" and "far from probable" (Squires, 2011).

Conclusion

The authority to arrest another person is one of the most awesome powers in our society. It also carries with it an awesome responsibility. Sometimes law enforcement authorities, believing they have the right person, will do anything to obtain a conviction. In some of the cases cited in this chapter, as well as many other exoneration cases, authorities still maintain they had the right person in the face of overwhelming evidence to the contrary. But rationalizing, playing with the facts, or lying in the name of justice cannot be condoned and can lead to unintended consequences that may tarnish the name of law enforcement and the sanctity of the justice system. An innocent person imprisoned for a crime he or she did not commit used to be the stuff of novels and dramas. As technology advances, it is the reality of the 21st century, and it is up to law enforcement authorities to prevent it.

References

Gross, S. R., Jacoby, K., Matheson, D. J., Montgomery, N., & Patel, S. (2005). Exonerations in the United States, 1989 through 2003. *Journal of Criminal Law and Criminology, 95*(2).

Squires, N. (2011, October 4). Amanda Knox freed: Tears of joy as four-year nightmare is over. *Daily Telegraph.* Retrieved August 24, 2012, from www.telegraph.co.uk/news/worldnews/europe/italy/8807836/Amanda-Knox-verdict-as-it-happened-October-4.html

Wambaugh, J. (1987). *Echoes in the Darkness.* New York: Bantam.

About the Editors

John E. Douglas, EdD, entered duty with the FBI in 1970 after serving four years in the U.S. Air Force. He received investigative experience in violent crime in Detroit and Milwaukee field offices and also served as a hostage negotiator. In 1977 Douglas was appointed to the FBI Academy as an instructor in the FBI's Behavioral Science Unit (BSU), where he taught hostage negotiation and applied criminal psychology.

In 1990 he was promoted as unit chief within the FBI's National Center for the Analysis of Violent Crime (NCAVC). Serving in that capacity, he had overall supervision of the Violent Criminal Apprehension Program (VICAP), Criminal Investigative Analysis Program (better known as criminal profiling), and the Arson and Bombing Investigative Services Program.

Douglas was a coparticipant in the FBI's first research program of serial killers and, based on that study, coauthored *Sexual Homicide: Patterns and Motives.* The University of Virginia awarded Douglas the prestigious Jefferson Award for academic excellence for his work on that study.

In 1992 Douglas coauthored the first edition of the *Crime Classification Manual* (CCM), the first study of violent crime to define and standardize techniques and terminology to be used by the criminal justice system and academia. Douglas again received the Jefferson Award for this research and the publication of the CCM.

Douglas has consulted on thousands of cases worldwide providing case analysis, interview and interrogation techniques, investigative strategies, prosecutorial strategies, and expert testimony. Included in the list of Douglas's cases are Seattle's "Green River Killer," Wichita's "BTK Strangler," the O. J. Simpson civil case, and the JonBenet Ramsey homicide.

Since his retirement in 1995 from the FBI, Douglas has been providing pro bono assistance whenever possible to police and victims of violent crime.

Douglas has coauthored both fiction and nonfiction books, including two New York Times best sellers, *Mindhunter* and *Journey Into Darkness.* He also coauthored *Obsession, Anatomy of Motive, Cases That Haunt Us, Anyone You Want Me to Be, Broken Wings,* and his newest book, *Inside the Mind of BTK.*

Douglas does numerous public presentations yearly, belonging to the Greater Talent Network (GTN) agency in New York. His personal Web site, johndouglasmindhunter.com, contains crime information as well as an active online discussion board.

Ann W. Burgess, RN, DNSc, is a professor of psychiatric mental health nursing at Boston College Connell School of Nursing. She received her bachelor's and doctoral degrees from Boston University and her master's degree from the University of Maryland. She, with Lynda Lytle Holmstrom, cofounded one of the first hospital-based crisis intervention programs for rape victims at Boston City Hospital in the mid-1970s. Her work expanded into the offender area when she teamed with special agents at the FBI Academy to study serial offenders of sexual homicide, rape, and child sexual offenses. This work advanced an understanding of the importance of the behavioral footprints in crime scenes and the profiling process.

Burgess served as the first van Ameringen Professor of Psychiatric Nursing at the University of Pennsylvania's School of Nursing for 17 years. She has been a sexual assault nurse examiner (SANE) since 1994 and continues as codirector of the SANE Training Program at the University.

Burgess served as chair of the first advisory council to the National Center for the Prevention and Control of Rape of the National Institute of Mental Health (1976–1980). She was a member of the 1984 U.S. Attorney General's Task Force on Family Violence and the planning committee for the 1985 Surgeon General's Symposium on Violence, served on the National Institute of Health's National Advisory Council for the Center for Nursing Research (1986–1988), and was a member of the 1990 Adolescent Health Advisory Panel to the Congress of the U.S. Office of Technology Assessment. She was elected to the National Academy of Sciences Institute of Medicine in October 1994 and chaired the 1996 National Research Council's Task Force on Violence Against Women. She was a member of the 2003 Archdiocese of Boston's Commission on the Protection of Children and is a member of the Cyril H. Wecht Institute of Forensic Science and the Law.

Burgess has been principal investigator of many research projects and has written textbooks in the fields of psychiatric nursing and crisis intervention and texts from her research in the crime victim area. She has coauthored over 160 articles, chapters, and monographs in the field of victimology. She also has testified in criminal and civil cases in over 30 states.

In 2000 she was appointed Professor Without Term at Boston College. She has received numerous honors, including the Sigma Theta Tau International Audrey Hepburn Award, the American Nurses' Association Hildegard Peplau Award, and the Sigma Theta Tau International Episteme Laureate Award, and Sigma Theta Tau International Nurse Researchers Hall of Fame.

Allen G. Burgess, DBA, is president of Data Integrity. He is a graduate of Massachusetts Institute of Technology and Boston University. He served in the U.S. Air Force and was assigned to the National Security Agency. His career spans 30 years beginning with computer design at Honeywell Information Systems, where he designed four computer systems and rose to the rank of chief engineer. He left Honeywell to join Raytheon, where he served as computer and displays laboratory manager and supervised the design of military computers. He left Raytheon to start Sequoia Systems, a manufacturer of fault-tolerant computers. In 1984 he started Data Integrity, where he holds a patent for a solution to the Y2K problem.

In addition to his industrial experience, Burgess has taught at Northeastern University, where he was an associate professor, and at Babson College, Boston College, Bentley College, and Boston University as a visiting professor. He currently teaches the Forensic Science Lab at Boston College and is a codesigner for interactive forensic simulation learning, where his specialty is digital forensics.

Robert K. Ressler, M.S., is a criminologist and codirector of Forensic Behavioral Services, a Virginia-based organization dedicated to training, lecturing, consultation, and expert witness testimony. He is an expert in the area of violent criminal offenders, particularly serial and sexual homicide. He is a specialist in the area of criminology, criminal personality profiling, crime scene analysis, homicide, sexual assaults, threat assessment, workplace violence, and hostage negotiation. He is a twenty-year veteran of the FBI, serving sixteen years in the Behavioral Science Unit as a supervisory special agent and criminologist, retiring in 1990. He developed many of the programs that led to the formulation of the FBI's National Center for the Analysis of Violent Crime.

Ressler became the first program manager of the FBI's Violent Criminal Apprehension Program in 1985. His academic affiliations have been as an instructor of criminology while at the FBI Academy, adjunct faculty at the University of Virginia, research fellow at the University of Pennsylvania, and adjunct assistant professor at Michigan State University's School of Criminal Justice. He has also been affiliated with Georgetown University's Program on Psychiatry and Law and the Department of Forensic Pathology at Dundee University, Dundee, Scotland.

He received the 1991 Amicus Award from the American Academy of Psychiatry and the Law, the 1995 Special Section Award from the Section of Psychiatry and Behavioral Sciences of the American Academy of Forensic Sciences, and two Jefferson Awards in 1986 and 1988 from the University of Virginia.

Ressler is a member of the American Society for Industrial Security, the International and American Academies of Forensic Sciences, the Academy of Criminal Justice Sciences, the International Association of Chiefs of Police, the International Homicide Investigators Association, the Vidoqu Society, and other professional organizations. He originated and directed the FBI's first research program of violent criminal offenders, interviewing and collecting data on thirty-six serial and sexual killers, resulting in two textbooks: *Sexual*

Homicide: Patterns and Motives (1988) and the *Crime Classification Manual* (1992). He also coauthored his autobiography, *Whoever Fights Monsters* (1992), *Justice Is Served* (1994), and *I Have Lived in the Monster* (1997).

Ressler's books and life experiences have inspired books authored by Mary Higgins Clark and others, as well as the films *The Red Dragon, Silence of the Lambs, Copycat,* and *The X Files.* Ressler has served with the U.S. Army, ten years of it active duty during the Vietnam era. He served in the military police and as a criminal investigation officer (CID), with the Army CID Command Headquarters in Washington, D.C. He retired at the rank of colonel with thirty-five years of service.

About the Contributors

Susan H. Adam, Ph. D., FBI, ret. Is a communication consultant for Adams and Associates, Washington, DC.

Anne M. Berger, Ph.D., M.B.A., M.S., R.N., is director of nursing systems research at Children's Hospital, Boston, MA.

Gregory M. Cooper, M.P.A., FBI ret., is consultant to Cristando House, Inc., Orange County, CA.

Lauren K. Douglas, J.D., vice president and general counsel, Hoffman Co, Alexandria, VA.

John P. Jarvis, Ph.D., is Chief Criminologist, Behavioral Science Unit, FBI Academy, Quantico, Virginia and chairman of the FBI Police Futures Working Group.

Carl J. Jensen III, Ph.D., FBI ret., is director of the University of Mississippi's Center for Intelligence and Security Studies, University, Mississippi.

Michael R. Napier, B.S.E., Ret. FBI, The Academy Group, Quantico, VA.

Stefan Treffers, BHSc, is a research assistant at a Canadian pharmaceutical research firm. His graduate studies are in criminology, sociology and the law.

Eric W. Witzig, M.S., Supervisory Intelligence Analyst at FBI (Ret.) Washington, DC.

Michael Welner, M.D., is chairman of the Forensic Panel in New York City, a clinical associate professor of psychiatry at New York University School of Medicine in New York City, and an adjunct professor of law at Duquesne University in Pittsburgh, PA.

Citation Index

Aas, 2007: 432, 433, 434
Allorge & Tournel, 2011: 50
American Psychiatric Association, 2006: 118, 504
Arasly, 2005: 466
Armagh, Battaglia, & Lanning, 2000: 412
Arnon et al., 2001: 501

Bales & Litz, 2005: 436, 437
BAU], 2008: 51
Beare, 2002: 447, 448
Bilger et al., 2006: 441, 443, 444
Black & Read, 2007: 458
Borja, 2008: 80
Bouton, 1990 46
Brandt & Sandler 2009 459
Bromberg, 1965 5, 6
Brown & Langan 4
Budowle et al., 2007: 454
Burke, 2007: 461, 462, 464

Cavanaugh, 2011: 439
CBC, updated 8/2/2012: 139, 140
CDC 2000 498
CDC, 2001: 500
Center for Civilian Biodefense Strategies, 2000: 502
Champeil, 2011: 50
Cieslak & Eitzen, 1999 498, 499
Cook, Cukier, & Krause, 2009: 449
Cook et al., 2009: 450, 451
Criscione 3
Cullen-DuPont, 2009: 435, 437, 438

Dembek, Pavlin, & Kortepeter, 2007: 455
Department of Justice 449
DeRosa, 2004: 46
Dickson-Gilmore, 2002: 449
Dietz, Hazelwood, & Warren 1990 354
Dietz et al., 1990: 222
DiNicola, 2005: passim
Dougherty 2004: 445
Douglas & Olshaker, 1995: 68
Douglas & Olshaker, 1995: 9, 68
Douglas & Olshaker, 1998: 352, 353
Douglas & Olshaker, 1999: 46
Douglas & Olshaker, 2000, 83
Douglas, Ressler, Burgess, & Hartman 1986: 114

Egger, 1990: 69, 70

Fairstein, 1993: 308
FBI BAU, 2008: 16, 53, 88
FBI, 2008: 115
FBI, 2008: 116, 455
Fuhrman, 2001: 75

GAO, 2011: 446
Garson & Vann, 2001: 47
Geberth 1981: 116
Gladwell, 2001: 465
Glassand Schoch-Spana 2002 502
Goddard, 1914: 5
Gorner 2001: 498
Government Accountability Office [GAO], 2011: 446

Greene & Ferslew 2009: 491, 492
Gudjonnson, 2003: 471
Gudjonsson, 1992: 518, 519

Haddal, 2010: 80, 89
Hagman, 2001: 501
Harr & Hess, 2006: 460
Harris, Thomas, Fisher, & Hirsch 2002 72
Hatcher, Mohandie, Turner, & Gelles, 1998: 460
Hawkins, 2006: 48
Hazelwood 113
Hazelwood & Burgess, 2009: 75
Hazelwood & Douglas, 1980: 118
Hazelwood & Douglas, 1980: 231
Hazelwood, 2009: 313
Henderson et al., 1999: 501
Holmes, 1995: 518, 520, 521, 524
Holmes, Comstock-Davidson, & Hayen, 2007: 49
Homeland Security Office of Intelligence & Analysis & FBI, 2008: 452
Hoover, Zhang, & Zhao, 2010: 47
Howlett et al., 1986: 71
Hurlbert, 1997: 497

Inglesby et al., 1999: 498, 499, 500
InGreggv.Georgia, 1976: 94
INTERPOL, 2011: 84

James v. State, 1952: 509
Jamieson, 1999: 448, 449
Jandl, 2007: 443, 445

Kalfrin, 1999a: 413
Keefer, 1998: 69, 70
Klotter, 1990: 509, 510
Knight & Prentky, 1990: 7, 324
Knight, Rosenberg, & Schneider, 1985: 7

Komoroski, Komoroski, Valentine, Pearce, & Kearns, 2000: 50
Krouse, 2011: 81, 82
Krouse, 2011: 81, 82

Leman & Janssens, 2007: 439, 444
Leo & Ofshe, 1997: 517
Lewis & Sigman, 2007: 51, 52
Liebowitz, 2011: 429
Lindesmith & Dunham, 1941 5
Lippin et al., 2006: 457
Liptak, 2011: 47
Loevinger, 1980: 508
Logan, Walker, & Hunt, 2009: 434
Logan et al., 2005: 438
Luk, Cohen, & Ferrence, 2007: 447
Luke, 1988: 14

Madsen, 2009: 447
Markman & Bosco, 1989 226
Marquise, 2006: 467
McAllester, 2010: 84
McAuliffe, 2001a: 413
McAuliffe, 2001b: 412
McDaniel & Ellis, 2009: 459
McGoey, 2010: 390
McGoey, 2012: 389, 390
McLaughlin, 2000: 412
Megargee & Bohn, 1979 7
Megargee, 1982: 118
Miles, 2007: 47
Miller, 2010: 450, 451
Minor, 1975: 465
Mittelman & Johnston, 1999: 432
Moossey, 2009: 439
Moossey, 2009: 440, 441
Moranv.Burbine, 1986: 508
Moreau, 1987: 14

Nance, 2008: 458, 462, 463
Nassar, 2009: 432
National Law Enforcement & Corrections Technology Center, 2011: 48

Nelson & Huff-Corzine, 1998: 227

Newman, Rayz, & Friedman 2004: 97

Newmanetal. 2004: 97

Newton, 1990: 69

Office for Victims of Crime, 2001: 412

Ofshe & Leo, 1997b: 517, 522

Payan, 2006: 451, 452

Regents of University of California, 1976 371

Reichert, 2004:

Reid, 2010: 468

Rennie, 1977: 5

Ressler et al., 1988: 118

Richardson & Kosa, 2001: 4

Rider, 1980: 279

Robert D.Keppel, 1995: 72

Roberts, 2001: 413

Roebuck, 1967: 7

Rule, 2004: 483, 485, 486, 487

Safarik & Jarvis, 2005: 227

Safarik, Jarvis, & Nussbaum, 2000: 228

Sapse, 2011: 49

Seto, 2001: 458

Smith, 2011: 47, 112

Spencer, 2002: 413

Spener, 2004: 445

Spener, 2009:

Spener, 2009: 442

Strickland, 2012: 53

Taeuber & Allen, 1990: 227

The Centers for Disease Control & Prevention CDC 2001: 497

The Victoria Advocate, 2003: 446

Tillery, 2007: 47

Tucker, 2011: 48

Turner & Koṣa, 2003: 78

U.S. Department of Justice, 2009: 82

U.S. ICE, 2012: 80

U.S.CIS, 2012: 80

U.S.Department of Justice, 2009: 81

United Nations, 2007: 84

Ushynskyia, 2010: 467

Van Liempt & Doomernik, 2006: 444, 445

Vessel, 1998: 518

Viano, 2010: 431

VICAP, 2002, 71

Viotti, Opheim, & Bowen, 2008: 80

Viotti et al., 2008: 80

Vorpagel, 1982: 116

Wallace, 2011: 50

Ward, Kiernan, & Mabrey, 2006: 80

Ward et al., 2006: 80

Welner & Mastellon, 2010: 102, 104

Welner, 2003: 97, 98

Welner, 1998: 100

Welner, 2001: 100

Welner, 2005: 104

Wilder, 1981 459

Witzig, 2006: 69

Wortley & Smallbone, 2006: 7

www.depravityscale.org, 2012: 99

Zhang & Chin, 2002: 442. 443

Name Index

Adams, Katherine, 139
Alberti, Pat, 257
Allen, Robert, 105
Anderson, Michael John, 426
Andrews, William, 155–157
Ansley, Michelle, 155
Arnder, Robert, 413, 414
Aron, Levi, 135
Avery, Dennis, 265–267
Avery, Rebecca, 265

Baehring, Franz
    Konstantin, 413–414
Bailey, F., Lee, 234, 388, 421
Bakoles, Nikole, 74
Barnet, Henry, 139
Bell, Larry Gene, 211
Bennett, William, 21
Benson, Margaret, 150–153
Benson, Steven, 150–153
Bissette, Patricia, 233
Bittaker, Lawrence
    Sigmund, 223–226
Blackburn, Robert, 273
Blake, Helen, 232
Bonaparte, Charles, J., 63
Bonner, Beverly, 42–43
Bosket, Willie, 159–161
Bowen, Earl Wayne, 172–174
Breivik, Anders Behring, 3
Bresette, Marian, 241
Bridgeford, Shirley, 69
Brooke, Edward, 233
Brooks, Pierce, 69–70
Brown, Dante, 241–242
Brussel, James A., 300–301
Bundy, Ted, 72, 75, 115, 217,
    484, 485, 515, 516

Carabbia, Ronald, 131, 132
Carlson, Allan Eric, 406
Carpenter, David, 117
Carpenter, Leona, 494
Chance, Rick, 426
Chapman, Mark David,
    168–169
Charga, Elizabeth, 123–124
Charga, Jamiel, 121–123
Charga, Jimmy, 121–123

Cisternino, Butchy, 132
Clampitt, Catherine, 44
Clark, Sophie, 233
Clemente, Jim, 9
Code, Nathaniel, 26–27
Coleman, Martha, 241
Comeau, Marie-France, 208,
    209
Corbin, Evelyn, 233
Cornish, Harry, 139
Costas, Kristen, 186, 189
Cunanan, Andrew, 479

Daneker, Kathleen, 140
Daniels, Anthony, vii
Darwin, 5
DeMier, Richart, 360
DeRungs, Robert, 105–106
DeSalvo, Albert, 232
DesLauriers, Richard, 62
Dilone, Miguel, 181
Dinh, Van T., 409–410
Douglas, John, 68
Dugard, Jaycee, 358–360
Dull, Judy, 69
Dunn, Kerri, 32

Ellis, Connie LaFontaine, 73
Elrod, Michael, 270
Elsroth, Diane, 140
Esposito, Danielle, 478
Evonitz, Richard Mark, 52
Ewing, Charles Patrick, 198

F. Coppinger Kevin, 62
Faherty, Kevin, 232
Fenton, Lynne, 371
Ferritto, Ray, 131–132
Fields, Ted, 242
Fink, Benjamin, 494
Foster, Marcus, 273
Franklin, Joseph Paul, 240–244
Freeh, Louis J., 65, 66, 67

Gaglia, Michelle, 426
Garrido, Nancy, 359–360
Giffords, Gabrielle, 247
Gilliam, Jackie Doris, 224–226
Gillmouth, Everson, 494
Glatman, Harvey, 69–70

Goddard, Henry, 5
Goldman, Ron, 170
Goldstein, Andrew, 197
Goring, Charles, 5
Graf, Joann, 233
Gray, Anthony, 413
Gray III, L. Patrick, 65
Green, Christina-Taylor, 247
Greene, Daniel, 130–132

Hall, Andrea Joy, 224
Hammond, Karl, 219
Hanssen, Robert, S., 65, 66
Harrelson, Charles, 123–124
Harrelson, Woody, 123
Harris, Eric, 268
Harvey, Donald, 255–256
Hasan, Nidal Malik, ii
Hayes, Steven, 390
Hearst, Patty, 273, 387–388
Heatly, Maurice D., 473, 474
Heckenkamp, Jerome T., 407
Hennard, George, 4
Hester, R. (Bob) S., 273–275
Hitchcock, Harry, 151
Holmes, James, 249–251
Hoover, John Edgar, 63–67
Huff, Yolanda, 162
Hyden, Christopher
    James, 91–92

Irga, Ida, 232
Ivanov, Alexey , V., 419

Jackson, Arthur
    Richard, 384–385
Jay, Matt, 176
Jenkins, Philip 251
Jiang, Juju, 421–422
Johnson, Martha Ann,
    172–174
Jones, Genene, 257–258
Jordan, Vernon, 241

Kaczynski, Theodore (Ted)
    J., 46, 299, 305–306
Katehis, John, 426
Katherine, Mary, 360
Kelley, Clarence M., 63–64

Kemper, Ed, 68
Kennedy, Robert, 238
Klebold, Dylan, 268
Kletzky, Esther, 134–135
Kletzky, Leiby, 134–135
Kletzky, Yehudah, 134
Komisarjevsky, Joshua, 390
Koster, Chris, 44

Lane, Darrell, 241–242
Lanza, Adam, vii
Layton, George, 105
Leah, Jacqueline, 224
Ledford, Shirley
    Lynette, 226–227
Lee II, Floyd, 249
Leffler, Trisha, 427
Leftkow, Joan, 195
Lennon, John, 168–169
Levy, Nathaniel, 417, 130
Lewicka, Izabela, 44
Lewis, James, W., 140
Licavoli, James, 130
Lisk, Kristin, 52–53
Little, Russell, Jack, 273
Lloyd, Jessica, 208–209
Lombrosos, Cesare, 5
Lougher, Jared Lee, 247–248
Loveless, Michael Jay, 106–107
Lundgren, Jeffrey, 265–268
Lynn, Carol, 151

Madson, David, 478–480
Maher, Colleen, 197
Maldonado, Susan, 257
Maleng, Norm, 486
Manning, Alphonse, 240
Markoff, Philip, 426–428
Martin, David, 242
Martin, Vera Faye, 494
Mateias, Calin, 421
McClenahan, Shawn, 75
McLane, Kendall, 159
McVeigh, Timothy, 3, 299,
    464–465
McWhorter, Stanley, 140
Meier, Shirley, 175–178
Meier, Torran, 175–178
Meling, Jennifer, 140
Meling, Joseph, 140
Mercado, Ruth, 69
Mercer, Melinda, 73
Metesky, George, 299–302
Mikula, Kathleen, 242
Miller, Dorothy, 494
Milliron, Jeanna, 41
Mitchell, Brian David, 360
Moore, Kristen, 299
Morgenbesser, Leonard, 315
Morrison, Paul, 43, 44
MuellerIII, Robert S., 65

Mullins, J., 74

Naisbitt, Cortney, 155–157
Naslund, Denise, 72
Nichols, Nina, 232
Nickell, Bruce, 140–143
Nickell, Stella Maudine,
    140–143
Nicoll, Daniel, A., 145–147
Norris, Roy Lewis, 223–226

Orlando, Dante, 322
Ortiz, Carmen M., 62
Osborn, Laura, 145
Ott, Janice, 72
Otto, John E., 67

Palmer, Betty, 494
Parker, James, 114
Parker, Richard, 176–179
Pennel, Steven, 29
Perez, Moises, 160
Petit, William, 114
Petrocelli, Daniel, 170
Pierre, Dale, 157
Pollard, John, 252
Prochair, Alfred, 161
Protti, Bernadette, 186–189
Puente, Dorothea, 494–496

Rader, Dennis, 46, 88, 409
Raines, Violetta, 181
Reedy, Janice, 59
Reedy, Thomas, 59
Reese, Lawrence, 241
Reese, William, 478
Reichert, David, 285–287
Remiro, Michael, 273
Rendell, Larry, 146–147
Resendez, Angel
    Maturino, 478
Ressler, Robert, 68
Ridgway, Gary, 482–489
Robinson Sr, John E., 41
Rogers, Joseph, 216
Ross, Bart, 194
Ruckelshaus, William D., 65,
    67
Rudolph, Eric, 299
RussellJr, George, 31

Saldana, Theresa, 384–385
Sanders, Lindberg, 274–275
Sandusky, Jerry, vi
Savio, Kathleen, vi
Scalish, John, T., 129
Schaeffer, Lucinda, 224, 225,
    226
Schwenn, Toni, 240
Sessions, William Steele, 65,
    66, 67
Shelton, Ronnie, 28

Shinrikyo, Aum, 456
Shipman, Harold, 251–252
Sidal, Jennifer, 214
Silva, Sophia, 52
Simpson, Nicole Brown, 170,
    66
Simpson, O., J., 9, 170
Sims, Anthony, 322–323
Skeem, Jennifer, 360
Slesers, Anna, 232
Smart, Elizabeth, 359–360
Smith, Adriane, Ione, 413
Smith, Christine, 73
Smith, Susan, 31
Smothers, Arthur, 242
Snow, Sue, 141
Spates, Herman, 160–161
Speck, Richard, 472
Stasi, Lisa, 44
Steinheimer, David, 413
Stout, Corinne, 427
Stuart, Carol, 21–22
Stuart, Chuck, 21–22
Sullivan, Jane, 232

Tagliamonte, Jackie, 358
Taylor, James, 172
Taylor, Raymond, 241
Trail, Jeffrey, 478
Trouten, Suzette, 41
Tulloch, Robert, 114

Unruh, Howard, 115

Vasquez-Garcia, 398
Versace, Gianni, 478–479
Vetter, Donna Lynn, 217
Vollmer, Scott, 270

Walker, Luis, 364, 365
Walker, Orren, 156–157
Walker, Stan, 155–157
Wason, Laurie, A., 75
Watkins, Leo, 241
Webdale, Kendra, 197–200
Webster, William H., 65, 66,
    67, 70
Weed, Steven, 388
Welner, Michael, 91
Wesbecker, Joseph T., 191–192
White, Jack, 130
Whitman, Charles, 472–476
Williams, Russell, 208
Wischniwsky, Heidi, 418
Wood, Judge John, 121
Wright, Jenny, Ann, 172–173

Yates, Robert, 73

Zantop, Susanne, 114
Zezev, Oleg, 403–405
Zimmerman, Gabe, 24

Subject Index

A

Abduction Rape (319), 358–360
Abduction Rape, Adolescent (319)
  Case Example of, 359
Abduction Rape, Child
  Case Example of, 358
Abductions, 73
Actus reus, 509, 510
Adult Domestic Sexual Assault, 321
Aerial Hijackings, 465–468
Aggravating factors, 94–96
Agroterrorism, 453
Anger Rape (314), 342–350
  Victimology of, 342
Anger Rape, Age, 344
Anger Rape, Child Victim
  Case Example of, 346
Anger Rape, Elderly Victim, 345
  Case Example of, 345
Anger Rape, Gender, 343
  Case Example of, 343–344
Anger Rape, Racial, 347
  Case Example of, 347–348
Anthrax, 453
Anthrax, 498–500
anti-social, 100
Argument/Conflict Murder (123), 183
  Crime Scene Indicators of, 184
  Victimology of, 183
  Investigative Considerations of, 184
Argument Murder, 185
  Case Example of, 185
statistics of, 278
Arson (200), 253. 277, 280–285
Attention Seeker,
  Case Example of, 285
Personal Revenge
  Case Example of, 288

  Victimology of, 279–281
Arson Willful and Malicious Mischief
  Case Example of, 282
Assault, (440), 392
ATF, 450–451
attempted homicides
  reporting of, 71
Authority Murder (124), 189
  Crime Scene Indicators of, 189
  Investigative Considerations of, 190
  Victimology of, 189
  Case Example of, 191–192
Authority Rape (313), 329
Authority Rape Adult, 330
Authority Rape Child, 331
Authority Rape of, a Child
  Case Example of, 332
Autoeroticactivities, 32
Automated data analysis, 45
Automated Fingerprint Identification
    Systems (AFIS), 50
Autonomous Migrant Entries, 432–433
Avenue King Crips, 61

B

Bank Robbery (421), 387
  Case Example of, 387–388
Battery/Abuse (450), 393
  Case Example of, 394, 396, 397
BAU, 78
Behavior, 22
Behavioral autopsy, 514
Behavioral Science Unit also see BSU, 113
Biological Attack
  Case Example of, 453
  Crime Scene Indicators of, 454
  Investigative Considerations of, 454
Biological Agents as Weapons, 497

Biological Attacks (603), 453
Biological Attacks and Bioterrorism, 452
Biological warfare, 50
blatant statements, 523
blitz attack, 32, 116, 212, 214, 229
bondage, 311, 351, 354
Boston College, 53
Botulism, 501
Britai,n 59, 251
BSU, 113
BTK, 88
BTK Strangler, 45
Burden of Proof 509
Bureau of Alcohol Tobacco and Firearms
    See ATF
Burglary, (430), 391
    Common Forensic Findings of, 391
    Investigative Considerations of, 391
    Case Example of,

C
Causation, 510
CDC, 497, 498
Central Intelligence Agency (CIA). See
    CIA
Chemical Attacks (604), 457
    Common Forensic Findings of, 458
    Victimology of, 457
Chemical Attacks and Terrorism, 457
Child Domestic Sexual Abuse, 323
Child Pornography (524), 59, 414–418
Child Victim Rape, 311
Chinese Human Smuggling Groups, 442
Cigarette Smuggling (602), 446–448
    consequences of, 449
    main modes of, 450
    Case Example of, 448
Classifying Crimes by Severity, 91, 94
Cleveland, Ohio, 28
CODIS, 51
Cold Case Analysis, 78
Columbine High School, 268
Combined DNA Index System
    (CODIS), 50
Commercial Profit (107), 149
    Crime Scene Indicators of, 150

Investigative Considerations of, 150
    Victimology of, 149
    Case Example of, 150–153
Communication Threats (401), 367
    Crime Scene Indicators of, 367
    Investigative Considerations of, 369
    Victimology of, 402
Communication Interoperability, 48
Computer Crimes (500), 399
Computer Data as the Target (512), 402
    Case Example of, 403
Computer Users as the Target (520), 406
Concealed weapon detection, 46
Confessions, 508
    challenges to, 516
Confessions
    Personal Dignity, 523
Confessions, category 2
    Case Example of, 519
Confessions, Category 2
    Traits, 517
Confessions, category 3
    Statements, 519
Confessions, category 3
    Case Example of, 520
Confessions, category 4
    Options, 521
Confessions, category 5
    Consequences, 522
Confessions category 1
    Behavior, 517
Conflict Murder, 186
    Case Example of, 186–189
Contract Murder (101), 119
    Crime Scene Indicators of, 119
    Victimology of, 119
    Common Forensic Findings of, 120
    Investigative Considerations of, 120
    Staging of, 120
    Case Study of, 121–124
Cookie Monster, 400–401
COPLINK, 49
Coprophilia, 311
COYOTE-ASSISTED BORDER
    CROSSING, 441–442
Crime analysis, assessment, 22, 36

Crime Concealment Arson, (230), 290
   Victimology, 292
   Common Forensic Findings of, 293
Crime case matching, 77
Crime Classification, 513
Crime Concealment, Murder (231), 291
   Case Example of, 291–293
Crimes Internet, 412
Crime Scene Redflags, 33
Crime scene search
   ten basic steps 15
Crimes of, anger, 32
CriminalCompetition (103), 128
   Common Forensic Findings of, 129
   Crime Scene Indicators of, 128
   Investigative Considerations of, 129
   Victimology of, 128
   case study of, 129–132
Criminal Act Requirements, 509–511
Criminal codes, 95
Criminal Enterprise, 119
Criminal Enterprise Homicide, 111
Criminal Enterprise Rape, 314
Criminal intent, 511–512
Cross-Border Smuggling of,
   Weapons, 449–451
CWD see also concealed weapon
   detection, 46–47
cyber crime, 60, 86, 403
cyber Crime scene, 401
Cyber criminals, 88
Cyber Security Enhancement Act, 87
cyber space, 40, 42
Cyber stalking, 411

D

Data collection, 512
Data mining, 46
Date rape, 308
Denial of Service (513), 405
   Case Example of, 406
Deoxyribo Nucleic Acid (DNA), 49, 50,
   51, 56, 77, 528, 536, 542
Department of, Homeland Security. See
   DHS
Depersonalization, 171, 214

Depravity Standard
   Case example of, 105
Depravity Scale, 101, 103
Depravity Standard, 99, 100, 102, 104, 105
DHS, 79, 80, 81, 446
Diagnostic and Statistical Manual of,
   Mental Disorders, See DSM 9
DNA torch, 291
Domestic Homicide (122), 169
Domestic Sexual Abuse (312), 322
   Case Example of, 322
Domestic Sexual Assault (312), 321
double homicide ,114
Drug murder (106), 143
   Victimology of, 143
   Crime Scene Indicators of, 144
   Investigative Considerations of, 144
   Common Forensic Findings of, 144
   Case Example of, 145
DSM, 9
DUTY TO WARN, 371

E

Elder Female Sexual Homicide (135), 227
   Common Forensic Findings of, 230
   Investigative Considerations of, 231
   Victimology of, 227
   Crime Scene Indicators of, 229
   Case Example of, 232–234
EMIF, 432
Enforcement and Removal Operations
   ERO. See ERO
Erotomania-Motivated Murder (121), 165
   Common Forensic Findings of, 167
   Crime Scene Indicators of, 166
   Investigative Considerations of, 167
   Victimology of, 166
   Case Example of, 168–169
European Union. See EU
EUROPOL, 85
Excitement-Motivated Arson (210), 283
   Crime Scene Indicators of, 284
   Investigative Considerations of, 284
   Victimology of, 283
Exhibitionism, 311, 326
Exploitation, 434

Exploitative Rape (313), 339
  offender characteristics of, 340
  Victimology of, 339–340
Exploitative Rape, Adult (313),
  Case Example of, 341
Explosive Attacks and Terrorism
    (606), 461
  Case Example of, 464
  Crime Scene Indicators of, 462
  Investigative Considerations of, 463
Extremist group murder (142), 268
  Common Forensic Findings of, 271
  Crime Scene Indicators of, 270–271
  Investigative Considerations of,
    271–272
  Victimology of, 270
Extremist group murder political,
  Common Forensic Findings of,
    272–273
  Crime Scene Indicators of, 272
Extremist groups
  Religious, 269
  Socioeconomic, 269
Extremist Homicide (142),
  Common Forensic Findings of, 239
  Crime Scene Indicators of, 238
  Investigative Considerations of, 239
  Political, 238
  Religious, 238
  socioeconomic/Hate crime, 238
  Victimology of, 238
Extremist groups
  political 239
Extremist Groups Using the
    Internet, 268–269
Extremist Homicide, 237, 240, 268, 273
Extremist Homicide religious,
    273
Extremist-Motivated Arson
  Crime Scene Indicators of, 298
  Victimology of, 297
Extremist-Motivated Arson (250), 297
'xtremist-Motivated Arson, Terrorism
    (251), 299
  'e Example of, 299
    ness testimony, 507–508

F
False Confessions 532
FBI 87, 88, 111, 113
  expansion of, 63
Federal Bureau of, Investigation (FBI), 74
Federal Emergency Management Agency
    (FEMA). See FEMA
Felony Murder (108), 153
Felony Rape (301), 314
FEMA, 81
Fixation, 312
Forensic botany, 49
Forenic Red Flags, 35
Forensic sciences, 49
Formal Gang Sexual Assault (331), 361
Formal Gang Sexual Assault, single
    victim
  Case Example of, 361
Fort Hood, 3, 4

G
Gang Motivated Murder (102), 124, 126,
    129
  Search Warrant Suggestions for 127
  Defining Characteristics of, 124
    Victimology of, 124–125
  Common Forensic Findings of, 125
  Crime Scene Indicators of, 127
  Investigative Considerations of, 128
Geographic information systems (GIS), 47
Global, 348
  Case Example of, 349–350
Global Crimes, 431
Global positioning Systems (GPS), 47
Godfrey v. Georgia, 46
Green River Killer, 74, 482
Green River Task Force, 73
Gregg v. Georgia (1976), 94
Group Cause Homicide (140), 263
  Crime Scene Indicators of, 264
  Investigative Considerations of, 264
  Victimology of, 263
Group Excitement (143), 275
  Common Forensic Findings of, 276
  Crime Scene Indicators of, 275
  Victimology of, 275

Group Cause Homicide, Cult (141), 263
  Case Example of, 264
Group-Cause Sexual Assault (330), 361
Group Excitement (143), 275

H

hate crimes, 32
heinous crimes, 97
heinous elements, 94
Hezbollah, 268
Home Invasion Robbery (422), 388
  Case Example of, 390
  Criminal profile of, 389
  Dangerous trends in, 389
  Method of, operation, 390
Homicide, 118
Homicide Injury Scale, 229
Hostage taking, 459
  Case Example of, 461
Human Smuggling (601), 443
  Crime Scene Indicators of, 443
  Victimology of, 443
Human Trafficking (601), 433
hyper religiosity, 245

I

Identity Theft (521), 407
  Case Example of, 407
  Signature, 24–32
Illegal Immigration Reformand
    Immigrant Responsibility Act, 433
Illegal migration (601), 432
Immigration and CustomsEnforcement
    (ICE). See ICE
Immigration and Customs Enforcement.
    See ICE
Indiscriminate Murder (108), 153
  Case Example of, 155
  Common Forensic Findings of, 154
  Crime Scene Indicators of, 154
  Search Warrant Suggestion 155
  Staging of, 154
  Victimology of, 153
Individual Domestic Terrorism,
    Socioecomonic Inspired (127),
  Case Example of, 249

Individual Profit murder (107), 147
  Common Forensic Findings of, 148
  Crime Scene Indicators of, 148
  Investigative Considerations of, 149
  Staging of, 148
  Victimology of, 147
Individual Domestic Terrorism Political
    Inspired (127), 247
  Case Example of, 247
Individual Domestic Terrorism, Religion
    Inspired (127), 244
  Case Example of, 249
Infantilism, 311
Informal Gang Sexual Assault (332),
    362
Informal Gang Sexual Assault, Single
    Victim (332),
  Case Example of, 362
information sharing, 47
information technology, 53, 66
Insurance Fraud (241), 296
  Case Example of, 296
Insurance-Related Death, 147
Internet, 37, 40, 44, 87, 399, 410, 411, 426
Internet child pornography, 7, 412
Internet Crimes Against Children. See
    ICAC
Internet Fraud Complaint Center
    (IFCC), 85
Internet serial murder, 41
Internet service provider (ISP). See ISP
INTERPOL, 83
Invasion of Privacy, 411
Investigative profiling, 116
ISP, 405, 412, 413

J

Junk Science, 535
Juvenile offenders, 231

K

Kidnap Murder (104), 14, 111, 118, 119,
    132, 134, 138
  Common Forensic Findings of, 133
  Crime Scene Indicators of, 133
  Investigative Considerations of, 133

Kidnap Murder (104), *(continued)*
Victimology of, 132
Search Warrant Suggestions 134

L

Law Enforcement Act of, 1994, 76
Law Enforcement Online. See LEO, 77
Long-Term Trends in Homicide Rates, 113

M

Malignant Software 400, 401, 402, 403, 406, 412, 423, 424
Investigative Considerations of, 401
Masochism, 311
Mass murder, 4, 16, 114, 471, 472, 474, 478, 481
Case Example of, 472
Classic Mass murder, 114
family mass murder, 114
McNaughton rule, 82
Medical Murders (128), 251
Common Forensic Findings of, 253
Crime Scene Indicators of, 253
Investigative Considerations of, 253
Staging of, 253
Victimology of, 252
Mens rea, 510
Military Sexual Assault/Rape (333), 363
Case Example of, 364
Military Sexual Harassment, 364
Military Sexual Trauma, 365
Minnick v. Mississippi, 512
missing person, 73
Mitigating factors, 92
Modus operandi (MO), 22, 23, 24, 25, 26, 72, 154, 225, 239, 272, 299, 310, 481, 489
MTC, 324, 325
R3, 325
murder, 10–14, 17, 56, 88, 92, 112, 124, 143, 153, 159, 165, 169, 183, 186, 189, 197, 291

⎩ Center for Missing and
⎩loited Children (NCMEC). See
MEC

National Center for the Analysis of,
Violent Crime see also
NCAVC, 35
National Crime Victims Survey, 8
National Cyber Crime Training
Partnership. See NCTP
National Integrated Ballistics
Identification Network
(NIBIN), 51
NCAVC, 30, 31, 67, 69, 78, 279, 516, 545
NCVS 8, 309
Necrophilia, 15, 19, 36, 100, 213, 311, 487, 488
neonaticidal mother, 179, 181
Neonaticide (122), 179
Case Example of, 181
Crime Scene Indicators of, 180
Investigative Considerations of, 181
Staging of, 180
Victimology of, 180
NICS, 450
non preferential killer, 117
Nonspecific Motive Murder (126), 196
Common Forensic Findings of, 196
Crime Scene Indicators of, 196
Investigative Considerations of, 196
Victimology of, 196
Case Example of, 197
North American Free Trade Agreement.
See NAFTA
North Shore Gang Task Force, 62
Nuclear magnetic resonance (NMR), 50
NW3C, 86

O

Objectivity, 36
Offender, 5–13, 23–26, 128, 133, 138, 143, 148, 150, 171, 193, 221, 228, 237, 239, 297, 321, 324, 327, 393, 412, 514
offender fantasies, 23
Oklahoma City, 3, 66, 73
Online Solicitation of, Children, 412
Operation Firewall, 87
Operation Melting Pot, 60
Operation Rio Grande, 433

Opportunistic Rape (313), 324
Over zealous Prosecution, 538

P

Paraphilias, 311, 326
Pedophile, 311
Personal Cause Homicide (120), 165
Personal Cause Religion-Inspired
   Case Example of, 201
Personal Cause Sexual Assault (310), 318
Personation, 25
Phases of a Crime, 11
PHYSICAL EVIDENCE, 508
Plague, 502
PLEA BARGAINING, 508
Poisoning, 492
   case examples of, 494
posing, 32
post Crime behavior, 12
Power–Reassurance Rape (313), 336
   offender characteristics of, 335
   Victimology of, 335
Power–Reassurance Rape, Adolescent
   (313), 338
   Case Example of, 338
Power–Reassurance Rape, Adult (313),
   Case Example of, 337
preCrime stage, 11
preferential child molesters, 311
Prescriptive interview, 512
prescriptive interviewing, 516
Primary Felony Rape
   Victimology of, 314
Primary Felony Rape (301), 314
   Case Example of, 315
Product Tampering, (105), 136, 140
   Common Forensic Findings of, 137
   Crime Scene Indicators of, 137
   Investigative Considerations of, 138
   Victimology of, 136
   Staging of, 137
   Case examples of, 139
profiling, 49, 67, 69, 116, 117, 118, 301
Profit-Motivated Arson (240), 293
   Crime Scene Indicators of, 293
   Investigative Considerations of, 294

Project Gun runner, 81
Project Safe Neighborhoods, 81
protection of, Children from Sexual
   Predator Act of 1998, 115
Pseudo-Hero Homicide (128), 257
   Case Example of, 257
Pseudo-hero killer, 237, 252, 254
pseudo-mercy/pseudo-hero killer,
   252–254
Pseudo-Mercy Homicide, 254, 255
pseudo-mercy killer, 253

R

rape 17, 18, 25, 26, 28, 35, 45, 55, 56, 75,
   93, 111, 215, 221, 226, 307–365
   General Forensic Evidence Collection
     of, 313–314
   Indirect offenses of, 319
   Isolated/Opportunistic Offense, 319
   Nonsadistic Types, 326
   Preliminary Offense, 320
   Sadistic Types, 325
   Transition Offense, 320
   Vindictive Motivation, 326
Rape and sexual assault kits, 313
Rapist, 26, 28, 68, 307–365
Rapist Types
   Comparison of, 326, 352
redflag, 33
Religion-Inspired Homicide (127), 244
   Crime Scene Indicators of, 245
   Investigative Considerations of, 246
   Staging of, 246
   Victimology of, 245
Revenge (125), 118, 165, 191, 192,
   193–195, 279, 286–289, 301, 302,
   303, 406, 464, 465
   Case Example of, 195
   Crime Scene Indicators of, 193
   Investigative Considerations of, 194
   Victimology of, 193
Revenge-Motivated Arson (220), 286
   Crime Scene Indicators of, 287
   Investigative Considerations of, 287
   Victimology of, 286
ritualistic behavior, 30

Robbery (420), 4, 21, 26, 69, 101, 105, 111, 120, 143, 147, 148, 153–158, 161, 162, 174, 202, 207, 221, 232, 243, 246, 273, 314, 315, 317, 318, 341, 343, 344, 367, 385–390
  Investigative Considerations of, 386
Robbery-motivated homicide, 143

S

Sadism, 100, 220, 311, 326, 348, 350, 354
Sadistic Rape (315), 350, 351, 353–355
Sadistic Rape Adolescent (315), 355
  Case Example of, 355
Sadistic Rape Adult (315), 354
  Case Example of, 354
Sadistic Rape Elder (315), 357
SAFECOM Program, 48
Safe Explosives Act, 82
Salt Lake City, 74, 242, 244
Stalking crimes, (410), 375, 377
  Investigative Considerations of, 377
Scatophilia, 311
Scotland Yard, 82, 83
Secondary Felony Rape (301), 317
  Case Example of, 318
Secret Service, 81, 87, 385
sentencing guidelines, 94
9/11/01, 65
Serial Arson (260), 286, 287, 288, 302–304
  Investigative Considerations of, 303
  Case Example of, 304
Serial Bomber 305
  Case Example of, 305
Serial murder
  Case Example of, 483
Serial Bombing (270), 305
Serial killer, 81
Serial murder, 16, 41, 51, 55, 78, 88, 115, 255, 471, 472, 477, 481
  offender, 47, 231, 232, 311, 320, 323, 336, 339, 344, 350, 355, 358, 363, 395, 412, 532, 536
  ial, 310, 311, 317, 318, 320, 327, , 332, 357

Sexual Homicide, Disorganized (132), 212, 214
  Common Forensic Findings of, 213
  Crime Scene Indicators of, 212
  Investigative Considerations of, 214
  Staging of, 213
  Victimology of, 212
Sexual Homicide, Organized (131), 205
  Common Forensic Findings of, 207
  Investigative Considerations of, 207
  Case example 210
Sexual Homicide, Sadistic (134), 220
  Common Forensic Findings of, 221
  Crime Scene Indicators of, 220
  Investigative Considerations of, 222
  Staging of, 221
  Victimology of, 220
Sexualization Motive, 325
sexually motivated murderer, 116
sexual sadist, 25, 68, 220, 222, 351, 354
SHR, 491, 492
Shreveport, Louisiana, 26
Signature, 22, 24, 25, 26–32, 145, 271, 272, 299, 300, 302, 303, 306, 481, 483
  analysis of, 31
single homicide, 114
Situational Murder (108), 158
  Case Example of, 159
  Crime Scene Indicators of, 158
  Investigative Considerations of, 159
  Victimology of, 158
Situational Murder Elder (108),
  Case Example of, 161
Small pox, 497, 498, 500, 501, 503, 504
snake heads, 442
Social Acquaintance Rape (313), 327, 328
  Case Example of, 328
Software piracy, 402
Spam, 400, 402, 406, 410, 423
Spokane, Washington, 73, 75, 89
Spontaneous Domestic Homicide (122), 170, 172, 175
  Common Forensic Findings of, 171
  Crime Scene Indicators of, 171
  Investigative Considerations of, 171
  Case Example of, 172

Spotsylvania County, Virginia, 60
spree murder, 16, 114, 115, 477
Staged Domestic Homicide (122), 10, 17, 165, 170, 174–175, 471
  Common Forensic Findings of, 175
  Investigative Considerations of, 175
  Staging of, 174
  Case Example of, 175
Staging 14, 18, 21, 22, 31–33, 36, 37
Stalker, Domestic (411), 377, 378
  Case Example of, 380
  Crime Scene Indicators of, 278
Stalker, Erotomania (413), 382, 383, 384
  Case Example of, 384
  Crime Scene Indicators of, 382
  Investigative Considerations of, 383
Stalker, Nondomestic (412), 379
  Case Example of, 381
  Crime Scene Indicators of, 380
Stalking Crimes
  Victimology of, 371
  Crime Scene Indicators of, 376
  Surveillance, 45, 46, 47, 56, 57, 133, 135, 161, 207, 220, 234, 270, 271, 273, 364, 376, 381, 382, 383, 386, 389, 390, 427, 432, 433, 449, 463
SWAT, 47, 248, 387, 477, 479
symbolic gestures, 28

T
The Bloods, 54, 61, 62, 124, 195
The Computer User as the Target, 399, 406, 407
  Case Example of, 407
the International Law Enforcement Academy (ILEA), 66
the Law Enforcement Assistance Administration (LEAA). See LEAA
the Massachusetts Treatment Center (MTCR3). See MTC:R3
Theorizing, 513
The Patriot Act, 87
Threat Delivery, 373, 374, 375

Threat Symbolic, 375
Threat Delivery Verbal Communication, 373
Threat Delivery Written Communication, 374
Threats, 78, 79, 85, 122, 133, 160, 251, 282, 299, 368
  Physical Communication of, 375
Threats Conditional, 371, 372
Threats Direct, 372
Threats Indirect, 372
Threats Nonspecific, 373
Through-the-wall surveillance, 47, 58
Toxicology, 35, 36, 57, 253, 260, 477, 495
Trafficked victims (601), 437
Trafficking Migrants (601), 438
  Investigative Considerations of, 438
  Victimology of, 438
  Process of, 436
Trafficking of, Narcotics (602), 451
Trafficking Operations, 81, 435, 440
  Types of, 436, 439
Trailside Killer, 116
Training and Research Institute of NW3C 86
triple homicide, 114, 422
Trojan horse, 181, 400, 401, 403, 405, 407, 409, 423

U
U.S. Customs and Border Protection (CBP), 80, 446
U.S. Customs Service, 59
U.S. law enforcement agencies, 60
Uniform Crime Reporting (UCR), 8, 111, 112, 121, 163, 306, 308, 491
Unabomber, 46, 299, 305, 306, 374
  see also Ted Kaczynski
undoing 30, 31, 36, 37, 171, 473
  Case Example, 30
unidentified dead persons, 75
Union, SouthCarolina, 31
unknown subject (UNSUB), 22, 30, 36, 37, 116, 118, 132, 170, 484
urophilia, 311

U.S. Department of, Justice (USDOJ), 61,
    162, 163
Justice for All Act, 527

V

Vandalism-Motivated Arson (200),
    280
Investigative Considerations of,
    281
typical offender of, 281
Victimology of, 280
VICAP, 69–79
    Crime Analysis Report, 75
Victim Contact, 311
victim risk, 151, 206, 368
Virtual Crime scene analysis 53

case examples 54–56
Viruses, 400, 452, 453, 497

W

Walton v. Arizona, 96, 107
West Side Rapist, 28
Wireless Communications, 48
World Health Organization, 502
Worm, 399, 400
wrongful convictions, 527–543

Y

Yersiniapestis, 453, 502

Z

Zoophilia, 311